Introduction to Sociology

A Canadian Focus

Seventh Edition

Edited by

James J. Teevan
UNIVERSITY OF WESTERN ONTARIO

W.E. Hewitt
UNIVERSITY OF WESTERN ONTARIO

Prentice Hall

A Pearson Company

Toronto

Dedicated to our students—past, present, and future.

Canadian Cataloguing in Publication Data

Main entry under title:

Introduction to sociology: a Canadian focus

7th ed.
Includes bibliographical references and index.
ISBN 0-13-017010-0

1. Sociology. 2. Canada - Social conditions. I. Teevan, James J., 1942- . II. Hewitt, W.E. (Warren Edward), 1954- .

HM51.I57 2001   301   C00-930211-5

0-13-017010-0

Vice President, Editorial Director: Michael Young
Acquisitions Editor: Jessica Mosher
Marketing Manager: Judith Allen
Developmental Editor: Lisa Phillips
Production Editor: Sherry Torchinsky
Copy Editor: Dennis Mills
Production Coordinator: Wendy Moran
Page Layout: B.J. Weckerle
Photo Research: Susan Wallace-Cox
Art Director: Mary Opper
Interior Design: Lisa Lapointe
Cover Design: Lisa Lapointe
Cover Image: The Special Photographers Co./Photonica

2 3 4 5   05 04 03 02

Printed and bound in Canada.

Statistics Canada information is used with permission of the Minister of Industry, as Minister responsible for Statistics Canada. Information on the availability of the wide range of data from Statistics Canada can be obtained from Statistics Canada's Regional Offices, its World Wide Web site at http://www.statcan.ca, and its toll-free access number 1-800-263-1136.

Chapter 15, Demography and Urbanization is adapted from Kevin McQuillan, "Population," in Robert Hagedorn, ed., *Sociology*, 5th edition, pp. 229-259. Copyright © 1994 by Harcourt Brace & Company, Canada, Ltd. All rights reserved. Adapted by permission of Harcourt Canada, Ltd.

Prentice
Hall

A Pearson Company

Table of Contents

Part I   Introduction   1

1   What Is Sociology?   *James J. Teevan and Marion Blute*   2

2   Research Methods   *James J. Teevan*   19

7   Gender Relations   *Lesley D. Harman*   168

8   Race and Ethnic Relations   *Carol Agócs*   194

9   Aging   *Ingrid Arnet Connidis*   228

Part IV   Social Institutions   253

10   Families   *Roderic Beaujot*   254

11 Religion *Lorne L. Dawson* 289

12 Media *Nick Dyer-Witheford* 319

Part V Social Organization 349

13 Work and Organizations *Jerry P. White* 350

16 Social Change *Edward Bell* 430

Preface

In this seventh edition of *Introduction to Sociology: A Canadian Focus* we have added a number of new chapters reflecting changing interests and concerns within the field of sociology, and made a few structural changes to the text. Added to the line-up are chapters dealing with aging, media, and social change. Aging and media are essential topics today, due to their growing importance in contemporary Canada. Social change is probably a topic we should have always included in the text. To make room for these new topics, we deleted the chapters on education, political sociology, and urbanization, incorporating their essentials into Chapter 4, Socialization, Chapter 6, Social Inequality, and Chapter 15, Demography and Urbanization. Chapter 4, Socialization, Chapter 11, Religion, and Chapter 13, Work and Organizations have new authors; so does the now expanded Chapter 15, Demography and Urbanization. Much of the old material is there but the viewpoint is fresh and updated. In all of this change, however, we have remained faithful to our original concept: having specialists in touch with the most recent research in their areas each contribute a part of the text. As editors, our job has been to integrate this material into an accessible resource that will inform and interest beginning students in the sociological enterprise.

This edition is divided into five parts. Part I introduces the field of sociology and its major variants, and includes a brief history of the discipline in Canada. It then discusses the research methods or strategies sociologists use to collect the data for their analyses. Part II focuses on society and the individual—the core of sociological thought—and includes discussions about culture, the shared way of life that is passed from generation to generation; the learning of culture through a process called socialization; and deviant behaviour (such as crime or mental illness), which some sociologists believe is due to failed attempts at socialization. Part III considers social differentiation and inequality in Canada. Here, the text examines social inequality, briefly defined as the relatively enduring differences in resources existing between social groups; gender roles, a major form of social differentiation and a source of considerable current interest in sociology; Canada's racial and ethnic groups; and our aging society. Part IV looks at social institutions, and contains chapters on the major structures of society: families, religion, and the media. Social organization is examined in Part V, with discussions of formal organizations and work, social movements, demography and urbanization, and social change.

As you will soon see, there is more than one sociological perspective on these various topics. The variety of sociologies is demonstrated throughout this volume, as the authors analyze their subjects and apply these various perspectives to the study of past and present Canadian society.

Acknowledgments

We would like to take this opportunity to express our appreciation to the various authors included in this text for their cooperation, hard work, and patience. We also gratefully acknowledge the many friends and colleagues who assisted our authors and us in putting the volume together, as well as the University of Western Ontario's Department of Sociology for its support. Many thanks as well to Dennis Mills for his assistance in editing the manuscript, and to Ann-Marie Anie, Michelle Tse, and Catherine Leblanc for their word processing skills.

We would also like to thank the reviewers, who offered many helpful suggestions: Pat Burman, University of Western Ontario; Howard Doughty, Seneca College; Rick Holmes, Mohawk College; Robert Lewis, Memorial University of Newfoundland; Nancy Netting, Okanagan University College; and Peter Poole, Okanagan University College. Finally, we would like to acknowledge the professional help from the staff at Pearson Educational Canada. Our thanks to Nicole Lukach, Lisa Phillips, and Sherry Torchinsky, for assisting us in developing this fine volume.

Contributors

Carol Agócs

Roderic Beaujot

Danièle Bélanger

Edward Bell

Marion Blute   Nick Dyer-Witheford
Michael P. Carroll   Edward G. Grabb
Samuel Clark   Lesley D. Harman
Ingrid Arnet Connidis   Kevin McQuillan
James Côté   James J. Teevan
Lorne L. Dawson   Jerry P. White

For the Instructor

The contributions of our constituent authors, combined with an editorial emphasis on clear language and minimal overlap, have resulted in an instructive text, consistently praised for its uniformity in level and consistent writing style. In this latest edition, significant updating and re-writing, plus the addition of new chapters covering a range of current topics in sociology now make this seventh edition tighter, smoother, and more current than ever.

Features of this Edition

1. *New chapters:* New chapters have been added in key areas including aging, media, and social change.

2. *Thoroughly revised chapters:* Chapter 4, Socialization, Chapter 11, Religion, and Chapter 15, Work and Organizations have been entirely re-written and updated. Demography and urbanization are now combined in a newly written chapter.

3. *Balanced approach to theoretical perspectives:* In this edition we have continued our efforts to inject a sound knowledge of sociological theory throughout the text. Chapter 1 provides an even more balanced introduction to the major theoretical paradigms of the discipline, dealing with structural-functionalism, conflict theory, symbolic interactionism, and feminism. These theoretical approaches are also applied more consistently to the specific areas addressed in subsequent chapters.

4. *Feminist theory:* Wherever possible, coverage of gender issues has been enhanced and integrated throughout the text.

5. *Up-to-date research:* The multi-author approach offers a degree of accuracy and a wealth of information attainable only through specialization. As in the past, this edition cites the most recent studies possible from Statistics Canada and other sources.

6. *Improved readability:* Once again, throughout the book, passages previously identified as difficult by students and expert reviewers have been rethought and rewritten to produce a clear, concise, and comprehensive text.

7. *More thought-provoking boxed inserts:* Many of the boxed inserts have been replaced with contemporary and topical material of interest to students. Many boxed inserts are now presented to promote discussion through the inclusion of questions related to the material presented.

8. *Predictive focus:* By way of conclusion, all chapters now include an important discussion regarding future trends and developments on the topic in question. Not only are students made aware of past and present tendencies in sociology, they are encouraged to think about what might come next, reinforcing the predictive dimension of the discipline.

Established Features

1. *Multi-author perspective:* This text combines the expertise and research base of thirteen sub-field specialists with a strong editorial focus to bring you the best of both worlds: the most up-to-date and accurate information—in a dynamic world and ever-developing discipline—explained by experts in each area, presented at a consistent level of difficulty.

2. *Accessible writing style:* The editorial team has always exercised strong control to produce an attractive and complete text with a focus on clear language and uncluttered phraseology. The result is a text that engages and motivates students to read on.

3. *Canadian perspective:* Through distinctly Canadian examples and applications, this volume brings students a view of their own sociological environment and areas of particular interest. The text absorbs students through real-world illustrations and discussions of personally and culturally

relevant issues. The objective is to focus on the Canadian context; because of course time constraints, instructors can best do justice to that material most immediate and familiar to students.

4. *Content coverage:* The volume covers the full spectrum of sociological theory, providing an excellent, balanced view of the major paradigms of the discipline. Core subject areas covered include: research methods, culture, socialization, deviant behaviour, social inequality, gender relations, race and ethnic relations, aging, families, religion, media, social organization and work, social movements, demography and urbanization, and social change.

5. *Part introductions:* The editors have included an introduction at the beginning of each part, designed to help students tie individual chapter topics together by providing context and perspective, and suggesting a focus to guide student learning and emphasize particular concepts. Students develop an understanding of the general picture and of the relationships between separate sub-fields in an overall sociological context.

6. *Pedagogical aids:* This text is designed to provide a firm informational base while capturing the excitement of sociology. Photos, tables, figures, charts, and extensive use of boxed articles make the book visually stimulating while supplementing written information. The boxed articles present a number of special-interest items and commentary, allowing real-world applications of theoretical perspectives through in-depth discussion of topical cases and viewpoints. Each chapter ends with a discussion of future trends, a summary, a list of key terms, a series of critical thinking exercises composed to spark student interest and debate, a list of suggested readings, and Internet web sites for further exploration. Key terms appear in bold print in the text for easy identification and reference. A full glossary appears at the end of the volume, with page numbers to guide readers to the place in the text where the term is first discussed.

Supplements

This edition is accompanied by a range of instructional aids, designed to meet student and instructor needs.

1. *Instructor's Manual and Test Item File:* This resource has been developed by co-editor Ted Hewitt. The instructor's manual has been designed to ensure maximum utility to the intro-level teacher. The Introduction includes general tips on teaching introductory level sociology, especially in large class format—now a fact of life on most university and college campuses. Chapter sections comprise: (1) a list of chapter headings; (2) a summary of *Introduction to Sociology* chapter contents; (3) a list of learning objectives; (4) a summary of key terms and concepts; (5) issues for class discussion; and (6) a list of NFB videos relevant to the topic. The test item file includes four basic types of questions, most new to this edition: (1) fill-in-the-blank; (2) multiple choice; (3) short essay; and (4) true-false. Answers are provided and page numbers appended to each question for easy reference to the text.

2. *Computerized Test Item File:* This computerized file is available in both Windows and Mac format. The test item file contains four basic types of questions, and most questions are either new or re-edited for this edition. Questions include: (1) fill-in-the-blank; (2) multiple choice; (3) short essay; and (4) true-false. Answers, page numbers, and difficulty level are appended to each question for easy reference to the text.

3. *Study Guide:* Prepared by co-editor James Teevan, this guide provides students with a study aid designed to complement the text. Chapter sections comprise: (1) a summary of objectives; (2) a summary of key terms and definitions; (3) self-quiz multiple choice questions; (4) fill-in-the-blank questions; and (5) answers. Students can pinpoint areas of weakness and return to the text for review, as necessary.

Introduction

In the first part of this book we provide an overview of sociology as a discipline. In Chapter 1 we examine its origins and varieties, and also present a brief history of sociology in Canada. How sociologists conduct their research is the subject of Chapter 2. Although the process generally involves the collection of data to describe or explain social phenomena, there are many specific research strategies from which to choose. Each is explained in a general way, followed by a discussion of its actual practice. An assessment of the relative strengths and weaknesses of the various research methods is also presented. Give each option a careful reading, and then, as the various research problems in need of research are suggested throughout the text, think about the option you might choose.

CHAPTER 1

What is Sociology?

James J. Teevan and Marion Blute

Introduction

One of the major concerns of sociology is to explain why members of some groups behave differently than members of other groups. The groups that affect human behaviour include whole societies, collectivities that share a common territory and way of life, such as Canada and the U.S.; smaller groups that share the same status, such as trade unionists, doctors, or right-to-life advocates; and even social categories, individuals who may not see themselves as forming social groups at all, but who possess some social characteristic in common, such as having no children, being over six feet tall, or living in the same province. Thus, sociology attempts to answer such questions as why the U.S. has more crime than Canada (see Chapter 3, Culture), why the crime rate in B.C. is higher than Newfoundland's (see Chapter 5, Deviance), why fewer women than men are in certain professions (see Chapter 7, Gender Relations), how cohabiting couples differ from those who are married (see

Chapter 10, Families), or why some Quebecers are attracted to separatism (see Chapter 14, Social Movements).

In seeking to explain such differences, many sociologists adopt a viewpoint developed over a century ago by the French sociologist Émile Durkheim (1858–1917) in his investigation of suicide. Many of Durkheim's contemporaries thought that mental illness, inherited tendencies, or unhappiness were causes of suicide. Although each of these explanations had merit, Durkheim believed that they focused too much on the person as an isolated individual. Durkheim argued that social factors—factors pertaining either to group structure or to the relationships between individuals in groups—also affect suicide.

Durkheim called these social sources of behaviour social facts. **Social facts** point to social or group-level explanations of behaviour, such as ethnicity, gender, place of residence, and marital status. They are thus unlike psychological factors, which emphasize individual, internal processes such

CHART 1.1   Sociology and the Social Sciences: A Comparison

Sociology	The study of social behavior and relationships, it examines the effects of society and group membership on human behaviour, as well as people's perceptions of their social environment, and the effects of these perceptions on social interaction. There is much overlap between sociology and the other social sciences described below.
Psychology	Primarily the study of individual sources of behaviour, its emphasis is on processes internal to the individual, such as motivation, cognition, learning, perception, and personality.
Social and cultural anthropology	Traditionally the study of small, nonindustrial societies, it has been extended to communities in industrial societies. This discipline tends to study these groups in totality, from their organization and culture, to specific institutions, including their political, economic, familial, religious, and legal systems. Sociologists are more likely to study only some of these topics at any one time in an attempt to achieve a more detailed view of a more limited subject area.
Political science	This discipline looks at government and political life, including the exercise of power and voting. Political sociologists study these issues as well, but usually examine them as they affect and are affected by selected aspects of the broader social context.
Economics	This discipline studies the production, distribution, and consumption of goods and services. As with political sociology, sociologists interested in the economy study these issues in a wider social context.
History	Generally focusing on past human behaviour, history includes both careful description and examination of causal processes, usually in narrative form. Although many historians seek generalizations that hold across several specific historical instances, much historical analysis is confined to the study of individual events or sequences. Historical data, although less accessible than current data, can be used by sociologists for their analyses, but often are not.

as drives and motives. (For a comparison of sociology, psychology, and other social sciences, see Chart 1.1.)

In his classic study of nineteenth-century suicide, Durkheim uncovered several differences that pointed to a social cause of suicide: men had higher suicide rates than women, Protestants higher rates than Catholics and Jews, older people higher rates than the young, and single people higher rates than the married (Durkheim, 1897). Durkheim saw the greater frequency of suicide among men, Protestants (see van Poppel and Day, 1996), the older, and the unmarried as due in part to the relative social isolation they experienced. As a group, men were more independent than women; Protestants on average were less integrated into religious communities than Catholics and Jews; the older and the unmarried generally had fewer ties to friends and family than the young and the married. Durkheim argued that these social links, found more frequently in some groups than in

others, act as buffers against suicide. He called the suicides that occur because of the lack of such social ties *egoistic suicides.*

Excessively strong social ties, claimed Durkheim, can also lead to higher suicide rates. This kind of suicide, called *altruistic suicide,* is exemplified by the World War II kamikaze pilots, who chose death for the glory of Japan, or by the members of the Branch Davidian religious sect, who committed suicide in Waco, Texas, in 1993.

Durkheim identified other types of suicide, also with social origins. *Anomic* suicides are found in those societies marked by insufficient rules and regulations, a condition that might arise in times of extensive and rapid social change. In anomic societies individuals experience feelings of unpredictability and of being without limits, and thus may be prone to suicide. *Fatalistic* suicides occur in societies having too many rules and too few options. Individuals in such societies may feel that they are trapped and see suicide as the only way out.

The degree of regulation in society, like the strength of the ties in social groups, is a social and not an individual variable. (Indeed, individuals may be little aware of these conditions.) Thus, in his explanation of suicide, Durkheim demonstrated how social conditions affect human behaviour. Note how sociologists are concerned with *rates* of behaviour—for example, suicides among men, and not the suicide of any one man—and with group differences, comparing, for example, the suicide rates of married versus single adults (Trovato, 1991).

At the same time, neither Durkheim nor sociologists today argue that behaviour is fully determined by the common experiences that may arise from group membership. Sociologists accept individual free will; people can and do make choices. But the social environment also affects behaviour, and if the conditions found in some groups are unlike the conditions in other groups, different behaviour may result. Thus, rates of behaviour (e.g.,

of suicide, divorce, or alcoholism) in various groups (e.g., men and women, Canadians and Americans) may differ according to these differing circumstances.

Suicide is obviously only one of the topics examined by sociologists. In later chapters, additional social facts will be examined in depth. But first let us present a brief discussion of the historical forces that led to the development of sociology and then take a look at its major theoretical approaches.

Sociology: Its Modern Origins and Varieties

Although sociology existed in various forms in the Western world prior to the eighteenth century (and probably in other parts of the world as well), the

Sociology—A Very Broad Field

Sociologists can and do study just about all aspects of human behaviour. The topics of their research range from the difference between birthday cards intended for women and those intended for men (Brabant and Mooney, 1989) to such crucial issues as the relationship between race and ethnicity and disease (see Clarke, 1990). This text will offer you many sociological insights, including how watching television affects people, the myths and reality of gender differences, how wealth is distributed in our country, the changing face of immigration, the effects of divorce on children, New Age religion, First Nations' protest movements, and the forms of work organization. Below is a selection of other discoveries taken from papers presented at recent conferences of sociologists. As you will

see, they all reflect Durkheim's belief that social structure and group membership affect behaviour.

- Infants born to women with higher education, economic status, and autonomy are more likely to survive their first year of life.
- While parents in Korea prefer the birth of a son, those in Jamaica prefer the birth of a daughter.
- Protestant fundamentalists are becoming more accepting of equality for women.
- Self-identified lesbians are no more likely than other women in the population to have suffered childhood or sexual abuse, suggesting that such mistreatment is not a cause.
- People who feel that they are worse off than others have a greater tendency to exhibit neg-

ative attitudes toward new immigrants.
- Negative experiences with condoms discourage many men from subsequent use, even those men with multiple sexual partners.
- Regardless of academic ability, children born closely spaced together in time are less likely to pursue higher education than those children born at longer intervals.
- Gossip is a weapon likely to emerge where the principals to the conflict are equals, intimate, and socially homogeneous and where there is no formalized authority structure.

Source: *Adapted from various recent Sociological Abstracts, San Diego, CA: Sociological Abstracts Inc.*

The Industrial Revolution heralded a new economy and a radically new organization of work.

French and Industrial revolutions kindled its modern development. Each caused upheavals in traditional European life: the French Revolution expanded the potential for democracy; the Industrial Revolution led to a new economy, the further growth of trade and cities, and a radically new organization of work. One result of these two upheavals was that relatively small, simple, rural societies—based on family and tradition, an accepted hierarchy of authority, and at least an outward appearance of consensus—gave way to more urbanized, heterogeneous, dynamic societies, marked by increasing conflict and growing social problems.

At about the same time as these social changes were occurring, science and scientific explanations, products of the Enlightenment, were increasingly supplanting religion and theological explanations of natural phenomena. Where earlier explanations were rooted in religious dogma based on authority and faith, scientific explanations were based on observation and on reason. (For one view of science, see Chart 1.2.) Many people optimistically felt that, just as science had revolutionized industrial

production, a science of society, applied to the ills and growing pains of the emerging societies, could bring them to new heights of cooperation, good will, and orderly growth. Credited by some as its founder, Auguste Comte (1798–1857) saw sociology as both a secular religion and a science. Sociologists would be its "priests" who would guide societies through turbulent times and suggest solutions to their social problems. The decline of traditional religion, which tended to see society as divinely fixed and unchangeable and social ills as part of God's will, made possible this new discipline. The excesses of the French Revolution—exemplified by the reign of terror and mass executions—and of the Industrial Revolution—as seen in the conditions of early factories—made the development of this new discipline seem mandatory. Thus was born the modern science of sociology (see Curtis, 1992).

Almost immediately after its birth, disagreements arose concerning the approach to research that sociology should take. (This topic will be discussed more fully in Chapter 2, Research Methods.) There were also disputes over the extent to which group membership determines behaviour

CHART 1.2   Characteristics of Science[1]

Empirical
Science is empirical, that is, based on observation and experience. Faith, intuition, and common sense may be sources of ideas, but science demands that such insights be subjected to empirical testing.

Explanatory
Science not only describes empirical reality but also uses laws and theories to explain why events occur, and in so doing, follows the rules of logic. For example, if groups with few social ties have relatively higher suicide rates, and if Protestants are such a group, then it is predicted that Protestants will experience higher suicide rates. This is sometimes called the "covering law" model of scientific explanation.

Simple, parsimonious, and elegant
Science prefers simple to complex explanations and seeks to explain the largest number of diverse kinds of observations with the fewest possible laws and theories. Hence Durkheim, for example, explained higher suicide rates among very diverse groups—men, Protestants, the elderly, and singles-with a single theory. Simple, parsimonious explanations are often said to be elegant and are admired by scientists in the same way that a work of art is admired.

Predictive
Science generally involves stating with a certain degree of probability that if certain events occur, others will follow. In sociology these predictions are not predictions of any one individual's behaviour but focus on group rates of behaviour, for example, on suicide rates among Protestants.

Pure versus applied
Science can be pure, seeking only the acquisition of knowledge, or it can be applied, concerned with putting that knowledge to use. Sociologists do not fully agree on this issue: some seek only descriptions and explanations, others use sociological insights in their attempts to solve social problems.

[1]The above description is best seen as only one view rather than as a universal description of scientific practice. In recent years historians and sociologists have compared this ideal with studies of how science actually is, and has been, conducted in practice, revealing significant discrepancies (see Dupré, 1993).

and how societies are structured. We shall discuss this last topic first.

Some early sociologists, among them Durkheim, argued that society is based on consensus and cooperation. A modern society is structured like a human body: a collection of organs, each performing a necessary function. Implicit in this view was the idea that the various segments of society (organs) work for the benefit of society as a whole (the body) and, hence, that social ills are temporary phenomena curable by appropriate "medicines" and "repairs."

Others, such as Karl Marx (1818–1883), rejected this analogy and saw society as made up of individuals and groups held together by society's strongest members, who use their power to coerce the weaker elements of society. In this account, social ills are chronic and serious, built into the very structure of society. Cures can only come from radical social change in which the powerful are forcibly overthrown and a more cooperative society established.

Put more simply, some believe societies to be founded upon consensus and cooperation, while others assert that power, coercion, and conflict mark their existence. Proponents of these two alternatives, historically known as **functionalism** (or structural-functionalism) and **conflict theory**, respectively, became major protagonists, each fighting to make their perspective dominant in the new science of society. Later, a third ("micro") approach emerged, called **symbolic interactionism**, followed by a range of feminist approaches. In the sections that follow, we shall examine each in turn.

Functionalism

Functionalism generally accepts the cooperation viewpoint and originally borrowed three major concepts from biology and medicine: function, equilibrium, and development. The term *function*, first of all, means that social arrangements exist because they somehow benefit society, and points to the importance of each part of society for the functioning and health of the whole. (Note the biological analogy with the parts of the body working together for the benefit of the whole organism.) Following this logic, functionalists could even argue, for example, that female prostitution (male prostitution was generally ignored) is beneficial and functional for society (see Davis, 1937). The general functionalist position is that if something persists in society, especially, as in the case of prostitution, in spite of widespread disapproval, then it must serve a function. If it served no function it would disappear.

Specifically, the argument that prostitution is functional begins with the assumption that men possess more sexual energy than can be accommodated in marital structures. Prostitution is seen as an outlet for some of this excess sexual energy—a business arrangement, quickly concluded, and demanding little or no emotional involvement. Affairs with single women or women married to other men, on the other hand, while satisfying such sexual needs, also would generally require greater emotional attachment and last longer. As such they pose a greater threat to family stability. Therefore, prostitution is beneficial or functional for a society in that it decreases the potential for family disruption and divorce. We shall return in a few paragraphs to a viewpoint that soundly rejects these arguments. A functionalist explanation of sexual jealousy among males will also be examined in Chapter 3, Culture.

Peace and consensus are seen as the natural states of society. Its ability to adapt to occasional, temporary, and minor problems, called **dysfunctions**, and return to a balanced arrangement is called **equilibrium**. Furthermore, because society is in equilibrium, the effects of a change in any one part of society will be felt in other parts of society. For example, eliminating prostitution might lead not only to more family disruption, but also, according to functionalist logic, to greater premarital sexual activity and even to increased rates of sexual assault.

Finally, the concept of development or progress is often, although not always, implied in functionalist thought. Social change is seen as gradual and usually in the direction of both greater *differentiation*, the development of new social forms, and functional integration. Through time, society adapts to its problems and is improved in the process. Thus, to return to our prostitution example, excess sexual energy is a dysfunction; society differentiates (creates) the occupation of prostitute to provide for a return to equilibrium; the family remains intact, and society is even improved, since unbroken families are presumed to raise happier, healthier, more productive children than do disrupted families. Once created, prostitution survives only so long as it is functional; should it cease to be so, it would disappear.

Sociology—A Liberal Discipline?

Informal reports suggest that the social sciences, and sociology in particular, encourage liberal thought. Is this true?

Baer and Lambert (1990) concluded, based on responses from a national sample of Canadian adults, that people who have studied social sciences at university are indeed less likely than people who studied business and the professions to endorse a conservative ideology with respect to the profit motive, the military, big business, and rights of labour. They are also more likely to support government expenditures for social welfare programs.

Baer and Lambert pointed out, however, that business and professional schools may encourage conservative views, pulling their students to the right, rather than social science courses pulling theirs to the left. They also caution that francophone sociology may be more critical and more activist than sociology in other parts of Canada, and thus more radical. For those interested in reading more on this topic, see Baer and Lambert in Vol. 27: 487–504, of the *Canadian Review of Sociology and Anthropology*, and a rejoinder in that same journal, Vol. 31: 184–195.

Conflict theory

In contrast to theories of cooperation like functionalism, **conflict theory** suggests that power, not functional interdependence, holds a society together; that conflict, not harmony, is society's natural state; and that revolutions and radical upheavals, not gradual development, fuel social change and improvement. According to this view, inequality is the major source of social conflict and is something to be eradicated, not applauded as in the functionalist argument, which sees inequality as necessary to ensure that society's difficult jobs will be filled (see Chapter 6, Social Stratification). Society is viewed as composed of groups acting competitively rather than cooperatively, exploiting and being exploited rather than each fulfilling a function for the whole society.

Reacting to functionalists, a common question raised by conflict sociologists is, "Functional for whom?" Conflict sociologists believe existing social arrangements benefit the powerful—such as capitalists and religious or political leaders, usually men, struggling among themselves for dominance—

certainly not all of society. Whatever the split, whether it be environmentalists and loggers, anglophone and francophone Canadians, students and teachers, there is division and conflict. At the same time, conflict theorists generally do admit to some degree of consensus and cooperation—otherwise society would fall apart—but then suggest that this agreement results from coercion and domination.

In perhaps the best-known example of conflict theory—and it should be emphasized that Marxism represents only one of several conflict perspectives—Marx argued that contemporary society is held together by capitalist domination, which pits the proletariat (workers) against the bourgeoisie (owners of capital) in a constant struggle for the profit from labour. He saw the relative calm of such societies as based not on consensus or functional interdependence, as functionalists might argue, but on the capitalists' coercion of the proletariat and the workers' lack of awareness of their own exploitation. Only through revolution, Marx argued, can workers ever hope to change the capitalist-dominated structure of society. (These themes will be explored in Chapter 6, Social Stratification.)

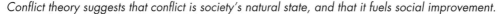

Conflict theory suggests that conflict is society's natural state, and that it fuels social improvement.

Going back to the female prostitution example, a conflict view would see prostitution not as serving a social need but as marked by power and coercion. Prostitutes are victims forced to work under degrading and dangerous conditions, competing for clients. They are paid as little as possible by their male customers, and much of that is taken by male pimps. Male police officers arrest female prostitutes more often than their male clients. Thus, from a conflict perspective, prostitutes are best viewed as another example of females exploited by males (Lowman, 1992). A radical overhaul of sex roles in society is required to modify the traditionally male-dominated arrangement of prostitution. Such an overhaul might lead, if not to an end to sexual exploitation, then at least to the decriminalization of soliciting or to equal treatment, by the police and judiciary, of prostitutes and their customers.

Symbolic interactionism and the micro perspective

Despite their different views of society, one emphasizing cooperation, the other conflict, both functional and conflict theorists share a tendency to downplay the influence of individual actors in their analyses. These theorists have a "macro" focus, concerned more with groups or societies and their interrelationships. Moreover, both functionalist and conflict theorists generally see individuals as shaped by the groups and societies to which they belong, rather than the other way around.

There is much truth to the macro point of view. After all, each of us is born into a preexisting society with its own way of life, and into particular groups such as families, ethnic/linguistic communities, social classes, and even nations that shape us. At the same time, we know that individual actions can and do affect the larger group. Compare the leadership provided by Nelson Mandela in urging South Africans to overcome racial divisions with that provided by Slobodan Milosevic in exploiting ethnic divisions in Yugoslavia. Obviously we are dealing here with a "chicken and egg" situation; societies and cultures make individuals who make societies and cultures that make individuals, and so on. Unlike most functionalist and conflict theorists, however, some microsociologists prefer to begin their analyses with individuals and their interactions.

Rather than viewing individuals in terms of a mechanical analogy in which they are pushed and pulled around by social forces as did Durkheim in his work on suicide for example, microsociologists view individuals as active *agents*. Individuals have goals, objectives, purposes, intentions, motives, or

Symbolic interactionism focuses on individuals and the autonomy of their behaviour.

utility functions (the precise terminology hardly matters) as well as knowledge and expectations about which kinds of behaviours are most likely to achieve them. As a much-quoted aphorism puts it, "People act from reasons not causes" (Landman, 1967).

In conducting their research, many micro-sociologists emphasize the subjective over the objective. If we were in a room together looking at the furniture, we probably would not have much difficulty in agreeing that X is a table and Y is a chair. Variation in these observations (table versus chair) would be largely attributable to differences in what is being observed rather than among observers. In other instances, however, the reverse is the case. The same falling snow can be seen happily by a groups of skiers, fearfully by others who have to drive in it, romantically by still others who watch it coating the trees, and resentfully by those who must shovel it. Behaviour and attitudes therefore can depend upon how individuals *perceive*, *define*, or *construct* their social world. In sum, variations in observations can be attributed to variations in the observed, or the observers, or some proportion of each.

While to some, all this may simply suggest popular ideas about "free will," a variety of schools of microsociology have explored more sophisticated understandings of the nature of individual-level processes and interaction, including their subjective aspects. One of the earliest and still influential schools of microsociology, **symbolic interactionism**, was founded by George Herbert Mead (1934). Symbolic interactionists claim that, unlike other animals, humans think and interact on the basis of information encoded in strings of symbols, such as sentences in a language like French or American Sign Language. A symbol is something that stands for or represents something else and in which there is no intrinsic connection between symbol and what it signifies. Hence, while a red light means stop and a green light means go, it could conceivably have been the reverse; the connection is an accident of history. According to Blumer (1969) the premises of symbolic interactionism are that humans act toward things on the basis of the meanings that the things have for them; meanings arise out of social interaction with others; and meanings are handled and modified through an interpretive process.

Later, other microsociologists such as Homans (1950) took their cue about the nature of individual-level processes and interaction from the psychology of *learning*. According to **learning theory**, individuals learn in a variety of ways, for example, by association, or through reward and punishment. Such individual-level learning processes can form the basis of a social theory to explain social life by noting that, beyond the physical environment, those with whom we interact are the source of most of the rewards and punishments that people experience. We mutually shape each other's behaviour. Moreover, in addition to such individual-level learning processes, psychologists have also investigated social learning processes such as observation and instruction. Through prodding, reinforcing, and punishing each other in myriad subtle and some not-so-subtle ways, we show each other and tell each other what and how to do things.

Still more recently, other microsociologists such as Coleman (1990) took their cue about the nature of individual-level processes and interaction from the *rational choice approach* of microeconomists. According to **rational choice theory**, the principles of microeconomics are applicable whatever the objective, including explaining social behaviour. At issue may not be money, but power, prestige, even motherhood or a reputation for saintliness. Among these principles, the most important is the *marginal value theorem*. According to this theorem, a rational actor will allocate energy, time, or other resources among alternative courses of action in such a way that the satisfaction received from the last (i.e., marginal, or least desirable) unit (course of action) allocated is equal to the others. Typically, although the satisfaction received per unit allocated to any one course of action may increase initially, sooner or later it tends to decline (think of how the amount of satisfaction you receive from eating an ice cream cone declines with each additional cone eaten and may even become negative, i.e., make you sick).

If, in addition, the outcome for any one individual depends upon what others choose, a more complicated theory called *game theory* is required to predict behaviour. For example, if professors tend to teach more successfully or give higher marks in smaller classes, then your choice of a psychology or a sociology course might be influenced not only by their relative costs (e.g., how much work is required) and their relative marginal utility (e.g., how much more knowledge or contribution to your academic record would be gained from an additional course in one or the other), but also by what others are choosing. You could thus be influenced to choose what is least popular to get into a smaller class and get a higher grade.

In their analyses, micro sociologists are as interested in cooperation and conflict as are macro sociologists. Rational actors may choose to cooperate with other actors, working together or engaging in exchanges of various kinds, or they may choose to exploit others, depending upon the conditions. The rational choice approach and the individual learning approach present yet another chicken and egg situation. What we want and think influences what we learn, which influences what we want and think, and so forth. Different theorists, however, choose to begin the story at different points.

Elements of various sociologies (such as symbolic interactionism, learning theory, and rational choice theory) are present in the work of some classical nineteenth-century social theorists. Gabriel Tarde (1903), a French sociologist and contemporary of Durkheim, opposed Durkheim's rather mechanical conception of social forces in his work on suicide. Instead, Tarde argued that *imitation*—what today we would call social learning—is the basic social fact. Tarde was a judge for many years and became convinced that criminals learn to be criminals from other criminals—that being a criminal is a profession. A German sociologist, Georg Simmel, was very interested in exchange processes in social interaction (Wolff, 1950). Another, even better known German sociologist, Max Weber, believed that sociologists must be able to empathize (to put themselves in the place of those they study) and attempt to understand, given the actor's goals and interpretations of their situation, the reasons for their actions. For example, in his classic study of the origins of capitalism, *The Protestant Ethic and the Spirit of Capitalism* (1904–05), Weber argued not only from a societal or macro perspective that the doctrine of Protestantism was associated with capitalism (in the same sense that Durkheim argued that Protestantism was associated with suicide) but also from a micro perspective that the link between

the two was subjectively understandable and traceable to Protestants' interpretation of their worldly role. While elements of various micro theories were present in the nineteenth century, these were more fully developed in the twentieth century. In recent years sociologists have become very interested in whether and how macro sociological approaches dealing with groups and entire societies and micro sociological approaches dealing with individuals and their interactions can be integrated with each other, or at least used to inform each other. Much remains to be accomplished in this respect.

Feminist theories

As you will read in Chapter 7, Gender Relations, there is no one "feminism." While all feminists would agree that gender inequality exists, they may disagree on its causes and thus on any "solutions." Some seek radical measures, others pursue more minor adjustments to current arrangements. Correspondingly, there is also no one feminist sociology. Still, it is the most important of the recent perspectives in sociology. Feminist sociology may be broadly defined as one "of" women from their standpoint and "for" women in the political sense of change (cf. Madoo-Lengermann and Niebrugge, 1996). The first question asked in this approach is always, "And what about the women?" The most general answer is that women are different, unequal, and oppressed, although their differentness, inequality, and oppression may vary by women's other characteristics such as race, social class, age, and sexual orientation, among others. Feminist sociology also does not treat gender as one variable among many, as for example Durkheim did in his study of suicide. Instead, the main focus is directly on gender, because gender crosscuts all aspects of social life.

Along with its focus on women, there is within feminist sociology a general consensus in at least four other areas. First, it tends to be more politically activist than other types of sociology; for example, it has been successful in raising public consciousness. Certainly everyone is more aware of spousal violence, date rape, and stalking, with growing numbers aware of the genital mutilation of women practised in some societies.

Second, feminist sociology is more inter-disciplinary than other types of sociology. Gender is important in all fields, including economics, history, anthropology, literature, science, and art. As a consequence, feminist sociologists are linked to scholars in these and other fields, more so than is the case for other sociologists. (According to Eichler and Tite [1990], they also tend to be the leaders in these interdisciplinary approaches.)

Third, feminist sociology is more accepting of a broader range of approaches to research. (For a discussion of female-friendly science, see Chapter 2, Research Methods.) Practitioners see knowledge as partial and interested, affected by power relations and discovered from a point of view, not total and objective. Thus it would be related as "I learned" rather than "the data revealed."

Finally, feminist approaches are less constrained by traditional divisions in sociology and often use aspects from different sociological perspectives. While very few feminist sociologists claim to be functionalists—it would be very difficult to find one who would defend a division of labour based upon gender as representing a consensual and mutually beneficial arrangement—many feminist sociologists are comfortable with some aspects of both symbolic interactionism and the various conflict approaches. Using the former, some practitioners might be concerned with how women and men learn to be feminine and masculine. But there are important disagreements too. Symbolic interactionism is not political enough for many and, worse, it distorts the experience of women, too often assuming that male perceptions of reality are the "norm."

From conflict theory, some focus on political economy and capitalism, as did Marx, and others on the system of male dominance or patriarchy; still others look to both as sources. (These topics are further discussed in Chapter 7, Gender Relations.) But compared with other conflict theorists, feminist sociologists examine the oppression of women more than the oppression of class, and expand "production" to include noneconomic forms ignored by traditional Marxists, including housework, mothering, and "invisible" work—those informal, hidden, and often devalued aspects of social life more often assigned to women.

All four models—cooperation theories like functionalism, conflict theory, micro sociologies like symbolic interactionism, and feminism—are popular in sociology today. A sociologist's specific choice of model depends in part on the phenomenon being examined. A conflict approach may best explain far-reaching and rapid social change, while functionalism may be used to understand long-lasting, stable, and widespread phenomena. The area of study is important too. Symbolic interactionism is frequently applied to the subject of learning (see Chapter 4, Socialization) while conflict theory is generally not stressed, although it could be. In the case of inequality (see Chapter 6, Social Stratification; Chapter 7, Gender Relations; and Chapter 8, Race and Ethnic Relations) the position is generally reversed. Feminist perspectives are appearing more frequently in all areas of sociology. Generally speaking, however, more than one approach is usually necessary for a full understanding of human behaviour.

Sociology in Canada

In its earliest phase, sociology in both English and French Canada scarcely existed as a discipline. While in American universities, under the influence of the Protestant-based "social gospel" movement for social reform, sociology was widely established by the turn of the century, the same movement in English Canada initially produced only a few courses in some Baptist colleges, along with some Methodist- and Presbyterian-sponsored social research (Campbell, 1983). Similarly, in French Canada, although the French Catholic sociologist and social reformer Frédéric LePlay gained an audience among some French Canadian intellectuals interested in Catholic social doctrines, the church-controlled educational institutions in Quebec were hostile to Durkheimian-style sociology (Rocher, 1977).

Eventually, however, sociology took hold in both English and French Canada. Both communities were influenced by the "human ecology" approach of Robert Park at the University of Chicago and his student Roderick McKenzie, eventually at the University of Michigan (Shore, 1987). While some Canadians obtained early Ph.D.s at Columbia University in New York City as well, their influence was, however, less far-reaching (Cormier, 1997). The human ecology approach studies the geographical distribution or zones and natural history (succession and change) of the components of communities. With reference to our earlier discussion, this school's approach to sociology is a mixture of conflict and functional approaches. Change begins with an "invasion" from one zone to another, for example, when a shopping mall is built in a residential neighbourhood. Competition ensues between developers and residents (both conflict phenomena), but eventually an accommodation is reached. This accommodation could involve a buffer zone—for example, the planting of trees and the construction of small hills to separate the two areas. A symbiotic (mutually beneficial) relationship and equilibrium are then restored, both functional phenomena (see Shore, 1987: 109–112).

The first sociology department in Canada was established at McGill University in 1925 under Charles A. Dawson, trained at the University of Chicago and co-author of the first Canadian sociology textbook, although the extent of the department's independence continued to fluctuate for some years thereafter (Helmes-Hayes, 1994; Palantzas, 1991). It was not until some years later that a group of francophone social scientists assembled at Laval, where a department encompassing ethics and sociology was founded in 1943 (becoming a Sociology department in 1951). In the 1940s the Laval group came under the leadership of Jean-Charles Falardeau, the first professionally trained sociologist in francophone Canada. Falardeau declared, "We ought to start looking at French Canada as no longer an entity to save, but as a reality to know" (quoted in Dumas, 1987: 122).

From these two Quebec departments, the first classics of Canadian sociology emerged. In subject matter they examined a range of national issues including, for example, Dawson's studies of the settlement process in western Canadian communities, and the work of Everett Hughes (first affiliated with McGill and later with Laval as well) on modernization and ethnic relations in "Cantonville" (Drummondville), a textile town in Quebec. Hughes came to be known as one of the great sociologists of his time, and his *French Canada in Transition* (1943) remains an international classic in the discipline.

Not surprisingly, like other aspects of Canadian history, society, and culture, the early American influence on sociology was supplemented with a British one. In addition to Dawson and Hughes, the McGill department in its early years included Leonard Marsh. Marsh had been educated at the London School of Economics, founded to conduct empirical social research and education in the service of socialism. Marsh's teacher there, William (later Lord) Beveridge, became the architect of the British social security system. Similarly, Marsh's early research at McGill, on Canadians "in and out of work" during the Great Depression, had a lasting impact on Canadian society (Helmes-Hayes and Wilcox-Magill, 1993). In 1932 he helped found The League for Social Reconstruction, a forerunner of the CCF and, hence, the New Democratic Party. The recommendations of his *Report on Social Security for Canada* (1943) for the federal government laid the foundation for the Canadian social security system, including family allowances and unemployment insurance.

In 1949, John Porter returned from the London School of Economics to Carleton College (now Carleton University) in Ottawa. Sixteen years later he produced *The Vertical Mosaic: An Analysis of Social Class and Power in Canada* (1965), which became another international classic of Canadian sociology. In it Porter argued that although Canada may be an ethnic and cultural mosaic (a picture made up of small pieces), it is an unequal or vertically stratified one-hence the "vertical mosaic" of the title, a phrase that Marsh had used many years before. We shall have more to say on these topics in Chapter 6, Social Stratification, and Chapter 8, Race and Ethnic Relations.

A second legacy of the British influence on Canadian sociology was to slow its spread beyond Quebec. In Britain, sociology was commonly viewed as an ahistorical and "shallow American discipline" (Hiller, 1982: 3; see also Clark, 1975). Thus, although from the 1930s through the 1950s research that can be viewed as sociological was performed in anglophone Canada, it was usually conducted in history, political economy, and even humanities departments; sociology departments just did not exist. The most important stream of this research, and one usually considered native to Canada, was performed at the University of Toronto by Harold Innis and later by S.D. Clark and Marshall McLuhan. Even there, however, the Chicago connection was stronger than has sometimes been supposed (Shore, 1987).

Harold Innis, a historical and institutional economist whom you will encounter in Chapter 16, Social Change, was trained at the University of Chicago economics department and influenced by Chicago-style sociological theory. In a trilogy of monographs on mining, the fur trade, and the cod fishery published after 1930, Innis argued that changes in demand for staple products (such as fur, fish, timber, iron ore, and wheat), the physical properties of the staples themselves, the technological means by which they are processed, and their geographical locations relative to transportation and markets shape not only economic but also political and social organization. For example, Innis maintained that the political boundaries of Canada were created by the demand for furs in Europe, the ease with which they were over-exploited in any particular area, the geography of the pre-Cambrian shield and river systems, and the canoe as a means of transportation. He also

argued that the perishability of cod, the coastal location of the resource, and the technology for curing it created the characteristic geographical distribution and social organization of Canada's east coast, with its numerous, small, scattered fishing villages.

Late in his life, Innis turned from the study of the transportation of goods to the communication of information. He concluded that the physical properties of media, like those of staple goods, had enormous consequences. He contrasted, for example, the relative permanence but unportability of stone and clay tablets with the relative portability but impermanence of papyrus and paper. Innis's work on communications media then influenced a fellow University of Toronto professor, an English professor, who became (along with Northrop Frye, the literary critic) Canada's most internationally celebrated scholar—Marshall McLuhan.

In *The Gutenberg Galaxy: The Making of Typographic Man* (1962) and *Understanding Media: The Extensions of Man* (1964), McLuhan argued that

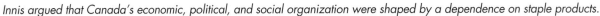

Innis argued that Canada's economic, political, and social organization were shaped by a dependence on staple products.

the dominant force in political, social, and cultural change in human history had been changes in the dominant medium of communication—from oral to written to electronic (see Chapter 12, Media). Various media are extensions of specific human senses; whatever medium predominates distorts perceptions in favour of a specific sense. Consequently, media shape not only the economic, political, social, and cultural environment but also the very nature of human consciousness. McLuhan's thesis was almost instantly recognized as the most original idea since Marx's attempt to explain all of human history with the concept of class conflict. "The medium is the message" briefly and clearly stated its central thesis, while phrases such as "the Gutenberg galaxy" and "the global village" succinctly communicated McLuhan's view that those steeped in a print rather than an electronic culture to all intents and purposes inhabit different universes (see Marchand, 1989). Although McLuhan himself always maintained a rich network of multidisciplinary contacts, friends, and associates, the fairly rapid creation of separate communications departments within universities caused the study of communications to have less influence on sociology and the other social sciences than it might otherwise have had.

Meanwhile, a student of Innis's, Samuel D. Clark, led a small group of sociologists out of the department of political economy at the University of Toronto to establish the first department of sociology in Canada outside of Quebec. For many years, Clark was Canada's best-known sociologist. Educated first at the University of Saskatchewan and then at the London School of Economics, McGill's sociology department, and finally under Innis in political economy at Toronto, Clark owed something to all of these influences. *Church and Sect in Canada* (1948) and *Movements of Political Protest in Canada* (1959), for example, include an Innis-style setting of new areas of economic exploitation (in the Canadian west), social disorganization (religious sects and political protest), and a Chicago-style focus on restoration of equilibrium in social organization.

By the early 1960s, sociology was tenuously established in Canada. Institutionally it was still limited to Quebec and Toronto. Intellectually it had inherited an interest in the structure of entire communities from the Chicago-style sociology of the 1920s. Yet it often combined this focus with political economy and with a historical approach, to take into account change on much longer time-scales than was common in Chicago-style sociology.

In the 1960s, the baby-boom generation came of age and, simultaneously, governments decided that continued economic prosperity depended on a higher proportion of university-educated people. As a consequence new universities, including new sociology departments, sprang up around the country, creating an unprecedented demand in Canada for university teachers of sociology. Large numbers of foreign sociologists, primarily American, immigrated to Canada to take up the newly created positions. By 1970–71, 60 percent of sociology and anthropology professors in Canada were not Canadian citizens (Hiller, 1982: 25). Such mass immigration could not fail to be disruptive, as any community- and ecology-minded sociologist would predict. Conflicts were initiated, some of which have never been resolved entirely.

In English-speaking Canada, the new faculty members came into conflict with those already there, and not infrequently with each other, as the imported American sociologists were not a homogeneous group. They reflected the many sociologies being practised in the United States. At Harvard, for example, Parsons had been producing his grand theoretical synthesis, integrating a free will/voluntaristic (as opposed to deterministic) view of human action with the kinds of social forces emphasized in the European classics (1937, 1951). At the opposite pole from such "grand theory," a whole technology of polling and survey research had been developed and had spread outward from Columbia University to many other American universities. If some Canadian sociologists thought Chicago-style studies of communities were too ahistorical, one can imagine what they thought of sociologists whose idea of research was almost exclusively to administer surveys of attitudes and beliefs! (This and other research options will be discussed in Chapter 2, Research Methods.) Political conflicts, too, were not uncommon. For some of the newcomers, the move to Canada was a straight-forward professional one. For others it was an abandonment of a society they viewed as hopelessly racist and war-mongering (this was the period of America's involvement in Vietnam). For still others it was an escape from the protesting students on American campuses. One can imagine the sparks that flew when protesters and the protested-against sometimes found themselves colleagues in the same department. And last but not least, both the old and the newly arrived professors often came into conflict with their students—the old because the sociology of communities did not seem to address the conflict-ridden times adequately, and the new because their knowledge of and sometimes even interest in Canadian society was often elementary at best, at least initially (Hiller, 1979).

As a result of some of these problems, the Association of Universities and Colleges of Canada established a commission on Canadian Studies in 1975. Their report, *To Know Ourselves*, stated that "a curriculum in this country that does not help Canadians in some way to understand the physical and social environment that they live and work in...cannot be justified" (Symons, 1976: 13). This in turn led to federal attempts to place limits on the hiring of foreign academics by Canadian universities. To this day the movement of the 1970s to "Canadianize" university curricula and personnel remains contentious—viewed as hurtful by some and too cautious and incomplete by others (Hofley, 1992).

In Quebec the changes and conflicts were somewhat different, but equally dramatic. The same demographic and economic forces were at work as in English-speaking Canada, but during the "Quiet Revolution" (see Chapter 14, Social Movements) the state took over responsibility for education from the Catholic church. As a result, the number of sociologists increased and departments were added—first at the Université de Montréal and later elsewhere, for example at the Université du Québec at Montreal (Dumas, 1987). Because of the language difference, however, Quebec imported fewer Americans and relied more on people without doctorates and on French Canadians trained in France or the United States. Conflict in Quebec was often associated with the addition of new departments, which tended to put forth, in their early days, different interpretations of Quebec society (Renaud et al., 1989). The earlier "modernizing" view, which had predominated at Laval, was displaced by various Marxist interpretations and by an analysis of Quebec as at once

a distinct ("global") society and an ethnic minority—even an "ethnic class" within Canada (Dumas, 1987).

Rocher described how, until about the mid-1960s, "among most of my Quebec francophone colleagues, there was the sense of belonging to a Canadian Sociology and the desire to establish ties and active relationships with anglophone colleagues in other provinces. We felt the need to share with them the fruits of our research and our endeavours" (Rocher, 1992: 66). Gradually, however, English-language and Quebec sociology in Canada went their own ways, with different journals, professional associations, and intellectual concerns. Rocher (1992) documented this decline in interaction, which he viewed as mirroring the crisis of the "two solitudes" in the larger Canadian society. He related it to a growing preoccupation by Quebec sociologists with changes within Quebec society, their increasing interaction with francophones beyond Canada, and the increasing anglophone unilingualism of Canadian professional meetings (although Canadian Sociology and Anthropology Association (CSAA) publications remain bilingual). Today there exist major differences between the two sociologies. For example, sociology proper in Quebec has remained concerned almost exclusively with macro sociological questions (Breton, 1989: 563). Associated with this emphasis, according to Béland and Blais (1989), is the infrequent use of quantitative methods in sociology in Quebec. Morris (1991) also found in Quebec sociology a greater emphasis on social policy and on applied rather than pure sociology. For a final example, perhaps because of the greater availability of funding for social research at the provincial level in Quebec, sub-specialties of sociology (such as criminology, demography, and urban and regional studies) have tended to become independently institutionalized there (Juteau and Maheu, 1989: 371).

Future Challenges

French Canada in Transition, The Vertical Mosaic, and *Understanding Media,* among others, are classics of social scientific and sociological scholarship, each contributing in its time to our understanding of ourselves. It remains to be seen whether sociologists

Careers in Sociology

Later in this book you will read about postsecondary education. For now, let us assume that you are attending school not only for the enjoyment of learning and to gain the credentials necessary to validate your claim to be an educated person, but also as an avenue to an interesting, well-paying job, one that will give you freedom to express your creative talents.

Sociology graduates work in a wide variety of occupations, especially in education, social service agencies, and other government departments. They apply the critical and creative thinking skills they developed in sociology to teaching and research, helping to explain social phenomena; to social welfare programs, seeking to improve people's lives; to the criminal justice system; and to social movements and private organizations working for a better society. Whether as personnel or communications managers, as designers or analysts of opinion polls, they generally share an appreciation for the social factors that affect individual behaviour and an optimism for the possibility of social change.

Source: Adapted from Scott Davies, Clayton Mosher, and Bill O'Grady, 1992. "Canadian sociology and anthropology graduates in the 1980s labour market." Society, 16: 39-46.

of this generation in Canada, many of whom began their careers in the 1960s, will be able to leave a comparable legacy. Clearly, the time for judgment is fast approaching: the wave of retirements that is underway among university sociologists is coinciding with astonishing changes both internationally and nationally. Can this generation of sociologists, Canadian or otherwise, provide insights into such issues as:

- the consequences of accelerating globalization and the continuing gap between rich and poor countries;

- the weakening of existing nation-states, combined with a resurgence of conflict among ethnic/linguistic groups in Europe, the former Soviet Union, and Canada;

- the future of Canadian federalism;

- the continued existence of racial, gender, and age discrimination; and

- last but not least, the consequences of the potential incompatibility between the current and projected size of the human population (and its way of life) and the continued existence of a variety of other species on this planet (see Marchak, 1990).

As you read in the subsequent chapters of this book about the facts that generations of sociologists have already uncovered, and the theories they have offered to explain these facts, perhaps you will make your own tentative judgments.

QUESTIONS FOR REVIEW AND CRITICAL THINKING

1. To what extent should sociology be used to ameliorate the problems of society, rather than simply "study" them?

2. In the study of social phenomena, is objectivity possible? What are some examples of how subjective experience may bias a sociologist's observations?

3. How would a conflict explanation of divorce differ from a functionalist one?

4. Ask your instructors how they became sociologists. Where were they educated? In what kinds of sociology were they trained? What kinds of sociology do they prefer now? How have they experienced the conflicts and changes in Canadian sociology since its beginning

KEY TERMS

conflict theory, p. 6

dysfunctions, p. 7

equilibrium, p. 7

functionalism, p. 6

learning theory, p. 10

rational choice theory, p. 10

social facts, p. 2

symbolic interactionism, p. 6

SUGGESTED READINGS

Carroll, William K., Linda Christiansen-Ruffman, Raymond Currie, and Deborah Harrison (eds.)

1992   *Fragile Truths: 25 Years of Sociology and Anthropology in Canada.* Ottawa: Carleton University Press.

This work contains articles on a variety of topics about sociology in Canada, including its relationship to social change, how sociological knowledge is made (including a look at feminist alternatives and the differences between English and French Canadian sociologies), its academic milieu, and finally its professional association.

Hoecker-Drysdale, Susan

1990   "Women sociologists in Canada: the careers of Helen MacGill Hughes, Aileen Dansken Ross, and Jean Robertson Burnett." Pp. 152–176 in Marianne G. Ainley (ed.), *Despite the Odds: Essays on Canadian Women and Science.* Montreal: Véhicule Press.

This article about the lives and careers of three early Canadian women sociologists tells an all-too-familiar story of obstacles, potential contributions frustrated, and accomplishments made but then often poorly (or only belatedly) rewarded and recognized.

Ritzer, George

1996   *Sociological Theory.* (4th ed.) New York: McGraw-Hill, Inc.

This theory text, although a bit advanced, describes the major early sociologists as well as perspectives in contemporary sociology including functionalist, conflict, symbolic interactionist, and feminist views.

WEB SITES

http://www.sosig.ac.uk/welcome.html

Social Science Information Gateway

This page provides links to dozens of sites of interest and potential use to students of sociology, from sociology associations worldwide, to electronic journals, to information on famous sociologists such as Durkheim.

http://www.mcmaster.ca/socscidocs/othdepta.htm

Sociology and Anthropology Organizations and Departments

At this site, you will find a complete listing of and links to sociology departments at post-secondary institutions in Canada, Canadian sociology journals online, and the Canadian Sociology and Anthropology Association.

CHAPTER 2

Research Methods

James J. Teevan

Introduction

Suppose you wanted to know if Canada's divorce rate is changing, if people are more or less happy after they divorce, what types of people tend to remarry more quickly than others, or what happens to children after their parents get a divorce. One way to find answers to these questions would be to look to your personal experiences (or to those of your friends) or to ask authorities such as your parents, teachers, or religious leaders.

Sociologists are reluctant to use such strategies because of their potential for distortion. For example, though there may have been fewer divorces recently among your family and friends, that does not mean the national rate is going down. Just because it was better for your cousins to be away from the constant fighting of your uncle and aunt does not mean that most children feel better after divorce. The fact that Aunt Liz remarried quickly does not mean that women remarry more quickly than men (the opposite is true). Personal

experience is usually not general enough and, worse, is too often based on selective perception— seeing what you want to see—for it to produce accurate statements about the larger society. Authorities, too, can be wrong or biased in the answers they provide. And finally, what happens when one person's experience or authorities contradict those of another? How is that resolved?

Sociologists thus argue that questions about divorce, and social life in general, require a research project of some sort. They want to collect and analyze data from a wide variety of settings before drawing any conclusions. The different ways that sociologists conduct their research is the topic of this chapter. It begins with an overview of two basic approaches and then presents in more depth an example of each, examining its relationship to theory, its model, forms of measurement, sampling, and data analysis—terms that will be defined below. An evaluation of the advantages and disadvantages of each approach ends the chapter.

Quantitative and Qualitative Methods

As you read in Chapter 1, Durkheim and Weber had quite different ideas on how to conduct research. Durkheim adopted a position called **positivism**, meaning that he wanted to use the research methods of the natural sciences, appropriately adapted, for the social sciences. Durkheim's followers favour what we today call *quantitative* methods. Counting and precise measurement of observable behaviour, concentration on a limited number of variables, and prediction are all hallmarks of a quantitative approach. In an example of quantitative research, Cook and Beaujot (1996) found that while marriage and the presence of young children tend to reduce the probability of leaving the workforce for men, the presence of children increases the chances of work interruptions for women, especially if they are not married.

Most quantitative sociologists never actually observe the behaviour of the people they study. Survey researchers, for example, take only verbal reports of that behaviour from their respondents. Experimenters observe laboratory behaviour, not that found in the real world (see the box "Does Drinking...?"). Thus others advocate an alternate approach, one often now called *qualitative*. An early exponent of qualitative methods, Weber argued that the social sciences should not copy the research methods and experimental designs of the natural sciences but should have their own research methods. Human behaviour is unique, he argued, because of the subjective meanings and motivations attached to it. Human beings are complex and make choices based on these meanings, making any discussion of marriage, children, and work much more involved than was described above. Moreover, sociologists need also to *understand* human behaviour, not just to be able to predict it. Because humans give meanings to their behaviour, because they engage in what Weber called *social action*, or meaningful goal-directed behaviour, the predictions would be incomplete without some understanding and some explanations of the behaviour from the actors' point of view.

To get at these meanings, qualitative sociologists can attempt to understand behaviour using a variety of strategies. For example, they may talk at length and in depth with informants (field interviews) or observe while participating themselves and then perhaps asking the actors about the meaning of their behaviour. This last method is called **participant observation**.

Having introduced quantitative and qualitative approaches generally, let us now turn to a specific quantitative approach.

One quantitative option: Survey research

Survey research is the most common type of research undertaken today and is familiar to most of you in the form of interviews or questionnaires. (See the box on "Content Analysis" for another quantitative option.) It involves asking people questions, either in written or oral form, and recording their answers. Let us now examine its relationship to theory, its model, and strategies for measurement, sampling, and analysis.

Theories and hypotheses

At its most general level, theory refers to the basic approach taken to a subject matter, such as a conflict or feminist approach, mentioned in the last chapter. But these are often very abstract. At a middle level, **theory** gets more specific and is composed of a set of interrelated statements that organizes and summarizes knowledge about some part of the social world. There could, for example, be a theory of crime, or a theory of prejudice. The statements found in these theories are often taken from the conclusions of prior research in which variables are linked to one another or shown to be related. A **variable** for sociologists is something (like income or religion) that takes on different values (varies) in different groups. A relationship between two variables means that they go together in some way, that changes in one accompany changes in the other. For example, level of integration and suicide rates are related, as pointed out in the last chapter, with the over- and under-integrated more prone to self-destruction. Integration and suicide are the variables, and the fact that extremes in integration may encourage suicide constitutes the relationship between them.

Female-Friendly Science

Rosser (1990) studied some of the ways in which women scientists conduct science differently than men do. As part of her research, Prof. Rosser attended conferences, talked with and read biographies and autobiographies of practising women scientists, and consulted the emerging literature on "women's ways of knowing." A more "female-friendly science," she concluded, would change currently dominant practices in observation, data-collection techniques, and analysis.

With respect to observation, she encouraged an expansion of the kinds of observations beyond those traditionally carried out by males to include various interactions, relationships, or events (such as midwifery) not seen or considered worthy of observation by traditional scientists operating from an androcentric (male-centred) perspective. Gender would always be a crucial

part of the questions being asked, but at the same time the context would be widened to encompass a more holistic, global scope along with a greater awareness of other sources of bias such as race, class, sexual orientation, and religion. Finally, more females would appear as subjects in research designs.

Re methods of data gathering, an increase in the number of observations and remaining longer in the observational stage (vs. analysis) would change, along with the use of a combination of qualitative and quantitative, even interdisciplinary, methods. These would be accompanied by the use of more interactive methods that shorten the distance between observer and the object being studied. The key is a sharing of power, less hierarchy, and a participatory construction of knowledge with those being studied.

Re analysis, the development of

theories that are at various levels (e.g., both the individual and social) and multicausal, including reciprocal causes, rather than simpler cause-effect models would be more common.

Finally, female-friendly science would be less competitive, making the role of scientist only one facet to be integrated with other aspects of life, including family life. A greater emphasis on strategies such as teaching and communicating with non-scientists to break down the barriers between science and the layperson would also be apparent.

For more on this and related topics, see work by Canadians such as Eichler (1988) and Reinharz (1992).

Source: Adapted from Sue V. Rosser, 1990. Female-Friendly Science: Applying Women's Studies Methods and Theories to Attract Students. New York: Pergamon Press (Chapter 4).

Testable hypotheses can then be derived from such theories. A **hypothesis** is a statement of a *presumed* relationship between two or more variables, usually stated in the form, "Other things being equal, if A, then B." If the A variable occurs, then the B variable also occurs. The B variable is the one being explained, the A variable the explanation. In causal statements, A is the cause or **independent variable**, B the effect or **dependent variable**. We might hypothesize that, other things being equal, gender (A) is related to a choice of research methods (B), with men more often favouring a quantitative approach and women more often a qualitative one (see Mackie, 1991 and the box "Female-Friendly Science").

Axiomatic and deductive logic are combined to derive such hypotheses from any theory. **Axiomatic logic** involves making connecting links

between related statements, as in, "If A→B and B →C, then A→C." For example, consider the following:

Theoretical statements:

1. Birth order (A) is related to closeness to parents (B) (first-born children are more closely tied to their parents than are later-born).

2. Closeness to parents (B) leads to conservative values (C).

Axiomatic logic:

3. Therefore, birth order (A) is related to conservative values (C) (first-born children more conservative than later-born).

Deductive logic involves deriving a specific statement from a more general statement. Thus, given the general statement that birth order (A) is related to conservative values (C), we can hypothesize that it is related to sexual permissiveness (C1), with first-borns less sexually permissive. The process could continue, with marijuana use being another dependent variable (C2), with the hypothesis that birth order (A) is related to marijuana use (C2) and, specifically, that proportionally fewer first-born children would use marijuana than would later-born.

But remember that hypotheses include the phrase *other things being equal*. That means that, at least *collectively*, the groups studied should be similar in other social characteristics too. In the current example, first- and later-born children should be the same in terms of age, sex, and religiosity, etc. To compare 15-year-old, religious, first-born girls with 20-year-old, atheist, later-born boys would be an unfair test of the effect of birth order on sexual permissiveness. The ideal of "other things being equal" may be difficult to achieve, but must be attempted because some of these variables are also related to sexual permissiveness.

Model

Models show how variables are related to each other, and are built by combining two or more "if A, then B" statements filling in or extending the chain. Thus, one could develop the following model to explain the relationship between social class and violent crime: Social class is related to age of parents at birth of first child (poorer parents have children at a younger age); age of parents is related to marital breakup (the earlier the onset of family responsibilities, the higher the separation rate); broken families are related to children's school difficulties, especially to failing grade one; early school failure is related to delinquency; and finally, delinquency is related to violent adult criminality. For any two variables in this chain, the variable that occurs first is generally assumed to be an independent variable, the later one a dependent variable, and the others the control variables. We shall explain control variables more fully later.

Measurement

Measurement of their variables is probably the most difficult task survey researchers have to perform. Generally it involves transforming the *theoretical* language of the hypothesis into the operational language of measurement. **Operational definitions** describe the actual procedures or operations used to measure theoretical concepts. For example, an I.Q. score is an operational definition of the theoretical concept of intelligence; counting the number of times per month people attend religious services can be an operational definition of religiosity.

The general strategy in operationalizing variables is to devise simple, directly observable or *empirical* measures of things that may be complex, difficult to measure directly, and hard to observe. Operational definitions, therefore, are what researchers look for or listen to in order to measure their variables.

How would you measure prejudice? Can you operationalize that variable? Suppose some of you said that you would measure prejudice by seeing if people did not like certain groups. Would that be an operational definition? No, because you still would not know what to look for. How do you see "not liking"? Would laughing at jokes that make fun of certain groups be an operational definition of that prejudice? Yes it would, because it is observable and relatively clear—both major requirements of an operational definition. It is an empirical measure that can be heard. Alternatively, you could ask: "Are you prejudiced against (insert name of group), yes or no?" That question is also an operational definition, providing an empirical indicator: the "yes" or "no" response.

Some of you probably do not like either of these operational definitions, the first because unprejudiced people may laugh at these jokes, and the second because people may be evasive in their answers or even lie. These objections raise the issue of the **validity** of operational definitions—the degree to which they actually measure what they claim to measure. Validity is always an issue in constructing and using operational definitions.

Besides being valid, operational definitions must also be reliable. **Reliability** means that measures of a variable should be consistent and not change over time or with the person using them. Thermometers, for example, are generally reliable. Operational definitions, however, may lack reliability, as when respondents (1) admit to certain attitudes early in a questionnaire but later on, perhaps because they are growing tired, deny the same attitudes; or (2) tailor their responses to the person asking the questions, for example when female interviewers get different answers than male interviewers. If a measure is unreliable, yielding inconsistent results, it cannot be valid. One of the differing results might represent a valid measure, but researchers would be unable to specify which one it was. Would it be the first? The last? The one given to a male or the one given to a female interviewer? On the other hand, although reliability is necessary for validity, it cannot guarantee it. Even fairly reliable measures such as income may not be valid measures of lifestyle or social class.

Sampling

Rarely do survey researchers have the time or resources to study everyone they want to. For this reason they usually draw a *sample*, selecting a subset of individuals from the population they wish to study. There are really only two rules of sampling. First, a sample should be *representative* of the population from which it is drawn. Second, conclusions should not be *generalized* beyond the group from which the sample is drawn.

The second rule is simpler, so we shall discuss it first. It means that if researchers fail to sample from some groups, they cannot say their findings hold for such groups. For example, if researchers draw a sample from sociology students at the University of Alberta and ask them to fill out a questionnaire about Quebec separatism, they cannot then discuss the attitudes of *all* students at the University of Alberta on this topic. They would not

Researchers usually draw a sample of individuals from the group they wish to examine.

know the views of non-sociology students because they omitted them from their sample.

Non-sociology students may be unlike sociology students in many ways, including their attitudes toward Quebec separatism. Similarly, the researchers cannot generalize from Alberta sociology students to all sociology students. York and Dalhousie sociology students, among others, were not sampled, and may be quite different from Alberta sociology students in their feelings about Quebec.

The goal of representativeness involves drawing a sample that "looks like" and thus can be used to represent the total population. To accomplish this, researchers could take, for example, a **random sample**. In simple random sampling, all individuals are listed (the result is called a *sampling frame*) and then some are selected for study purely by chance, just like names from a hat or numbered balls from the cages on television lottery shows. For an alternative to this listing, see the insert "Hello, I Am Calling...."

Although preferred in theory because every individual has an equal chance of being selected, random samples in practice are often difficult to achieve. Listing all the individuals from which the sample will be drawn, for example all Canadians, is time consuming, often difficult, and sometimes impossible. Therefore, researchers may opt for a process called cluster sampling or multistage random sampling, to simplify the task.

In **cluster sampling**, researchers first randomly sample large units. Then they randomly sample medium units within the large units. Finally, they randomly sample even smaller units within the medium units. For example, they could list all the geographical areas (tracts) used by the census to facilitate enumeration in Canada, and select 100 at random. Then they could list all streets in these census tracts and randomly select 500 of them; and finally, list all residents who live on those streets and randomly select 1000 for interviewing.

Both simple random sampling and cluster sampling permit generalizations to the population— a major goal of researchers. Anyone can be chosen and thus the samples should be representative, reflecting the population from which they are drawn. But, in reality, researchers using random sampling techniques often cannot generalize to the total population because many of the randomly chosen individuals refuse to be interviewed. For this and other reasons, some researchers turn to also imperfect, but easier to execute, quota samples.

Quota sampling is a less expensive alternative to random sampling and involves a conscious, as opposed to chance, matching of the sample to certain proportions in the population. For example, if researchers know that 35 percent of a population

"Hello, I Am Calling to Ask Your Opinion...." Sound Familiar?

Telephone interviews are an increasingly popular survey research technique because of their unique advantages: lower cost, a better response rate than mailed questionnaires, easier access (many people will not admit interviewers into their homes and many interviewers do not feel safe entering the homes of strangers), and a greater feeling of anonymity. On the down side, people can easily hang up, and the overall response rate is lower than for personal interviews. Nevertheless, these are seen as small costs in this increasingly popular alternative to personal interviews (for a discussion see Neuman, 2000).

Random Digit Dialing (RDD) is a sampling technique whereby the telephone numbers to be called are randomly generated by a computer. Since most Canadians have phones, RDD is, in effect, a much cheaper alternative to a listing of all Canadians. It is also better than using a phone directory because it gets around the problem of unlisted and newly listed numbers. On the other hand, it misses some of the very poorest people, who cannot afford a phone.

are women in the labour force, 19 percent women at home, 40 percent men in the workforce, 6 percent men at home, they can interview people in exactly those same proportions, thus insuring that the sample is "representative" of the population. The actual respondents are generally chosen by availability—that is, from those who are close and willing to be interviewed, until the final list of respondents conforms to the 35, 19, 40, and 6 percent figures. The major drawback to quota sampling is that those who are nearby and cooperative may be quite different from the further-away and/or uncooperative segments of the population.

Quota sampling is really a sophisticated version of *accidental sampling*, in which researchers talk to anyone at a selected location, regardless of their social characteristics. Shoppers in a mall and students in introductory sociology classes often form accidental samples. Their strength is their low cost, and this makes them a popular choice; their drawback is the inability to generalize to the larger unsampled population.

In conclusion, limited resources mean that not everyone can be studied. If researchers have substantial funds, they will draw simple random or cluster samples; if less money, quota samples; and with little money, accidental samples. The ability to generalize the findings to the population decreases in the same order, due to increasing doubts concerning representativeness.

Analysis

After collecting their data, researchers must begin analysis, the process of examining the data to look for relationships among the variables. The exact type of analysis depends on the complexity of the hypotheses being studied, but the basic process in survey research involves an examination of relationships between independent and dependent variables. For example, suppose a researcher collected data (see Table 2.1) on perception of punishment and shoplifting among adolescents.

The independent variable (here placed at the top of the table) might be the expected severity of punishment, the dependent variable frequency of shoplifting, and the hypothesized relationship that those who expect severe punishment are less likely to shoplift than those who expect only light punishment. N refers to the number of individuals

University students often form accidental samples. Their drawback is the inability to generalize to the larger population.

Table 2.1   Relationship Between Perception of Punishment and Shoplifting

Categories of the dependent variable	Categories of the independent variable	
	Expect severe punishment	Expect light punishment
Shoplift	36% (21)	78% (38)
Do not shoplift	64% (37)	22% (11)
N	100% (58)	100% (49)

in each category of the independent variable: 58 who expect severe punishment and 49 who expect light punishment, called *marginals* because they fall outside of the actual table. Of the 58 who expect

Content Analysis

Content analysis involves the examination (analysis) of themes (content) from communications such as conversations, letters, newspapers, books, or movies. It is often like survey research in its assumptions and practices. It tends to use deductive logic to derive hypotheses, and to focus on a limited number of variables.

Because it generally uses operational definitions, content analysis also resembles a survey research approach to measurement. This practice leads to quantifiability, reliability, and replicability. But the method is less strong on validity. Researchers cannot know whether the values and meanings they as-

sume to lie behind the communications are the actual values and meanings of the original communicators, or whether the audiences understood these values and meanings. Subtle, hidden, or between-the-line meanings, known perhaps only to the communicators and their audiences, are also problematic for content analysts. Finally, researchers cannot tell if the people actually acted as their communications would suggest.

As for sampling, content analysis generally involves some form of random sampling procedure, allowing generalizability at least to the sampling frame. Authors, their books, and then certain pages may

be cluster-sampled, for just one example. The analysis tends to be quantitative and statistical, much like survey research analysis.

The great strengths of content analysis are (1) because the data are inanimate, researchers do not affect them, a potential error in most quantitative methods; (2) it is inexpensive; and (3) it lends itself to historical and cross-cultural analyses. The main drawbacks concern validity, a potentially serious flaw, and selective survival of documents and other communications. For example, while formal works may survive, day-to-day writings, especially those of the less privileged, are less likely to do so.

severe punishment, 21 shoplift and 37 do not. Of the 49 who expect light punishment, 38 shoplift and 11 do not. These numbers appear in the *cells* where the independent and dependent variables meet. As a general practice, researchers do not examine these numbers, called the *raw* data, in their analysis. Percentages allow for better comparisons. The only rule to remember about these percentages is that *each category of the independent variable must add up to 100 percent*. To calculate a percentage, divide the number in any cell by its corresponding column marginal (or N) and multiply the result by 100; e.g., $37 \div 58 \times 100 = 64$ percent. Here it can be seen that those who expect a more severe punishment are less likely to shoplift (36 percent) than those who expect only a light punishment (78 percent). Again, notice that *each* of the categories of the independent variable adds up to 100 percent.

On the basis of these data, it can be concluded that there is a relationship between perception of severity of punishment and shoplifting. Note, however, that the relationship is not perfect. Some who expect light punishment do not shoplift, while some who expect severe punishment do. Most

sociological relationships are like this, incomplete and imperfect. Sociological research usually finds that two variables *tend* to be related under *certain* conditions for *some* people. Collectively, human beings are too complex, have too many pressures acting upon them, and possess too many options to exhibit the simpler relationships more characteristic of the natural sciences.

The conditions and kinds of people are the "other things being equal" of the hypothesis. As mentioned, sociologists call these "other things" **control variables**, and survey researchers take these into account *statistically*. To do so, they take the original data and divide them into additional tables, one table for each category of the control variable. Suppose we think that threats of punishment work more for girls than for boys, who more often allow peer pressure to make them ignore such consequences. When researchers "control" for sex, they make two identical tables, one for boys and one for girls. The new tables look exactly like the original, with the same headings and the same categories, and all categories of the independent variable still add up to 100 percent, but in each table

The Conservatives Are Ahead;
The Liberals Are Ahead....

All of us have seen polls reported in the media, and what is noteworthy is how different, even contradictory, some seem—especially at election time. How can the Liberals and the Conservatives both be leading by 10 percentage points? One quick answer is that polls never claim to be exact. That is indicated in the phrase "+/–" so many percentage points. So a 55% is really between 51% and 59%. Sometimes a result may be completely off; the "19 times in 20" figure means there is a 5% chance they are wrong.

But what else happens? First, and very rarely, outright fraud may be operating. More likely, however, a more subtle bias may be in evidence. This may occur in how "not at homes" are treated. Replacing these respondents by others means that those more likely to be out (and thus employed?) may be under- represented. Repeated attempts to contact until the chosen respondent is home may mean the opposite. Or suppose the first question in one survey asks about high taxes while in another it asks about overcrowded hospitals. Won't some (especially undecided) people in the first move to the political right, while in the latter they will move to the left? And finally, recall that most polls talk about decided voters. There is always some chance that a 40/40 dead heat with 20% still undecided, could become a 60/40 landslide.

Does Drinking Lead to Date Rape?
Social Science Experiments

Experiments are better than survey research in demonstrating cause. In the simplest social science experiment (Neuman, 2000 describes more complex designs), subjects are divided by chance into two groups—for example, by the flipping of a coin, with heads to one group and tails to the other. Once the subjects are in separate groups, a cause (independent variable) is introduced into one of them, called the **experimental group**. Since the cause is introduced to the experimental group only, any effect (dependent variable) should be found in that group only and not in the second or **control group**, which does not experience the cause.

Suppose researchers were interested in the relationship between alcohol and date rape. After random assignment of dating males to either group, alcoholic beverages would be served to the experimental group and soft drinks to the control group. Then both groups could be given a series of hypothetical situations to examine their dating behaviour. They could be asked, "Your date has just said 'no' to sexual intercourse. Would you: (a) respect her wishes, (b) ask again, (c) pressure her to change her mind, (d) continue a bit further to see how serious she is, (e) ignore her and go ahead?" If alcohol reduces inhibitions, the males in the experimental group should more often choose the latter options (c, d, or e) than the males in the control group. If alcohol is not a factor, there would be no difference in answers between the two groups.

A crucial difference between survey research and experiments occurs in their models. The effects of all potential control variables are supposed to be eliminated through the random assignment of subjects to the experimental or control conditions. Such randomization attempts to make true the statement "other things being equal" and means that the experimental and the control groups should be quite similar except for one thing: the independent variable. For example, there should be approximately similar numbers of the very religious, the going-steady, and children of professional parents in each group.

continued

Even variables in which the experimenters are not interested—for example, dancing ability—should be approximately the same as a result of this chance assignment. With these "other things being equal," their influence on the dependent variable is then ignored and the model made quite simple, involving only the independent variable, here alcohol, and the dependent variable, response to a date's "no." You will recall that in survey research, control variables must be included in the model because they may affect any relationship between the independent and dependent variables.

Analysis in experiments is then done by comparing the experimental and control groups on the dependent variable. But what if, by chance, the random assignment did not make the two groups equal in all ways? To examine this possibility, most experimenters take two measures of their dependent variable (here, dating behaviour) although perhaps with slightly different but equivalent questions. The first is called a *pre-test*, which comes before the introduction of the independent variable (here, alcohol). The second is a *post-test*, since it comes after. Analysis

involves looking for changes in predicted dating behaviour between the pre- and post-test in both groups. Any difference in the control group could have been caused by many factors, such as boredom or greater familiarity with the questions on dating, but should not have been caused by alcohol, which its members did not drink. The difference between the experimental group's pre- and post-test, minus any difference in the control group, thus represents the net effects of the independent variable. As in survey research, however, the relationship will not be perfect, and additional causes of date rape can be examined in additional experiments to explain why this is so.

While experiments are good in demonstrating cause and effect, they have their downsides. First, ethical considerations make many experiments impossible. Researchers cannot, for example, force people to attend religious services to examine the effects of such attendance on racial prejudice. They have no control over whether a person is born male or female, to a large or small or rich or poor family—all key variables in social research. Turning to measurement, in the current example a battery of

hypothetical questions is used to measure actual dating behaviour. Merely being in an experiment can alter people's behaviour as they try to please the experimenters, doing things they think the experimenters want. This is sometimes called the *Hawthorne effect*. So experimental measures are sometimes even more removed from real behaviour than the measures used in survey research, and thus they have the potential for even greater invalidity. In fact, **external validity** refers to whether experimenters can generalize from their experiments to the real world.

Finally, with respect to sampling, experimenters generally need more cooperation than do survey researchers, because subjects in experiments have something done to them. Moreover, many subjects have to return for several sessions of such manipulation. Because of these greater costs in time and effort, subjects for experiments tend to be drawn from accidental samples, with paid volunteers and university students frequent choices. Generalizing experimental results to non-volunteers and to non-university populations should therefore be done only with caution.

the control variable is constant or controlled, meaning that it is the same for everyone in the table, all boys or all girls, allowing examination of the sexes separately. These tables could show that the predicted relationship between severity of punishment and shoplifting holds better among girls and less well among boys.

The examination of control variables still does not complete the analysis stage. Sociologists must inspect the cases in the control tables that still do not support their hypotheses, and look for factors that make them exceptions. They must attempt to

find out why, for example, some boys who expect light punishment still do not shoplift. Perhaps it is because they are very religious. The researchers also must attempt to explain why some girls who expect severe punishment nevertheless do shoplift. Perhaps extreme poverty is a factor in these instances. This finding must also be added to any conclusions drawn.

The list of control variables that serve to qualify the generalizations suggested by the original analysis can be lengthy. Researchers, however, ordinarily collect and analyze data on only those variables logically and closely connected with their independent and dependent variables, and use their knowledge of the field to decide which variables are relevant. The purpose of these controls is to approximate the conditions of the natural-science controlled experiment, a basic goal of positivism, to make all other things equal except for variations in the independent and dependent variables. A quite different approach marks the qualitative alternative of participant observation, to which we now turn.

A qualitative strategy: Participant observation

Real-life behaviour is rarely seen directly in most quantitative research. Qualitative researchers, in contrast, generally make such observation a central requirement in their research strategies. For example, in **participant observation** a researcher asks permission to join and observe a group and to question its members about the meanings of their behaviour. It is this strategy we shall describe in the next section, examining theory, models, measurement, sampling, and analysis, as we did for quantitative research.

Theories and hypotheses

Many qualitative sociologists feel that because most theories about social life are incomplete, *perspective* is a better word than theory. The use of that term allows a greater flexibility. In addition, the ideal of much participant- observational research is to begin a study with minimal preconceptions and to allow the data whenever possible to speak for themselves. These perspectives, then, are sensitizing devices, showing researchers where to look but not limiting their investigations.

Many participant observers thus refuse to derive hypotheses as do survey researchers, but instead use inductive logic, allowing the facts they observe eventually to lead to theoretical gener-alizations. As deductive logic goes from the general to the specific, **inductive logic** goes from specific facts to general statements. Thus, participant observers tend to collect their data first and conclude with what they call **grounded theory**, theory rooted in and arising from their data. For example, researchers might note that some women tend to

ask more questions and try to extend rather than limit conversations compared to men. Researchers can then end up with a generalization about how gender affects conversation. The theories come after examining the data, not before as in most quantitative approaches. (In practice in both qualitative and quantitative methods the relationship between data and theory is more like a circle, with data forcing revisions of theory and theory affecting the type of data collected, in a continuous loop.)

Model

Participant observation rarely deals in simple one independent/one dependent variable models. Instead, models involve many variables acting at once, as happens in the real world. One common strategy in participant observation is to look initially at many things and over time to focus on fewer variables, thereby simplifying the model as the research progresses. Even with such simplification, however, participant observation ordinarily involves more complicated models than either experiments or survey research. Variables are not isolated, either artificially, as in laboratory experiments, or statistically, as in the control tables of survey research, and thus the models are correspondingly more complex. In addition, the models of participant observers are often more general than specific, in the form of themes and motifs, and arise as the researchers become immersed in the data. A second difference between participant observation and more quantitative methods concerns cause. Qualitative researchers are satisfied in many instances with associations—that is, relationships between variables—without any idea of cause or talk of independent and dependent variables. When they do look at cause, multiple causes and longer causal chains are stressed.

Measurement

The most important difference in measurement between quantitative methods and participant observation is that participant observers view real behaviour, going beyond both survey research's verbal reports of that behaviour and the artificial behaviour of laboratory experiments. They can also see behaviour the actors are unaware of, behaviour

Qualitative Methods

Qualitative methods are not just an alternative or a supplement to quantitative methods. Originally borrowed from anthropology and applied to the study of urban life by the Chicago School in the 1920s, qualitative or *interpretative* sociology has enjoyed a fluctuating popularity in North American sociology. While the 1940s and 1950s saw the rise of positivism in social research, the publication of *The Discovery of Grounded Theory* by Glaser and Strauss in 1967 heralded a new era in qualitative methods, today the preferred approach to doing sociological research for many. In the 1990s and into the millennium, sociology is changing to embrace questions of voice and standpoint (see below), traditionally silent in positivist sociology. Today, many sociology departments in North American universities offer courses in qualitative methods, and the publication of ethnographies in book form and in journals such as the *Journal of Contemporary Ethnography* and *Qualitative Inquiry* is burgeoning. Below are some definitions and examples:

Qualitative Methods Social research methods that come from a humanistic orientation to society, based on Weber's notion of **verstehen** (understanding rather than prediction) as the goal of sociology.

Humanistic Orientation A humanistic orientation to social research stresses *involvement, interpretation,* and *value orientation.* In contrast, a positivistic orientation emphasizes *detachment, objectivity,* and *value neutrality.*

Involvement Qualitative methods require that the researcher become involved with research participants. This usually involves face-to-face contact in the form of interviews, participant observation, or non-participant observation, although it may also involve non-face-to-face contact such as telephone interviewing. Even in historical research, to be a qualitative researcher requires "taking the role of the other," or in other words attempting to see the world through the eyes of those who are being studied (see *historical research* below).

Interpretation Qualitative data are never meant to be seen in an objective way, for it is understood that all that is known of the social world is a consequence of interpretation. Thus, the perspective and standpoint of the researcher are significant in determining how the data will be interpreted. Today it is essential for the researcher to state her/his standpoint before presenting any research findings. For example, the researcher must position herself or himself according to race, class, sex, age, sexual preference, ability, etc., as well as explain how access to the group in question came about, thus highlighting the researcher's privilege as a courtesy member of the group.

Value Orientation Since qualitative research involves taking the role of research participants, the interpretation may take on a moral quality. Researchers are often confronted with the opportunity or even necessity of making a moral evaluation of issues surrounding social justice, oppression, marginalization, or powerlessness of their research participants. Some researchers choose to embrace a value orientation and use their position as an advocate for oppressed groups (see *participatory action research* below).

Types of Qualitative Research

Biographical Method Recognizing that one's own life experiences define one's interests and topic in sociology, the biographical method emphasizes the biography of the researcher. According to Denzin (1994: 510), "Interpretive research begins and ends with the biography and the self of the researcher. The events and troubles that are written about are ones the writer has already experienced and witnessed firsthand."

Ethnographic Interview Individual structured, semi-structured, or unstructured interviews with members of the community in question can provide life stories and insights into the experience of being a member of a particular group. They are usually audiotaped and transcribed verbatim. There are several qualitative analysis software packages, such as *The Ethnograph* and *QSR NUD*IST,* that facilitate the organization and analysis of qualitative data.

Feminist Methods While it is theoretically possible to do feminist research using quantitative methods (Reinharz, 1992), qualitative methods tend to be more consistent with the feminist project of dismantling the oppressive relations of patriarchy, for they allow for the hearing of previously silenced and marginalized voices such as those of women and other minorities. Indeed, some argue that positivist sociology has been an instrument of the domination of women by white, middle-class males (Olesen, 1994).

Historical Research When reading/writing social history, the lives and worlds of people long gone are subject to interpretation just as much as, if not more than, those currently living. The dead do not have an opportunity to challenge or correct "misinterpretations" of historical events. As Tuchman (1994: 312) pointed out, "In historical research, as in all other kinds of research, the data to be used depend upon the question the researcher wishes to answer and the information the researcher can find to answer the question." Histories have traditionally been written from the vantage point of the dominant group, and as such have reflected contemporary realities. "To read the works of Marx and Weber, one must also under-

stand how nineteenth-century historians interpreted the past" (Tuchman, 1994: 307).

Participatory Action Research Research that is consciously conducted with the aim to use the privileged position of the researcher to advocate for social change among oppressed groups is known as participatory action research. Frequently embracing a Marxist orientation, researchers within this tradition do not subscribe to the idea that social research should simply describe social life, and they seek to correct social injustice through the research process (Whyte, 1991).

Postmodern Research With the growing popularity of postmodern approaches to society, some qualitative methodologists (Denzin, 1994) require that the authority of voice be subjected to strict questions, such as "which voice" is authoritatively speaking for a community, and how does the voice of

the interpreting researcher unavoidably negate the authority of the heard voice? Questions such as these may lead to questioning the entire process of doing social research.

Standpoint Research Dorothy Smith (1987), a well-known Canadian feminist, is generally credited with being the originator of "standpoint" sociology. Simply put, Smith argued that the standpoint of the researcher will determine the questions brought to research and ultimately the findings of any research project. While her major contribution has been to highlight the importance of gender in research, sex, class, race, age, ability, and sexual orientation are each "standard standpoints" to be considered. As noted above, all qualitative researchers must now state their standpoint before providing the findings of their research.

Source: Lesley D. Harman, 1999. [Written for this volume.]

---

the actors are unable to describe adequately, and even behaviour the actors might not admit to in an interview. If clarification is needed to interpret these observations, explanations from the actors themselves can supplement the researchers' interpretations. Indeed, in their reports, participant observers often allow the actors to explain their behaviour as it makes sense to them. The researcher-controlled "objective" and standardized measures more typical of quantitative researchers become less important, while the subjective definitions of the actors become more important. Thus, participant observers more often begin with actor-defined definitions, in contrast to the researcher-defined operational definitions of quantitative methods.

Sampling

Obviously, if researchers live with a group of people to observe them, they cannot study a large number of such groups. The time, money, and effort required would be too costly. Thus, participant observation usually involves only a small number or even just one case, generally chosen because of availability. Sampling considerations extend beyond the choice of group to be studied, however. Inside the group there is much sampling involved; observers cannot be everywhere at all times, or watch all things even in one place. Thus, they sample times, places, people, and behaviours. These samples can be taken randomly or on a quota basis. Often they are not, however, and instead are

Public behaviour is most amenable to secret observation by a researcher who takes the role of outsider.

determined by chance, by the unpredictable flow of the interaction. Still, deliberate bias, including choosing data to support the researchers' preconceived notions, must be avoided whatever the sampling procedure.

Analysis

As previously stated, participant observers often let the actors explain their own behaviour. Some of the actors' explanations may be rationalizations, and in fact their subjective perceptions may be objectively inaccurate, but the explanations still are recorded as motivations behind the actors' behaviours. The participant observers can then add their explanations to those of their informants.

Analysis in participant-observation research is often descriptive, attempting to make a coherent portrait of a complex social reality. Numbers are less apparent and words more so. Causal relationships may or may not be specified, but if they are they must be fitted into a larger overall description of the subject matter. In fact, one problem that arises with participant observation is the researchers' inability to describe all that is going on, to complete the picture fully. This occurs because there are just too many facts and too much data to include. Thus, inevitably, participant observers must be selective and edit the information with which they attempt to describe their subject matter. Such decisions are based on their familiarity with the topic, logic, guidance from both colleagues and the actors themselves, and the feelings and intuitions of the researchers. Such a process is hard to plan fully in advance, and must be partly determined in the field.

One common analytical strategy is to examine the data while still in the field, while the research is still going on, with the early analysis rather unfocused and the later increasingly limited. In this way, models and hypotheses that become apparent in those earlier stages can be tested in later ones. This sequential practice is a good way to test grounded theory. Negative case analysis, examining those cases that fail to support the generalizations drawn, can then force their revision. Thus, like most social scientists, participant observers use both inductive and deductive logic in examining social reality.

This concludes our brief description of participant observation. More unstructured and flexible than survey research, its exact operations are harder to specify. Still, after reading this section, you should at least be familiar with its logic and rationale. The next section compares participant observation with the previously discussed survey-research approach.

The Methods Compared

Survey research and participant observation can be compared in many ways. Each is strong in some ways and weak in others. Thus let us compare them on the same criteria: validity—whether their measures are accurate reflections of social reality; generalizability—whether the conclusions hold beyond the actual group studied; and ability to reveal causes of behaviour.

The issues of validity and generalizability are related and are at the heart of the debate between quantitative and qualitative researchers. Participant observers argue that much survey research is invalid, because survey researchers get only verbal reports of that behaviour, and respondents may slant their answers to what they think the interviewers want to hear. They may even lie, giving socially approved answers that reflect well on them and avoiding responses that place them in an unfavourable light. A related criticism is that survey researchers often examine *attitudes* instead of *behaviour*, and people often do not act as their attitudes would predict (explaining why husbands think they *should* share more household tasks than they actually *do*). Finally, in quantitative research, operationalization lets the researcher rather than the actor define and measure behaviour, again raising validity issues.

Survey researchers counter these claims by arguing that careful research design can minimize some validity problems. Self-administered (and cheaper) anonymous questionnaires, as opposed to interviews, for example, can decrease lying and the effects of respondent-researcher interactions. To increase validity, interviewers can be trained to detect misunderstandings and resistance and to encourage candour and honesty. Survey researchers suggest, moreover, that participant observation also yields invalid data, first, because the observers, just by being there, change people's behaviour. People will not act naturally while being observed. Even if they learn to trust their researchers, knowing that they are being watched will still affect their behaviour. Second, quantitative researchers believe that participant observation data are too vulnerable to potential biases, needs, and unconscious distortions of the observers themselves and that different observers will "see" different things, and thus the measures are unreliable. And while a need for validity checks is all the more important in such instances, the flexibility of the method (seen as a strength by its practitioners) makes **replication**, or the repeating of a study, difficult in participant observation. Thus any invalidity would be harder to uncover than would be the case for quantitative researchers.

A difficulty in making generalizations is another significant criticism survey researchers make of

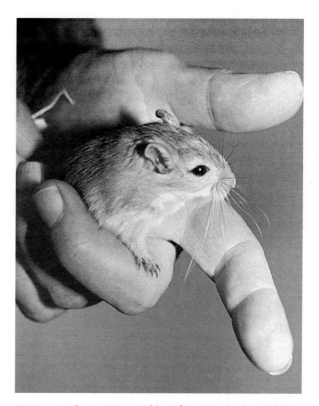

Many social scientists would prefer to apply the methods of natural scientists to their data.

participant observation. With few groups (or sometimes only one group) studied, the chance that the observations may not be representative of other groups is increased. Thus generalizations from participant-observation data to the wider but unstudied population should be made only with caution.

Needless to say, this participant-observation/survey-research debate continues. Qualitative participant observers, while admitting that their small non-representative samples may permit only limited generalization, still lay claim to greater validity, because they observe actual behaviour, over time, and in a natural setting. Moreover, given a choice between validity and generalizability, participant observers feel that validity is the more important criterion to satisfy. A valid picture of even a nonrepresentative sample is preferable to an invalid description of a perfectly random sample. Survey researchers, on their part, point to their improvements in validity and reject this argument.

Turning to cause, to demonstrate that A causes B, researchers must show not only a logical connection between them, but that A is prior to B and that A and B are not connected only through C, a variable causing both A and B. The random assignment in experiments attempts to rule out all such C variables by making all of them equal, thus insuring that A is the only cause operating. Survey research and participant observation cannot rule out other causes as easily, if at all.

In most survey research, data on independent and dependent variables are collected at the same time, a procedure called **cross-sectional research**. This is quite efficient in terms of cost, but a negative side effect is that researchers often cannot demonstrate which variables come first, which are causes, and which are effects. For example, as will be discussed more fully in Chapter 12, Media, does exposure to television violence cause violent behaviour? Or do violent people choose to watch violent television? Or is it both?

In addition, survey research often deals in **correlations**, demonstrations that changes in one variable are concurrent with changes in another. But variables may "go together" without the correlation between them being causal. Survey researchers must be especially careful about **spurious relationships** in these correlations— assuming that a relationship is causal when it is really only through a third variable, (C), that (A) and (B) are linked. For example, there is a correlation between the amount of money spent in dating relationships (A) and sexual activity (B). Survey research data would reveal that other things being equal, the more money spent, the greater the sexual activity. Is money, an independent variable, causing sexual activity, a dependent variable? No—the real relationships are between involvement (C) and money spent (A), and between involvement (C) and sexual activity (B). The greater the involvement, the more money is spent and the more sexual activity occurs. Interpreting the correlation to mean that money leads to sexual activity is spurious. Survey researchers generally do manage to see through such spurious relationships. Exactly how they accomplish this is a question best left to a more advanced text, but it generally involves examining the types of control variables on the original relationship. Thus, spuriousness is not an insur-mountable problem, but an issue with which survey researchers must deal.

Participant observers, because their research is done over time (called **longitudinal research**), may be better able to see which variable comes first, but they have a problem in that many variables happen at once, making it hard to determine which are causal. Their full, rich picture may make it difficult to isolate the specific causes of behaviour. This is one reason some participant observers choose not to focus on cause and instead deal mainly with descriptions.

In sum, validity is potentially stronger in participant observation than in survey research. For generalizability, survey research may be better. Each has difficulty in demonstrating cause and effect. Because no method is without flaws, some researchers engage in **triangulation**, the application of several research methods to the same topic, in the hope that the weaknesses of one method can be compensated for by the strengths of the others. For example, the findings of a participant-observation study may be confirmed by survey research or vice versa.

Quite often the subject of inquiry will point to a choice. Studies of national voting behaviour generally require survey research, and much of the research in stratification and religion reported in this book used survey research. On the other hand, culture, social movements, and emerging topics about which little is known are often examined with participant observation, because of its flexibility.

A common omission: Historical and comparative issues

The qualitative and quantitative research techniques described so far collect data over a short period of time, making it difficult to examine long-term trends. In addition, most researchers confine their work to their own society. *Historical* and *comparative analysis* of different societies attempt to fill these gaps. Both allow a special type of replication, a retesting of hypotheses in new settings, leading researchers either to greater confidence if similar results appear, or to reformulations if conflicting data are uncovered. Because of these strengths, let us examine these methods more closely.

Since it is undertaken after the fact and must rely on whatever data were collected at the time,

Following Their Own Path: Marxist Research Methods

There are several research strategies that appeal to conflict sociologists, reflecting the diversity of conflict approaches outlined in Chapter 1. As a group they may have little in common except for a rejection of Durkheim's positivist stance—that natural-sciences methods should be used to study social reality. Here we shall focus on a Marxist conflict model.

Generally those who adopt a Marxist approach are critical of subjective perspectives on social life, such as that of symbolic interactionism. Marxists argue that people are constrained by (and are not the makers of) social reality. But they could be free if someone, perhaps social scientists, would reveal to them their oppression. People have potential but they are deceived and exploited, and have lost control over their own destiny.

Theory is useful to Marxists to the extent that it reveals the causes of the problems faced by the oppressed and helps people see the path to an improved life. The model

used in Marxist research concentrates on the potential for change and generally sees the amount of power and resources held, especially economic power and resources, as the major independent variable affecting all other aspects of life. Attention to history, something missing in much functionalist research, is especially important because change, which results from the conflict that arises over ownership of resources, rather than stability, is the focus. A *dialectical* approach, which sees history as a series of conflicts over existing material arrangements, is attractive to Marxists. This approach maintains that the seeds for its transformation exist in every society, with the new society that results, in turn, containing the seeds for its own transformation.

Measurement and sampling are not key methodological elements to Marxists, who tend to prefer a critical approach. They like to ask embarrassing questions, to uncover exploitation, and to expose

hypocrisy. Marxists look for the conflicts surrounding the unequal distribution of resources, in the hope of encouraging large-scale changes to the status quo. And they prefer to do this in the real world, as opposed to the laboratory.

Nor is analysis, at least in the form of hypothesis testing, so important. Marxists generally "know" what is going on. Instead their role is to act upon their research, a strategy they call **praxis**. They reject Weber's recommendation, that it is not the role of the scientist to suggest social policy, as too passive. Instead they see the role of social scientific analysis specifically as one of unmasking the unjust conditions in the world in order to help the downtrodden see the sources of their ills. Thus research should be action-oriented, a step taken to empower the weak and then to improve the world. Smashing myths and uncovering contradictions are just the first part of that process (see Neuman, 2000).

---

historical analysis actually entails a variety of research methods. Thus, researchers can perform a qualitative study of diaries or letters written a hundred years ago or can do a statistical quantitative analysis of census data originally collected through survey research. In comparative research too, any method can be used, with the one chosen used repeatedly across cultures.

As a by-product of the versatility of their methods, historical and comparative analysts can use deductive and/or grounded theory. Their models can be simple or complex. Still, it would probably be fair to say that historical analysis is especially attractive to conflict theorists because it

best allows a focus on change. We know also that positivists, especially survey researchers, tend to avoid historical sociology. The more problematic issues for historical and comparative analysis relate to measurement and sampling. We shall discuss each in turn.

In collecting their data, historians distinguish between primary and secondary sources. **Primary sources** are records produced at the time, described by a contemporary of the event, including eyewitness accounts, diaries, and official records. **Secondary sources** are created when individuals report what a primary source said. The potential problems surrounding the validity of secondary sources are readily apparent. The greater the distance in time, in space, and in perspective between the primary and secondary sources, the greater the chance for misinterpretation. But the primary source may be invalid as well. Who wrote it down and why? Did the person deliberately or unwittingly distort the data to tell a certain story? And worse, while the validity of current data can be checked against other current or new data, historical data often cannot be. Thus, validity is always an issue in historical analysis.

Cross-cultural researchers can collect new data or use available data. One excellent source of existing, generally participant observation, data is the anthropological reports found in the *Encyclopedia of World Cultures*, ten volumes summarizing over 1500 ethnographies of societies around the world. One of the problems with using someone else's data, a procedure called **secondary analysis**, however, is that they may be incomplete, since the original collectors were not aware of the information later researchers would need.

Sampling remains the final stumbling block in historical and comparative research. In the latter, how many societies are to be included? Costs multiply quickly. Inside the countries chosen, a representative national sample might be impossible, leading to questionable generalizability. The preference in historical analysis for a complex picture also generally results in a small number of cases and a limited time frame. (Historical studies using census or other official data—see for example Chapter 15, Demography and Urbanization—are an obvious exception to this generalization.) The problems of missing or incomplete data may then further reduce the sample size. The end result of these factors is a difficulty in generalizability.

Summary

The discussions of Durkheim and Weber begun in the Introduction were continued in this chapter, this time with respect to their different research strategies. Durkheim was associated with quantitative research and specifically survey research, Weber with qualitative research and participant observation. The place of theory and hypotheses, types of models, measurement issues, sampling, and simple analysis were presented for both, and their strengths and weaknesses compared. Included in boxes in the chapter were alternative strategies such as content analysis and experiments, along with Marxist and feminist comments on methods, and a further elaboration of qualitative methods.

If you decide to become a sociologist and to conduct research, you thus have many options open to you. Whatever method you choose, the most anyone can reasonably ask of you is honesty, competence, and a healthy scepticism. You should never deliberately choose one method over others because its data will most likely support your preconceived biases; you should be willing to undergo the training that will allow you to be expert at whatever method you choose; and you should be aware of the weaknesses, especially concerning validity and generalizability, of your method. This is a big order, one best saved for an advanced course in research methods.

But before going on to the next general topic of the book, Culture, finish this chapter by reading the following short section. If a research paper is required in an introductory sociology course, it will probably involve library research rather than the collection of new data. Consequently, this section deals with writing library research papers.

Writing a Sociology Library Research Paper

The first task in writing any research paper is to define a topic broadly. Students should choose one in which they are interested, as it will make the work easier. The second requirement involves a review of the literature, that is, an examination of existing studies on the chosen topic, for example, homosexuality. Bring a set each of 5×7- and 3×5-inch cards for taking notes. Recent books can be found by looking up "homosexuality" in the library's subject catalogue. The locations of scholarly articles on homosexuality can be found by using a software called *Sociological Abstracts*, saving you much time. For popular articles in print, *The Reader's Guide to Periodical Literature* is useful.

The amount of information available will probably be overwhelming. (In the rare instances when little is written on a topic, introductory students should probably choose a new topic.) How can your review be made more manageable? Restricting the search to the last five years or so could help, and will make the paper more timely as well. But there probably will be still too much to read. The task is to narrow the subject down sufficiently to make it more manageable. Here the options are many: the focus could be the lifestyles or culture of homosexuals, how the role is learned, the difference between gays and lesbians, or why homosexuality is considered deviant and the extent of hidden homosexuality, whether social class affects homosexual lifestyles, with the rich living one and the poor another, or the discrimination and prejudice homosexuals face. Each of these topics might come out of the next few chapters of this book. What about homosexual families? How does religion treat homosexuality? The possibilities are endless, and the earlier stages of even this narrowed review will probably reveal the need for an even more restricted focus.

The next step is to decide the type of research review to be written. Choices here include an integrative review that summarizes what is known on a topic, showing points of agreement and disagreement and issues needing further research; a historical review tracing what has been learned about a topic over time; a cross-cultural review comparing the subject in different societies (Neuman, 2000).

The next step involves the two sets of cards. For all relevant articles, the author, title, date, name of journal, volume number, and pages should be entered on the top of one of the smaller cards. These cards can be alphabetized later to become the bibliography. Use the larger cards for relevant notes on the chosen topic, listing the author's name and enough of the title to identify definitively the source recorded in its own section at the very top. Specific page numbers for all quotes and for any specific ideas borrowed should also be clearly written there for later documentation. For long quotes or whole sections, making photocopies of the relevant pieces and then taping them to cards may be appropriate, *with the page number prominently recorded.*

As the cards accumulate, patterns begin to emerge. There seems to be agreement on some matters, disagreement on others. Links between certain aspects of the general topic become clearer, and an order becomes apparent. Sorting the cards into categories is the final step before the actual writing. The categories become the basis for an outline of the paper. Avoid the error of poor organization by outlining carefully, re-outlining, and using subtitles freely, according to the information found. Proper organization allows movement from point to point in a systematic and non-repetitive way. It also helps to avoid the error of lack of focus. Students who do not have a specific objective in mind may end up merely citing scattered findings, or they may include irrelevant facts, perhaps in the hope that including every fact possible will impress their instructors. The opposite is more often true; students should include only the material directly relevant to the focus of the paper.

The following suggestions about structuring your report are not rigid rules, but general guidelines.

1. *Introduction.* The introduction to a paper should indicate why the paper is being written. Why is the topic important—is there a need to solve a problem in society, to test a theoretical position, to reveal or discuss a contradiction? The introduction should begin with the most general rationale for the paper and logically proceed to a more specific problem. The last paragraph of this section should indicate what the paper will accomplish, giving a very brief outline of the contents.

2. *Results of literature review organized according to purpose of review.* Students should decide which sections of the works they are going to use, and enter them into a computer file (or tape them to larger sheets of paper) along with any necessary bibliographical information, adding their own analysis and summaries as appropriate. Failure to reveal sources and omitting quotation marks is called *plagiarism.* Findings should be clearly presented, supported when necessary with tables, charts, and graphs. (Again, if these are taken from the work of others, proper credit must be given.) Each finding should be explored within the

framework of the arguments originally developed in the introduction.

3. *Discussion.* In this section, the student must discuss the meaning and importance of the points made in the previous section and show how they relate to the purpose of the investigation as stated in the introduction. In many ways, the discussion is the most important part of the paper as it represents the student's original thoughts, not an organization of the insights of others. Thus, a great deal of thought and care is required for this section. It should make sense out of the sometimes disparate information included in the previous section. To make linkages between ideas, transitional phrases such as "thus," "moreover," "however," "nevertheless," and "on the other hand" make the writing smoother, although they will not suffice if the connections are also not apparent in the text itself.

4. *Summary and Conclusion.* Students should briefly summarize the paper here, in so doing showing the progress in knowledge made since the introduction. Suggestions for research that would provide answers to unanswered questions raised in the paper may be included here.

Finally, about the writing itself, consistency is important. Choose a tense and stick to it, for example, "Mundy *says* that homosexuals *are...*" Also choose a person. In general, it is best to write in an impersonal style (avoiding "I," "me," "my," etc.), keeping some distance between author and topic. Plurals ("they," "their") help to avoid the awkward "he/she" construction and the sexism of relying on the singular pronouns of "he" or "she." On the other hand, particularly in discussion sections, students should not be afraid of an occasional "I think" or "I believe." Writing should also be somewhat formal; some students become so informal that rigour and organization suffer. A thesaurus and dictionary are useful to help avoid repetition. Finally, the pages must be numbered, and proper footnoting and referencing used. Scholarly journals, for example, the *Canadian Journal of Sociology* or The *Canadian Review of Sociology and Anthropology*, provide good examples of proper reference style. The purpose of references is not to impress readers with the writer's depth of reviewing the research, but to enable them to find the sources used.

Several revisions are usually necessary. Showing a draft to someone who has experience with this type of assignment can help. If you're using a word processor, the spell check function will catch obvious errors, but it misses such things as confusing *their* for *there*, and *too* for *to*. A friend can help with such proofreading. Finally, papers must be typed and a copy should be kept.

Writing papers is always hard. We hope these suggestions will make the process a bit easier.

QUESTIONS FOR REVIEW AND CRITICAL THINKING

1.   Design an experiment to test the advantages and disadvantages of assigning qualified minority teachers to teach children of their own ethnic group, as opposed to having any qualified teacher instruct the children.

2.   Which research strategy would be most useful in studying why some of your friends continued their education after high school while others did not? Defend your choice.

3.   Design a questionnaire to examine the extent of and reasons for drug use among students.

4.   What topics would you like to study in sociology? Do personal values affect your choice? Should you be value-neutral or an activist, using research as a tool to improve the world?

KEY TERMS

axiomatic logic, p. 21

cluster sampling, p. 24

content analysis, p. 26

control group, p. 27

control variables, p. 26

correlation, p. 34

cross-sectional research, p. 34

deductive logic, p. 22

dependent variables, p. 21

experimental group, p. 27

external validity, p. 28

grounded theory, p. 29

hypothesis, p. 21

independent variables, p. 21

inductive logic, p. 29

longitudinal research, p. 34

operational definition, p. 22

participant observation, p. 29

positivism, p. 20

praxis, p. 35

primary versus secondary sources, p. 35

quota sample, p. 24

random sample, p. 24

reliability, p. 22

replication, p. 33

secondary analysis, p. 36

spurious relationship, p. 34

theory, p. 20

triangulation, p. 34

validity, p. 22

variable, p. 20

verstehen, p. 30

SUGGESTED READINGS

Lofland, John and Lyn Lofland

1995   *Analyzing Social Settings.* (3rd ed.) Belmont, CA: Wadsworth.

This volume is an excellent presentation of field research methods. It is readable and contains many illustrations of actual field research.

Neuman, W. Lawrence

2000   *Social Research Methods.* (4th ed.) Boston, MA: Allyn & Bacon.

This text provides a thorough overview of the research methods discussed in this chapter.

Nock, David

1993   *Star Wars in Canadian Sociology.* Halifax: Fernwood.

This book examines how the personal lives of Canadian sociologists affect their scientific "knowledge." It stands as an attack on positivism and points to the need to examine the geographical region of the researcher as it affects sociological research.

Thompson, Linda

1992   "Feminist methodology for family studies." *Journal of Marriage and the Family* 54: 3–18.

Short and easy to read, this article examines feminist methods in the area of family research. Values and both quantitative and qualitative methods are discussed.

WEB SITES

http://129.97.58.10/discipline/sociology/research.html

Doing Research in Sociology

This site contains useful information on doing research in sociology. Learn how to search for research material in periodicals, newspapers, and social science databases, as well as how to prepare your research report.

http://www.statcan.ca

Statistics Canada

Interested in doing quantitative research on Canadian subjects? At the Statscan Web page, you can find the most recent census data on various aspects of life in Canada.

Society and the Individual

In this section of the book, our central concern is to expand and illustrate Durkheim's claim that social structure and membership in social groups are important determinants of human behaviour. In Chapter 3, culture is defined as the general way of life that is shared by a group of people, is passed on to later generations, and affects their behaviour and perceptions in some way. Culture includes the values and norms that shape social conduct, the rules and conventions of everyday social life. Culture also includes the social roles that people play, and the variety of social conditions under which people live. Values, norms, and roles vary from one society to another. Even within a society, cultural features vary. For instance, the social unit called Canada is composed today of various subgroups whose different racial and ethnic origins and regional locations have given rise to correspondingly different *sub*cultures.

Cultures may be analyzed from various viewpoints. To a functionalist, cultural elements help to make society stable and viable. On the other hand, conflict sociologists analyze culture with reference to power differences in society. Research here focuses on questions such as which groups benefit from the way of life that is adopted and who determines the norms and values. As you read the chapter, try to think of alternative explanations that could be substituted for some of the arguments offered.

For culture to affect behaviour, it must be internalized or learned by individual group members. Such internalization may occur when members learn to play roles, for example, the roles of teacher or farmer or daughter. The acquisition of culture is the focus of Chapter 4, Socialization, which argues that there are biological, social, and environmental influences that affect human learning. Social factors are especially important in shaping identity, or a sense of self, which is in turn an important determinant of behaviour. Without such social input, humans would be little different from animals. The Socialization chapter also focuses on how individuals adapt to their social environment. While symbolic interactionism and conflict theory are discussed, the chapter does make a number of assumptions about human adaptation drawn from the functionalist perspective. Who benefits and gains from the socialization experience should be a constant question in your reading of the chapter. Socialization agents and contexts are examined historically.

The failure of certain individuals to internalize the norms, values, and "appropriate" social roles contained in their culture is discussed in Chapter 5, Deviance. Crime, considered by many to be the ultimate deviant act, is a major concern here. The chapter examines the social origins of definitions of deviance, including functional and conflict explanations, and shows how these definitions vary across cultures. The role of power and societal reaction are also discussed as factors in the labelling of acts as deviant. The general sociological perspective again is applied: social structure and group membership affect rates of behaviour, this time deviant behaviour.

3

Culture

Michael P. Carroll

Introduction

In observing individuals in a social group—whether a nation, a family, or a classroom—it soon becomes clear that their behaviour is not random. Not all possible behaviours actually occur, and if you were to observe the group long enough, you would notice that certain behaviours tend to occur with a great deal of regularity. Obviously, there is something that produces such order in social life.

Much of that "something" is what sociologists call *culture*. The use of this particular word may confuse some of you because culture also has a perfectly legitimate everyday meaning that has nothing to do with the orderliness of social life. In everyday language, people are "cultured" if they have sophisticated or refined tastes. What this usually means in actual practice is that they enjoy those activities favoured by the educated élite but not by the general public. Hence, drinking French wines is a mark of culture, drinking domestic beer is not; watching a ballet is cultured, watching stock-car racing is not.

Social scientists, however, use the word culture in quite a different sense. The most common definition found in sociology texts is one constructed by a nineteenth-century anthropologist named Edward Tylor. For Tylor, culture included "knowledge, belief, art, morals, law, custom, and any other capabilities and habits acquired by man as a member of society" (1871: 1). Notice that this definition gives no clue as to what all the things listed (knowledge, belief, art, etc.) have in common. Upon reflection, though, it turns out that each of the items listed by Tylor is something that (1) is shared by all or almost all the members of some social group; (2) the older members of the group try to pass on to the younger members; and (3) shapes behaviour (as in the case of morals, laws, and custom), or at least structures perceptions of the world (as in the case of the other items listed in Tylor's definition). If we call anything that meets these three criteria a **cultural element**, then we can define the **culture** of a given group very simply as the sum total of all the cultural elements associated with that group.

Sociologists consider certain elements of culture to be particularly important. They are values, norms, and roles.

Some Basic Concepts

Values and norms

Values are shared, relatively general beliefs that define what is desirable and what is undesirable; they specify general preferences. A belief that divorce is only a last resort for troubled marriages and a preference for abstract paintings are both values. **Norms**, on the other hand, are relatively precise rules specifying which behaviours are permitted and which prohibited for group members. Note that in everyday usage, norm has quite a different meaning—it means average. Here, again, sociology has constructed its own vocabulary by attaching a new meaning to a familiar word. When a member of a group breaks a group norm by engaging in a prohibited behaviour, other group members will typically *sanction* the deviant member. To sanction is to communicate, in some way, disapproval to the deviant member (a topic to which we shall return in Chapter 5, Deviance).

When asked to give examples of a norm in our society, most students tend to think of laws, such as those against murder and physical assault. Most laws in a society are indeed social norms. The more important point, however, is that your life is governed by many norms that are not laws.

Consider the following case. You feel very close to people who have given you every reason to believe that they are close friends. You then find out that they have systematically lied to you in order to gain some advantage. How would you feel? Quite hurt, probably, and most of you would also feel that their behaviour was wrong. Why? Because most people in our society believe that close friends should neither deceive nor exploit, and a behavioural norm that flows from this belief is that people claiming to be your friends should not lie to you to gain some advantage. Note that your friends have probably not done anything illegal (that is, no laws have been violated), but a norm—in this case an important one—has clearly not been respected.

You are usually not aware, in any explicit way, of many of the norms that structure your behaviour. For instance, there is one particular norm that regulates your daily behaviour, and that is so strongly held that for me to even suggest that you might violate it will make most readers of this chapter somewhat ill. Although students can rarely guess what norm I am talking about, it is easy to express: in our culture, there is a strong prohibition against coming into contact with the bodily discharges (a polite term for such things as urine, feces, pus, vomit, and mucus) of other individuals. Consider how many times in a given day you go to great lengths to make it unlikely that others will come into contact with your bodily discharges. Think, too, of how sick and repulsed you would be if this norm were broken, if you actually did come into contact with the bodily discharges of others.

"Society": Defining an Important Term

Society is probably one of the most commonly used words in all of sociology. Despite that (or more likely because of that), there is no single definition found in all sociology textbooks. Generally, however, sociologists apply the term to any fairly large group of people who (1) share a common culture, (2) think of themselves as having inherited a common set of historical traditions, (3) interact with other group members frequently, and (4) see themselves as being associated with a particular geographic area. The term society is often applied to nations (Canadian society, U.S. society). It can, however, be applied to sub-groups within nations (French-Canadian society), or to groups that cut across national boundaries (Western society).

Most readers would likely justify their strong reaction to contact with the bodily discharges of other people in terms of hygiene; that is, they would see it as a reaction that helps to avoid disease and for that reason would be very sensible. This is actually a fairly typical sort of rationalization, since people in most societies like to believe that their particular norms make "good sense," and that if the norms were violated something bad would happen. It is fairly easy to demonstrate, however, that our norms relating to bodily discharges involve more than just hygiene.

First of all, the aversion to bodily discharges was present in our society long before we became aware that diseases could be transmitted by germs. Second, many nonindustrial societies had the same strong aversion to bodily discharges and yet never developed a germ theory of disease. Third, even now, in our own society, there are patterns that are hard to explain on the basis of hygiene alone. Clark and Davis (1989), for instance, found that among Canadian university students some patterns are directly the reverse of what a hygiene hypothesis would lead one to expect. Asked what would be more upsetting to find in the bathtub of a newly rented hotel room, hair near the drain or a dirty footprint, most people choose the hair, although washed hair is less likely to contain germs than dirt.

As another example of the implicit norms governing your behaviour, consider the norms regulating sexual behaviour. What exactly are those norms? Don't respond with the norms that you attribute to supposedly unenlightened people (like your parents). What norms govern your sexual behaviour? Some students might hold to the norm that says that sexual intercourse is acceptable only in a marital context, or at least only when marriage is expected to occur in the near future. Most students do not (Hobart, 1993). Certainly one of the minimal conditions you would impose is that, to be acceptable, sexual intercourse must occur with the consent of both partners. The vast majority also believe that there must be "informed consent," which in effect means that both parties must be of a certain age and aware of what they are doing. But in this liberal age, are there any other conditions? Yes. One survey, reported in Chapter 10, Families, indicates that many Canadian

university students do add another provision: sexual intercourse is most acceptable when there is evidence of strong affection. This is not to say that sexual intercourse without affection does not occur, but that the preferred behaviour for these students is sexual intercourse between consenting individuals who have a strong affection for one another.

These few examples, of course, do not begin to exhaust the list of norms that regulate daily behaviour; undoubtedly, readers can think of many norms not mentioned here. But as soon as you begin to list the norms that regulate your behaviour, it becomes clear that some seem more important than others. For sociologists, the crucial difference between important and less-than-important norms lies in the nature of the reaction of group members when the norm is violated by an individual member. Sumner (1940) long ago introduced two terms, folkways and mores, to capture this distinction. **Folkways** are those norms that do not evoke severe moral condemnation when violated. The requirement to wear clothes is probably a folkway for most people. If you saw someone running around campus naked, you might feel embarrassed, amused, or titillated, but not morally outraged. **Mores** are those norms whose violation does provoke strong moral condemnation. Our strong moral condemnation of sexual assault, arson, and murder, for instance, suggests that the norms prohibiting these behaviours are mores.

It must be emphasized that the difference between mores and folkways lies in the nature of the *reaction* produced by the violation of the norm, and not in the *content* of the rule. For instance, one of the norms in our society is that dogs should not be eaten, while one of the norms in contemporary Hindu society is that beef should not be eaten. These two norms are similar in content, but one is a folkway, the other a mos (singular of mores). You may be very upset if you hear that someone has eaten a dog, but you are unlikely to be morally outraged. Yet that sense of moral outrage is exactly what would be evoked among Hindus were someone to openly slaughter, cook, and eat a cow. We shall have much more to say about the importance of audience reactions to norm violations in Chapter 5, Deviance.

A social role is a cluster of expectations about the behaviour that is appropriate for a given individual in a given situation.

Social roles

A **role** is a cluster of behavioural expectations associated with some particular social position within a group or society. For instance, the two social positions of importance in most classroom situations are "teacher" and "student." Most of us expect that a teacher will come to class prepared, will not assign grades arbitrarily, will not show up to class drunk, etc., and so these expectations, taken as a sum, define the teacher role. (As an exercise, you might try to think of the expectations that define the student role.)

A moment's reflection will indicate that one person can occupy several different roles at once. What roles have you occupied during the past week? Brother? Sister? Student? Friend? Enemy? Female? Male? Son? Daughter? This occupation of multiple roles opens the door to **role conflicts**, that is, situations in which the behavioural expectations associated with one role are inconsistent with those associated with another concurrent role. Some of the clearest contemporary examples of role conflict involve the parent role. The need to care for children—physically, emotionally, and otherwise, or even to arrange for others to care for them on a regular basis—quite often interferes with the demands of a full-time occupation, especially one in a competitive environment. Thus, there is the potential for conflict between the parent role and the full-time worker role, a role conflict that perhaps falls more frequently upon women. (We shall have more to say on this topic in Chapters 7, Gender Relations, and 10, Families.)

In studying roles we must always keep in mind that, without exception, they are social definitions, and thus, to a certain extent, they are arbitrary. This means that roles we take for granted in our own culture may not exist in the same form in other cultures. Here the "mother" role is a particularly good example for making the general point.

In our culture, the traditional definition of the mother role suggests that mothers are supposed to provide their children with emotional support, especially when the children are hurt and frightened, to nurse them when they are first born (with either breast or bottle), and to provide them with guidance as they grow. Some members of our society might even regard these behaviours as natural, as resulting from an innate tendency in most women towards mothering. But let us look at some evidence.

In many European societies prior to the nineteenth century, it was common for biological mothers to send their newborns for care and feeding to a "wet nurse" and her family for a period of one to two years. When these children were returned by the wet nurse, they were often cared for by older siblings or by other relatives, and not by the biological mother. In the case of peasant families, in which the mother had to work alongside the father in the fields, a pattern like this might reflect only economic necessity. It happens, however, that this same pattern was especially strong among the middle and upper classes in traditional Europe. But obviously, if the behaviours that for us are all associated with the single role we think of as "mother" were split up and allocated to a range of

On Defining the "Mother" Role

A social role is a cluster of expectations about the behaviour that is appropriate for a given individual in a given situation.

Ask yourself the following question: "Is the increase in the number of married women with families, working outside the home, having a harmful effect on family life?" The odds are that you have a definite opinion on this subject. When a recent Gallup poll asked a similar question of a national sample of Canadians, 53% said that a woman working outside the home did have a harmful effect on family life, 43% said it did not, and only 4% expressed no opinion at all (Bozinoff and Turcotte, 1993).

Now suppose I asked you a second question: "Does the large number of married men with families in the working world have a harmful effect on family life?" Likely you would be taken aback. In this case, the odds are that you do not have a definite opinion on the subject, if only because it's a question you've never asked yourself. In fact, it's a question that sociologists themselves almost never ask. While there have been hundreds, possibly thousands, of studies on the effects of maternal employment outside the home on children, there have been few on the effects of paternal employment outside the home.

But why does changing "married women, with families" to "married men, with families" convert the question from one on which you have a firm opinion (one way or another) and which has been well-studied by sociologists into one that is puzzling, about which you do not have a firm opinion, and which has not been particularly well studied? The answer, presumably, is that you, along with most sociologists, still see the raising of children as being primarily a mother's responsibility, that is, as an expectation that is part of the definition of the "mother" role. Consequently it "makes sense" to you to think about the possible "harmful effects" of something (like working outside the home) that might diminish the amount of time that a mother devotes to her children. Because "primary responsibility for raising children" is not an expectation that you have for the role "father," it does not occur to you to think about the "harmful effects" of a father working outside the home.

different people, then in these societies there was no role that can be said to correspond precisely to the mother role in our own society.

The general point to be made here is that every role is a cluster of expectations about behaviour, but this clustering varies from culture to culture. That our own culture groups together certain behavioural expectations in order to form a particular role does not guarantee that other cultures will group those same expectations together in the same way to form the same role.

Some additional terms

At this point, it will be useful to introduce a few additional terms. The first of these is **subculture**, a group of people within a single society who possess, in addition to the cultural elements they share with the other members of their society, certain distinctive cultural elements that set them apart. Thus, Ukrainians, Jews, Italians, or Iranians residing in Canada are often called subcultures because they share among themselves certain religious or ethnic beliefs and customs that are not characteristic of the Canadian population as a whole. Canadian subcultures will be discussed more fully in Chapter 8, Race and Ethnic Relations.

When the members of a society or a subculture agree that a specific set of norms and values should regulate some broad area of social life, such as the economy, family life, religion, or politics, then that set of norms and values is called an **institution**. Institutions are discussed in later chapters of this text.

The term **material culture** refers to all the physical objects used and produced by the members of a society or a subculture. Thus, for instance, the material culture of a nonindustrial society would

Popular culture refers to those preferences and objects that are widely spread across all the social classes in a society.

include its pottery, the tools it uses to gather and process food, and its sacred objects, while the material culture of our own society would include our clothes, books, automobiles, and houses.

The term **popular culture** refers to those cultural objects and beliefs that are widely distributed across all the social classes in a society, such as comic books and horror films. It is often contrasted with the culture associated with one particular group in society. Since popular culture is by definition widely distributed, larger societies do not usually develop a popular culture until they develop mass media, including print, radio, and television (see Chapter 12, Media). Also, since relatively expensive things are not likely to achieve a wide distribution, the elements of popular culture are generally inexpensive. For instance, the fact that comic books are relatively inexpensive compared with other sorts of books undoubtedly accounts in part for their popularity, just as the low cost of the dime novel accounted for its popularity during the nineteenth century. For sociologists, the study of popular culture is important because it can provide insights into societal values and norms that are implicit, that is, that structure our thinking and behaviour but whose content is not something that we think about in any precise way. The inserts "More Than Just a Toy" and "Urban Legends" are examples of how the study of popular culture can provide insight of this sort.

Aspects of Culture

Ever since the nineteenth century, three observations have consistently forced themselves upon virtually every investigator concerned with the study of culture. They are that (1) cultures exhibit enormous variation with regard to their values, norms, and roles; (2) few cultural elements are common to all known societies; and (3) the elements of culture in a given society are often interrelated.

Urban Legends

Urban legends are stories that have the following characteristics: (1) they are passed along mainly by word of mouth; (2) the people who repeat these stories believe them to be literally true; (3) the stories are set in the recent past and associated with some nearby geographical location; and, most importantly, (4) the stories are almost always completely false. Some of the best-known urban legends include stories about albino alligators in the sewers of New York, about snakes found in blankets imported from the Orient, about 5-year-old boys who are found castrated in shopping centres, about pets put into microwave ovens, about corpses that are mislaid, about Mexican dogs that turn out to be rats, etc.

Such stories can tell us something about the fears that characterize urban societies. For instance, the story about the young boy found castrated in a shopping centre (which has been recorded at hundreds of locations all over North America) usually includes racial overtones, since the alleged perpetrators are often said to be black. Attributing such an act to a minority group is by no means something new. During the Middle Ages, for instance, Jews were regularly accused of the ritualistic castration and killing of Christian boys, just as, during the early days of the Roman Empire, Christians were regularly accused of the same thing. It seems obvious that the popularity of this modern version of the castrated boy story (and it is a story that is certainly well known to my students) says something about the fears of the dominant white population in North America.

Often urban legends reflect more than one cultural attitude simultaneously. For instance, in the past few years there have been a number of urban legends about AIDS. In one of the most common of these stories, a man meets an attractive woman in a bar, they go to his hotel room, and they have sexual intercourse. The next morning, when he awakes, the man finds the woman gone and a message scrawled in lipstick on the mirror in the bathroom: "Welcome to the wonderful world of AIDS." At one level, the story can be seen as reflecting our very real worries about this disease. But notice that in the story the disease is knowingly spread by a woman to a man. While this pattern of transmission is possible, it is far more common—in the real world—for a man to spread the disease to a woman or another man. Furthermore, while there have been people with AIDS who knowingly spread the disease, most have been males, not females. The fact that the urban legend reverses the observed pattern in order to make a woman the source of danger says something, it has been argued, about prevailing cultural attitudes toward women in our society.

Another common sort of urban legend involves what Fine (1992) calls "redemption rumors." The core of the story here is that a large company is willing to redeem tokens taken from one of its products by making a donation to some medical charity. In the two most common versions of this urban legend, the tokens are usually (1) pop-can tabs or (2) cigarette packages. When these legends first began circulating several decades ago, they suggested that the charitable donation made by the corporation(s) in question would be used to purchase wheelchairs, iron lungs, and Seeing Eye dogs; more recent versions suggest that the donations would be used to purchase kidney dialysis machines. Quite often these stories will also include the name of a particular person, usually a child, who will benefit when the tokens are redeemed. Despite the detail that usually goes into these stories, they are generally false. Yet, as Fine points out, despite the denials routinely put out by tobacco companies and soft-drink companies, as well as by any number of charitable organizations, these redemption rumors persist, and any number of people find themselves with a lot of pop-can tabs or cigarettes packages and nobody to give them to. What accounts for the popularity of these stories?

Fine himself suggests two possibilities here. First, the fact that redemption rumors attach themselves to things like cigarettes and soft-drinks, people may simply be trying to rationalize their continued use of products that are otherwise perceived to be unhealthy. Second, and more important, redemption rumors may be an attempt to recapture or reestablish a "folk community," that is type of society in which everyone was honestly concerned with the well-being of everyone else and worked together to ease human suffering. On the other hand, the fact that we feel the need to manufacture stories aimed at recapturing such a folk society implies that there is a widespread sense that our society has become something else, that is, that we have become a society in which individuals and groups are generally concerned with their own special interests and NOT with the interests and well-being of the society as a whole.

Cultural variation

If we take an overview of the hundreds of societies in the world, past or present, the first thing that strikes us is that there is tremendous variation with regard to the cultural elements found in them. In fact, many societies have values and norms that are directly opposite to those that we might take for granted here.

Some of this cultural variation was apparent in our earlier discussion of the mother role, and other examples of such variation are not difficult to discover. In our society many individuals believe that there exists one god, responsible for all of creation, and they typically describe this god using imagery that is male. Swanson (1960) found that about half the nonindustrial societies in the world also believe in a single god, responsible for creation, although that god is not always seen as a male, or even as having a human likeness. Among the Iroquois, for instance, god was female, while among the South American Lengua, god is a beetle. But the remaining societies in the world either believe in many gods, no one of which is responsible for all creation, or do not believe in personalized gods of any sort (see Chapter 11, Religion).

Documenting cultural variation has always been a special concern of anthropologists, and one of the most famous of all the anthropological studies concerned with cultural variation is still Margaret Mead's *Sex and Temperament in Three Primitive Societies* (1935). In this book, Mead described three societies in New Guinea (a large island just to the north of Australia) that she studied in the early 1930s. Mead was concerned most of all with gender roles, and in the first of her societies, the Arapesh, she found that both males and females were cooperative, mild-mannered, and gentle, and very much concerned with helping their young. Among the Arapesh, in other words, both males and females seemed to embody the traits that Western societies associate with females. Mead's second society, the Mundugumor, was quite different. Here, both males and females were aggressive (and that included being sexually aggressive), uncooperative, jealous, hostile, and relatively unconcerned with parental tasks. To Mead it seemed as if both males and females among the Mundugumor conformed to the gender stereotype associated with males in Western

societies. But, for Margaret Mead, it was her third society, the Tchambuli, that was the most important. Among the Tchambuli, women were confident and efficient, very much involved in economic activities, cooperative (as least with other women), and central to the organization of the household. Tchambuli men, by contrast, seemed relatively passive and peripheral. They concerned themselves mainly with artistic activities of one sort or another, argued among themselves, and—to Mead—seemed maladjusted. Among the Tchambuli, Mead claimed, the gender roles associated with males and females in our own society had been reversed.

For several generations now, Mead's work has been held up as evidence that there are no "fixed" cultural elements, that in the end all cultural arrangements are arbitrary and so, in principle, subject to change. This does not mean, however, that Mead's work has not been criticized. In reviewing the responses to Mead's work, Ward (1996: 47–51) noted two criticisms in particular. First, Mead ignored history in studying the Tchambuli (which was, remember, her most important case). It turns out that at the time of Mead's visit, the Tchambuli had only recently been transferred from one location to another. While Tchambuli women quickly rebuilt the trading networks that had always been their special domain, Tchambuli men were still in the process—while Mead was there—of reestablishing the web of ritual activities that traditionally had been their domain and the source of their prestige. The result was a society in which women seemed more "dominant" than they usually were. Quite apart from her inattention to recent history, Mead has also been criticized for using global terms like "aggressive" and "passive" to describe an entire class of people. More recent feminist thinking suggests that how males and females behave, even within a single culture, can vary from context to context. On the other hand, despite the criticisms that have been levelled at Mead's work, no one denies that the three societies she studied—despite being in close geographical proximity to one another—were strikingly different from one other and so her work continues to provide clear evidence of just how different cultures can be. We shall return to Mead in the next chapter.

One advantage of becoming aware of cultural variation is that it often gives us a new perspective on things that are happening in our own society. A great many students, for example, seem to think that the high divorce rates associated with contemporary industrial societies are evidence of a declining commitment to traditional "family" values that are characteristic of life in a more traditional society. But the fact is that high divorce rates occur not only in industrial societies. In their study of nearly 200 nonindustrial societies, Broude and Greene (1983) found that divorce was almost universal in about 8 percent of these societies and that it was a relatively common event in another 37 percent. In other words, many traditional societies are more similar to our own society than we think.

Something else that we can "learn" about ourselves in studying other cultures is that many of the behaviours we consider to be deviant (deviance will be considered at length in Chapter 5) are normative elsewhere. For instance, in the late 1800s an anthropologist studying a Native society in New Mexico, the Zuni, brought a Zuni woman to Washington, D.C. The woman, whose name was We'wha, was quickly dubbed a "princess" and soon became the toast of Washington society. There was just one thing: her physical appearance seemed a bit unusual. One newspaper account of the time suggested that We'wha had a relatively broad face, a massive body, and parted her hair strangely (Ward, 1996: 176). In fact, We'wha was a biological male who had adopted the behaviours and dress more usually associated with females in Zuni society. The Zuni, like many indigenous societies in North America, recognized that some biological males had an affinity for the female role and encouraged such individuals to take on traits normally associated with females. Sometimes as well, biological females took on male roles. Early anthropologists used the term *berdache* to describe these individuals and the roles they occupied. More recently, Native scholars have suggested that such people be called "two-spirited." Whatever the term used, these individuals were regarded as engaging in behaviours that were perfectly in accord with Zuni norms. In our own society, by contrast, "two-spirited" individuals would almost certainly be labelled either transvestites or transsexuals, and their behaviour would be seen as deviant, that is, inconsistent with prevailing cultural norms.

Canadian/American value differences

So far, we have been talking about cultural variation that exists among relatively distant societies. What happens if we move closer to home, and simply consider Canada and its closest neighbour? There is a fairly extensive descriptive literature on Canadian/American value differences, but the theoretical argument that is most discussed and cited (by sociologists at least) is one put forward by Lipset, an American sociologist, who has presented his argument in a number of publications over a quarter of a century (e.g., Lipset, 1990).

Reduced to its simplest form, Lipset's argument includes two basic hypotheses. The first is that the differing historical experiences of Canada and the United States in the late eighteenth century had a profound and lasting influence on the culture of each region. One part of British North America, the United States, underwent a revolution. That experience, Lipset argued, produced a basic distrust of government and a great emphasis upon individualism. The other part of British North America, Canada, underwent no such revolution and—just as important—became the haven for many who left the United States, having rejected the American Revolution. The result was that in Canada there was a greater trust in government and a greater emphasis upon the group and maintaining harmony within it.

These initial cultural differences were reinforced by other institutional differences between the two countries. Lipset noted, for example, that throughout most of the nineteenth century the two dominant religious organizations in Canada were the Anglican Church in English Canada and the Roman Catholic Church in Quebec. Both of these organizations were hierarchically arranged and had a long history (especially in Europe) of close cooperation with the state. These historical ties made it even more likely that Canadians would have a greater trust in their government and would be less individualistic. In the United States, by contrast, the dominant religious organizations were those Protestant sects that stressed the separation of church and state, and that promoted a religious individuality.

Lipset's second hypothesis is that, once established, these cultural differences between

Canada and the United States contributed to a range of other differences. Rates of violent crime, for example, are three to four times higher in the United States. This is true, Lipset noted, even though the number of police officers per 100 000 population is substantially lower in Canada. Lipset argued that Canada has lower rates of violent crime with fewer police because Canadians are less individualistic and have a greater respect for the state. He used the same basic argument to explain why Canada has fewer riots and fewer deaths from political violence; why Canadians are more willing to endorse laws restricting various behaviours (Canadians, for instance, are more likely to endorse laws restricting the ownership of handguns, the consumption of alcohol in public, the activities of door-to-door salespeople, etc.); and why Canada has more government-run welfare programs.

Lipset consistently maintained that his argument is supported less by any one piece of data than by the way everything seems to fit together. The problem is that everything does not fit together. For example, part of Lipset's argument is that value differences between the United States and Canada were exaggerated because Canada became a haven for those who rejected the American Revolution. Yet, some have suggested that many of the settlers who came to Canada were neither especially pro-British nor anti-American, but simply individuals seeking unclaimed land (Grabb, 1998).

Lipset also reported that Americans are more likely to join voluntary organizations and that this reflects their greater distrust of government. That is, since they distrust their government, they are more willing to get things done through voluntary organizations. But more extensive tests of Lipset's claim here (reviewed in Grabb, 1998) indicate that the greater American commitment to voluntary organizations is due mainly to the fact that Americans are more likely to join church-related organizations. With regard to other sorts of voluntary organizations, such as conservation groups, human rights organizations, charities, etc., there are no systematic differences between the two nationalities.

In other places, Lipset clearly identified very real differences but offered interpretations that do not stand up to direct testing. He was quite correct, for example, in saying that there are more government-run social services in Canada. For Lipset this reflected the greater degree to which Canadians trust their government. But when attitudes are assessed directly, the situation is quite different. For instance, surveys suggest that Americans are more likely than either English- or French Canadians to be confident about their governmental institutions (e.g., Congress or Parliament) and more likely than either English- or French Canadians to respect established authority (Grabb, 1998). This is hardly what the Lipset thesis would lead us to expect.

Often Lipset seems determined to hold on to his theory even when aware of data that do not support his views. Thus, Lipset argued that the greater emphasis upon individualism in the United States hinders the development of class consciousness, which is why a strong socialist movement never developed in that country. In Canada, by contrast, the emphasis upon the group promotes class consciousness, and Canada did develop a strong socialist party in the form of the NDP. The problem is that support for the NDP has been lowest in precisely those regions of Canada, like Quebec and the Maritimes, where even Lipset admitted that a cultural emphasis upon the group has been especially strong. Lipset's response was to equate the Parti Québécois with the NDP in Quebec and to suggest that extensive patronage in the Maritimes has created a web of personal loyalties that encourages the population to support the traditional parties.

Baer, Grabb, and Johnston (1993) have suggested that part of the difficulty in testing Lipset's theory is that regional differences *within* Canada and the United States are more important than national differences *between* the two countries. Using a variety of attitudinal measures, for instance, they argued that Quebeckers have become relatively liberal on most issues and that people from the U.S. South are especially conservative. When these two groups (Quebec and the U.S. South) are excluded from the analysis, these authors failed to find any significant attitudinal differences between Canadians and Americans.

Some commentators have rejected Lipset's theory simply because it seems implausible (to them) that historical events occurring two hundred years ago could have the strong and continuing influence that Lipset alleged. These commentators suggest that whatever differences might exist between Canada and the U.S. are more easily explained by things happening now, in the present, than by things that happened so long ago. For instance, crime rates are lower in the Canada than in the U.S., but Grabb (1998) suggested that this pattern is more plausibly explained by linking such rates to the greater disparity between rich and poor in the U.S. and to fact that the U.S. is more characterized by deep-seated racial antagonisms. Similarly, rates of religious participation are higher in the U.S. than in Canada, but this is part of a global pattern that has nothing to do with the American Revolution per se. Rates of religious participation are almost always higher in the presence of religious diversity, that is, where a wide range of religious groups are competing with one another (Finke and Starke, 1992), and the U.S. is currently more religiously diverse than Canada (see Chapter 11, Religion).

Yet, as shaky as Lipset's theory seems, it is probably premature to reject it entirely. As we shall see in a few pages, most of the important theoretical perspectives on culture have been developed by anthropologists, not by sociologists. In all cases, anthropological assessments of cultural values in a society have been based on an analysis of things like mythology, religion, literature, folklore, etc., and not upon surveys, or at least surveys of the sort conducted by sociologists. It has seemed obvious to anthropological investigators that a myth or a folktale that has been passed along from generation to generation, for example, is far more likely to say something about cultural values than are the standardized responses (strongly agree, agree, disagree, strongly disagree) to a fixed set of questions created by an investigator. This has seemed especially true when the concern has been to detect those cultural values that people hold strongly but do not consciously think about-those of which they may not be fully aware.

If we wanted to assess Canadian culture using the more traditional anthropological methods, what would we look at instead of survey data? One obvious possibility is Canadian literature. Indeed, a number of commentators (mainly writers and literary critics, not sociologists) have called attention to certain themes that do distinguish Canadian literature from American literature. Lipset (1990) himself reviewed much of the research here, since some of the differences lend support to his theory. Several commentators have suggested, for example, that there is more emphasis upon generational conflict (especially between fathers and their rebellious sons) in American literature and a greater emphasis upon the maintenance of harmonious relationships in Canadian literature. In other cases, the systematic differences identified by previous commentators seem less relevant to Lipset's theory, but are nonetheless interesting in themselves. A higher proportion of the important writers in Canada are women, for instance, and strong female characters may be more likely to appear in Canadian fiction.

The moral? There may be deep-rooted differences between Canadian culture and American culture that are undetectable using the survey research so prominent in sociology, and so anyone seriously interested in the study of Canadian culture would do well to supplement quantitative sociology courses with courses in qualitative sociology, anthropology, Canadian literature, and Canadian art.

Cultural universals

So far, we have been concerned only with cultural diversity. But among all the diversity, are there any **cultural universals**? That is, are there any elements of culture found in every single, known society? There do seem to be a few. Every society, for instance, has rules limiting sexual behaviour, though the content and number of these rules vary greatly from society to society. In every known society, there is a division of labour by sex, with certain tasks allocated to females and others to males, although the task assignments to either men or women vary among societies.

Some students might think that an incest *taboo*, a norm prohibiting sexual intercourse between parents and children and between siblings, is universal, and they would be right—almost. It turns out that there are about a half-dozen or so societies in which incestuous relationships were permitted for members of the royal family as a way to maintain the purity of the royal lineage. Indeed, in some it was actively encouraged. For instance,

Anthropologists often attempt to detect cultural values that are strongly held but not consciously conceptualized.

between 325 B.C. and 50 B.C., Egypt was ruled by the Ptolemies, a royal dynasty founded by Ptolemy I, one of Alexander the Great's generals, and eleven of the thirteen Ptolemaic kings married either a half- or full sister. There is also evidence that brother/sister marriage was widely practised among commoners in ancient Egypt. One estimate (Roscoe, 1996) suggests that in certain Egyptian communities at least one-sixth of all marriages were between full siblings. The incest taboo, then, is only a near universal.

One of the most important of all cultural universals concerns the relative status of men and women. There are many societies in which men, on average, have more political power and more social prestige than women; these are usually called *patriarchies*. Then there are a fair number of known societies in which men and women are roughly equal in social status, either because one group does not, on the average, have more power and prestige than the other, or because greater male power and prestige in certain areas of social life are balanced by greater female power and prestige in other areas of

social life. Yet, amid the diversity known to exist among all the societies of the world, there has never existed a true *matriarchy*, that is, a society in which women have more political power and more social prestige than men. The Amazons of myth and legend are just that: myth and legend. What we are dealing with here, then, is a negative universal; that is, with something—matriarchy—that is universally absent from all known societies.

The most important point to make in connection with cultural universals, however, is that the number of such universals is relatively small, at least as compared with the number of ways in which cultures vary.

Cultural integration

Before closing this section, it is necessary to point out that many of the elements that comprise a given culture are interrelated, so that a change in one element can produce changes—often quite unintended changes—in other elements. This inter-relationship is known as **cultural integration**. The

On Defining the "Father" Role:
An Example from Nuer Society

The patriarchal Nuer, an African society, accept two types of marriage that we usually do not. In each, the person who plays the role of father for a child is not the biological father. In the first case, a Nuer widow remains bound until her death to transfer rights to her children to her husband's group. This contract becomes effective when her father accepts cattle from her husband's group at the time of her marriage.

Ideally, she will remarry her deceased husband's brother or some other member of his group. But even if she simply takes lovers, any children born of those unions will be defined as offspring of her dead husband (hence the term "ghost marriage"). In a rarer form of Nuer marriage, an older wealthy woman may give cattle to a father to "marry" his daughter. The young woman then takes lovers and any children born are defined as the children of the female "father" and belong to the older woman's father's group, even though membership in it is transmitted along the male line. Here we have an exception to the near cultural universal that "fathers" must be males.

Source: Adapted from Roger M. Keesing, 1981. Cultural Anthropology: A Contemporary Perspective. (2nd ed.) New York: Holt, Rinehart and Winston (pp. 216–217).

---

best way to illustrate this process is to consider the extreme case, in which a single cultural change, made with the best of intentions, had ramifications that were massive and utterly disastrous.

An instance of this sort is provided by considering an aboriginal society in Australia called the Yir Yoront. Traditionally, the Yir Yoront travelled throughout various regions of Australia in small bands, each band a cooperative unit that gathered plants for food and hunted animals. In the early decades of the twentieth century, the Anglican Church set up a mission with the goal of converting the Yir Yoront to Christianity. To reward those individuals who came to the mission and took instruction, these missionaries passed out something that they thought would be useful: axes with steel heads. Before this time, the Yir Yoront had used stone-headed axes they had made themselves. A few years after the advent of the Anglican mission, many Yir Yoront bands had ceased to function as cohesive social units and their members had become completely dependent upon handouts from the mission. What happened? For Sharp (1952), the key lay in the impact of those steel axes upon Yir Yoront culture; but to understand this impact you need to know more about that culture.

Most of us probably formed our initial impression of what life in a nonliterate culture is like from the movies, and most movies portray tribal societies as having a chief of some sort. The notion that a small band of individuals should have a single leader strikes us as being perfectly natural and obvious. But, in fact, small bands do not always have a single leader. The Yir Yoront did not have chiefs. In this society, any two individuals would determine who had authority over the other by using a complicated system of rules. Basically, these rules specified that older people had authority over younger people, that men had authority over women, and that some blood relatives had a measure of authority over other blood relatives. Though these rules tended to concentrate authority in the hands of the older males within a given kinship group, the system was complicated enough that the lines of authority were not always clear. To solve this problem, the Yir Yoront had devised a very concrete procedure for constantly reinforcing these lines of authority; this procedure involved their traditional stone-headed axes.

These axes were used for a variety of tasks that confronted the average Yir Yoront. But, while everybody might need an axe, the axes were the property of the older males within each kinship group. This meant that anyone needing an axe would have to go to one of these individuals. In effect, asking one of these older males for permission to use his axe became a way of acknowledging that male's authority.

Now enter the European missionaries, filled with the typically Western attitude that superior technology (steel axe-heads rather than stone, for instance) is always a good thing. They distributed axes with steel heads to the Yir Yoront who came to the mission, but it turned out that it was mainly women or young men who did so; therefore, these were the people who got the new axes. Having their own axes meant, of course, that they no longer had to go to the older males for the use of an axe. While this might seem very fair and egalitarian to us, the fact remains that, lacking the concrete procedure to reinforce the lines of authority in the society (asking for permission to use an axe), the authority system fell apart, and nothing arose to take its place. Without an authority system, it became difficult to maintain the cooperation among band members necessary for successful hunting and gathering activities. Consequently, the bands ceased to function as independent social groups because some missionaries gave axes to a category of individuals (young men and women) who, under their culture's prevailing social norms, should not have owned them.

Within more differentiated societies, the interrelationship of cultural elements often ensures that the same change will have quite different consequences for different groups. Di Leonardo (1991) presented a good example of this in a discussion of a social movement calling itself the "Great Way of Former Heaven," which arose in Kwangtung, China, around the turn of the twentieth century, and which defined heterosexuality and childbirth as polluting. A great many women saw this movement as a way of liberating themselves from the restraints of a patriarchal society. The movement's ideology allowed single women to resist traditionally arranged marriages and to take jobs in the local silk industry. Women already in arranged marriages who joined the movement were able to avoid sex (with their husbands and other males) and childbirth, and were able to live with other women. In this case, however, avoiding sex and childbirth meant purchasing other women, concubines, who were obliged to be available for sex with the husbands. The women who became concubines hardly benefited as a result of this social movement. Here then is a case in which a change

that raised the status of one group of women had the opposite effect for another group of women in the same society.

The point concerning cultural integration should not be over-emphasized. Cultures are never so tightly integrated that any change will have widespread effects. Whether a particular cultural change introduced within a group will have further cultural ramifications depends upon the particular pattern of interrelationships among the cultural traits found in that group. Tracing out the relationships linking the cultural traits in various groups is one of the primary tasks of the sociologist and the social anthropologist.

Conceptual Dangers in the Study of Culture

The "scientific ideal" suggests that decisions to reject or accept arguments have to do with the fit (or lack of fit) between arguments and the relevant empirical data. But those of you who read the fine print at the bottom of Chart 1.2 in Chapter 1 were told that this ideal is not always met. What we accept as sociological knowledge is sometimes determined as much by our pre-existing biases as by the data that we gather. This bias is an example of what we call ethnocentrism. In its most general sense, **ethnocentrism** refers to the tendency to see things from the point of view of the observer's culture rather than from that of the observed. It occurs frequently, not only among students, but even among social scientists. But this general definition masks degrees of ethnocentrism.

At its worst, ethnocentrism can refer to the tendency to view other cultures as inferior rather than just different. This type of ethnocentrism was especially prevalent during the nineteenth century. For instance, most social anthropologists of the time accepted a view of social evolution which held that societies passed through three stages: savagery, barbarism, and civilization. They also believed that most nonindustrial cultures were stuck at the levels of savagery or barbarism, indicating the low esteem in which they held these cultures.

Though far less common today, ethnocentrism of this sort still crops up now and again. For instance, someone who uses the term "primitive society" to refer to what is really a nonindustrial society might be accused of ethnocentrism, since "primitive" now carries negative connotations that go far beyond a simple consideration of the type of economy found in a society.

A more subtle type of ethnocentrism, harder to spot and probably more common among the readers of this book than the one just described, is the tendency to believe that what is true of your culture is also true of other cultures. Given the nature of our society, two specific biases that flow from this type of ethnocentrism are Eurocentrism and androcentrism.

Eurocentrism is a bit of a misnomer, since it refers to a bias that goes beyond the borders of modern Europe. Basically, a theory or theoretical perspective is said to be Eurocentric when it has been shaped by the values and experiences of the white, middle class in Western industrialized societies. In the simplest case, Eurocentrism means assuming that these values and experiences are universally shared. This happens more often (and more easily) than you might expect.

In the early part of this century, archeologists investigating the Ice Age in Europe began discovering female figurines carved out of stone. They were found over a wide area that stretched from France to the Ural mountains, with most being found in Central Europe. In the majority of cases, the breasts, hips, and buttocks of the woman depicted seemed especially large, something which suggested to the (mainly male) archeologists involved that the figurines were associated with fertility. The figurines were promptly dubbed "prehistoric Venuses" (after the Roman goddess of beauty) and accepted as evidence that a fertility goddess had been worshiped in prehistoric Europe.

Over the past few decades, professional archeologists, including most feminist archeologists, have challenged the fertility-goddess interpretation of these figurines. First, it seems unlikely that the figurines represent a single goddess or a single anything. Rice (1981), for instance, demonstrated that the figurines display the same diversity with regard to physical traits (some are pregnant, some are not; some are young, some are old; etc.) that you would expect to find among a living population of prehistoric women. This would suggest that the figurines are more likely representations of individual women. But more importantly, nothing in the archeological record itself suggests that the figurines were used for a religious purpose. Indeed, other possible explanations exist.

Townsend (1990) pointed out, for example, that human figurines have been used for a variety of purposes in non-Western societies. In certain First Nations societies in Alaska, shamans had dolls that

More Than Just a Toy: Barbie as Cultural Icon

In Greek mythology, Athena sprang fully grown from the head of Zeus and went on to acquire a reputation for cleverness. In 1959, Barbie emerged as a fully formed teenager from somewhere within the Mattel Corporation to become the best-selling toy in the world. Athena was born wearing a suit of armour; Barbie came equipped with a hard plastic body. Athena was virginal but worked with males on a number of difficult tasks;

Barbie is virginal (at least semi-virginal) and paired with Ken. But Barbie and Athena differ dramatically in at least two ways: Barbie has lots more stuff and a whole lot more fun!

Barbie's success is phenomenal. In the United States and Canada, the vast majority of girls under the age of twelve have at least one Barbie, and it's common for a girl to have several Barbies. What accounts for Barbie's popularity?

Partly, it's due to the fact that Barbie and the merchandising package that surrounds her mesh so well with the dominant culture in most capitalistic societies. Barbie, after all, is the quintessential consumer, and in the never-ending task of acquiring for Barbie her own special cars, horses, furniture, jewelry, clothing, etc., young girls learn to become the sort of

continued

consumer upon whom capitalistic societies depend. Barbie also embodies qualities that have long been favoured in middle-class families: she's pretty, neat, always anxious to have the proper outfit for the proper occasion, and (it goes without saying) intensely heterosexual. Finally, Barbie works to reinforce the traditional gender roles that so many members of the middle class now see as under attack by feminists. She is, after all, concerned with her appearance (her hair in particular), likes nice clothes, and gravitates towards occupations (stewardess, teacher, candy striper, fashion designer, perfume designer, etc.) traditionally associated with women. True, she does occasionally break away from the traditional gender stereotype. In the early 1970s, for instance, Barbie became a medical doctor. The fact is, however, Dr. Barbie never did sell very well (Urla and Swedlund, 1996: 283).

As a cultural icon, however, Barbie is most distinctive on account of her impossible body. Although she has undergone many transformations over the last few decades, and although there are now a variety of Barbies that differ from one another in regard to skin colour and facial features, two things have remained constant: her elongated body and her large breasts. Urla and Swedlund (1996)

compared the measurements taken from a sample of different Barbies with the measurements of the statistically "average" female in the United States. Needless to say, they discovered that if Barbie were scaled to the height of the average female, and her bodily proportions remained constant, then she would be clinically anorexic to an extreme degree-albeit unusually buxom. These same authors did a similar study with Barbie's friend Ken. They found that Ken's proportions were also unrealistic when compared with the statistically average male, but (and this, they argue, is the important point here) far less so than Barbie's. To the extent that Barbie's body sets a standard that is impossible for real-life girls to meet, she reinforces a cultural climate in which women must inevitably be considered inferior. Moreover, Urla and Swedlund pointed out, in the midst of the excesses characteristic of capitalistic societies, that a slender body is something that can be achieved only through self-discipline and control; Barbie's hyper-slender body therefore suggests that females are in special need of control and discipline and this, too, may reinforce male domination or patriarchy (see Chapter 7, Gender Relations).

But nothing is ever simple, and Urla and Swedlund went on to suggest further that we should also pay

attention to what Barbie is not. For instance, although Barbie has many accessories, a husband and (her own) children are not among them. Barbie is not, in other words, a wife and mother. Nor is she, like so many other dolls, a child to be cared for as a child. On the contrary, Barbie is a strongly sexualized female who conveys an aura of independence. There is, in short, little about Barbie or Barbie's merchandising that can be seen as socializing young girls for a traditional role as mother and wife. To paraphrase the authors: Barbie owns an expensive car and isn't married; she can't be doing everything wrong!

Finally, we must not fall into the trap of regarding young girls as purely passive consumers of what confronts them. Whatever Mattel may intend Barbie to be, young girls are capable of associating their Barbie dolls with a range of roles and personalities. What is needed, these authors suggested, is more research into just what these different roles and personalities are.

In the end, then, Barbie turns out to be surrounded by a fairly complex set of cultural values. These values may not all be consistent with one another, but they are all very much reflective of the cultural milieu from which Barbie sprang and in which she flourishes.

were thought to travel to another world to retrieve lost souls. Women in Tanzania were often healed by driving their illness into a figurine. In other societies, human figures are used in magical procedures designed to harm somebody. In short, there is a range of meanings that the Venus figurines could have had for prehistoric peoples in Europe.

So why has the interpretation of the Venus figurines as prehistoric goddesses become so

popular with Western audiences? Most likely because this interpretation conforms to two preexisting biases that are both Eurocentric. First, in a number of European societies—from the Classical civilizations of Greece and Rome, to the Christian societies of the Middle Ages, to contemporary Roman Catholic societies—people have routinely made statues of the supernatural beings in whom they believe. The practice is familiar

The idea of a "fertility goddess" conforms to a Euro-centric gender stereotype of women as nurturing beings.

to us, it "makes sense." But there's more. Part of the traditional gender stereotype associated with women in the Western tradition is that women are most of all supposed to be mothers, whose primary goal is to bear and nurture children. The idea of a nurturing "mother goddess" responsible for fertility is consistent with this Western stereotype, and so once again the idea of a prehistoric mother goddess seems to "make sense" to us and for that reason seems plausible. In both cases, then, we are assuming that what makes sense to us would have made sense as well to prehistoric peoples. That is Eurocentric thinking.

Another common Eurocentric bias has to do with power. When parties of unequal power meet, those with less power often find it necessary to adapt their behaviour to the dictates of those with more power. Since this is something that the more powerful parties rarely have to do, it is something that they can easily miss or overlook. Given the power differences that exist between Western and non-Western societies, this means that contact with the West can (and has) produced changes in non-Western societies that have been overlooked by Western commentators.

For instance, when Europeans made contact with First Nations communities in eastern Canada, they reported that these communities were dominated by males, and these early reports were taken at face value by later commentators. By contrast, Leacock (1983) suggested that in the period just before European contact, First Nations communities in eastern Canada were most likely egalitarian, with the political and economic importance of males and females being roughly equal. But the European males who contacted these communities were used to dealing with other males. Because Europe was the more powerful culture, First Nations communities had to adapt to this fact. The result was that as these communities fell under European influence, the economic and political importance of their males increased relative to females. In short, if Leacock is right, the social inequality of males and females in these particular First Nations societies came into existence only after European contact, and this process went entirely unnoticed by European observers.

An unwillingness to acknowledge the ways in which power shapes our interaction with other cultures, and the accounts that we construct of other cultures, is by no means limited to the distant past. Patai (1994) pointed out that the sociological and anthropological investigators who pour out of North America to study the societies of the developing world are usually white and middle class and almost always perceived (correctly) by the people they study as having access to all sorts of resources (including simply being on good terms with the local authorities). This may raise expectations on the part of the people being studied (expectations, for instance, that the investigator may "help" them in some way) and this in turn can shape their response to the investigator's queries.

Androcentrism means "male-centredness." It is a bias that involves (1) seeing things from a male point of view or (2) seeing things in a way that reinforces male privilege in society. One form of androcentric bias, for example, is to systematically develop cultural interpretations that see men as active and women as passive even when the available data are consistent with other interpretations.

For instance, it is routine (and has been for more than a century) for anthropologists to see the manufacture of stone tools by our prehistoric ancestors as one of the first and most important technological innovations in the history of our species. Gero (1991) noted that almost all discussions of stone tool production have assumed that these tools were made by males. But why? Modern experiments have demonstrated that making stone tools does not require great upper-body strength, which if it did might give males an advantage. Furthermore, the very sites where archeologists found most stone tools—house floors, base camps, village sites—are quite plausibly areas in which women congregated to carry out their work. This suggested to Gero that at least some stone tools are likely to have been used by women. But if women used stone tools, she argued, there is no particular reason not to suppose that women also made stone tools.

In short, there is no evidence that rules out the possibility that women were as active as (or even more active than) men in the manufacture of stone tools. Why then have anthropology textbooks consistently seen "man the tool-maker" standing so prominently at the dawn of human prehistory, and why have the students who have read these texts been so willing to accept this image? Gero's answer is that we have projected a current androcentric image—men as the active inventors of important technologies—back on to the past.

Androcentrism also can mean a tendency to prefer theories that proclaim innate differences between males and females and which therefore provide a rationale for gender inequalities in society. Implicit in much sociological thinking in the nineteenth and early twentieth centuries, for instance, was the notion that individuals had a limited amount of "vital force" that could be used for thinking and biological reproduction. Since women devoted so much of their vital force towards reproduction, there was less of it available for thinking. This explained (so the argument went)

why women were less intelligent than men. The androcentric bias here seems evident. But before you laugh aloud and conclude that modern audiences would never be so gullible as to accept a theory like this, keep in mind that it is still widely believed—both by a number of social scientists and by many university students—that males are more likely to use the right side of their brain than females, and that this is why males are better at mathematics than females, even though there is much controversy surrounding this view (see Chapter 7, Gender Relations). Is talking about unsubstantiated differences in "brain lateralization" really all that different from talking about unsubstantiated differences in the allocation of "vital force"?

Androcentric bias also leads us to choose the male experience over the female experience for study. Traditional anthropological accounts of hunting and gathering societies, for example, devoted far more space to describing hunting activities (usually done by males) than to gathering activities (usually done by females) even when gathering provided most of the food consumed in a society. The simple fact that we call these societies "hunting and gathering societies" rather than "gathering and hunting societies" is for some feminist anthropologists an indication of androcentric bias.

Finally, androcentrism seems evident in those cases where theories that purport to be about society in general are really about the male experience in society. Gilligan (1982: 18) pointed out, for instance, that the index to Piaget's influential *Moral Development of the Child* (see Chapter 4, Socialization) has four entries under "girls." By contrast, there is no entry at all called "boys." This is because, she argued, "the child" that Piaget discussed at length throughout the book is implicitly assumed to be male. Similarly, Kohlberg (also in the Socialization chapter) used a sample of male college students to develop a theory of moral development and subsequently declared that theory to be universal. Gilligan's (1982) own research demonstrated how starting with a sample of females produces a quite different model of moral development.

Theoretical Perspectives on Culture

Sociologists who study culture have used a range of theoretical perspectives. The most important and best-known analyses of culture, however, have each drawn upon one of four quite different perspectives. These are: (1) functionalism, (2) conflict theory, (3) cultural materialism, and (4) feminism.

Functionalism

Functionalism is a perspective you encountered in the introductory chapter, and one that you will see again many times throughout this book. The essence of functionalist explanation, when applied to culture, is that a given norm or value is explained by showing how it contributes to the overall stability or survival of the society in which it is found.

One of the first investigators to use this functional explanation in an explicit way was a social anthropologist named Bronislaw Malinowski. His work, even today, provides some of the clearest examples of functionalist explanation. Malinowski (1954 [1925]) was at one point studying a society located among the Trobriand Islands in the South Pacific. The Trobrianders derived much of their food from fishing in the ocean waters surrounding their islands. What Malinowski found was that every aspect of such ocean fishing was surrounded by an elaborate system of magic. But why did they use magic? At first glance the answer might seem obvious: the Trobrianders used magic because they believed it would help them catch more fish. But, Malinowski argued, if magic is used simply to ensure success, then every society should use magic extensively to ensure success at whatever activity is important to its members. Such widespread use of magic, however, is simply not the case. Some societies, like the Trobrianders, make extensive use of magic; others do not. What accounts for this cultural difference?

In beginning his explanation, Malinowski noted that ocean fishing is an extremely uncertain activity. The Trobrianders had no control over the weather or over the locations at which fish might be caught. Added to this, of course, was the fact that taking a canoe on to the ocean was a relatively dangerous activity. How would you feel if you had to engage in a dangerous and uncertain activity day after day? You would probably feel quite anxious, and Malinowski assumed that the Trobrianders felt the same way. This anxiety would be reduced if you felt, however incorrectly, that you could control your environment. This is precisely the feeling that magic provides. The use of magic allowed the Trobrianders to believe that they could control both the weather and the locations at which fish were to be found. Malinowski's conclusion, then, is that magic is likely to be used whenever people face dangerous and uncertain environments. The Trobrianders faced such an environment, and therefore used magic. Other societies face relatively safe, certain environments, and therefore they do not use magic.

Malinowski had one final bit of data that provided an especially convincing conclusion to his argument. Besides fishing on the open ocean, the Trobrianders also fished in a sheltered lagoon. Unlike ocean fishing, fishing in the lagoon was relatively safe, and since the lagoon was a relatively small place, finding the right place to fish was less of a problem. Given Malinowski's argument, one would expect that magic would not be associated with lagoon fishing. That is exactly what he found. Although the Trobrianders surrounded ocean fishing with much magic, none was associated with lagoon fishing.

Notice how Malinowski's explanation fits the basic functionalist pattern. He explained a given cultural element, in this case the use of magic, by showing how it contributes to the overall stability of the society: magic reduces the anxiety produced by the dangers and uncertainties associated with open-ocean fishing.

The functionalist perspective used by Malinowski influenced not only social anthropologists, but sociologists as well. Perhaps the best examples of functionalist explanation in sociology are contained in a book entitled *Human Society*, written by Kingsley Davis. Published originally in 1949, the book has been reprinted many times. *Human Society* was intended to be an introductory text, though one that explicitly adopted a functionalist perspective. As a result, most of Davis's discussion is devoted to those fairly standard topics, such as socialization, religious institutions, and marriage and the family, that tend to be covered in every introductory textbook. But Davis also devoted an entire chapter to something that would strike many as an unlikely candidate for functionalist explanation: sexual jealousy among males.

Most people probably regard such jealousy as somehow pathological, as resulting from, say, the basic insecurity of males concerning sexual matters. Nevertheless, sexual jealousy among males is found in every known society, and for the functionalist, like Davis, that means that it probably contributes to social stability. But how?

Davis started off by making a very crucial assumption-crucial in the sense that if it were false, his entire argument would fall apart. He assumed that, unless a society placed some restrictions upon sexual intercourse, most males would be constantly competing with other males for sexual access, producing much conflict. The conflict, in turn, would prevent the cooperation that must be maintained if society is to survive. This assumption led Davis to conclude that every society must have norms of some sort regulating sexual intercourse. But how are these norms enforced? That is, what ensures that most members of society obey most of the norms most of the time? There has to be some type of deterrent. That is where sexual jealousy comes in.

Jealousy is an emotional response that fosters aggression. Specifically, it fosters aggression against people who have given others a reason to be jealous. Given this fact, Davis argued, a community will encourage its members to be jealous whenever their sexual rights have been violated, sexual rights being those rights guaranteed under the prevailing sexual norms. The fact that the community encourages people to be jealous whenever their sexual rights have been violated will deter individuals who might think of violating those rights. For instance, suppose

Re-Reading Mother Teresa: A Conflict Approach?

If I asked most of you reading this book to list ten public figures you admire and respect, Mother Teresa would probably appear on a great many lists. Born in 1910 in the former Yugoslavia to Albanian parents, Mother Teresa founded an order of Roman Catholic sisters who today minister to the poor in over eighty countries. From the early 1950s until her retirement for reasons of health in 1990, she personally gathered the dying from the streets of Calcutta, India, and brought them to her hospital where they could die with dignity. As a result, Mother Teresa was often called a "living saint," and in 1979 was awarded the Nobel Prize for Peace.

Although it rarely makes the news, Mother Teresa was criticized by a number of Roman Catholic activists, in India and elsewhere. In an interview published in an Italian magazine (L'Expresso, September 9, 1990), a Catholic theologian who teaches near Calcutta suggested that it was the Western media that "created" Mother Teresa. He meant that it was the Western media—not the media in India or the rest of the Third World—that first raised her to mythic status. Certainly, it was a Western agency that granted her the Nobel Peace Prize.

Why the criticism? It relates to Mother Teresa's approach to poverty. For her, poverty is something to be alleviated by good works. In her many speeches, she never attacks the root causes of poverty, those social conditions that ensure that the mass of people in the Third World remain poor while relatively few remain rich. Her approach to poverty, in other words, does not threaten entrenched privilege. The conflict approach to religion, to be discussed in Chapter 11, Religion, makes the same point, that religion is a conservative force, one that can be used as a means to calm the masses, a flower on the chain of oppression.

So, how much of the West's regard for Mother Teresa is due to a sincere appreciation of her selflessness (and certainly no one doubts that as an individual she is selfless) and how much to the fact that the West controls and consumes most of the world's resources and finds in Mother Teresa someone whose approach to poverty does not threaten that pattern of control and consumption? Sounds to me like a good discussion question. It shows that in applying a conflict perspective, surprising issues can be raised, even about Mother Teresa.

that one of the sexual norms in a society is that the only person who has a right to sexual intercourse with a married woman is her husband. The foreknowledge that a husband will become jealous (and aggressive) if some other male has intercourse with his wife and the foreknowledge that this jealousy will be encouraged by the community at large would, according to Davis, deter to some degree both the wife and any potential lover from violating that norm. To convince yourself of the reasonableness of the Davis argument, you might think about things the other way around. If it were absolutely certain that people in this society would not get jealous if someone had intercourse with their spouse, would this make adultery more likely? If you answered yes to this question, then you basically agree with Davis's analysis.

A consequence of this formulation is that the only way to eliminate sexual jealousy is to eliminate sexual norms—and if Davis's initial assumption is correct, this cannot be done without producing much social instability. Functionalist explanations of this sort are still popular in sociology, but much less so than they once were. Thus, let us turn to other perspectives, beginning with conflict theory.

Conflict theory

Some conflict theorists, following Marx, lump cultural beliefs under the more general heading of "ideology," the system of thought that serves the interests of the dominant groups in society. This usually means that ideology is seen as something that legitimates existing inequalities of wealth and power, or as something that prevents the less powerful from seeing the true cause of this inequality. Conflict theorists also apply this same perspective to religion (also usually considered to be ideology). You will be considering the Marxist perspective on religion in Chapter 11.

A conflict approach to culture has been especially influential in connection with the *sociology of knowledge*. This is a subfield of sociology concerned with studying the influence of social factors on what passes for knowledge in a society. Sociologists of knowledge adopt the view that knowledge is a cultural element, and that we acquire knowledge in much the same way that we acquire other cultural elements. This runs counter to the commonsense view that what we accept as knowledge is determined mainly by rational criteria, such as the degree to which a piece of knowledge is supported by the available evidence. In any event, the conflict variant of the sociology of knowledge is that forms of knowledge—for example, scientific theories—often become popular in a society as much because they serve the interests of the dominant classes in that society as because they have a basis in fact or anything else.

Do you really think it is a coincidence, a conflict theorist might argue, that Darwin's theory of evolution first became popular in nineteenth-century England? Or are you willing to grant that Darwin's emphasis upon competition and survival of the fittest, as the keys to evolution, just might have been especially appealing in a society in which the rich favoured free economic competition and believed their high status to be mainly the result of their innate abilities?

Or take something closer to home: the theories presented in this book. You have been told—and will be told again and again in this textbook—that functionalism is a major theoretical perspective in sociology. By itself, that statement is true. But why? Why, in other words, has functionalism proven so popular with sociologists in North America? A conflict theorist might answer by pointing to the essentially conservative nature of functionalism. It is, after all, a theoretical perspective that emphasizes how cultural elements, such as values and norms, contribute to the stability and smooth functioning of society. Such a perspective, so the argument goes, would naturally be favoured by the dominant groups in society who have a stake in maintaining the status quo.

In Chapter 6, Social Inequality, you will be introduced to a particular functionalist theory dealing with stratification. (You might want to jump ahead to page 144 and read that theory before proceeding here.) This theory suggests that certain occupations both are "more functionally important" to the smooth running of society and require "more talent"—are "harder to fill"—than others, and therefore that the smooth functioning of society depends upon insuring that qualified people move into these more important and harder-to-fill occupations. And how is that done? Why, by insuring that these occupations are given more social rewards (read: money, prestige, and power) than other occupations. *Voilà*: an argument that suggests that stratification is valuable because it contributes to social stability. A conflict theorist would suggest that this theory has proven so durable in sociology (it first appeared in the 1940s) because it suggests that inequality is, well, *good* for society. It would thus be a theory favoured by some middle- and upper-class professors who teach it (and the middle- and upper-class students who learn about it).

The great value of the conflict perspective on culture is that it forces us to challenge a great many attitudes and beliefs that would otherwise be unexamined. Even if in the end we reject a particular conflict account, the exercise of considering it is very much in keeping with the purpose of education. With this in mind, you might try developing a conflict perspective on some of the many campaigns that are important in our society at the moment. Is there any basis for believing, for example, that the current cultural emphasis upon global ecology or upon household recycling works to divert our attention from prevailing injustices and from the groups that are responsible for those injustices? Or what about those campaigns against cancer that adopt a purely medical model, seeing cancer mainly as a disease for which a medical cure must be found, rather than, say, mainly as a condition brought on by things put into our environment by industry? You might surprise yourself.

Cultural materialism

Cultural materialism is a third perspective used to study and explain culture. Cultural materialists de-emphasize ideas and ideology as determinants of cultures, and instead see cultures as adaptations to the needs forced upon social groups by the specific physical environments in which they live.

The essence of cultural materialism is best conveyed by examples, and the best examples of this approach are to be found in the applications developed by Harris (1985). One of his concerns was to explain the Hindu ban on the slaughter of cows. To many Western observers, this ban may seem utterly senseless, a classic example of how religion and the inertia of tradition can stand in the way of rational behaviour (religion and rationality

Cultural materialism sees culture as an adaptation to the needs forced upon people by the nature of the physical environment in which they live.

will be discussed in Chapter 11, Religion). Nothing seems more tragic than for Hindu farmers in India to see their families starve rather than kill the sacred cows that wander the countryside. Nevertheless, Harris argued, if you think that the Hindu farmers are in a tragic situation right now, that is nothing compared with the misery and human devastation that would result if those farmers started to slaughter their cows.

How did Harris come to this very counter-intuitive position? He started by noting that there are two basic types of agricultural systems in the world today. One, the type used in Canada and most Western nations, is a highly mechanized system that relies on tractors for motive power. Such a system also relies heavily upon petrochemicals, both to fuel the tractors and to provide synthetic fertilizers. The second type is a nonmechanized system that relies on draft animals like oxen for motive power and uses dung for fertilizer. This is the system that characterizes modern India.

There are three reasons why India cannot convert to the more mechanized system of agriculture. First, India currently has insufficient capital either to purchase the required machinery or to establish a system for the distribution of petrochemical products. Second, the experiences in Western nations make it quite clear that one effect of agricultural mechanization is the displacement of people from the country to the city. India's urban areas are already overcrowded and simply cannot absorb a massive influx from the country. Third, although Westerners think that tractors are more efficient than oxen, Harris argued that this is not always true. In India, a tractor can plough a field about ten times faster than can a pair of oxen, but the initial cost of that tractor is something like twenty times the cost of the oxen. Given this fact, tractors are more cost-effective than oxen only in the case of large farms that require a lot of ploughing. In the case of small farms—and the vast majority of farms in India are small—oxen are more cost-effective than tractors. India, then, will probably continue to use the nonmechanical type of agriculture for some time to come.

At this point, Harris came up with an interesting statistic from Indian government reports: in an average year, the number of oxen available for use by Indian farmers is only about 66 percent of the number of oxen needed by those same farmers. This chronic shortage of oxen is one of the major reasons why thousands of Indian farms fail each year. If Western farmers want new tractors, they go to a dealer, but if Indian farmers want a new ox, they go to—a cow.

We begin to catch a glimmer of the reasoning behind Harris's position. Only by insuring that most of its farms are productive can India feed itself. Only by maintaining a large population of cows can India's farmers be assured that sufficient oxen will be available to make the farms productive. Even with the current ban on the slaughter of cows, there are not enough oxen to go around. Think of how much greater the problem would be if a significant percentage of those cows were slaughtered.

But wait. Isn't there a flaw in the argument? If maintaining a large population of cows is so much in the farmers' self-interest, why do things have to be formalized under the guise of a religious ban? Wouldn't farmers just naturally not slaughter their cows? Harris's response to this criticism is simple. Rains in India are irregular and thus famine is recurrent and unavoidable. Indian farmers are like you or me; if they see their families starving, they will be strongly tempted to kill their cows to feed their families. Yet if they do kill those cows during a time of famine, there will be an even greater shortage of oxen than normally occurs, and it will be difficult for agriculture to recover when the famine ends. In fact, killing the cows might easily mean that the famine will never end.

The only solution is a total, absolute, and religiously inspired ban on the slaughter of cows. Only a ban of this sort has the remotest chance of overcoming the farmers' temptations to feed themselves and their families during times of famine.

Students who have found this example of cultural materialism interesting should consult Harris (1985), in which he also provides explanations as to why North Americans won't eat horsemeat (though most of Europe does) but love milk (regarded as something like cow spit in traditional China), why Europeans don't eat insects but people living in the Amazon basin do, and why the Aztecs ate other human beings on a scale unheard of anywhere else in the world. Lunch anyone?

Feminism(s)

As you read in the last chapter and will read in Chapter 7, Gender Relations, feminism is a very diverse movement using a variety of theoretical approaches. Many of the contributions made by feminist investigators over the past three decades have been in the area of gender studies, and these will be discussed in Chapter 7. Another important feminist goal has been to uncover the androcentric biases mentioned earlier in this chapter. Beyond this, the most important feminist contributions to the study of culture have been concerned with (1) searching for the cause of female subordination throughout the world, and (2) importing into the study of culture a greater emphasis on women and the female experience.

With the rise of what was then called the Women's Liberation Movement in the 1960s,

Feminism is a term that encompasses a wide variety of very different things.

feminists became concerned with finding "the" cause of female subordination. In contrast to the theories popular with non-academic publics (which usually emphasize male/female differences in physical strength), most of the feminist theories developed during this period trace female subordination to the fact that woman conceive and give birth to children. In one particularly influential theory, for example, an anthropologist (Ortner, 1972) suggested that "Female was to Male as Nature is to Culture." What Ortner meant is that all societies make a distinction between things that "belong to nature" and things "that belong to culture," and that all societies invariably value the Culture category more highly than the Nature category. Since women were so closely tied to a biological process, like giving birth, in all societies, Ortner argued, women would universally come to be associated with Nature—and this in turn insured that men would come to be associated with the more highly valued Culture category. We shall return to nature/culture issues in the next chapter.

Unfortunately, as anthropologists went on to investigate gender relations, it became clear that there was a diversity and subtlety to gender relations in different societies (and often in the same society across different historical periods) that did not seem explainable in terms of any one, unitary variable. Ortner herself, for example, eventually repudiated her own theory since it became clear that there are many societies that do not associate woman with Nature. Even in our own culture, there have been many periods in Western history when the "mother nature" metaphor so familiar to us today has been absent. Generally, as Di Leonardo (1991) pointed out, anthropological and sociological theories positing a single, universal cause for female subordination had been discredited by the late 1980s. Since then, feminist investigators have preferred to explain gender inequality in a particular society by careful consideration of the distinctive cluster of social and economic conditions prevailing in that society.

The second important contribution made by feminist investigators was to foster a greater emphasis on women and the female experience in studying culture. This has meant overcoming the view, latent in most traditional accounts, that what is important about a culture are the things that men do and the things that men care about. It has also meant interviewing both men and women in a particular society to find out how their experience of the same institution (say, the family or religion) differ. Finally, it has meant paying attention to things like rape and other forms of gendered violence that have often been overlooked in traditional anthropological accounts.

This new emphasis on the female experience in the study of culture also affected the study of human prehistory. Traditional accounts of human prehistory, for example, had always argued that hunting (presumed to have been a male activity) and the technology surrounding hunting (arrowheads, spears, etc.) were the most important elements in human social evolution. A number of feminist scholars, by contrast, have argued that the gathering of food by females was far more important to the development of human social institutions than the hunting of animals by males. Not only did gathering provide most of the food in earliest human societies (just as it provides most of the food in modern hunting and gathering societies), but there are solid reasons for believing that systematic food-gathering would have given rise to complex patterns of group cooperation and communication.

Other feminist scholars (like Conkey, 1997) have challenged the presumption that there was a *gendered division of labour* (i.e., a pattern in which men do certain tasks and women do others) in our prehistoric past. There is nothing in the archeological record, they point out, that suggests men were more likely to be hunters (and less likely to be gatherers) than women. What we have done, they argued, is simply to project the sort of division of labor that emerged in historic societies (like our own) back onto the prehistoric past in order to make the present seem more "natural." After all, the traditional argument goes, if men and women have always engaged in different tasks, then that makes assigning them different tasks in the present seem, well, natural. The feminist argument, by contrast, is that once we recognize that there is no solid evidence for a gendered division of labour in our prehistoric past, then it becomes easier to imagine changing the division of labour by gender that exists in our own society.

Feminist investigators working in this tradition also forced a reevaluation of those many studies that used observations on modern primates (a group that includes all the various species of apes and monkeys) to make inferences about early human societies (Sperling, 1991). Different types of primates have different types of social organization, and it just happened that traditional (male) investigators have devoted most of their attention to the study of those particular primates, like baboons, whose social organization centres around males defending territorial space. Intensive study of other primate species, like chimpanzees (who are in fact much closer to us in an evolutionary sense), reveals that in these groups the mother-child bond is the most important social relationship.

From sociology to cultural studies

By the 1960s, the study of culture had slipped to the margins of sociology in North America. The reasons for this are still not entirely clear, though Smith (1998) has suggested that it was part of a general reaction against theoretical frameworks (like functionalism) and theoretical concepts (like culture) that emphasized social stability over social change. Over the past thirty years, however, the study of culture has once again become popular in sociology. One reason for this, Smith suggested, is that during the 1970s and 1980s sociologists in Canada and the United States came more and more to be influenced by various European theorists who share a common commitment to tracing previously unrecognized links between culture and other aspects of our social and mental experience.

One of the distinctive contributions made by these European theorists was that many things previously taken to be "natural" are in fact cultural inventions that arose at a particular point in historical time in response to particular societal conditions. For example, we now take it for granted that certain people are predisposed toward sexual activity with members of the same sex. We can debate whether this is the result of biology, the social environment, or some combination of the two, but that some people are homosexual seems obvious. Given this, it will seem strange to realize—as Foucault (1978) pointed out—that in Western societies the category "homosexual" was an invention of the nineteenth century. Prior to this, of course, people knew about "homosexuality" (the activity).

Furthermore, although homosexuality was regarded as immoral, Western publics recognized that some people did sometimes engage in homosexual activity, just as some people sometime robbed, murdered, and so on. Even so, the *idea* that there is a category of persons who are generally predisposed (by their nature or their personality) to engage in homosexual activity simply cannot be found in the writings of Western thinkers prior to this time.

Foucault's argument is that the cultural invention of the homosexual was an attempt at social control. In other words, by defining a deviant activity (in this case, homosexual behavior) as resulting from a person's biology or personality, people engaging in such acts could now be defined as "sick" and so brought under the control of a powerful medical establishment. The invention of the "homosexual," in short, allowed the power of medical science to be coopted in the service of regulating what was then a culturally devalued activity.

Foucault's general argument here has been especially appealing to scholars interested in the interplay between gender, sex, and sexuality. Groneman (1995), for example, pointed out that it was only in the nineteenth century that medical doctors began to apply the term "nymphomaniac" to some of their female patients. Supposedly, this term referred to a medical condition that caused women to be characterized by excessive sexual desire. In principle, there was a corresponding term for males, satyriasis. But if you look at what medical doctors of the period took as indicators of nymphomania and satyriasis, it quickly becomes clear that the two terms were not symmetrical. In the case of women, things like adultery, wanting more sex than their spouses, excessive flirtation, and masturbation were often enough to merit a medical diagnosis of nymphomania. These same things were never enough to justify a diagnosis of satyriasis in men. Groneman, following Foucault, suggested that the category "nymphomaniac" was invented so that women who stepped outside the rigidly defined gender roles of the Victorian period (which characterized women as sexually passive) could be defined as "sick" and so treated (and brought into line) by a male-dominated medical establishment. The preferred method of treating nymphomania, incidentally, was surgical removal of the ovaries. To fully appreciate the horrific significance of this, imagine a society in which men who committed adultery, masturbated, or flirted excessively were routinely subjected to castration.

These two examples do not capture the diversity that exists in the new tradition of cultural studies that has taken root in North America and Europe. Interested students might want to consult the various essays in Smith (1998) and Long (1997) and learn, among other things, how the public discussion over AIDS has been shaped selectively in order to reinforce prevailing notions of heterosexual monogamy; how popular childrearing manuals continue to promote a model of childrearing that is perfectly suited to the needs of a capitalistic society, but which works against the economic interests of women; and why the merger of animals and children in shows like the Muppets is so appealing to us. Hint: in the Western tradition, undomesticated animals are often seen as a threat to human society but, even so, are rarely defined as inherently "bad."

Those working in this new tradition of cultural studies have never been too concerned about disciplinary boundaries and have borrowed freely from sociology, anthropology, literature and film studies, history, linguistics, philosophy, and psychoanalysis for their insights. One consequence of this interdisciplinary emphasis, it would appear, is that the increasing popularity of cultural studies has worked to destabilize "sociology" as a distinct and separate category. Academic departments of sociology continue to exist, of course, as do specialized journals of sociology. Even so, sociology has quite literally vanished in some areas. Almost all large bookstores, for example, used to have a section entitled "sociology." In many cases, that is no longer the case (you might want to check this out for yourself in your local area). So where do you find sociology books? Most often in a section called— what else?—"cultural studies." Even Durkheim's *Suicide*, which has always been considered the prototypical study in sociology, is now often found in a "cultural studies" section. So what does the future hold? Are the subject headings posted in Chapters and other large bookstores quite literally the "writing on the wall" for sociology? Is "sociology" itself just a cultural construct that has served its historical purpose and is now in the process of being discarded?

Summary

Social life is patterned, not random, and much of this patterning can be attributed to the fact that every social group possesses a culture. A cultural element is something that is held in common by the members of a group, that affects their behaviour or the way they view the world, and that is passed on to new members. A group's culture is simply the sum total of all the cultural elements associated with that group. There are many types of cultural elements, but the three most important ones for sociologists are values, norms, and roles.

Most students of culture are concerned with three observations: (1) that the content of culture varies greatly across the totality of the world's societies; (2) that very few cultural elements are found in all the world's societies; and (3) that the elements of a given culture are often interrelated. However, much of what we see when studying cultures, whether our own or some other, is vulnerable to distortions produced by pre-existing biases. Ethnocentrism is always a danger, and Eurocentrism and androcentrism are especially common.

The most important theoretical perspectives used in the study of culture are: (1) functionalism, (2) conflict theory, (3) cultural materialism, and (4) feminism. Cultural studies is an interdisciplinary approach to the study of culture that is becoming increasingly popular among sociologists.

QUESTIONS FOR REVIEW AND CRITICAL THINKING

1. Make a list of at least twenty norms and beliefs you hold and/or activities in which you engage. How would you defend them to an ethnocentric person from another culture? Could you explain smoking cigarettes, drinking alcohol, shaving, dieting, and watching summer reruns or baseball on television to such a person?

2. Choose a set of popular toys and for each toy identify the cultural beliefs and attitudes that it seems to reflect.

3. Read again the argument about Mother Teresa presented in one of the boxes of this chapter. Then identify other individuals who are widely admired in this society, and develop and discuss conflict interpretations of why these individuals are so widely admired.

4. Why might a cultural studies approach to culture be more appealing than a conflict or functionalist view? How might a cultural studies approach incorporate a functional viewpoint?

KEY TERMS

androcentrism, p. 57

cultural element, p. 41

cultural integration, p. 52

cultural materialism, p. 62

cultural universals, p. 51

culture, p. 41

ethnocentrism, p. 54

Eurocentrism, p. 55

folkways, p. 43

functionalism, p. 59

institution, p. 45

material culture, p. 45

mores, p. 43

norms, p. 42

popular culture, p. 46

role, p. 44

role conflict, p. 44

society, p. 42

subculture, p. 45

urban legends, p. 47

values, p. 42

SUGGESTED READINGS

Harris, Marvin
1985   *Good to Eat.* New York: Simon and Schuster.
Harris applies cultural materialism to a wide range of food taboos and food preferences and, in the process, responds to criticisms made of earlier versions of his arguments. Some of his analyses seem stronger than others, but all are informative and thought provoking.

Lipset, Seymour Martin
1990   *Continental Divide: The Values and Institutions of the United States and Canada.* New York: Routledge.
Lipset systemically compares Canada with the U.S. along a number of different cultural dimensions and relates the differences he finds to the history of each country. His analysis should be read in conjunction with the critiques mentioned in the text.

Mead, Margaret
1935   *Sex and Temperament in Three Primitive Societies.* New York: Morrow.
This is one of the all-time classics in social science. By considering in depth three cultures radically different from our own, at least with regard to sex roles, Mead very forcibly establishes just how much the content of cultures can vary.

Ward, Martha C.
1996   *A World Full of Women.* Boston: Allyn & Bacon.
This book mixes anthropology and sociology in order to focus on activities involving women in a variety of societies, including our own, while simultaneously developing various critiques of the ways that these activities have been viewed by traditional anthropologists and sociologists. It is written for the beginning student.

WEB SITES

http://pubweb.web.co.za/arthur/leglist.html
Legendary Site of the Week
Legends are an integral aspect of society's culture and one of the most intriguing. At this site, read about the latest in mythology, folklore, and urban legends from around the world.

http://www.yahoo.com/text/Regional/Countries/
Yahoo! Country Index
Ever been to Benin, Djibouti, or Mongolia? Make a virtual visit and learn all about cultures from around the world courtesy of this Yahoo! site.

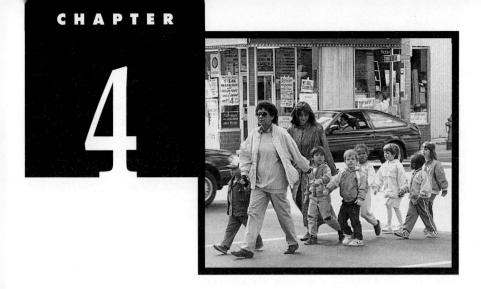

CHAPTER 4

Socialization

James Côté

Introduction

On April 22, 1999, two young men walked into their high school in Littleton, Colorado, heavily armed with pistols, rifles, and dozens of homemade bombs. By the time they finished their violent rampage, they had murdered twelve fellow students and a teacher, and left twenty-three other students wounded, some critically. Then they killed themselves. Following this carnage, a similar, if less spectacular, act of violence took place in a high school in Taber, Alberta, and hundreds of threats of violence involving bombs and guns were made in schools around Canada and the U.S., causing class cancellations and evacuations. In the year and a half preceding the Littleton incident, six mass murders took place in American high schools (Phillips, 1999).

Just how do we make sense of such grotesque acts? Certainly, the news media and talk shows were abuzz with efforts to explain each incident, but little consensus emerged on which to base any concerted efforts to prevent such acts in the future. Part of the difficulty in dealing with complex problems of this sort is that too often simplistic answers are given. For example, some people want to blame television; others want to restrict access to firearms. Although both of these factors likely play a role, any explanation of such a large problem needs to be comprehensive enough to include the myriad of factors involved, both immediate and more removed.

Within the social sciences generally, the socialization perspective holds the most promise for explaining these types of behaviours. In this chapter, we define this concept and examine a range of current perspectives in socialization. In the conclusion of this chapter, we shall see how well the various socialization theories examined below account for the Littleton incident. In this way, the Littleton incident will constitute a "social specimen" for evaluating the utility of socialization theories.

Defining Socialization

There are several possible definitions of socialization. Perhaps, however, it would be helpful to note what socialization is not. Socialization does not mean to put something under the control of the government or the state, as in socialized medicine; and it does not mean to mingle with others, as in attending raves.

Most generally, **socialization** refers to the means by which someone is made "fit" to live among the other humans. These socialization processes are intended to ensure both the physical survival of individual members and the survival of the group or culture. This means that when someone is socialized, he or she has the motivation, skills, and knowledge necessary to live with others in group relationships. When any of these three factors is missing or deficient, a person can experience difficulties in getting along with others.

In order for cultures to perpetuate themselves, members need to be enticed in some way to conform to their rules and values. As far as we know, this goes for all cultures and subcultures, including those found in extreme situations like prisons. When socialization processes are most effective, the enticements for conformity involve the *learning* of skills, roles, norms, and so forth. Sometimes, however, enticements for conformity involve *pressuring* people to obey in a variety of ways, from simple looks of disapproval by strangers to charging people with criminal offences.

In addition, some social scientists use socialization to refer to how people are *conditioned* so that inborn temperaments and capacities are moulded to produce the desired traits that complement a given group or culture. This view of socialization takes a more complex form when people are viewed as having a number of preset stages through which they pass during their life course. In this more complex view, socialization contexts and processes differ at each stage of the life course, and the final outcome of socialization for a particular person is dependent on how well socialization contexts match the characteristics of that person "unfolding" at each stage. Some view these stages as largely cultural in origin, while others view them as "constitutional" in nature—part of an **epigenetic** makeup of individual, in which the person is likened to a flower, with genetically preset stages of growth, the outcome of which depends on how well, or poorly, the environment nurtures it during that stage.

We shall see below how each of the various perspectives on socialization utilizes one or more of these underlying assumptions.

Socialization begins at birth and continues throughout life.

Issues in the Study of Socialization

Implicit in the above discussion of the nature of socialization are several issues that represent disputes in the field, or at least disagreements about how to analyze specific circumstances. For example, one issue pertains to whether, or the extent to which, socialization is inherently benign or coercive, and for whom in specific contexts. This is an issue that often separates functionalists and conflict theorists. Do some, or even all, socialization processes help people "find themselves," or do they "force-fit" people, and make people only think they have been fulfilled? From a conflict perspective, much socialization simply involves getting people to want to do what they otherwise must do, without using excessive force. If this is true, and functionalists are mistakenly assuming that socialization processes are benign, then functionalists may simply be contributing to the oppression of human beings by studying how to perfect coercive socialization processes. Such questions loom large today in attempts to understand what is happening in the various contexts in which young people now spend much of their time, especially high schools. Many people thrive in these environments, yet others react in a variety of negative ways, from social withdrawal to rampages of violence. Are those who do not thrive somehow personally deviant, or is the school to blame? Or both? In this case, we run the risk of "blaming the victim" if we focus only on individuals' reactions, because the deviant behaviour may simply be a result of socialization into a culture or subculture that we do not understand. Certainly, adults run the risk of doing this when dealing with those young people who have formed their own subcultures with different sets of rules. Deviance and rules are discussed in the next chapter.

A second issue concerns the extent to which people can resist attempts to socialize them. Regardless of whether the socialization attempts are benign or coercive, there are disagreements regarding how much free will people are capable of exercising in their dealings with the social structures that lie behind socialization efforts. This issue is more broadly known as the *structure-agency* debate.

Structure and Agency: If Everybody Is Cool, Is Anyone Cool?

Most people today want to be hip or cool, or at least it seems that way. But what does it mean to be hip or cool? The term "hip" came into usage in the 1950s; born of urban-American black culture, "hip" made its way into mainstream English through the music and drug subcultures of that decade. For jazz musicians, it meant being tolerant. For drug users, it implied a unique understanding of the world. In general, for Beatniks, being hip meant a laid-back attitude. Whatever the take, the basic idea was to be nonconformist. Moreover, these meanings had relevance only in the context of anti-establishment subcultures, because they represented a rejection of mainstream society, which, by implication, cannot be hip.

In the 1960s, the desire to be hip spread, and a substantial proportion of a generation (hippies) adopted the knowledge and attitude representing hipness, which they referred to as being "cool." During this period, hippies could readily identify one another by means of their simple dress and hair styles, neither of which had a commercial basis. But, cool still remained an intangible state of mind.

Beatniks and hippies never really posed a threat to capitalist society, in spite of their rejection of it, but ironically it was capitalist society that learned to appropriate the disdain these groups held toward it. Playing on the young people's rebellious spirit and desire to be "in the know," marketers learned in the 1970s how to turn countercultural symbols into fashion trends. As Bellafonte, Gross, and Cray (1994) argued "[C]apitalism proved itself well-suited to absorb whatever was hip that might fascinate consumers, while discarding the uncomfortable parts. For every counterculture, there emerged the corresponding sales counterculture."

These marketing techniques have been around for several decades now, and have convinced millions of people that they can buy hipness or coolness. But, as Bellafonte, Gross, and Cray (1994) noted, "[W]hen hipness is embraced from mainstream, much of the life gets squeezed from it. If the signs of hip—goatees, pierced nipples, and calf tattoos—are everywhere, what's so hip about them? If the attitudes of hip...are officially sponsored by the major media, what's so special?" In short, hip and cool cannot exist among the mainstream, yet literally billions of dollars and endless hours of leisure time are spent in pursuit of them by many mainstream youth.

This phenomenon is well illustrated in the three Woodstock music festivals held over the last 30

continued

years. The first Woodstock in 1969 was largely a spontaneous event in which the organizers lost money, but made history and a cultural statement. The second Woodstock, held in 1994, is noted as being "history's largest convergence of the mass market," whose organizers test-marketed the lineup of bands, sold official refrigerator magnets and condoms, and were sponsored by several multinational corporations including Pepsi and Apple Computer. The organizers made lots of money, but there was no cultural statement—only several hundred thousand conformists pretending to be cool by getting high. Woodstock '99 likewise made lots of money, will be remembered for the riots in which a dozen truck trailers—containing T-shirts and other official merchandise, as well as exorbitantly priced food and soft drinks ($4 for a Coke)—were set on fire. This may have been a "cultural statement" to the effect that some young people are tired of being exploited, but it is hard to see how a rampage of violence is hip or cool, regardless of how one is dressed.

What do you think? Has the agency originally represented by hipness and coolness been transformed into a new form of structured conformity, or is it still possible to use attitude and appearance as anti-establishment statements?

On the one hand, the social structures responsible for socialization can be quite imperceptible, and even though no physical force is used in enforcing these structures, a high degree of conformity can result (e.g., conventions of personal appearance). Is our widespread conformity in dress simply a matter of people not having the willpower to resist social pressures? Is it a matter of people being unable to create their own behaviour patterns? Such questions have a relatively long history in sociology, and are related to an *oversocialized conception of humanity* held by previous generations of sociologists (Wrong, 1961), where people are viewed as not having the agency to resist, or deviate from, social pressures.

On the other hand, if people are capable of deciding things, even partly, on their own and exercising a free will, where does this agency come from? Is this an inherent mental capacity; is it something that we learn; or is it a combination of both? Is it a trait that varies among people, so that some people have more of it than others and are therefore more able to resist social pressures? Is it something that we use only when the opportunity arises? Or, is it exercised only when we are faced with a lack of guidance and structure from our culture?

These questions have a long philosophical history, so we cannot hope to answer them in this chapter. But raising them helps us to better understand the tasks faced by those who attempt to grasp the nature of socialization and to apply socialization theory to real-life events. You may find yourself thinking of one or more of these questions as you read this chapter, as for example when it considers the effects of television and mass culture (see the box "Structure and Agency").

The nature/nurture debate

We can see in the above discussion of definitions and issues that a full understanding of socialization requires a firm grasp of the essentials involved. The starting point in this respect concerns the raw materials that form the basis of human behaviour. Understanding their nature has been the object of a long and lively controversy known as the **nature/nurture** debate. Different positions on the fundamental causes of human behaviour can be traced as far back as the ancient Greek philosophers, Plato and Aristotle. However, the nature/nurture debate in modern science dates back only one century, with its heyday in the first few decades of the twentieth century.

The eugenics movement, which sought to perfect the human gene pool, caused an outrage that drew a number of academics into the nature/nurture controversy. This movement has its roots in Darwin's concept of *adaptation* and his theory of biological evolution into "higher" species. Eugenecists argued that if Darwin was right, we should be able to direct evolution. And, out of this line of thinking, the movement grew, stimulating efforts to develop techniques of genetic engineering involving the control of breeding within and between the "races." Most disturbing was its goal of race improvement through "selective breeding," with an implication that the "weak" should be left to die, or at least should not be allowed to reproduce. These ideas affected immigration policies in the first part of the century and were key to the Nazi movement in Germany (see Broad and Wade, 1982).

To a large part, it was the racism inherent within the eugenics movement that drew opposition from social scientists who had been studying nurture, or environmental, influences on human behaviour. For example, in the 1920s *behaviourism*, how human behaviour can be conditioned from birth, and modified later in life, through a series of rewards and punishments, made great advances. In fact, while behaviourism promised a science of behaviour that directly contradicted the claims of eugenicists regarding the need for genetic engineering and selective breeding, it replaced them with social engineering. The early part of this century saw much experimentation in principals of learning by behaviourists like Pavlov and Watson, who believed that humans are "responding organisms"—animals without free will—that can be conditioned to do just about anything if the appropriate rewards and punishments are provided on the right reinforcement schedules. Much of their research was carried out on dogs, pigeons, and so forth, and they had considerable success with children. Adults, however, have proven be more complex "organisms," as we see below.

The racist implications of the nature side of the controversy also caught the attention of anthropologists like Boas, Benedict, and Mead, who attempted to show how the facts of extreme culture variations made it unlikely the humans have genetic predispositions strong enough to fully determine how they structure their societies (see, for example, Mead, 1928). Instead, they argued that cultures produce patterns of human behaviours that cannot be traced to genetic makeup (e.g., Benedict, 1934).

Although it does not receive much explicit attention today, this debate is still important because of its political implications. To appreciate the implications of this debate, ask yourself what is at

stake? If the "nature side" is true, and behaviour is predetermined genetically, societies do not have to take responsibility for social problems because by implication these problems are unavoidable. If genes cause people to commit crimes, rehabilitation will not work. Moreover, economic privileges may be justified on the belief that the wealthy are genetically superior and that is how they (or their ancestors) acquired their wealth. Hence, the nature position in this debate calls for the preservation of the status quo. To the extent that the status quo preserves privileges of powerful groups, beliefs in the genetic basis of behaviour will likely be more popular among their members.

In contrast, if nurture arguments are true, then economic privileges may be the consequence of preexisting social inequalities that favour some people over others. Accordingly, the nurture position tends not to favour the status quo, but rather calls for social reforms to address social inequalities and to remedy the social ills that are at the root of criminality and others forms of deviance. Given the left-wing implications of the nurture position, and its implicit challenge to the status quo, this position should be less popular among the upper classes and more popular among those without economic privilege.

Thus, when we ask what is at stake in terms of how we explain the essentials of human behaviour, the answer is that much is at stake, and this is likely why the nature/nurture debate has been such a persistent controversy. Among the important issues at stake are: social-class distinctions, the justifications for capitalism and socialism, immigration policies, the existence of social programs to remedy social ills, and human rights. Even the nature of adolescence is implicated in this debate.

One of the major issues in the early nature/nurture debate was the question of whether or not adolescence is inevitably a period of storm and stress caused by genetically based hormonal disturbances, as was argued by proponents of the nature position (Hall, 1904). This is an issue to which anthropologists such as Boas, Benedict, and Mead turned their attention, arguing that some cultures exist in which adolescence is not a turbulent period (Mead, 1928). Although Mead's work has been criticized (Freeman, 1983), subsequent research has supported her argument that adolescent turmoil is not found in all cultures. Moreover, within cultures there is a great degree of variation in how adolescence is experienced, with many young people experiencing little emotional turbulence (Arnett, 1999; Côté, 1994).

In fact, strictly speaking, while puberty is a biological phenomenon, adolescence is a cultural phenomenon. This does not mean that adolescence is some sort of fiction, but rather that adolescence is a socially structured period of life produced by cultural reactions to puberty and the requirements associated with transition to adulthood. Most cultures provide some sort of transitional period between childhood and adulthood, but in most pre-industrial societies this is a relatively short period, serving as a signal that it is time for the person to begin the move toward adulthood. Beyond the near universality of the rites of passage and initiation ceremonies (like bas mitzvahs, confirmations, graduations) that institutionalize the passage out of childhood, Schlegel and Barry (1991) found evidence of a "social stage" of adolescence in virtually all of the 186 pre-industrial societies they studied, with adolescence defined as "a period of social role learning and restructuring, away from the behavioural modes of childhood and toward adult modes" (1991: 8). However, this "social stage" was often as short as one year, especially for females. Such practices argue against any biological definition of adolescence. In most pre-industrial societies, adolescence ends at age 16 for females (between 16 and 18 for males). It almost always ends with marriage in a girl's teen years.

Has the nature/nurture debate been resolved? In a sense, yes, because virtually all researchers agree that human behaviour is determined by both. However, most scientists still study behaviour from one position or the other, and very few study the interaction or simultaneous effects of nature and nurture, in part because it is extremely difficult to do so (the exception to this is the emerging field of evolutionary psychology; Buss, 1999). Still, most researchers agree that a number of abilities and traits are jointly influenced, like intelligence, aggression, risk avoidance, and shyness (Rice, 1998), with initial genetic dispositions modifiable to some degree in most persons. For example, about 5 to 10 percent of children are born with a disposition to be fearful of unfamiliar people, objects, and

Both genetic and environmental factors affect human personality and behaviour.

situations. Researchers have found that this shyness can be mitigated in almost 40 percent of these children (although some children [10 percent] will become even shyer) with parental efforts to reduce the shyness (Rice, 1998).

Attempts to demonstrate that human societies are strongly structured by genetically based, evolutionary influences remain controversial, with alternative explanations yet to be eliminated scientifically. For example, evolutionists interpret various sexual and mating behaviour patterns as genetically programmed survival mechanisms, whereas learning theorists argue that people may simply be making rational calculations based on rewards and punishments.

Still, sociobiology (Wilson, 1975), and more recently evolutionary psychology (Buss, 1999), have strong and vocal adherents. Sociobiologists try to show how human behaviour patterns are affected by the processes of natural selection, with some even arguing for a "gene-culture coevolution" whereby "cultural fitness" and "genetic fitness" are interrelated (e.g., Rushton, 1988). Evolutionary psychologists make the more modest claim that humans have "evolved psychological mechanisms" that affect their dispositions to think in certain ways, but which can be overridden by cognitive activity (Buss, 1999).

In terms of where the "battle lines" have been drawn, then, we are somewhere but not much further along than we were in the early part of the century, when the nature/nurture debate was at its height. Part of the problem has been that the search is for a single "human nature," when in fact humans are manifestly multifaceted (Gamson and Modigliani, 1974). For example, most scholars and scientists have pursued the question of the essential nature of the species with singular images in mind. Some have an image of human as "animals" who live with ever-present, powerful, instinctive, biological drives, especially sexual and aggressive ones (e.g., Plato, Freud); others fundamentally conceive of humans as "profit-seekers," who attempt to maximize their rewards and comforts, and to minimize their costs and discomforts (Adam Smith and B.F. Skinner); still others view humans as "meaning seekers," who need to make sense out their world, and have therefore established culturally specific means of communicating (languages) about shared meanings (e.g., Aristotle, Locke, Mead); still and yet others see humans as "noble savages," born inherently good, with intrinsic potentials to be creative, spontaneous, caring, loving, and potential-seeking, but who can be corrupted by society (Rousseau, Maslow).

Each of these images of the essential nature of humans has generated an enormous amount of thought and research. So, which one is right? Well, in a sense all are right to a certain degree. The problem is that, out of a need to simplify, each focuses on one image and filters the world through a single lens, eliminating information that does not fit through that lens. In fact, it is perfectly plausible to accept elements from all four models, for each can be empirically demonstrated to some degree, and each seems to represent different facets of human potential and limitation. In other words, it appears that there is no *one* human nature, but rather a multitude of human needs, potentials, and limitations that are found in varying degrees in all of us. In turn, these come into contact with cultural pressures (socialization forces) that affect the final shape taken in each of us (see Buss, 1999; and the box "People as Meaning Seekers and Profit Seekers").

Reviewing these positions on nature and nurture helps clarify the definitions of socialization provided earlier because it suggests a number of comparisons with other animal species. For example, it becomes immediately obvious that there are fewer limits to the socialization possibilities in humans than in other animal species. Another way to put this is to say that other animals are less responsive to conditioning from their environments. Animals that live in the wild (e.g., lions and wolves) are very difficult to condition, both in terms of

People as Meaning-Seekers and Profit-Seekers

A large-scale longitudinal study of the life goals of hundreds of thousands of first-year college students in United States (Astin et al., 1994) shows how populations can change over rather short periods of time in their primary goals in life. They found that while in the mid-'60s, only about 45 percent of college students rated "being very well off financially" as a very important objective, by the mid-'80s this figure reached about 75 percent. In contrast, in the mid-'60s "developing a meaningful philosophy of life" was endorsed by over 80 percent of incoming students, but by the mid-'80s this dropped to just over 30 percent. In other words, profit-seeking goals and meaning-seeking goals have traded places among those undertaking the transition to adulthood.

These findings cannot be explained in terms of a changing genetic make-up over such a short period of time (nature). Instead, it appears that certain socialization influences (nurture) have changed, so that more university-attending people believe it more rewarding to be materialistic than philosophical or spiritual. Is this anticipatory socialization, or is something that has already been learned from the socialization contexts to which these students were exposed before attending university, or both?

learning new behaviours and living among humans. However, there are a number of species that have been domesticated by humans (e.g., cats and dogs, distant cousins of lions and wolves), which are much more open to conditioning, and much more compatible with human societies. Still, these domesticated animals show sharp limits in the extent to which they can be taught new behaviours —cats more so than dogs, probably because of their different genetic dispositions related to their evolutionary histories.

Humans, in contrast, have long since domesticated themselves in terms of their animal natures, although these "animal natures" continue to show themselves in ways that can disturb human cultures, as in the Littleton incident. Indeed, one is hard-pressed to find any instincts in humans as strong and directed as those even in domesticated animals. The long period of dependency of human infants attests to the fact that we have little of the instinctual equipment of other animal species associated with survival (Williams, 1983). Whatever instincts remain in us have become weak and diffuse, and are modifiable through socialization processes—hence the great diversity in cultures around the world. Moreover, humans possess an intelligence far greater than any other animal species (as far as we know) that enables them to adapt to new situations, and to create symbolic meanings that help them live in cooperative groups (see the boxed insert entitled "Nature without Nurture? 'Girl Acts like Chicken'").

Perspectives on Socialization

The concept of socialization is fundamental to the social sciences, especially sociology, psychology, and cultural anthropology. As we shall see, sociologists are interested in the content of what people learn, the contexts in which this learning takes places, and how the contents and contexts of socialization change over the life course (Hewitt, 1994: 3). In contrast psychologists are more interested in how people learn, and anthropologists study how these learning processes differ among cultures while still producing well-functioning humans. In this section, we briefly review how human socialization is viewed within each of these disciplines.

Sociological perspectives

Within sociology, we can find three distinct conceptions of socialization corresponding to the three classical theoretical perspectives: functionalism, conflict perspectives, and symbolic interactionism.

Nature without Nurture? "Girl Acts like Chicken"

Davis (1947) reported the case of a girl who for six years lived alone in a dark room apart from the rest of her family. When discovered, she could only croak and in many ways behaved like a frightened animal. But with professional care, she quickly took on human characteristics and within a year, she could speak, write, and add. At the age of 8½, she had caught up with her peers. While there are no well-documented cases of feral children (children raised by animals), a 9-year-old girl was found after having spent most of her waking hours in a chicken coop (London Free Press, 1 July 1980). Living with chickens, she acted like one; she could not talk, took very small and quick steps, and flapped her arms like wings. She received professional help, but showed no real progress.

According the Bettelheim (1967), most reports of feral children are likely of autistic children who have been abandoned by their parents, because they do not react to socialization processes like other children. Autism is not well understood, but the manifestations of this condition do give us some idea of what humans would be like without the capacity for, or receptivity to, socialization influences. Given that human infants are so vulnerable and take such a long time to develop self-sufficiency, do you think it is really plausible that infants could survive with the help of animals only?

Functionalism

Functionalists tend to view socialization as a necessary and benign process inherent in all groups and societies. From this perspective, socialization performs several vital *functions* that maintain the structure of groups and societies, particularly from one generation to the next. Three major purposes to these processes are identified.

First, socialization plays a major role in the formation of the individual personality, while moulding people's attitudes and behaviours to conform to group values and needs. As a result, within groups people develop similar sets of outlooks and habits that make it easier for them to interact with each other. Second, socialization represents a set of processes and contexts responsible for cultural transmission. For example, within a particular group or culture, a common language is transmitted to all new members. Without socializing group members to speak a common language and to internalize a common set of symbols, cultures would be unable to support the cooperative activities necessary for an effective division of labour. Consequently, it would be difficult for members to share customs and traditions, or to agree upon a set of norms or laws. And, third, socialization performs the function of social integration. With their common personality characteristics and common language, people come to share common conceptions of their place in the world, as well as their places in their own cultures. These similarities help people to identify with one another, and to recognize their similar interests.

The process by which language development occurs is central to socialization.

Of course, these functions of socialization are not necessarily perfectly or uniformly fulfilled among all members of a group. Within a culture, each person has a slightly different socialization history, even within the same family. Moreover, in the contemporary world, people from a variety of cultural backgrounds mix with one another, making socialization processes highly complex and often incomplete. For example, if you have travelled to a different culture, you might have encountered problems as simple as knowing how to eat a meal "properly" or how to express thanks for acts of kindness without offending someone.

Conflict approaches

Conflict theorists do not disagree with functionalists regarding the basic nature of socialization processes, but they tend to disagree about how benign some of these processes are, how neutral their outcomes can be, and even how necessary some socialization is. Instead, conflict theorists focus on the concept of **social reproduction**, namely, the ways in which societies reproduce themselves in terms of privilege and status. Conflict theorists argue that people do indeed learn about appropriate attitudes and behaviours, but these attitudes and behaviours vary by social class, gender, and race/ethnicity, so people within each of these social categories tend to learn things that perpetuate those categories. Thus, people with less privilege and status (e.g., in the working class) tend to be taught to accept their position and not question who benefits from their uncritical acceptance of the class structure.

This reproduction can be compounded when the categories overlap, for example, when working-class males and females reproduce the socioeconomic outcomes of their parents, which are equal in terms of class, but not gender (e.g., male father but female daughter). Moreover, this acceptance can be at a great price for the individuals concerned, as when schools treat those from less privileged backgrounds in an unsympathetic manner. Research has shown that public schools tend to be structured for students from middle-class backgrounds who have different language conventions than working-class students (Bernstein, 1973), and they tend to be taught by those from middle-class backgrounds. Accordingly, working-class students may be subtly, or even harshly,

"cooled out," namely, made to believe that they do not possess the intelligence or abilities to succeed academically. As a result, they may stop trying and eventually occupy social-class destinations similar to, or lower than their parents. In contrast, middle-class students are more likely to be "warmed up"— encouraged to excel. If so, they are likely to think more highly of themselves (and therefore have higher self-esteem), to try harder, and therefore to stand a better chance of occupying social-class destinations equal to or greater than that of their parents.

Feminist sociologists have many of the same concerns as conflict theorists with respect to the nature and outcome of socialization processes. Feminist sociologists are particularly concerned with gender socialization, as specific sets of "processes through which individuals learn to become feminine and masculine according to expectations current in their society. In particular, individuals develop gender identity and learn to express gender norms. Especially important is the internalization of norms specifying gender inequality and gender division of labour" (Mackie, 1999: 75). Most researchers believe that adolescence is a time of particular vulnerability to gender socialization processes, with femininity and masculinity being an intensified target especially in peer groups (Côté and Allahar, 1994).

Given these concerns, conflict theorists and feminist sociologists are interested in first recognizing social inequalities and then modifying socialization processes to help address those inequalities (see the box entitled "Youth, Social Control, and the Mass Media: A Conflict View").

Symbolic interactionism

This approach to socialization takes the position that *interactions* among individuals are mediated by *symbols*, in the form of language and gestures, that form and shape the self—hence the term *symbolic interactionism*. Symbolic interactionists argue that individuals constantly monitor themselves and others in attempts to give meaning to events. In doing so, they observe the actions and reactions of other people towards them, and they then incorporate these responses into their self-structures. (For example, if individuals perceive that other people regard them as aggressive or smart or good-

Youth, Social Control, and the Mass Media: A Conflict View

Young people are enthusiastic consumers of the mass media, and over the years such enthusiasm has often been cause for concern. Today, for example, magazines directed at young women—"teenzines"—often send the message to girls that they should intensify their feminine characteristics with cosmetics and fashionable clothing. On the one hand, one could argue that these magazines are simply meeting a market need, insofar as young women want these things. Another, more critical perspective, however, is that such magazines are specifically engineered to create a consciousness among young women that only then becomes defined as a need.

An analysis of the content of the various mass media aimed at adolescents showed that all such organizations share this vested interest. Some of these media do so as agents for other economic interests (e.g., television programs, teenzines, and fashion magazines). Others, however, do it directly for themselves (e.g., the music industry, with television channels devoted entirely to this task). At the heart of much of this activity is the attempt to sell young people some element of an identity they have been taught to crave. With this accomplished, identities are sold back to them as products whose purpose is to provide a means of demonstrating their "individuality," however illusive or fleeting.

As a result of decades of influence (and practice), the "leisure industries" that sell music, fashion, and cosmetics now have a largely uncritical army of consumers awaiting the next fads, which often seem more and more outlandish. In spite of their seemingly anti-establishment guise, these activities are tolerated by larger economic interests because the army of willing consumers is the same group that serves as a massive reserve of cheap labour, willing to work under poor conditions, for little pay and few benefits. In addition, distracting young people with these trivial identity-pursuits constitutes a form of social control because it helps prevent them from actively protesting their own disenfranchisement, lack of adult privileges, and the loss of a meaningful identity, denied them through a series of laws, customs, and institutional practices. Instead of attempting to condition young people to spend money they do not have, the media might have focused on helping them to develop their intellects and their sense of social responsibility.

Source: Adapted from James Côté and Anton Allahar, 1994. Generation on Hold: Coming of Age in the Late Twentieth Century. Toronto: Stoddart.

looking, they may come to define themselves as such.) They then take the meanings about themselves and others they acquired from previous interactions and use them to give their current conduct meaning. In other words, for symbolic interactionists, people are meaning-seeking and self-referential, and through these activities they both create societies and socialize each other (Hewitt, 1994).

As mentioned in the introductory chapter, this theory has been a popular perspective in sociology for some time. Its basic ideas were developed by several philosophers and social scientists during the early years of this century, especially by Cooley (1902), who introduced the notion of the **looking-glass self** (the idea that personality is shaped as individuals see themselves mirrored in the reactions of others), Thomas (1923), who is noted for the idea of the *definition of the situation* (if a situation is defined as real, it is real in its consequences), and George Mead (1934), who developed a theory of how the self forms. Mead has been particularly influential, and is often considered synonymous with symbolic interactionism, so we will focus on his work.

At the centre of Mead's theory is the concept of **role-taking**. Mead asserted that effective communication between individuals requires that one "take the role of the other." Mead believed that people would try to put themselves in others' shoes,

Cooley argued that we come to see ourselves as others see us, much like the view in a mirror.

to imagine their thoughts and perceptions. As a result, they would be able to see themselves as others see them. This is possible because of the uniquely human ability to interact symbolically. The use of language and the ability to take the role of the other then allows the self to develop.

Mead contended that the development of the self takes place in two stages. When children acquire a sufficient vocabulary to begin naming people and objects they observe, they begin to play-act roles. In this *play stage*, they pretend to be a mother, father, firefighter, or teacher. For the first time, they practice taking the roles of others that they have observed, and are in a position to reflect upon themselves behaving in a variety of roles. For the first time, children can think of themselves as *objects* with specific qualities and capacities. They can now imagine how other people view them. Playing at roles in this way provides exercises in "being another to one's self" (Mead, 1934: 151). Thus, the

basis of behaviour moves from mere imitation to more reflective self-direction.

In the *game stage*, children develop more unified conceptions of themselves as they learn to simultaneously take the role of multiple others. For example, in a game of baseball, a child might alternate roles between batter and pitcher, but also learns to appreciate the importance of all of the other players on the field. As this is experienced, the children imagine how those in the other roles think about their actions. As this is practised, the children learn to imagine themselves in terms of other children's perspectives towards them. By appreciating the interrelations of a set of roles rather than one isolated role, children develop a generalized conception of what is expected of them and how others will react to them. Thus, through informal and formal play, children learn how to conceive of a **generalized other** rather than of single, specific others. Eventually, children's perceptions of generalized others represent their ideas of what is expected in terms of social norms and provide a unified basis for self-reference. Hence, the self develops more fully and is capable of self-reference in terms of generalized others, or multiple viewpoints.

Mead also thought it useful to think of two complementary processes associated with the functioning self: the I and the Me. The **I** represents the impulsive side of the self, which is spontaneous and creative. In contrast, the **me** is the more deliberate, reflective side of the self; it takes time to evaluate how others might react to the actions of the I. For example, the I might want to make a joke during a lively conversation, but the me might inhibit it by reflecting on how the joke might be received by others, mulling over whether the audience might think it off-colour or politically incorrect.

Finally, in addition to the generalized other, Mead also believed that people are influenced by **significant others**, persons who are well known and whose attitudes and opinions affect one's life. Significant others include family members and friends as well as persons of high prestige, like teachers and celebrities. People are motivated to impress these others in certain ways, and engage in a number of techniques to manage how others perceive them. These techniques of *impression* *management* have been intensively studied by later symbolic interactionists like Goffman (1964).

In sum, symbolic interactionists are interested in how people cognitively construct and manage realities about themselves and others. The developmental product of this cognitive activity is the self, which represents the "human capacity to exert control over conduct—to coordinate behaviour with that of others and create complex social acts and social objects" in a self-referential manner (Hewitt, 1994: 72).

Psychological perspectives

As noted above, psychologists are more interested in how people learn and how this learning changes them, whereas sociologists are more interested in the content of, and the contexts governing, what people learn. Psychologists often prefer to speak in terms of the concept of "human development" instead of socialization, because they tend to see the human organism as active in the process of its own growth. This more active role is possible either through people's cognitive participation, or through the unfolding of **ontogenetic** stages that are part of an *epigenetic* "ground plan." These stages represent "developmental change" or the structural reorganization of the mental make-up of the person (the psyche).

Social learning approaches

The guiding principle behind these theories is that human behaviour is largely determined by the consequences people expect to follow from their behaviours. These expectations are thought to be based on individuals' past experiences in similar situations and on their observations of others in similar situations (Bandura, 1986). The outcomes of a behaviour can be negative or positive, trivial or important, and they may not be immediate. We can see from this account how learning theory is also referred to as "behaviourism."

The key to learning theory is an understanding of how people assess the consequences of their choices of behavioural options. The consequences are of varying degrees and have varying probabilities of occurring. For example, punish-

ments for stealing vary in severity, and the odds of getting caught range from zero to one hundred percent, depending on the circumstances. Obviously, then, severe punishments and a high likelihood of being apprehended should strongly discourage people from deciding to steal something. However, people are not always conscious of the factors they consider, and many activities are repeated so often each day as to be automatic, with no conscious awareness that information is even being processed, as in driving a car and using a familiar computer program.

Learning principles thus are straightforward and commonsensical. When the outcome of a behaviour is positive, the probability of a person repeating that behaviour is increased. For example, if you receive a good grade in a subject like literature (a positive reinforcement), you are more likely to take additional literature courses. Conversely, a poor grade in a subject (a negative reinforcement) reduces the probability, for many, of taking further courses in that subject. Similarly, if a person is socially rewarded for being aggressive and violent (e.g., approval by peers and a successful outcome), the likelihood of those behaviours being repeated is increased. If peers (and others) socially punish (e.g., through disapproval or a reduction in social status) aggressive and violent behaviours, they are less likely to persist.

Finally, learning theorists also study indirect methods of learning, like *modelling*. Modelling is an important process by which people indirectly learn new behaviour patterns. In it, people observe how someone else (especially someone they admire) is rewarded or punished for a specific behaviour in a specific context. If the model is rewarded, the person will attempt to imitate the model's behaviour in the hope of obtaining a similar reward (e.g., approval, sex, money, status, or fame). However, if the reward is not forthcoming, the new behaviour is less likely to be repeated. Moreover, the person imitated may become less highly regarded, and cease being a role model (see the box entitled "Learning Through Imitation").

In summary, learning theorists are interested in the mechanisms of learning and how various factors affect how behaviours are shaped, maintained, and extinguished.

Learning through Imitation: A Hockey Analogy

Much of human behaviour is learned through modelling others. In The Game, Ken Dryden (1983) recalls some examples of modelling.

In the late 1950s, the CBS network televised NHL games on Saturday afternoon. Before each game, there was a preview show in which a player from each of the teams involved that day would compete in two contests, one of which was a penalty-shot contest. The goalie they used each week was an assistant trainer for the Detroit Red Wings named Julian Klymquiw. Short and left-handed, Klymquiw wore a clear plexiglass mask that arched in front of his face like a shield. None of us had ever heard of him, and his unlikely name made us a little doubtful at first. But it turned out that he was quite good, and most weeks he stopped the great majority of shots taken at him. So, during backyard games of "penalty shots," we pretended to be Julian Klymquiw, not Terry Sawchuk or Glenn Hall. And before each of our contests began,

we would perform the ritual that Klymquiw and announcer Bud Palmer performed each week:

"Are you ready, Julian?"

"Yes, Bud."

But the backyard also meant time alone. It was usually after dinner when the "big guys" had homework to do and I would turn on the floodlights at either end of the house and on the porch, and play. It was a private game. I would stand alone in the middle of the yard, a stick in my hands, a tennis ball in front of me, silent, still, then suddenly dash ahead, stickhandling furiously, dodging invisible obstacles for a shot on net. It was Maple Leaf Gardens filled to wildly cheering capacity, a tie game, seconds remaining. I was Frank Mahovlich, or Gordie Howe, I was anyone I wanted to be, and the voice in my head was that of Leafs broadcaster Foster Hewitt: "… there's ten seconds left, Mahovlich, winding up at his own line, at centre, eight seconds, seven, over the blueline, six—he winds up, he shoots, he scores!" The mesh that had been tied to the bottoms of our

red metal goalposts until frozen in the ice had been ripped away to hang loose from the crossbars, whipped back like a flag in a stiff breeze. My arms and stick flew into the air, I screamed a scream inside my head, and collected my ball to do it again—many times, for many minutes, the hero of all my own games.

It was a glorious fantasy, and I always heard that voice. It was what made my fantasy seem almost real. For to us, who attended hockey games mostly on TV or radio, an NHL game, a Leafs game, was played with a voice. If I wanted to be Mahovlich or Howe, if I moved my body the way I had seen them move theirs and did nothing else, it would never quite work. But if I heard the voice that said their names while I was playing out that fantasy, I could believe it. Foster Hewitt could make me them.

Source: K. Dryden, 1983. The Game. Toronto: Macmillan (pp. 55-56). Reprinted by permission of Macmillan of Canada, A Division of Canada Publishing Corporation, Toronto.

Cognitive-development approach

Some psychologists focus on specific aspects of human development, namely, people's ways of thinking, and of seeing the social world. Cognitive-developmental theories explain behaviour in terms of the development of these perceptions and thought processes.

Piaget (1965), a Swiss psychologist, is perhaps the best-known pioneer of these theories. Through systematic observations, he discovered that as

children mature they use increasingly complex cognitive processes, and can process more information. He also argued that all individuals potentially pass through the same four stages of cognitive development: **sensorimotor** (in which the infants concern is to understand how its needs can be met by the external environment), **pre-operations** (the early use of concept formation and intuition), **concrete operations** (learning basic logic and perspective taking), and **formal operations** (using propositional thinking and abstract reasoning, along with full role-taking capacities, the ability to "project" self and others into hypothetical situations), although the speed at which they do so may vary greatly, and many, if not most, may not complete the cycle. As people pass through these stages, they grow to understand the world in more complex and abstract ways, they come to appreciate the rights and roles of others, and they become less egocentric about their own place in the world.

Moral development proceeds in tandem with cognitive development, Piaget maintained, and it occurs in stages too. During the earliest stage (from about ages 4 to 7) children believe that norms and ethical rules are rigid and absolute, coming from some higher external authority such as parents. Piaget called this stage the **morality of constraints**, or *moral realism*. External restrictions (e.g., from caregivers) on behaviour and the consequences of actions are of prime importance, while intentions matter little. Children believe that wrong acts are always punished, and thus punishment plays a major part in defining an act as wrong.

Between the ages of about 7 to 9, most children mature into what Piaget called the **morality of cooperation**, or *moral relativism*. Rules (and later on, laws) come to be seen as products of negotiation and compromise, such as the give-and-take in peer groups, discussions within families, and debates in legislative assemblies. At this stage motives become increasingly important, and actions are judged not so much in terms of absolute principles as on the basis of particular situations. Children learn that actions are neither always wrong nor always right, but must be judged individually according to the circumstances involved.

Finally, **moral autonomy** becomes a possibility sometime after puberty. The sense of moral autonomy is based on a unified system of abstract principles regarding right and wrong. At this stage, individuals can operate and think independently of authority, rules, and laws; but they do so after considering the perspective and needs of others. Moral principles universally applicable to all are adopted, and it is accepted that individuals have an obligation to act as their consciences dictate (i.e., autonomy has obligations).

Kohlberg (1984) elaborated on Piaget's work by studying how people can pass through up to six stages of moral development. In his expansion of Piaget's formulations, Kohlberg also showed how individual styles reflect sociopolitical and moral philosophies. In particular, Kohlberg's stages represent the transition from egocentrism to a sociocentric perspective-taking. People mature beyond the egocentrism and strict self-interest of Kohlberg's Stages 1 and 2 by expanding their points of reference to include social order and social convention. At his Stage 3, there is a desire to win social approval (the "good boy/girl–bad boy/girl" stage), and at Stage 4, deeds are done out of duty (the "law and order" stage), Piaget's moral relativism. Kohlberg's upper stages expand on Piaget's moral autonomy: they are concerned with self-chosen moral-ethical principles, rather than selfish needs (Stages 1 and 2) or approval-seeking (Stages 3 and 4). Moreover, they involve principles that transcend the immediate and concrete, and go beyond a particular society. At Stage 5, there is a concern with the preservation of human rights, while at Stage 6, the preservation of equality, dignity, and life, regardless of consequences for oneself, is the overriding principle. Research shows that few operate at this level, although many people can conceive of it, because it is extremely difficult to put into practice, especially when most other people operate at lower levels.

Cognitive-developmental theorists are interested in how people develop more complex, differentiated, and mature ways of thinking about the world, with the hope of stimulating people to move to higher levels of development, and therefore improve themselves and the world. Moreover, although we know much about how to stimulate these forms of development, this work is largely ignored by schools and educators (Muuss, 1996). Recently, Kegan outlined an even more elaborate theory, but the title of his book—*In over Our Heads: The Mental Demands of Modern Life*—reveals how poorly he thinks we are doing in terms of stimulating people to achieve their cognitive potentials.

Psychoanalytic approaches

Writers who adopt the psychoanalytic point of view analyze the workings of psychic structures and processes. The two best-known psychoanalytic theorists are Freud (1935) and Erikson (1968).

Freud postulated that the personality consists of three major components. The instincts and drives with which humans are born form a major portion of what he called the physiologically based **id**. It is impulsive, selfish, and pleasure-seeking. It is also a source of psychic energies, such as aggressive and sexual, that can be used or repressed. The **ego** begins to emerge early in childhood as the id encounters obstacles to its impulse-gratifications, usually from parents, but also from the infant's own helplessness (the infant needs help from its environment to satisfy its needs, like nourishment). Thus, the ego constitutes those cognitive processes that help the individual figure out how to achieve satisfactions based on the constraints and opportunities of its immediate environment. As individuals mature, these ego processes become more complex, and give people attributes that make them unique in terms of their own ideas, beliefs, memories, hopes, and fears. The ego's interactions with the world are guided by the *reality principle*: ideas initially associated with impulses are modified into actions to fit the real world, depending on actual opportunities. The third component of personality—the **superego**—consists largely of what is generally called "conscience." Children acquire the many values and rules of their culture, largely by internalizing their parents' superegos, which usually contain society's norms. These norms then guide the ego in reconciling id impulses with the limitations and requirements of culture and society.

For Freud, people can pass through several stages: *oral, anal, phallic, latency,* and *genital,* conforming to the process of physical maturation. If each is successfully resolved, and no serious fixations occur, the person develops a healthy, mature (non-neurotic) personality consisting of a strong ego and a well-developed superego. People who do not develop sufficiently strong egos and superegos can encounter considerable difficulties later in life in terms of impulse control, reality testing, and their ability to empathize with others. In fact, these individuals often show up as not having been adequately socialized.

Erikson did not significantly modify Freud's basic ideas, but instead built upon them, showing how culture is relevant to ego development over the entire life span. One of his major contributions is an eight-stage description of ego development. He considered his theory "psychosocial" because each stage involves the interaction of the individual's gradually maturing psychological characteristics with the social contexts the individual experiences. Some people pass through them faster than others, but generally the tasks associated with an earlier stage must be successfully completed before going on to the next stage. Incomplete tasks may mean that the individual later has to return to that stage, or at least will have considerable trouble when presented with situations requiring skills that should have been previously mastered.

The first years of childhood include four stages in which specific ego strengths are acquired: during the first stage, children need to develop the ego strength of basic trust (versus distrust); in the second, autonomy (versus shame and doubt); in the third, initiative (versus guilt); and finally in the fourth, industry (versus inferiority).

During adolescence and youth, the task is to develop a viable sense of identity (the fifth stage) with which to move on to the tasks of adulthood. This is frequently a period of identity confusion and identity crisis, as we shall see below. During the sixth stage, young adults face the challenge of developing a sense of intimacy (versus isolation), while during the seventh stage people face the problem of nurturing a sense of generativity or caring for others, instead of being drawn into a sense of self-absorption and stagnation. In the last stage, usually entered in old age, individuals must evaluate and come to terms with the overall quality of their lives. Here the major alternatives are integrity or despair.

Of the eight stages, Erikson wrote most about the identity stage, in part because he believed it is the most difficult stage to resolve for people in modern societies. Erikson originally conceived of the notion of the "identity crisis" when treating identity loss among war-trauma victims during World War II. Later he drew a parallel between this type of disturbance and the experiences of "severely conflicted young people whose sense of confusion is due to a war within themselves" (Erikson, 1968: 17). He also wrote about the identity problems of adulthood, which he saw to be "normal" responses to the *anomie* or lack of norms associated with modern societies.

Erikson's writings suggested that the psychosocial identity that emerges during the identity stage is comprised of three interrelated components: the subjective/psychological component (ego identity); the personal component (behavioural styles that differentiate individuals); and the social component (recognized roles and statuses within a community or society). These components need to come together during the identity stage, and when they do not, or as they are doing so, an identity crisis is evident. The *identity crisis* is characterized by a subjective sense of identity confusion, behavioural and character-ological disarray, and a lack of recognized role or roles in a community. Accordingly, resolution of the identity stage is facilitated when (1) a viable community role is acquired, (2) behaviour and character become stabilized, and (3) a relatively firm sense of ego identity is developed (Côté, 1996).

Another way to express the problems people face in forming an adult identity is to speak of three forms of continuity: between the self and itself; between the self and other; and between other and other. The first type of continuity is what Erikson had in mind when he coined the term "ego identity" (i.e., a sense of self-sameness over time or personality constancy). The second type of continuity pertains to a person's relationships with others. A continuity here maintains the stability of personal and social identities, whereas a discontinuity threatens the stability of those identities. The third type of continuity represents the stability of relations in a particular community or group. When these community relations are stable and continuous, people's personal and social identities within the community are safeguarded. However, when these relations are unstable, people's personal and social identities come under pressure and may undergo revision. What is particularly important to note, however, is that unstable community relations (problems in "other-other" continuity) make it difficult for those attempting the transition to adulthood to do so in an easy fashion. This is especially so for those younger members of society who do not have a sense of "self-self" continuity (ego identity) and unstable "self-other" relations.

These three forms of identity problems are now commonplace among adolescents in modern, industrial societies, in part because these societies have experienced such a protracted period of social change in which their key institutions have become relatively disorganized (as we explore below). Yet, we can see in Erikson's work just how important a stable and structured society is in aiding the formation of adult identities. Thus, we can see why socialization problems can make identity, in its various forms, problematic for the individual. Also, we see why the types of socialization contexts found in modern societies can create a variety of problems for many individuals, leading some to undertake a "negative" identity formation, in which they invert the values of their parents and culture, out of "a desperate attempt at regaining mastery in a situation in which the only available positive identity elements cancel each other out" (Erikson, 1968: 176). We see below how important Erikson's work on identity is when we attempt to account for the Littleton incident.

Cultural anthropology

Cultural anthropologists help us better understand the relationships among socialization practices, cultural patterns, and personality characteristics. Their influence was greatest in the first half of the twentieth century, when anthropologists travelled to far-flung places on the globe, reporting on the tremendous variations in cultural arrangements. Common to all of these distant cultures are rites and rituals that provide concrete structure for the life course, while at the same time ensuring the continuity of the culture through the shaping of specific behaviours and personality characteristics compatible with the needs of the culture. Anthropologists found that the more individuals are integrated into a culture, both behaviourally and emotionally, the greater the chance of a culture perpetuating itself. In addition, cultures adopt childrearing practices that are consistent with their own institutional and behavioural patterns, but these childrearing practices can be very different from those found in other cultures. They can range from coddling children to being very harsh to them. It should be evident that cultural anthropologists share many assumptions with functionalists. In fact, as we saw in Chapter 3 on Culture, a number of the early functionalists like Malinowski were anthropologists.

Because they sought out cultures that differ from Western ones, cultural anthropologists enjoyed a special place in the public's imagination. Through their efforts, Westerners have developed less ethnocentric and less racist attitudes and learned to accept the legitimacy of other cultural arrangements. Such tolerance, referred to as *cultural relativity*, involves "an awareness that different cultures have different ways of meeting life's demands. Different cultures have various guidelines regarding important decisions such as choosing a marriage partner, raising children, taking care of the infirm elderly, and so forth" (Brislin, 1993: 33). While this perspective involves a suspension of disparaging judgments, thereby opening one's mind and expanding one's awareness, it does have its limitations. It is difficult not to pass judgment on certain cultural practices, as in the obvious case of Nazi Germany, nor is it appropriate to suspend judgment when one sees obvious injustices (e.g., forced female circumcisions). However, by appreciating that there is no one right way to socialize people, Westerners have come to appreciate how they can learn from other cultures in this regard.

Benedict (1938, 1980) did just this in a landmark essay on adolescence. She argued that most pre-industrial societies provide for a continuous passage from childhood, through adolescence, and into adulthood. By doing so, cultural continuity was safeguarded, and individual members of the society did not experience serious personal difficulties in making transitions through these social statuses. Western societies, however, are age-graded, largely segregating children, adolescents, and adults from each other. In pre-industrial societies it is thus easier for younger members to learn over a period of time the skills necessary for adult functioning, and experience the realities of life, like sex, work, and death. This occurs during the mid- to late teens in most of these societies (Schlegel and Barry, 1991). By the time they reach adulthood they are prepared for their adult roles.

Western societies have introduced three sets of discontinuities into the socialization process, according to Benedict. First, Western children are socialized into non-responsible roles, even though adulthood ostensibly requires a self-regulated responsibility. Second, children are socialized to be submissive, despite adults being expected to be dominant. And, third, children are shielded from sexuality (she first wrote about this in 1938), while Western adulthood requires a complex awareness of sexuality. Benedict's question was just when, where, and how are people to learn these three essential aspects of adulthood? Benedict did not believe Western societies have good mechanisms for transmitting these things, and saw adolescents as left on their own to learn them. Consequently, Western adolescence can be a difficult period of adjustment.

Margaret Mead, Benedict's colleague, took up this issue in a series of studies in the South Pacific. She was specifically interested in the belief that adolescence is inevitably a time of "storm and stress." As noted above, this idea was popular at the time among those who supported nature arguments about human behaviour. Based on the work of Hall (1904), many people believed that adolescence was a period in which everyone inevitably went through a period of development that essentially reproduced human evolutionary history, in this case the long period in human history of "barbarism," preceding "civilization" of the adult stage. Given the absoluteness of this claim (i.e., that everyone in every culture experiences adolescence as stressful), if one culture could be found where this was not the case (the *negative instance* method), then a cornerstone of the nature side of the nature-nurture debate would be upset.

Before reviewing what Mead reported, it is instructive to review Hall's claims about the origins and symptoms of adolescent storm and stress. He defined storm and stress in terms of the *emotional instability* associated with swings between opposite feelings: "alternations between inertness and excitement, pleasure and pain, self-confidence and humility, selfishness and altruism, society and solitude, sensitiveness and dullness...." (1904: 40). Hall made the following assertions regarding evolutionary basis of these symptoms (1904: 71):

Early adolescence is...the infancy of man's higher nature, when he receives from the great all-mother his last capital of energy and evolutionary momentum.

Thus the child is father of man....These years again, like infancy, should be sacred to heredity, and we should have a good warrant indeed before we venture to interfere with its processes.

Hall was so convinced about the absoluteness of evolutionary influence over adolescence that he advised adults to stand back and let the processes unfold, because he believed that emotional instability was inevitable in all adolescents. But it was Hall's racism and patronizing view of non-Western societies that drew Mead's interest as an anthropologist.

Mead tackled this issue of the universality of adolescent storm and stress on the remote islands of Samoa. She reported her findings in a book that has been the best-selling book in the history of anthropology, *Coming of Age in Samoa* (1928). In it Mead compared three groups of females: those who had not yet experienced puberty, those who were experiencing it, and those who were past it. She reported that the experience of puberty made no significant differences in the character of these females. In her words: "The adolescent girl in Samoa differed from her sister who had not reached puberty in one chief respect, that in the older girl certain bodily changes were present which were absent in the younger girl. There were no other great differences to set off the group passing through adolescence from the group which would become adolescent in two years or the group which had become adolescent two years before" (1928: 196).

Mead attributed the lack of adolescent storm and stress in Samoa to its consistent and continuous socialization practices. In contrast, she argued, the difficulties affecting the adolescent of 1920s America were caused by conflicting standards of conduct and morality, and "the belief that every individual should make his or her own choices, coupled with a feeling that choice is an important matter." In contrast, she asserted that in 1920s Samoa (1928: 273):

The gap between parents and children is narrow and painless, showing few of the unfortunate aspects usually present in a period of transition...essentially the children are still growing up in a homogeneous community with a uniform set of ideals and aspirations.

This evidence of cultural differences in the prevalence of adolescent difficulties led Mead to conclude that adolescent "storm and stress" cannot be considered a biological inevitability.

Although her work in Samoa has been the subject of considerable controversy, it appears that the source of much of the criticism lies with residual disputes associated with the nature-nurture debate and not with her chief conclusion about the source of adolescent turmoil, because subsequent research confirms that conclusion (Côté, 1992). Nevertheless, the legacy of Hall's work lives on in the public mind to the extent that people still hold stereotypes about adolescent turmoil and "raging hormones."

Socialization Contexts and Agents

Now that we have examined the underlying assumptions regarding the nature of socialization, and the perspectives that various social scientists have taken toward it, we can move to a consideration of the question of how socialization takes place. Simply put, socialization takes place within a variety of social contexts, and within each context there are various socialization agents. We examine five contexts below, but do not focus on agents of socialization per se, such as teachers and parents. This is in part because agents are imbedded in the contexts and in part because we are all socialization agents. That is, each of us participates in socialization processes in one way or another through our very participation in groups. In groups, we express our approval and disapproval that shape the subsequent conduct and thought of others, as both symbolic interactions and learning theorists argue. Thus, we are all informal socialization agents.

The term *socialization context* refers to social settings that affect socialization processes, thereby influencing the individuals involved. In this sense, there is a concern with stable patterns of social interaction in groups through which common symbols are transmitted. Socialization contexts vary according to the characteristics of groups (e.g., size and boundaries), as well as the characteristics of group members (e.g., age, gender, race, and class). When undertaking this sort of analysis, the focus is on how socialization contexts (settings) set the stage for socialization processes and how individuals are affected by these contexts.

Most socialization takes place in subtle ways, so people do not recognize efforts to shape them, but in modern, industrialized societies many contexts are explicitly mandated to *change* people in ways that they may or may not want to be changed. In these contexts, specific socialization agents do so with **role systems**, an interrelated set of social positions based on a division of labour in which people share expectations about desired outcomes, and power hierarchies. Sometimes these efforts are successful, especially when people want to be changed, as when they volunteer for the military. However, socialization efforts can be less than successful when people resist in various ways. When the socialization mandate is only partly realized, unintended consequences can result that set up a series of events that create new contexts or distort the originally intended consequence. In contrast, some people are too motivated to change, or are too susceptible to certain influences, so that socialization occurs when it was not intended. This problem may arise with the mass media, where the intention is to entertain, but some people (even a very small percentage) take it as a learning experience or internalize role models. As we see below, this has become a serious problem in terms of the effects of mass culture, and is implicated in copy-cat and fringe incidents of violence, like school violence.

One way to understand how problems can arise in socialization contexts is in terms of differences in **socialization ratios**, namely, the number of *socializers* (agents) to *socializees* (those being socialized). The lower the ratio (fewer agents), the less the context will change through being socialized. For example, if a professor (the agent) has a class of four hundred students, chances are diminished that the professor will have an emotional or intellectual impact on any of those students. In contrast, a professor or teaching assistant with a class (or tutorial) of twenty students stands a much better chance of having an impact, other things being equal. What may not be equal is how willing or motivated the socializees are to being

A positive consequence and the context of an action are both significant determinants of behaviour.

affected by the teacher or the material in the course. Students who are keen on the subject matter can be highly affected, even in a class of four hundred, but those who are not keen may not be affected even in the smaller class (Côté and Levine, 1997).

The socialization ratio is also related to how much potential power those being socialized have in a given context. The lower the ratio, the more they can exercise power just by their sheer numbers (e.g., using class reactions to intimidate teachers they do not like, or to get course requirements reduced). This is especially relevant when factors of motivation are taken into account. If individuals are not motivated to change, less change will take place. In fact, it is common for "subcultures" (cliques and gangs) to emerge in these contexts, which in turn have their own socialization potential. In these cases, socialization agents may have to be authoritarian to maintain their control of the context and their power in the socialization hierarchy, but this recourse to coercion can simply feed the "subculture of resistance." The most obvious example of this socialization problem is in prisons where a few guards must keep large numbers of unwilling inmates under control. However, the problem can also be found in high schools, where a few teachers are supposed to be teaching (stimulating cognitive development in) large numbers of students. To the extent that mass education at the secondary level is resisted by a segment of the student body, the task confronting teachers becomes more difficult and the need for authoritarian measures increases. This only feeds the growth of "peer subcultures" in the schools that express their resistance in various ways, toward both the teachers (and what they represent) and the other peer subcultures that emerge. The recent rise in high-school violence, including the Littleton incidence, attests to the problem of trying to change, with inadequate resources, people who do not want to be changed. The peer subcultures that emerge under these conditions, as with the "Trench-coat Mafia" at Littleton (the group of students to which the killers were attached) tend to be so small (15 to 20 members in this case) that they can more appropriately be called "peer-cults."

Related problems associated with social contexts can be identified that seem to be particularly common in societies that have dismantled many of their social control mechanisms, or have had them disrupted, as in modern, industrialized societies. For example, socialization can be **inadequate** or incomplete when people are not exposed to all experiences necessary to function in certain roles, as when educational systems fail to provide sufficient job training. It has also been identified as a problem by anthropologists like Benedict and Mead, with respect to the transition from adolescence to adulthood. Socialization can also be **defective**, when unintended outcomes or consequences arise. Some video games—the point-and-shoot variety—actually provide training for murdering people. Training young people to be violent murderers is not the intention behind these media (making money is), but it seems to be happening with increasing frequency. A number of the mass murderers in the recent high-school rampages experienced this form of "gun training."

Finally, socialization can be **disjunctive** in the ways that Benedict described above. In fact, a lack of continuity of experience in moving between institutional settings is now common in modern societies, so much so that it is accepted as normal and of not much concern. For example, large numbers of people are regularly released from mental hospitals and prisons, with little support or means for re-entry into the community. When back in the community, they may find themselves stigmatized and shunned, and therefore with no useful social roles to play. For many in this situation, life back in the hospital or prison may be preferable because they have a means of subsistence there, as well as a sense of place and identity.

Of course, formal socialization agents are not unaware of these problems, but modern societies have increasingly opted to leave the solutions up to the individuals affected, rather than providing collective solutions, like providing the means for effective *resocialization*, or the replacing of old behaviours and attitudes with new ones. However, individuals are often at a loss concerning what to do to fill the gaps within and among social contexts, and are left on their own to make their way into the social and economic institutions that establish security and fulfilment (e.g., securing a long-term profession or career). One individual response is **anticipatory socialization**, whereby people project themselves into the future in the hope of acquiring the characteristics appropriate to the institutional destination they hope to reach.

One way to understand how we have come to the point where we accept a society with so many socialization problems is with a model developed by Mead late in her career. She provided it in her book *Culture and Commitment: A Study of the Generation Gap* (1970). In it Mead postulated a theory of intergenerational relations that reflects three stages of cultural change and associated patterns of commitment between children and parents: "*postfigurative*, in which children learn primarily from their forebears; *cofigurative*, in which both children and adults learn from their peers; and the *prefigurative*, in which adults learn also from their children" (1970: 1).

Mead's theory of changing intergenerational relations is straightforward, yet profound, because it encapsulates what appears to have happened in most world cultures in recent history. Indeed, Mead was fascinated with how preliterate societies had been affected by contact with technological societies. She noted how deep these effects ran, down to the day-to-day relations between children and adults, as both attempted to make sense out of their changing worlds.

In **postfigurative** cultures, the relations between parents and their offspring are governed by traditional norms beyond questioning by either parent or child. Child-disciplining practices are long-established and not open to discussion. The postfigurative culture is stabilized by the

Social Change and Childrearing

Mead's theory of changing intergenerational relations sheds light on a number of issues. For example, with Mead's theory we can make better sense of a recent incident in Troy, Ohio, where a 33-year-old man was spanked by the police ("Spanker Spanked," *The Globe and Mail*, 9 February 1995). Why? Well, it appears that he bruised his 10-year-old son while spanking him with a wooden paddle. The incident was brought to the attention of the local police, who charged the father with domestic violence. As part of a plea bargain, the police humiliated the father by spanking him with the same paddle and then destroying it.

The legitimacy of a parent to discipline a child generally would not be questioned in a postfigurative society, where child discipline is often severe. In fact, in nonindustrial Western societies, not disciplining a child in a strict manner was often seen as cruel and negligent. In an increasingly prefigurative society such as Canada, we are witnessing a reversal of this, in which the act of physical discipline is viewed as negatively as not disciplining was in the past. Now, parents do not have as much authority rooted in tradition; and there is less faith that they possess the wisdom to raise their children properly.

In prefigurative societies, the well-being of the current and future generations of children has been largely divorced from past practices. Consequently, there is now great confusion about how to raise children effectively. And, there is even more bewilderment about what the future holds for generations brought up with very little discipline, physical or otherwise. Mead would not be surprised, therefore, to hear that today these issues are of increasing concern. As Underwood ("Are Your Kids Driving You Crazy?" *The Globe and Mail* 17 April 1999) wrote, "[S]omewhere along the line, things got little off track....[Parents] began to let their youngsters call the shots. Children today are not only seen and heard, they expect to be obeyed: their war cry, 'You are not the boss of me!' is ringing out across the continent." In response to this increasing tyranny of childhood, bewildered and frustrated parents are looking for help in dealing with children, who they feel are behaving like spoiled brats who cannot control their impulses, take responsibility for their actions, or empathize properly with others. Bookstores are stocking titles like *Who's in Charge?* and *I'll Be the Parent, You Be the Kid* that offer advice to beleaguered parents.

In the past, strict disciplining practices were believed to build character; now they are viewed as abusive. How would you go about studying whether children are getting out of hand, or is this generation of parents just unable to handle normal problems of childrearing?

coresidence of three generations (including grandparents) and the assignment of most social roles. Consequently, change is slow and intergenerational continuity great, even revered. These cultures often engage in ancestor worship and instill a sense of responsibility for many generations to come. Postfigurative cultures bear clear similarities with pre-industrial societies.

In **cofigurative** cultures, the intergenerational linkage becomes tenuous because of social change brought by technological advancement, economic transformation, immigration, war, and so forth. One (or more) of these forces affect the culture, giving children a different set of experiences than their parents had, if only for a brief time. Consequently, to some extent, offspring look to nontraditional sources for components of their sense of meaning, particularly from among their contemporaries. Thus, there is a fundamental change in the relations between parents and children, whereby the authority of the parent can be questioned, and the child can actually give direction to the parent in certain instances. As a result, the eventual adult roles of offspring are no longer as taken for granted by either parent or child. However, the schism between parent and child is limited because offspring are obliged to observe and respect significant elements of the traditional culture shared with their parents.

Finally, **prefigurative** cultures are characterized by rapid and massive social change. Because of the extent of social change, parents have little conception of what the future holds, so their past life-experiences are of little use to their offspring with respect to their present sense of meaning and future roles. As a result, parental guidance is not well regarded by children. Moreover, parental belief systems (and traditional culture, if applicable) are often dismissed as invalid by offspring. In fact, Mead argued that in prefigurative cultures the young can actually teach their parents about the ongoing social changes, or achieve a level of social status, to the point where their parents can become subservient to them in various ways. Hence, the gap between parents and offspring that opened in the cofigurative culture is widened in the prefigurative one (see the boxed insert entitled "Social Change and Childrearing").

We can see how socialization becomes more problematic as societies pass through these three stages, and we can see how it becomes more *reciprocal*, with offspring socializing their parents to increasing degrees (reciprocal socialization happens in all societies, but is minimized in postfigurative ones).

Social context and the life course

To illustrate some of the above principles, we shall now examine the changes in the socialization contexts governing the transition to adulthood, contrasting the present with the past, beginning over one hundred years ago. Five contexts will be examined, each of which provides some of the normative structure for the transition to adulthood (i.e., what to do, when to do it, why, where, and with whom). The contexts governing the transition to adulthood since about 1800 include: the family, religion, education, the peer group, and mass (or popular) culture. We see below how the relative importance of each has shifted dramatically. These shifts can help us understand how incidents like Littleton have become possible.

At the beginning of the twentieth century, the mid- to late-teen years were quite different than they are now. Around 1900, only a small number of teens attended secondary schools, almost half were involved in agricultural labour, and the rest were employed in the labour force, often making a living wage or close to it. While many lived with their families, there was paid work available for them (without the age prejudices we now witness) and, for those who lived with their parents, considerable financial contributions were made to the family. For working-class families, their most prosperous years were often when their children worked and lived with them (Allahar and Côté, 1998).

In the year 2000, in most Western nations, the vast majority of teens attend secondary schools. In Canada and the U.S. today, over one-half of secondary-school graduates go directly to postsecondary institutions (Nobert and McDowell, 1994). Thus, only a minority (less than one-third) of those in this age group (18 to 24) is engaged in employment that is sufficiently well paid to afford them independence from their parents. Those who stay with their parents rarely contribute much financially, and make only minor contributions to household labour (although young females do more housework than young males), leaving them free to pursue various leisure activities (White, 1994). In addition, their parents often subsidize them with free or cheap room and board, or allowances, and their mothers often provide "domestic" services for them. Referring to Canadian youth, Lindsay, Devereaux, and Bergob (1994: 5) found that those "aged 15-19 devote less time than the general adult population to productive activities, while they have more free time and spend more time sleeping." Similarly, Arnett (1996: 162) argued that "adolescents in many American households are treated not like equal adults but like indulged guests." Moreover, if they have a decent job, and do not pay room and board, some young people can have more discretionary income than their parents (Mogelonsky, 1996).

What has happened over this century to transform young people from being productive citizens to dependents on their families and educational systems? And on what basis are they denied their right to contribute to the society and economy to their full productive capacities? Answers to these questions can be found in the shifting importance of socialization contexts.

Some two hundred years ago, the family and religion were the contexts providing most of the normative structure in the transition to adulthood for the vast majority of the population. The family most likely exerted the greatest influence for most people at the time, especially in frontier communities. Since then, however, the family has been in steady decline as a direct overriding influence (see Chapter 10, Families). Some two centuries later, the family provides more of a "safety net," protecting the young from an unwelcoming economy.

For many people, then, the family is no longer the strongest influence in determining major life choices relevant to future adulthood, or what to do along the way (e.g., what to do for a living, whom to marry, and so forth). American teens on average now spend five minutes a day alone with their fathers and twenty minutes with their mothers (Bennett, 1994). Moreover, when they interact with their parents, they are not necessarily spending

"quality time," because they usually meet in front of the television. This is hardly an ideal situation for adults of one generation to guide and relate to the next generation, especially in terms of communicating common cultural symbols. Television enters the picture even more, as we see below.

By the mid-1900s, religion had begun a sharp decline in influence as well (see Chapter 11, Religion). In Canada, only 12 percent of young people attended services regularly in the 1990s (Clark, 1998; cf. Bibby, 1993; Bibby and Posterski, 1992), down precipitously from mid-century. People are now more likely to "pick and choose" their religious beliefs independent of organized religions.

Around 1850, education began to emerge as an influence for the children of affluent parents. Since then, its influence has grown, so that now it is one of the most important institutions providing structure to the transition to adulthood. Currently, in most Western countries, the majority of teens are in school, and in some countries between one-third and one-half of those in their early twenties are still in school. By the end of the twentieth century, mass and private educational systems had become enterprises in their own right, occupying up to one-third of the population, and holding a monopoly in the training of workers.

But critics say that the system of mass education created resembles too much the system of mass production developed to maximize industrial production. People are not products that can be manufactured on assembly lines, but rather need individual care and attention. The large, factory-like schools that most young people must now attend can breed feelings of alienation and resentment, creating the conditions for clique formation and problems in identity formation. Smaller schools, critics argue, can avoid these problems, because teachers and students know each other better, and there are more resources per student for sports, music, and other extra-curricular activities. Even Al Gore, while vice president of the United States, recognized this, when he said in a speech that we need to stop herding students "into overcrowded, factory-style schools [where] it becomes impossible to spot the early warning signs of violence, depression, or academic failure" (quoted in Christian, 1999: 19). In fact, students who attend smaller schools get better grades, attend more, and participate in more extra-curricular activities. They are also less likely to be part of a clique or gang, to fight or be attacked, and are more likely to discuss their problems with teachers (Christian, 1999).

To provide one more contrast, in 1940, things like chewing gum, making noise, and talking out of turn were considered top problems by high-school teachers in the U.S. In 1990, the same question put to teachers found the top problems to be drug and alcohol abuse, pregnancy, suicide, rape, robbery, and assault (Bennett, 1994). Have teenagers suddenly become afflicted with some genetic defect or biological epidemic? No, so nature is not at fault; it is the socialization contexts provided for adolescents by adults, or nurture, that are far different than in the past.

Peer groups have also changed over the last two centuries. In earlier times, especially in rural settings, peer groups had a minimal influence on the transition to adulthood; they were difficult to form, and small and on an *ad hoc* basis when formed. By the 1950s, peer groups were increasingly affected by the technologies of industrial society, especially, the automobile, which gave young people greater opportunities to interact independently of their parents, and the mass media, which transmitted youth-culture symbols to wide audiences, so young people in far-away places were given a common language with which to bind their peer groups together independent of their parents' cultures. This is not to say that young people and their parents live in entirely separate worlds, but that the amount of common culture shared has diminished considerably, leaving young people open to other influences. Those who are more cognitively developed, self-confident and autonomous, and with more mature forms of identity are able to participate in, and learn from, all of these influences without any apparent difficulty (Conger and Galambos, 1997). However, a significant number of young people today show adverse effects from being too involved in peer cultures and mass culture, as evidenced by the high casualty rate among this age group (e.g., suicides, youth-on-youth violence, car accidents, and the like; Arnett, 1996; Côté and Allahar, 1994) through their involvement in the seamier side of mass culture.

Mass culture, or popular culture(s) disseminated through the mass media, rose to ascendence along with, and through, peer groups. In fact, mass culture may require segregated groups in order to thrive. In the past, more members of society shared a popular culture, which represented their common roots (as contrasted to an élite culture, in which only the rich could afford to engage). Popular-culture activities involving song and dance brought people of all ages together in community celebrations, binding communities through the sharing of common symbols (note the annual celebrations of "folklore" and other "ethnic" activities in many Canadian cities—these are leftovers from "pre-mass culture"). Over the twentieth century, however, driven primarily by the mass media, popular culture has become increasingly segmented by age, with each age group adopting its own forms of song and dance as they make the transition to adulthood (see Chapter 12, Media). This has introduced a symbolic wedge between successive generations of the twentieth century, reducing the amount of time they spend with others and the cultural symbols they share.

Since the mid-1900s, the transition to adulthood has been increasingly affected by mass cultures whose promoters seek out wide audiences, largely based on age. Mass culture is delivered to the widest audience through a "dumbing down," whereby the lowest common denominator is targeted, namely, passive and uncritical consumers who prefer not to expend mental energy during their leisure time. We can see, therefore, that it will not be effective in influencing everyone.

Television has become the main medium by which mass culture reaches its intended audiences. Strasburger and Donnerstein (1999: 129) argued that "an increasing number of studies document that a serious problem exists" with respect to "children, adolescents, and the media." Part of their concern is over the expansion of the media into video games and videocassettes. When the time spent with these media is added to that of television, some American teens spend as much as 55 hours per week in front of a cathode-ray tube. One problem, they believe, is that these media exert a behavioural and psychological *displacement effect*. Behaviourally, the time spent watching television takes away from other activities, like physical exercise, reading, and face-to-face interaction with other people. Psychologically, the *content* (those ideas that occupy people's minds and to which they have ready access) of what is viewed can affect the consciousness of the viewer—and the younger the viewer, the greater the effect. The more one is exposed to certain ideas, or ways of thinking, the more likely these are to affect choices made and beliefs held.

But, mass culture uses television as only one of its conduits for affecting consumer behaviour. All of the mass media have been exploited in one way or another as part of the attempt to make profits. And, again, it is not that people mindlessly buy into the mass-cultural messages that are bombarding them. People, including many young people, are able to resist these messages if they are so motivated. However, marketers have learned how to feed off this resistance, especially from young people, in the various youth-oriented industries that emerged in the latter half of the twentieth century. Now, many symbols of youth resistance to mainstream society and market forces are commodified and sold to younger cohorts so they too can feel "hip" or "cool." Frank (1997a) documented these marketing tricks and showed ironically how marketers have used the concepts of "cool" and "hip" to trick mass consumers into believing that they can show others how much they are their own "individual" by wearing, using, driving, or consuming something that has been mass marketed.

Marketers have developed a variety of strategies to make people think that consuming their product is hip or growth enhancing. The chief marketing strategy documented by Frank (1997b) is "liberation marketing": it presents ads critical of mindless, middle-class consumers, who are depicted as dumb suburbanites, trapped workers with sadistic bosses, or executive automatons in grey uniforms. Liberation ads tacitly admit that business now rules the world, but its own products or services can liberate consumers from this oppression, if only momentarily (e.g., the advertising of shampoos that give women orgasms in public or soft drinks that enable impossible risk-taking adventures). Marketers have also nurtured new brand loyalties that provide models of existential rebellion, in which a product is used as an expression of resistance against, or escape from, the drudgeries of work and urban life. Companies have also worked to create brand identities, which help consumers assimilate a product into their own sense of identity (e.g., Apple computers attempt to appeal to those who have a humanistic vision of the future).

Marketing strategies now also involve multimedia penetrations of consumers' lives (products presented not only in explicit ads, but also in movies, music videos, television programs, and magazine articles) and merchandised spinoffs that often involve the consumer voluntarily advertising products (e.g., names brands stamped on clothing, or other products like knapsacks and personal CD players). Frank contended that the attempts to appropriate youth culture have been highly successful, noting that contemporary "youth culture is liberation marketing's native tongue" (1997b: 45).

One way to gauge how much effort has been put into influencing the mass-consumption of the youth population is to consult the marketing literature, where we find that not only is there tremendous attention directed at understanding how young people think, but also great interest in influencing their thoughts. But this stands to reason, given the vested interests of marketers. Because they make their wages by predicting and affecting future consumption patterns, they need to be able to chart out *current* consumption patterns. Within the past few years, articles with the following titles have appeared in *American Demographics: Consumer Trends for Business Leaders:* "Marketing to Generation X" (Ritchie, 1995), "Talking to Teens" (Zollo, 1995), "The Rocky Road to Adulthood" (Mogelonsky, 1996), "Getting Inside Kids' Heads" (McGee, 1997); and "College Come-ons" (Speer, 1998). Even more telling of the motivations of marketers are some of the captions for these articles, like "The teenage market is free-spending and loaded with untapped potential;" "Don't assume 18-to-24-year-olds are adults. The pre-adult life-stage is here to stay;" and "Today's college students have more money than their predecessors, and they don't mind parting with it. Product and service providers want a piece of the spending now, but the ultimate goal is to cultivate long-term customers."

Are mass marketers successful? Well, the youth market in the U.S. is estimated at almost 300 billion dollars per year. One-third of this money is from young people's discretionary income and two-thirds comes from their parents (Palladino, 1996). Inasmuch as mass culture is a potent socialization context to which people are now exposed on their way to adulthood, the expert advice is "buyer beware."

Explaining Youth Violence: The Littleton Incident in Context

We have covered a number of diverse perspectives in this chapter, each of which offers some insight into the nature of, and problems associated with, socialization. We conclude with an analysis of the Littleton incident based on a mix of these perspectives as they bear upon the issues raised by this incident. First, we will gather together several facts from similar incidents and compare them with facts about the Littleton incident, and then we need to pause to consider alternative explanations from "nature" causes.

What can we say about elements common to the rash of mass murders in high schools? First, they generally occurred in larger high schools. Second, all shooters were males between the ages of 11 and 18 with easy access to firearms. Third, all were deeply affected by mass culture in some way, including movies like *Natural Born Killer*, video games like *Mortal Kombat*, death-themed music like that produced by *Marilyn Manson*. Fourth, all were experiencing some psychological difficulties, especially depression. And, fifth, all were triggered by something related to peer involvements, like being excessively teased or having a girlfriend break up with them (Cloud, 1999).

These five factors apply to millions of Canadian and American teenagers, but they do not mass-murder their peers, so why did those handful of teens choose to do so? The two Littleton murderers, Harris and Klebold, were both from middle-class, two-parent families, and were apparently fairly intelligent. However, they had no active religious involvements or if they did, they were willing to go to Hell together. It also appears that their parents were "distant" in the sense that they did not talk with them much, or monitor their behaviour;

otherwise they would have seen the guns lying around and the bombs being made. But, many teens have minimal contact with their parents and no contact with religious figures or ideas. So, why did they engage in such a destructive, including self-destructive, rampage?

Could it be that we do not even need any sort of "nurture" explanation? Is it possible that these mass murderers were just "that way" because of their genetic makeup? The answer is no, because a purely genetic or biological explanation is implausible by the mere fact that anything instinctual or genetic needs to be expressed through some sort of supportive environmental medium (Buss, 1999). Still, all of the perpetrators were teenaged males who are in the high-risk age-sex category for violent behaviours, and many had histories of aggressive behaviour (Arnett, 1999; Males, 1996).

Alternatively, why can we not simply argue that these incidents represent extreme forms of adolescent storm and stress? The reason is that these outbursts would not have taken place, or may have taken other forms, in different cultural settings. Note, for instance, that the availability of guns like assault rifles in the U.S. makes these phenomena distinctly American (in the Taber incident in Canada, a small hunting rifle was used). Although these young men may have reacted as angrily in another culture, without these readily available weapons, they could not possibly have carried out such carnage, and their anger may have been taken out in some other way. Moreover, this particular expression of aggression must be viewed developmentally. These young men were at a stage in their lives—the identity stage—when they needed to find positive outlets for their aggression and energy, but apparently none was available. Instead, they invested their aggression in culturally provided fantasy outlets that encourage exactly these forms of violence. In the Littleton incident, one of the assailants had just been turned down by the U.S. Marines. Again, millions of young men, many of them prone to aggressive behaviour, go through this age period without carrying out mass murders, so the explanation for these specific incidents of violence needs additional factors to be found elsewhere.

Thus, turning to the Littleton incident, we need to understand how the mental lives of these two young men interacted with their particular social circumstances. We know about the social circumstances, and since these are widespread, the adult community (socialization agents) needs to be alert to them because they apparently constitute a powder keg. Most prominent is the existence of large, factory-like schools that breed the forms of alienation and resentment felt by all of these murderers. These schools give rise to clique formation and the setting of peers against one another. That is the "keg." The "powder" seems to be the mass culture to which all are exposed, but to which some take so seriously that they alter their identity formation to incorporate it. This mass culture teaches hate and alienation, for those who are looking for it, and it shows people how to take revenge for perceived personal injustices, from point-and-shoot video games to instructions on bomb-making over the Internet. Harris and Klebold had even made a video for a class project in which they dress-rehearsed their carnage, and they customized a *Doom* game that "computer-modelled their crime" (Pooley, 1999: 20). No adult socialization agents took note. In fact, both had been through an "anger management" course at their high school, receiving glowing reviews (Phillips, 1999: 20).

But, the "match" that sets off the powder keg needs to be found in the mental state of these young men who choose these particular outlets for their frustration and aggression. For this we will have to surmise from these individuals' behaviours using psychological perspectives. Obviously, these individuals were unable to empathize properly with others, otherwise they would not have been so cruel. Their level of moral development could not have been high, or else they would have adopted a sociocentric view of others that would have inhibited them from hurting others in this way. Apparently, their superegos were not well developed, or else they would have experienced guilt and anxiety while even contemplating such acts. Obviously, they learned how to do these things by observing and imitating others. But less obvious are the identity problems they experienced that we now take to be "normal" because they are so widely experienced. These young men were experiencing an adolescence in which there are few meaningful and socially validated roles to play, and, given how prolonged adolescence has become, they likely felt

that the end of their adolescence was an eternity away (a sense of temporal distortion is a common symptom of ego identity problems). With little identity validation from their peers or adults, they likely turned to a "negative identity" (Erikson, 1968) as a way to avoid overwhelming feelings of identity confusion (evidence for Harris's negative identity can be seen in the fact that his father was in the U.S. Air Force and he chose Hitler's birthday to commit the crime). In doing this, they inverted the values of their parents and culture, flaunting their rebellion in their parents' and community's faces, adopting once and for all the negative identities of the "Littleton murderers."

If we backtrack to what was absent in their lives, we find that in terms of traditional socialization contexts, these young men had no buffers to keep them from going over the edge: there were no socialization agents from their family, from a religion, or from a school who could bring them back from the edge, or who even saw them on the edge. They apparently only had influences from their peers and mass culture pushing them further and further toward that edge. Unless things change in terms of the institutional configuration governing the transition to adulthood, we can expect more incidents like these, along with a spreading of violence to places we have not yet considered. Further, we can expect a spreading of this alienation and identity confusion to people who otherwise would have made the transition to adulthood in a problem-free fashion, had they been raised in another culture where socialization agents take seriously their obligations to guide the next generation into adulthood in a safe and benign fashion.

Summary

We began and ended this chapter with an examination of a recent mass murder committed by two young men in a high school. We used this incident as a social specimen for evaluating and illustrating the socialization perspective and the various socialization theories. We found that the perspective and the theories combined help us to understand and explain a complex and growing problem in modern society.

Socialization was defined from a variety of perspectives, all of which involve teaching or inducing people to fit into, and cooperate with, human groups. From these definitions arose a number of issues associated with how much influence societies have in determining people's behaviour and how much personal control people can exert over their own behaviour in the face of cultural influences and societal pressures. In addition to cultural influences, scientists have also argued that evolutionary-based genetics plays a role in how people behave, both in terms of personality traits and in terms of how societies are structured. Referred to as the nature/nurture debate, positions have been adopted along the range, from total genetic influence to total cultural influence. Given the focus of this chapter, the impact of culture was emphasized with the acknowledgment that much remains to be learned about genetic influences and how they interact with cultural ones.

Within sociology, three perspectives have dominated the field. Functionalists emphasize the integrative function of socialization in maintaining existing social structures. Conflict theorists question how benign these socialization processes are, arguing that they often serve to perpetuate inequalities and injustice. Symbolic interactionists, in contrast, focus on the micro level of analysis in terms of how individuals learn to interact with each other through negotiating and sharing symbols embodied in the language and role playing.

While sociologists tend to be interested in the contexts and content of socialization, psychologists focus on how people learn and how this changes them. Three psychological perspectives were examined: social learning theory, which emphasizes how people react to the consequences of their behaviours; cognitive- development theory, which studies how people's thinking changes over the life course; and psychoanalytic theory, which looks to the structure of mental functioning to explain behaviour patterns.

Finally, some contributions of cultural anthropology were discussed, showing how variations between cultures, and within cultures historically, help us appreciate the diversity of ways in which socialization practices can be carried out.

The substantive portion of this chapter focused on socialization contexts and agents, illustrating them in terms of how the periods of adolescence and youth have come to be structured in contemporary Canadian society. Socialization contexts vary in the extent to which they can and do exert influence over people. In many contexts, people resist attempts to influence them, leading to unintended consequences and a variety of socialization problems. Socialization contexts also vary over the life course of the individual, and they have changed over the course of history. Using a one-hundred-year time frame and five social contexts, it was argued that the family and religion have declined in the extent to which they socialize young people for adulthood and their place in the community, while education, peers, and mass culture have increased in influence. It appears that, increasingly, the socialization of new recruits to adulthood is in the hands of bureaucracies and businesses, rather than parents and other concerned adults.

QUESTIONS FOR REVIEW AND CRITICAL THINKING

1. Can you list instances from your own experiences that would be examples of defective socialization? Can you think of any examples in which you experienced anticipatory socialization?

2. Besides your parents and teachers, who were your significant others? What were their effects on you?

3. In your own family, is there evidence of a preconfigurative world?

4. Observe the behaviour of children for a few hours. Is there evidence that some of their behaviour has been shaped by television?

KEY TERMS

anticipatory socialization, p. 89

cofigurative culture, p. 91

concrete operational stage, p. 82

defective socialization, p. 89

disjunctive socialization, p. 89

epigenetic, p. 70

formal operational stage, p. 82

generalized other, p. 80

I and me, p. 80

id, ego, superego, p. 84

inadequate socialization, p. 89

looking-glass self, p. 79

moral autonomy, p. 83

morality of constraints, p. 83

morality of cooperation, p. 83

nature versus nurture, p. 72

ontogenetic stages, p. 81

prefigurative culture, p. 91

pre-operational stage, p. 82

postfigurative culture, p. 90

role system, p. 88

role taking, p. 79

sensorimotor stage, p. 82

significant others, p. 80

socialization, p. 70

socialization ratio, p. 88

social reproduction, p. 78

SUGGESTED READINGS

Erikson, Erik H.

1968   *Identity: Youth and Crisis.* New York: Norton.

Erikson's seminal statement on human identity and how it has been made vulnerable by social change and the disruption of communities.

Gergen, Kenneth

1991   *The Saturated Self: Dilemmas of Identity in Contemporary Life.* New York: Basic.

Gergen argues that the self and identity are becoming "multiphrenic" and "relational" as a result of the changes in people's lives, brought on by the penetration of modern and "postmodern" technologies into their lives.

Kegan, Robert

1994   *In Over Our Heads: The Mental Demands of Modern Life.* Cambridge: Harvard University Press.

Kegan takes us beyond Piaget and Kohlberg to show us how far we have yet to go cognitively if we are to "get" what it means to understand the opportunities and limitations of contemporary society.

Strasburger, Victor C.

1995   *Adolescents and the Media: Medical and Psychological Impact.* Thousand Oaks, CA: Sage.

This up-to-date study examines the effect of various forms of media upon the mental and physical well-being of young people.

WEB SITES

http://www.demographics.com

American Demographics

Visit a journal where the efforts to shape people's consumption behaviour are reported.

http://www.adbusters.org

Adbusters

At this site, online efforts to draw people's attention to the attempts to shape their consumption behaviour are reported.

http://www.stanford.edu/group/adolescent.ctr

Stanford Center on Adolescence

This site that reports on the efforts of experts who are attempting to improve the transition to adulthood and counteract some of the deleterious effects of contemporary American society.

CHAPTER 5

Deviance

James J. Teevan and Lesley D. Harman

Introduction

When Canadians read about a robber or hear about the depression of a friend, most picture the individuals involved. Reactions range from fear to moral outrage to victim blaming. Less often do people think about how the behaviour of these individuals is affected by the social environment— such as the province in which they live, the unemployment levels they face, their families and peer groups, and the relative disadvantages posed by sex, class, race, disability, age, and sexual preference. Such social factors are of primary concern to sociologists, who attempt to discover the role of society in **deviance**, the general term given to any behaviour that is perceived to violate social norms. The various sociological perspectives concerning society's part in the origin and development of deviant behaviour is the subject of this chapter. It begins with a topic essential for any understanding of deviance: how do societies decide what is deviant and what is not?

Definitions of Deviance

The behaviours and conditions that people may consider deviant are quite diverse, ranging from murder, arson, and anarchy to mental and physical illness, obesity, and extreme thinness, to breaches of etiquette or over-politeness, to genius. One thing these examples of deviance have in common is that each is perceived as somehow not "normal." Normal behaviour is that which conforms to a particular society's norms or rules.

The inclusion of genius in the list of deviant behaviours reveals that some "positively" sanctioned behaviours may be considered deviant as well. Indeed, there can be a **stigma of excellence** (Posner, 1975). Being overly attractive, excelling at sports, or performing saintly acts carry a social price and may lead to exclusion on the basis of not being "normal." So, then, it is possible to conceptualize a continuum of deviance ranging from the most severely sanctioned, embodied in a person such as Paul Bernardo, to the most positively sanctioned,

99

embodied in a person such as Mother Teresa (recall Chapter 3, Culture).

A second characteristic shared by many behaviours defined as deviant is that each is morally devalued, at least somewhat (Sacco, 1992), surrounded by negative feelings, and thus seen by some people as an acceptable target for social control. This control can range from simple staring and mild ostracism, to more serious reactions such as medical treatment and corporal punishment. Deviance, then, is the "conflict between those who behave in particular ways and those who seek to control their behaviour...and the problems each group creates for the other" (Sacco, 1992: 3).

Not only does deviance include a broad range of behaviour, there is also great variation within and across societies, in time and space, in what each considers to be deviant. In her short life, Joan of Arc was considered both a "saint" and a "sinner." In 1429 she led the French army to victory, in 1431 she was burned at the stake as a heretic and a witch, and in 1920 she was canonized. In Chapter 3, Culture, we saw how some societies ban the eating of cows, others pigs, and still others, neither. Indeed, anthropologists have shown that most behaviours have been designated as deviant somewhere, at some time, or under certain circumstances, and yet have been accepted elsewhere, at other times, or under other circumstances. For example, in traditional Inuit culture, infanticide and the killing of old people were seen as acceptable means to protect a limited food supply (see Edgerton, 1985). Most other Canadians would have severely condemned such behaviour. Although the different outlooks are understandable given the unique conditions facing the Inuit, they illustrate the relative definition of deviance, that what is deviant is specific to time, place, and circumstances.

Additional evidence for this variability can be found by looking at homosexual behaviour and suicide. Although considered deviant by many (if not most) Canadians, both homosexuality and suicide have been tolerated and even encouraged elsewhere. Male homosexual behaviour was accepted and practised in quite a number of societies and was so much the norm in parts of ancient Greece that they did not even have a special word for homosexual (Downing, 1989). Today it is estimated that 5 percent of the Canadian population

is gay or lesbian (Blum, 1997). For many of these people, as for any individuals engaging in behaviour that others define as deviant, to them their chosen lifestyle is normal. Suicide was preferred to dishonour by Japanese samurai and also practised by Brahmin widows, who threw themselves upon their husbands' burning funeral pyres—an Indian practice called suttee (see Edgerton, 1985). Suicide by modern "freedom fighters" who attach bombs to their bodies is also seen as honourable: their gift to the cause. Closer to home, people dying of various painful or degenerative diseases have fought for the right to assisted death. The list could go on. The point is that even suicide is not always considered deviant. Indeed, in twenty-first-century Canada it may become common for the terminally ill to examine the option of suicide, even assisted suicide, with the blessing of family, friends, and medical care-givers, to escape lives sustainable with modern technology but defined as "without quality."

The existence of deviant subcultures also points to the relativity of norms. A **deviant subculture** is a group of individuals who share a trait defined as deviant by the larger society. Homosexuals, bikers, Satanic groups, and nudists are obvious examples, but the category may also include left-handed people, religious orders, the rich and famous, and extremely intelligent people who join Mensa. For Brake (1980), a subculture is a collective solution to collectively experienced problems. Its distinguishing feature is that what the members have in common is defined as deviant by the broader culture, but that same common element is not only normal to them but intensely important to their identity, to their sense of who they are. The support provided by a subculture moves one from being a lone deviant to an accepted member of a group.

Who then makes the decisions as to what is or is not deviant? For example, who made marijuana, but neither alcohol nor tobacco, illegal? Who decided that government lotteries, sometimes described as voluntary taxes on the ever-hopeful poor, should be legal, while bookmaking should not? Who said that prostitutes should be routinely viewed as deviant for their trade yet their clients less so? Further, why were these decisions made? There are several answers to these questions, depending upon how society is viewed, whether more in a functionalist manner, seeing relative harmony and consensus, or more in terms of symbolic interactionism, seeing societal reaction and labelling, or more in terms of the conflict perspective, seeing power relations and social inequality, or more in terms of a feminist perspective, seeing gender relations within patriarchy.

A functionalist position

Durkheim (1949) took a functionalist position, arguing that definitions of deviance arise out of the **collective conscience**, the values held in common by the vast majority of a society's members. For example, most Canadians would agree that arson, murder, and robbery are deviant acts, and that to weigh 300 kilograms is not normal. According to Durkheim, then, the source of definitions of deviance is society itself.

Moreover, deviance can serve positive functions for society (recall the discussion of prostitution in Chapter 1, What is Sociology?). Deviance, so long as it is not so widespread and/or serious enough to undermine the basic fabric of society, can be beneficial in several ways (Coser, 1964). First, deviants can be used as scapegoats, and serve to unify the rest of society. They can be targets for pent-up tension and aggression. Serving as common

enemies, deviants can unite conformists, especially when no external enemies exist, increasing the conformists' cohesion, productivity, and well-being. As such, deviance sets the moral boundaries between groups, dividing between "us" and "them."

Second, deviants can be used to mark the bottom layer of society and to illustrate clearly the meaning of abstract rules. Viewing deviants enables non-deviants to see exactly what is not allowed (proscribed) or demanded (prescribed), and by comparison allows non-deviants to feel like saints, comfortable and secure in their conformity. In fact, Erikson (1966) argued that if there were no deviants to rally against and to serve as "inferior" comparisons, society would redefine new behaviours as deviant in order to satisfy these needs. He explained accusations of witchcraft in the Puritan settlements of colonial New England in this way.

Third, deviance can call attention to flaws in the social system, serving as an early warning that something is wrong. Thus, like smoke detectors, deviance can help society avoid other potentially larger problems that could prove more damaging.

Fourth, deviance can begin a process of social adaptation and progress to new and better norms and values. Many advocates of values now commonly accepted were once defined as deviant when, ahead of their time, they pressed for social

Acceptable Deviance

Harman (1985) argued that most of us engage in what she calls "acceptable deviance" at least part of the time. **Acceptable deviance** is deviance that is tolerated and in some cases encouraged by the majority of the group. Let us illustrate this with the example of speeding. On most Canadian highways, the posted speed limit is around 100 kph. Any speed higher than this violates the law. However, the collective experience of driving on a highway is quite different. Individuals driving on Toronto expressways, for example, may notice that the average speed driven is closer to 120 kph. In fact, in busy traffic, one may feel "forced" to speed. What is going on here? The group has defined a different norm from the stated law, and this is acceptable deviance. Ironically,

to drive at the posted speed may invite hostility from other drivers. A footnote to this example is that the police also honour the grassroots definition of speeding by ticketing only those drivers who exceed 120. In this case, then, we see that the formal agents of social control have yielded to the collective definition of deviance.

The minor deviance associated with Hallowe'en may actually prevent the greater deviance that could erupt without such an outlet.

change. Jesus and Gandhi were deviant in this sense. Nineteenth-century feminists who demanded equality for women were similarly labelled deviant.

Finally, minor forms of deviant behaviour can take the pressure off and serve as safety valves. They permit individuals to let off steam, almost as if in a "time out," and in the process perhaps prevent more serious disruptions. For example, the minor deviance associated with Hallowe'en (or even the major destruction after a home-team world championship) may actually prevent the greater deviance that could erupt without such an outlet. For all these reasons, then, it can be understood why Durkheim actually argued that deviance is "normal" and "good" for societies.

Symbolic interactionist perspective

The sociology of deviance changed significantly in the 1960s and the 1970s when a micro sociological emphasis became popular. From the symbolic interactionist perspective, it became apparent that so much of deviance-defining is determined by societal reaction and not necessarily by the behaviour itself. Becker (1963) went so far as to argue that it does not really matter whether a person has committed a deviant act; if she or he is perceived to have committed an act then she or he will be treated accordingly. Certainly, there are many examples of the Guy Paul Morins and David Milgaards who, accused of crimes that they did not commit, spent years in jail until they were finally found innocent. Countless women were burned at the stake during the witch hunts of the Middle Ages, simply on the basis of rumour and innuendo. There is also the grim reality that some individuals continue to be treated as if they are normal, law-abiding citizens while carrying on illegal activities. Paul Bernardo lived a "double life"—as an accountant by day and the Scarborough Rapist by night—for months before he was finally detected and captured. It all boils down to the social construction of reality, and who is in a position to do the defining. We have already been introduced to this concept in Chapter 1 and in Chapter 4, Socialization. What does social construction mean in terms of deviance?

Lippmann (1922: 81) argued that, "[W]e do not first see, then define, we define first and then see." As an observation about the human tendency to treat objects as well as other people on the basis of labels, this is very accurate. Imagine for a moment going to a church bake-sale and seeing a grandmotherly-type woman with a table of glass jars. On those jars are labels that say "Raspberry Jam." How likely would you be to question the contents of the jar? Probably you would think, "Well of course it's raspberry jam, she's not the kind of person who would poison me." Indeed, symbolic interactionists note that groups tend to define others as "kinds of people." When we meet a stranger, we base our subsequent behaviour to a large degree on the way the person is dressed, the social context in which we meet, what they tell us about themselves, and on what other people tell us about them. We even allow our views of others to be influenced by rumours. A man is rumoured to be having an affair, a teacher is rumoured to have sexually assaulted a student, a politician is rumoured to have stolen public funds. In each of these cases, it ultimately may not matter whether the rumour is true or not. It is the societal reaction that defines the person as deviant.

Thus the "labelling perspective," as it has come to be called, recognizes that deviance is socially constructed. As Becker argued, "[S]ocial groups create deviance by making the rules whose infraction constitutes deviance, and by applying those rules to particular people and labelling them as outsiders. From this point of view, deviance is not a quality of the act the person commits, but rather a consequence of the application by others of rules and sanctions to an 'offender'" (1963: 9).

Conflict perspectives

Conflict theorists believe that society is held together by coercion rather than cooperation, and argue that definitions of deviance arise out of special interests. Those with power get to have their definitions of deviance prevail while those without power, under constant threat of disapproval from those in control, must get along as best they can.

This general position has two main variants. According to the first, a more Weberian position sometimes called **pluralism**, various segments of society, such as the wealthy, the religious, or even bureaucrats in the criminal justice system, compete to have their definitions of deviance accepted. Becker (1963) called these individuals **moral entrepreneurs**, people and groups who seek to influence the passing of rules and the setting of standards. Although benefit to society is often cited as the rationale behind the definitions of deviance proposed—and these people often see themselves as social reformers—there are sometimes self-serving reasons of equal or greater importance. For example, early twentieth-century Canadian narcotics legislation had labour groups among its supporters. They saw in the anti-opium laws the potential for deporting Chinese immigrants, whom they viewed as a threat to their own employment because they would accept lower wages (Solomon and Madison, 1986). Giffen, Endicott, and Lambert (1991) added that once on the books, anti-narcotics legislation is often amended to include additional drugs, not necessarily because the drugs newly proscribed are dangerous but because the drug-enforcement bureaucracy needs a broader mandate to justify its continued budget and existence. In Chapter 13, Work and Organizations, we shall explore Weber's view of the growing power of bureaucracy in modern life.

The second variant of the conflict position accepts Marxist principles and originates from what is sometimes called the *radical* or **critical school**. It sees an economic élite as the major force behind definitions of what is and what is not deviant (see Comack and Brickey, 1991). With either variant of the conflict position, whether it is a single economic élite or several competing groups that define

Difficulties in Moral Entrepreneurship

Sociologists have a long history of opposing censorship. For decades they have been most vocal when conservative moral entrepreneurs have tried to limit freedom of expression. For example, they have fought against those who would limit birth-control information and those who would ban communist writings, having little sympathy for claims that such expressions might be offensive to religious views, or serve as the basis for subversive attacks on existing political economy. But today sociologists increasingly face difficult dilemmas in their defence of freedom of expression. When moral entrepreneurs include feminists who seek to suppress pornography and minority groups who do not want certain literary works to be taught in schools because of the unflattering way the groups are depicted, many sociologists are caught in a bind. Will they lend their support to the oppressed, whom they traditionally champion, or will they continue to fight censorship? Are liberal (or radical) expressions of censorship different from their conservative counterparts? Can this apparent dilemma for sociologists be resolved?

deviance, the general conflict argument is that definitions of deviance often represent special interests. Conflict theorists do not deny that consensus can exist, but they recognize that as long as social inequality exists, those in power will use their position to ensure that their own interests are met. Relations of domination, then, ensure that those "on top" are in a position to define "the other" as deviant. Their investigations are directed less towards individual deviants, as might be done by functionalists, than towards the rules and standards themselves and the groups that profit, economically or otherwise, by providing definitions of deviance. Finally, conflict theorists do not see deviance as functional. Deviance divides rather than unites, as it encourages people to be judgmental, sometimes distrustful of one another, even afraid of whole groups of people. It also deflects attention from the larger issues of inequality, racism, sexism, and the consequences of capitalist greed.

A feminist perspective

A feminist perspective on deviance begins from the understanding that the history of the sociology of deviance has mirrored the larger discipline of sociology in that it has, until recently, been written for, by, and about men. Historically women have been ignored in deviance studies, with the exception of interest in their sexuality (Schur, 1984; Chesney-Lind, 1989). As such, studies of women's deviance has been limited to studies of so-called "bad girls" (prostitutes, strippers, "promiscuous delinquents") and their relations with men. Beginning in the early 1980s, however, feminist research began to focus on the victimization of women in and by patriarchy. Behaviours hitherto trivialized and not considered deviant, such as sexual harassment, some sexual assault, homelessness, and other forms of violence against women, such as the oppressiveness of body norms, became the subject of a growing literature in which the sociology of deviance was called upon to make room for the experiences of women.

If deviance is any variation from what is considered normal, then this phenomenon can be explained by Daly (1974: 65), who claimed that "[T]o be female is to be deviant by definition in the prevailing culture." In other words, as de Beauvoir (1953) noted, in patriarchal society the "normal"

human being is male, and the female is constituted as "The Other." As we shall see in Chapter 7, Gender Relations, patriarchy is a system of masculine domination. This means that traits and attributes normally associated with masculinity become the distinguishing characteristics of "normality." So, within this model, anything associated with femininity is by definition deviant. As Schur (1984) once put it, even when they are normal, women are deviant.

In the area of psychiatry, Rohde-Dascher and Price (1992) wrote about the patriarchal origins of psychoanalysis and its sexist view of women's roles. Kaplan (1983) noted that many traditional definitions of mental health are biased against women, with "normal" being equated with male behaviour. To illustrate her point, she devised, only somewhat tongue-in-cheek, a female-defined form of mental illness: "Restricted personality disorder." It is marked by limited emotionality, even denial of emotional needs, a refusal to admit to being hurt much less to cry, a need always to appear self-assured, the choice of physical or intellectual activities over emotional experiences, and finally a preoccupation with work. How many men suffer some degree of this "illness?" Indeed, it is male psychiatrists who have created categories of mental illness. *Penis envy* was not a term defined by women; indeed, a wish for women's creative capacities might have led to the condition of *womb envy* had psychoanalysis been female-dominated (see Rohde-Dascher and Price, 1992). The fact that the word *hysteria* is derived from the Greek word for uterus is another example of the underlying masculine bias in psychiatry.

A feminist perspective on deviance, then, will tend to highlight the experiences of women and to focus on ways in which they are labelled deviant for both conforming to and deviating from gender norms. The primary focus of this research is on perceived violations of appearance norms, maternity norms, sexuality norms, and occupational norms. So through this approach it is possible to understand how it is deviant to be both obese or anorexic, to be both childless or a mother, to be both a "good girl" or a "bad girl," to be both employed in traditional and untraditional jobs or to do unpaid domestic labour. In turn, a feminist analysis also recognizes how agencies of social control tend to reproduce relations of patriarchy by keeping women "in their place."

Other perspectives

Very few sociologists take either an extreme functionalist or an extreme conflict view concerning definitions of deviance. Most would reject as naïve the view that capitalists make all of the laws—if so, how did laws against price-fixing and unfair competition get passed? Most also could not accept a view of a collective conscience without conflict. Witness the amendments to sexual assault legislation made a few years ago. Feminists had to battle long and hard to change the legal system, to reduce police reluctance to lay charges, to lessen the need for corroborative evidence, to increase sentences for offenders, and to allow husbands to be charged. Even in the case of murder, about which many think there is consensus, there are disputes: Is abortion murder? euthanasia? execution of criminals? killing in time of war?

In between functionalism and a critical perspective are several compromise views on definitions of deviance. One argues that although conflict explains the origins of some definitions of deviance, consensus explains their continued support. Briefly put, over time the originally less-than-impartial definitions of deviance become widely accepted. A second position softens the idea of conflict between a powerful and a powerless group, and points to *negotiation* between and among groups with varying degrees of power (see Kent, 1990). For example, people with physical exceptionalities fought for and won the right not to be called "the disabled," and homosexuals have made gains in recent court decisions concerning equal rights, including same-sex spousal benefits.

In the end, each type of deviance should be examined separately to see which explanation best fits. For example, rules about which society is not in full agreement, such as rules against gambling, adult pornography, drug abuse, and other activities that involve willing participants and make "society" the main victim, are often explained by a Weberian conflict perspective.

Gusfield (1986), for example, argued that 1920s prohibition legislation in the U.S. was promoted by rural Protestants who disliked and distrusted a growing urban Catholic population. Fearful that their way of life was threatened by these Catholic immigrants, the Protestants lobbied successfully to make the alcohol (which was drunk mainly by Catholics) illegal (see Maxim, 1993, for a similar investigation of Ontario dry versus wet counties). Finally, a lack of power may explain why some things fail to get defined as deviant. Was, for example, the federal government guilty of kidnapping when it "relocated" Japanese Canadians during World War II? Leroux and Petrunik (1990) also made this argument with respect to elder abuse, which, compared with spousal and child abuse, receives much less reaction from society.

Forms of deviance such as assault and driving while intoxicated, which most people would think of as harmful, may be better explained by Durkheim's consensus position. Property crimes, especially theft, may need the two-stage explanation: conflict for origin, consensus for current support. The laws were originally made by wealthy property owners who made them after their paying of low wages, creation of unemployment, and a general refusal to share may have encouraged theft. Today, however, most Canadians have some property they would like protected and so most would support the law. Finally, the relative nonenforcement of laws against "capitalist crimes" such as environmental pollution, lack of worker safety, and price-fixing may need a critical analysis.

Whichever theory best fits any specific example of deviance, the general point to remember is that society, either the whole or its more powerful segments, is a crucial variable to consider in examining definitions of deviance. Societies choose to worry about homosexual behaviour or to focus attention on the destruction of endangered species and rainforests, to open new prisons or to emphasize the creation of more jobs. Such decisions determine what is deviant. Definitions are not absolute, and thus it would be wrong (and ethnocentric) to assume that what is now considered deviant in Canadian society has everywhere always been so, or will everywhere always be so.

TABLE 5.1   Police-Reported Incidents, by Most Serious Offence, Canada and the Provinces/Territories, 1996

CANADA Population: 29,863,600	Actual Number	Adults Charged		Youths Charged	
		Male	Female	Male	Female
First degree murder	369	197	13	13	–
Second degree murder	203	153	29	27	2
Manslaughter	60	42	13	7	1
Homicide—Total	**632**	**392**	**55**	**47**	**3**
Attempted Murder	**848**	**563**	**65**	**81**	**6**
Sexual assault	25,821	7,814	133	1,430	35
Sexual assault with weapon	651	271	14	36	4
Aggravated sexual assault	290	149	7	9	2
Sexual Assault—Total	**26,762**	**8,234**	**154**	**1,475**	**41**
Assault	177,728	58,509	8,890	7,712	3,441
Assault with weapon/ causing bodily harm	35,194	16,309	2,843	3,180	790
Aggravated assault	2,731	1,625	282	271	49
Unlawfully causing bodily harm	2,390	1,346	157	208	76
Discharge firearm with intent	263	86	7	13	–
Police	5,566	3,343	815	271	126
Other peace-public officers	860	435	88	57	26
Other assaults	2,946	909	145	115	33
Non-Sexual Assault —Total	**227,678**	**82,562**	**13,247**	**11,827**	**4,541**
Robbery with Firearms	6,646	1,635	105	410	24
With other offensive weapons	10,322,	2,154	260	1,007	167
Other robbery	14,274	2,451	272	1,578	383
Robbery—Total	**31,242**	**6,240**	**637**	**2,995**	**574**
Crimes of Violence—Total	**291,437**	**99,097**	**14,258**	**16,589**	**5,187**
Business Premises	110,073	9,236	404	4,622	345
Residence	242,132	14,937	1,159	10,280	1,167
Other	43,880	2,079	86	1,784	130
Breaking and entering—Total	**396,085**	**26,252**	**1,649**	**16,868**	**1,642**
Motor Vehicle Theft —Total	**178,580**	**8,491**	**509**	**6,105**	**789**
Bicycles	83,603	724	30	919	45
From motor vehicles	347,890	5,242	257	3,070	177
Shoplifting	111,174	33,795	19,493	11,857	8,865
Other	306,682	14,464	3,662	5,720	1,292
Theft—Total	**849,529**	**54,225**	**23,442**	**21,566**	**10,389**
Have Stolen Goods—Total	**30,599**	**14,388**	**2,170**	**5,290**	**1,062**
Cheques	40,343	7,062	3,307	341	184
Credit Cards	17,405	3,381	1,148	472	202
Property Crimes—Total	**1,555,800**	**123,324**	**36,005**	**51,242**	**14,593**

TABLE 5.1   *continued*

CANADA Population: 29,863,600	Actual Number	Adults Charged		Youths Charged	
		Male	Female	Male	Female
Prostitution—Total	**5,912**	**2,742**	**3,197**	**20**	**165**
Gaming and Betting—Total	**710**	**409**	**138**	**2**	**1**
Offensive Weapons—Total	**16,132**	**5,336**	**444**	**1,338**	**137**
Arson	12,865	665	140	509	55
Counterfeiting currency	19,650	394	58	71	7
Disturbing the peace	54,519	3,439	498	461	127
Indecent acts	6,431	1,213	117	67	4
Kidnapping	1,876	1,002	55	110	21
Trespass at night	5,434	613	22	246	10
Mischief	364,021	13,816	1,793	6,743	960
Other Criminal Code Offences	205,847	37,187	5,696	6,321	1,864
Other Crimes—Total	**776,911**	**108,389**	**20,065**	**24,011**	**6,116**
Criminal Code Traffic—Total	**161,805**	**82,834**	**9,310**	**–**	**–**
Total Criminal Code	**2,785,953**	**413,644**	**79,638**	**91,482**	**25,896**

Source: *Statistics Canada, 1998. Canadian Crime Statistics 1996, Catalogue No. 85-205E, Table 3.3.*

Applying a Deviant Label

Whatever acts or conditions a society decides to define as deviant, common sense says that not everyone who fits the definition is discovered. This brings up a second aspect of definitions of deviance: once the definitions exist, the reaction of others (the audience) are crucial in deciding who is and who is not a deviant. Hence, not only are the definitions of deviance social, their application to specific individuals is social too. Official counts of deviance, such as crime (see Table 5.1) and mental illness rates, are then also social products. These ideas are illustrated in Figure 5.1 and the discussion that follows.

In box (1) are *deviants*, so-called because they perform deviant acts or are unusual in some way, and because their audiences respond to their deviance. (For convenience, from here on, the words "or are unusual in some way" will be omitted.) In box (4) are *innocents*, who perform no deviant acts and receive no audience reactions. So far, there are

FIGURE 5.1   Audience Reactions and Deviant Actors

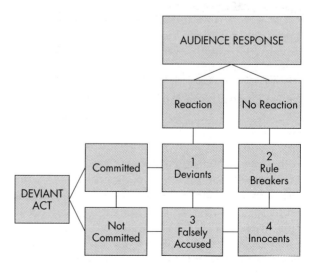

Source: *Howard S. Becker, 1963. Outsiders. Studies in the Sociology of Deviance. New York: Free Press (p. 20).*

Society's reactions are important aspects of a person's deviance, in some ways even more important than the person's actions themselves.

FIGURE 5.2   Crime Funnel

the number of crimes decreases as one moves down through the funnel

actual crime
crime detected
crime reported
crime recorded
arrests
trials
convictions
dispositions
(fine, probation, institutionalization)

no major problems, except perhaps for the previously mentioned issue of who gets to define deviance in the first place. The picture is more complicated in boxes (2) and (3), rule breakers and the falsely accused, respectively. **Rule breakers** commit deviant acts, but no one responds to them for some reason. If you ever shoplifted, lied at customs, or sucked your thumb in bed after childhood and either were not caught or if caught were excused for some reason, then you are a rule breaker (see Gabor's [1994] book *Everyone Does It: Crime by the Public* from the University of Toronto Press). If you are secretly homosexual, you are a rule breaker, at least in contemporary Canada. Compare these rule breakers to the *falsely* accused in box (3) who, although they commit no deviant acts, are reacted to as if they have, perhaps even suffering punishment and segregation from innocents and rule breakers alike. Mistakes like this do happen.

Looking at actions and reactions, then, it becomes clear that society's reactions and application of the label deviant are important aspects of a person's deviance, in some ways even more important than the person's actions themselves.

Conflict sociologists argue that there may be as many or even more rule breakers than deviants, with actual amounts (rule-breaking rates) of alcoholism, drug abuse, crime, and mental illness in Canada all much greater than official data (deviance rates) indicate.

The **crime funnel** (Figure 5.2), as it is called, is the process of loss that takes place from the actual number of crimes committed to the final number of convictions (Silverman, Teevan, and Sacco, 2000). At each point in the crime funnel, losses occur due to fear, bias, discretion, and human error. Let us take the example of sexual assault, a highly underreported crime. At the top of the funnel are the total number of sexual assaults committed. However, many are not even detected. Partly what is meant here is that there is some variation in how one defines sexual assault. One woman on a date with a man with whom she has nonconsensual sex may define it as sexual assault, another may not. So the crime funnel begins to lose cases as soon as there is a difference in how one defines a crime. The next crucial point is that of reporting. Fear keeps an estimated 90 percent of sexual-assault victims from reporting their crimes. Historically, women repeatedly experienced the shame of sexual assault throughout the criminal justice system, at the hands of police and defence lawyers. Although attitudes are changing, and women are being given more permission to speak up against their assailants, many victims still prefer to suffer in silence. Even once sexual assaults have been reported to the police, however, a certain number are thrown out as "unfounded"; for example, if the victim has been drinking, has worked as a stripper or a prostitute, or has been "morally discredited" in the past; those whose morality is in any way questionable are thus less likely to be seen as "legitimate victims." Further along the crime funnel, more losses occur at the points of arrests, convictions, and finally dispositions. In the end, some researchers estimate that only about 1 percent of the total number of sexual assaults committed are resolved through a disposition. For mental illness, too, Hagan (1991) estimated that as many as 25 percent of Canadians suffer psychological impairment. Only about 13 percent of the population sees a doctor for such problems in any one year, however, and an even smaller percentage is hospitalized (Bland, Newman, and Orn, 1990).

These omissions are revealed when researchers ask respondents to report their rule breaking, regardless of whether reactions by others have turned it into deviance. For example, in the past year how often have you driven while even slightly intoxicated? Did you ever shoplift, drink under age, or use illegal drugs? The answers, called self-report data—along with victimization data responses from victims about their crime experiences—can then be compared with police data. Both sources reveal a great undercounting of crime. For example, self-report data reveal that 24 percent of Canadians have cheated on their income tax at least once, a percentage quite at variance with official data (Brooks and Doob, 1990).

A related point is that any change in the number of labellers and their resources can create corresponding increases or decreases in deviance, without changes in the actual rule-breaking rates of behaviour. Such was the case when the addition of more police to a force led to a higher official crime rate (see Koenig, 1991). In another context, provincial governments are quite aware that the greater the number of doctors licensed, the more illness that is treated, and researchers have argued that the greater availability of psychiatric facilities in urban areas is part of the cause of higher mental illness rates in cities compared with rural areas (Kates and Krett, 1988).

Finally, even with a constant number of labellers, any change in their focus can affect deviance rates. For example, the recent decline in arrests for marijuana use is only partly due to fewer users; another factor is the turning of police attention from marijuana to harder drugs and from users to pushers (Wolff, 1991). Crimes defined as less serious routinely lose priority to more serious ones. The general point to be taken from these examples is that counting deviance is a social activity involving more than the individual deviants themselves. Reactors are a crucial part of the process. Therefore, caution must always be exercised when interpreting official statistics of crime and deviance.

The next issue is whether labellers are biased. Do reactions to the same deviance fall equally upon all people, especially on all groups of people? Most of us can think of examples of rule breakers who were caught and were excused for various reasons. Indeed, there are some fairly widely accepted criteria and rules for excusing deviance (Edgerton, 1985). To illustrate, children under the age of 12 cannot be tried in criminal court. In fact, children, along with the very old, are often excused from obligations that are applied to the rest of society. Drunkenness (though less frequently accepted today), transient physical or mental illness, and being temporarily under the influence of an overwhelming emotion may excuse people from being labelled deviant. Finally, Hallowe'en, funerals, and stag parties are settings that may allow behaviours not normally tolerated.

Despite some grumbling, this lack of uniformity in the application of labels is not generally perceived as a major problem. Sometimes it is even given a positive connotation and called *discretion*, giving officials the *choice* to react or not to react, for example when young offenders are given a second chance. On the other hand, when discretion gives rise to accusations of prejudice and discrimination on the basis of gender, race and ethnicity, or social class, then there is a big problem. For example, if police expect more delinquency in poorer areas, and look for it there, they will then find it there in what is partly a self-fulfilling prophecy. Had the police been equally observant in wealthier areas, they would have found higher rates of delinquency there as well (see Wordes and Bynum, 1995).

In the area of mental illness, some conflict theorists argue that all people do things definable as insane, but only some are labelled that way. Do you

Poverty may lead to mental illness. On the other hand, mental illness may lead to poverty via unemployment and a history of unskilled jobs.

ever talk to yourself, feel claustrophobic in elevators or crowds, or believe in fantasies because they make you happy? Any one of these could be signs of mental illness. Conflict theorists argue that a lack of power is often an important factor (although not the only one) in using the mental-illness label. Thus, part of the higher, official mental-illness rates found among single or lower-class individuals, compared with those who are married or middle class, may be due to their relative lack of resources and their greater vulnerability to being labelled (Scheff, 1984). Similar behaviours engaged in by the rich and famous may be simply passed off as "eccentric."

Similar arguments are made about the higher rates of mental illness among women. In this case, however, demonstrating bias is a bit more complicated. First, women are more open about their problems and may seek treatment more than men, thus inflating their rates of mental illness

(Rhodes and Goering, 1994). Just think who is more likely to ask directions when lost, your mother or your father, and you will see the logic of that statement. (See also Mirowsky and Ross [1995] for a discussion of whether women are more mentally ill, perhaps owing to the heavier burdens they bear, or more often labelled, another manifestation of male control, or both.) Second, the distinction between institutionalized and noninstitutionalized care is quite important in this debate. In out-patient treatment, there are more mentally-ill women than men, but men outnumber women in psychiatric hospitals, partly because men suffer more often from substance abuse, organic psychoses, and those personality disorders that require (often lengthy) hospitalization (Statistics Canada, 1996, *Health Reports, Mental Health Statistics, 1982-83 to 1993-94*). Thus, although women are more frequently perceived to suffer mental illness than men—approximately a 5:4 ratio (see Bland, Newman, and Orn, 1990)—in counts of serious mental illness, men exceed women (Mowbray, Herman, and Hazel, 1992), an argument against the general conflict position regarding bias. Finally, in a particularly interesting study, Rosenfield (1982) found that women who suffer substance abuse or personality disorder (illnesses more frequently found among men) and men who suffer depression or neuroses (more frequently found among women) are hospitalized more often than if they suffer forms of mental illness more "appropriate" to their gender. What all of these points suggest is that, going back to the feminist approach to deviance, the label of "mentally ill" is generally seen as more appropriate for women than for men. Some argue that, in a society characterized by women's subordination and institutionalized low self-esteem, women are more likely to internalize definitions of themselves as deviant and to look to others, particularly experts (psychiatrists, physicians) for help (Ehrenreich and English, 1979). Indeed, the widespread proliferation of self-help books, heavily directed toward women, provide advice on how women can "improve themselves" to be "more acceptable" and thus less deviant.

Critics of the conflict perspective argue that the bias in the system that reduces the official rates of deviance among the more advantaged, given the same behaviour, is smaller than first appears. Much of the deviance committed by the better-off that gets ignored is both minor and infrequent. Various studies support this conclusion and suggest that for serious crime or delinquency there is little bias. It is mainly for less serious infractions that unequal treatment inflates the rates of deviance among the disadvantaged. In fact, Henshel (1990: 179) made the point that this potential for bias is greatest in minor crimes, where the language of the law is deliberately vague (e.g., disturbing the peace, loitering, and being a common nuisance), or where enforcement is haphazard (such as possession of minor drugs and less serious traffic infractions). Thus, these crimes, rather than homicide, arson, and robbery, may be most vulnerable to biased handling. Indeed, in the area of crime, a general

Race and Ethnicity as Factors in Crime and Delinquency

Any search for relationships between racial or ethnic status and crime raises some thorny issues. Historically, Canadian crime statistics routinely included information on occupation, education, and religion, along with place of birth, a crude measure of ethnicity. Criminologists used this information to discuss group differences in crime, just as Durkheim did in his study of suicide. In fact, ethnic differences in crime and delinquency were expected, a natural product of the inequalities symbolized by the vertical ethnic mosaic that is called Canada. Sociologists wrote volumes on the culture conflict arising from the widespread immigration that took place earlier this century and thought it an important explanation of some crime (Sellin, 1938).

Today, however, there are many, and not only minority group members, who think that crime statistics based on race or ethnicity will be used to promote hatred and discrimination (Yi, 1991) and thus should neither be collected nor reported. Too often, they argue, people forget that most members of any racial or ethnic group are not criminal. Below are some of their arguments against collection.

1. Deviance, as pointed out earlier, requires a reaction as well as an action. Since victims, the police, and the courts may react more to criminals from some groups than to others, some of any racial or ethnic differences found in official crime rates may be due to these differential responses or bias, and not to actual crime differences.

2. Some of any differences found will be due to the crimes chosen for attention. For example, some crimes, especially white-collar crimes, often get no official reaction. Thus, if ethnic or racial variations are reported, then the specific crimes to which the generalization applies and does not apply should be mentioned.

3. Not only is measuring crime an issue, but rigorous definitions of race and ethnicity are also hard to achieve (see Roberts and Gabor, 1990). For example, a lack of agreement on the traits that distinguish the races and the effects of changing political boundaries, in the case of ethnicity, lead to difficulties in unambiguously classifying many individuals into distinct ethnic and racial groups. In addition, increasing intermarriage rates have meant that there are fewer and fewer people in Canada and elsewhere who can claim that all of their ancestors came from only one group.

4. Finally, even if the crime rates of only those individuals who can demonstrate only one racial or ethnic background were collected, which would leave out many Canadians, it would be important to examine the rates of these groups in their homelands, as immigrants to other lands besides Canada, and over time, to see if similar rates occurred. If they did not, then something besides ethnicity and race must be operating.

Taken together, these measurement issues should have warned you that great care should be used in examining variations in crime among racial and ethnic groups. If you decided that such data should not be collected, think now about the criminal justice system's practice of reporting crime statistics by gender and age. Is this practice defensible, or is it sexist and ageist? Should crime statistics even be reported by province or city?

conclusion is that the poor generally do commit the more serious (predatory) crimes, more often (see Hartnagel, 2000).

Similarly, in the area of mental illness, most research concludes that level of impairment is more important than power in treatment decisions (see Link and Cullen, 1990). As generally is the case for crime and delinquency, the less powerful may be more often labelled for minor forms of mental illness than the more powerful, but for serious psychiatric impairment such bias is less apparent.

In conclusion, when official data are used, be aware that differences in the secrecy and processing of deviance can affect the rates for some groups compared with others. Pay special attention when the less powerful are listed as having higher deviance rates. They may in fact be more frequently deviant, a result perhaps of their poorer living conditions and lack of legitimate opportunities, points to which we shall return. On the other hand, it may be that they are being singled out for special treatment. But also be critical of those champions of the disadvantaged who say that it is only official bias and attempts at social control that inflate the deviance rates of the poor (also see the box "Race and Ethnicity as Factors in Crime and Delinquency"). In effect, they are arguing that poverty and disadvantage have no effect on deviance. But examination of illness, suicide, and mortality rates, especially infant mortality rates, reveals that there are real differences among social groups that probably have little to do with biased audience reactions. In short, there are costs to being disadvantaged, including higher rates of some forms of deviance. Then the debate turns to what causes these real differences, the topic of the next section of this chapter.

Theories of Deviance

Introduction

Before presenting theories of deviance, a few general points are in order. First, the behaviours included within the general area of deviance are too diverse for any one theory to fully explain why people engage in them. It would be surprising if crime, mental illness, and drug abuse, along with the various other things called deviant, shared exactly the same set of causes. Even within the same area of deviance, different theories are required to explain, for example, embezzlement versus arson, schizophrenia versus depression, and dependence on tranquillizers versus alcoholism. Second, any one form of deviance may be best explained by a combination of factors taken from several theories, rather than by a single theory. For example, Ratner and McKie (1990) found that violent crime was best explained by ethnicity (it was especially high among Native peoples), but also by unemployment, especially that experienced by males over age 25. The first section will look briefly at several examples of biological and psychological theories, and then we shall move on to their sociological competitors.

Biological and psychological theories

Almost by definition, biological theories of deviance look to individuals. For example, Sheldon (1949) hypothesized that body type is related to crime. He argued that muscular individuals or **mesomorphs** are more likely to be assertive, dynamic, and aggressive, and that these personality traits are related to greater criminality. Thinner **ectomorphs** and fatter **endomorphs** are less criminal, the former depicted as complainers who withdraw from society, the latter luxury-loving extroverts. A more recent variant of this biological explanation examined the effects of levels of testosterone on deviance. Dabbs (1990) concluded that testosterone level is related to: violence and crime at a young age, trouble with parents and school, drug use, a greater number of sex partners, being absent without leave from the army, and being a fraternity "party animal." He also checked for the effects of social class and found that subjects from lower socioeconomic backgrounds have, on average, higher levels of testosterone and are more vulnerable to its effects than their better-off counterparts.

Turning to mental illness, researchers conclude that biology is more important in some forms of mental illness than in others. For example, schizophrenia is more genetic than social in origin, and biological factors are certainly important in the senile psychoses of the elderly. But other forms of mental illness, such as borderline personality disorder, are more likely caused by social factors such as physical abuse, quality of parental care, criminal parents, etc. (Byrne et al., 1990).

In most cases, however, *both* social and biological factors are seen as important. Beisner and Iacono (1990), for example, noted that a predisposition to schizophrenia is biological (and more common among males) but that environmental factors such as poverty and adverse working conditions play a role in bringing it on. And part of higher mental-illness rates among the elderly has to do with their loss of social status and their loneliness, not just biological aging.

By now you should have a taste for how biological theories look at individual factors in deviance. Several selected psychological theories of deviance may also be noted, even more briefly. They, too, focus on individuals. For example, criminal behaviour may be traced to individual personality, with the view that criminals are more impulsive and crave excitement more than do noncriminals (see Polakowski, 1994). Similarly, Freudians might see some mental illness as the result of an inability of the ego, as mediator, to handle conflicts between the id, the superego, and the external world.

This presentation of psychological theories is deliberately incomplete. It is intended merely to provide points of comparison for the sociological theories to come, which examine society's role in deviance.

Sociological criticisms of biological and psychological theories

Biological explanations of deviance (see Walsh and Gordon, 1995) are generally rejected by sociologists because they too often pay insufficient attention to the social factors that interact with their explanations. Thus, males with high levels of testosterone (biological variable) may be more rewarded and encouraged by others (social variable) for their aggression and therefore learn to be more criminal. Also, because of their extroversion, they may be watched more closely by society (social variable) and thus others are more aware of their deviance. This scrutiny will inflate their deviance rates. Mesomorphs, due to their body shape and size, may be more likely to be recruited to

delinquent gangs, while fat and skinny males who might secretly dream of belonging to a violent gang might be overlooked. More importantly, on their own grounds, biological theories have problems. For example, what about the many mesomorphs who become athletes or RCMP officers rather than criminals? Moreover, why don't individuals with the same genes (monozygotic twins) exhibit the same deviance? Although there is great overlap, there is not a 100 percent concordance in the area of mental illness (Cockerham, 1996). Even though adopted children are more like their biological fathers than their adoptive fathers (with whom they live) in criminality, suggesting a biological link, it cannot be the only factor as many do not follow the path of their criminal biological fathers. And what about their mothers, whose genes they share, who are less frequently studied?

Another serious deficiency concerns the sometimes wide fluctuations over time in the amounts of deviance. Most official data show, for example, that crime-especially violent crime (Silverman, 1992)—increased dramatically from 1962 to the 1990s and now is decreasing somewhat. Hartnagel (2000) points out that conviction rates for indictable crimes were especially high from 1910 to 1920, a time of immigration and mobility, and much lower in the 1950s compared with earlier and later decades. Delinquency was lower during the Depression, when fathers were home, and higher during World War II years (McCarthy and Hagan, 1987). To take another example, alcoholism, measured indirectly through liver cirrhosis rates, has generally increased throughout the century, at least until the mid-1970s (Newman and Bland, 1987). Since then, even though alcohol consumption has continued to rise, alcoholism appears to have decreased (see Eliany, 1991). Did biology change in the same way during these times? No, biological factors, whether they be genes, hormones, or body type, just cannot show the parallel fluctuations that would be expected if they were the major causes. So something more than biology is responsible.

Although psychological theories of deviance are generally more appealing to sociologists than biological ones, they are also criticized for the difficulty of measuring some of their concepts and for underestimating the influence of the social factors that precede psychological factors in deviance. Thus, there is a difference in focus. Psychologists hold social variables such as race, sex, age, and social class constant, and then look for differences in psychological variables, while sociologists focus directly on those social variables. Sociologists thus take a step further back in the causal chain; they want to know what social factors are related to inadequate egos or to extroversion and impulsiveness. They want to study the social conditions that would damage even the healthiest mind.

Before leaving this topic, it should be noted that interdisciplinary explanations of deviance are becoming more frequent, and the fight for scientific turf among the various disciplines is becoming more sophisticated. It is less frequently seen as an either/or situation as researchers instead look at the roles that social, psychological, and biological factors play and how they can be combined to give the fullest picture of deviance, a process we noted as occurring in the nature/nurture debate.

Introduction to sociological theories of deviance

Before examining the sociological theories of deviance and seeing how deviance varies across groups and with differing social conditions—a task that Durkheim's analysis of suicide inspires—a methodological note is in order. In several places, the data supporting the theory are taken from official rates of deviance, not rule-breaking rates. This is because official data are both more readily available and more comprehensive than other sources. Self-reported data might lead to different conclusions. It is important to keep this rule-breaker versus deviant distinction in mind when evaluating explanations of deviance, because the causes, correlates, and explanations can be quite different, depending upon whether the smaller number of deviant individuals or the larger number of rule breakers is studied. Thus, always pay attention to the type of data being presented before drawing conclusions. Second, the classification of the theoretical approaches presented is somewhat arbitrary. Different researchers make different distinctions, and some of the theories to be presented have aspects that would allow them to fit into more than one category in the scheme (Silverman, Teevan, and Sacco, 2000).

In the early 1920s, Shaw and McKay (1942) were among the first modern researchers to use a sociological approach to explain deviance. They called it *human ecology*, a study of how different areas or zones in cities exhibit different rates of various types of deviant behaviour. They found that official delinquency rates, along with crime, infant mortality, tuberculosis, mental illness, and truancy rates, were highest in the centre of cities and steadily decreased in concentric circles drawn further away from the centre, reaching their lowest point in the suburbs. This pattern occurred regardless of the individuals and racial or ethnic groups that lived in these zones; that is, as new people moved in and others moved out, they took on the rates of the area into which they moved. Thus, Shaw and McKay concluded that something to do with the area affected deviance rates, that social rather than individual explanations were needed, and specifically that the level of disorganization of the area was behind the differences. Signs of this *disorganization* include the amount of poverty and unemployment, the presence of condemned buildings, crowding, transiency, and a low rate of home ownership. Combined, these factors lead to low levels of cohesion and social control among whomever lives there.

Today the original ecological approach is criticized for paying insufficient attention to the reactions needed to create deviance (are the police more active in the core?), for the ethnocentrism implicit in the term disorganization (perhaps it is just a different type of organization), and for difficulties in deciding the causal direction, involving the issue of *social selection* versus *social causation*. Perhaps in some instances these areas attract deviants to them (selection) rather than produce them (causation).

We still see applications of an ecological approach today (although current researchers are more aware of its faults) in studies that reveal that crime rates are generally higher in urban than in rural areas (Sacco, Johnson, and Arnold, 1993). The excess is due mainly to property and vice crimes, which are more common in our cities, and not to crimes against the person, which are found everywhere. According to a recent U.S. study

(Dawson, Grant, Chou, and Pickering, 1995), alcoholism, too, is found more often in urban than in rural areas, partly as a result of availability. Further, there is generally more mental illness in urban settings than in rural areas (see Dekker, Peen, et al., 1997). Perhaps the more traditional life and greater community spirit combined with the slower pace and lesser crowding of rural areas work against crime, alcoholism, and mental illness, while the problems found more often in cities increase them. On the other hand, sometimes the data do not fully support, or even contradict, urbanization theories. Canada's territories are not urban, yet their deviance rates are generally higher than the rest of a highly urban Canada. This may reflect the special problems faced by the Inuit (we will discuss this in later chapters). Whatever the explanation, however, difficulties in relying on urbanization as an explanation of deviance are clearly revealed.

Along with urbanization, mobility is also important in deviance (Timms, 1998). Deviance rates tend to be higher where there is migration and a consequent decrease in the stability of neighbourhoods and social ties. Thus, the highest rates of crime in Canada are found in the territories, British Columbia, and Alberta, where migration is greatest, with lower rates in relatively stable provinces or those facing out-migration such as Newfoundland, New Brunswick, and Prince Edward Island (Statistics Canada, 1996, *Canadian Crime Statistics, 1996*). This general east-to-west pattern (see Kennedy, Silverman, and Forde, 1991) was also discovered by researchers looking at alcoholism and use of alcohol (Eliany, 1991) and suicide (Hasselback et al., 1991). All of these are findings Durkheim would have predicted.

In the next section, we shall look at several of the most prominent sociological successors to this basic ecological explanation. Please keep in mind that each theory to be presented may be able to supply some insight into some aspect of some of the many forms of deviance; so the question is not which theory to choose, but how much each can add to the whole picture.

The theories are divided into two types, those that emphasize social structure (a macro focus) and those that emphasize social process (a micro focus). The former range from functionalist theories, which see deviance as a temporary, correctable issue, to conflict and radical theories, which see deviance as built into the very structure of society and thus less easily corrected. The specific focus of these structural explanations, moreover, can be on all of society or on certain parts, such as families or the school system. Social-process explanations, in contrast, are generally symbolic interactionist, concentrating on how structure is perceived and then translated by individuals into behaviour. They examine the learning and meanings of behaviour and its unfolding in stages over time. What these structural and process theories have in common is a perception that society is important in creating deviance.

Social-structural explanations

Anomie theory

In Canadian society the achievement of wealth and material success is a widely shared goal. The education system, the mass media, parents, and peers all may encourage this pursuit, but these objects of material success are in limited supply and there are not enough legitimate means available for everyone to own an expensive car, nice clothes, and a large house. The discrepancy between the goals a society instills and the legitimate means it provides to achieve those goals can lead to a state of normlessness, a large-scale breakdown of rules, called **anomie**. According to Merton's (1957) functionalist model, the greater the discrepancy, the greater the anomie, and the greater the amount of deviance that can be expected.

Most readers of this book are using an acceptable means, higher education, in their attempt to achieve material success, a legitimate goal. Merton called such behaviour *conformity*. Conformists accept the goals of society and possess the means to achieve them. Individuals without such access to legitimate means have four options, each considered deviant in some way. First, they can lower their goals to the level of their means, and engage in **ritualism**. Ritualists are the honest, hard-working people, often of the lower-middle and working classes, who live in modest, rented homes, own older cars, make some of their own clothes, and take few holidays. Their deviance is

The discrepancy between the goals a society instils and the acceptable means the society provides to achieve those goals leads to anomie.

that they have given up on the fancy success goals, not that they have broken society's rules.

The second option for those who lack legitimate means is to keep the goals but to engage in what Merton called **innovation**. Innovators range from criminals to plagiarists and cheaters on exams—individuals who use deviant means to achieve non-deviant ends. Rather than becoming bankers and lawyers, innovators become thieves and con artists, in a parallel race to material well-being.

Retreatism, a third category in Merton's anomie model, involves rejecting both the means and the goals of society and, instead, withdrawing from society. Drug addicts, for example, are considered retreatists and are often scorned by conformists, innovators, and ritualists alike. (Yes, even criminals do not like drug users, finding them too unreliable for the cooperation needed for criminal activity.) On the other hand, retreatists also include members

of religious groups who substitute equally valued goals, e.g., salvation or contemplation, for the more common goal of worldly success. Such retreatists generally are more positively viewed than others, but if they become too public or controversial in their activities, as in the case of some religious sects (see Chapter 11, Religion), their behaviour may then be seen as **rebellion**, the final type of deviance in the model. Rebels are in essence active retreatists, individuals who are vocal in their rejection of society's means and goals and who advocate a new social system.

Merton's four types of deviance vary, but they share a common cause according to him: not flaws in the individual, but flaws in the structure of society.

Social deprivation and deviance

In support of Merton's ideas, most research shows that official crime rates are higher among the disadvantaged, those with less access to legitimate means such as higher education and full employment (see Hartnagel, 2000). For example, Schissel (1992) found unemployment related to homicide. A lack of means and crime often then reinforce one another in a vicious cycle. For example, for the disadvantaged, a record of delinquency leads to difficulties in finding adult employment, which in turn leads to more crime (Hagan, 1992) and even fewer legitimate opportunities, etc.

Looking specifically at violent crime, we see that the disadvantaged tend not only to be more frequently criminal, but to be more serious and violent in their crimes as well (Ratner and McKie, 1990). As before, there may be some bias behind the actions of some agents in the criminal justice system that inflates the rates, but the assaults and murders you read of in the paper are found more often among the underprivileged. Although Native peoples are only a small percentage of the population, they are greatly overrepresented among criminal suspects and victims—a cost of the poverty, crowding, substance abuse, and discrimination they experience.

If hospitalization (official) records are used, social class is related to mental illness, as it is to crime. The data generally suggest that for serious forms of mental illness, the higher the social class, the lower the incidence of mental illness (Lundberg,

1991). Divorce, single parenthood, low education, and multiple disadvantages are also associated with a greater likelihood of mental illness. Less serious forms of mental illness, on the other hand, tend to be relatively more prevalent in the advantaged classes.

The interpretation of this association between mental illness and social class, however, is not straightforward. There is dispute over whether poverty leads to serious mental illness (social causation), or mental illness leads to poverty, via unemployment and unskilled job histories (social selection), with Ortega and Corzine (1990) favouring the latter. We mentioned these ideas in the discussion of the ecological approach. There is some truth in each explanation, but right now the evidence is leaning towards causation. The overriding effects of poverty and abuse that lead to stress and mental illness cannot be dismissed (Dohrenwend et al., 1992). Consistent with this finding is the fact that mental illness rates, as measured by hospitalization discharges, are generally higher in the poorer east than the west (Statistics Canada, 1992, *Health Reports, Mental Health Statistics, 1989-90*).

For just one more example of the relationship between deprivation and deviance, although education and income are positively related to the use of alcohol, with the poor and less educated more often abstaining (Eliany, 1991), unemployment is generally related to higher levels of consumption, especially for young males (Temple et al., 1991), assuming they can afford the alcohol. Also, when the poor do drink, they often drink in greater quantities (Eliany, 1991).

Merton's focus on the discrepancy between widely accepted goals and the supply of adequate legitimate means for their achievement set the stage for still other theories. For example, Cohen's (1955) theory of gang delinquency argues that many adolescents, especially lower-class boys, do not have the values and skills (means) necessary to succeed on the criteria (goals) demanded by the middle-class school system. Sensing failure and feeling disapproval from teachers and peers alike, the boys band together to seek a group solution to their problem. Rejecting the schools' middle-class standards, which they find so hard to achieve, they establish a **contraculture**, a way of life exactly opposite to the middle-class ideal, but one in which

they can succeed. If middle-class values include politeness, promptness, care of property, and reluctance to fight, these boys will be rude, late, destructive, and belligerent. They will measure their self-worth in how malicious, how negative, how useless—in short, how delinquent—they can be. Thus, in a way they are similar to Merton's rebels. Cohen called this inversion of middle-class values **reaction formation**. For a more recent discussion of adolescent subcultures and delinquency, see Tanner (1992), who argued that such subcultures are less likely to occur in Canada than in the U.S., because of opposition here to rigid educational streaming, and the presence of varied ethnic groups, which retards the creation of a unified working-class culture.

Merton's model can also be extended to other applications. He wrote about material success, but his idea of anomie can be applied to all scarce or restricted commodities, from sexual satisfaction, to beauty, to honour and prestige. Often the means to achieve these socially encouraged goals are not sufficiently available. Even when they are, structured inequality or inaccessibility to opportunity prevents many from using them. So it is not just a lack of means to achieve material success that encourages innovation. Let us look further at the variables of age and gender in this broadened context of anomie.

Virtually all studies reveal that younger people commit more crimes than older people. Children aged 12 to 17, for example, are 10 percent of the population but 23 percent of those charged with crimes (Statistics Canada, 1998, *Canadian Crime Statistics, 1996*). And the gap between young and old, especially in property and drug offences, may be increasing. How is this relevant to anomie? Simply stated, youth more frequently lack means than do older people. They are marginal and segregated in adolescence, awaiting adult status, which is increasingly postponed since they are the frequent victims of unemployment. Many become dependent, even hopeless, and as a consequence turn to drugs and steal what they need. Eliany (1991) found young males the most frequent users of marijuana. On top of this, as a group, youth are more rebellious than their seniors and always vulnerable to being labelled deviant, sometimes even "asking for" such a reaction after having found it difficult to fit in.

But when the relative powerlessness of youth coincides with a need in young males to assert what they perceive as adult masculinity, an explosive situation too often arises. One report suggested that youths are becoming more violent in their crimes, especially with respect to common assault (Gabor, 1999; Statistics Canada 1998, *Canadian Crime Statistics, 1996*, Catalogue 85-205E). Alder (1992) claimed that young men, especially those unemployed and without hope, use fighting both among themselves and against women to demonstrate their masculinity, to show that they are in control (and thus in possession of means).

Nor is this theme new. Lack of means to achieve adult status was used to explain male delinquency by Bloch and Niederhoffer (1958), who argued that boys will try to act strong, cool, independent, and smart, all traits they think adult males possess. Denied or lacking the means to those ends, however, boys' versions of those behaviours often end up as delinquent. Strength is translated into fighting, coolness into alcohol and drug use and dangerous driving, independence into disrespect for authority, and smartness into being a con artist.

Problems with anomie theory

Merton's anomie theory generated much criticism. Some objected to his unproven assumption that everyone shares common success goals. Another criticism is that anomie theory was developed in the U.S. Lipset's (1990) comparison of Canada and the U.S. described in Chapter 3, Culture, would suggest that Canadians' greater respect for authority should result in less anomie here. Others focused on whether anomie is the effect of absolute poverty or of the contrasts of inequality. As already mentioned, the poorer east has lower crime rates than the wealthier west. Long-standing and widespread poverty, as in the Maritimes, may lead the poor to ritualism, the lowering of goals, and not to crime. The inequality of poverty amidst relative affluence, however, coupled with transiency, as in Alberta and British Columbia, may encourage innovation and crime as a response to the contrast (Kennedy, Silverman, and Forde, 1991). Finally, Ratner and McKie (1990) did not find unemployment a predictor of property crime as anomie theory would predict, and Schissel (1992) found only

inflation, but not unemployment, related to robbery and theft.

A larger criticism concerns Merton's apparent acceptance of official crime rates, data that may reflect lower-class crime better than middle- and upper-class crime. These critics argue that anomie theory holds up less well when self-report studies are conducted. This type of data reveals that many of the rich, although law-and-order advocates, are innovators rather than conformists, such as the officials who accept bribes or kickbacks for work contracts or the corporate executives who fix prices or falsely advertise. Their deviance cannot be explained by a lack of means in any usual sense of the word. Only by arguing that these people lack legitimate means to allow them to achieve *extraordinary* goals would anomie theory work (see Snider, 1992). In their personal lives, more expensive cars and clothes; larger, more luxurious homes; and longer, more exotic holidays could be the lofty achievements that motivate the innovation of the rich. A similar explanation could be used for doctors who overbill (see the box "Medifraud").

Other, conflict-oriented theorists have noted Merton's failure to examine the forces that cause the inadequacy of means. Anomie theory views crime in functionalist terms, as a dysfunction that greater opportunities can correct. But to many conflict critics, the inherent greed of the capitalist system is the cause of inadequate means. To these critics, only an extensive reconstruction of society, one that could remove inequality, will suffice. Welfare and unemployment insurance—state interventions to create means—are just insufficient (Schissel, 1992).

Merton's theory is also sexist, although it would not have appeared so in 1938 when it was first published. Where do women fit in anomie theory? More often denied means than men, they should be highly criminal. Yet perhaps with the exception of Native women, whose crime rate is especially high (La Prairie, 1990), women generally have low crime rates. Indeed, in all societies young males are more criminal by far than any other group. For example, Ratner and McKie (1990) found that young males aged 16 to 17, followed by males aged 18 to 24, were the groups most implicated in property crime in Ontario. Merton never really dealt with this apparent contradiction. Part of the answer,

Medifraud

Physician fraud, like other white-collar crimes—those illegal activities committed by people in the course of their routine business or professional lives—is infrequently studied. Media attention, public fear, demands for police action, and even criminological research are much more likely to be focused on robbers and burglars. But is this emphasis misplaced? Certainly, if the monetary losses are compared, medifraud is probably one of today's more expensive crimes. Wilson, Lincoln, and Chappell (1986) estimated that Canadians were losing between $300 and $400 million annually to physician dishonesty. The figures would be higher today. Worse, such fraud is hard to detect, with the result that these criminals are infrequently prosecuted and punished.

The forms of medifraud are varied but easy to describe. Physicians can charge for extended (counselling) visits when they actually give regular service, provide extra and unnecessary treatments, make medically unnecessary referrals in return for commissions, or make claims for treatments not given. What is a bit harder to understand is the motivation. After all, physicians' incomes are not at poverty levels. Wilson, Lincoln, and Chappell (1986) argued that some physicians engage in medifraud simply because they want more money, just like other thieves. The rationalizations are different, however. Because their tax bills are high, some of these doctors feel that they deserve the extra compensation. Others, tired of bureaucratic rules and what they regard as government interference in their profession, engage in such dishonesty to gain what they feel is a fair wage. The high probability that they will get away with the fraud simply reinforces such perceptions.

Before you ask your doctor about such practices, remember that most doctors do not abuse the system, and that those who do are not the only white-collar professionals who criminally abuse their positions. University and college teachers, lawyers, accountants, and others all contain within their ranks some white-collar criminals.

Finally, generalize a bit and ask yourself whether there is a parallel situation for white-collar violent crime. Is there a similar inattention to the deaths caused by corporations that pollute the environment and provide unsafe working conditions, while the media, public, police, and criminologists focus on gun-toting or knife-wielding killers?

See Snider's 1993 volume, *Bad Business: Corporate Crime in Canada* for more on this topic.

Source: Adapted in part from Paul Wilson, Robyn Lincoln, and Duncan Chappell, 1986. "Physician fraud and abuse in Canada: a preliminary examination." Canadian Journal of Criminology, 28 (pp. 129–46).

---

however, lies in the next criticism. (We shall return to women and crime in other sections as well.)

Cloward and Ohlin (1960) questioned Merton's apparent assumption that deviant means are available to all. They argued, instead, that individuals need access to illegitimate means if they are to become innovators, for example, role models, or some other means to learn the required skills, and then access to opportunities to innovate (1960: 168). Not everyone has the ability, or the chance, to become an embezzler, prostitute, or con artist, they pointed out. If denied that access, some would-be innovators are forced into ritualism or retreatism. In another context, Cloward and Ohlin's argument concerning the need for opportunities to innovate explains the decline in alcoholism experienced during World War II, when supplies declined because the army needed alcohol for the war effort.

The most important application of this idea of access to illegitimate means, however, may be to explain some of the relationship between gender and crime. Part of the great underrepresentation of women among criminals may be due to women being given fewer opportunities (Reitsma-Street, 1999). They may not be accepted by men criminals; they do not spend as much time in places where crimes occur, such as areas around bars; and they are less often in the positions of responsibility needed before one can engage in white-collar crime. Such a view might explain why, in eighteenth-century Britain, women were 45 percent of the felons (serious criminals), but only 15 percent by the early twentieth century (Feeley and Little, 1991). The growth of industrialism that occurred during the period and the arrival of the Victorian age coincided to restrict women more to the home and thus away from criminal opportunities. We shall return to this subject in Chapter 10, Families.

As you will read several times in this book, however, today women increasingly work outside the home for pay. On the one hand, the increase in the use of such legitimate means should decrease their crime. On the other hand, being in the work environment should increase their opportunities for learning crime. What is the truth? The reality is that women are appearing more frequently in criminal statistics. Whether, as a result of feminism and its effects, women will eventually equal men in their criminality (the convergence hypothesis) is doubtful (see Hartnagel, 2000). It has not happened in the area of alcoholism; female alcoholism rates are still less than those of males (Lo, 1995). Moreover, it is generally not the women who support the women's movement who become criminals. The fact is that when women become criminals, they are different from men criminals: their crime tends to be less violent, with more shoplifting and petty thefts, and fewer assaults, robberies, break and enters, and murders (see Alder, 1992). Silverman (1992) calculated a 9:1 ratio for men to women among those charged with violent crimes. Girls' delinquency seems to be less serious as well, more theft-oriented but not violent (Reitsma-Street, 1998), although there is some sign of convergence with that of boys (Statistics Canada, 1999, *Juristat Service Bulletin*, Vol. 19.2).

Social-control theory

Social-control theory is a structural theory, too, but one quite distinct from the anomie position. The biggest difference is that it sees all people as potential deviants, and then argues that social bonds constrain most individuals into conformity. Rather than asking why people deviate, it asks why *don't* people deviate. For example, Gelles (1983) argued that men abuse women *because they can*. Because patriarchy tends to protect abusive men and make it difficult for women to leave abusive marriages, Gelles argued, society implicitly gives permission for men to be abusers. From a social-control perspective, then, *all* men would abuse women. Its

focus is narrower than anomie theory as well, looking not so much on society in general as on families, schools, and other groups that serve as socialization agents, provide the bonds that discourage deviance, and include role models for conformist behaviour.

Hirschi (1969) popularized this position and maintained that meaningful attachment to family and friends pulls people away from deviance. This occurs as they consider the opinions of those significant others before acting. Besides attachment, other ties include *involvement*, or investment of time and energy in conventional activities, and *beliefs* in pro-social values. Like attachment, they lead to a *commitment* to and respect for the value of conformity, and thus less deviance. Correspondingly, such things as alienation from family, empty time and leisure, and pro-deviant sentiments weaken social control and permit deviance (see Brownfield and Thompson, 1991; Gottfredson and Hirschi, 1990). Here we shall examine the effect of a few specific ties only—family, school, social support, and the changes associated with old age.

Let us begin with families, a potentially important resource for both children and spouses. Regarding children, a *meta-analysis*, one that examines all previous research on a topic to reach a general conclusion, found that broken homes are related to delinquency, for both boys and girls. They are more of a factor in minor than in major forms of delinquency and, parallelling this, they are more strongly related to self-report than official data (Wells and Rankin, 1991; LeBlanc et al., 1991).

For adults, the major familial social tie is marriage. Becoming unmarried has effects on drinking (Temple et al., 1991) as does single status generally, especially among males. At the same time, marriage and job stability inhibit criminal behaviour (Sampson and Laub, 1990). Being married also reduces the risk of suicide, as does religious affiliation, another social tie (Hasselback et al., 1991). In addition, marriage reduces chances for mental illness, but its effects vary by type of illness (Williams, Takeuchi, and Adair, 1992) and perhaps gender. Married women have higher rates of mental illness than single women (see Gove, 1990).

Feminist theorists argue that it is the very institution of traditional marriage, with its tendency to reproduce patriarchy, with a male household head and submissive female, which shelters abusers and encourages female economic and emotional dependency, all producing conditions in which depression is a predictable outcome (Ehrenreich and English, 1979).

Turning to the school as a source of social ties, Hartnagel and Tanner (1986) found that school experience is even more important than social class in predicting delinquency. A weak attachment to high school, found more frequently among boys in lower-ability groups, is related to delinquency regardless of social class. LeBlanc, Vallieres, and McDuff (1993) also found the school experience, including weak performance by the student and discipline by school authorities, to be an important factor in both delinquency and adult crime. Working part-time while in school may also be a factor. Tanner and Krahn (1991) argued that low attachment to school leads to the part-time work, which in turn leads to drinking and also to association with deviant peers who have sought a similar escape from school activities in their part-time work.

With respect to age (see Chapter 9, Aging), older people generally have fewer social ties and thus a greater potential for deviance, according to social-control theory. Their crime rates, however, are very low. This may partly reflect a lack of means, but the

A weak attachment to high school is related to delinquency regardless of social class.

other social ties mentioned by Hirschi are also a factor. For example, conventional activities and prosocial values, both generally associated with increasing age, inhibit crime. The data for suicide are more in tune with control theory, however, as rates do increase with age (Hasselback et al., 1991). The relationship between alcoholism and age is more difficult to interpret. Data on alcohol use (not alcoholism) reveal that as age increases alcohol use decreases (Eliany, 1991). Still, alcoholism is a problem in the older population, with older people, especially retired men, more likely to drink alone (Eliany, 1991).

With respect to mental illness, rates peak at ages 35 to 44 (Bland, Newman, and Orn, 1990) and then jump again in old age (Statistics Canada, 1992, *Health Reports, Mental Health Statistics, 1989-90*), although patterns vary with specific forms of illness. For example, schizophrenia begins earlier in life and depression generally occurs later. Old age may be an especially vulnerable time as senile psychoses increase in prevalence. Part of this is biology, but the loss of status, jobs, friends, and vitality, along with increased poverty, also take their toll.

Finally, we should add that social support in general may be an important variable in reducing deviance. This theme parallels Durkheim's discussion of suicide discussed in Chapter 1. For example, the availability of confidants and friends can buffer the effects of stress for individuals and can help them avoid mental illness (Noh, Zheng, and Avison, 1994). A similar tendency occurs in the case of alcoholism: loneliness is an important cause, one that hinders attempts to give up drinking (Akerlind and Hornquist, 1992). The higher proportion of completed suicides (versus attempts) among males compared with females can be attributed to the lack of social support as well.

There are several main criticisms of the social-control position. Some critics reject its assumption that all people would be deviant if they could. They do not believe that a release from social ties is all that stands between most people and robbing banks, or sexually assaulting or killing others. Rather than focusing on the absence of restraining factors as a cause of crime, these critics still want to look at push factors, at differences in individual motivation to commit crimes. They argue, for example, that anomie theory's concept of strain and the frustration of being encouraged to achieve what turn out to be unachievable goals must have some effect on individual decisions to commit crimes. A related criticism is that social-control arguments may be better suited to minor forms of deviance, while other explanations may be needed for serious forms.

In one feminist critique of the social-control argument, Chesney-Lind (1989) discovered that 50 percent of victims of child sexual abuse leave home before the age of 18, and that many female runaways are fleeing sexual victimization at home. Once on the streets, they are forced into crime to survive. Other research (Chesney-Lind and Rodriguez, 1983) indicated that almost all adult women in prison had been sexually victimized in childhood, routinely followed by running away from home, prostitution, drug use, and the attendant reduced opportunities for higher education, career training, and a "stake in conformity," which Hirschi and others argued is so important to maintaining a law-abiding existence. Thus the feminist critique of the social-control approach emphasizes that "social control" is assumed always to be in the best interests of the child, and "lack" of social control leads to delinquency. As both Gelles and Chesney-Lind indicated, however, it is the very lack of control over the controllers that allows abuse to continue unchecked in families, leading to lasting and often irrevocable damage to the children affected.

From another point of view, however, conflict theorists want to know what weakens the social bonds. Perhaps poverty and other societal flaws weaken the bonds that might otherwise constrain deviance, with any resulting deviance further straining the social bonds. Critics also ask how control theory can account for the crimes and other deviance of the powerful, those who are closely attached to others, are deeply involved in conventional activities, and appear to be committed to conformity. Are these people tied perhaps to their corporations and not to society at large? For answers to these questions, we turn to structural theories that are more conflict oriented.

Conflict-structural explanations

In their explanation of deviance, radical conflict theorists see much bias in the criminal justice system, focus almost exclusively on capitalism, and often proclaim the necessity for revolution. Less radical conflict theorists are aware of things like capitalist pollution and price-fixing, but also include crimes not specific to capitalists in their analyses, like the daily physical assaults to which the oppressed are so frequently vulnerable. These theorists also place somewhat less blame on the police and courts, and accept the possibility of reform. The two views do agree, however, that power is a crucial factor in any explanation of deviance. For radicals, it is economic power; for the less radical, other sources of power are important too. Let us start with the less radical position.

Hagan's (1988) approach to deviance uses Marx's measure of class—control over one's labour—in explaining the relationship between social class and deviance, whether it be delinquency, computer crime, homicide, or even fear of crime. This approach also includes noneconomic variables, such as gender of child and family patriarchy. The crucial assumptions in his power-control model are that mothers have a greater role in socializing children than do fathers, and daughters are more controlled than sons. The result, claimed Hagan, is higher deviance rates among boys. This gender difference is least pronounced in homes where both mother and father have jobs where they are in control. In these generally wealthier and more egalitarian families, mothers have more power and they treat their daughters and sons more similarly. The daughters, in turn, are more like the sons in their deviance.

Gender differences in deviance are greatest in patriarchal households, which are common when the father is controlled at work and the wife is either not employed outside the home or, if so, is also controlled. Note how the structure at work affects family structure. In patriarchal families, mothers control their daughters more than their sons, leading the girls to be less inclined to take risks and less frequently deviant. Risk-taking is the key intervening variable (see Tanner and Krahn, 1991). Data for less serious forms of delinquency support this interpretation and may help to explain why wealthy adolescents engage in some forms of delinquency more than those less well off. They are less coerced, take more risks, and see themselves as above the rules and with freedom to deviate (Hagan and Kay, 1990). On the other hand, for more serious forms of delinquency and crime, it may be

that patriarchy leads to male aggression and violent sons (Simpson, 1991), not among the rich, but among the under-classes.

Turning to more radical theorists, we see that they focus more on problems created by capitalism, like unemployment and reduction in buying power for those with jobs, increasingly found in the developed world. Capitalists, they argue, use the law to remove the under-classes from a glutted labour market and to render them tame (Schissel, 1992). The purpose of the law, according to Spitzer (1975), is to transform "social dynamite," like unemployed youth, into what he calls "social junk," a category in which he included the elderly and mentally ill, also potentially costly but less of a threat to the capitalist order. From the nineteenth-century's arrests for drunkenness (Brown and Warner, 1992) to current drug laws, some see the legal system as a tool to control the poor. Rather than legalize drugs, capitalists use the government to keep them illegal in order to reduce the potential of the "dangerous" classes for large-scale organized civil disturbance (Christie, 1993).

The other distinguishing mark of the radical position is its demand for a total restructuring of society, one that would eradicate inequality and replace current short-term and inadequate solutions to the problem of deviance by making more legitimate means available. Critical theorists think that researchers should be part of this transformation, to put their theories into action in what they call *praxis*, a term introduced in Chapter 2, Research Methods.

Before leaving this brief discussion of structural theories, a note is in order. Intellectual opponents as they are, functionalists and radicals often assess each other's position too harshly. Radicals see functionalists as right-wingers, law-and-order advocates, even bigots who blame the true victims of inequality and oppression (the criminals) and seek only minor adjustments to what are major structural faults. Functionalists see radicals as hopeless idealists who blame the rich for everything; as philosophers more than sociologists, holding theories that the data contradict; even as hypocrites whose revolutionary zeal is cushioned by the frequent affluence of their university lives.

The truth is less extreme. The two groups do emphasize different aspects of deviance, but

Wife Abuse

Smith (1990a) examined some of the social factors associated with wife abuse in Toronto. His results parallel a number of other recent studies on the topic and some of what you have already read in this chapter about deviance. Briefly, he found that low family income, husband unemployment, and low educational and occupational attainment of either spouse are related to physical abuse. Younger women are also more vulnerable. On the other hand, ethnicity and religious affiliation are not significantly related to such abuse.

But there is much dispute surrounding such studies. A primary issue is measurement: many abused women just will not admit, due to shame, fear, or other reasons, their experiences. Thus such abuse always will be undercounted. A second problem concerns the types of abuse to be counted. Restricting the concept to physical abuse, as is often done, makes it easier to study but ignores its other forms such as mental

abuse, verbal attacks, economic blackmail, and tyranny, and thus underestimates the magnitude of abuse. Broader definitions and better reporting might have revealed that wife abuse occurs everywhere, under all circumstances, and in all groups, and that the search for correlates is misleading. Indeed most husbands have engaged in some form of it at some time (see DeKeseredy, 1992; Lupri, Grandin, and Brinkerhoff, 1994). Abuse is not limited to a few rotten apples; it may instead be built into the very fabric of society, in patriarchy or in capitalism, for example.

Smith (1990a) and others are aware of such criticisms. Indeed, in another article (1990b) he pointed out that an ideology of patriarchy is related to abuse and that lower socioeconomically situated men are more likely to accept that ideology. Men's need to be in control, perhaps especially prominent among those denied control at work, often leads to assault, he argued.

Finally comes the issue of how to eradicate wife abuse.

Widespread restructuring of society will not come easily or quickly, and time is a luxury women suffering today and tonight cannot afford. While capitalism and patriarchy continue to exist, more specific programs, like arresting abusers, may offer some relief. Why do police daily ignore some domestic violence but virtually no bank robbery (see Dobasch and Dobasch, 1992)?

But the police cannot protect everyone, and many women do not want their spouses jailed. Some abused women bring charges and later drop them, not because they are weak, but to use as leverage to improve their situation (Mendel-Meadow and Diamond, 1991). They use the threat of the police only as a bargaining tool, to pressure for better treatment—an alternative they prefer to the imprisonment and loss of income offered by the criminal justice system. No strategy pleases everyone in this widespread and difficult problem.

---

generally each is aware of its complexity. For example, radical theorists admit that Marx wrote little about crime and, as mentioned earlier, they know that not all laws favour capitalists. Some are modifying their views in what is called *left realism* (see Young and Matthews, 1992). Functionalists, for their part, are aware of the costs of inequality and of the relativity of law. They also know about the extent of white-collar crime and are fully aware that sanctions for the crimes more frequently committed by the affluent are weak—sentences for auto theft, for example, are often more severe than those for tax evasion—and that the regulatory agencies that

police the powerful are overworked, underfinanced, and vulnerable to funding cutbacks (see Snider, 1992). What is harder to reconcile are the means each group would use to remedy the situation. One looks more to major restructuring, the other more to individual rehabilitation. Whereas functionalists might increase prison sentences to deter crime, and more conflict-oriented criminologists push for decent wages and day care (Snider, 1991a), radicals still see the need for a revolution.

The major contribution of structural theories, in general, is to point out that factors beyond individuals are important in explaining deviance.

These theorists focus attention on society, on its expectations and the means it provides to individuals to achieve those expectations, and on social ties as constraints on deviance. They have greater difficulty in answering why, given the same social structure, some individuals become innovators while others become ritualists, or why some with few social ties conform while others deviate. Additional answers to these questions come from the social-process theories, which follow. In general, they argue that the choices depend upon individual definitions of the situation, a symbolic interactionist concept.

Social processes and deviance

Differential association

The basic symbolic interactionist position explains deviance by examining how it is experienced and interpreted by individual deviants. Each act of deviance is seen as unique, and a subjective interpretation by the person who performs it will explain even its seemingly irrational aspects (Katz, 1988). One of the earliest symbolic interactionist theories of crime was advanced by Sutherland (1939), who argued that individuals learn crime the same way they learn conformity—in an interactional setting with others. He maintained that if behaviour—normal or deviant—is rewarded, it will be repeated. You read about this in Chapter 4, Socialization. The key to the learning of conformity as opposed to deviance is the groups with which individuals interact. If individuals interact more with others who socialize them to value deviance, either directly by rewarding it or indirectly by providing role models and perhaps vicarious reinforcement, they may develop an excess of pro-deviance definitions of the world and become deviant (see Heimer and Matsueda, 1994). If, on the other hand, they interact more with others who socialize them to value conformity, they should learn pro-social definitions of the world and become conformist. Thus the name of his theory is **differential association**: learning through association with groups having differing values, such that, in the end, pro-deviant definitions of the situation exceed conformist definitions. Clinard and Yeager (1980) found differential association theory

applicable even to white-collar crime, with executives indoctrinated into a corporate culture that includes definitions and rationalizations favourable to the commission of corporate crime.

Expanding on Sutherland's ideas, Sykes and Matza (1957) argued that most delinquents feel guilty about violating the law and can engage in such illegal behaviour only after rationalizing their guilt through **techniques of neutralization**. These techniques, which are learned and shared among delinquents, permit them to define their behaviour as somehow acceptable and in turn allow them to stay basically committed to conventional society. (Such a view is quite at odds with Cohen's view of delinquents.) Sykes and Matza outlined five such techniques:

1. Denial of injury; for example, "No one gets hurt by shoplifting."

2. Denial of the victim; for example, "The victims deserved what they got."

3. Denial of personal responsibility; for example, "I was drunk when it happened."

4. Condemning the condemners; for example, "Everyone is doing it"; or, "Other people do worse things and get away with it."

5. Appeal to higher loyalties; for example, "I couldn't let my friends down; I had to help them."

Doctors who overbill, it is argued, use a variant of the second technique, claiming that government bureaucracy and artificially low fees force them into this fraud (Wilson, Lincoln, and Chappell, 1986), while some male hustlers may use a variant of the third, arguing that when they engage in homosexual behaviour it is just for the money, not for sexual pleasure. The point is that individuals *drift* in and out of deviant activities, back and forth between conformity and deviance, in contrast to the views of functionalist and conflict theorists alike, who tend to see determinism and a deviant-conformist dichotomy (Matza, 1990).

Evidence against this drift position includes Sampson and Laub's (1990) findings that childhood delinquency is linked to adult crime, alcohol abuse, school failure, unemployment, divorce, economic dependency, and other deviance. No drift is apparent in that overall deviant pattern, and instead social deprivation may be involved. Perhaps drift theory is less applicable to the socially disadvantaged. It is middle-class juvenile delinquency that is more often transient and disappears in adult conformity. Bias may be a factor here. If caught (Hagan, 1992), middle-class delinquents are given a second chance, thus allowing them to return to respectable society. Poorer delinquents live under more adverse conditions and are less frequently given those second chances. As a consequence, they cannot drift out as easily.

A more serious criticism of the whole differential association perspective is that it is circular. What causes the culture that is passed on in intimate groups that then encourages or allows crime and deviance? Answers to this question may require a return to structural theories such as anomie. Also, why do some learn to define deviance as acceptable, while others who live in similar circumstances do not? There are no definitive answers to this issue, but the next symbolic interactionist position attempts to provide at least a partial social-process answer to this question.

Labelling

Another quite popular symbolic interactionist perspective on deviance, developed after Sutherland's efforts, is called **labelling theory** (see Schur, 1971, 1984). We mentioned it briefly earlier. It poses a challenge to the idea of deterrence (using punishment to stop deviance) and maintains that society creates deviance through its reactions to people who break its rules. For example, if adolescents have taken some beer from neighbourhood garages, the victims can react in a number of different ways. First, they can just forget about it. Most research shows that many crime victims choose not to report their crimes (including some serious ones), especially if they define them as trivial or as something about which the police can do nothing. On the other hand, they can treat the theft as a crime and call the police. If they do so, they may have begun what labelling theorists call the **deviance amplifying process** (Wilkins, 1964). It refers to the belief that reacting to deviants, whether this be called treating, rehabilitating, or punishing, may actually increase rather than stop the deviance

Labelling theory maintains that society creates deviance through its reactions to people who break its rules.

and may even lead to more serious forms of it. The reactions backfire because of the way in which they are subjectively experienced and are dysfunctional rather than functional. Exactly how this happens is outlined in a series of propositions, most of which can be traced back to the work of Lemert.

Lemert (1951) examined stuttering behaviour (cf. Petrunik and Shearing, 1988). He said that many children pause in their speech and have irregular or deviant (as defined by adults) speech patterns. He believed that if adults ignore these speech problems, many children will outgrow them. On the other hand, calling their attention to the problem may make the children self-conscious. They may become anxious about their speech, may pause, and may speak even more irregularly, perhaps even stutter. This may lead to more reactions from others, and then more stuttering, in a vicious circle. The children may eventually define themselves as stutterers, and the stuttering become permanent.

These same ideas were then applied to other forms of deviance: delinquency, mental illness, and even physical incapacity. The general model is one of a *self-fulfilling prophecy*:

1. Deviance occurs. It is widespread and caused by many diverse factors.

2. The audience reacts to some of this deviance, thus beginning to transform the actors involved from rule breakers into deviants.

3. Additional deviance occurs and again it has many sources—anomie, differential association, etc.

4. This deviance is followed by a stronger reaction from others, who begin to take steps to segregate the deviants from conformist others. On their part, the deviants seek out others, similarly or previously labelled, who in turn welcome the new recruits as allies and provide them with additional opportunities for deviance.

5. Still more deviance may occur, and more reactions follow. Those labelled complain about being singled out and direct hostility at those who label them, even stereotyping them in return, as when police are called "pigs."

6. These acts generally bring on even stronger audience reactions. In a process called *role engulfment*, "deviant" becomes the master status of those so labelled. Their conformity is ignored or misinterpreted and their deviance magnified out of proportion. Thus, for example, when many people see homosexuals, that is all they see. Their occupation, education, charity, ability at sports—all other aspects—take a second place to the homosexuality. In another context, those never labelled as mentally ill can be nervous and tense some days, even lose their tempers, while recovered mental patients would be "suffering a relapse" were they to behave in a like manner. Basically, the audiences expect deviant behaviour, look for it, and are not disappointed. Even past behaviour may be redefined as deviant in a process called *retrospective interpretation*.

One result of these activities by reactors is a deviant-versus-conformist dichotomy. People are frequently perceived as one or the other, when the reality is they all fall somewhere along a continuum, in at least two senses. First, most deviants conform most of the time: most criminals dress the same way, eat the same foods, and watch the same television shows that conformists do. Second, and more importantly, most people are neither pure deviants nor pure saints. In the area of theft, for example, between professional thieves and absolute law-abiders are those who lie to customs officials, neglect to return money when too much change is given, do not report all income on their tax forms, etc. Between homosexuals and heterosexuals are not only bisexuals but also those who have engaged, as adults, at least once, although perhaps under special circumstances, in homosexual behaviour. In the area of mental illness, too, there is no mentally ill/mentally well dichotomy; the distribution of individuals is a continuum from the most to the least mentally healthy.

7. The process continues as the labellers further isolate the deviants, who in turn spend more and more time with others similarly labelled. The deviants, starting perhaps with the weakest and most vulnerable among them, begin to define themselves as deviant. The stronger are more successful in this battle, and hold out longer before defining themselves as deviant.

8. Finally, deviant behaviour arises from those deviant self-concepts. The acts of this last stage constitute **secondary deviance**—deviance that arises not from the original various causes of primary deviance, but out of the deviant self-concepts that result from the isolation, segregation, alienation, and even self-hatred of those labelled deviant. Isolated acts of deviance, to which perhaps the individuals initially are not fully committed, can thus become regular and stabilized, changed into *deviant careers* because of the reactions of others.

Lemert's original ideas on the potential negative effects of audience reactions to deviance were oversimplified by many, some even arguing that reactions cause deviance and that society should therefore never punish or label anyone as deviant. But these are distortions of labelling theory. Its originators wanted to caution official reactors to deviance, to warn them that those who commit deviant acts that are minor and common may turn to rarer, more serious acts if they are cut off from conventional society. For example, if children are segregated for being disruptive at school, a common and minor form of deviance, they may become hostile and angry; they may become truants, incurring greater penalties; eventually they may turn to theft and other less common but major forms of deviance. In the area of mental illness, Scheff (1984) argued that some bouts of mental illness are transitory, but they can become longer-lasting if others react to them. For example, people labelled mentally ill may be rewarded for playing sick roles, as when psychiatrists encourage them to accept their illness. On the other hand, their attempts at non-sick roles, to return to previous occupational and family roles for example, may be rebuffed. Confused, ashamed, and anxious, they may eventually accept the role of insanity as the only alternative open to them, and the initially transient mental illness may become chronic (see Link, 1991).

In short, labelling theorists seek to investigate the effects of audience reactions. Being symbolic interactionists, these theorists argue that the deviants' definitions of self and of the situation are crucial, and that treatment or punishment, subjectively experienced, may move the individuals in an unintended direction. Moreover, they argue, a deviant does not emerge full-blown but must be developed over time in a process of exchange with the larger society.

In research of this proposition, the effect of imprisonment, perhaps the most extreme form of reaction, has been examined to see whether it deters further crime or whether it increases secondary deviance and criminal careers. Handleby et al. (1990) found in a sample of 180 boys released from Ontario training schools that 80 percent were soon incarcerated again, provincially and/or federally, some as many as five times. These data could be used to support the labelling theorists' position. Additional support comes from Letkemann's (1973) classic study of federal prisons, which found that some inmates learn criminal technical skills in informal relationships with more skilled prisoners,

and make the contacts and alliances that will serve to advance their criminal careers after release. If, in addition, employers are reluctant to hire ex-criminals, the resulting unemployment may in turn encourage further criminality. Finally, Kaplan and Fukurai (1992) studied drug use among adolescents and found that negative sanctions lead to self-rejection, then to reduced motivation to conform, to greater interaction with deviant peers, to reevaluation of deviant identities, and finally to an increased predisposition to use drugs. Taken together, these and other studies lend some support to labelling theory's concept of secondary deviance (see also LeBlanc, McDuff, et al., 1991; LeBlanc et al., 1993).

Critics of the proposition that labelling increases deviance argue, first, that it is too broad. Types of reactions, types of deviants, and types of deviance should be examined to see specifically in which cases the proposition holds true and in which cases deterrence takes place. Perhaps informal reactions from friendly peers can deter rather than lead to secondary deviance. Perhaps those individuals with the most ties to society and thus more to lose can be deterred by treatment and punishment, rather than pushed to secondary deviance by them. For example, first-time, younger offenders, especially those who value the opinions of their labellers, may be deterred; similarly, Berk et al. (1992) found arrest worked better on spouse abusers who were employed and legally married than on those who were unemployed and not married. Finally, perhaps punishment can deter certain types of deviance; it does deter much shoplifting, and imprisonment appears to deter many robbers and thieves (Schissel, 1992) from repeating their crimes.

On the other hand, labelling is less relevant to alcoholism (Combes-Orme et al., 1988); gender and other issues are more important. Together these arguments point to the need to qualify the theory, to make it less general. As before, it should not be a choice between either deterrence or labelling; both may be applicable in different circumstances to different forms of deviance.

A final major criticism of labelling questions the existence of secondary deviance. Cannot the causes of primary deviance continue to cause what only appears to be secondary deviance? Critics thus question the transiency of the primary deviance, often arguing that it has deep-seated origins and would have continued with or without labelling. Most of the previous structural theories would support this argument.

Putting it all together

In general, the types of deviance discussed in this chapter are more frequently found among males, the single, the very young or very old, the poor, in cities, and in those provinces with high levels of population mobility. All of these factors share the common condition Durkheim uncovered in his study of suicide: a relative lack of integration. You can see that this social variable is as relevant today as it was over one hundred years ago.

In concluding this section on theories of deviance, it must be repeated that the specific causes of deviance are complex, including both individual factors and social factors. To focus on individuals and ignore the role of society gives an incomplete and inaccurate picture. Remember that sociological insights must be added to those of other disciplines that seek to explain the same behaviour. They were never meant to stand alone. Thus, given social conditions such as anomie, poverty, illegal opportunities, and contact with groups that value deviance, the fact that not all individuals who experience these conditions experiment with

deviance may call for an examination of individual factors and perhaps social ties. The fact that, after experimenting, only some individuals continue their deviance may also suggest an examination of individual factors. Social variables, like reinforcement, social ties, and labelling, may also be relevant here, however (see Tittle, 1995).

Given this qualification, in the general sociological model shown in Figure 5.3, most of the arrows leading to deviance still come from the social factors highlighted in our previous discussions of the effects of social structure and process on deviance. But, as pointed out in Chapter 1, What Is Sociology?, that is what sociology is all about: it seeks social explanations of social rates of behaviour.

Three final cautions are in order. First, the factors discussed in this chapter are sometimes only correlated with deviance and not necessarily causes. Sociologists cannot conduct the experiments necessary to establish causation absolutely. This issue was raised in Chapter 2, Research Methods. Second, there is often more variation within groups than between groups, meaning that the range and variation of behaviour are generally greater inside a group than between groups. For example, the difference between the number of crimes committed by the most and least criminal men is greater than the gap in average crime rates between men and women. This brings us to a third warning: the

FIGURE 5.3   Model of Factors Encouraging Deviant Behaviour

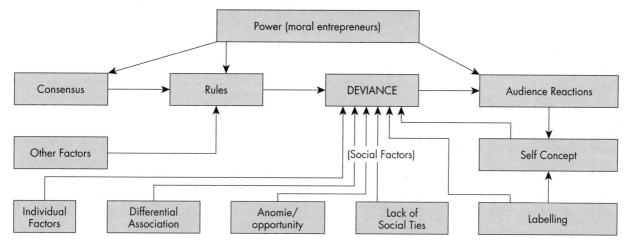

Victims and Crime

Criminologists have long been aware that crime victimization is not random, that some individuals are more likely to be victimized than others, and that a few people even suffer repeated victimization (Sacco and Johnson, 1990). This knowledge has led some researchers to focus on the interaction between criminal and victim, and to examine victims and their role in crime. An implicit assumption in their work is that everyone is a potential criminal and what needs to be explained are the factors that turn that potential into reality.

Early studies found that many victims know their criminals, and the term *victim precipitation* (victims being part of the cause of crime) was even used. Although victims were not seen as a general cause of crime—anomie and other sociological theories were better explanations for that—victims in some circumstances were seen as having a role in their specific victimization. Think about those who leave keys in a running car while they run into a store, leave their houses unlocked, get drunk and then pick a fight, or walk in certain neighbourhoods after dark. Although this conclusion provided hope to some citizens that they could protect themselves from crime, by locking their doors, for example, it was also quickly criticized for coming too close to blaming the victims. Think of date rape—few today accept the view that whatever happened before the assault, from drinking to displays of affection, caused the lack of consent to be ignored.

A more recent focus of such research is the *routine activities* approach, which says that the coming together in time and space of suitable victims, motivated criminals, and the absence of effective social control (a lack of police, for example) are needed for crimes to occur (Kennedy and Baron, 1993). Again, focus is not exclusively on criminals and includes victims. Thus, researchers might examine the effects of the growing number of unattended houses (related perhaps to dual-wage-earner families or increased affluence allowing more holidays) on burglaries, or the number of bars in which young people congregate (combining alcohol and the gathering of crime-prone groups) on assaults. They would look to "hot spots," those specific addresses and intersections that have more than their share of criminal incidents (see Gabor, 1990).

While the addition of victims to the equation perhaps adds to an understanding of crime, many, especially conflict theorists, are critical of this type of research. They point out that it would omit much of corporate crime, in which victimization is so diffuse that a focus on specific victims is rare. Worse, it takes attention away from the larger and more general causes of crime: inequality and patriarchy, perhaps. Rather than preventing crime by attacking these overriding issues, looking at the role of the victim can lead only to a temporary solution; for when some people learn how to reduce their chances of victimization, the chances of others are increased. Crime is merely displaced onto different, more available victims (Gabor, 1990).

application of any of the generalizations made in the chapter to any specific individuals would be inappropriate. Being a young male in trouble at school may not have caused your brother's theft spree. Being a married female may not have caused your aunt's depression. Sociology deals with groups, not individuals. These cautions should be added to the previously discussed issues concerning the (often wide) discrepancy between official and self-report deviance rates.

Summary

Deviant behaviour is a designation given by a society to the things it considers somehow not normal and which it sees as worthy of some form of social control. These designations are culturally relative; almost every behaviour has been defined as deviant in some place or at some time, and as nondeviant at other times or in other places. Thus, deviance is a status conferred by society, not a quality intrinsic to the acts themselves.

Sociologists have long debated the sources of these definitions of deviance. Some emphasize a shared, society-wide consensus as the main source. Others focus more on the various social groups that compete to make such decisions. Still others feel that economics is the major force behind definitions of deviance. All three viewpoints and some compromise positions have merit, depending on the type of deviance being considered.

Counting deviance is also an issue. Deviance requires a reaction as well as an action. This rule breaker-versus-deviant controversy goes beyond the obvious idea that not everyone who is deviant gets caught, and looks at bias in the application of the label "deviant."

Explanations of deviance include biological, psychological, and sociological theories. Sociological explanations examine social structure, including the idea that society does not provide enough means for everyone to achieve the lofty goals it instills, thus opening the door to deviance. Social-process theories view deviance as learned in group interactions with others. Either way, social factors "cause" deviance.

Most sociologists prefer their societal explanations of deviance to those that emphasize the individual deviants, including most of those derived from biology and psychology. In questioning the structure of society, the making of social rules, the application of the rules, and specific social conditions including the effects of punishment, they seek social explanations. Still, deviance is to be understood as a complex interaction between the individual and society. Theories that claim to explain deviance must incorporate this fundamental principle.

The future? Deviance defining is a political process, and changes to the moral boundaries of any society come slowly, usually involving an interaction between public consciousness and formal social control in the form of laws. For example, prior to the 1980s it was legally impossible for a man to be charged with raping his wife. Her consent was assumed. But legislation in 1984 made rape in a marriage illegal. This dramatic change allowed for a further gradual shift in consciousness to take place at the individual and collective level toward less tolerance of violence against women. Men's groups, the White Ribbon campaign, and other grass-roots organizations attest to some of these changes. At the same time, we are a long way away from the eradication of this social problem. Drinking and driving were social norms in the 1970s, until the lobbying of groups such as MADD (Mothers Against Drunk Drivers) served as a wake-up call for police and legislators to tighten the penalties against drinking and driving. The current generation of young adults reading this text has been brought up to believe that drinking and driving is wrong.

The current politics around decriminalization of marijuana and prostitution point to the possibility that a loosening of some of the rigid definitions of deviance may also be on the horizon. "Victimless" crimes (there is no victim who might call the police) may follow the pattern that gambling did—from deviance to being defined as an alternative lifestyle. So less tolerance of victim-involved crimes, including toughening of the Young Offenders Act, and more tolerance of victimless crimes may be the future.

Finally, the economics of deviance includes government expenditures. With balanced budgets and concern for the national debt, we can probably see the continuation of efforts to keep people out of prisons and mental hospitals. Expect the non-violent to be increasingly "treated" outside of expensive, publicly-run institutions.

QUESTIONS FOR REVIEW AND CRITICAL THINKING

1.   If the poor had power to write the laws, what changes would you expect to see in the legal system of Canada? What might be the changes if only women made the laws?

2.   Think of examples of how success can turn some of yesterday's terrorists and villains into today's revolutionary heroes, and even into elected leaders? How did this happen? What theories could be used to explain such a turnaround?

3.   Apply labelling theory to growing old in our society, using the attainment of age 65 and retirement as the primary deviance.

4.   Consider one or two examples of your own behaviour that others consider deviant. Which theory or theories of deviance best explain them? Which theory or theories are least applicable?

KEY TERMS

acceptable deviance, p. 101

anomie theory, p. 115

collective conscience, p. 101

contraculture (counterculture), p. 117

crime funnel, p. 108

critical school (also radical school), p. 103

deviance, p. 99

deviance amplifying process, p. 126

deviant subculture, p. 100

differential association, p. 125

ectomorphs, endomorphs, mesomorphs, p. 112

innovation, ritualism, retreatism, rebellion, p. 116

labelling theory, p. 126

moral entrepreneurs, p. 103

pluralism, p. 103

reaction formation, p. 117

rule breakers, p. 108

secondary deviance, p. 127

stigma of excellence, p. 99

techniques of neutralization, p. 125

SUGGESTED READINGS

Gomme, Ian
1998   *The Shadow Line: Deviance and Crime in Canada.* Toronto: Harcourt Brace.
A comprehensive text with sections on both theory and specific examples such as murder, sexual assault, prostitution, drug use, organized crime, corporate crime, and mental illness.

Linden, Rick (ed.)
2000   *Criminology: A Canadian Perspective.* (4th ed.) Toronto: Holt, Rinehart and Winston.
A multi-authored, comprehensive venture, this excellent volume includes discussions of law, criminal statistics, theories of crime, and patterns of criminal behaviour.

MacLean, Brian (ed.)
1996   *Crime and Society: Readings in Critical Criminology.* Don Mills, ON: Addison-Wesley.
The readings look at things like white-collar crime, dating violence, and gangs, using a critical perspective.

Sacco, Vincent and Les Kennedy
1998   *The Criminal Event.* Scarborough, ON: Nelson.
Deals with the criminal event (the victim, perpetrator, and police setting), theories, and responses to crime.

Silverman, Robert, James Teevan, and Vincent Sacco (eds.)
2000   *Crime in Canadian Society.* (7th ed.) Toronto: Harcourt Brace.
Collected here are some of the best examples of Canadian research on crime. Included as well are a section on the sociology of law, a discussion of criminal statistics, and summaries of crime theories.

WEB SITES

http://www.sscf.ucsb.edu/soc/honors/deviance
Socioweb
At this site, you will find links to many sites that explore topics related to various aspects of criminality and deviance.

http://www.copnet.org
The Copnet Homepage
The Copnet site provides links to information on crime and law-enforcement agencies in Canada and around the world.

Social Differentiation

The previous chapters looked at culture and its acquisition, or lack of acquisition, by society's members. Research strategies to investigate these and other social phenomena were also examined. In this next section of the book, we focus on social differentiation. The sources of inequality and the fact that various groups are unequal in their power and privileges are the central concerns of Chapter 6, Social Inequality. The learning of male or female roles is a major focus of Chapter 7, Gender Relations. Various feminist perspectives are offered as the chapter discusses the differences between gender and sex, examines cultural definitions of "masculine" and "feminine," and describes the costs of being a female or male in contemporary Canada. Sexuality, poverty, and deviance are examined, in turn, as they relate to gender. Another major topic in this area, especially for Canadians, is the study of the various racial and ethnic groups in society. This topic is examined in Chapter 8, Race and Ethnic Relations. A topic of increasing importance in the twenty-first century will be Aging, the title of Chapter 9.

The analysis of social differentiation is central to all of sociology. First, as a dependent variable (recall Chapter 2, Research Methods), differentiation arises in part from, and then reinforces, various subcultures that are passed on to different groups and individuals in the socialization process. Individuals learn different roles, values, norms, and aspirations by virtue of their being born male or female, into different families, going to different schools, living in different geographical areas, and becoming members of different groups. When this differentiation becomes the basis of a ranking system and of inequality among the groups, it is relevant to the study of social stratification.

Second, social differentiation clearly can act also as an independent variable, with important consequences for the lives of individuals in society. Membership in a gender group, in a minority or majority subculture, and the occupation of different social ranks can affect aspects of family life, for example one's age at marriage and chance of divorce. It can affect religious practices, participation in social movements, and the size of one's family. These topics will receive greater attention in the next two sections of the book. For now, remember that social differentiation is a key factor explaining much of human behaviour. Keep this in mind as you read the rest of the book.

6

Social Inequality

Edward G. Grabb

Introduction

Modern societies are complex entities, filled with all kinds of people working at various jobs, living in different circumstances, and engaging in a wide range of activities and behaviours. Social scientists usually refer to this great diversity and complexity in social life as **social differentiation**. While societies vary in the degree to which social differentiation occurs, it seems that, in the course of human history, social differentiation has increased.

Logically, social differentiation involves only a distinction of duties and responsibilities in a social structure. An example would be the distinction between the various jobs performed in a factory or office. In virtually all but the simplest structures, however, this *division of labour* gives rise to a difference in the ranking and evaluation of the individual tasks and those who perform them. This process by which individuals, or categories of individuals, are ranked on the basis of socially differentiated characteristics gives rise to relatively

enduring structures of **social inequality** among individuals and groups.

In this chapter, we examine basic concepts and definitions, and then consider classical theories of social inequality and some recent developments in the field. Subsequently, we look at the eight most important factors or patterns of social differentiation that give rise to the unequal distribution of privilege and prestige in Canadian society.

Concepts and Definitions

Power

Lenski (1966) asserted that the study of social inequality is concerned mainly with who gets what and why. In this view, social inequality is a *distributive process*, in which some people receive more of the valued things in life, especially wealth and prestige, than do others. In addition, social inequality is concerned with examining the *relations between* those groups who receive different amounts of wealth and prestige. Here, we argue that **power**—the ability to command resources and thereby control social situations—is the basic concept to consider when attempting to explain both the distribution of these valued things and the relations between unequal groups in society. Hence, power is the essential determinant of social inequality.

Most sociologists are interested in studying structured or **institutionalized power**. Power is structured or institutionalized when it becomes a regular and recurring part of everyday existence, usually because it is established in formal laws or in accepted conventions and customs (Lenski, 1966; Grabb, 1997). We can identify three major forms of structured power in society: *economic power*, which stems mainly from control of material resources like property or wealth; *political power*, which arises largely from control over human resources or the activities of other people; and *ideological power*, which comes from control over the ideas, beliefs, knowledge, or information that guides social action (Giddens, 1981; Grabb, 1997, 1999a).

Status and stratum

How is power established or institutionalized in society? One approach to this question is to examine how power derives from the rights of individuals or groups occupying a certain position, or **status**, in the various spheres of social life. Social inequality represents institutionalized power differences in a set of these statuses. In earlier European societies, for example, the status of king had greater power than the status of duke, which in turn had greater power than the status of serf.

Sometimes those performing different functions and occupying different statuses are, nevertheless, of similar rank in terms of their command over resources. For example, carpenter, plumber, electrician, and auto mechanic are distinct occupational statuses, yet they are often considered of about equal rank in the system of inequality. This cluster of occupational statuses, which we might label "skilled labourers," is an example of a **stratum**, or status category. Those researchers who view social inequality as a series of ranked groupings of people, somewhat like geological strata or the layers of a wedding cake, are especially likely to use the term, stratification, to denote the system of social inequality.

Obviously, every individual can and does hold many statuses simultaneously. Consider a person who is female, 30 years old, married, a high-school graduate, and a real-estate agent. These traits are, respectively, that individual's sex status, age status, marital status, educational status, and occupational status. The combination of all such statuses is a person's **status set**.

Status hierarchies and power dimensions

Those statuses that translate into significant power differences in society are the most crucial for the study of social inequality. We can isolate at least eight **status hierarchies** that seem most important in Canadian society: the three socioeconomic hierarchies of wealth (including income and property), occupation, and education; race or ethnicity; region or rural/urban location; gender; age; and political status. These hierarchies represent eight power rankings that define most of the structure of inequality in Canada. As we shall see in Chapter 14, Social Movements, some of these rankings may also provide the basis for group cleavage or integration in society and, hence, for collective action.

Social inequality in Canada can thus be seen as a multiple hierarchy phenomenon (Hurst, 1996; Curtis et al., 1999). **Status consistency** grows when individuals have consistently similar status levels within all or most of these hierarchies. Some individuals rank relatively high on all or most power rankings. An example might be a white, male, Ontario lawyer who earns over $100 000 per year, has a university education, and serves as a deputy minister in the federal government. A high degree of status consistency in a society tends to be indicative of a "closed" inequality system, one in which certain groups dominate and benefit most from the society.

The opposite of status consistency is **status inconsistency**, which occurs when an individual's ranking on one status hierarchy has little or no relationship to rankings on other hierarchies. An example might be a wealthy doctor living in a large Ontario city whose parents were poor immigrants when they came to Canada. A large degree of status inconsistency in a society may indicate a more "open" stratification structure in which traditionally disadvantaged groups, such as racial minorities or women, are able to achieve high status in other hierarchies, for example in the educational or occupational hierarchies.

Ascribed and achieved status

The difference between open and closed systems of inequality relates to another pair of concepts: ascribed versus achieved status. An **ascribed status** is a feature assigned to an individual by circumstance rather than by accomplishment. These features tend to be characteristics an individual acquires at birth and cannot change. Race, ethnic origin, sex, and age are examples of ascribed statuses. **Achieved status** refers primarily to

Race, ethnic origin, sex, and age are examples of ascribed statuses.

performance characteristics, traits attained by individual action. Perhaps the best examples in a society like ours are education and occupation. A society can be characterized as open if achieved statuses are more important than ascribed statuses in determining a person's rank in the overall system of inequality.

Some earlier social thinkers argued that the modern age is one in which achievement criteria have indeed become of increasing importance (Parsons, 1951; McClelland, 1961). "What you know" not "who you know," "what you do" not "what your background is," are said to be the key factors. While there may be some evidence for this argument, we shall see that achieved statuses and ascribed statuses tend to go hand in hand. In other words, while achieved statuses play a more important part in social inequality than was the case in centuries past, the opportunity to achieve, particularly in the education and occupation hierarchies, is strongly influenced by ascribed traits such as race, sex, or inherited wealth. Hence, ascribed statuses have considerable influence, even in supposedly achievement-oriented societies such as Canada. A similar position is stated in Chapter 7, Gender Relations.

Social mobility

The question of an open system of inequality is also relevant to the concept of *social mobility*. If a society is open, there should be considerable opportunity for individuals to change their positions over time on the important status hierarchies. Consider occupational mobility, for example. This movement can involve changes in the occupation of the same individual during his or her life, or **intragenerational mobility**. Or it may entail differences between the occupational status of child and parent, that is, **intergenerational mobility**. While we usually discuss **vertical mobility**, movement up or down a status hierarchy, as most indicative of an open system, we can also examine **horizontal mobility**, movement between positions within the same rank or status category. An example would be a person who leaves a job as a government economist to teach economics in a university. Both jobs fall into approximately the same stratum in the occupational status hierarchy.

Class and social class

The final major concept to consider is class. This is probably the most frequently used term in the field of social inequality. However, because of the many different meanings attached to the concept, it is difficult to offer a single definition acceptable to everyone. In this chapter, we use the class concept in a way more or less consistent with its use by the two principal classical theorists of inequality, Marx and Weber. For clarity, we can distinguish between the terms *class* and *social class*. Class refers only to one's position in the general economic hierarchy. As discussed later in the chapter, this corresponds to Weber's view of class as position in the economic "marketplace." It also parallels approximately Marx's concept of a "class in itself." In all cases, **class** refers to a category of individuals with a similar degree of economic power, as indicated by any of the following: property ownership, educational qualifications, labour power, or occupation (see Giddens, 1973).

For a **social class** to exist, however, more than just similar economic position or market capacity is required. The individuals involved must also have a common sense of identity, an awareness of their shared characteristics and interests, and a tendency to act together as a real group. As we shall see, this definition corresponds closely to Weber's view and approximates what Marx called a "class for itself." Whereas simple economic classes are often identifiable in societies, genuine social classes rarely exist. Marx expected that the class of wage labourers in the capitalist system eventually would become a social class in the complete sense: a class conscious, politically mobilized, revolutionary proletariat that would act as a group to produce fundamental change in the social structure. Our findings in Canada and other modern societies, however, suggest that this particular social class, this proletariat, has yet to take shape. Instead, the closest approximation to a real social class in modern times may be at the top of the system, among an upper set of controlling élites with the group consciousness and regular interaction necessary for a real group to exist (Porter, 1965; Clement, 1975; Carroll, 1986; Francis, 1986).

Now that we have considered the key concepts and definitions, we can examine more closely the theories that sociologists have offered to explain social inequality. We begin with the classical views of Marx and Weber. Then we compare these theories with a quite different school of thought, structural functionalism. Finally, we look at some recent attempts to combine the most important ideas from these earlier approaches into new explanations.

Major Theories of Social Inequality

Marx: Class, conflict, and the power of property

Historical roots

Marx's theory of classes and class conflict is the key starting point for understanding structured inequality in modern societies. Both supporters and opponents alike have devoted considerable effort to a critical evaluation of his ideas.

Marx was born in Germany in 1818 and died in England in 1883. His life spanned a period of great social change and political and economic turmoil in Europe. In the first half of his life, Marx witnessed and supported unsuccessful revolts in Germany and France, events which he saw as attempts by the less privileged to achieve social justice and a more equitable share of the wealth in those societies. The latter part of Marx's life was spent in England, where industrial capitalism had developed most fully. The so-called "industrial revolution" taking place in Britain was transforming the social structure in a way that both fascinated and saddened Marx. Tremendous surplus wealth was generated by the efficient capitalist economic system, yet this wealth was largely given over to the owners of business while the great majority of working people lived in poverty. Dickens's novels, such as *Hard Times*, are perhaps the best-known illustrations of this period of British history.

It was out of this social and historical context that Marx's ideas emerged (and also the science of sociology itself, as mentioned in Chapter 1). The great gap between rich and poor in that period, and the fact that capitalism could produce such extraordinary wealth yet leave so many people impoverished, were, for Marx, contradictions that required explanation. Marx tried to arrive at an explanation by analyzing societies from previous ages: ancient Greece, ancient Rome, and medieval Europe, in particular. He concluded that each major societal form is characterized by a clear split between "haves" and "have-nots": master and slave; feudal lord and serf; capitalist and worker. Moreover, each of these forms of social organization is marked by struggle, either open conflict or underlying antagonism, between the two main groups.

The means of production and class structure

For Marx, what really underlies the division of societies into two opposing groups, apart from obvious differences in wealth and prestige, is the power that comes from the ownership or non-ownership of property. In particular, Marx focused on private ownership of productive property, or what he called the "means of production." Under capitalism, productive property refers to natural resources necessary to produce the essentials of life (e.g., food, material for clothing, housing, tools) and to the factories and machinery that transform raw materials into finished goods.

Marx argued that, historically, the dominant group in any society was the one that owned the means of production. It was precisely because some people could claim possession of productive property that inequality among social groups and the formation of classes occurred. Private property meant that owners could determine the distribution of all wealth. Thus, under the capitalist system in Marx's time, the propertyless majority, who owned only their own labour power, had no choice but to rely on those who owned property to employ them as wage workers, often with only sufficient income to keep themselves and their families alive.

Marx believed that a basic contradiction in this system would become more and more apparent to the people as capitalism developed and expanded.

Marx argued that the propertyless majority, who owned only their labour power, had no choice but to rely on those who owned property to employ them as wage workers.

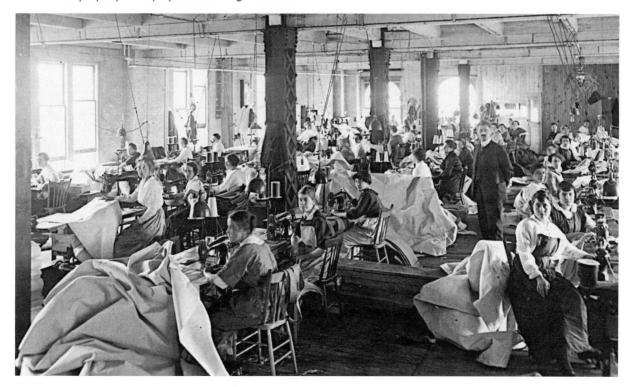

The contradiction, in Marx's view, was that the mass of workers, the majority of the population, gained little benefit from the great wealth they themselves produced. In other words, those who generated the riches of the society through their labour received only a small portion as a living wage, with the remainder going to the capitalist owning-class.

Marx claimed that under feudalism, the economic system that operated prior to capitalism, a similar contradiction had existed. The ruling class of feudal lords, who contributed little to the creation of wealth in their system but reaped most of its benefits, was opposed by the then new class of capitalists, who were a rising, dynamic force seeking social change and a new economic system. Likewise, Marx expected that the working class, or **proletariat**, would become the rising new force under capitalism, one that would oppose the now obstructive and superfluous class of capitalists, the **bourgeoisie**. Just as the bourgeoisie had triumphed over and transformed feudalism, so too would the proletariat realize its potential, overthrow the bourgeoisie, and transform capitalism into socialism.

Revolt of the working class

The change from capitalism to socialism was, for Marx, the culmination of this historical process of class struggle. For socialism to triumph, however, the working class would have to become more than just a **class in itself**, a category of people sharing the same economic position as non-owners of productive property. In addition, an awareness of common position and a willingness to mobilize as a force for change would be essential if the proletariat were to become a genuine **class for itself**, a group that would transform society.

To achieve the mobilization of the working class, several obstacles would have to be overcome. For example, apart from their economic power, the owners of property, in Marx's view, had great influence in various ideological structures: religious institutions, the communication media (see Chapter 12, Media), the educational systems, and so forth. We shall return to this argument in subsequent chapters. The owning class could use each of these structures to manipulate or indoctrinate the workers and to justify its privileged position. Also, the owning class had effective control of the political structure, or state, and so could use legal, military, and police power to maintain its position if necessary.

Despite these obstacles, Marx believed that a successful revolution by the proletariat was possible, and that the circumstances necessary for this change would eventually be realized. While Marx offered no precise predictions as to how the revolution would come about, he did expect a number of processes in the development of capitalism to spur the working class to action (Giddens, 1973). To begin with, capitalism encourages the rise of urban centres, since large numbers of propertyless rural inhabitants migrate to the cities in search of employment (see Chapter 15, Demography and Urbanization). This growing concentration of urban labourers is a key initial step towards working-class awareness. A second important process in capitalism is the increasing expansion of production into large-scale factories employing many workers. This process also means a concentration of workers in close proximity to one another and a further basis for awareness of their common class position.

In addition, workers are made more aware of their common plight and their separation from the owning class by the workings of the capitalist economy. In Marx's view, capitalism is based on a rational and efficient, but relentless and self-interested, pursuit of profits by the owning class. The quest for increasing profits frequently has unfortunate consequences for the society as a whole. For example, in their desire for greater gain, owners often produce more goods than they can sell. This practice means a loss of money for the capitalist, whose most obvious recourse is to lay off workers to save money. But laying off workers means less money for the workers to purchase the capitalist's products. Hence, the demand for these goods falls, and the capitalist loses even more money. In this downward-spiral fashion, economic crises tend to occur in the capitalist system: overproduction, high unemployment, and slow economic growth. After each crisis there is a period in which the economy stabilizes, but always at the expense of the lower strata.

Several additional developments occur in the stabilization period to widen the gulf between the working and owning classes. First, the smaller capitalists, or *petite bourgeoisie*, who are the most vulnerable in bad economic times, either sell out their businesses or fail, and are taken over by larger capitalists. This leads to a growing concentration of ownership within a shrinking group of large-scale capitalists. This concentration, coupled with the gradual disappearance of the middle class of small owners, makes it more and more clear that workers and big capital are the only two classes of consequence in the system. Second, it is increasingly evident to the workers that they are the losers in economic crises, while most of the large-scale bourgeoisie prosper. As capitalism matures, *absolute* living standards for everyone, even the workers, are likely to rise because of the tremendous surplus wealth that is amassed. However, in Marx's view, the *relative* difference in economic well-being between owner and worker will continue to widen. This widening gap and the realization by workers that they are the first to suffer in bad times stimulate class polarization still further.

One final factor that Marx believed would promote working-class consciousness and the polarization of the bourgeoisie and proletariat was the rise of the joint-stock company. In the earlier stages of capitalism, owners do play an active role in the production process by managing operations and making administrative decisions. Under advanced capitalism, however, businesses are increasingly owned only on paper, with individuals buying shares in companies. Marx believed that, in such a system, it would become even more obvious to the workers that mere ownership is essentially superfluous to productive activity. That is, owners as shareholders control the means of production and accumulate rewards from it, but offer nothing constructive or valuable in return, not even managerial or administrative effort. Thus, the distinction between the productive proletariat and unnecessary capitalists would become increasingly clear.

Marx believed that all of these processes would produce an awareness among the workers of their exploitation and oppression by the bourgeoisie. The far greater numbers and, consequently, the potential power of the working class, coupled with its consciousness of class position and its desire to eliminate class inequalities, would set the stage for the workers to mobilize to overthrow the capitalist class. We should note that Marx did not see this revolution by the proletariat as automatic, in the sense that it would come about of its own accord. The basic conditions for the change were, in Marx's view, inherent in the capitalist mode of economic and social organization. However, the ultimate fate of the revolution depends on the actions of the proletariat and its desire and willingness to change society.

Classless society

What system would replace the capitalist order? Marx avoided specific predictions about this new system, but he generally suggested two stages would follow the revolution. First, Marx foresaw a socialist phase, a "dictatorship of the proletariat," with the leaders of the revolution heading the political apparatus of the society, the state. The state would abolish private property, thus eliminating any distinction between owning and non-owning classes. The tremendous productive capacity of the old system would be retained, but the state would ensure that the wealth created by the economy was distributed equitably to the productive members of society, to the workers themselves.

In the second stage after the revolution—communism—the state as a political force would become unnecessary and would die away, although some individuals would still be required to remain as administrators of the productive and other spheres of society. Communism would represent the first system without class distinctions, without a class structure, and without class conflict (Giddens, 1973).

Whether the classless society Marx envisioned will ever come to pass remains an open question. For many observers, the disappearance during the 1990s of communist regimes in the former Soviet Union and other countries raises doubts about Marx's projections, at least for the foreseeable future. It is also notable that, even in societies in which a socialist system has been implemented or still exists, inequality has not been eradicated. The need for a group of administrators to oversee the complex operations of any advanced society is probably one major reason why inequality has not yet been eliminated.

Program for Revolution: Key Points in *The Communist Manifesto*

In 1848, Marx and Engels outlined the key changes that they believed were required in the transition from capitalism to socialism. The following passage is taken from their famous document, The Communist Manifesto.

...in the most advanced countries, the following will be pretty generally applicable.

1. Abolition of property in land and application of all rents of land to public purposes.
2. A heavy progressive or graduated income tax.
3. Abolition of all right of inheritance.
4. Confiscation of the property of all emigrants and rebels.
5. Centralization of credit in the hands of the state, by means of a national bank with state capital and an exclusive monopoly.
6. Centralization of the means of communication and transport in the hands of the state.
7. Extension of factories and instruments of production owned by the state; the bringing into cultivation of wastelands, and the improvement of the soil generally in accordance with a common plan.
8. Equal liability of all to labour. Establishment of industrial armies, especially for agriculture.
9. Combination of agriculture with manufacturing industries; gradual abolition of the distinction between town and country, by a more equable distribution of the population over the country.
10. Free education for all children in public schools. Abolition of children's factory labour in its present form. Combination of education with industrial production, etc., etc.

When, in the course of development, class distinctions have disappeared, and all production has been concentrated in the hands of a vast association of the whole nation, the public power will lose its political character. Political power, properly so called, is merely the organized power of one class for oppressing another. If the proletariat during its contest with the bourgeoisie is compelled, by the force of circumstances, to organize itself as a class, if, by means of a revolution, it makes itself the ruling class, and, as such, sweeps away by force the old conditions of production, then it will, along with these conditions, have swept away the conditions for the existence of class antagonisms and of classes generally, and will thereby have abolished its own supremacy as a class.

In place of the old bourgeois society, with its classes and class antagonisms, we shall have an association in which the free development of each is the condition for the free development of all.

Source: *Karl Marx and Friedrich Engels, 1848. The Communist Manifesto. New York: Washington Square Press (1970, pp. 93–95).*

Weber's critique of Marx

One common criticism of Marx's theory of classes is that it paints too simple a picture of social inequality, especially in modern societies. Critics claim, first of all, that Marx over-estimated the economic structure as the source of power in society. Secondly, many writers feel that Marx's splitting of society into two classes, the propertied and the propertyless, ignores the existence of other identifiable classes.

Multiple power sources

One of the first to raise such issues was another German thinker, Max Weber. Weber lived and wrote in a time after Marx's death and was able to observe certain developments in capitalism that Marx could not. Weber accepted Marx's emphasis on economic class and property ownership as fundamental to social inequality. However, Weber pointed out that economic class by itself was not the only source of power or criterion for ranking in the social structure. Weber noted that power or influence could also be gained from status honour, or prestige, deriving from membership in certain groups. Such *status groups*, which may include ethnic, religious, or similar entities, involve exclusive membership; awareness of like tastes, lifestyles, and interests; and a tendency to act and interact as a unit. Similarly, Weber saw parties as an additional basis of power or command over resources in society. Party, in this sense, refers both to political parties and to other "special-interest" groups (e.g., trade unions, lobby groups) that can also operate in and influence political decisions. Weber was one of the first to view power in this multifaceted way. Each of the three factors—economic **class**, **status group**, and **party**—serves as a source of power and a basis for group formation in society (Giddens, 1973).

Weber conceded that these three aspects of inequality are frequently closely related, so that those who dominate the economic system tend also to have considerable status honour and political control. However, he disagreed with what he believed was Marx's contention, that all power derives ultimately from the control of the economy and the production process. Weber did not accept the view of some Marxists that the political, religious, educational, and other structures of society act only to serve the interests of the ruling economic class. To Weber, each of these structures possessed some power in its own right, some recognized sphere of influence and control. In this sense, Weber's view is one of the first *pluralist* conceptions of power in social theory. Power is pluralist here in the sense that it derives from more than one single source or structure.

The existence of "middle classes"

Weber's pluralist view of power is also revealed in his discussion of class structure. Weber argued, in opposition to Marx, that there were more than just two main economic classes, the bourgeoisie and proletariat. As discussed earlier, Marx also was aware of the existence of middle classes in capitalism, but he believed that these groups were transitional and would eventually become part of the two major classes. In his work, Weber included a range of middle classes, people who lack the privilege of large property ownership but who have more than just labour power to sell in the capitalist marketplace. These middle classes possess one or both of the following: (1) small amounts of productive property, such as shops, small businesses, or small farms; (2) valued skills, such as the special training or education of a physician, lawyer, or artisan.

Weber agreed with Marx that the small business segment of the middle classes was in decline. However, the other major segment, those people with specialized skills or training, would not decrease but expand and flourish under capitalism. Many of these people would fill positions as technical and administrative workers in the huge, developing bureaucratic structures of modern society. According to Weber, the need for managers, accountants, bookkeepers, supervisors, engineers, architects, teachers, and so on in the business, government, and educational bureaucracies would ensure that the middle classes would not be a transitional group, but a rising force in modern society.

Classless society and bureaucracy

You will recall Marx's expectation that future societies would see the end of classes and inequality. If we employ Marx's criterion for defining classes—the ownership or non-ownership of property—it is possible to envision the disappearance of classes. We need only abolish private property, and the basis for class formation would not exist. This is the approach that was taken officially in socialist countries like China or the former Soviet Union. It appears, however, that the abolition of private property is insufficient to eliminate inequality between identifiable groupings in society. Whether we call these unequal groupings classes or strata, the fact of inequality persists, even with private property eliminated. In socialist societies, the bases for power differences and group formation have simply shifted from property ownership to other factors, particularly access to valued education or skills and to political power. Those who dominate these sources of power tend to dominate the society (Giddens, 1973, 1981; Parkin, 1979).

Weber's analysis of bureaucracy (see Chapter 13, Work and Organizations), provides some explanation for the persistence of structured inequality in both socialist and capitalist societies. In any social structure, people in decision-making positions must have the legitimate right or power to decide, if they are to ensure that their chosen course of action will be followed by others. By definition this means that hierarchies based on unequal power and control will arise. In the modern era, these power hierarchies have increasingly taken the form of bureaucracies. Bureaucracies are designed for the administration and performance of various important tasks—policy-making, allocation of economic resources, health care, job placement, defence, and so forth. While socialism may attempt to remove material inequalities, it cannot eliminate the need for these administrative structures in making and implementing important decisions.

The problem of attaining individual equality and freedom in the face of bureaucratic dominance in societies of every type is probably the major dilemma facing Marxist and socialist theorists in the present day. In fact, Weber argued that bureaucracy would be even more common in socialist systems in which so many more aspects of life are regulated by government. Hence, power differences and inequality could be even greater in a socialist system than under capitalism. Certainly, the recent history of current and former communist countries points to this problem.

Weber clearly recognized the threat bureaucracy poses to equality and freedom, but believed the bureaucratic form was necessary for the efficient coordination and management of essential tasks in complex societies. Unlike another theorist, Michels (discussed in Chapter 13), Weber did not believe that an *iron law of oligarchy* operates in social structures, in which those in power inevitably abuse their position to gain special benefits for themselves at the expense of the masses. Nevertheless, Weber believed that the potential for such abuse of power is basic to modern social organizations, whether capitalist or socialist.

Structural functionalism: Consensus, individualism, and pluralism

While Marx stressed conflict, group (class) action, and the singular importance of economic power in understanding social inequality, the structural functionalist school of thought emphasizes consensus, individual action, and the pluralism of

power in social structures (Davis and Moore, 1945; Parsons, 1953). Let us consider these three points.

Consensus or conflict

Marx believed that conflict and struggle between groups are basic to the operation of all known societies. In contrast, structural functionalist theorists, as mentioned in Chapter 1, concentrate on what they perceive as the harmony and agreement that mark social interaction. They argue that social groups could not survive as they do without considerable consensus on the norms and values that govern social life. Rather than viewing structured inequality as something imposed upon the people by those in power, structural functionalists argue that this inequality is based largely on an underlying awareness and agreement about the value put on various positions in the social structure.

The value given to each position or status depends on two factors: its functional importance for society and the relative scarcity of people with the talent or training needed for the position. Some statuses, such as doctor, scientist, or judge, are said to be both more important and harder to fill than, for example, the positions of parking-lot attendant or file clerk. Hence, the rewards attached to the more crucial positions and those requiring rare skills must be proportionately greater than the rewards attached to the less valuable statuses. Otherwise, the most qualified individuals would not aspire to the key positions or, if in them, would not perform their important duties properly. The rewards used to motivate individuals in this system are of three types: (1) "sustenance and comfort," which are most readily attainable from material and economic gains such as money or property; (2) "humour and diversion," which may come from material returns but also include such benefits as extra leisure time or a flexible and varied work schedule; and (3) "self-respect and ego expansion," which tend to stem mainly from the prestige and honour accorded those who occupy important positions.

Several assumptions underlie this functionalist argument, but a central one is the presupposition that there is a high level of consensus among social actors: first, on the functional importance of each status—that is, on what the important jobs are; second, on what constitutes a "reward" in social

Some statuses are said to be more important and harder to fill than others.

understanding inequality in societies, structural functionalists focus almost solely on individual action and individual status as the factors in social inequality. In modern societies, the most important status determining a person's position is occupational status. The functional importance of this status and not, for example, inherited wealth and privilege, indicates the rank of any single individual.

Pluralism or property

While the structural functionalist analysis of social inequality differs considerably from the Weberian perspective, one view they share is that societies are pluralist or multifaceted structures. In the structural functionalist conception, social organization involves the coordination of interdependent subsystems, each with its own functions to perform if the overall system is to survive. The major subsystems, or *institutions*, of society include the economy, the polity (or political institutions), religion, education, and the agents of social control (police, military), among others. Each institution is said to operate in harmony with the others, to ensure social stability, maintenance of the system, and the general well-being of the population. The contrast between this formulation and Marx's focus on the overriding power of property ownership is apparent. For Marx, those who dominate the economy through ownership of the means of production ultimately hold sway in all other spheres and, moreover, can bring the power of the political, social control, and other structures into play to protect their domination.

life; and, third, on how rewards should be allotted to the various positions in the social structure.

The further assumption that different rewards are essential to motivate human beings leads to the conclusion that social inequality is inevitable and, in fact, performs a positive function for society by providing incentives for people to develop their talents to the full and to find their "proper" places in the system. It is alleged that those who are willing to work hard and apply themselves, and who can forego present rewards to achieve special skills and training, will achieve privileged positions and be rewarded with greater material benefits, prestige, and life satisfaction. It is assumed, once again, that there is general agreement on the importance of hard work, on the existence of opportunity for all, and on the rules that regulate the contest for success.

Individualism versus class action

The second aspect of structural functionalist thinking that distinguishes it from Marxian theory is its general avoidance of the concept of class. Rather than proposing a class or group basis for

Combining the major theories to explain modern systems of inequality

We get very different views of social inequality depending on which theoretical perspective we consider. The differences exist primarily because each approach emphasizes different factors to explain structured inequality in modern societies. It can be argued that no major theory by itself gives a complete picture, and that each applies better to some situations than to others. Consider the Marxian perspective. Marxism originated in nineteenth-century Europe and seems particularly suited to describe the group struggle and class divisions of that time and setting. Since then, however, Marxism has achieved its greatest following in the less industrialized countries of the world, and may not be as applicable to industrialized societies as it once was. In the less industrialized countries of Africa, Asia, and Latin America, for example, the continued sharp contrast between rich and poor has enabled class polarization and revolutionary potential to remain strong. In the industrialized capitalist countries of North America and Europe, however, absolute living standards have risen significantly for virtually everyone, the middle strata have not disappeared, and opportunities for mobility are still at least perceived to exist by many people. Hence, complete class polarization and outright revolution seem like distant and unlikely developments in advanced capitalism at this time.

Nevertheless, many elements of Marxian theory are useful for understanding modern systems of inequality. The role of conflict and struggle in human affairs and the great power invested in those who own and control property are undeniably important facets of modern life that affect inequality.

The structural functionalist view of inequality originated in the United States where, historically, such ideas as equal opportunity, free competition, and individual achievement were cherished and accepted as realities by much of the population. It is unlikely, however, that anything resembling complete equality of opportunity has existed in any known society. Discrimination on the basis of race, gender, and family class background, for example, continues to play a significant role in defining inequality, even in supposedly egalitarian societies. However, certain aspects of the structural functionalist perspective do ring true. Some consensus, not just conflict, does operate in social systems; otherwise, social organization would not be possible. In addition, the expansion of the labour forces of most modern societies has provided opportunities for individual success on the basis of merit and training.

Some theorists have attempted to reconcile these disparate theoretical approaches by bringing together elements of each perspective that have the greatest merit. Dahrendorf (1959) and Lenski (1966),

for example, attempted to show how both conflict and consensus operate in social systems. It is likely that a complete synthesis of theories is not possible. However, key features of the major theories can be combined to provide a more inclusive model for representing social inequality (Grabb, 1997). We suggest, first of all, that individual action, especially through educational and occupational attainment, does play a role in defining social inequality in countries like Canada. At the same time, group memberships play a major part in determining the structure of inequality. Most notable is membership in the upper class, and in that small set of élites that dominates the major institutions of society. Other group affiliations, such as race, ethnicity, and gender, also represent different bases of inequality, both inside and outside the élites, and are related to differences in command over scarce resources, including wealth, education, and prestige. The recognition of individual and group factors indicates that both the structural functionalist and Marxist approaches are relevant for understanding the overall pattern of social inequality.

Acknowledging that there are multiple bases for social inequality is consistent with both Weberian and structural functionalist theories. Each theory stresses the pluralist nature of power in systems of inequality. However, each ranking does not play an equally important role. Following Marx, we shall argue that control of property and wealth, particularly by large business enterprises, is the most important source of power in modern societies. We shall examine Canadian research on this point later in the chapter. At the same time, following Weber, we suggest that the other two socioeconomic status hierarchies, education and occupation, also are crucial in shaping the system of inequality.

Taken together, these three hierarchies have tended to promote the formation of a structure of three classes or strata in capitalist countries like Canada. This structure is made up of an upper class, which dominates large property ownership; a middle class, which, because of highly marketable skills, education, and training, holds the more powerful and rewarding jobs; and a working class, which has few skills other than labour power and so occupies the less powerful and less rewarding positions in the labour force. Of course, within these three broad groupings, many finer distinctions could be drawn. For example, sociologists sometimes speak of the "lower-middle class" or the "upper-working class" as subcategories in this three-class system. Some also include a fourth grouping, an "under class" of very poor and disadvantaged persons. This category includes people who may possess no property, education, or labour power and who may, for instance, be frequently unemployed because they cannot find work or are unable to work (Giddens, 1973; Grabb, 1997, 1999a).

In addition to the three socioeconomic hierarchies discussed above, five other hierarchies form Canada's overall system of social inequality. First, political power is crucial, especially when we consider that, officially at least, the ultimate power in society, even greater than that of the economic élite, is invested in the political leadership and the state. Generally speaking, it is the interplay between those who control political power and those who dominate the economic sphere that is the key process shaping the system of inequality in Canada and other modern societies. Second, differences in power and privilege between men and women are large in our society, so that gender has an important bearing on structured inequality. Recently, age has received increasing recognition as an important factor in social inequality. As for the remaining two rankings, based on ethnic and/or racial origin, and region or rural/urban location, these are of particular importance in describing inequality in Canada, with its image as a "vertical mosaic" of diverse cultures and geographic areas (Porter, 1965).

While other possible bases of social inequality could be considered, such as religion, for example, they will not be examined here because they are less salient in contemporary Canada than are the eight hierarchies suggested above.

In the next section of this chapter, we shall take a detailed look at each of the eight rankings. We shall see that there are connections in many cases between the rank of individuals and groups in one hierarchy and their ranks in others. An understanding of these interrelationships among hierarchies, taken together, should give the reader a relatively complete picture of the nature of social inequality in Canadian society.

Social Inequality in Canada

Socioeconomic hierarchies I: Wealth, income, and property

Wealth, including various forms of income and property, plays at least two major roles in social inequality. First, wealth is clearly a result or indicator of a person's position in the system of inequality. Wealth or income is the return people receive from their position in the economic structure. This return usually involves income from a job, but may include earnings from investments or property ownership. In all of these cases, wealth comes as a reward that can be high or low, depending on the market value of a person's job or property holdings. The distribution of wealth, then, is the most direct measure or indication of how groups or individuals rank in the overall structure of inequality.

Nevertheless, wealth plays a second key part in social inequality, at least in capitalist societies like Canada, where private property and inheritance are protected by law. Wealth is itself a form of property that can be used through investment to acquire more wealth and property. In this sense, wealth is not only a consequence but also a cause or means by which a person's position in the system of inequality is maintained or changed.

Distribution of income and wealth

How are wealth and property distributed in Canadian society? Are these sources of power widely diffused throughout the population or are they concentrated in a small group of people? There is no doubt, first of all, that people in most industrialized societies in this century have enjoyed an *absolute* increase in real wealth. In Canada, between 1951 and 1989, earned income increased by 198 percent for men and 284 percent for women, even after the effects of inflation were taken into account. It is important to note that this increase was most pronounced prior to 1980. By the early 1990s, growth in real income had levelled off and at times declined, although there was evidence of a slight upturn again by the late 1990s (Statistics Canada, 1994, *Income Distributions by Size, 1994*, Table 1; Urmetzer and Guppy, 1999: 57–58).

But the real issue of inequality for students to consider is the distribution of this income. The question, in other words, is one of *relative* income, of how well certain strata have been doing compared to others. In one study of this topic, all families or individuals who earned money in a particular year were ranked by their total income for that year and then divided into *quintiles* (five strata of equal size). Results showed that the top quintile, the top 20 percent of the hierarchy, earned about 42.8 percent of all the before-tax income made in Canada in 1951, while the bottom quintile earned only 4.4 percent. By 1996, this unequal distribution of income had remained almost unchanged, with the top quintile's share at 44.5 percent and the bottom quintile's portion at 4.6 percent (Urmetzer and Guppy, 1999: 59–60). The same study showed that, if the higher income taxes paid by the top quintile are taken into account, the amount of income inequality between the top and bottom decreases, but only slightly. This study also found that income inequality would be far greater if it were not for the relatively higher amounts of "social transfers," such as employment insurance and welfare payments, that are given to poorer Canadians (see also O'Connor, 1999). Overall, then, the rich have generally remained rich and the poor remained poor during this period.

These figures for Canada, which correspond approximately to those reported in the United States and other developed countries (e.g., Chawla, 1990;

World Bank, 1997), thus suggest that the unequal distribution of income has not changed much in recent decades. To establish a more complete picture of economic inequality in Canada, however, we must look beyond earned income alone. It is important to consider all the accumulated assets— stocks, real estate, durable goods, and the like—that together form the total wealth of an individual or group. The most recent data available (for the mid-1980s) show that the top 10 percent of Canada's population held over half of all wealth, while the top 20 percent retained about 70 percent (Davies, 1999: 69). Thus, the distribution of wealth is even more unequal than the distribution of income.

Distribution of property

Besides income and wealth, the other major means for achieving economic power in a capitalist society is through ownership or control of property. Under the capitalist system, large property, especially in the form of giant corporations, is rarely owned outright by one person or even a few people. Instead, corporations are owned by shareholders, each "owning a piece of the rock." This is a popular image, suggesting a dispersion of economic power to the wider population. However, studies indicate that ownership tends to involve a relatively small number of shareholders in many cases. Moreover, even where ownership is dispersed, minority shareholdings rather than majority ownership are

Do the Rich Really Get Richer?

The gap between the incomes of Canada's top business executives and those of other workers has grown dramatically in recent years. A study by the consulting firm KPMG looked at the Chief Executive Officers, or CEOs, of 268 major companies listed on the Toronto Stock Exchange. The study showed that, from 1992 to 1995, annual incomes for CEOs rose by 32 percent, to an average

of $776,000 per year. During the same period, the average income of Canadian workers increased by less than 3 percent. The survey also revealed that pay increases for executives were not related to how well their companies had performed. In fact, the CEOs of less profitable businesses actually received larger average raises than those running the more profitable companies. Such is an indication

of how people with wealth and power in our society are able to protect and enhance their advantaged economic positions, sometimes regardless of their performance or contributions to the nation's economy.

Source: From a Southam News story by Bertrand Marotte, published in the London Free Press, September 25, 1996 (p. D5).

often all that is needed to achieve effective control of decision-making in the corporations. Frequently, the shares in a company are spread across a large number of isolated individuals, most of whom do not attend shareholders' meetings, and some of whom may not have voting rights for electing company directors. In such instances, control of a small block of shares, perhaps only 10 or 20 percent, may be sufficient to determine how the company is run (Francis, 1986; Grabb, 1999b). Therefore, ownership or control of property, and hence economic power, can be concentrated in a small group of people.

Perhaps even stronger evidence of the concentration of property ownership has been offered by various studies of corporate control in Canada. Francis (1986) concluded that a small group of thirty-two wealthy families, along with five "conglomerates," or clusters of companies, controlled one-third of Canada's non-financial assets in 1985. Carroll (1986) has also identified a powerful set of six "cliques" that form the inner circle of the Canadian corporate structure. It appears, then, that economic power deriving from property ownership is more highly concentrated in a smaller set of individuals than ever before.

More recent government statistics confirm this high concentration of property control and suggest that it has increased with time. For example, in 1987, there were more than 400 000 companies operating in Canada, yet the largest twenty-five enterprises by themselves accounted for over 41 percent of all corporate assets. By 1993, economic ownership had become even more concentrated, with the top twenty-five enterprises owning 46 percent of Canada's total business assets (Grabb, 1999b: 6; see also O'Connor, 1999).

We can see, then, that Canada's system of inequality is marked by large differences in economic power, in the form of wealth and property holdings. A relatively small group of people at the top possesses much of the wealth. In addition, within this "upper class," an even smaller élite, including the owners and directors of dominant corporations, controls most of the society's economic resources.

These findings are broadly consistent with a Marxist interpretation of social inequality. The continued unequal distribution of wealth, the relative decline in wealth and property holdings among the lower strata, and the concentration of economic power in a small élite all support such a view. However, these realities apparently have been insufficient to produce the class polarization and proletarian revolution Marx expected under advanced capitalism. While the explanation for this failure is complex, three possible reasons should be considered. First, the general population has done better economically, at least in absolute terms, than Marx anticipated. Such developments as worker unionization and the institution of government social programs—health insurance, old age pensions, and the like—have meant at least modest increases in living standards for most people. Despite spending cuts by all levels of government that have weakened social programs in recent years, it may be that most workers still feel their material position is adequate. Second, even those workers who are discontented may believe that they lack the power to change the situation. As a consequence, rather than becoming a unified force for revolution, much of the working class has remained passive, accepting their disadvantaged position in the system. Finally, despite the serious inequalities existing in Canada, perhaps there is sufficient real or perceived upward mobility to maintain the belief among many workers that opportunities continue to be there for those who will take them. Such optimistic beliefs would tend to reduce class polarization.

We shall consider the question of mobility later in this chapter, but whatever the opportunity structure, economic inequalities in Canada in recent decades have apparently not been sufficient to promote a concerted move for change among the working and middle classes. In the next section, we examine occupation's role in the distribution of economic power, particularly for these two classes.

Socioeconomic hierarchies II: Occupation

Except for wealthy property holders, occupational status is the major source of economic power for most individuals. Because occupation correlates with other key variables—income, education, gender, ethnicity—it is sometimes viewed as the best single indicator of an individual's overall rank in the system of inequality. Thus, it is useful to examine trends in the occupational composition of the labour force. In this section, we consider some of the transformations in Canada's workforce and then look at changes in the distribution of income by occupational status over time. This will help us to assess how the market capacities of various occupations have changed in recent decades. Finally, we also look at research on occupational mobility in Canada. This will help us to evaluate the degree to which social inequality in our society is an open or closed system.

Occupational shifts

The first major historical development to note is the great increase in the types of jobs that exist today compared with earlier times. Nuclear physicist, computer scientist, X-ray technician, and jet pilot are just a few of the many jobs that have come into being in the relatively recent past. The growing variety of occupations is a prime example of the increasing social differentiation in modern societies, a process discussed earlier in this chapter.

In addition to the greater number of occupations, there has been a notable shift in the relative size of occupational categories over time. Occupations can be divided roughly into three groups: manual or blue-collar jobs, non-manual or white-collar jobs, and agricultural or farm occupations. Manual jobs normally entail physical labour or working with the hands, as the name implies. In social research, these jobs are sometimes equated with the working class, and include such occupations as construction worker, factory labourer, miner, logger, and mechanic. Non-manual jobs typically involve working with symbols and ideas, rather than with the hands. Non-manual jobs are sometimes used as an indication of middle-class position by social scientists, and include such occupations as doctor, lawyer, teacher, nurse, business manager, salesperson, accountant, and clerk.

An examination of historical shifts in these three job categories is quite revealing (see Table 6.1). First, the proportion of agricultural occupations has declined greatly, from over 40 percent in 1901 to

Table 6.1   Canadian Labour Force, Percentage Distribution by Major Occupational Groups, 1901–1996

	1901	1921	1941	1961	1981	1991	1996
All occupations	100	100	100	100	100	100	100
White collar	15	25	25	39	53	57	55
Managerial	4	7	5	8	9	12	13
Professional/technical	5	5	7	10	16	18	18
Clerical	3	7	7	13	19	18	14
Sales	3	6	6	8	9	9	10
Blue collar	45	42	49	49	43	38	39
Manuf./mech./construction	21	16	21	22	29[1]	23[1]	24[1]
Labourers	7	10	6	5			
Transport/communication	5	5	6	8			
Service	8	7	11	11	12	13	14
Fishing/logging/mining	4	4	5	3	2	2	1
Agriculture	40	33	26	10	4	3	3
Occupation not stated	–	–	–	3	1	4	3

[1]Because blue-collar categories differed after 1971 from previous years, these three occupational categories are combined for the years 1981 to 1996.

Source: Kubat and Thornton (1974: 153-55); Statistics Canada, 1981 Census of Canada, Catalogue No. 92-917, Table 1; 1991 Census of Canada, Catalogue No. 93-327, Table 1; 1996 Census of Canada, Catalogue No. 92-364.

Table 6.2   **Average Incomes of Major Occupational Groups (full-time employed), as a Percentage of the Average Income for all Occupations, 1931–1996**

	1931	*1941*	*1951*[1]	*1961*	*1971*[2]	*1981*	*1963*[3]
All occupations	**100**	**100**	**100**	**100**	**100**	**100**	**100**
White collar	**209**	**172**	**134**	**120**	**130**	**109**	**103**
Managerial	314	253	169	184	204	179	127
Professional/technical	214	176	141	150	144	127	113
Clerical	125	112	102	92	89	72	76
Sales	140	122	107	106	108	90	91
Blue collar	**86**	**90**	**93**	**87**	**91**	**90**	**86**
Manuf./mech./construction	101	102	106	99			
Labourers	53	61	73	60	97[4]	105	96
Transport/communication	115	104	100	94			
Service	97	85	84	76	80	60	66
Fishing/logging/mining	63	69	90	71	79	107	108
Agriculture	**35**	**30**	**37**	**38**	**51**	**68**	**57**

[1]Median income 1951.

[2]Figures after 1971 exclude those with no employment income and those whose occupations were not stated or included in the major categories.

[3]Figures for 1996 are based on average earnings for full-time, full-year workers.

[4]Because blue-collar categories differ after 1971 from previous years, these three occupational categories are combined from 1971 on.

Sources: Derived from N.M. Meltz, 1965. Changes in the Occupational Composition of the Canadian Labour Force: 1931–61. Ottawa: Queen's Printer (pp. 64-65); Statistics Canada, 1971 Census of Canada, Catalogue No. 94-765; 1981 Census of Canada, Catalogue No. 92-930; Statistics Canada, 1998, Earnings of Women and Men 1996, Catalogue No. 13-217.

about 3 percent in 1996. Blue-collar occupations recently have declined somewhat, but still formed close to 40 percent of the workforce in 1996. However, there have been shifts within the blue-collar group, including a move to more service work, such as food preparation, hairdressing, and housekeeping, plus a decline in unskilled labour and primary labour, such as fishing, logging, and mining. The white-collar sector has expanded the most, from 15 percent to more than 50 percent of the Canadian workforce. Much of the white-collar growth, however, involves lower positions—sales clerks, typists, file clerks—which, in terms of income, power, and work activities, are similar to working-class occupations (see Braverman, 1974; Rinehart, 1996; Lowe, 1999). Thus, part of the non-manual expansion may be indicative of a rising "new working class" of low-paid, semi-skilled, white-collar workers.

Occupation and income

As Table 6.2 reveals, blue-collar relative earning power has changed little since 1931, with incomes staying at about 10 percent below the national average. At the same time, white-collar incomes have declined from 2.09 times the national level in 1931 to 1.03 in 1996. On the surface, this relative income decline in the white-collar sector lends some support to the new-working-class view. That is, with many white-collar incomes becoming more like blue-collar incomes, we might conclude that today's non-manual employees, in their market capacity and perhaps other traits, are more like the working class than the middle class. Even so, several points should be noted here.

First, the white-collar income decline, as Table 6.2 indicates, appears to be most significant for clerical workers, who now earn incomes that are

Labour in the Working Class

In his book *The Tyranny of Work*, Rinehart (1996) assessed the nature of labour for the modern working class. He suggested that in more and more industries the jobs of blue-collar workers have gradually undergone a significant reduction in skill requirements in this century. Due to ever-improving technology, especially computers, and an increasing division of labour, their work has become routine, easy to learn, unskilled, and repetitive. Even what was once skilled labour, such as machining, has been affected by these trends, thus blurring the previous, more clear-cut distinction between skilled and unskilled workers.

"Semiskilled and unskilled workers literally sell their capacity to work: they sell the ability to learn a specific job, any job, in a particular work organization. When they change jobs, their 'skills' are not ordinarily transferable (unlike those of crafts[people] or professionals) and they are obliged to acquire new 'skills' for new jobs" (Rinehart, 1996: 28).

well below the Canadian average and that are also lower than those of blue-collar workers as a whole. Managerial and professional incomes, on the other hand, continue to be higher than those of blue-collar workers, although their incomes, too, have moved closer to the Canadian average over time.

A second important point about the general decline of white-collar incomes is that much of this trend is due to the flow of poorly paid women into many of these positions (Krahn and Lowe, 1998; Lowe, 1999; Creese and Beagan, 1999 and see also Chapter 7, Gender Relations). White-collar males outside the clerical sector have maintained a significant edge over blue-collar workers. For example, in the full-time workforce in 1996, males in managerial and administrative jobs earned almost 50 percent more than the Canadian average, while males in upper-tier professional areas, such as the medicine and health fields, for example, earned incomes almost 70 percent above the average (Statistics Canada, 1998, *Earnings of Women and Men 1996*, Catalogue 13-217, Table 5).

Finally, it should also be noted that these income figures give only a partial picture, since they do not include other economic advantages—job security, fringe benefits, and promotion opportunities—which have traditionally been more likely to benefit white-collar workers, especially those in the professional-technical and managerial categories (Lowe, 1999: 121).

Occupation and social mobility

The previous discussion of the occupational structure leads to another important issue: the process of social mobility in systems of inequality. Earlier, we described social mobility as any shift in status by an individual or group within a status hierarchy. Analyzing vertical intergenerational mobility is particularly helpful in assessing how open or closed a system of inequality is. If we can show that parents' statuses do not really affect their adult children's statuses in a particular system, this would suggest the system is open. In an open system, individuals are neither helped nor hindered by the power of their parents, or by such ascribed characteristics as their family's race, ethnic origin, or class background. On the other hand, when children do gain or lose chances for success largely on the basis of their family backgrounds, we have a more closed inequality system.

The most general approach to the study of social mobility is to take into account all of the eight major power dimensions considered in this chapter. Thus, social mobility may be defined as a change in the relative amount of all "power resources" held by a person or group. In most cases, however, social scientists have concentrated on the occupational status hierarchy alone when assessing social mobility. This is probably because, as was noted earlier in this chapter, occupation may be the best

Occupation may be the best single indicator of overall class position for most of the population.

single indicator of overall class or stratum rank for most of the population.

One early study showed that occupational mobility patterns in Canada were similar to those of other industrialized nations. This analysis found a moderate relationship (a correlation of about .40) between fathers' and sons' occupational status (Goyder and Curtis, 1977: 304-308), suggesting that family class background, as measured by fathers' occupation, has a notable but not overwhelming impact on sons' adult occupational attainments. Goyder and Curtis also found that, if intergenerational mobility is traced over four generations, the association disappears. In other words, the effect of family class background on occupational attainments seems not to accumulate from great-grandfather through to great-grandson. Hence, the authors concluded that there is an "impermanence of family status over non-adjacent generations," suggesting that Canada is "an achievement society rather than an ascriptive one" (Goyder and Curtis, 1977: 316).

More recent research on occupational mobility reveals other interesting patterns. One study found

that the relationship between fathers' occupational status and the occupational status of both sons and daughters declined significantly from 1973 to 1986 (Wanner, 1993: 171–74). This implies that people are increasingly less likely to inherit occupational privileges now than in the past, and suggests some increase in overall mobility, openness, and equality of opportunity in Canada's occupational structure in recent years. Of course, these findings do not mean that inheritance of occupational advantages has disappeared (Wanner, 1993: 175; see also Wanner and Hayes, 1996). Moreover, such research applies mainly to the broad range of individuals in the middle of the class structure, and not to the very poor and the very wealthy. For example, other evidence indicates considerable inheritance of privilege among wealthy families, for example (Clement, 1975; Davies, 1999).

In conclusion, mobility does occur in our society, even though the overall opportunity structure is far from completely open. The major mechanism providing the chance for mobility across generations seems to be the education system. Especially for that large central group from middle-

and working-class backgrounds, the acquisition of skills and training through the schools is probably the best bet for individual advancement. In the next section we consider just how equally or unequally educational advantages are distributed in Canada.

Socioeconomic hierarchies III: Education

Education is included among the set of socio-economic status hierarchies because it is closely linked to the acquisition of income, wealth, and occupational status in modern societies. In Canada and other countries, the education system is the primary means by which most people achieve upward mobility and material success. Education plays a crucial role in sustaining the belief that our system of inequality is neither closed nor totally determined by ascribed status characteristics such as race, gender, or inherited wealth. If individual achievement in the education system is consistently translated into higher incomes and better jobs, then the argument that an open, competitive, and fair system exists is made more convincing.

Recall that structural functionalist theory is most closely identified with the view that inequality is the result of a contest in which education and training are the key means to success. In Canada, there is some evidence to support such an assertion. Generally speaking, higher education has a significant connection with higher income and occupational attainment. In 1995, for example, university graduates in Canada earned almost double the employment income of high-school graduates, although this difference was not as large among younger age groups (1996 Census of Canada, *Employment Income by Highest Level of Schooling and Age*). As for occupational differences, one recent study demonstrates clearly that higher education tends to be associated with better jobs (Baer, 1999). Using 1991 Census data, this study found that more than 77 percent of university graduates and more than 90 percent of post-graduates had "discretionary" occupations. This term refers mainly to employment in upper-level professional, technical, managerial, and administrative fields, where people typically have more control over their work and do more interesting tasks. In contrast, the same study found that about 75 percent of high-

school graduates and more than 80 percent of those with less than a high-school diploma were engaged in "routine" jobs, involving less personal freedom and less stimulating work activities. Other employment data indicate that university graduates enjoy additional advantages. Compared to non-graduates, graduates are less likely to be unemployed, less likely to remain unemployed if they do lose a job, and more likely to earn higher salaries when employed (Picot and Wannell, 1993; Anisef and Axelrod, 1993). Clearly, while higher education by itself is not sufficient for success and does not guarantee a better job to everyone, it is still a necessary prerequisite in most cases.

An important question to ask when discussing education and social inequality is, who does and who does not acquire higher education, and why? For educational attainment to be truly an achieved status, there must be equal opportunity for all citizens to acquire education, assuming they have the motivation and the ability to do so. Otherwise, education becomes much like an ascribed characteristic, something that one possesses or lacks as a result of the inherited advantages or disadvantages of gender, race, or class background.

Canadian data indicate that, in the past, ascribed traits such as class background were significantly related to educational attainment. For example, Porter's (1965: 184) early research from the 1950s showed that individuals whose families earned above-average incomes and whose fathers had high status occupations were greatly overrepresented in the university student population. More recent studies have found increases in the proportion of post-secondary students coming from lower socio-economic backgrounds. These results indicate that Canada's educational structure has become more "meritocratic"—more accessible to people on the basis of ability rather than class background—than it was before (e.g., Ali and Grabb, 1998; Fournier et al., 1999). Nevertheless, these studies and others also reveal that students from the lower strata are still underrepresented compared to their proportion of the population (Nakhaie and Curtis, 1998; Guppy and Davies, 1999).

Of course, inequality of educational opportunity may not be the only reason why people from the lower strata are underrepresented in Canada's post-secondary institutions. Some studies indicate that other factors probably have an impact. Parents' and children's perceptions of the chances for education, their knowledge of educational programs, and their evaluation of the utility of education in the job market all reduce the likelihood that lower-class children will go on in school. In addition, differences in parental encouragement of children's educational aspirations may make it more likely that middle- and upper-class children will continue in the education system (Davies, 1999; Guppy and Davies, 1999).

Even if all of these factors are taken into account, it is likely that much of the difference in education in the population is due to inequality of access. Despite the availability of government assistance and student loans, post-secondary education remains an expensive undertaking that low-income people often cannot afford. There is also reason to believe that continued government underfunding of higher education is beginning to restrict access to post-secondary education once again. All of these factors suggest unequal educational opportunity and threaten the major avenue of upward mobility for a large number of Canadians (Wotherspoon, 1991).

This completes our discussion of the major socioeconomic status hierarchies. We have seen that wealth and property, occupational status, and education all play important parts in shaping the system of inequality or class structure. In the remaining sections of this chapter, we examine some of the interrelationships between these aspects of inequality and the five other key hierarchies.

Racial and ethnic inequality

Racial background and ethnic origin (discussed in Chapter 8, Race and Ethnic Relations) are important factors distinguishing people from one another in Canada. It is also apparent that racial and ethnic diversity, or "multiculturalism," has important implications for the overall structure of inequality.

Various factors have operated to make race and ethnicity important factors in the analysis of social inequality. First, different groups arrived in Canada at different times, so that some groups were able to make prior claims on power and property rights. Second, some cultures may put less stress than others on the importance of acquiring wealth and power; hence, differences in values may have contributed to racial or ethnic inequality. In addition, ethnic or racial background frequently has been used as a basis for favouritism or discrimination, making it difficult for some groups to enter the upper strata while allowing others ready access. These factors and others have produced in Canada what Porter (1965) called a "vertical mosaic," a social structure involving many diverse racial and ethnic groups, ranked along a hierarchy of power and privilege.

We begin our examination of the links between racial or ethnic background and social inequality by assessing the relationship between these factors and the three major socioeconomic rankings. Then we look at the racial/ethnic composition of the economic élite. Finally, we focus on two groups that occupy unique positions in the system of social inequality, the French Canadians and Native peoples.

Race, ethnicity, and socioeconomic status

Table 6.3 shows the rankings of twenty-three self-identified racial or ethnic categories in 1991, on three socioeconomic indicators: average income, the percent of each category with upper white-collar occupations, and the percent of each category with some university education. Perhaps the most surprising result is that those of British origin, while above the total population average on all three factors, rank only sixth in income, ninth in occupation, and sixteenth in education. These figures suggest that, at least in the general population, the British no longer enjoy the dominant position they once did.

Some of the ethnic groups that rank above the British on the three socioeconomic indicators are other Europeans, particularly Ukrainians, Hungarians, and Poles. However, people who identify themselves as Jewish rank the highest in most cases, while several "visible" minorities, including Filipinos, Arabs, South and West Asians, the Chinese, and others, also do very well. The situation of Jews and visible minorities is notable if we consider that all of these groups have been viewed historically as victims of significant

TABLE 6.3   Socio-Economic Status of Selected (self-identified) Ethnic Groups,[1] Canada, 1991

Rank	Average income[2]	Percentage in upper white-collar occupations[3]	Percentage with some university education[4]
1.	Jewish ($45,523)	Jewish (52.3)	Filipino (54.2)
2.	Ukrainian ($33,923)	Ukrainian (36.1)	Jewish (47.2)
3.	Hungarian ($33,072)	Arab (36.1)	Arab (40.2)
4.	Polish ($32,890)	Chinese (35.6)	West Asian (35.6)
5.	"Canadian" ($32,714)	Hungarian (34.6)	Chinese (35.1)
6.	British ($31,498)	German (33.6)	South Asian (34.5)
7.	German ($31,276)	Polish (33.4)	Polish (28.9)
8.	Balkan ($31,225)	Dutch (33.2)	Hungarian (27.8)
9.	Italian ($30,525)	British (31.6)	Ukrainian (27.6)
10.	Dutch ($30,377)	Filipino (29.8)	Latin, Central, South American (27.5)
11.	Arab ($28,656)	West Asian (29.6)	Vietnamese (27.1)
12.	French ($28,509)	French (29.6)	Spanish (25.8)
13.	Chinese ($28,099)	"Canadian" (29.4)	German (25.1)
14.	West Asian ($27,832)	S. Asian (29.2)	Balkan (23.2)
15.	South Asian ($27,580)	Black, Caribbean (26.7)	Dutch (22.3)
16.	Greek ($26,347)	Balkan (26.3)	British (22.0)
17.	Spanish ($26,316)	Italian (25.8)	"Canadian" (20.1)
18.	Portuguese ($26,105)	Spanish (25.1)	Black, Caribbean (19.4)
19.	Black, Caribbean ($25,416)	Vietnamese (24.6)	Italian (18.3)
20.	Vietnamese ($23,792)	Aboriginal (24.5)	Greek (17.8)
21.	Filipino ($23,321)	Greek (22.5)	French (17.2)
22.	Aboriginal ($22,242)	Latin, Central, South American (20.8)	Portuguese (8.7)
23.	Latin, Central, South American ($21,032)	Portuguese (15.5)	Aboriginal (8.6)
Full Population	**($30,157)**	**(30.4)**	**(20.6)**

[1]Total origins, including single and multiple mentions of each group.
[2]Annual employment income in 1990, full-time employed only.
[3]As a proportion of all occupations. Upper white-collar occupations include professional, technical, managerial, and administrative positions.
[4]As a proportion of the total population fifteen years old and over.

Source: Adapted from Statistics Canada, 1991 Census of Canada–Ethnic Origen, Catalogue No. 93-315.

discrimination and prejudice in Canada and elsewhere. Of course, their high socioeconomic rankings should not be seen as evidence that discrimination and prejudice no longer exist in Canadian society (see Reitz and Breton, 1994; Allahar and Côté, 1998; Satzewich, 1998; Henry, 1999). As well, the high position of many visible minorities partly reflects Canadian government policy, which did not encourage large-scale immigration of such groups until the 1960s, and which until recently has allowed mainly those with recognized skills and training into the country. As a consequence, many highly educated middle- and upper-stratum members of these groups have come

to Canada from elsewhere (Breton et al., 1990). There is also evidence that certain visible minorities are still overrepresented in lower-paying jobs (Agócs and Boyd, 1993: 337–38). This is consistent with research suggesting that non-whites as a group still make lower incomes than whites in Canada (Li, 1992; Lian and Matthews, 1998). The 1990 data shown in Table 6.3 also suggest that visible minorities tend to be below average on income, even though many such groups rank above average on education level and on the proportion holding upper white-collar jobs (see Hou and Balakrishnan, 1996). On balance, however, recent research suggests that there are real opportunities for socioeconomic success for many ethnic minorities in Canada today (see also Ali and Grabb, 1998).

Ethnic composition of the economic élite

Historically, the British dominated Canada's economy. Information from 1885 and 1910 indicates that more than 90 percent of Canada's industrial leaders were of Anglo-Saxon background (Clement, 1975: 73). French Canadians made up 29 percent of the population but only 6 to 7 percent of the élite, and other ethnic groups were virtually excluded.

By 1951, Porter's research showed almost no change from these figures (Porter, 1965). Clement's subsequent research (1975: 234), revealed some erosion of British dominance between 1951 and 1972, with the Anglo-Canadian proportion of the economic élite dropping slightly (to 86 percent), the French rising somewhat (to 8 percent), and "other" groups, especially Jews, increasing moderately (to 5 percent). One recent summary of evidence on this question indicates some shifts in the composition of the economic or business élite. The British still predominate, but depending on the estimate, they now form between one-half and two-thirds of the Canadian élite or upper class. The French make up another 14 or 15 percent, while other ethnic groups, especially Jews, now account for as much as one-third of the élite (Ogmundson and McLaughlin, 1992). Even so, it has been pointed out that the growth of non-British representation in Canada's economic élite is no greater than the growth of non-British representation in the population as a whole (Nakhaie, 1997).

Overall, then, people of Anglo-Saxon background continue to have an advantage at the élite level. However, as we have seen, outside this upper stratum, British origin has considerably less significance, with several other groups ranking higher in socioeconomic status. We turn now to a discussion of French Canadians and Native peoples, who historically, at least, have been in a disadvantaged position in the overall system of inequality.

French Canadians and social inequality

Until recently the French did not occupy a particularly privileged position in Canadian society. (This issue will be discussed more fully in the next chapter.) Even now, the French rank below average on education and are only in the middle on the other two socioeconomic indicators (see Table 6.3). In the past, various reasons have been put forth to explain the French position. Some have said that the French needed time to recover from the initial shock of the British economic and political takeover in the eighteenth century (Milner and Milner, 1973). Others saw the past avoidance by the French of "English-style" business and economic activity as a cause of their lower socioeconomic status (McRoberts, 1988: 178). Some have suggested that differences in values and upbringing put French Canadians at a disadvantage in the competition for material success, especially in business careers (Harvey, 1969; Richer and Laporte, 1971). Finally, ethnic prejudice and discrimination have been cited at times as an obstacle to French progress (Archibald, 1978).

Probably a combination of these factors contributed to the historically low position of French Canadians in our society. However, in the 1960s, during the "Quiet Revolution," there was a move in Quebec to catch up with English Canada. Since then the French have come to dominate the Quebec government and civil service (McRoberts, 1988). The French now form an increasing portion of both the salaried middle class and the new business class in Quebec (Ogmundson and McLaughlin, 1992; Nakhaie, 1997). Evidence also suggests that the economic advantages of the English over the French in Quebec have diminished considerably. By 1990, French Canadians who worked full-time made about 9 percent less than their British counterparts, and about 5 percent less than the overall Canadian average (see Table 6.3). Within Quebec, in fact, French Canadians now earn just a bit more than English Canadians (Canadian Press, 1994). Other recent evidence indicates that opportunities for occupational attainment, social mobility, and educational achievement have become increasingly similar for French and English (Agócs and Boyd, 1993; Guppy and Arai, 1993; Ali and Grabb, 1998). One analysis of income differences, using 1991 Census data, has shown that, as long as they have the same education level (and if the effects of other variables, like age and gender, are controlled), French Canadians actually "now earn significantly more than those of British ethnicity" (Lian and Matthews, 1998: 461–462).

These developments suggest that ethnic inequality involving French Canadians is changing, with the English becoming less powerful than before. Nevertheless, the English—both Canadian- and American-born—continue to hold somewhat greater economic power at the élite level in Quebec, through their positions in dominant corporations (McRoberts, 1988; Nakhaie, 1997). For this reason and others, many French Canadians continue to call for greater economic control and political autonomy. Some favour the Parti Québécois program of sovereignty or outright independence for Quebec. Others support a new version of Canadian confederation, in which Quebec is formally acknowledged as a distinct society, and French rights and powers are given greater recognition than before. Quebec's 1995 referendum, in which almost half of the province's population voted for sovereignty, is a clear indication that French Canada's position within our society is still a serious and largely unresolved issue (see Chapter 14, Social Movements).

Inequality and Native peoples

Native peoples also occupy an exceptional position in Canada's vertical mosaic. The erosion of their power, through the loss of land and natural resources, had a devastating initial impact on Native inhabitants (Menzies, 1999). The subsequent separation of many Natives from the rest of the population, due to voluntary avoidance, geographic isolation, and the government's policies of wardship for indigenous peoples, helped sustain and institutionalize their low status (Frideres, 1988; Wotherspoon and Satzewich, 1993). Such isolation may have helped to preserve Native identity, but probably at the expense of Native participation in the quest for jobs, education, and material affluence. Perhaps more than any other group, Native people face the dilemma of having to choose between preserving their ethnic identities and succeeding in the larger society. Racial prejudice must also be seen as a factor, although in recent years this appears to have declined somewhat. Some Canadians still perceive Native peoples as being low in "social standing" (Pineo, 1986). Other Canadians also hold negative stereotypes of Native groups. However, evidence suggests that, overall, the Canadian public has often been sympathetic towards, though also poorly informed about, Native peoples (Langford and Ponting, 1992: 141; Ponting, 1998).

Some recent developments suggest that the position of Canada's Native peoples may improve. Funds derived from the settlement of Native land claims, as well as the increasing political awareness of Native leaders (see Chapter 14, Social Movements), may provide a means for Natives to achieve greater prosperity (Wotherspoon and Satzewich, 1993). The socioeconomic attainments of Natives have also improved in recent years, although serious inequalities remain (see Table 6.3). Natives increasingly hold white-collar jobs, though they are still under-represented in such positions. And although their unemployment rates are far above average, among employed Natives, income differences have declined somewhat. Native workers made over half the national average in 1980, compared with only a third of the average in 1971, while those employed full-time earned about 74 percent of the national average income in 1990. Some educational improvements are also evident: in 1971 only 3 percent of the Native adult population had some postsecondary education, but by 1981 this figure had risen to 19 percent (Siggner, 1986: 71–76). By 1991, about 9 percent of Native people had attained at least some university education.

Nevertheless, the prospects for Native peoples still hinge primarily on fuller acceptance of Native rights by political leaders and the general population. The effects of the 1990 confrontation at Oka, Quebec, as well as subsequent incidents at Ipperwash, Ontario, and elsewhere, are still being felt. In the long run, the Native position will probably be determined by how the dilemma of identity preservation versus participation in the larger structure is resolved.

Regional and rural/urban inequalities

Regional and rural/urban differences, perhaps as much as racial and ethnic diversity, give Canada its image as a mosaic of distinct parts. Canada's variability on these dimensions is illustrated in the contrast between major urban centres like Toronto, Montreal, or Vancouver, and the less populous and more isolated areas of the Maritimes, the Prairies, and the North.

Overall, geographic location has an important impact on social inequality among Canadians. In a sense, location is another source of power affecting the distribution of wealth and resources, because those who live in the urbanized, strategically located centres have considerably greater opportunity to achieve high positions in our society.

One theoretical approach that helps in thinking about such differences is the *metropolis-hinterland* perspective (Davis, 1971). In this view, Canada's social structure involves a complex network of regions and communities in which the rural and peripheral areas, or hinterlands, are ultimately connected by a series of intermediate links to a few major urban centres, or metropolises. The intermediate links in the system include local outposts, small towns, and middle-sized cities, all acting at different levels as depots between the outlying districts and the large population centres.

The metropolises are the focal points for industry, economic activity, politics, and education in the nation. Large-scale business enterprises, the major corporations, the seats of political power, and the largest universities are situated in the metropolitan centres. Economically, the hinterlands serve as sources of raw materials—primary resources like fish, wheat, petroleum, lumber, and ore—most of which are processed in the metropolises and then sold to hinterland inhabitants

as finished goods. People constitute another resource that flows out of the hinterland and into the metropolis. More and more Canadians have left the hinterland areas for jobs in the big cities, taking with them their labour power and skills, their potential political affiliations and voting power, and their intellectual abilities (see also Chapter 15). All of this resource potential is lost by the hinterlands in favour of the large centres. Those who stay behind, near their family roots, historical heritage, and traditional communities, suffer considerably in terms of their relative power in the system of inequality. The local economy typically has little industry, so that job prospects are poorer and unemployment is more prevalent. In addition, isolation from the central political power and from greater educational opportunities helps to perpetuate and accentuate this lower position.

Metropolis-hinterland disparities are illustrated by differences in average incomes by geographic location. In Table 6.4, the average family income of all Canadians in 1997 has been assigned a score of 100. The other numbers in the table represent the average income in each location as a percentage of the Canadian average. This procedure allows us to observe a number of interesting differences in income, by region and rural/urban category. First, we see that, in both Canada as a whole and in each separate region, income generally increases with an

TABLE 6.4   Average Family Income by Region and Community Size, as a Percentage of the Average Family Income for Canada, 1997[1]

| Region | Rural areas | Urban areas | | | Total |
		under 30 000	30 000–99 999	over 100 000	
All Canada	**87**	**88**	**92**	**107**	**100**
Atlantic provinces	71	76	85	88	79
Quebec	75	75	85	96	90
Ontario	103	93	96	116	111
Prairie provinces	89	93	96	102	98
British Columbia	96	96	98	109	104

[1]Average family income for all Canada in 1997 was $57 146 and is set at 100 in this table for comparison purposes.
Source: *Statistics Canada*, Income Distributions by Size in Canada 1997, *Catalogue No. 13-207, Tables 2, 3, and 4.*

increase in community size. In other words, the most highly urbanized areas are the places in which average incomes are greatest, while rural districts show the lowest income levels. This result is consistent with the view that wealth is more highly concentrated in the metropolis. A second finding that conforms to the metropolis-hinterland argument concerns regional differences. The most economically developed and industrialized areas, particularly the urbanized areas of Ontario, British Columbia, and the Prairies, appear to provide the highest standard of living. As of 1997, both Quebec and the Atlantic region were below the Canadian average. This was especially evident in the rural parts of these two areas, where families earned only about 70 to 75 percent of the national average (see Swan and Serjak, 1993; Forcese, 1997: 58–81; Wien, 1999).

Other evidence related to business ownership and corporate concentration indicates that the metropolitan centres of Ontario form most of Canada's economic core. Toronto stands as the most influential financial and industrial centre in the nation, with Montreal a distant second (Semple, 1988; see also Britton, 1996). In and around these cities, most of Canada's major corporations are located and directed. Not only in terms of current residence, but also with respect to place of birth, urban southern Ontarians have for some time made up the large majority of the economic élite (Clement, 1978; Newman, 1981; Francis, 1986).

In general, then, economic power is heavily concentrated in the established urban locations of the nation. As noted earlier, these same locations are also the seats of political power and higher education. In combination, all these factors have promoted great inequalities between regions in Canadian society.

Gender inequality in Canada

In recent decades, gender has come to be seen as one of the major factors in the study of social inequality. Previously, gender differences in socioeconomic rank, power, and prestige were not given a great deal of attention by students of inequality. When these topics were discussed, the analysis tended to focus on traditional female roles in marriage and family life. Marriage, rather than

career, was the principal means of female social mobility, and a woman normally was assigned her social rank on the basis of her husband's command over resources, not her own.

The changing roles of women in modern society (see Chapter 7, Gender Relations) have done much to shift the focus towards women themselves in current research (Mackie, 1991; Wilson, 1991). The major change in women's roles in this century has been their influx into the labour force. In Canada, women made up over 45 percent of the paid workforce in 1996, compared to only 13 percent in 1901 (Statistics Canada, *1961 Census of Canada and 1971 Census of Canada, Historical Tables*; Statistics Canada, 1996, *The Labour Force: Annual Averages*). In 1980, for the first time in history, more than half of Canadian women were in the paid labour force. By 1996, this proportion had reached 57 percent (Creese and Beagan, 1999: 200). The great shift of women into the work world has provided society with a whole new pool of previously untapped talents and skills. However, the economic benefits gained by the average woman entering the workforce have often been limited. Female workers have consistently earned far less than male workers, even in advanced capitalist and socialist societies. In Canada, there has been a gradual improvement over the past few decades, but, by 1996, full-time working women still earned just over 73 percent of the male average (Statistics Canada, 1998, *Earnings of Women and Men 1996*).

Research also indicates that the lower socio-economic rank of women cannot be fully explained by their lesser training and experience. Canadian studies have shown that, when the greater training and experience of male workers is taken into account, women still make only 80 to 90 percent of what men make (Calzavara, 1993: 315–16). Data for the 1990s suggest that, among those under the age of 25 who have university degrees, there is a much smaller difference in the average wages or incomes of males and females; however, a clear female disadvantage is still evident among the older and less-educated age cohorts (Beauchesne, 1994; see also Statistics Canada, 1998, *Earnings of Women and Men 1996*). These income differences have continued, even though, for some time now, women's average educational attainment has been catching up with, and in recent year surpassing, that of men

In Canada, full-time working women in 1996 still earned just 73 percent of the male average.

(Guppy and Arai, 1993). It seems likely, then, that certain forms of gender discrimination, rather than differences in educational qualifications, are at the root of some of the income difference between men and women.

Some writers have suggested that female subordination in the system is so serious that the women's position is almost like that of a minority group, such as blacks or Native peoples. (We will discuss the feminization of poverty in Chapter 7, Gender Relations.) While there are problems with such a claim, some aspects of the women's situation do parallel that of minority groups. First, sex, like ethnicity or race, is an ascribed trait that affects opportunities and life chances. Second, just as minorities are sometimes negatively evaluated, both by others and by themselves, so too are women (Mackie, 1991: 26–29). In addition, women share with racial and ethnic minorities a high degree of exclusion from the economic élite. As Clement has argued, "[W]omen are probably the most under-represented social type in the economic élite" (Clement, 1990: 184; Fox, 1989). Such findings suggest that many women continue to be disadvantaged in our society.

Age and social inequality

The study of age and aging has been of increasing interest to sociologists in recent years (McPherson, 1990; Novak, 1997; see Chapter 9, Aging). Like sex or ethnicity, age is an ascribed attribute over which the individual has no control, but which has important implications for determining a person's rank in society.

Most research suggests that age has an up-and-down, or *curvilinear*, association with social inequality. In other words, as we move from the youngest to the oldest ends of the age spectrum, we generally find that people in the middle-age range enjoy the highest incomes and socioeconomic rank, with younger and older people ranking lower in most cases (Guppy et al., 1999: 248–250). For young people, this is often because their recent entry into the labour force means they begin at lower salary or wage levels in their occupations. For elderly people, the lower economic standing is largely the result of retirement from the labour force and having to live on reduced income from pensions and savings.

One obvious difference between young and old is that young people generally can hope to improve their position in society over time, as part of the normal process of joining the workforce and moving towards a future career. Most elderly people, however, must hope that their fixed incomes will not be eroded too severely over time by inflation and rising living costs.

This difference between young and old may explain why some researchers see the problems of the elderly as more serious, even though there is evidence that young people also face an uncertain economic future these days (Côté and Allahar, 1994). In fact, not all elderly Canadians live in impoverished circumstances. Although more than 40 percent of families headed by persons over age 65 were living below the official low-income line in 1969, by 1995 this figure had dropped to only about 11 percent (Guppy et al., 1999: 252). This trend indicates the success of government programs in alleviating the economic problems of Canada's elderly. Still, evidence shows that elderly women in Canada, especially those living alone, continue to endure economic difficulties (see also Chapter 7, Gender Relations). In 1995, for example, 51 percent of all elderly females who lived alone were below the low-income line (Guppy et al., 1993: 251). This finding illustrates how two distinct inequality variables—gender and age—can combine to produce more complicated and more acute patterns of inequality. It also reveals the important impact of age on a person's life circumstances, even in an advanced and affluent society.

Political power and social inequality

The final component to consider in Canada's system of social inequality is the political power hierarchy. We have saved this topic until the end because, in a sense, political power may be viewed as the ultimate manifestation of power and the ultimate determinant of structured inequality in society. In nominally democratic countries, the political structure, or *state*, is the official representative of the power of all citizens. Thus, in theory at least, the political structure can act as the key mechanism for shaping all the major forms of inequality.

The concept of the state includes numerous substructures: the political leadership and elected representatives, the courts and judiciary, the civil service, the police, the military, and so forth (see Grabb, 1997). Virtually all societies are organized around the principle that the state is the means for creating and implementing laws, and thus the sanctions and rights that define power differences in society.

The state can establish and maintain political power differences, but the state can affect the distribution of power in other realms, as well. The creation of economic power advantages for the propertied over the propertyless, through the legally recognized institution of private property, would be an illustration of how the political structure can be used to affect power differences outside the political sphere itself. Of course, political power also has the potential to remove or reduce power differences, through the creation of laws prohibiting race or sex discrimination in hiring practices, for example.

In these and other ways, position in the political hierarchy can be a source of power in itself and a potential means for establishing, enforcing, or altering power relations in other spheres. This is the basis for the argument that political power is a binding element, related to and interacting with all of the power sources that form the overall system. In addition, some observers see political power as the ultimate power source because, in a formal sense, those with power in other spheres must answer to those holding political power. Of course, other analysts have questioned whether the full authority of the state is really exercised when it confronts those in power in other areas, particularly the economic élite.

The state and the economic élite

We have noted that the state has the legally sanctioned power to control the actions of individuals and groups, even those who dominate the other institutions of society. In the economic sphere, for example, the government has acted against large corporations found guilty of price gouging, false advertising, environmental pollution, or making unsafe or defective products. Nevertheless, while we can think of specific instances in which political leaders have opposed the economic élite for the "common good" or the "public interest," it often appears that the state favours the economic élite and makes decisions on the basis of particular, rather than general, interests (Clement, 1988).

It is from this point of view that Porter once criticized Canada's political leadership. To him, the major political parties have long engaged in "brokerage politics," making policy decisions based on what will get them reelected rather than what is best for the nation (Porter, 1965: 373–77). This may mean advocating policies favourable to the powerful and to special interests, in exchange for the campaign funds and voting power these groups can provide.

What is the significance of this alleged tendency for the political structure to favour the interests of the powerful, particularly the economic élite? Most social scientists would reject the extreme view that the state is merely a tool in the hands of the economic élite, doing the bidding of big business at every turn. What seems to occur instead is that both state and economic leaders agree on the general goals and values that should guide the operation of society. Among these common goals are the need for political stability, economic development, and a continued promotion of capitalist expansion. State leaders accept the idea that the economic élite should make large profits. At the same time, however, the state must try to maintain social harmony and appear not to favour the economic élite too much, at the expense of other classes. Such

Hilary Weston, Lieutenant-Governor of Ontario, is the wife of Galen Weston, head of George Weston Ltd. Individuals who are nearer the top of the various power rankings are also likely to exercise above-average political power.

action would undermine the state's basis for popular support, perhaps leading to severe disruptions in both political stability and economic development (Fox and Ornstein, 1993; O'Connor, 1999).

Composition of the state élite

Our previous discussion suggests that state leaders and the economic élite have much in common, at least in regard to goals, interests, and values. Another way of assessing the links between élites is to examine the social origins of state leaders. We might expect a considerable overrepresentation of individuals from upper-class backgrounds in the Canadian state élite. Porter's early analysis in the 1950s and a subsequent study by Olsen using 1973 data did find that the upper class was

overrepresented compared to its proportion of the general population (Porter, 1965; Olsen, 1980). However, the level of upper-class representation declined during the period between the two studies. Furthermore, the majority (almost three-quarters) of the state élite in 1973 was from middle-class origins. While the working-class representation was low in both cases, these findings indicate that the state leadership is clearly open to those with non-élite origins. More recent evidence shows that, while numerous political leaders in Canada have served as directors of large businesses (and vice versa) over the years, these linkages are not nearly large enough to produce corporate domination of the government (Fox and Ornstein, 1993). This suggests that there is little direct dominance of the political leadership by those controlling wealth and property in Canada. Instead, the state and big business are two separate but compatible forces in our society.

Political power and the individual

To this point, we have discussed political power mainly at the élite level. However, in liberal democracies, even those dominated by élites, some power exists in the hands of the people. Voting, joining political parties and other voluntary associations, and, of course, running for election are some of the ways in which the individual can exercise political power. But what groups are most likely to use these means of political expression? In particular, which social strata are most likely to participate in the political structure?

Given the general pattern of social inequality suggested in this chapter, it may be no surprise that individuals who are nearer the top of the various power rankings are also likely to exercise above-average political power. Research has shown that Canadians from higher socioeconomic backgrounds are more likely to vote, join political organizations, and take an interest in politics (Grabb and Curtis, 1992; Chui et al., 1993; Curtis et al., 1999). Several studies have found that those with higher positions are more likely to run for public office. For example, people in upper-middle-class (professional and managerial) occupations made up roughly 20 percent of the labour force in the period between 1964 and 1985, but they accounted for over two-thirds of the federal election candidates and over 80 percent of the elected MPs in the same period

How Does Your Rank Affect You?

The importance of social inequality in sociology is apparent from the wide use of social inequality variables as explanatory factors in social research. Each of the eight power hierarchies discussed represents a distinct variety of structured inequality that can have consequences for many social phenomena. The literature that has developed around the effects of social inequality is massive. Here, we briefly examine some of the work that has been done, to illustrate the effects of social inequality on the lives of Canadians. We focus specifically on differences across socioeconomic groupings in life chances, lifestyles, values, and beliefs.

Life chances
Probably the most crucial consequence of social inequality concerns the life chances of people from different socioeconomic backgrounds. Generally, the term *life chances* refers to the ability to lead a healthy, happy, and prosperous existence. Studies show consistently that life chances decline as one moves down the socioeconomic ladder. As will be discussed in Chapter 15, Demography and Urbanization, lower-status individuals have shorter life expectancies and they are more susceptible to a broad spectrum of physical and mental health problems (National Council of Welfare, 1993; Health

Canada, 1999). The poorer strata also are more likely to suffer malnutrition, are less likely to use medical facilities and services, and experience poorer and more hazardous working conditions (Forcese, 1997). All of these elements, coupled with lower economic resources and fewer educational opportunities, lessen the quality of life in the lower strata and make the chances for a satisfying and rewarding existence less likely than they are for the higher strata.

Lifestyles
Social inequality also has a bearing on lifestyle. Differing economic resources, education levels, and life experiences lead to variations in a host of phenomena: consumption habits, manner of dress, speech patterns, and leisure activities, to name just a few. Generally, life in the lower strata is more restrictive than in the upper strata: less leisure time, less freedom of action, less flexibility in daily routine, and less variety in experiences and interests. The limited activities and experiences of working-class people are revealed in a number of ways. People from the lower strata are less likely to belong to clubs and organizations, do less reading, and participate less in community life than do other people (Eichar, 1989; Kohn et al., 1990; Chui et al., 1993; Curtis et al., 1999). Instead, home life tends to receive

greater emphasis. Nevertheless, even home activities often are disrupted by the need for working-class parents to work overtime or take part-time jobs to supplement incomes (Rinehart, 1996: 122).

Values and beliefs
Another important consequence of social inequality is the tendency for different values and beliefs to be generated within social strata. Some studies suggest that greater economic deprivation and occupational instability in the working class lead its members to place a high value on material success, good pay, and financial security (Form, 1985).

Other research indicates that differences in the nature of the jobs done by people from different classes can lead to important differences in values and beliefs. For example, studies in several countries suggest that, because members of the working class have little personal freedom at work or control over their job environment, they place a lower value on individual independence or "self-direction" than do people in middle-class occupations. It appears that working-class parents are, in turn, more likely than middle-class parents to teach their children such values as obedience and conformity, rather than self-direction or independence (Kohn et al., 1990; see also Baer et al., 1996).

(Guppy et al., 1988). Individuals who are more centrally located in terms of socioeconomic status, ethnicity, and region are also more likely to express a feeling of personal political power and efficacy (Grabb, 1988; Baer et al., 1990).

In various ways, then, the political power structure is closely bound up with the more general configuration of social inequality in Canada. At the élite level, and for the whole range of individual Canadians, political power is associated with the other sources of power that determine the distribution of wealth, prestige, and other resources in this country. Those who tend to dominate the other status hierarchies—especially the economically privileged, but also men, central Canadians, and those of British background—tend as well to hold sway in the political sphere (Ogmundson and McLaughlin, 1992; Nakhaie, 1997). Although there are exceptions, the consistency in this pattern is a striking feature of social inequality in Canadian society.

Summary

This chapter has introduced you to the topic of social inequality in Canadian society. We looked at basic concepts and definitions and discussed the major theories advanced to explain the process of social inequality in modern societies. We proposed eight principal components to consider when examining Canada's system of inequality: wealth (including income and property),occupation, education, race or ethnicity, region or rural/urban location, gender, age, and political status. Each of these is the basis for a status hierarchy and corresponding power ranking, reflecting the distribution of resources and privileges in the population.

Our analysis indicates some fairly close linkages among the eight status hierarchies, with high status on one hierarchy often associated with high status on the others. Certain rankings seem to have a relatively greater influence. In particular, power deriving from wealth and property tends to have the greatest impact on the overall system of social inequality. The group that dominates in this hierarchy, the economic élite, is the single most powerful entity in the structure. Along with the political leadership, or state élite, they make most of the major decisions affecting the operation of the country, the distribution of wealth and resources, and the extent of inequality experienced by other Canadians.

And what can we say about the future of social inequality in Canada? Is it possible to predict whether the current patterns will continue as they are, or change in dramatic ways as we enter the new millennium? Different researchers are bound to offer different answers to such questions. However, the evidence we have reviewed in this chapter indicates that social inequality will remain a significant problem in our society for many years to come. Of course, there is reason to be optimistic that there will be some decline in the amount of inequality on certain dimensions. For example, the gradual increases in women's occupation, income, and especially education levels that we have seen in recent decades seem likely to be sustained in the future. At the same time, though, the evidence offers little basis for expecting much improvement in other areas. This is illustrated by the absence of any real change in the unequal distribution of income and wealth to the rich and the poor in Canada over the last half-century or more, and by the increasing concentration of ownership among large-scale business enterprises in this same period. Taken together, these patterns suggest that Canada, like other capitalist societies, will continue to be a country in which major inequalities exist between the powerful and the powerless, or the haves and the have-nots. These are much the same inequalities that sociologists have been studying since the time of Marx and Weber, and they seem destined to be subjects of concern to us for the foreseeable future.

QUESTIONS FOR REVIEW AND CRITICAL THINKING

1.   Structural functionalists argue that social inequality, or what they usually refer to as social "stratification," is necessary to motivate the best or most qualified individuals to seek the most important positions in society. What does this view imply about the motivations or abilities of those individuals and groups that do not attain high positions? How would they respond to this argument?

2.   Some have said that Marx's theory of classes and revolution is not relevant to modern societies such as Canada. Can you think of some ways in which this statement is true and some in which it is false? How might recent events in the former Soviet Union, China, and elsewhere influence your response?

3.   You have learned in this chapter that the structure of inequality in Canada has remained fairly constant over the years, with both rich and poor maintaining their relative proportions within the total population. What main proposals or programs do you believe could be instituted to eliminate or decrease persistent inequality in Canada?

4.   Sociologists have always debated the precise meaning of the concept of social class. Less often do they consider what people in general think about social class. What important characteristics and behaviours, in your opinion, distinguish social classes? Is there one key criterion or are there many? In a mini-research project, ask a sample of your friends or fellow students what social class means to them. See if there are any differences of opinion among them. For example, do men and women give different responses? Older and younger people? Poorer and richer people?

5.   How hard is it to "get ahead" in Canadian society? What are some of the principal barriers to social mobility in Canada? How might these be removed?

KEY TERMS

achieved status, p. 137

ascribed status, p. 137

bourgeoisie, p. 140

class, p. 138

class for itself, p. 140

class in itself, p. 140

class, status group, party, p. 143

horizontal mobility, p. 137

institutionalized power, p. 136

intergenerational mobility, p. 137

intragenerational mobility, p. 137

power, p. 136

proletariat, p. 140

social class, p. 138

social differentiation, p. 135

social inequality, p. 135

status, p. 136

status consistency, p. 136

status hierarchy, p. 136

status inconsistency, p. 136

status set, p. 136

stratum, p. 136

vertical mobility, p. 137

SUGGESTED READINGS

Allahar, Anton, and James Cote

1998   *Richer and Poorer: The Structure of Inequality in Canada*. Toronto: James Lorimer.

The authors use a framework that centres on the role of dominant ideology to examine social inequality in Canada, with a special focus on class, gender, age, and race/ethnicity.

Curtis, James, Edward Grabb, and Neil Guppy (eds.)

1999   *Social Inequality in Canada: Patterns, Problems, and Policies*. (3rd ed.) Scarborough, Ont.: Prentice Hall Allyn and Bacon Canada, Inc.

This book, a collection of articles dealing with all the major social hierarchies in Canada, also considers some of the important consequences of social inequality for people, as well as policies that could be implemented to alleviate problems of inequality.

Grabb, Edward G.

1997   *Theories of Social Inequality: Classical and Contemporary Perspectives*. (3rd ed.) Toronto: Harcourt Brace Canada.

This book reviews and evaluates the major perspectives on social inequality that have emerged from classical and contemporary social theory.

Krahn, Harvey, and Graham Lowe

1998   *Work, Industry, and Canadian Society*. (3rd ed.) Toronto: Nelson.

This book reviews a range of sociological issues pertaining to the study of work and industry in Canada, including labour force trends, women's employment, the organization of work, and questions of power and control at work.

WEB SITES

http://www.hewett.norfolk.sch.uk/curric/soc/marx/marx1.htm
The Karl Marx Page
Read more about the man and his work at this site.

http://www.achilles.net/~council/facts.html
The Canadian Council on Social Development
This site provides a wealth of statistical and other data on income inequality, poverty, and welfare in Canada.

Gender Relations

Lesley D. Harman

Introduction

Try to imagine yourself without your body. If you find this difficult, it is because so much of your sense of self comes from your physical presence. Next, try to imagine yourself having been born a member of the other sex. What would you look like? How would you dress? How would you act? How would your opportunities and life chances be different? The difficulty you experience in undertaking these exercises speaks to the social significance of gender.

People experience gender as a condition that partly determines their opportunities and life chances, happiness and sadness, definitions of success and failure. It influences many actions, decisions, and choices made on any given day: what to wear, what to eat, how to interact with others. In fact, most behaviour is greatly affected by what is "gender appropriate." Moreover, because gender norms are so pervasive, they are often invisible. Men rarely question why they do not wear dresses; women are often unaware of why it is that they

avoid walking alone at night. Most people rarely think about the way they see themselves during the countless times they look in the mirror. If opportunities are offered or held back because of their maleness or femaleness, individuals may accept this state of affairs as "the way it is" rather than consider it unjust.

Yet it is the very pervasiveness of gender norms that makes them of interest to the sociologist. Why is it so important whether people are female or male? How are life experiences influenced? What are some ways in which these arrangements could be changed? These are just a few of the questions that will be addressed in this chapter.

We shall begin with a discussion of the gendered order and the gendered identity, two levels of analysis that can be applied to the study of gender. Then, we shall define the term gender, and examine the dominant theoretical perspectives applied to its study. That is followed by a consideration of the nature and implications of several prevalent myths of biological determinism, and a discussion of their implications. We shall then look at the ways in which language serves to support an ideology of gender inequality. The process of gender socialization will also be discussed, along with substantive areas concerning the body and sexuality, work and reproduction, health and aging, the feminization of poverty, and gender and deviance.

Gendered order and gendered identity

As with other social phenomena, gender can be analyzed at different levels. At the macro level, we speak of the gendered order; at the micro level, we speak of the gendered identity.

The **gendered order** refers to the different treatment individuals are accorded on the basis of gender. This usually takes the form of opportunities offered or opportunities blocked. It is supported by a fairly rigid set of **gender norms**, an integral part of most cultures, specifying appropriate behaviours for males and females, including a heterosexual assumption that sex between males and females is the only kind acceptable. The gendered order is also supported by an **ideology of gender inequality**. In this belief system, it is generally understood that males are superior to females. Men are more entitled to make decisions, to control resources, and to occupy positions of authority. Although this ideology has been challenged in recent years, particularly through the consciousness-raising of the women's movement, it continues to exert great influence in Canada and elsewhere.

At the micro level of analysis, sociologists are concerned with how the gendered order is transmitted to and internalized by individual members of society. The **gendered identity** refers to the self as it develops in accordance with an individual's gender and the social definitions of that gender. **Gender socialization** is the process of acquiring a gendered identity, and begins at birth. Almost all infants are born either male or female (with a few exceptions mentioned later), but through the process of socialization they become masculine or feminine. Through taking on the socially appropriate gender roles, children become integral parts of the larger gendered order. This often occurs in so unconscious a fashion that people may be blinded to its existence. It can be said, then, that the gendered order is socially reproduced through the process of gender socialization.

The two levels of analysis, order and identity, are intimately linked. Structures are reproduced through identities; identities tend to accept structures more or less uncritically. Yet it is clear that neither the gendered order nor the gendered identity are "natural" phenomena in the sense of being universal and immutable. Rather, they are cultural, and hence socially constructed. And the relevance for sociology is that anything that is socially constructed may be reconstructed. In other words, the existing set of relations can be changed.

Defining gender

Sex and *gender* are terms that are often confused, but for sociologists they have distinct meanings and are used to distinguish between biological and social categories. **Sex** is a biological category. With very few exceptions, humans are born decidedly male or female. Sex refers to physiological differences, the most pronounced of which involve hormones, the reproductive organs, and body size.

Males are born with reproductive organs (penis, testes) that enable them to impregnate females. Males also have the capacity to develop greater muscle mass and strength than females. Females are born with reproductive organs (ovaries, uterus, vagina, and latent mammary glands) that enable them to bear and nourish babies. They live longer than males and have the capacity to withstand greater pain and stress (Blum, 1997).

Gender is a social category, referring to the social expectations that are developed and placed upon individuals on the basis of their biological sex. Different gender roles exist for males and females. They are socially created and then learned; people are not born with them. In taking on these roles individuals are expected to become "masculine" or "feminine" and to act in a "masculine" or "feminine" way.

Because it is culturally specific, gender will vary in time and space. In our culture, masculinity entails a set of expectations that, in Canada, often includes dominance, aggression, rationality, physicality, and strength. Femininity entails a set of expectations that often includes submission, passivity, intuition,

Gender roles are socially created and then learned; people are not born with them.

emotionality, and weakness. While these definitions are slowly changing, they remain fairly strong and distinct.

The **nature/culture dualism** (recall Chapter 4, Socialization) is often used in mythology and cultural archetypes, such as recurring images in legends and fairy tales, to describe the dichotomy between femininity and masculinity. Nature is associated with the feminine—earth, reproduction, the cycles of life, mystery, sexuality. *Culture* is associated with the masculine—science, domination, control, reason. Western imagery is full of this dichotomization. *Cinderella*, the classic fairy tale, shows Cinderella as living close to nature and waiting to be rescued by her Prince Charming, the epitome of patriarchal culture. *My Fair Lady* celebrates the stories of the "uncultured" woman who is rescued and transformed by the "cultured" man.

Others argue that gender can be a blend of traits, and that acquiring a gendered identity means finding a place somewhere along the continuum between various "masculinities" and "femininities." Bem (1974) argued that individuals may be classified as feminine, masculine, androgynous (a blend of feminine and masculine), or undifferentiated

(neither feminine nor masculine). Among the Zuni, gender is seen as an individual trait that one develops during one's life, and until age 6 children are referred to as "child" rather than "girl" or "boy." *Berdaches*, then, are those who continue to live, work, and dress as members of the opposite sex without stigma (Roscoe, 1991). These different views demonstrate how we are in a time of significant social reorganization. But however one classifies gender, one thing is clear: there is a distinct differential valuation of the masculine and the feminine traits within patriarchy, in which masculine traits are more highly valued and rewarded in males than they are in females. This translates to a decided preference for male offspring globally, resulting in dramatic demographic trends in societies such as China in which fertility is restricted (see insert on "Missing Women").

What this means is that women are perceived as dangerous, often evil, for their sexuality and closeness to the mysteries of reproduction. Men are perceived as the ones whose role it is to control and transform women. Such ideas are so deeply embedded in our culture as to often provide an unrecognized legitimation for the subordination of

Missing Women

In most Western countries, there are more males than females born, perhaps 105 males to 100 females. By age 25 or so, the numbers even out and from then on there are more women than men, especially at older ages. Some of these ideas will be expanded in the Aging and Demography/Urbanization chapters. Our point here is discrimination against women. In China, for example, the 1990 census found 93.8 females for every 100 males, down from a previous census. The figures for other Asian countries are similar, from India to Bangladesh, from Nepal to Turkey, and other societies that still nurture a traditional preference for sons.

Up to 60 000 000 females may be missing. "Millions of women have died because they're women," said Sharon Capeling-Alakija, director of the United Nations Development Fund for Women, adding that mothers as well as fathers are responsible (Kristoff, 1991). Despite governmental edicts against the practices, ultrasounds are routinely used to determine the sex of the foetus, with girls frequently aborted. Girls born may be abandoned or given less care than boys. Pro-life groups would be appalled. How could pro-choice groups respond?

Source: *Adapted from Nicholas D. Kristof, 1991. "Stark data on women: 100 million are missing." New York Times, November 5, 1991, B5-9.*

women and the stigmatization of all that is feminine within patriarchy.

Stereotypes are changing, although slowly. In 1976, David and Brannon suggested that there were four themes that came together in the traditional Western stereotype of masculinity: "no sissy stuff" (repulsion toward anything "feminine"); "the big wheel" (the premium placed on material success and power); "the sturdy oak" (the appearance of confidence, strength, and toughness); and "give 'em hell" (the celebration of violence). They came together in the theme of the "warrior." Pleck (1981) argued that the "new" male role model included economic achievement, intellectual and interpersonal skills, heterosexual gentleness, and intimacy. What does it mean to be a man today? In 1993, Kaufman maintained that masculinity is a paradox of pain and power. Men enjoy the power that their dominant social position gives them, but experience pain as they are not permitted to fully evolve as human beings with emotional lives. Boys growing up in contemporary society look around and see that they will have to develop a coat of armour to "be a man," and that sensitivity is a sign of weakness.

Themes concerning "femininity" have tended to focus on women's bodies and the social roles they engender, particularly sexuality and motherhood.

The madonna/whore dichotomy speaks to the contradictory celebration of motherhood as "good" and the moral prohibition against women's non-procreative sexuality as evil. The good-girl/bad-girl split results. Wolf (1997) argued that for young girls growing up in contemporary society, this sends out conflicting messages: in a society that celebrates women's beauty and rewards women for being attractive, the very same traits are seen as evidence of immorality.

It can be argued that sex is an ascribed characteristic while gender is an *achieved* characteristic, terms you saw in the last chapter, Social Stratification. Such an argument suggests that people are born either male or female, but they become masculine or feminine. The process of becoming gendered is one that may be more or less successful, depending on a number of factors including role models, sanctions, and opportunities to deviate from gender norms. Yet the notion that gender is achieved also suggests that there is some degree of freedom of choice about one's gender. From a sociological perspective, it should become clear in the pages that follow that the power of the gendered order to influence and shape identity is so great as to suggest, however, that gender may also be seen as ascribed or assigned by society.

Theoretical Perspectives on Gender

A functionalist perspective

Functionalists generally take the biological differences between the sexes as evidence that males and females are suited for different types of work. Indeed some, fewer today than previously, see role differentiation between males and females as necessary and positive, and use biological differences to justify what is called the *gendered division of labour*. Such functionalist thought often looks to "the family" as the basic functioning unit of society (Parsons and Bales, 1955). The Parsonian family followed the "head-complement" nuclear family arrangement (see the discussion in Chapter 10, Families) in which the father (the patriarch) is the dominant figure and the decision-maker. The mother in this arrangement is submissive and the conflict mediator.

For Parsons and Bales, this nuclear family arrangement reflected an essential division of labour conforming to broader dimensions of social life. The **instrumental dimension** includes tasks of the **public realm**—the realm of paid labour and commerce, which they argued is the preserve of men. Instrumentality includes rationality, aggressiveness, strength, and domination. Males are socialized within the family into instrumental roles, making them most suited for the competitive world of the workplace when they become adults. The instrumental "superior" in the family (the father) serves as the breadwinner and protector of the family in the public realm. The **expressive dimension** consists of the traits necessary for the demands of the **private realm**—the realm of unpaid domestic labour and biological reproduction—and is the preserve of women. Females are socialized within the family into expressive roles, making them most suited for the nurturing demands of the domestic sphere when they become adults. Expressivity includes emotionality, and passivity, even weakness. The expressive "superior" of the family (the mother) serves as the unpaid homemaker, nurturer, and caregiver in the private realm. She is expected to give birth and then to care for the needs of the offspring, as well as those of the instrumental superior.

The gendered division of labour as portrayed by Parsons and Bales further assumed that males and females are naturally suited for their respective spheres, and that the distinctiveness of these spheres is both natural and necessary. Instrumental and expressive roles are seen to be complementary, that is, necessary to each other, as well as being necessary to the continued functioning and survival of society. Arguments concerning complementary roles also tend to overlook the fact that these roles are unequal. Within the typical Parsonian family, the male has financial autonomy and decision-making power. He has a position in the public realm that gives him access to status and resources unavailable to a woman. The female, on the other hand, is isolated in the home, frequently devalued in her role as homemaker, and dependent both emotionally and financially on the male breadwinner. This state of affairs may indeed be complementary, but it certainly gives an advantage to males, to the systematic disadvantage of females. Indeed, a major criticism of the functionalist view is that it justifies an ideology of gender inequality.

This functionalist view of the gendered division of labour has been criticized on many grounds. First, in today's society it is simply not representative of the way that most people live. Whether out of choice or necessity, most Canadians find other living arrangements more suitable. These alternatives challenge the assumptions that households must include both a father and a mother and their biological offspring, and that the division of labour should be such that women work in the home while men work outside of the home. In 1996, 15 percent of Canadian households were lone-parent households, 83 percent of these headed by females, and over half of married women worked outside of the home for pay (*Canadian Social Trends*, 1999). Increasingly, same-sex couples are raising children. Clearly, contemporary trends do not bear out the picture painted by Parsons and Bales in the 1950s.

Nevertheless, the ideology represented by the functionalist perspective continues to have an impact. In the mass media, education, religion, law, and policy, there is a tendency for women to be portrayed in less instrumental roles, and for men rarely to be portrayed in expressive roles. The view that these roles are somehow natural dies hard, although, as we shall see, there is little evidence for such a claim.

The symbolic interactionist perspective

The fundamental premise of symbolic interactionism is that reality is socially constructed, and that the social world is in a constant state of negotiation and renegotiation. Unlike functionalists, symbolic interactionists see nothing natural or deterministic about the relationship between sex and gender. Rather, they focus on the ways in which masculinity and femininity are socially constructed (Mackie, 1991). For symbolic interactionists, the process of becoming gendered is a social one that involves the development of a gendered identity. The impact of gender socialization, then, is seen as great indeed.

As evidence for the view that sex and gender need not necessarily be related in a deterministic and immutable way, symbolic interactionists often cite cases in which the acquisition of a gendered identity is not as straightforward as is usually the case. For example, in certain rare instances, male infants are born apparently without an apparent penis and testes. Assumed to be girls, they are raised as such. When a penis later appears and they discover that their genitalia are in fact those of males, gender confusion often results (Blum, 1997). Transsexuals provide another example. Here individuals find themselves physically male or female, but socially define themselves as the other sex. Thus their sense of self as a gendered identity is different from their biological sex. People who think of themselves as of one gender, but feel biologically trapped in bodies of the other, may even seek the radical measure of sex-change operations. (See the boxed insert on "Gender Confusion".)

"Gender blenders" (Devor, 1989) are individuals who are born anatomically female but who are routinely mistaken for men. Devor reported that for the women she studied, rather than causing a sense of confusion, being mistaken for men leads to certain revelations about gender relations. These women realize that being mistaken for a male can

"Gender Confusion": The Case of Transsexuals

In the 1950s the world was shocked by Christine Jorgensen's sex-change operation in Denmark. The reaction was not much lessened a generation later when Richard Raskind, once captain of the Yale tennis team, army officer, and father, underwent similar surgery and became Renée Richards, professional tennis player and coach of Martina Navratilova.

For men—and many more men undergo this operation than women—the process involves electrolysis, estrogen therapy, the removal of male sexual parts, and sometimes the construction of a vagina; for women it involves a hysterectomy, breast removal, and additional hormones, and, less frequently, the creation of a penis is attempted.

The numbers are not large, but they do relate to what we have been discussing—that gender is a socially constructed phenomenon. Transsexuals are people whose biological sex is inconsistent with their gendered identity. Anatomically they are one sex, but they feel like and want to be defined as a member of the other sex. Needless to say, transsexuals can never create children, but in virtually all other ways they seek to adopt a new sexual identity. It is much more than transvestism, the wearing of clothes of members of the other biological sex. Transsexuals identify with members of the opposite sex so much that they are willing to endure physically and socially painful operations to become members of the other sex.

Why do more men than women undergo this process? Mackie (1987) speculated that sexism is one answer. Men acting in a feminine manner in our society—in their dress, for example—are less tolerated than women who act in a masculine manner. Men beyond a certain age cannot live together without questions being asked. Thus some of the men undergo surgery to avoid the stigma of homosexuality.

Source: *Adapted from Marlene Mackie, 1987.* Constructing Women and Men: Gender Socialization. *Toronto: Holt, Rinehart and Winston (pp. 12 ff.).*

Gender Blending

Sociologist Holly Devor studied fifteen women whom she called "gender blenders": women whose physical appearance caused them to routinely be mistaken for men. The life of a gender blender reveals surprising pleasure and liberation from the constraints of traditional "femininity."

The gender blending females in this study learned well the tenets of the patriarchal gender schema, which dominates North American society. They learned that their female sex was supposed to be the irrefutable fact that made them into women and that, as women, they were supposed to behave in a feminine fashion. They also learned, early in their lives, that femininity was patriarchy's way of marking a portion of the population for a secondary status in the service of men.

At the same time as they were learning that femaleness was a stigmatized condition in their society, they were also learning to be proficient at, and take pleasure in, the ways of masculinity. By accident, they discovered that if, as adults, they practised the degree of masculinity to which they had become accustomed as youngsters, they could neutralize some of the stigma of their femaleness as well as enjoy some of the privileges usually reserved for men.

This realization served to reinforce their tendency to masculinity in three ways. Firstly, their masculinity was an accustomed stance that had been with them since their childhoods. They had little desire to change their habits and were thus pleased to find reasons to support their continuance of that behaviour. Secondly, the contrast between their status as women, on the one hand, and the freedom and respectableness they acquired when mistaken for men, on the other, only confirmed and solidified their awareness of the stigmatized condition of womanhood. Their sense of femininity as a contaminant to be avoided was thus enhanced. Thirdly, they simply found joy in the sense of power that walking the streets with the freedom of men imparted to them. That sense of freedom of movement and security of person, on an everyday individual basis, gave them a feeling of exhilaration unmatched in their experience of femininity. They learned that, as men, they were free to do the things they enjoyed most, where they wanted to, and when they wanted to. As women, they felt humiliated, constrained, and vulnerable to sexual attack and violation. Their choice was to buy their public dignity and freedom at the price of their womanhood.

Source: Holly Devor, 1989. Gender Blending: Confronting the Limits of Duality. Bloomington, IN: Indiana University Press (p. 145).

have its advantages. It exempts them from the subordinate treatment given to the "feminine" women they see all around them. "They learned that, as, they were free to do the things they enjoyed most, where they wanted to, and when they wanted to. As women, they felt humiliated, constrained, and vulnerable to sexual attack and violation" (Devor, 1989: 145). (See the boxed insert on "Gender Blending.")

An either/or duality between masculinity and femininity is widely accepted in Canadian society as normal and natural. However, it is becoming increasingly clear that socialization into rigid roles is often neither consistent nor enduring and that a blending of the two roles is common. Nowhere is this issue more evident than in the case of homosexual behaviour. It is now estimated that up to 15 percent of the population may reject exclusive heterosexuality, instead engaging in same-sex relationships (homosexuality) or in both homosexual and heterosexual relationships (bisexuality). For these individuals, the social sanctions meted out may be more than outweighed by the new-found freedom of sexual expression. Indeed, the challenge posed by gays and lesbians to the gendered order and its **heterosexual assumption**, that the only natural and appropriate sexual activity is heterosexual, is a profound example of the social construction of gender.

The greatest contribution of the symbolic interactionist perspective to the study of gender is that it recognizes that the process of becoming gendered is a social one, not a natural one. For symbolic interactionists, what can be negotiated can also be renegotiated. This view provides the possibility that the existing gendered order can change, just as gendered identities can be shaped in altogether different ways.

A Marxist conflict perspective

Not surprisingly, most Marxist theorists see gender as a source of social inequality, but they have been unwilling, for the most part, to relinquish the view that social class is the dominant cause of oppression in capitalist society. Patriarchy, or the system of male dominance, is seen to be a product of capitalism, and hence to play a secondary role. The oppression of women, then, is only one manifestation of the injustice of a class-based society.

In his writings, Marx tended to take a position very similar to that of the functionalists on the question of the gendered division of labour. Like functionalists, Marx saw biology as destiny and wrote of women "primarily as mothers, house-keepers, and members of the weaker sex" (MacKinnon, 1989: 13). MacKinnon (1989: 256) went so far as to claim that "no distinction exists between these views of Marx and those of contemporary 'pro-family' conservatives." For the most part, Marx's writings on work in capitalist society were exclusively about men.

Engels's much discussed *The Origin of the Family, Private Property, and the State* (1972 [1884]) did give an account of the subjugation of women, arguing that it had its origins with the introduction of private property. With private property came the nuclear family, with men as breadwinners and property owners and women as propertyless reproducers. Engels likened women in the family to the working class, in their economic oppression, and men in the family to the capitalist class.

The historical accuracy of Engels's theory has been questioned (MacKinnon, 1989). His work has also been criticized for its functionalist presupposition that the original gendered division of labour had its roots in the division of labour in heterosexual sexual intercourse (men and women performing different roles), implying a universality and permanence to these relations—in other words, that they cannot be changed. Thus, for the most part, it is left up to more recent feminist theories to provide a systematic critique of the nature of patriarchy in capitalist society.

Feminist perspectives

Feminist perspectives are widely misunderstood. There are in fact many feminisms, and sociologists calling themselves feminists do not always agree. Most feminist perspectives do agree, however, that Canada is a patriarchal society and that gender relations are the dominant tool for the oppression of women. **Patriarchy** is the system of masculine dominance through which masculine traits are privileged and males are systematically accorded greater access to resources while women are systematically oppressed.

Maternal feminism was a movement that took hold in Canada toward the end of the last century. Maternal feminists, such as Nellie McClung and Emily Murphy, held that women's real strength lay in their reproductive capacities. Women's roles as wives and mothers were seen, as in the functionalist perspective, as their true calling and source of status. Efforts to dilute women's maternal role, through the limitation of biological reproduction and work outside of the home, were regarded as threats to male power. Such a view is not widely shared by feminists today, since it is precisely the rigid equation between femaleness and reproduction that is seen to be oppressive.

Liberal feminism takes the view that structural inequality between women and men is the consequence of a lack of equality of opportunities, rights, and education. Liberal feminists tend not to question inequality in society generally, only women's place in existing unequal social structures. They hold that this inequality can be eradicated through the creation of laws and social policies that will alter power relationships. For example, liberal feminists argue that governmental provision of universal daycare would free women from the demands of childcare and allow them to enter the paid workforce. Liberal feminists also argue that legislation calling for "equal pay for work of equal value" would be effective in eliminating structural inequality in the workforce, so that women and men would be equitably paid for their work outside the home. A major criticism levelled against liberal feminism, however, is that it does not recognize that structural inequalities are rooted in deeper material (capitalist) and ideological (patriarchal) relations, which must be challenged and overcome before true equality between the sexes can be achieved. Governments cannot change these relations so easily.

Socialist feminism seeks to meld Marxism and feminism. Those taking this perspective see the roots of gender inequality in the combined oppressiveness of capitalism and patriarchy. Socialist feminists argue that capitalism produces isolating and alienating domestic roles for women in which they occupy a low status and are systematically devalued. It is only through a direct challenge to capitalism that the roots of patriarchy can be destroyed. According to this view, "Oppressed women must unite with oppressed men to fight against their common enemy—the powers of capitalism" (Kourany, Sterba, and Tong, 1999: 413). Some authors (MacKinnon, 1989) have pointed out that this perspective is, in fact, an "unhappy marriage" between two incompatible views. As we have seen in the discussion of the Marxist perspective, there is a fundamental antagonism surrounding issues of class and gender between Marxists and feminists. This antagonism is not resolved but rather held in tenuous balance by those who call themselves socialist feminists.

Radical feminism is a perspective that sees women's oppression as fundamentally rooted in the system of patriarchy. The approach calls for equality between the sexes through the abolition of male supremacy. Radical feminism has been responsible for raising consciousness and inspiring changes in a variety of areas aimed at reducing the oppression of women. For example, its recognition that violence against women is fundamentally unacceptable has moved Canadian society from one in which the problem of wife battering was laughed out of the House of Commons in the early 1980s to a quite different climate, in which significant government funding has been directed towards education and change in the area of family violence. Awareness that women's voices have been systematically silenced in culture, education, and politics has led to efforts to open up new avenues for expression including women's culture, women's language, women's literature, women's music, and women's "ways of knowing." Some radical feminists argue for the end of women's reproductive role, for it is seen as the most widespread source of oppression. The search for alternative reproductive technologies, such as *in vitro* fertilization, may also be seen as an avenue for the permanent liberation of women from the masculine domination of their bodies. Others in this category advocate "separatism"—that is, the establishment of separate spheres for women and men.

Generally speaking, the different feminist perspectives address to varying degrees the main sources of female oppression in society, and come to very different conclusions about how gender inequality can be resolved. They all share, however, a recognition that it is in the areas of biological reproduction and paid labour that the main problems, and their solutions, seem to lie.

Nature versus Nurture: Myths of Biological Determinism

The nature/nurture debate, which you saw in Chapter 4, Socialization, is at the root of much of the current confusion and debate over the question of sex and gender. Biological determinism suggests that individual potential is patterned before birth by ascribed hereditary factors, as found in genetic makeup. When applied to the question of gender relations, this appears as the highly controversial "sex is destiny" argument: social roles and gender are predetermined by biological sex.

But to arrive at such views, people must take a cultural product and treat it as if it were "natural"—from nature. The is called the **naturalization of history**. Some myths reflecting this tendency include "It is natural for boys to be strong and girls to be weak"; "It is not natural for boys to cry"; "It is not natural for women to have body hair"; "It is not natural for men to stay home with children while women work outside of the home"; etc.

A frequent implication of biological determinism is that most highly valued social roles in the public domain are seen to be natural for men because they require "masculine" traits, such as rationality, for their successful performance. Women, on the other hand, are encouraged to be

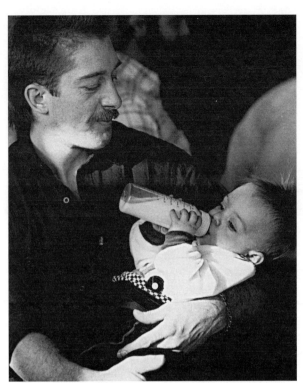

Biological determinism applied to gender relations is seen increasingly as myth.

more emotional than men, which in turn may lead to expectations that they are less capable of rational thought and decision-making. Systematically devalued roles, such as caregiving and unpaid domestic labour, are then seen to be natural for women because they require "feminine" traits, such as nurturing, for their successful performance.

The biological determinist argument is fundamental to the functionalist perspective and to most conservative arguments against changes aimed at greater gender equality. It can serve as the basis for discrimination and can inhibit social change, as can the "nature" (as opposed to nurture) position in general. As one might imagine, researchers have devoted a great deal of effort to determining the validity of this view. The basic issue is the extent to which social traits can be traced to biological sex, if at all. Some questions that researchers have pursued include "Are males superior at spatial abilities?"; "Are males better than females at math?"; "Are males more aggressive than females?"; "Are

females adversely affected by hormonal shifts?"; and "Do females have better verbal abilities than males?" Caplan and Caplan point out that such research is inherently biased, simply by the way that the questions are put. As they note, "The answers we get always depend partly on the way we ask the questions" (1999: 2). Such research is based on two essentially flawed assumptions: "1. that if we find a 'sex difference' in some ability or kind of behavior, that means that all males do a particular thing and all females do some quite different thing (e.g., all males are aggressive and all females are passive and peace-loving)" and "2. that sex differences are biologically based and, therefore, inevitable and unchangeable" (1999: 3) The former would mean that all boys do better than all girls at math, the latter that girls' worsening performance in math relative to boys around grade eight or so is a biological and not a cultural phenomenon. The Caplans would reject each argument.

In seeking answers to such questions, researchers in the 1970s tended to study very young children because they are not very far along in the socialization process, and thus it is assumed that any sexual differences uncovered should be due more to biology than to culture. The conclusions of this research indicated that while there are certainly physical and hormonal differences between girls and boys, there is no evidence to suggest that these differences lead to either the "natural" complementarity of females and males or the "natural" superiority of males over females. The Caplans also pointed out an interesting observation about published research findings; that research on sex differences that finds no difference is less likely to be published than research that supports prevailing cultural beliefs (1999).

Probably the most compelling question of innate sex differences concerns the belief that males are more aggressive than females. This has variously been attributed to the amount of testosterone in the male body, the greater capacity of males to develop strength, and the persistent belief that males have a greater sex drive than females.

This highly controversial issue is made more complex by difficulties in defining and measuring aggression, particularly among infants. The interpretation of what is an aggressive act is clearly influenced by cultural definitions of passivity and aggression, which may interact with gender. Condry and Condry (1976), in a classic study, showed a videotape of a baby responding to a jack-in-the-box to female and male college students. The sequence of the baby's response involved being startled, then agitated, and finally starting to cry. The observers who were told that the baby was a boy described it as angry, while those who were told that it was a girl described it as frightened. The authors suggested that such attributions of sex differences tend to be "in the eye of the beholder."

Other researchers have tended to focus on the "activity level" of infants in order to establish innate tendencies towards aggression, and have repeatedly found no sex differences. As children learn and are exposed to role models, their behaviour comes to conform more and more with societal expectations. That is, under the influence of socialization practices, boys become more aggressive and girls less so. Other researchers who claim that the higher rate of adult male participation in violent crimes indicates greater aggression overlook distinctly sociological reasons for this, such as socialization and the gendered division of labour (Blum, 1997). It has also been pointed out that the assumption that there is a causal relationship between hormones and behaviour is flawed, because research has shown that in fact behaviour can influence hormones, in both women and men (Caplan and Caplan, 1999.)

Are male and female brains organized differently? There has been much debate over the question of brain lateralization, or the belief that the two hemispheres of the brain are responsible for different functions. The left hemisphere is generally thought to be responsible for speech, while the right hemisphere is thought to be responsible for visual perception. Believing that males and females perform these functions at different levels of ability because of biological causes, some scientists have attempted to demonstrate that male and female brains are actually differently organized, and more specifically that females are left-brain dominant, males right-brain dominant.

The research findings have been inconsistent, and demonstrate little more than that the current understanding of the human brain by science is still incomplete. However, it is interesting to note that, in addition to the aspects of brain lateralization mentioned above, "The left hemisphere, as well as

being verbal, has also been characterized as intellectual, analytic, and businesslike, while the right hemisphere has been characterized as spontaneous, intuitive, and experiential, as well as spatially skilled" (Frieze, Parsons, Johnson, Rubble, and Zellman, 1978: 93). To find that females are left-brain dominant and males are right-brain dominant, then, would not be in the interest of those who seek to maintain current gender stereotypes that support male superiority in all traits that are considered highly valued. Indeed, it would suggest precisely the opposite: that females would be biologically superior in terms of "masculine" traits, while males would be biologically superior in terms of "feminine" traits (Renzetti and Curran, 1992).

More recently it has been pointed out that female brains tend to be less lateralized and more "balanced" than males (Blum, 1997). There may indeed be differences in the ways in which male and female brains work. For example, the corpus callosum, the tissue connecting the two hemispheres, is up to 23 percent thicker in women than in men (Gorman, 1992). While such differences may exist, it is also a matter of cultural interpretation to assign meaning to them. A leading authority on "brain sex" provided the following insights into the study of sex differences in brains: "They are few, they are slight; we don't know what causes them, and in many cases we don't know what they do. On the other hand, they are real" (Blum, 1997: 46), just as men and women have different bodies and hormone levels.

While much research focuses on testosterone and its role in aggression, other attention has been directed at the role of female hormones in behaviour. Women's exclusion from social roles requiring responsibility, sound judgment, and rational decision-making has historically been justified by the claim that women's menstrual cycles interfere with their ability to function rationally. Premenstrual syndrome (PMS) refers to the physiological changes that may occur just before a woman's menstrual period. "Symptoms" may range from physical discomfort to mood swings. Researchers have suggested that the majority of North American women suffer from PMS, but exact numbers vary with one's definition of the condition.

The "discovery" of PMS has brought mixed reactions from feminists. On the one hand, many women are pleased that there has been recognition by the medical community of the role played by hormones in the monthly rhythms of the female body. Women who feel they suffer from PMS now may get help more easily from various clinics. Yet others criticize what they call the "social construction" of PMS. They suggest that the "discovery" of the disorder has inadvertently put more power in the hands of the medical community, by giving physicians yet another condition they can diagnose and use to label women as deviant, and by providing the pharmaceutical industry with yet another market for the selling of drugs. PMS is now listed by the American Psychiatric Association as a psychiatric disorder. As Caplan and Caplan (1999: 76) concluded, "This is a perfect Catch-22; the normal female is driven by her hormones, and female-hormone-impelled behaviour is crazy; therefore, the normal female is 'naturally diseased'." The main danger, critics suggest, is that using biological explanations for behaviour can and does result in the legitimation of unequal treatment of women (Laws, Hey, and Eagan, 1985). Indeed, others have argued that there is a social-psychological basis to PMS, suggesting that women's attitudes to their menstrual cycles are culturally produced. In North American culture, where menstruation is devalued and even called "the curse," women may develop negative feelings about their monthly periods.

What all of these discussions of the "myths" of biological determinism point out is how readily scientists, physicians, lawyers, and judges will accept biologically based explanations of behaviour that tend to support gender stereotypes. Because of this tendency, it is likely that the search for answers in this nature-and-nurture discussion will continue.

Language and the Gendered Order

One way to understand the cultural valuation of masculinity and femininity is to examine the way that language is gendered. The English language is not gender neutral, nor are the common usages of that language. Language, through persistent patterns, communicates more than just meaning; it also communicates cultural values.

Language use reproduces the gendered order primarily by suggesting that male experience is either universal or more important than female experience. There are several ways in which this occurs. First, the use of "he" or "man" to refer to anyone and everyone suggests that "he" or "man" includes everyone, perhaps even that anyone worth talking about is male. Yet this excludes the experiences of over half of the population. Second, the use of suffixes like "man," although less common today, similarly defines important roles as male roles. For example, "chairman," "workman," and "fireman" could seem to exclude the possibility that females could occupy such roles. The tendency to communicate sexist messages, such as male superiority or the assumption that certain roles must be occupied by either males or females, through language is known as **linguistic sexism**.

Even linguistic usages that do not explicitly exclude may have the same effect in terms of the cultural messages conveyed. When referring to occupations, there are some which are clearly assumed to be held by males, others by females. For example, how many times have you mentioned to friends that you have been to see your doctor and they have responded, "What did he say?" This question implies that the role is occupied by a male. Similarly, if you were to say that the nurse had given you an injection, your friend might ask, "Did *she* hurt you?"

When asked to change their usage to include women, many argue, "It's only language; what's the fuss?" From a sociological perspective, however, there is really no such thing as *"only* language." Language conveys a set of structural relations that are passed on to the young through the process of socialization, the topic of a previous chapter. One way in which our perceptions of gender might change is through the gradual move towards what is known as *gender-inclusive language*: language that recognizes and attempts to overcome the sexism contained in the tendencies mentioned above. "What did the doctor say?" and "Did the nurse hurt you?" are examples.

Considerable research has been devoted to the question of male and female differences in conversations (for a summary see Tannen, 1990). Most concur that gender relations are reflected in conversational patterns. They look to many aspects of conversations to support this, including the use of tone, loudness of voice, use of interruptions and silences, body language, as well as the actual content of conversations.

Tannen (1990) found that men's conversational styles reflect their socialization into a world where they are expected to achieve power and dominance. "In this world, conversations are negotiations in which people try to achieve and maintain the upper hand if they can, and protect themselves from others' attempts to put them down and push them around" (1990: 24). Many women, on the other hand, are socialized to seek relationship, nurturing, and consensus. "In this world, conversations are negotiations for closeness in which people try to seek and give confirmation and support, and to reach consensus" (1990: 25).

Getting Gendered: The Development of the Self

If there is little evidence to support the "natural" superiority of males over females, then how is it that the gendered order is structured systematically to give males advantage? The answer is gender socialization, the process through which the gendered order is socially reproduced in the young. Through it, the continuity of the gendered order is ensured. Upon the birth of a child, the proclamation of the child's sex is usually the first piece of information verbalized. With the claim, "It's a boy" or "It's a girl," the process of gender socialization begins. Most people do not like to refer to a child as "it." So the establishment of whether "it" is a "he" or a "she" takes on paramount importance, and sex is communicated in socially coded ways.

One common way in which sex is proclaimed is to dress babies and young children in clothing and colours considered to be sex-appropriate. It may even be difficult to purchase clothing in gender-neutral tones or styles. Parents may wait to discover the sex of their child before decorating the nursery or accumulating too many clothes, for fear of "making a mistake" by having pink in a boy's room or perhaps too much "masculine" clothing for a little girl. Hair styles also are highly gendered, with

girls being encouraged to grow long, curly locks, sometimes adorned with ribbons and barrettes, while boys' hair is more often kept shorter and unadorned. Boys tend to be dressed in a way that suggests readiness for "rough and tumble" play—in rugged, hardy clothing. Girls more often are dressed in a way that suggests a need to stay clean and out of the mud—in lighter colours, more delicate fabrics, and ribbons and bows. Why such conformity? The social disapproval that people would expect for dressing a boy in a pink dress, for example, speaks to the strength of our gender norms. The parent or caregiver who must explain to children that "Boys don't wear dresses" is passing this on. Today, however, more children are being dressed in "unisex" sweatsuits and overalls, suggesting a change from the more rigid patterns of the past. Yet, a glance at any advertisement for children's clothing will also reveal that attitudes have not changed completely.

Another code applied very early to newborn children involves their naming. Parents anticipating the birth of a child usually develop two separate lists of names—one "if it's a girl," the other "if it's a boy." It is seen as socially important to convey sexual identity through names. There are very few truly androgynous names, that is, names that could be equally applied to a male or a female. The naming of a child in a gender-inappropriate way may lead to the child having to endure endless teasing from peers, and, as we have seen, the reactions of others are important for the development of identity.

The toys chosen for babies and young children also suggest definite ideas of gender-appropriate play. A visit to a toy store will confirm that the children's toy industry remains highly gendered. Many boys continue to be offered battle-oriented toys, construction toys, cars, and trucks, suggesting socialization into instrumental traits. Girls, on the other hand, are surrounded by stuffed animals and dolls dressed in pink and lace, as well as toys pertaining to household tasks such as baking and cleaning, suggesting socialization into expressive traits. While there is some evidence of crossover and the use of gender-neutral toys, a glimpse at Saturday morning television advertisements directed at children will confirm that even today this important source of gender socialization remains strong.

Young children are encouraged to behave in ways considered sex-appropriate.

Some more subtle ways in which boys and girls are shaped for their gender include the ways in which parents convey their own expectations to children. For example, parents describe their newborns in gender stereotypical ways, describing boys as tall, large, athletic, and serious, while girls are small, pretty, with delicate features (Reid, 1994). Parents tend to handle children differently, from the newborn stage on, depending on their sex. Boys tend to be handled more roughly, girls more gently (McDonald and Parke, 1986). Even the tone of voice used to address newborns differs, with a softer tone for girls and a stronger tone for boys. Research indicates that mothers tend to speak more clearly to their sons than to their daughters, and tend to teach their sons more actively than they do their daughters (Weitzman, Birns, and Friend, 1985). In the same study, it was shown that even those parents who claimed to be committed to treating

their boys and girls exactly the same were actively, albeit unconsciously, socializing them into different gender roles.

As seen in Chapter 4, Socialization, individuals tend to respond to the expectations and activities of significant others by repeating behaviours for which they are given approval. The most significant others in early childhood socialization belong to the immediate family. Primary socialization into gender roles is reinforced in turn by agents of secondary socialization, such as schools, the media, religious institutions, and the workplace. Consistency of expectations is thus maintained throughout the gendered order.

Through the process of gender socialization in Canadian culture, boys are consistently rewarded for emulating the "masculine," while girls are generally, if not consistently, rewarded for emulating the "feminine." Negative sanctions—for example, names like "wimp," "sissy," or "tomboy"—are given to those who deviate, suggestive of the fear of parents that their child might be homosexual. Interestingly, the least forgiving dispensers of these labels are often children's peers—evidence of the power of their own gender socialization. Gradually, children internalize the gender norms so that they are inseparable from their sense of self. Boys will come to view it as unthinkable ever to wear a dress; girls may be convinced that they should not be too assertive.

Trapped in Our Bodies: The Body and Sexuality

The relationship between the gendered order and gendered identity becomes readily apparent when we examine cultural norms for physical attractiveness. All individuals are trapped in their bodies, and the body becomes a very important factor in social development at an early age. Others perceive individuals according to cultural appearance norms—as cute or pretty, plain or ugly, fat or thin, tall or short. From subtle differences such as whether they have blonde, brown, or red hair, to more significant ones such as whether they are differently "abled," the social meanings attached to physical attributes all become early components of the self. Indeed, it would not be an exaggeration to say that the foundations of a sense of self-worth are often built on how bodies conform to appearance norms.

For the most part, ideas of beauty and attractiveness are culturally produced. The mass media and fashion industries play a large role in this process. Successfully socialized males and females internalize these norms and attempt to emulate them. One systematically consistent aspect of this is the *objectification of females*. Females learn at an early age that they are objects to be looked at. Long before they understand the meaning of sexuality, young girls are encouraged to emulate the seductive appearance of adult women, while young boys are encouraged to appreciate this appearance and to respond in an active way.

Indeed, historically, women's worth has been embodied in their appearance—women's assets

Ideas of beauty and attractiveness are culturally produced, especially by the mass media and fashion industry.

have been culturally defined in terms of physical attractiveness and childbearing capacity. Females have been taught that it is through these means that they can achieve status in the adult world—by marrying men who will then support them through male access to the public world of work and industry.

In turn, males have been socialized to view themselves as subjects—autonomous actors whose success depends on initiative, assertiveness if not aggressiveness, and persistence. The male body should reflect this by being strong and tough. The ways in which men dress, walk, and talk all mirror these societal expectations. "Masculine" traits are applied to the pursuit of females, the objects.

Moreover, masculine qualities are more highly valued and may be seen to improve with age, while feminine "assets" fade over time. Women become increasingly devalued, particularly as they pass out of the childbearing years. On aging men, grey hair and wrinkles are a sign of distinction, suggesting wisdom and experience, while on women they suggest unattractiveness and diminished worth. With menopause, Greer (1992) pointed out, many women experience a kind of social "invisibility," suggesting that their value to society has vanished with their youth.

It would be wrong to suggest that, just because the body is so important for women's gendered identity, appearance norms are not oppressive for males in our society. The rigid norms governing how males and females must present themselves are oppressive to both sexes. A rugged, "masculine" body conforms much more closely to societal norms than does a smooth, soft, "effeminate" one.

Sexual performance also is somehow implied by how masculine one appears. Penis size, muscle development, height, and profusion of facial and bodily hair all may be criteria on which males compare themselves, and in each case bigger or more means more "manly." Penis size is mythologized to be directly related to the amount of pleasure a male can give a female in intercourse, and hence a large penis is a source of status among males, while one that "doesn't measure up" may be a source of shame. Muscular development is seen to indicate strength as well as sexual prowess. Height is significant given the cultural requirement that in heterosexual relationships males should be taller than females. Facial hair, especially among adolescent males, is seen to be evidence of virility, as is hair elsewhere on the body, particularly the chest. Balding at any age, but particularly "premature" balding, is a dreaded sign of failing virility. Any indication of impotence or lack of virility will bring shame to most males.

Although body awareness is a constant source of concern for both males and females, research has shown that females in our culture tend to be more concerned than males about their bodies, and that this concern tends to take the form of negative feelings about their bodies. Males, in contrast, tend to feel more positive about their bodies (Franzoi, Kessenich, and Sugrue, 1989). For females, the high premium placed on appearance often leads to an almost obsessive pursuit of beauty according to cultural definitions—a goal that is unattainable by most, but made to appear within reach by the cosmetics and fashion industries—and to a cultural obsession with achieving a desired weight.

Recently, sociologists and psychologists have noted the widespread occurrence of eating disorders. *Anorexia nervosa*, a condition affecting mostly females, takes the form of voluntary starvation in the pursuit of thinness. The obsessive quality of this disorder leads those suffering from it to have a distorted perception of their bodies, such that they always feel fat, even when severely malnourished and underweight. Bulimia is a related condition in which sufferers alternatively binge and purge, frequently aided by the use of laxatives and diuretics. These conditions have reached epidemic proportions in North America among female high-school, college, and university students, and are severely debilitating, in some cases even leading to death. While the psychological explanations for such eating disorders are complex, many researchers attribute their massive increase to the "cult of thinness," in which women's self-worth is defined particularly through their appearance (Wolf, 1990).

Less life-threatening, but nonetheless telling about contemporary cultural values, is the current emphasis on physical fitness for both males and females. On the one hand, some argue convincingly that fitness is important for health. On the other hand, many individuals become obsessed with fitness, suggesting that there is more to it than simply a concern for health. Indeed, the social meanings attached to fitness translate into definitions of self-worth. Individuals who "work out" regularly and are seen to be fit are somehow interpreted as being more desirable and worthy. This has allowed fitness centres and aerobics classes to become the "meet markets" of today.

Change in the arena of body and sexuality has been slow. Indeed, not only does female objectification persist, but the objectification of the male body, through the use of cosmetics and fashion, seems to be on the increase (Wolf, 1990). While many might argue that there is greater room than ever for the exercise of individual choice, for example in clothing, the high rates of eating disorders, combined with the cultural obsession with fitness, lead one to wonder whether fundamental patterns have changed at all.

The Effects of Gender

Work and reproduction: The gendered division of labour

Masculine and feminine roles also affect adult norms of biological and social reproduction. In the gendered order, gender differences are manifested in expectations regarding motherhood, fatherhood, and paid and unpaid labour, known as the **gendered division of labour**.

The idea that women are biologically more suited for the social role of parenting has historically led to limitations on the possibilities for both women and men. If mothering should come naturally to women, then it follows that it will be expected that all women will be mothers, willingly, lovingly, and competently. Along with these expectations go sanctions against those who would rather not have children, or those for whom mothering is difficult. Such women may find themselves labelled deviant, as "selfish" or "bad mothers" respectively (Schur, 1984). Yet the role is contained within a web of relations that limit women's other roles, particularly in the public sphere of paid labour. Women who wish to "have it all," for whom a complete life includes both a career and a family, may find the expectation that they will stay at home for at least the early periods of a child's life inhibiting to progress in their careers. In turn, some women may sacrifice childbearing potential in order to become established in their careers. Still, for many women, the combination of mothering and working outside the home, while stressful and trying at times, remains a satisfying combination (Crosby, 1991).

Men too are limited in terms of the expectations surrounding parenting. It is only in recent years that males have become more involved in fathering. Far more prevalent during the decades of the 1950s through to the 1980s was the model of the "absent father"—perhaps physically present in the family, but emotionally uninvolved in the expressive sphere of family life. For authors such as Miedzian (1991), the pressures placed on males to "be a man" channelled their socialization away from nurturing. Masculinity, when rigidly interpreted, excludes warmth and caring. So it stands to reason that boys raised on such a model will not be encouraged to take an active part in parenting.

There is a tendency to associate the concept of work with paid employment, and it is only recently that distinctions have been made between paid work outside the home and unpaid work in the home (see Chapter 10, Families). Women's work in the home may be divided into three categories: "wifework," "motherwork," and "housework" (Rosenberg, 1990). *Wifework* refers to the work expected of women in their roles as wives: seeing to the emotional, physical, and sexual needs of their husbands. Motherwork refers to the work expected of women in their roles as mothers: seeing to the emotional as well as physical needs (feeding, clothing, and healing) of their children. *Housework* refers to the work expected of women in their roles as homemakers: cooking, cleaning, shopping, and overall maintenance of the sense of order and appearance of the home.

Within the paid workforce, there has historically been a wide disparity between "men's work" and

Many women occupy the double ghetto of paid pink-collar labour and unpaid domestic labour.

"women's work," in terms of the perceived social value of the work and its remuneration. In keeping with their gender socialization, men have typically occupied higher status, white-collar jobs or more physically demanding blue-collar jobs, while women have been relegated to the pink-collar ghetto of women's work. Indeed, women have been said to occupy a **double ghetto**: the pink-collar ghetto of paid labour and the domestic ghetto of unpaid labour. Women who work outside of the home full-time are still expected to do wifework, motherwork, and housework when they are home. They are the ones who must take time off from work if a child is sick, and they are blamed if there are problems at home (Luxton, 1990). In 1992, of all parents working outside the home for pay and having primary responsibility for childcare, 95 percent were mothers (Logan and Belliveau, 1995).

Women's work outside the home is frequently in lower-status occupations that mirror women's training as caregivers and homemakers. The largest number of employed women continue to hold positions in the clerical field, while other "typical" female occupations include teaching, nursing, and social work. In recent years the trend has been towards greater crossover between typical men's work and women's work. Between 1982 and 1994, women's employment in the clerical field dropped from 34 to 28 percent, while women's employment in managerial and administrative occupations jumped from 6 to 13 percent (Best, 1995: 33). But while women's representation in traditionally male-dominated professions has increased greatly in the last decade, there is still substantial room for change.

Historically, men's wages have been significantly higher than women's, even when men and women worked in the same occupation. This reflects the societal assumption that men's work was more important than women's work, and was necessary to support a family. The discrepancy between men's and women's salaries has been explained by the idea of the "family wage": historically it has been assumed that a male breadwinner would be earning the money to support an entire family (with the female staying at home, doing unpaid domestic labour). If women did work outside the home, this work was not taken seriously but treated as work for "pin money."

Objectification of women in the work world has been an unfortunate fact of life as well. Wolf (1990) chronicled how the "professional beauty qualification" has been the generally unstated, single most important factor in a woman's success in the paid labour force. There are whole categories of work in which physical attractiveness is a prerequisite for success—the so-called "display" jobs that permeate the entertainment and service industries. But women in all lines of work have experienced sexual harassment on the job—unwanted attention of a sexual nature. When this occurs in a work setting, it is experienced as a confusion between being treated as a worker and as a sex object. For women who may already have low self-esteem, the message is that their looks are more important than their brains. In addition, sexual harassment usually involves a power differential, with the majority of incidents involving males in a superior position harassing subordinate women. The fear of job loss, stalking, or other reprisal has kept women silent in the past. Recognition that sexual harassment was widespread in the workplace as well as in the educational system led to greater regulations and penalties for this behaviour. As a result, it is less threatening today for individuals experiencing harassment to come forth and seek justice.

Ideas concerning women's work outside the home have changed in recent years. The majority of married women now work in the paid labour force, mostly for economic reasons (Calzavara, 1993). Yet disparities in remuneration have been slow to adapt to the changing realities. Even in 1996, women's full-time earnings were only 73.4 percent of men's (*Canadian Social Trends*, 1999; and recall Chapter 6, Social Stratification). Policy initiatives such as pay equity are important steps in the direction of rectifying these inequities.

Health and aging

Not surprisingly, men and women experience health and aging differently. Historically, men's life spans have been significantly shorter than women's (a topic to which we shall return in Chapter 15, Demography and Urbanization). This means that women often outlive their partners, and indeed, in old age there are far more widows than widowers.

FIGURE 7.1   Employment Concentration and Occupational Distribution of Women, Canada, 1996

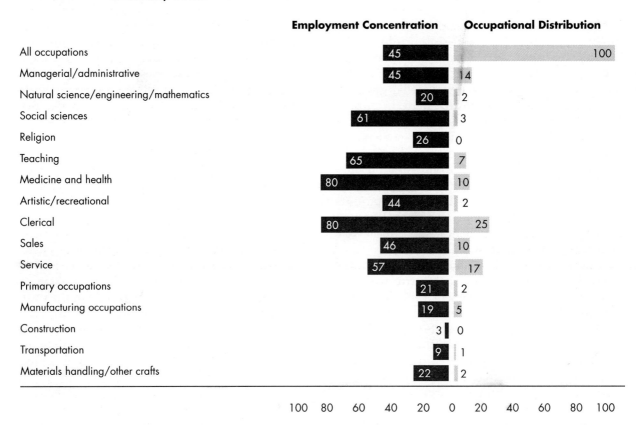

Source: Statistics Canada, "Employment Concentration and Occupational Distribution of Women, Canada, 1996," adapted from "Labour Force Annual Averages," Catalogue No. 71-220.

In 1996, the average life expectancy was 75.7 years for males and 81.4 for females (*Canadian Social Trends*, 1998). Several explanations have been advanced for these differences. In keeping with the biological tendency for women to endure stress better than men, some argue that females may simply be biologically favoured for longevity.

Others suggest that these differences are environmentally produced. Many of the diseases and ailments that cause an early death in males are related to the paid workforce and the stresses it produces. Cardiovascular disease, the leading killer of Canadian males aged 45 to 64, is often the result of a stressful lifestyle and not enough emphasis on proper nutrition and exercise (Parliament, 1990). Striving executives who put in many hours of

overtime per week to the neglect of their physical and emotional well-being may be prime candidates for such an early death. And given the fact that, to date, fewer women have been employed in the types of paid jobs that are seen to require such commitment, it is not surprising that they are less frequently casualties of such work-related diseases. Other work-related illnesses, such as cancer, may have their origins in poor working conditions associated with typical blue-collar "men's work," such as factory work and mining. Time will tell if, as more women enter the paid labour force, they will come to suffer from such work-related diseases.

Because of the dependency that many women experience in their roles in the private realm during their childbearing and childrearing years, many are

Homeless Women: A Tragic Consequence of Patriarchy

Homelessness among women has become increasingly visible in our society in recent years, and this visibility has led to a general alarm that something should be done about it. Women are generally seen to belong in homes—and within our culture, the "home" implies private property and family. Women without homes are therefore seen as deviant. In a study of homeless women in a large Ontario city, Harman (1989) found that most of those who stayed in a hostel for homeless women had in fact been "domestically fixed" at one time, and had become homeless when their ties to family and property were severed. "At least half of those seeking shelter at one hostel for women are former mental patients. Others are widows; married women escaping from violent and/or alcoholic husbands; wives left alone as a result of desertion, commitment, or incar-

ceration of their husbands; teenage runaways; and single mothers" (Harman, 1989: 20).

To understand the feminization of poverty, look at what happens to some women when economic support is removed from their lives. Suddenly they are without income, and it is the rare homemaker who will have sufficient financial resources to continue to make mortgage payments and keep up a house. From there, the descent to poverty is a rapid downward spiral, facilitated by the stigma attached to being a female lone parent. Childcare for preschool children is expensive and subsidized places are limited. Paid employment is hard to find if one is unskilled and has been out of the workforce for a number of years. Even women who have careers find it next to impossible to sustain the same standard of living on one income. Social services are inade-

quate and shelters are often overcrowded. Affordable housing is limited. The "Catch-22" of the welfare system—one must have a fixed address to receive welfare payments, and consequently one must have enough money to cover first and last months' rent and other related expenses such as moving costs—means that some women cannot make use of affordable housing even if it is available to them. Welfare payments may provide for a subsistence lifestyle, but certainly do little to help a woman "get back on her feet." Literally on the street, without a fixed address, without an income, and unable to acquire housing, these women join the ranks of the homeless. One woman poignantly expressed her experience of rapid loss of status and income when her husband died: "I remember waking up one morning and realizing, 'Oh God, I'm on the skids'" (Harman, 1989: 20).

ill-prepared financially and emotionally for growing old as widows. Pension plans are geared to members of the paid workforce, often excluding women who have devoted their adult lives to the demanding task of being a full-time homemaker. Yet it is this segment of society that lives longer. It is not surprising that a large proportion of elderly females end up in poverty, some so destitute as to make up part of the growing category of "homeless women" (see the boxed insert on "Homeless Women"). Aged women, particularly the "older elderly" (those over 75 years of age), account for a significant proportion of Canada's poor.

Recently, the longevity gap between males and females has diminished slightly. This may be a product of both better healthcare for men and

greater involvement in the paid labour force for women. It is interesting that, while cigarette smoking in Canada has been in an overall decline, the group in which it has been slowest to fall is women (McKie, 1990). And while mortality rates continue to drop, cancer is still the leading cause of death for women aged 45 to 64, with the percentage of female deaths due to cancer increasing (Parliament, 1990).

The feminization of poverty

One of the most profound cumulative effects of the gendered order on the life experiences of women in Canadian society is that, at all stages of the adult life cycle, women are more likely than men to be

Many women are ill-prepared financially and emotionally for growing old alone.

poor, and they are more likely than men to be trapped in a life of poverty. This is known as the **feminization of poverty** (Harman, 1992). The reasons for it have to do with the blocks to opportunities experienced by women, as well as the ways in which the Canadian state operates to keep poor women in a condition of dependency on government assistance such as welfare and family benefits.

Much of this is a consequence of the broader patriarchal ideology through which females are socialized to aspire to the roles of wife and mother. In Canadian society, these roles are devalued and provide women with a "legitimate" livelihood only when couched within a traditional nuclear family arrangement. Yet, a glance at recent statistics indicates that lone-parenting is the fastest-growing category of household arrangement in Canadian society. And within this category, 83 percent of lone-

parent families are headed by females (*Canadian Social Trends*, 1999), many of whom live in isolation, without support from their former or estranged husbands, forced to rely on government assistance.

The stereotypical "single mother" on government assistance is often a target of criticism, stigmatized for deviating from the conventional role of mother. Her morality may be called into question even if she is single as a result of leaving an abusive husband, or is alone due to the desertion of a husband. If the woman has not been educated or trained for paid employment, or is unable to secure it, she must receive some kind of financial support to provide for her family. The amounts provided are barely sufficient to cover minimal food and housing. Childcare is expensive and a luxury not all can afford, with subsidized daycare spots limited and waiting lists long. Thus, women in this situation are tied to the home; any work that they do find tends to be menial and low-paying. The result is often a vicious circle of poverty that is difficult to escape. The road to change must include the opening up of opportunities for education, childcare, affordable housing, and decently paid labour for those who want it, and the provision of adequate support for those whose choice is to engage in full-time mothering at home.

Gender and deviance

Gender norms affect definitions of male and female deviance. In the realm of sexuality, the heterosexual assumption is predominant. Males and females who choose same-sex partners and homosexual lifestyles are labelled deviant. Individuals may also be labelled deviant for violating work norms—for example, males who choose to stay at home to care for their children while their wives work outside of the home, or those who choose unconventional occupations such as nursing or social work. More generally, males who are not "masculine" and females who are not "feminine" meet with social disapproval. Males who do not conform to the demands of "masculinity" may be labelled "wimps." After being told at a very young age that "boys don't cry," and being encouraged to be rough and aggressive, males who swim against the tide and develop their "sensitive" side often pay the heavy price of peer disapproval.

The study of gender and deviance also reveals some interesting paradoxes. The first paradox is that violence is considered normal, not deviant. It is generally agreed that ours is a culture of violence (Miedzian, 1991). Some, such as Kaufman (1993), have observed that learning to be masculine is analogous to learning to be violent. Little boys are often encouraged to fight, and are sometimes taught that violence is the swiftest form of conflict resolution.

Ruth (1990) observed that training into the Arnold Schwarzenegger mode of masculinity is similar to training into the role of soldier. Soldiers cannot do their job if they feel compassion for the persons they are expected to kill. So, cold objectification of others, including women and children, may be as "normal and natural" to a man raised to idealize the "Terminator" as any other feature of the taken-for-granted world. Indeed, in some circles using violence to control women is even celebrated. On the other hand, males who reject the association between masculinity and violence may meet with resistance from other men and even some women, for whom their choice poses a threat. Present concern with the tolerance of violence in society led Miedzian (1991) to conclude that perhaps if society socialized boys to develop their nurturing side, things such as war, child abuse, and violence against women would be unthinkable. But at the moment, sensitivity among males is often considered deviant. At an early age boys learn that the full experience of human emotions is a sign of weakness and femininity.

A second paradox is that, for women, to be "normal" is often to be deviant. Women who deviate from male-established norms, such as Devor's gender blenders, are labelled deviant. When females exhibit strength and assertiveness, their behaviour may be met with social disapproval and labelled "unladylike" or "unfeminine." Females who aspire to nontraditional occupations, who do not marry, or who opt out of the motherhood role may all experience definitions of themselves as socially unacceptable. Lesbians may be labelled deviant precisely because they refuse to accept subjugation to male dominance.

In the area of crime, males are overwhelmingly represented in violent crimes, crimes against the person, and crimes against property. Females more often commit shoplifting, and are more often charged with "morals" crimes such as soliciting, stripping, and other behaviours involving their sexuality. When women are the victims of crimes by men, most notably battering and sexual assault, too often society responds by questioning their complaints—asking what the women did to provoke the crime.

This "blaming the victim" represents a third paradox. Domestic violence has until very recently been considered a private matter of discipline and social order (men's work). If women were battered, they were probably not performing their roles adequately in some way. Regrettably, some police and judges still retain this view and act upon it. Sexual assault is another area in which females have often been blamed for their own victimization. Accusations that a woman "asked for it" or detailed questioning of her personal morality too frequently continue to be responses to charges of sexual assault. This is particularly true of women such as prostitutes or strippers, whose occupations lead many to assume that they are always sexually available and hence cannot be "raped."

Working Towards Change

This chapter has suggested that a sociological analysis of gender relations must take into account the development of the self as well as the larger gendered order that structures the experience of being male or female in Canadian society. As we have seen, the gendered order is a pervasive one. And while its existence has clearly favoured men, it must also be seen as largely oppressive of both women and men. Expectations of masculinity and femininity are both pervasive and consistent, with enormous pressure to conform and a ready-made stigma system for those who deviate. The general tendency to avoid ostracism keeps most males and females conforming more or less to the social expectations of the gendered order. And it is this very tendency to conform that inhibits social change.

But change has begun. Primarily through the efforts of the women's movement, social organizations at all levels are now forced to be aware of gender issues, at least nominally. Consciousness of the dangers of sexism is gradually

Masculinity and the "Men's Movements"

As with the diversities in "feminisms," it is important to recognize that there are many "masculinities" present in Canadian society today. The "macho" image has given way to a broader range of choices. Among these, at least three "men's movements" have come onto the 1990s gender politics picture: the profeminist movement, the gay rights movement, and the men's rights movement.

The profeminist movement

Men supporting the profeminist movement are concerned with eradicating the system of patriarchy, which has systematically privileged all men. Some adherents of this perspective feel that feminism is the political movement that will liberate men and women alike from the oppression of patriarchy (Salutin, 1993) and permit men to embrace less traditional models of masculinity. One recent, highly visible expression of this movement in Canada has been the "White Ribbon" campaign, in which men across the country have organized against violence against women. This is a significant part of the general societal response to the 1989 Montreal massacre, in which fourteen women were murdered at École Polytechnique, and its anniversary has become recognized across Canada as a time for men to express their support of women's right to be free from violence and to show that not all men are violent.

The gay rights movement

Male homosexuals pose a particular challenge to definitions of masculinity. The choice to engage in same-sex relationships violates the heterosexual assumption of patriarchal society, and continues to be regarded as unnatural and immoral by many citizens. Yet, gay activists have fought against the discrimination and the "gay bashing" that have often resulted from a climate of homophobia, or the fear of homosexuality. Although the Canadian Supreme Court refused, in a close vote, to recognize homosexual marriages, Canada took a leadership role in the liberalization of regulations concerning homosexuals when, in the late 1980s and early 1990s, it lifted its ban on homosexuals in the military, some of its provinces and municipalities extended benefits to same-sex couples, and most provinces extended human rights protection to gays and lesbians.

The men's rights movement

In contrast to the profeminist and gay rights movements, the men's rights movement has emerged to oppose feminist efforts. For some men, strides towards equality for women and gays have been experienced as a form of "reverse discrimination" in which they have begun to feel victimized for being heterosexual males. Various groups have organized to express dissatisfaction with women's rights, and have demanded theirs back.

filtering through. But feminism, and gender consciousness in general, has been disproportionately a white, middle-class, urban social movement. It is for these groups that things have improved the most. The voices of women of colour and poor women, however, are increasingly being heard. They are changing the face of feminism as it takes into account the historical tendency of the movement to ignore their issues—racism in particular.

In any event, as with all dimensions of society, any change at the structural level must be met with some comparable change at the level of individual behaviour—the gendered identity. It is necessary for all members of the society to examine ways in which they have benefited as well as ways in which they have been oppressed by the gendered order, and to begin to work for change in their own arenas.

Summary

Whether one is born female or male in Canadian society will have significant implications for identity and life chances. Socialization, identity, sexuality, position in the paid labour force, longevity and general health, relative poverty, and many other variables are determined in part by gender. Gender is the socially constructed set of expectations associated with a particular sex.

Canadians live in a patriarchal society—one that generally favours males and disadvantages females. Functionalists regard the patriarchal arrangement as useful and necessary. Symbolic interactionists maintain that it is a negotiated order and one that may be changed. Marxist theorists see it as a consequence of oppressive social structures, primarily capitalism.

In addition, there are a variety of feminist perspectives. Maternal feminism views motherhood as a source of women's status; liberal feminism looks to law and policy to remedy social inequality; socialist feminism regards the combined effects of capitalism and patriarchy as constituting the basis for women's oppression; and radical feminism advocates the abolition of patriarchy. Similarly, there is no one male response to feminism. Responses range from sympathy to antagonism.

The question of biological determinism has been hotly debated. To date, studies have revealed little compelling evidence to suggest that males and females are differentially suited for social roles on the basis of biological factors alone. Yet this argument continues to be made, and is frequently used to justify social inequality.

The gendered order is structured by many invisible means, one of which is language. Linguistic sexism suggests that male experience is either universal or more important than female experience. Conversational styles tend to reflect socialization into gender norms. A conscious, increased use of gender-inclusive language may help to overcome some of these inequities.

Gender socialization is a powerful force in the perpetuation of gender inequality. Through this process, males learn to be masculine and females learn to be feminine. Clothing, names, toys, physical handling, and tone of voice all reflect parental and societal expectations that children will learn and conform to accepted gender norms. Deviations from these norms are heavily sanctioned.

The body and sexuality are the stage for a clearly visible gendered drama. Females and males alike find that the expectations for the shape and presentation of their bodies are difficult to ignore. Particularly for women, the body is objectified and seen to be a critical source of status, leading in some cases to obsessional disorders such as anorexia nervosa and bulimia. Conforming to rigid codes for masculinity and femininity in a structure of compulsory heterosexuality is highly restrictive.

Gender inequality is also evident when it comes to reproduction and paid labour, in the gendered division of labour. Because females are biologically equipped for reproduction and the devalued role of mother, they have also been ghettoized in devalued roles as homemaker and pink-collar worker. Males, on the other hand, have tended to have greater access to high-status positions in both the home and the workplace. While there is some evidence of change, distinctly male-dominated and female-dominated occupations persist.

Men and women experience health and aging differently in Canada. Much of this has to do with the social roles into which they are cast, and the resultant toll taken on the body. Males tend to have shorter lives than females; however, females are more likely to grow old alone and poor. As the working lives of men and women become more alike, for example when they move into occupations traditionally held by the other sex, these tendencies may even out.

The feminization of poverty is one striking consequence of patriarchy in Canadian society. Women are more likely than men to be poor during their adult lives, and to be trapped in a life of poverty. This situation is not likely to change until more opportunities are open to women in the paid labour force and programs such as universal daycare are instituted to free women from domestic obligations.

Social sanctions for deviating from gender norms are strong. The heterosexual assumption can make the choice of an overtly homosexual lifestyle a costly one. Other deviations from the rigid expectations of masculinity and femininity in the areas of the body, sexuality, reproduction, and paid and unpaid labour may lead to social stigma. Most Canadian adults find it costly to go against the grain and tend to prefer conformity. This in turn reinforces the gendered order and keeps the rate of change slow. But change is occurring, and many hope that the social basis for gender inequality may one day disappear.

If we had a crystal ball to predict what changes might be in store for this new millennium, perhaps it would show a world in which the Zuni way of raising children to be who they will be rather than making rigid definitions for them would prevail. What would the consequences be for gender roles? Free choice for occupation, procreation, relationship, and sexual preference are a few. Governmental-legal recognition could mean final equality for all. However, what we know about the power of socialization tells us that change is slow. Children so often become what their parents are, that we might have to wait for several generations for change to be firmly implemented in the social fabric. Sociological research might help speed up the process by examining the role of education, media, religion, and state in the structural reproduction of gender relations.

QUESTIONS FOR REVIEW AND CRITICAL THINKING

1.   What groups are the major promoters of gender equality today? Should they be funded by government or by private fundraising?

2.   How might you, as an elementary school teacher, go about changing the current system of gender socialization?

3.   Suppose that somehow the English language could be rendered completely gender neutral. Would this mean the end of gender discrimination? If not, why not?

4.   Can women be sexist? What, if any examples can you think of?

5.   Will the day ever come when structural inequalities between men and women completely disappear? If not, why not?

KEY TERMS

double ghetto, p. 185

expressive dimension, p. 172

feminization of poverty, p. 188

gender, p. 169

gender norms, p. 169

gender socialization, p. 169

gendered division of labour, p. 184

gendered identity, p. 169

gendered order, p. 169

heterosexual assumption, p. 174

ideology of gender inequality, p. 169

instrumental dimension, p. 172

liberal feminism, p. 175

linguistic sexism, p. 179

maternal feminism, p. 175

naturalization of history, p. 176

nature/culture dualism, p. 170

patriarchy, p. 175

private realm, p. 172

public realm, p. 172

radical feminism, p. 176

sex, p. 169

socialist feminism, p. 176

SUGGESTED READINGS

Blum, Deborah

1997 *Sex on the Brain: The Biological Differences between Men and Women.* New York: Viking.

A review of the scientific literature on biological differences between males and females.

Caplan, Paula J. and Jeremy B. Caplan

1999 *Thinking Critically about Research on Sex and Gender.* New York: Longman.

This very readable book is a valuable tool in learning to be an informed consumer about research on sex and gender. It highlights the sources of research bias, provides a history of research on sex and gender, and focuses on key questions that have been asked in the past.

Kaufman, Michael

1993 *Cracking the Armour: Power, Pain and the Lives of Men.* Toronto: Viking.

A sensitive discussion of the paradox of being male in a patriarchal society, a role Kaufman identifies as one of power and pain.

Renzetti, Claire M. and Daniel J. Curran

1999 *Women, Men and Society* (4th ed.). Toronto: Allyn and Bacon.

A comprehensive textbook on gender relations in contemporary patriarchal society.

WEB SITES

http://www.herplace.org

Canadian Women's Internet Association

The homepage of the Canadian Women's Internet Association, this site contains many useful links to information for and about women. Topics range from Gender and Sexuality, to Women and Technology, and Health and Fitness.

http://www.infocan.gc.ca/facts/women-e.html

Facts on Canada—Women

This site provides a detailed overview of women's participation in Canadian society from an historical perspective.

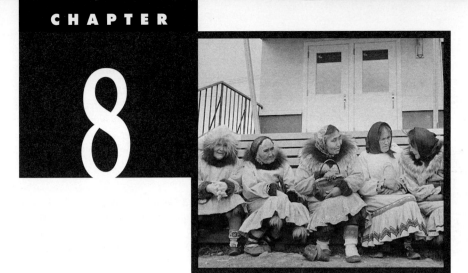

Race and Ethnic Relations

Carol Agócs

Introduction

Canadians often describe their society as an "ethnic mosaic," a varied composition of many peoples whose distinctive cultures give colour and texture to the whole. The image of the mosaic symbolizes the reality of the ethnic and racial diversity that has been increasingly characteristic of Canadian society in recent decades.

At Confederation, Canada's total population was approximately 60 percent of British origin, 31 percent of French origin, and 8 percent of other ethnic origins. Since then the Canadian population has become much more diverse, with a significant increase in the representation of ethnic origins other than British and French. Census definitions of ethnic origin have changed over time and, recently, the census has collected data on multiple as well as single ethnic origins of Canadians, making it problematic to compare data from various census years. The 1996 census found that 31 percent claimed Canadian origin, 52 percent reported some British ethnic origin, 20 percent indicated some

French ancestry, and 4 percent reported Aboriginal origins. The other most frequently mentioned ethnic origins in 1996, in order, included German, Italian, Ukrainian, Chinese, Dutch, Polish, and South Asian. The 1996 census found that visible minorities comprise about 11 percent of the Canadian population, including in order of size, Chinese, South Asian, black, Arab/West Asian, and Filipino populations (Statistics Canada, *1996 Census of Canada, The Nation*, Catalogue nos. 6002-6606).

Canada's mosaic exists within the structure of a **pluralistic society**, a social system of coexisting ethnic groups. To some degree each group maintains its own distinctive culture and social organizations, such as clubs and religious institutions. At the same time, each participates with Canada's other ethnic groups in common cultural, economic, and political institutions.

However, ethnic populations in Canada, as in most pluralistic societies, are hierarchically ranked. Some ethnic groups, such as the British in Canada, have historically dominated positions of economic, political, and social power, while others, such as

Native peoples, have been and remain relatively powerless. In referring to Canadian society as a **vertical mosaic**, Porter (1965) called attention to the fact that ethnicity is a major source of inequality, cleavage, and conflict in Canadian society. More recent research (e.g., Agócs and Boyd, 1993) has documented the growing importance of racial diversity as a basis of inequality in this country. You will recall that we discussed such inequality in Chapter 6, Social Inequality, and we will do so again in Chapter 14, Social Movements.

We begin this chapter on race and ethnic relations in Canada with a discussion of the processes involved in the formation and development of immigrant communities. Once we have an understanding of local ethnic communities as social entities, we shall consider the meanings of the concepts of ethnic group, race, and minority group, and some of the manifestations of ethnic and racial inequality. We shall then discuss the historical processes of colonialism, conquest, and migration, forces that laid the foundation for Canada's vertical mosaic. Finally, we shall examine three influential interpretations of the past, present, and future of ethnic and race relations—assimilationism, two-category perspectives, and pluralism—and consider some of the implications of each for social policy. Our concluding theme will be the continued importance of racial and ethnic pluralism and conflict in the modern world, and in Canada in particular, and the challenge this social reality poses for this generation.

The Local Ethnic Community: Formation and Development

One day in 1962, a young man stepped off a plane in Toronto, having flown all night from Rome. He had torn up his roots for the promise of a steady job, a house, a good standard of living for his family, and an education for his children—things less attainable at home. He was welcomed by his uncle, who drove him to a tidy duplex in a predominantly Italian neighbourhood. There his aunt, cousins, and other relatives from his home village of Gagliano, in the barren mountains south of Naples, waited to celebrate his arrival.

His aunt and uncle had sent money for this journey, the fruit of several years of saving and planning. They had arranged for their nephew to work as a labourer for the same construction firm where the uncle worked as an equipment operator, and for him to share temporarily the upstairs apartment with another young man who had arrived from Gagliano the year before. The new immigrant was to learn some English and to try in the next year or two to save enough money to repay his aunt and uncle and to buy a one-way ticket to Toronto for his wife, who was waiting in Gagliano.

The experience of this man was far from unique; after World War II, approximately half a million Italians immigrated to Canada, part of a much larger immigration from all countries, but especially from Europe, to Canada (see Figure 8.1). Between 1991 and 1996, over a million immigrants came to Canada, more than half from Asia and the Middle East (Statistics Canada, *The Daily*, Dec. 2, 1997: 2). For all immigrants, settling in a new country means cutting ties with relatives and lifelong friends in the "old country" and trying to become part of a sometimes confusing world of strangers.

Studies of the immigration experience suggest that migration is frequently a social act, with primary social relationships as strong influences upon the decision to migrate and the subsequent process of settlement. (We shall discuss the reasons for migration more fully in Chapter 15, Demography and Urbanization.) The migrant's destination is often a place where relatives, friends, or others from the same town have already settled. **Chain migration** is a sequential movement of persons from a common place of origin to a common destination, with the assistance of relatives or compatriots already settled in the new location (Campani, 1992). Assistance may take the form of information helpful in weighing the decision to migrate, money for transportation, a place to stay upon arrival, job offers, or legal sponsorship.

In the years since World War II, Canadian immigration policy has encouraged family reunification through the chain-migration process, by freely admitting some relatives of persons settled in Canada, and by classifying immigrants who receive legal guarantees of support from relatives or others in Canada as family class, assisted relatives, or *sponsored immigrants*. Sponsorship of

FIGURE 8.1   Immigrants and Visible Minorities: Percentage of Census Metropolitan Areas, 1996

	Immigrants	Visible Minorities
Toronto	42	32%
Vancouver	35	31
Hamilton	24	8
Kitchener	22	9
Windsor	21	10
Calgary	21	16
Victoria	19	8
St. Catherines–Niagara	18	4
London	19	8
Edmonton	19	14
Winnipeg	17	11
Oshawa	17	6
Montreal	18	12
Ottawa–Hull	16	12
Thunder Bay	12	2
Regina	8	5
Saskatoon	8	5
Sudbury	8	2
Halifax	7	7
Saint John	4	2
Sherbrooke	4	2
St. John's	3	1
Quebec	3	1
Trois-Rivieres	2	1
Chicoutimi-Jonquiere	<1	<1

Source: Statistics Canada, The Daily, Catalogue No. 11-001, Nov. 4, 1997, Chart 5; Feb, 17, 1998, Chart 1.

new immigrants by relatives has been the characteristic pattern among some ethnic populations such as Italians, Greeks, and Portuguese. Conversely, 63 percent of newcomers to Canada from Asia, 75 percent from the Caribbean, and 71 percent from South America immigrated as members of the family class or as assisted relatives during the years 1981 through 1985 (White, 1990: Table B4).

Through chain migration, separated family members and friends may be reunited, and a supportive community is often formed that may help the immigrant to cope with the inevitable experience of alienation associated with confronting a new and strange culture. Whole families, even entire villages, have been transplanted from Lebanon, Italy, Portugal, Greece, and many other

Around a widening network of chain migration, an ethnic community takes shape.

parts of the world to urban neighbourhoods in Canada (for example, see Campani, 1992).

Chain migration is an adaptation and extension of traditional kinship and friendship ties and reciprocal commitments. The new arrival from Gagliano, resettled in Toronto with his aunt and uncle's aid, paid rent to them, helped them to build an addition to their house, and was a frequent and welcome visitor for evening chats. Perhaps in time, the newcomer in turn assisted other relatives to resettle in Toronto. Around a widening network of such exchanges over a period of time, an ethnic community takes shape.

Most ethnic communities develop *institutions*— organized, patterned ways of behaving and carrying on social interaction in order to accomplish specific goals of the group and meet its collective needs. Institutions such as religious organizations, separate schools, shops and professional services, social agencies, political or advocacy organizations, and cultural and social organizations may appear to

parallel and duplicate organizations already present in the larger society. But Rosenberg and Jedwab (1992) suggested that ethnic groups develop organizations as a means of coping with community needs that are not otherwise met within the context of Canadian society. In a study of the Italian, Jewish, and Greek communities of Montreal, they found that each group developed and used ethnic organizations in different ways, depending upon how the group was treated by the surrounding Quebec society. In a survey of nine ethnic groups in Toronto, Breton (1990) also found considerable variation among the groups in degree of involvement in ethnic organizations. However, most groups preferred to use mainstream organizations, such as human rights commissions or unions, to deal with discrimination, rather than turn to ethnic community organizations.

The degree to which an ethnic population develops a strong sense of solidarity and ethnic identity and a self-sufficient range of ethnic institutions parallelling those of the larger society, referred to as **institutional completeness**, depends upon many factors. These may include the group's cultural values and social patterns, the treatment it receives from the society around it, the size of the city and of the ethnic population, its prosperity, and the nature of the employment opportunities offered by the region in which the community is located. If an ethnic community builds a secure niche within a local economic structure, it may grow in size and affluence, be able to support ethnic organizations, and develop common economic and political interests as well. For example, in postwar Toronto, Italian immigrants established themselves in the construction industry as labourers and craftspeople, and increasingly, as contractors and developers (Reitz, 1990). As a consequence of such occupational specialization, ethnic community members may come to share values that go beyond language, culture, and social ties, to encompass well-defined economic and political interests. Many other examples of occupational specialization within a local economy could be mentioned, including Toronto's Macedonians, who concentrated in the restaurant and catering business (Herman, 1978); postwar immigrants from the Netherlands, who have been well represented in agriculture (Ishwaran, 1977); and recent immigrants from Hong Kong, many of whom are entrepreneurs in Canada.

Perhaps to some degree occupational specialization is rooted in the desires of immigrants themselves, who may come to Canada seeking opportunities to farm, own a business, or practise a trade or profession—goals that may be difficult to achieve in their homelands. It has also been Canada's policy to encourage the immigration of experienced and trained farmers, entrepreneurs, tradespeople, and professionals.

Occupational specialization and exploitation may result in part from discrimination or limited opportunities in the local economy. Although discrimination in employment on the basis of ethnicity, race, or religion is legally prohibited in Canada, job opportunities for some racial and ethnic groups, and for immigrants in particular, may be limited. Reitz (1990: 178–79) found that, for immigrants in Toronto who had low educational qualifications, ethnic specialties provided opportunities to earn income, but in jobs of low status. For example, Portuguese women were ten times more likely than other women to work as cleaners (Reitz, 1990). At the same time, access to an ethnic labour market can contribute to the business success of ethnic entrepreneurs. For Germans, Jews, and Ukrainians, Reitz (1990: 181) found that ethnic occupational concentration had no negative effect on income or status, and for Italian men, working in an ethnic business had a positive effect on income. Thus some members of ethnic groups seem to derive benefits from ethnic specialization, but its impact on occupational status and income varies, depending on a particular group's or individual's circumstances.

There is evidence that occupational differences among white ethnic groups have declined over time (Isajiw, Sev'er, and Driedger, 1993), although some distinctive ethnic occupational concentrations persist. Thus, white ethnic groups have experienced upward mobility in the occupational structure, to the point where they have reached income equality with the majority population, provided they have adequate qualifications. A growing body of Canadian research, however, suggests that race and Aboriginal status are associated with disadvantage in occupational status and income (Agócs and Boyd, 1993; Lautard and Guppy, 1990). Satzewich and Li (1987) found that immigrants who are members of racial minorities in Canada have lower incomes and occupational status than European and U.S. immigrants who arrived in Canada at the same time, even when sex, age, English proficiency, and level of education are statistically controlled. Reitz (1990: 160–61) found that in Toronto, men of West Indian and Chinese ethnicity had much lower incomes than the majority white population and the other five ethnic groups in the study, when education, work experience, and hours worked were taken into account. (Further evidence of racial discrimination in employment will be discussed later in this chapter).

We have begun our discussion of Canadian race and ethnic relations by trying to understand something of the origin, development, institutional framework, and economic base of the local community that originates as a consequence of migration. It is now necessary to address the more general questions of the meanings of ethnicity, race, and minority-group status.

Ethnic Group, Race, and Minority Group: Some Definitions

The ethnic group

The Turks of Germany, the Scots of Canada, the Italians of Australia, and the Kurds of Iraq all may be seen as examples of *ethnic groups*. They all exist within pluralistic societies in which peoples of various cultural, religious, or racial backgrounds live side by side, however uneasily, within a single social, economic, and political system. Such societies exist as a consequence of the historical processes of colonialism, conquest, and migration. Before we turn to an overview of the ways in which these processes have shaped the evolution of ethnic and race relations in Canada, it is necessary to explore the meaning of the concept ethnic group.

An **ethnic group** is a highly variable and complex social entity that has assumed various forms in different societies and historical eras; scholars, therefore, disagree on its defining characteristics. The influential theoretical perspectives of Weber (1946) and Barth (1969) suggest, however, that ethnicity has four major dimensions, listed in Chart 8.1, with their manifestations at the individual and group levels.

Ethnicity as an ascribed status

To say that membership in a social group is an ascribed status means that it is *usually* conferred at birth, a social attribute inherited from parents and other ancestors. Ethnicity, like race, gender, and age, is not something that individuals aspire to, strive for, choose, or achieve in life, except in rare and controversial instances. Like other gifts or accidents of birth, ethnicity is a relatively enduring identity, rather than something that can be set aside or changed, as an occupation can be. It is one of those givens of social existence that become deeply embedded within individual identity. Of course, individuals will vary in the degree to which ethnicity is central in this respect.

The fact that ethnicity is ascribed means that ethnic groups are self-perpetuating, an important characteristic differentiating ethnic groups from other kinds of social groups such as religious sects or voluntary associations. The ethnic group, then, includes ancestors long dead, as well as those who are the present-day carriers of the group's culture, and probably at least some of their children as well. Because the ethnicity of parents and ancestors is visited upon their children and grandchildren, the ethnic group itself continues to exist from generation to generation, at least as a potential that may be realized under certain conditions.

To say that ethnic identity is ascribed and that ethnic groups are self-perpetuating does not mean that ethnic groups are biological entities, or that individuals inherit behaviours or cultural patterns or even combinations of physical traits. Ethnicity is not a matter of biological inheritance, but of social definition and experience.

CHART 8.1   Some Defining Characteristics of the Ethnic Group

	Dimensions of ethnicity			
	An ascribed status	A form of social organization	A subculture	A focus of identity
Individual ethnic group members	inherit ethnic group membership	are involved in interaction and a shared institutional framework	tend to share some fundamental values	feel a sense of belonging with other members
The ethnic group as a whole	is self-perpetuating	has boundaries	transmits a culture rooted in historical experience	is recognized as a collectivity by others in the society

Ethnicity as a form of social organization

From the perspective of its individual members, the ethnic group may be viewed as a set of social relationships originating within a family, and radiating outward to include primary ties with kin, friends, neighbours, and others with whom interaction is frequent. If informal interaction and communication patterns tend to be particularly intense among persons of the same ethnicity, then these relationships may be said to form an *ethnic network*. Members of a network frequently share a set of values and way of life, and individuals may identify their personal fates with these people. For some, being part of an ethnic group may meet needs for social relatedness and belonging.

As one element of a pluralistic society, then, the ethnic community is a product of social interaction rather than formal organization. The ethnic community has no rules of membership, no coordinating agency, no official leadership. Yet it does have norms that regulate membership, an internal social hierarchy, and formal organizations that promote group solidarity and meet collective needs.

An important feature of the ethnic group as a form of social organization is that it has boundaries that include some individuals but exclude others. If a social group is to have an identity, it must have boundaries that are set and maintained by patterns of interaction. Some kinds of social interactions may be confined largely within the group while others are not.

In part, ethnic group boundaries may be culturally defined; for example, an Irish Protestant who marries a Jew may be included within the boundaries of the Jewish community by converting to its religion. Sometimes geographic concentration and isolation from other groups can contribute to the maintenance of ethnic boundaries, as among the Old Order Mennonites and Hutterites, who choose to minimize contact with others by separating their communities both geographically and socially from the surrounding population. Spatial separation or segregation may reinforce discriminatory social barriers between ethnic populations and the rest of society. The isolation of Native peoples as a result of the reserve system has helped to maintain boundaries between them and other Canadians, and has contributed to their lack of access to educational and occupational opportunities, health care, and the standard of living generally available to other Canadians.

However, the survival of an ethnic group usually does not depend upon physical isolation. An ethnic group's boundaries may persist even when its members live side by side with other groups, and participate with others in economic, social, and political activities. For example, the Jewish community retains a high degree of ethnic identity, solidarity, and community involvement within the context of a highly urbanized and cosmopolitan lifestyle (Isajiw, 1990; Breton, 1990).

Boundaries are perhaps most effectively maintained not by physical isolation or separation, but by social norms that influence behaviour in interpersonal relationships. Norms, or expectations about role behaviour, are learned during socialization within a family and community, and are continually reinforced through daily interaction and experience. While norms may regulate or restrict inter-ethnic contacts in intimate relationships, contacts that do not threaten group boundaries may be permitted more readily. In many plural societies, ethnic groups meet in the marketplace, at work, or in school. Ethnic *endogamy*—that is, marriage within an ethnic group—is perhaps the critical factor in the maintenance of ethnic group boundaries. Isajiw (1990: 77–81) found that Toronto ethnic groups differ in their emphasis on marriage within the group. For the Jewish group, endogamy remained an important value into the third generation, while for Ukrainians, Germans, and Italians, it decreased in importance with each generation in Canada.

The ethnic group as a subculture

An ethnic group as a social organization, with boundaries maintained by social norms governing interaction, has an existence of its own, independent of its individual members. It persists from generation to generation; it has a history. The sharing of experience over time gives specific cultural meanings to the social relationships that ethnic group members have with one another. These historical experiences are unique to each group, and are an important dimension of the ethnic identity that is passed down to succeeding generations during socialization. They shape understandings of what it means to belong to the ethnic group. Shared understandings growing out of a group's historical experience give support to a complex of shared values as well as to personal identity.

Generally speaking, the sharing of cultural traits such as food preferences or distinctive styles of musical expression need not be a defining characteristic of an ethnic group. Italians may remain Italians even if they do not enjoy the opera, read no Italian newspapers, and belong to no church. And Poles who do these things, nevertheless, will not be defined as Italians. While ethnic group members may tend to share certain cultural traits and many values, it would be a misconception to define ethnic group membership in these terms.

The sharing of language is a bit different. The maintenance of language has been considered a fundamental aspect of collective existence for French Canadians and Ukrainians, but has not been as strongly emphasized by German, Italian, or Jewish Canadians (Isajiw, 1990: 51). Among some Aboriginal peoples, there is currently a strong interest in teaching their original language to the young as a part of cultural survival and spiritual renewal (e,g., Lawrence, 1999: 1).

The 1980s and 1990s saw a growing presence in Canada of people whose mother tongue is a language other than English or French, primarily as a result of immigration. The Census of Canada defines mother tongue as the first language a person learns at home in childhood and still understands. In 1996 about 17 percent of Canadians reported mother tongues other than the two official languages. The most frequently reported languages are Chinese, Italian, German, Spanish, Portuguese, Polish, Punjabi, Aboriginal languages, Ukrainian, Arabic, and Tagalog (Statistics Canada, *The Daily*, Dec. 2, 1997).

Ethnicity as a focus of identity

Socialization, discussed in Chapter 4, is the critical factor in the acquisition of ethnic identity. Ethnic identity is a part of self-concept. If both parents are members of the ethnic group, or if the family participates actively in the life of one ethnic community, children may form a strong identification with that group. Their individual personalities become firmly linked with the historical experience, values, way of life, and social patterns that are at the core of group life. Thus, personal identity and collective identity become intertwined.

However, the process of acquiring ethnic identity is usually not simple in contemporary pluralistic societies. As children grow up, they typically confront many influences that go beyond the home and primary social network to include educational, communications, government, and other institutions of the larger society, and a variety of informal social contacts. In such encounters, children may also learn that their group occupies a lower rank in the stratification system of the larger society, and that social mobility or acceptance by the larger society may demand compromising their ethnic identity. An extreme example is the treatment of Native children in Canadian residential schools, where they were forced to live apart from their families and communities, were punished for speaking their own languages or maintaining their communities' beliefs and values, and were often victims of abuse (Fournier and Crey, 1997; Miller, 1996).

Because of such oppressive experiences—and because it may be painful to be singled out for being "different"—children may experience considerable conflict between the two worlds in which they live: the home and ethnic community, and the larger society, including the school and peer group.

Children of immigrants sometimes live on the margin between two worlds, bearing two competing identities that are equally important.

Stonequist (1963) used the term **marginality** to describe the condition of personal identity whereby individuals function and identify themselves as members of the group into which they were born, while at the same time participating in another very different and sometimes hostile world (Streitmatter, 1988). Living on the margin between two worlds, full members of neither, they bear within themselves two competing identities.

Situations in which individuals assume a new ethnic identity represent interesting instances of marginality. The author and conservationist Grey Owl was born in 1888 in England, where he had a conventional Victorian childhood as Archie Belaney. Soon after his immigration to Canada in 1906, he settled with an Ojibway band, learned their language, married an Ojibway woman, and identified himself as Native for the rest of his life. Grey Owl's lectures and writings advocating the protection of Canada's wildlife commanded a large and enthusiastic following while he lived. But after he died, it was discovered that he had not been born an Indian, and there was public outrage about the fact that he had presented himself as one (Dickson, 1973). (A 1999 feature film *Grey Owl*, directed by Richard Attenborough, portrays these interesting events.)

Race and minority group

The public reaction to the discovery that Grey Owl was really Archie Belaney suggests the power of the social meanings attached to ethnic labels. Grey Owl lived in an Ojibway community as an accepted member, yet the general public to whom he addressed his writings ridiculed him as a white man masquerading as Native, a fraud who tried to present himself as a member of a social category to which they felt he did not really belong.

Inherited features such as family surname and physical traits, such as skin colour and hair texture, in themselves have no necessary consequences for behaviour. Yet such identifying features often become *socially defined* as very significant. All individuals who have a particular characteristic, such as dark skin, may be seen by others as members of a single **social category**, which is defined as a collection of individuals all of whom share a single trait that is regarded as socially

meaningful. The social meaning attached to racial or ethnic categories often includes the assignment of a rank within the hierarchy of society. This position is not necessarily subordinate; ethnicity is not always stigmatizing, nor always associated with oppression. It is quite possible for an ethnic group to occupy an élite or privileged status, as English Canadians have done until recently in the economic life of Quebec.

Frequently, however, racial or ethnic labels become criteria for assigning individuals or groups to subordinate positions within a social hierarchy. Moghaddam and Taylor (1987) studied the effects of this process on women who had immigrated to Canada from India. These women tended to perceive themselves as "women," "individuals," and "Canadian." But they felt they were perceived by most Canadians as "Indian," "women," "immigrants," "coloured," and "South Asian"— labels associated with lower status in Canadian society.

Members of a social category may not have anything in common beyond their shared identifying features. However, if as a consequence of their treatment and position in society they become involved in social interaction with one another, and come to share values and a sense of identity and common interests, they may *become* a social group. This process of *ethnogenesis* has occurred among the First Nations of North America, who lived as separate and frequently warring groups, each with its own culture, until Europeans forced upon them a common label and identity. It was only because Columbus thought he had arrived in India that the label "Indians" was applied to Aboriginal peoples of the Americas.

Race and racism

A primary example of an arbitrary social category is a **race**, which is thought to consist of persons who share inherited physical characteristics such as skin colour and facial features, characteristics charged with social meaning in many societies. Indeed, an enormous amount of scientific evidence has invalidated notions that genetically separate races of human beings ever existed. A recent comprehensive review of evidence from genetic research (Templeton, 1999: 632) concludes that human "races" are not pure and that this is not due to recent intermarriages. "Instead, human evolution has been and is characterized by many locally differentiated populations coexisting at any given time, but with sufficient genetic contact to make all of humanity a single lineage sharing a common evolutionary fate."

Moreover, research in genetics has established that the physical attributes that have been considered the markers of race, such as stature, skin and eye colour, or hair texture, are inherited quite independently of one another and are not always found together. The so-called "races" thus can best be understood as social constructs defined by dominant groups in a society (Li, 1988: 23) to justify exploitation and their oppression of minority groups.

Racism is an ideology that regards racial or ethnic categories as natural genetic groupings, and

that attributes behavioural and psychological differences to the genetic nature of these groupings. Biological traits are used to label some human beings—invariably those belonging to categories other than the one doing the labelling—as inherently inferior, and therefore proper objects of exploitation and domination.

During this century, racist notions have been used to rationalize the oppression of Aboriginal peoples, the Nazi extermination of Jews and Gypsies, and laws restricting the immigration of southern European and Asian peoples to Canada and the United States.

Social scientists, like others who influence public opinion, have contributed their share to racist

A Comment on the Terminology of Race

The term race refers not to "real" social groupings whose membership can be specified objectively or empirically, but to arbitrary categories that reflect a social process of labelling and classification. The concept of race has changed through time, and has taken on various social meanings that have had profoundly negative effects upon the lives of individuals and groups of people. So while race is a product of human decisions that have no scientific basis, the reality of "race" as a social concept cannot be denied; nor can the fact that the concept of race has been used as the basis for social stratification, oppression, and the denial of the humanity of the majority of the world's people. As the sociologist W.I. Thomas pointed out: "[W]hat is perceived as real is real in its consequences" (Merton, 1957: 421).

In today's pluralistic society, a variety of terms are used to refer to the concepts of race, colour, or mi-

nority status based upon physical characteristics. It is probably true that all of these terms create discomfort and misunderstanding, especially to the degree that they are words used primarily by dominant white majorities to refer to people whom they consider to be different. For example, in Canadian legislation, government policy, and data reported by Statistics Canada, the term *visible minorities* is used. This phrase is commonly used to refer to people who look different from the white majority in Canada because of the colour of their skin or facial characteristics, and who often are disadvantaged in the workplace as a consequence. A great variety of peoples are lumped into the category of visible minorities, including Chinese, South Asian, black, Arab/West Asian, Philipino, Southeast Asian, Latin American, Japanese, Korean, and Pacific Islanders <**www.statcan.ca/ english/Pgdlo/People/Popul ation/def/defdemo40h.htm**>.

Clearly, the term visible minority does not refer to a social group. Other terms including *people of colour* and *racial minorities* are also used to refer to this category.

It should be noted that aboriginal peoples in Canada do not see themselves as a "visible minority" or an ethnic group within the multicultural population of Canada, but as Canada's First Nations—sovereign peoples whose relationship to the government and people of Canada has yet to be defined.

Deconstructing the various terms that refer to race and to Aboriginal ancestry, and subjecting them to historical and critical analysis, is an important project for interdisciplinary research. Any terminology that is imposed upon minorities by dominant majorities, rather than developed and proposed by these groups to refer to themselves, will be problematic and implicated in the structure of racism in society.

thinking (Gould, 1981). In North America, for example, ethnic groups were called "races" throughout the early decades of this century, and Canadian political leaders and social scientists argued in favour of restricting the immigration of U.S. blacks, Chinese, and other groups, on the grounds that they were undesirables, or not biologically equipped to adapt to the Canadian climate (Krauter and Davis, 1978). The term "race" was used in the Canadian census to refer to the French- as well as the English-origin population until 1941. However, largely through the efforts of later generations of social and biological scientists and of human rights, ethnic, labour, and community organizations, racist ideas have been challenged and have weakened their hold on popular thinking in Canada, although they are far from disappearing. Indeed, racist conceptions continue to be put forward in both academic and political contexts, in Canada as in other parts of the world.

Minority groups and patterns of subordination

A **minority group** is a social category that occupies a subordinate rank in a social hierarchy; such a group is accorded unequal treatment and excluded from full participation in the life of society. The term *minority* refers not to the size of the group—a minority may outnumber dominant groups, as in South Africa under apartheid—but to its position in a context of power relationships. In post-Confederation Canada, Japanese, Chinese, First Nations, Inuit, and blacks have suffered restrictions on their freedom of access to employment, housing, education, and citizenship (Boyko, 1998). The right to vote has at some time been denied to each of these groups.

In the modern world, extreme forms of social control have been used to subordinate minorities of all types. Such measures include *expulsion*, the forcible removal of a minority from its homeland—a fate suffered by Canada's First Nations during the settlement of the country, and by west-coast Japanese Canadians during World War II. Soon after Canada declared war on Japan, all persons of Japanese origin living within one hundred miles of British Columbia's coastline, the majority of them Canadian citizens, were forcibly evacuated from their homes. They were stripped of their property

and placed in "relocation centres" in Alberta, Ontario, and other provinces, where they lived in camps and worked as farm labourers. After the war, many Japanese remaining in Canada were not able to return to their west-coast communities, but remained dispersed in other areas (Sunahara, 1981).

The modern world has also seen instances of *annihilation* or *genocide*—the intentional massacre of peoples. The destruction of certain aboriginal groups as a result of the European conquest of the Americas, of European Jews and Gypsies by the Nazis, of Armenians in Turkey, and of Muslims in Bosnia-Herzegovina are but a few items in a catalogue of horrors (Chalk and Jonassohn, 1990). The "ethnic cleansing" operations directed against the Kosovars in Yugoslavia in 1999 is a more recent example.

Dominant groups frequently control and restrict the economic, social, and political participation of minorities by means of **discrimination**, the practice of denying to members of certain social categories opportunities that are generally available within the society. Discrimination may in some instances occur by legal means (*de jure*). For example, until 1960 an article of the Indian Act withheld the vote from Indians in all provinces except Newfoundland. More common in Canada today is *de facto* discrimination that occurs as a matter of common practice, often in violation of the law, as in the case of a landlord who, in contravention of provincial human rights statutes, finds an excuse for refusing to rent an apartment to someone of another race.

Considerable Canadian evidence on the prevalence of discrimination against members of minority groups exist. Driedger and Mezoff (1981) for example, found that two-thirds of Jewish high-school students in their Winnipeg sample had experienced discrimination, in the form of verbal abuse, ethnic jokes, language ridicule, and other acts. Almost half the Polish-, Italian-, and French-origin students also reported these experiences. In another study, approximately two-thirds of women who had immigrated to Canada from India felt they had been badly treated in Canada because of their race (Moghaddam and Taylor, 1987: 134). Finally, a 1995–96 survey of 1081 graduates of York University in Toronto tracked experiences with the job market a few months after graduation. Looking just at graduates who had found or were looking

Land of Opportunity for Whom?

A telephone poll of 1 575 adults in the greater Toronto area conducted by Goldfarb Consultants for the *Toronto Star* found that racial minority groups are much more likely than other Toronto residents to personally experience discrimination. The *Star* reported that 62 percent of blacks, 37 percent of Chinese, 40 percent of Filipinos, and 37 percent of Hispanics say they have experience discrimination, compared with 29 percent of the non-minority Torontonians surveyed.

Discrimination was found to affect the search for a job, wage levels, and access to raises and promotions. Respondents from the black, West Asian/Arab and South Asian groups are most likely to state that finding a job is their most serious problem; these communities also report the lowest household income, and the least satisfaction with life in Toronto. In contrast, 80 percent of Italian and Portuguese respondents indicate that they feel they have fair and equitable pay, access to jobs, promotions and

raises. While 86 percent of the general population feels their community is treated fairly by the media, only 32 percent of blacks and 49 percent of South Asians feel that their communities get fair treatment in the media. (Results from the total sample are considered accurate within 2 percentage points, 19 times out of 20; the margin of error is higher for individual minority groups).

Source: Adapted from "Opportunity knocks...but not for all." Toronto Star, 2 May 1999.

for full-time jobs, the researchers found that both parents' income and ethno-racial origin made a large difference. While 58 percent of graduates of European origin had found full-time employment, only 40 percent of black, 54 percent of South Asian, and 35 percent of Chinese origin were employed full time. The impact of class and ethno-racial origin strongly influenced success in getting full-time work, even when skills, area and type of degree, grade-point average, and other factors were considered in the regression analysis (Grayson, 1997). See the box "Land of Opportunity for Whom?".

Systemic or **institutionalized discrimination** occurs as a by-product of the ordinary functioning of bureaucratic institutions, rather than as a consequence of a deliberate policy or motive to discriminate. Systemic discrimination consists of patterns of institutional practices that perpetuate majority-group privilege and create disadvantage for minorities simply by conducting "business as usual." For example, by setting a rule that recruits must be at least 1.8 m tall, a police department may effectively exclude many ethnic applicants, for reasons unrelated to their ability to do the job, since the average height of members of these groups is less than the Canadian average. Systemic discri-

mination may also take the form of exclusion of minority women and men from informal communication and social networks, or biased decision making about promotions, job assignment or pay (e.g., Burke, 1991; Ibarra, 1993; Karambayya, 1997).

There is strong evidence that minorities in Canada also face wage discrimination. In an analysis of 1991 census data, Li (1998) found that native-born and foreign-born white Canadians have an earnings advantage, while native-born and foreign-born visible minorities and Aboriginal peoples have an earnings disadvantage when year of education, age, nativity, full-time vs. part-time employment, gender, industry, occupation, and number of weeks worked are statistically controlled. The most severe pay disadvantage was suffered by foreign-born visible minorities, despite their higher than average level of education (Li, 1998: 123).

Research in Toronto has demonstrated the existence of direct discrimination by employers against black job-applicants. Pairs of job applicants, matched in all respects except that one was black and the other white, applied for over 430 advertised jobs. The whites received three job offers for every one received by the black applicants, who experienced many instances of discriminatory treatment (Henry and Ginzberg, 1985; 1993). Similar field trials in Washington, D.C., and Chicago found levels of discrimination comparable to those found in the Toronto study, suggesting that "discriminatory practices are not widely different in the two countries" (Reitz and Breton, 1994: 84–85).

Many other studies in Canada and the United States have shown how discriminatory employment practices restrict access to jobs, promotions, and equal pay for North American-born black and Asian minorities (for example, see Duleep and Sanders, 1992). Analyses of data for Toronto (Reitz, 1990: 151) and Canada (Boyd, 1993; Christofides and Swidinsky, 1994; Li, 1992) demonstrate that when education and other productivity factors are taken into account, minority women face even more income disadvantage than minority men in the workplace. Women who are members of minority groups, then, are doubly disadvantaged in employment due to the effects of both gender and minority- group discrimination (Das Gupta, 1996; Neallani, 1992).

Discrimination in employment is reinforced in some societies by the practice of segregation on the basis of minority status. **Segregation** is a form of social control whereby physical distance is maintained in order to ensure social distance from groups with whom contact is not wanted. Segregation involves the exclusion of ethnic, racial, or other minorities from the facilities, residential space, or institutions used by dominant groups.

For most of this century in South Africa, under an elaborate system of legislated racial segregation known as *apartheid*, or "apartness," every individual was classified by race; interracial sex and marriage were banned; and racially separate public facilities, educational systems, residential space, and work arrangements were enforced. After a struggle that lasted for generations and cost the deaths, imprisonment, and torture of thousands, the key segregation laws were repealed in 1991. Democratic elections in which all races voted were held for the first time in 1994, and Nelson Mandela was inaugurated as president, with a mandate for governance based on principles of reconciliation, democracy, and equality (Sparks, 1995).

Rates of residential separation among ethnic and racial groups are high and persistent in Canadian cities, even when socioeconomic status

Nelson Mandela has become a symbol of determination to end institutionalized segregation in South Africa.

is taken into account. Indexes of residential segregation are highest for the Jewish and Portuguese populations and moderate for the black, Chinese, Hungarian, Russian, and Italian groups (Kalbach, 1990: 98). In Toronto, the Chinese and black populations show a pattern of scattered pockets of concentration (Kalbach, 1990: 130). Research suggests that people's desire to live near others of the same background, discrimination, and poverty are causal factors in ethnic and racial residential separation (Agócs, 1979).

Explaining discrimination

In their attempt to explain discrimination in modern societies, social scientists have studied various kinds of influences. Before the 1960s, there was much interest in the role of ideas and beliefs in motivating

The Mass Media and Racial Minorities: "The Prism of Whiteness"

Few would dispute the prominence of the media in guiding, shaping, and transforming the way we look at the world...how we understand it...and the manner by which we experience and relate to it.... A media-dominated society such as ours elevates the electronic and print media into an important source of information on how to shape an operational image of the world... Those in control of media information define the beliefs, values, and myths by which we live and organize our lives. They impose a cultural context for framing our experiences of social reality, in the process sending out a clear message about who is normal and what is desirable and important in society....

Media values are designed around those priorities that can capture as large an audience as possible for maximizing advertising revenues.... Media messages come across as safe, simple, and predictable in order to appeal to the lowest common denominator in society. Information about the world, if it attracts a broad audience, is included. Otherwise it is excluded, especially if any potential exists to offend significant markets. Especially in advertising, the media acknowledge the necessity to cater to dominant attitudes and prejudice. The logic of these circumstances dictates media mistreatment of racial (and other) minorities as the norm rather than the exception....

The media in Canada relay information about who racial minorities are, what they want, why, how

they propose to achieve their goals, and with what consequence for Canadian society. How responsibly have the media acted in this respect?...

Certain patterns can be extrapolated from media (mis)treatment of racial minorities. Minorities are defined and categorized (a) as invisible, (b) in terms of race-role stereotyping, (c) as a social problem, and (d) as amusement....

(a) Minorities as Invisible

Racial minorities are reduced to invisible status through underrepresentation in programming, staffing, and decision-making. Minorities are deemed unworthy of coverage unless caught up in situations of conflict or crisis... This marginalization continues into advertising, where they are excluded because of minimal purchasing power or low socioeconomic status and prestige... A 1987 ACTRA (Alliance of Canadian Cinema, Television and Radio Artists) study found that minority members accounted for only 3 percent of the actors on Canadian stages, less than 3 percent of those in commercials, and 5.5 percent of the actors on television. This compares with the average of 16 percent representation in American television.... Media "whitewashing" (especially in advertising) contributes to the invisibility of minorities in society. Racial minorities are restricted in [a] way that "denies their existence, devalues their contribution to society, and trivializes their aspirations to participate, as fully-fledged members"....

(b) Minorities as Stereotypes

Minorities have long complained of stereotyping by the mass media. Notwithstanding some improvements in this area, the report card on mass media stereotyping shows only negligible improvement. Race-role images continue to be reinforced, perpetuated, and even legitimized through media dissemination and selective coverage. When appearing in advertising, racial minorities are often cast in slots that reflect a "natural" propensity for the product in question. Who better to sell foreign airlines, quality chamber-maid service in hotels, or high-cut gym shoes?...

(c) Minorities as Social Problem

Racial minorities are frequently singled out by the media as a "social problem." They are described in the context of "having problems" that require solutions requiring an inordinate amount of political attention and consuming a disproportionate slice of national resources... In addition, the media are likely to define minorities in terms of "creating problems" by making demands unacceptable to the social, political, or moral order of society. For example, aboriginal peoples in Canada are portrayed time and again as "troublesome constituents" whose demands for self-determination and self-government are anathema to Canada's liberal-democratic tradition. This "us versus them" mentality fostered by the media is conducive to the

continued

scapegoating of racial minorities, who are blamed for an assortment of social ills or economic misfortunes....

(d) Minorities as Amusement
Racial minorities are often portrayed as irrelevant to society at large. This decorative effect is achieved by casting minorities in the role of entertainment by which to amuse or divert the audience. On-air television programming creates a situation where racial minorities find themselves ghettoized into

roles as sit-com comedians. The restrictive effects of such an orientation serve to trivialize minority aspirations, as well as to diminish their importance as serious contributors to Canadian society...

Racial minorities are victimized by media treatment that confirms and endorses audience prejudice... Compounding the difficulties is the absence of racial minorities in creative positions, such as those of director, producer, editor, or screenwriter. Fewer still are positioned in the upper levels of man-

agement where key decision- making occurs. The experiences and realities of racial minorities are distorted by the media, largely because of the inability of largely white, middle-class media personnel to perceive and understand the world from a different point of view.

Source: *Augie Fleras and Jean Leonard Elliott, 1992.* Multiculturalism in Canada: The Challenge of Diversity. *Scarborough, Ont.: Nelson Canada (pp. 234–43). Reprinted by permission of ITP Nelson Canada.*

discriminatory acts against minority group members. Of special importance was the concept of **prejudice**, an attitude that prejudges individuals because of characteristics assumed to be shared by all members of their group. Those characteristics may be based on **stereotypes**—mental images that exaggerate what are usually perceived to be undesirable traits of typical members of a group, and which are applied to all of its members.

A prejudice is not a product of experience, and may persist despite contrary evidence, particularly when prejudice serves to rationalize a position of privilege. One reason prejudice is often so deeply entrenched is that it is a part of culture that is learned early, and that it is a product of negative emotions as well as mental images (see Sniderman et al., 1993). The teachings of parents and teachers, the nursery rhymes and stories, the television shows and media children are exposed to all contain assumptions and evaluations concerning social groups and their attributes and social ranks. Indeed, the mass media in Canada continue to be criticized for ignoring ethnic and racial minorities and for presenting them in ways that are stereotyped, inaccurate, and insulting (Fleras and Elliott, 1992: 233). (See the box "The Mass Media and Racial Minorities.")

The connection between prejudiced attitudes and discriminatory behaviour has been the subject of a great deal of research over the past few decades.

The implication of many studies is that the relationship between attitudes and behaviour is extremely complex. A prejudiced person does not always act in a discriminatory way, and there is little evidence that discriminatory behaviour is caused by prejudiced attitudes.

Survey evidence has shown that, with the passing generations, the attitudes of whites towards minority racial and ethnic groups have become more tolerant and accepting. A 1990 survey by Decima found that 90 percent of Canadians and 86 percent of Americans agreed that "all races are created equal" (Reitz and Breton, 1994: 67–68). Yet often visible minorities in Canada continue to suffer from disproportionate rates of poverty, unemployment, menial occupational status, and poor living conditions as mentioned above (Small, 1998). Clearly, improvement in the attitudes of the dominant group is not in itself a solution to the problems of inequality and discrimination.

Race and Ethnic Relations in Canada in the Twentieth Century: An Overview

Intergroup relationships in Canada in this century have been shaped by the historical processes of colonialism, conquest, and migration, processes that continue to have influence generations after these events took place. Colonized groups such as the First Nations of North America became part of a plural society involuntarily, by coercion, and remain economically and politically marginal to that society. The military conquest of Canada's French by the British shaped subsequent relationships between the two majority groups. Migrating groups, such as the many of Asian, South or Central American, or those of European origin who now populate Canada, entered the society voluntarily, although economic need or political repression may have driven them from their homelands. The communities and institutions they have established in Canada are not transplants, but new social forms created in response to the challenges that confronted them in the new country. We shall discuss each of these historical processes in turn.

Colonialism and the First Nations

The struggles and accommodations that have characterized contacts between aboriginal peoples— or First Nations, Métis, and Inuit—and the rest of Canadian society reflect a system of inter group relations that grew out of **colonialism**. In colonial situations, whether in the Americas, Africa, or elsewhere in the world, a settler culture and society have invaded and dominated an indigenous population, controlling and exploiting the land, resources, and institutions of that population, and over time undermining or destroying its culture and way of life.

In the course of colonization, the settler country generally sends out representatives to extract resources from the colonized land, establish settlements, and administer the indigenous population. As institutions of the settler country are imposed on the native population, frequently by violent means, the erosion of their culture and economy proceeds. Thus, a social system becomes established that is characterized by external control and seizure of the indigenous population's property, and their oppression and enforced dependence— all of which is rationalized by a racist ideology.

During the earliest period in the colonization of Canada by the French and English, the First Nations provided for their own survival needs in traditional ways, through fishing, hunting, gathering, trading, and cultivating crops. But during the early sixteenth century, cooperative relationships in the fur trade were established between the Europeans, especially the French, and various First Nations. By the end of the century, the trading economy had undermined traditional subsistence activities and incited warfare among Native groups vying for exclusive trading alliances with the European powers.

Both the French and the British used trading relationships with First Nations for economic gain and to enlist them as allies against their enemies. But as political and economic realities changed, and these alliances and trade relationships became less useful and profitable, the British increasingly made war upon First Nations. They wanted Native lands for their land-hungry settlers. Some of these white encroachments were met with armed resistance, as in the 1869 and 1885 rebellions of Indians and Métis under the leadership of Louis Riel in the Red River and Saskatchewan River regions. The first rebellion ended with limited gains for the Natives, but the second ended in complete defeat and the hanging of Riel. By 1901, wars, forced resettlement, and disease had brought an absolute decline in the size of Canada's Indian population, from an estimated 200 000 to 1 000 000 at the beginning of European settlement to not much more than 100 000 (Beaujot, 1978: 36).

The practice of negotiating treaties with individual bands, begun by the British Crown and continuing after Confederation (1867), resulted in the surrender by some First Nations of their interests in their ancestral lands, sometimes in exchange for the right to live on reserves as wards of the state, segregated from the rest of Canadian society. Under the terms of the Indian Act (first passed in 1876 and subsequently revised), *registered* or *status Indians* are entitled to live on reserve lands and to receive certain government programs and services, such as education and health care. However, some First Nations have opted out of certain sections of the Indian Act and some are self-governing.

Since Confederation, the affairs of status Indians have been managed by various branches and departments of the federal government, which has administered the reserves, band funds, property, education, welfare, and the fulfillment of treaty obligations. As the reserve systems and residential schools became entrenched, First Nations

Nunavut: A Distinct Inuit Society

(Note that this article was published in 1993. Nunavut became a separate territory April 1, 1999.)

The map of Canada is being redrawn. The Inuit of the Eastern Arctic have reached a land-claim agreement with the Government of Canada. It is the largest and richest Native land claim ever in Canada, perhaps in the world. But it is even more than that, because tied to it is the creation of a new territory—Nunavut—Canada's third northern territory, which will be carved out of the Northwest Territories. Stretching from the Manitoba border to the northern tip of Ellesmere Island, Nunavut will be larger than any other province or territory, and twice the size of British Columbia. When the new territory is officially born on April 1, 1999, the working language of its government will be Inuktitut, since 80 percent of its 22 000 residents are Inuit....

For Canada, Nunavut represents a new relationship with an Aboriginal group. For the first time, a provincial or territorial government will speak largely on behalf of one group of Native people. While Nunavut will not mean self-government for Inuit in a constitutional sense, it will be self-government in effect, because of the Inuit majority. The Inuit will acquire responsibility for a host of social, economic, and political problems, and must hope that the solutions can be found with their powerful new tools of government and management. Defining how they will exercise these powers is the next major challenge facing Inuit leaders.

"Inuit will have enormous influence on issues that concern them," says John Amagoalik, who is sometimes called the father of Nunavut. He was one of a dedicated group of Inuit who devoted much of the last twenty years of their lives to the negotiations. Those issues of Inuit concern distill down to a sense of control over their own lives, and recognition of the right to self-determination. "We are very much a distinct society," he says. "The Nunavut government will have the responsibility of protecting and preserving that distinct society."

The accord gives the Inuit the same control over their affairs as other territorial governments have, and more autonomy than any other Native group in Canada. The land-claim settlement gives the Inuit outright ownership of about 18 percent of the land... The remaining 82 percent...remains Crown land, but the Inuit will have joint control with the federal government over land-use planning, wildlife, environmental protection, and off-shore resources. Inuit will keep the right to hunt, fish, and trap throughout Nunavut. The settlement also gives them $1.15 billion, which they hope will help generate economic and social revival.

It is not a perfect deal for the Inuit. To get it, they agreed to sign away forever any future claim to Aboriginal title to the land. But, to many, it was a triumph of patience and dedication, as more than a decade and a half of difficult negotiations came to fruition....

A key to Amagoalik's perseverance may lie in his own childhood experience of Inuit powerlessness. He was among the Inuit who were experimentally relocated by the federal government in 1953 from Inukjuak, in northern Quebec, to Ellesmere Island. He remains outspoken about the deception that led to his family's relocation into an area of poor hunting and wretched living conditions. The federal government, to this day, refuses to acknowledge the move was for sovereignty reasons....

For most Inuit, one appealing aspect of Nunavut is that government will be closer to the people, both physically and spiritually. But a major problem will be how to gather and hear opinions from such remote communities. A solution may lie in the fact that the North is already well linked through satellite television services. Such an instantaneous communications link could be used to connect communities to one another and the leadership forum to its people...

Today there are profound social problems in Nunavut. Jobs are scarce and Native unemployment is commonly in the 30 to 50 percent range. Only 15 percent of students complete high school... "We know that our culture is eroding, that spousal assault and drug and alcohol abuse are increasing, that the suicide rate among young Inuit is a tragedy of national importance." The detractors of Nunavut say it will be impossible to create a new government amid such social ills and low levels of education. The proponents argue that Nunavut itself is the answer to these difficulties, with its opportunities for jobs and training.

Source: *David F. Pelly, 1993. "Dawn of Nunavut." Canadian Geographic, March/April 1993 (pp. 21–26).*

communities manifested the demoralization that has affected powerless colonized peoples in many parts of the world. Indian residents of reserves had few ways to influence the paternalistic and quasi-colonial government bureaucracies. (See Chapter 14, Social Movements.)

Non-status Indians are those who do not meet the criteria of status Indians under the Indian Act, and are thus exempt from the Act's provisions. So too are the *Métis*, a people descended from marriages between Indian women and early settlers, traders, and trappers, mainly of French and British stock. Although these groups suffered many of the same injustices and deprivations endured by status Indians, they do not have the same entitlements.

Canada's 33 000 Inuit are also exempt from the provisions of the Indian Act, and no historic treaties were made between the Inuit and the Government of Canada. Sustained contact between Inuit and other Canadians has occurred only recently, beginning with the construction of large military installations in the North during World War II. Since that time, change in the Inuit way of life has been rapid and dramatic, involving impoverishment, social disorganization, and much disruption of traditional ways of life, as is usual with colonialism, when a settler society invades and dominates an indigenous population. In recent years, government policy, including the forced removal of communities, and economic change have led to the concentration of many Inuit in urban centres, where educational and social service facilities and housing are located. The rapid importation of southern workers, institutions, consumer goods, and social patterns has further transformed traditional Inuit culture, economy, and family life, and created marginality among the young.

As a result of a comprehensive land claim settlement in 1993 between the federal government and the Inuit people, Canada's third territory, Nunavut, was created in the central and eastern Arctic on April 1, 1999. Nunavut, which means "our

The need to implement an alternative to the reserve system and the movement towards self-government by aboriginal peoples present a major policy dilemma for Canada's pluralistic society.

land" in Inuktitut, constitutes more than a fifth of Canada's land mass. In 1999, Nunavut established its own elected legislative assembly and government within the Canadian parliamentary system (Platiel, 1993). (See the box "Nunavut: a Distinct Inuit Society.")

In the post–World War II years, the size of the aboriginal population increased substantially, to 799 010 in 1996 (Statistics Canada, 1996 Census, *The Daily*, January 13, 1998: 2). The increase in numbers of aboriginal people counted is due in part to improved census questions, as well as to a 1985 amendment to the Indian Act that ended its discriminatory impact on Indian women who had married non-Natives, and on their children. Moreover, among registered Indians, the rate of population increase is about twice that of the rest of Canada, resulting in an Indian population that is younger than the Canadian average.

Today, approximately 47 percent of registered Indians live on the more than 2000 reserves in Canada. Living conditions vary considerably from one reserve to another, but generally speaking the reserve population is impoverished and lacks opportunity for higher education and employment. The average income on reserves is less than half the Canadian average (Indian & Northern Affairs Canada, *Information*, November 1997: 1). Life expectancy for Indians is about eight years below the Canadian average, and infant mortality is 1.7 times the national average (*Globe and Mail*, June 14, 1990). Many reserve communities face severe environmental hazards resulting from industrial and resource development, which has polluted waterways and disrupted the fish and game stocks upon which many communities have depended for a livelihood.

Increasing numbers of Indians have been migrating to urban centres, and sizeable Native populations have settled in Vancouver, Calgary, Edmonton, Regina, Saskatoon, Winnipeg, Toronto, and Montreal, as well as in a number of smaller centres located not far from reserves (McDonald, 1991). Research on the experiences of Indians in various Canadian cities has found a pattern of stratification similar to that existing on many reserves. Most off-reserve aboriginal people live in family households, but suffer severe economic and social disadvantage. The unemployment rate for aboriginal people living off-reserve is roughly triple the rate for the Canadian population (McDonald, 1991). In many instances, life in the city appears to offer no more advantages than living conditions on reserves, and there is evidence that, to many, reserve communities are more attractive than cities, especially if some economic opportunity is available (Gerber, 1984).

For First Nations people in Canadian society, whether living on or off reserves, the past twenty years have been a time of collective commitment and action directed towards change and renewal, and ultimately self-determination. Native associations, community organizations, and individuals are engaged in struggles to reclaim and strengthen their cultures, languages, religions, lands, communities, and families, which have all been profoundly damaged by the impact of colonialism and its legacy of discrimination and racism.

French and British Canadians: Two majorities, two solitudes

Conquest is another historical process that brings pluralist societies into being. In Canada, the British conquest of New France was followed by a series of events that established the foundations of contemporary French-British dualism. The dominant metaphors in Canadian scholarship as well as in law and popular tradition have long described Canada as a bicultural country composed of "two societies," "two majorities," "two charter groups," "two founding races"—and, some have added, "two solitudes."

The French-British relationship has distant historical roots that should be familiar to all Canadians. New France after 1663 was a French colony that was to be developed into a flourishing agricultural society resembling rural France. In 1665, when the Crown's first administrator, Jean Talon, arrived, New France held about 3000 settlers, the majority of whom were men and boys. By making land grants to discharged soldiers, offering land and free passage to new settlers from France, and importing shiploads of young French women whose orphaned or impoverished state left them few alternatives, Talon oversaw the growth of New France to 7833 French inhabitants by 1675 (Lower, 1973: 22). After that time, there was very little immigration from France, and today's population of some six million Canadians of French ancestry are largely the descendants of those early settlers.

The pattern of French settlement, known as the *seigneurial system*, entailed the granting of lands by the French crown to landowners (seigneurs), who declared themselves vassals to the king. *Seigneurs* were obliged to parcel out the lands under their authority to *habitants*, or permanent settlers. Small groups of *habitants* lived in parish communities, each with its Roman Catholic *curé*, who performed many essential secular as well as religious functions.

The *habitants* farmed long narrow strips of land running back from the rivers, but for the most part agriculture remained a subsistence activity rather than a profitable commercial venture. As an economic activity, farming could not compete with the fur trade, which grew in importance. The primary economic value of New France as a colony became its resource of furs, readily available through trade with Native peoples. Trade relationships between European countries and their colonies in general can be described as a mercantile system, characterized by crown control of industry and trade. Colonies were treated solely as sources of raw materials and labour, dependent upon the parent country for manufactured goods, as well as for defence and religious and political authority.

It was primarily to control the fur trade that the British and French states struggled for possession of New France. The struggle intensified after the founding of the Hudson's Bay Company. This famous company was entitled under charter from the English crown to exclusive trading and commercial rights, and to the rights to govern and to make war, in the lands now called northern Ontario and Quebec and in parts of Alberta and the Northwest Territories, as well as Manitoba and Saskatchewan. The Hudson's Bay Company soon established trade relations with the First Nations, who then became involved in the armed struggle between the British and French.

Not only commercial rivalry but also differences of religion, economic life, and culture figured in the British-French conflict. The large and relatively prosperous population of British Protestants, initially concentrated along the Atlantic coast, spread westward into French territory and consolidated Britain's hold upon the east. In the early eighteenth century France lost both Newfoundland and Acadia to the British, Acadia becoming Nova Scotia.

The Treaty of Paris (1763) transferred virtually all Canadian lands under French control to the British, whose empire now stretched from the Atlantic to the Mississippi. Britain then faced the problem of governing some 65 000 French-speaking Roman Catholics, who possessed a distinct way of life, history, language, and set of institutions. The British chose to deal with this challenge by establishing a policy of cultural and political pluralism that recognized the "French fact," legally acknowledging the special status of the French in Lower Canada. This recognition was embodied in the Quebec Act of 1774, which reaffirmed the religious freedom of Roman Catholics, confirmed the Church's right to tithes, recognized the seigneurial system of land tenure, allowed the trial of civil suits by French law, and provided for an appointed legislative council with French representation whose ordinances were to be published in both French and English.

For nearly all of the century that followed, the history of Canada was a story of tense British-French relationships, with recurring challenges, especially by British merchant groups and Loyalist migrants from the United States, to the rights enshrined in the Quebec Act, and to customs generally followed in French-speaking parts of Canada.

With Confederation in 1867, the foundation of contemporary language rights was laid. Under Section 133 of the British North America Act,

Either the English or the French language may be used by any Person in the Debates of the Houses of the Parliament of Canada and of the Houses of the Legislature of Quebec; and both those Languages shall be used in the respective Records and Journals of those Houses; and either of those Languages may be used by any Person or in any Pleading or Process in or issuing from any Court of Canada established under this Act, and or from all or from any of the Courts of Quebec. The Acts of the Parliament of Canada and of the Legislature of Quebec shall be printed and published in both those Languages (Royal Commission on Bilingualism and Biculturalism, 1967: 47).

The constitutional basis for Canadian bilingualism, making French an official language equal to English in federal and Quebec law, resides in this legalistic language.

The Manitoba Act, passed three years later in the aftermath of the Métis rebellion, confirmed the official equality of French and English in the public life of Manitoba. However, this important legal guarantee of French language rights outside Quebec did not survive the rapid influx of English-speaking settlers. By 1890 the French were reduced to a small proportion of Manitoba's population, and the provincial legislature, reflecting the assimilationist and anti-Catholic mood of the time, abolished separate schools and adopted the English Language Act, making English the sole language of public affairs in the province. This act was not disallowed by the federal government nor tested in court until 1979, when the Supreme Court ruled that all legislative acts of the province must be rewritten in both languages, a decision reaffirmed in 1985.

Contemporary French-English relationships

Outside Quebec there has generally been little recognition by the other provinces of the "French fact." For example, at the present time New Brunswick, with less than 3 percent of Canada's population, is the only officially bilingual province. Federally, the Royal Commission on Bilingualism and Biculturalism was established in response to Quebec's Quiet Revolution of the 1960s (see also Chapter 14, Social Movements), which brought rapid modernization to the economic, political, and cultural institutions of the province and stirred nationalistic and separatist currents. As a consequence of the Commission's extensive research and public hearings, the federal government enacted the Official Languages Act (1969), which sought to extend the use of French within the federal civil service and to make public services available in French wherever concentrations of francophones reside.

The legal foundation of Canadian bilingualism and biculturalism is one essential ingredient of contemporary French-English relationships. Another is the territorial concentration of about 77 percent of Canada's single-origin French ethnic population in the province of Quebec, whose population was 41 percent of French ethnic origin in 1996, according to the census. Québécois influence over the province's territory and its major educational, religious, judicial, and governmental institutions has been a crucial resource in the struggle of French

Canadians to maintain their language and culture. The victory of the Parti Québécois in the Quebec provincial elections of 1976 reflected a widespread desire to maintain and extend this control. The first important initiative by the new government, the 1977 language legislation known as The Charter of the French Language, or Bill 101, specified that the language of Quebec's French majority would be the official language of Quebec, and the legal language of work, business, education, and all public functions within the province.

If we attempt to understand why the Parti Québécois government enacted such legislation as its first priority, we may gain insight into some of the dilemmas of the French position in Canada today. For French Canadians, legal guarantees and territorial concentration have not altered the fact of English cultural and economic dominance, and the erosion of the French language and culture outside Quebec. This erosion has complex sources, among them the fact that English-speaking immigrants to Canada have vastly outnumbered French-speaking immigrants, the adoption of the English language both by the French outside Quebec and by other ethnic groups in Quebec and in Canada as a whole, and the decline in Quebec's birth rate. We shall discuss each factor in turn, as well as the impact of the historical dominance of the British in the economy of Quebec.

From 1946 to 1971, eleven immigrants came to Canada from Britain for every one from France (Beaujot, 1979: 17) in part because of preferential treatment accorded English-speaking and British immigrants. However, even after the law was changed to extend greater opportunities to immigrants from other parts of the world, the number of French-speaking immigrants continued to be negligible. The federal Immigration Act of 1978 acknowledged this by broadening the provincial role in the selection and integration of immigrants, resulting in some increase in the number of French-speaking immigrants to Quebec.

However, French Canadians have continuing reason to be suspicious about the adverse effects of immigration on their culture. Even in Quebec, before Bill 101, the majority of postwar immigrants adopted the English language and culture rather than the French: in Montreal prior to Bill 101, for every immigrant who acquired French, three learned English (Beaujot, 1978: 35). Quebec sociologist Marcel Rioux estimated that in his province "something like 85 percent of the children of new arrivals attended English schools in the 1970s" (1978a: 144). This was possible because, until the passage of Bill 101, English and French had equal status as languages of Catholic and public instruction in Quebec. (In other provinces, provision has been made less often for the instruction of French-speaking children in their first language.)

Scholars of French Canada, such as Breton (1978) and Guindon (1977), have pointed out that French Canadians historically responded as a collectivity to their marginal position in Canadian political, cultural, and economic life by creating a complex system of parallel institutions and informal social networks within which many community affairs and social relationships were confined. French Catholic schools, parishes, credit unions, labour organizations, communications media, voluntary associations, and a wide range of other institutions, some with government support and others operating through custom and tradition, met the collective needs of French Canadians. British Canadians in Quebec also developed a fairly high degree of institutional completeness, and traditionally dominated the economic sector. As a result, in past generations British-French contacts in Quebec were largely confined to the public sphere, to formal bureaucratic settings such as the factory. But even within the factory, the presence of occupational stratification often meant that French assembly-line workers worked and ate lunch side by side with other French workers, and were linked weakly to English-speaking white-collar workers and management by bilingual supervisors.

However, the modernization of Quebec society, the Quiet Revolution, language legislation, and other reflections of national consciousness and political power changed the rules of the game in Quebec by opening up mobility channels to the French and extending the control of francophones over Quebec's economic, educational, and political institutions. After the passage of Bill 101, the use of French rapidly increased within business organizations. Most francophones are now able to work in their own language in Quebec, and the proportion of anglophones who are bilingual has increased greatly, according to census information.

One element of this change was the out-migration of many anglophones, especially unilingual people uncertain about their future in an increasingly French Quebec. Their departure in turn heightened a trend towards polarization in Canada. With French dominant in Quebec and English in the rest of Canada, with the English minority declining in Quebec and French culture weak in other provinces, many observers identified a social reality not of a bilingual Canada but of a Canada of two unilingual solitudes (see Lachapelle and Henripin, 1982). French immersion has been a very successful educational movement in Canada, but it has not stemmed the tide of assimilation of French as a living language and culture outside Quebec. Waddell (1986: 108) suggested that "within English Canada, French appears to be essentially a symbolic language that mingles class and national sentiments, or a souvenir of distant Quebec or Acadian origins." He argued that the federal government has adopted an institutional approach to language rights and services based on the concept of individual rights, while Quebec has endorsed a territorial principle based upon the notion of collective rights and national survival. Thus, the vision of a bilingual and multicultural Canada is in conflict with that of a francophone Quebec in a bicultural Canada.

Constitutional and political developments have not brought together the two solitudes. The 1982 Canadian Constitution was not ratified by Quebec partly because of the absence of a provision recognizing that province as a "distinct society." The failure of the federal and provincial governments in 1990 to approve the Meech Lake Accord, which contained such a clause, followed by the "No" vote in the 1992 national referendum on the Constitution, led to a reassessment of their relationship with Canada by many Québécois. In 1993 the separatist Bloc Québécois became the Official Opposition federally, and in 1995 a referendum took Quebec to the brink of a victory for separation and sovereignty. In recent years, public opinion in Quebec appears to have cooled somewhat toward sovereignty, but the relationship between the two majority groups in Canadian society remains troubled as the Québécois "nation" continues to evolve, in the face of resistance from the rest of Canada.

The relationship between the two majority groups in Canadian society has arrived at a critical turning-point, as witnessed by the 1995 referendum.

The "other ethnic groups": The shaping of the Canadian mosaic

It is inaccurate to think of Canadian society as nothing but two unified ethnic blocs in confrontation, complex as the implications of such an image may be. Along with the Native presence, a history of massive immigration has created a much more complex pluralism in Canada, one marked by a high degree of ethnic and class diversity. According to official figures, roughly twelve and a half million foreign-born people came to Canada between 1851 and 1991.

In the first decade of the twentieth century, the economy and society of Canada were still largely agrarian, and government policy was oriented towards agricultural development. The vast prairie lands had yet to come under the plough, and the Canadian government sought to promote immigration to "settle the empty west with

producing farmers," in the words of Clifford Sifton, then Minister of the Interior and architect of Canada's immigration policy in the early twentieth century (Royal Commission on Bilingualism and Biculturalism, 1969: 22). Government sponsorship of recruitment and transportation for immigrant peasants and farmers from Europe and the United States, and the availability of free land, combined to double the foreign-born population of the prairies from 1901 to 1911. The majority of immigrants in those years, as in earlier decades, came from Great Britain and the United States. While many of the British immigrants, like the Irish settlers of the nineteenth century, gravitated towards the industrial cities, large numbers of the Americans, among them people of German, Polish, Danish, and various other ethnic backgrounds, joined the stream of new farmers to the prairies. At the same time, the first heavy wave of immigrants came from central and eastern Europe; among those were Ukrainians, Poles, Hungarians, and Russians.

Early twentieth-century rural ethnic settlements in Manitoba, Saskatchewan, and Alberta frequently took the form of isolated and homogeneous communities, described by Dawson in a classic study called *Group Settlement: Ethnic Communities in Western Canada* (1936). The bloc settlements of such groups as Doukhobors, Mennonites, German Catholics, Mormons, and French Canadians constituted "culture islands," each occupying a territorial base set off from surrounding populations by distinctive language, institutions, and religious or national identity. They were relatively successful as settlers because of their group settlement patterns and the cooperative nature of their social organization, which differed from the myth of the individualistic pioneer homesteader.

The era of the farmer-immigrant was a relatively brief one in Canada's history, for the predominant pattern of immigrant settlement has long been urban. As early as 1921, the first year for which data are available, 56 percent of Canada's foreign-born were living in urban areas, compared with only 48 percent of the Canadian-born. The transformation of Canada from an agrarian to an urban-industrial society was already well under way at that time, and opportunities for industrial employment in the growing cities attracted both farm-reared Canadians and immigrants.

The heavy influx of new immigrants during the years since 1945 also contributed to urban-ethnic diversity, since the vast majority of these immigrants settled in the seven largest metropolitan areas of Canada. For example, in 1996, 42 percent of the population of Metropolitan Toronto and 35 percent of Vancouver residents were born outside Canada. Immigrants tend to gravitate towards destinations that offer economic opportunity. In an urban industrial society, job opportunities are most plentiful in the largest cities, and the effects of chain migration are also seen in the congregation of immigrants there. By 1996, nearly three-quarters of all immigrants to Canada were living in Toronto, Montreal, and Vancouver, compared with 26 percent of the Canadian-born population, according to the census (Statistics Canada, 1996 Census of Canada, *The Daily*, Nov. 4, 1997). Take another look at Figure 8.1, which shows immigrants as a percentage of selected city populations as of 1996.

Since the late '50s, the predominance of British immigrants has given way to a broader mix of peoples (see Figure 8.2). Before 1978, immigrants originating in Europe made up 70 percent of newcomers to Canada, but in 1996- 97, immigrants from Asia contributed 66 percent of total immigra-tion, while Europeans made up 17 percent (Statistics Canada data reported in Immigration Facts, *Transition*, September 1998: 8).

In addition, since the end of World War II, hundreds of thousands of people have come to Canada as refugees, having been displaced by revolutions and political oppression in their homelands. The numbers of refugees seeking asylum from violence and oppression grew throughout the 1990s, and as a signatory of the United Nations Geneva Convention, Canada has a duty to accept refugees (for details on recent immigration and refugees to Canada see Citizenship and Immigration Canada, "Facts and Figures 1998, Immigration Overview" at <http://cicnet.ci.gc.ca/english/pdffiles/pub/facts98e.pdf>).

Overall, before 1967 discriminatory immigration policies severely restricted the settlement of Chinese, South Asian, black, Japanese, and other racial minorities in Canada. With the refocusing of immigration policy in the 1970s to emphasize occupational skills, educational qualifications, demands of the economy, family reunification, and refugee criteria instead of national origin, the immigrant population has become increasingly heterogeneous and representative of Third World countries. The administration of policies regarding admission of immigrants and refugees, however, continues to adversely affect racial minorities. Domestic workers from poor countries, who are admitted to Canada on a temporary basis specifically to work in private households at low wages, are especially disadvantaged (Avery, 1995; Henry, Tator, et al., 1995: 75–78; Arat-Koc, 1992).

FIGURE 8.2   Immigrants From Top 10 Places of Birth, as Percentage of All Immigrants Arriving Between 1991 and 1996, Canada

Hong Kong	10.5%
People's Republic of China	8.5
India	6.9
Philippines	6.9
Sri Lanka	4.3
Poland	3.6
Taiwan	3.1
Vietnam	3.1
United States	2.8

Source: Statistics Canada, The Daily, Catalogue No. 11-001, November 4, 1997: 4.

Perspectives on Canadian Race and Ethnic Relations

We now turn our attention to three dominant perspectives on intergroup relations within a pluralistic society—assimilationism, two-category perspectives, and pluralism. Each perspective functions in two ways at the same time. First, each describes a social reality, and second, each contains suggestions about the future of ethnic and race relations, and as a result, has implications for social policy.

Assimilationism

The interpretation of ethnic group relations that dominated North American thought for at least the first half of the twentieth century was **assimilationism**—the view that ethnic diversity gradually and inevitably declines as ethnic group members are integrated or absorbed into the general population of the society. Ethnic groups are viewed as transitory rather than central and enduring features of modern society. This is partly because of the assumed irrelevance of ethnic diversity to the political, social, and economic life of modern industrial society, which is viewed as rational, achievement-oriented, bureaucratically organized, market-driven, and international in scope. Attach-

Assimilation is the process of becoming part of the larger surrounding society and culture by becoming more and more like the dominant group.

ments of sentiment, ascription, kinship, community, and shared culture, which are fundamental to ethnic identity, are seen as survivals of an earlier stage of societal development that are out of place in the modern age. This view of ethnicity is usually held by functionalists, but it could be argued that most of the great sociological theorists, from Marx to Weber to Durkheim, have reflected such a perception.

Assimilation is the process of becoming part of the larger surrounding society and culture by becoming more and more like the dominant group, so that in time Polish Canadians, for example, would be indistinguishable from the British or French Canadians with whom they live. As a group they are unique only while they are relatively recent arrivals. In time they will improve their social and economic position and disappear into the great melting-pot, in which various ethnic groups and cultures blend into a single culture and society.

The melting-pot image has been a prominent feature of national identity in the United States, but assimilationism as a description and social ideal has also had its adherents in Canada (see, for example, Porter, 1980). Assimilationist assumptions were reflected in official policy towards immigrants and ethnic groups before World War II. The preference for British immigrants and the existence of severe restrictions on the immigration of racially and culturally different peoples have already been mentioned. These restrictions were based, in part, on the assumption that those peoples who are most similar to the dominant Canadian population—the British—would most readily adapt to life in Canada, cause fewest problems for the dominant group, and ultimately assimilate.

The sociological theory of assimilationism is rooted to a large degree in the work of Robert Park (1950; 1952), one of North America's first and most important sociologists, and leader of the Chicago school of urban sociology between 1915 and 1940. As we saw in Chapter 1, What Is Sociology?, Park's theories became influential in Canada through the work of Charles Dawson, a scholar and teacher in the field of Canadian ethnic group relations, who was Park's student at the University of Chicago and later founder of the first Canadian department of sociology at McGill University.

Park viewed the modern world as a melting-pot, a total system characterized by large-scale geographic and social mobility that tended to break down the isolation of local cultures, causing cultural and social patterns in the global society to become uniform and homogeneous. Park considered the breakdown of small-scale, provincial societies and cultures, with their ascribed class and status distinctions, to be a positive development. He felt it would help to liberate individuals by making status dependent upon achieved rather than ascribed criteria. (Many of Park's contemporaries, on the other hand, interpreted these same developments as signs of a decline of community and a growth of alienation in society.)

Park developed the notion of a **race relations cycle** to describe four successive stages in the relationships between dominant and minority groups in any society. These stages are contact, competition, accommodation, and assimilation. Through exploration, migration, or conquest, groups come into contact, beginning a process of communication that breaks down the isolation of each. If these groups begin to draw from a common pool of limited resources, *competition* ensues between them. The competitive stage may eventually be resolved through the *accommodation* of the weaker group, which adopts the language and culture of the more powerful. In time, if the distinctive external signs that differentiated one group from another are erased, *assimilation* is complete. The peoples intermingle and the offspring of intergroup unions belong fully to neither group. Ultimately, the ethnic group member becomes "a mere individual, indistinguishable in the cosmopolitan mass of the population..." (Park, 1950: 208–209).

There would, however, be instances of intergroup contact in which the race relations cycle would not run full course, for Park believed that distinctions among peoples may be maintained when ethnic or racial characteristics are highly visible. He considered physical traits such as colour to be the chief obstacles to the universal assimilation he envisioned, for these external marks cannot be changed, and constitute lightning-rods for animosities and prejudice. Their presence perpetuates an endless vicious circle of majority prejudice, and minority withdrawal and defensiveness.

Other sociologists, after Park, contributed substantially to assimilationist theory, among them Gordon (1964), who noted that the concept of assimilation must be broken down to reflect the many-sided nature of individual and group life. It is especially important to distinguish between cultural assimilation, or **acculturation**, and **structural assimilation**. Gordon argued that individuals may acculturate quite readily—that is, they may learn the language, values, and customs of the dominant group and make them their own. But this does not mean that they will be assimilated into the social structure—that is, accepted into intimate or primary social relationships with the dominant group. The majority group may still hold back from entering into friendship, marriage, or neighbour relationships with the minority. Thus, even though a group may acculturate, it may never succeed in assimilating into the social structure of the larger society.

Assimilationist thinkers generally hold liberal, individualistic values, and assume that it is only through individual achievement that upward mobility in the social hierarchy can occur. They further assume, as in Park's thought, that maintaining one's ethnic culture and languages will hinder upward mobility because it reduces acceptance of the ethnic group member by the majority group. Thus, ethnic group members must accept a trade-off: giving up their ethnicity in return for social acceptance, improved status, and a good standard of living.

The notion that the assimilationist perspective provides a useful interpretation of the realities of ethnic group relations has been more widely held in the United States than in Canada, where the image of the mosaic has long been a national symbol of its ethnic diversity. As discussed previously, patterns of ethnic and especially racial inequality remain entrenched both for men and for women, even when level of education is considered. The Canadian mosaic continues to be a vertical one.

As a social goal and guide to policy, assimilationism has also been subjected to damaging criticism. The assimilationist perspective suggests that, if the goal is equality of opportunity for all, then public institutions must be universalistic rather than particularistic. That is, institutions must apply the same set of rules to every individual in the same way, "regardless of race, religion, or national origin." Groups, then, are officially ignored, and only the claims of individuals are recognized by assimilationist theorists. It is assumed that, in order to be equal, people must all be alike, and that equality means treating everyone alike, regardless of their differences.

It had become apparent by the 1960s that the condition of blacks and Native peoples as groups was not improving through the process of social mobility whereby individuals play by the universalistic rules of the game. The goal of bringing these groups into the mainstream of American and Canadian societies has seemed farther and farther away as census data chart the continuing gap between the incomes and unemployment rates of blacks and Natives, on the one hand, and the rest of the population on the other. The historical legacy of slavery, colonialism, discrimination, and cultural destruction weighs heavily upon present generations.

Many thoughtful observers in academic and public life concluded that extraordinary measures have to be taken to overcome the barriers to assimilation and integration that result from long-standing patterns of discrimination and disadvantage. The application of universalistic rules and standards is resulting in what we earlier called systemic or institutionalized discrimination. Inequality is built into the occupational structure, and many minority group members are not even getting to the starting-gate in the race for advancement. The rules of the game are not fair to all, since they were established by the majority and serve to maintain their position of privilege. It follows that the rules must be changed in order to remove those barriers that have excluded minorities from access to jobs, promotions, and career advancement.

Employment equity is a broad strategy for change in the policies, practices, and culture of the Canadian workplace (Agócs, Burr, and Somerset, 1992). Its objectives are to increase the representation of disadvantaged groups at all levels of the occupational structure, to remove barriers to their career advancement, and to create a workplace

A Reverse Brain Drain?

We read in the paper about the brain drain to the U.S. or other countries where taxes are supposedly lower. One response is that Canada actually gains in this exchange as educated people from other, especially developing, countries come here to work in ever greater numbers. Let us look at this issue a bit further.

In actual fact, many immigrants with advanced degrees do not get to use their training in Canada. Doctors and other professionals, for example, sometimes end up driving taxis. Why?

The federal government makes education and skills its paramount criteria for individual applications for immigration (this does not apply to family class or refugee immigrants). However, the educational credentials that immigrants received in their home countries may not be recognized by accreditation bodies and regulatory agencies in Canada as equivalent to Canadian degrees. Hence immigrants may not be permitted to practice their professions or trades in this country. Added to this barrier are the effects of discrimination, an uncertain economy, and in some cases lack of facility in English or French.

As a result, we see many foreign-trained university graduates working as sales clerks in stores, and in other kinds of jobs in which they are underemployed.

Immigrants are also more likely than the Canadian-born to be unemployed; as the last hired, they may be the first fired in economic downturns. The situation of racial minority immigrants is particularly difficult, as is suggested by data that reveal that visible minority immigrants earn less than while immigrants—most likely because of discrimination.

What, in your view, might affirmative action programs be able to do about this problem?

Source: Adapted from Mark McKinnon, *"Give us your highly educated."* Globe and Mail, 24 May 1999, p. B1.

culture free of discrimination. In Canada at the present time, the designated employment equity groups are Native peoples, visible minorities, women, and people with disabilities. Under the 1986 federal Employment Equity Act (as revised in December 1995), employers in the federal jurisdiction and the federal public service are required to implement employment equity programs and to report annually on their results. The Federal Contractors Program requires employers who sell goods and services to the federal government to implement employment equity requirements as well.

Employment equity requirements and enforcement from 1987 until 1995 were weak, and their impact on the representation of racial minorities and aboriginal people in employment was small (e.g., Leck and Saunders, 1996; Jain et al., 1997). There may be reason to hope for greater progress under the strengthened federal requirements. However, progress in eliminating systemic discrimination requires the enactment of strong employment equity legislation at the provincial level, since most work places fall within the provincial sector.

Two-category perspectives

Scholars who theorize a two-category system of race relations in North America have argued that the assimilationist perspective describes whites only. Blacks and Native peoples are in a separate category; they have not been part of the melting-pot because of the persistence of racism in society, which has its roots in the historical experiences of slavery and colonialism. They are viewed as minority groups who continue to occupy a disadvantaged position in a society dominated by whites, who constitute a single homogeneous social category. Rioux (1978b) argued that the Québécois are also a minority group in this sense, one whose destiny is unique because of its historical position as a people conquered, colonized, and dominated by the British.

Two-category perspectives on race relations are pluralistic in the sense that they view society not as a single body, but as two separate collectivities in conflict. These two distinct social categories are hierarchically ranked, and bound together in a relationship of dominance and subordination within a single society and culture.

Examining several nineteenth- and twentieth-century societies in which the institutions of slavery and colonialism were integral parts of the development of modern capitalism, Van den Berghe (1967) developed a two-category theory of relationships between the races. According to him, liberal democratic societies such as the United States faced the dilemma of reconciling their ideals of liberty and equality with their oppression of black slaves and their extermination of Native peoples. Van den Berghe reasoned that this reconciliation was accomplished ideologically by dividing humanity into two categories: "the civilized" (the human beings) and the "savages" (the inferior beings whose humanity was denied). The application of egalitarian and democratic ideas was restricted to those defined as "the civilized," that is, the dominant white group. The result in countries such as the United States and South Africa was what Van den Berghe called a "Herrenvolk democracy"— a system that was "democratic for the master race but tyrannical for the subordinate groups" (Van den Berghe, 1967: 18).

Could such a harsh image apply in any way to Canadian reality? Although slavery did not become entrenched in Canada, it did thrive until the passage of the Emancipation Act by the British Parliament in 1833. Blacks have been subject to discrimination not only under Canadian immigration law, but also in employment, public accommodations, housing, and education. Segregated black schools existed in Ontario and Nova Scotia until the mid-1960s (Krauter and Davis, 1978: 50). However, an all-encompassing system of de jure racial segregation like that of the southern United States never became established in Canada. The image of a distinct, racially defined social category standing in a relationship of legalized subordination to whites apparently does not apply to blacks in Canada in the same way that it did in the United States.

However, Canada is not without its own race-relations dilemma. The reserve system has long been the principal instrument of Canadian policy towards the First Nations. It is a policy that has treated the various Indian peoples as a single social category with "special status" under the law, excluded from the larger society yet dependent upon that society, and hence subordinate to it. While keeping Indians socially, politically, and economically separate and subordinate, the reserve system and the Indian Act have been instruments of forced acculturation to the religions, languages, values, and traditions of the larger society, and of the destruction of First Nations' cultures and social structures.

The First Nations are not merely one of the many racial and ethnic groups in the Canadian mosaic. Because of their aboriginal rights, and because of the history of colonialism to which Native peoples have uniquely been subjected, they are fundamentally different from other groups, and require recognition as autonomous peoples equal in status to the English and French. As such, the First Nations are entitled to control over their ancestral lands, self-determination, and the right to deal collectively with the government of Canada—a right implied in the government's traditional practice of making treaty agreements with aboriginal peoples as nations. Many bands and Native organizations such as the Assembly of First Nations (representing Indians), the Native Council of Canada (representing Métis and non-status Indians), and the Inuit Tapirisat have been negotiating for many years with the government of Canada and initiating court actions in attempts to gain self-government and ownership of lands traditionally occupied and used by aboriginal peoples, and never ceded under treaties. In pressing their land claims, the First Nations are attempting to ensure the survival of their peoples and cultures as distinct entities, and to improve their standard of living and access to opportunity for succeeding generations. Today, nearly all schools on reserves are administered by First Nations themselves, and there has been a large increase in the enrollment of aboriginal people in universities and colleges in the past decade.

The commitment of aboriginal peoples to self-determination challenges the assimilationist assumption, explicit in federal policy since Confederation, that First Nations should be absorbed into the larger society. The need to implement an alternative to the reserve system, and the movement towards self-government by aboriginal peoples, present a major policy dilemma for Canada's pluralistic society.

Pluralism

During this generation, the worldwide rise of nationalistic movements has shaken loose historic accommodations between dominant and subordinate ethnic and racial groups, not only in Canada and the United States, but also in many parts of Africa, Europe, Asia, and the former Soviet Union. Ethnic and Aboriginal communities across Canada have sought public recognition of their distinctive aspirations and ways of life, and racial minorities have demanded an end to discrimination.

Ethnic and racial diversity are very much a part of our contemporary society, and "assimilation" seems as far away as it ever has. From Québécois, First Nations, Jews, Chinese, Muslims, Sikhs, and many other groups come the questions: Can't we all enjoy equal opportunities as members of one

Pluralism is the view that ethnic diversity remains a central feature of modern urban society, and that ethnicity is an important aspect of individual identity and group behaviour.

society while maintaining our differences, our identities, and our communities? Can we not coexist as equals within a single society, even though we do not all look the same, or share the same values and culture?

Pluralism, the view that ethnic diversity and conflict remain a central feature of contemporary societies, and that ethnicity continues to be an important aspect of individual identity and group behaviour, has been widely accepted in the post–World War II era. The image of the ethnic mosaic has become integral to Canadian national identity, and a feature said to distinguish Canadian from American values and culture. It is generally understood today that "Canadian culture" itself is not a homogeneous whole, but an intricate tapestry of many hues woven from the strands of many ethnic and regional subcultures.

Since Canada is a pluralistic society, both assimilation and ethnic and racial differentiation are going on at the same time. While in some respects Canada's ethnic groups become more alike as time passes, in many ways their influence brings an increasing diversity to the cultural, social, and political life shared by all Canadians. For example, immigrants, by becoming citizens and voting, may show signs of assimilation. Yet in local elections they may support candidates who represent their own ethnic group's interests, thus bringing diversity to the political spectrum.

In fact, many pluralists contend that ethnic group members make progress and improve their positions in the social hierarchy not by individual achievement and dissociation from their roots, as assimilationists would argue, but by group efforts, using ethnic solidarity as a resource. It is collective action that benefits the group, and thereby its individual members. When members of an ethnic community vote in a bloc, they force the political system to recognize and respond to their concerns. When relatives pool their resources to start a business, they not only provide jobs for their kin, but also contribute to the economic life of their community. When members of the community patronize ethnic businesses, they strengthen the community's overall business climate. When successful ethnic businesspeople are able to assist their children to attend university, they help to provide the community's next generation of leaders.

In all of these examples it is the collective action of the community, rather than the efforts of isolated individuals to achieve upward mobility, that brings progress to members of the group.

A study of Iranians in Montreal suggests that different members of the same ethnic group adopt varied strategies in working out a relationship with Canadian society. In the study, those immigrants who chose a strategy of ethnic cultural maintenance were more likely to belong to Iranian organizations and to endorse collective means of getting ahead. Those who agreed with an assimilationist strategy tended not to belong to Iranian organizations and to have an individualistic view of mobility. Both groups had a high level of confidence in their ability to do well in Canada (Moghaddam, Taylor, and Lalonde, 1987). Many studies (e.g., Breton et al., 1990) have provided evidence that ethnic groups, as well as individuals, adopt a variety of different approaches as they integrate into Canadian society and improve their socioeconomic position, while retaining varying degrees of ethnic identity and community solidarity.

The increasing heterogeneity of Canada's population, the growing numerical strength and voting power of ethnic groups, and the acceptance of a collectivist strategy have coincided with a shift away from the official image of Canada as a bicultural country towards a recognition of it as multicultural. In 1971, Prime Minister Trudeau, with the support of all political parties, announced a policy of "multiculturalism within a bilingual framework," under which federal recognition and support would be extended to the various ethnic groups that constitute the Canadian mosaic (Government of Canada, 1971). The Multiculturalism Act of 1988 affirms the government's commitment to the preservation and appreciation of cultural diversity, and to the promotion of the full and equal participation of individuals and communities in all aspects of Canadian society (Fleras and Elliott, 1992). However, critics (e.g., Li, 1988) have noted a lack of results and questioned the government's real commitment to these principles.

The institutions of Canadian society have begun to grapple with the fact that ethnic and racial diversity and inequality are not just individual traits, but fundamental characteristics of the social system as a whole. Canadians now face the challenge and opportunity of learning to live in harmony and mutual respect in a society in which ethnic and racial diversity will continue to grow.

Summary

Canada is a pluralistic society, a social system composed of ethnic groups that coexist in both peace and conflict within a common cultural, economic, and political framework, while maintaining cultures and social institutions that are to some extent distinctive. Canada has been called a vertical mosaic in recognition of the fact that racial and ethnic groups occupy differing ranks within its stratification system: some groups enjoy relative privilege, while others lack access to power and opportunity in Canadian society.

A major form of ethnic group life in Canada, the local immigrant community, often develops through a process of chain migration, the sequential movement of people from a common place of origin to a common destination, with the assistance of relatives or compatriots who settled there earlier. In the ethnic community, the newcomers find a familiar social network and an array of institutions to meet their needs. As the community grows, it establishes a place for itself within the local economic structure. Economic interests combine with cultural and social patterns to shape the community's distinctive adaptation to the new environment.

As a concept, ethnicity has several dimensions. Ethnicity is an ascribed status, a potential conferred upon individuals at birth, which becomes a part of personal identity during socialization within an ethnic community. The ethnic group is self-perpetuating and has boundaries that are set and maintained by patterns of interaction rather than by formal structures, cultural traits, or isolation. The ethnic group is also a subculture, the product of shared historical experiences that shape present understandings about values important to the group.

While members of a social group share values, interests, and patterns of interaction, a social category such as a race is a collection of individuals who share certain physical features that are charged with social meaning. Racist ideologies have rationalized the exploitation of certain categories of human beings because of inherited characteristics.

Minority groups are categories of people that are oppressed and relegated to subordinate ranks in the social hierarchy, regardless of their numbers. Various forms of social control, including annihilation, expulsion, discrimination, and segregation, have perpetuated the oppression and subordination of minority groups in modern societies.

Canadian race and ethnic relations have been shaped by the historical processes of colonialism, conquest, and migration. Colonized groups such as aboriginal peoples become part of a plural society involuntarily, often suffer long-standing and severe discrimination and disadvantage, and remain economically and politically marginal to that society. The reserve system has been the cornerstone of Canada's Indian policy, although increasing numbers of Indians are migrating to cities, where they generally experience many of the same deprivations that drove them from reserve communities.

The conquest of the French by the British shaped the subsequent relationship between Canada's two founding peoples. Legal guarantees at the federal level provide for the perpetuation of the language, religion, and culture of French Canadians, and the concentration of the French within Quebec provides a powerful territorial and institutional base in the struggle of the French to perpetuate their culture. But, for a variety of reasons, the French language and culture have eroded in the rest of Canada, where English cultural dominance has accompanied the economic dominance of what was once British North America.

Immigrant groups enter a society voluntarily, although they may have been driven from their homelands by economic want or political oppression. The British and Americans have long been Canada's dominant immigrant groups, but in the post–World War II era, immigrant origins have been diverse, with increasing representation of Third World peoples. In recognition of the reality of ethnic diversity, the federal government in 1971 announced a policy of "multiculturalism within a bilingual framework."

Interpretations of ethnic and race relations encompass both the task of describing social reality and the need to formulate social goals or visions of what Canadian society should be like. Assimilationism is the view that diversity declines as ethnic group members achieve economic prosperity and are absorbed into the general population and culture of the society. This view of society as a melting-pot has proven to be an inaccurate description of social reality and a doubtful guide to social policy. Two-category perspectives, applied to North America, attempt to understand the experiences of white and racial minority peoples in very different terms. Whites are seen as constituting a single social category, one into which white ethnic groups are generally assimilated. The two-category perspective holds that, because of the historical experiences of slavery and colonialism, and/or a legacy of racism, racial minorities are socially defined as a separate category whose members generally occupy a subordinate status in society and therefore remain unassimilated. Pluralism, the perspective that recognizes the central place of ethnic diversity and conflict in modern societies, has long typified Canadian thought on ethnic relations, and is expressed in the policy of multiculturalism. But inequality remains a central feature of most pluralistic societies today, including Canada, and racism and ethnic conflict continue to pose dilemmas for Canada and the modern world.

QUESTIONS FOR REVIEW AND CRITICAL THINKING

1. Compare and contrast the historical experiences of the twentieth-century refugees who arrived in Canada with those coming today. Who is likely to arrive in future? What changes, if any, should be made to our refugee policy to make it fairer to all parties concerned?

2. Describe the historical development of a local ethnic community with which you are familiar. Examine the degree to which ethnicity continues to influence the attitudes and behaviours of members of this group. Compare your results with those who have studied other groups.

3. Are Canadian blacks an ethnic group? Your discussion should include a thoughtful analysis of what an ethnic group is.

4. Examine the migration, marriage, and occupational patterns in the history of your family by charting your genealogy and then listing the occupations, geographic movements, and marriages of as many family members as possible. Summarize any patterns you observe, applying concepts used in this chapter such as chain migration, occupational specialization, ethnic network, discrimination, ethnic stratification, occupational mobility, and ethnic endogamy.

KEY TERMS

acculturation, p. 219

assimilationism, p. 218

chain migration, p. 195

colonialism, p. 209

discrimination, p. 204

ethnic group, p. 199

institutional completeness, p. 198

marginality, p. 202

minority group, p. 204

pluralism, p. 223

pluralistic society, p. 194

prejudice, p. 208

race, p. 202

race relations cycle, p. 219

racism, p. 203

segregation, p. 205

social category, p. 202

stereotypes, p. 208

structural assimilation, p. 219

systemic or institutionalized discrimination, p. 205

two-category perspectives, p. 221

vertical mosaic, p. 195

SUGGESTED READINGS

Das Gupta, Tania
1996   *Racism and Paid Work.* Toronto: Garamond Press.
This Marxist analysis examines racial and gender inequality, and the dynamics of racism and sexism, in the paid workplace in Canada, with a focus on the health care and garment manufacturing sectors.

Henry, Frances and Carol Tator
1995   *The Colour of Democracy: Racism in Canadian Society.* Toronto: Harcourt Brace.
The authors, social scientists and long-time activists for racial equality, examine the dynamics and impacts of racism in Canadian society today.

Helms-Hayes, Rick and James Curtis (eds.)
1998   *The Vertical Mosaic Revisited.* Toronto: University of Toronto Press.
Leading Canadian sociologists provide a readable overview of the state of Canadian society and scholarship on ethnic and race relations since the publication of John Porter's classic, *The Vertical Mosaic* (1965).

Long, David Alan and Olive P. Dickason (eds.)
1996   *Visions of the Heart: Canadian Aboriginal Issues.* Toronto: Harcourt Brace.
Eminent First Nations scholars present analyses of a variety of current social and legal issues.

Purich, Donald
1996   *The Inuit and Their Land: The Story of Nunavut.* Toronto: James Lorimer.
Purich, a former director of the Native Law Centre at the University of Saskatchewan, examines the social, economic, and political history of Nunavut and the Inuit struggle for self-government.

WEB SITES

http://www.canada.metropolis.net
The Metropolis Project
This Web site provides research and information resources on migration, immigration, refugees, and ethnicity in Canada and other countries.

www.uottawa.ca/hrrec
Human Rights Research and Education Centre
This site, based at the University of Ottawa, provides information and links to many sources on human rights and equality issues in a wide variety of fields, in Canada and internationally.

www.crr.ca
Canadian Race Relations Foundation
This foundation's Web site provides information on examples of current research and community action on issues of racism in Canada.

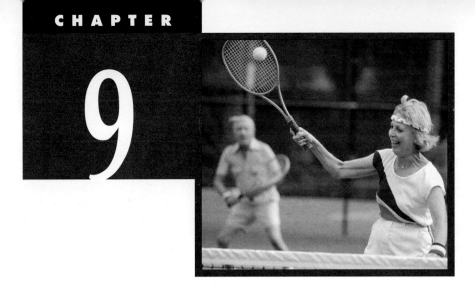

Aging

Ingrid Arnet Connidis

Introduction

Canada's population is aging. What does this mean? *Population aging* refers to the growing proportion of Canadians who are older, usually indicated by the percentage of the population aged 65 and over. Due primarily to a drop in the birth rate over several decades, Canada's population has been aging steadily so that, as this century begins, 12 percent of the Canadian population falls into this category. The proportion of Canadians 65 and over will peak at 23 percent in 2041, when the last of the baby-boomers have reached 65 years of age (see Chapter 15, Demography and Urbanization).

Canadians aged 85 years and over are the fastest-growing portion of our population. The average life expectancy of women born in 1997 is just over 81 years, and of men 76. This is good news, as it means more of us can look forward to an unprecedented long life. And yet, as we shall see, population aging is often treated as bad news, as a

serious problem to be solved rather than as an advance to be celebrated.

Interest in examining aging issues has increased as the population has aged. Two specialties, *geriatrics* and *gerontology*, focus on the study of aging. **Geriatrics** involves studying the physiological aspects of aging and the unique health concerns of older persons. **Gerontology** takes an interdisciplinary approach to studying aging that involves the physical, psychological, and social processes related to growing older and being an older person. More than most other fields in sociology, the study of aging has been multidisciplinary. Thus, works on aging from a variety of social sciences are published in journals such as the *Journal of Gerontology* and the *Canadian Journal on Aging* or presented at multidisciplinary conferences such as the annual meetings of the Canadian Association on Gerontology. A multidisciplinary approach has the advantage of accumulating broader knowledge on a given topic by tackling it from different vantage points (e.g., the physical, psychological, and social aspects of aging). However, this chapter focuses on the *sociological* study of aging, which means an emphasis on the social aspects of aging.

The objective of this chapter is to present a balanced portrayal of old age and aging by demonstrating that for most older persons, later life, like the rest of the life course, has both ups and downs, and that most older persons are able to enjoy the former and weather the latter quite effectively. At the same time, however, the aging of the population and the cumulative effects of inequalities over a lifetime mean that there are very important social policy issues related to studying the sociology of aging. The fact that older people tend to be resilient should not be the basis for downplaying their very real needs when formulating social policy.

Aging: A Personal Matter

Personalizing aging

Most subjects are more interesting to us if we can relate them to our personal lives. Before we begin our review, take a moment to reflect on your own life and key people in it. Is anyone in your family or social circle aged 65 or more? Sixty-five is the age typically used to delineate the old from the middle-aged but it is an arbitrary cutoff. However, 65 is a *social marker* of later life, as it has been the conventional retirement age and of entitlement to economic benefits in most Western countries. Perhaps you are thinking of a grandparent or parent. How often do you see this person? Do you enjoy each other's company? What is this person's marital status? How many children does s/he have? Siblings? Are there ways in which you help this person? Does she help you in any way? What was this person's life like when he was your age? Do you know his or her work history? Is this person retired? Happily? How would you describe this person's health? Does this person receive any social services or government benefits? How would this person compare this stage of life with earlier stages?

You might find yourself wanting to ask this person these questions directly; you will have an interesting conversation if you do. One thing that may strike you is how connected old age is to the rest of life. Our experience of later life is fundamentally shaped by the decisions we make and the lives we lead as younger persons. Now, as you read about various theories, issues, and experiences of aging in the sections ahead, think about the older person you know. Consider how your background (gender, class, ethnicity/race, the nature of your ties to your parents, siblings, or other family members), the decisions you make (e.g., which university to attend, where to live, which job to take, whether to marry and/or have children), and your experiences (not always in your control) are likely to shape your own old age.

Stereotypes of old age

"Life is trouble. Only death is not." This quote from *Zorba the Greek*, a novel by Kazantzakis (1952) and later a movie starring Anthony Quinn, is a good starting point for thinking about aging. Viewing population aging as a problem is reflected in our culture by a surprisingly negative view of old age itself. And yet, how many of us would choose an early death over a long life? Too often, aging is equated with trouble, leading us to feel that there is not much to look forward to in older age. Yet, older people have uniformly high scores in studies of happiness and life satisfaction, and rankings of the stress levels created by various life events show us quite vividly that life at all ages includes "trouble." For example, a traditional scale of stressful life events ranks the top ten stressful events, starting with the tenth, as retirement, marital reconciliation, being fired from work, marriage, personal injury or illness, death of a close family member, a jail term, marital separation, divorce, and the number one stressful life event-death of a spouse (Holmes and Rahe, 1967). While some of these events are more likely in older age (losing a spouse and retirement), others are more likely at younger ages (being fired, marriage, marital separation, and divorce). The others are not age specific. Yet, the changes associated with younger years tend to be treated as challenges to be met, while those of older age are portrayed more often as insurmountable setbacks. At all ages we confront change, and change, whether negative or positive, tends to be stressful.

The negative view of aging is also reflected in stereotypes of the old as sick, isolated, ignored, and lonely. Such a view of old age is often reinforced by researchers who are inclined to focus on problems as a way of establishing the importance of a particular area of study. There have been attempts to counter such a disheartening view by creating equally atypical positive stereotypes that focus on the 80-year-old marathon runner, or the woman who just completed her Ph.D. at age 75, or the wealthy, globe-trotting, retired couple. These images are indeed heartening, but they can minimize some of the real benefits of older age by essentially exalting old age as long as it is youthful. As well, in exaggerating the virtues of aging, positive stereotypes deny some of its harsher realities, impeding the development of creative and effective coping strategies by individuals and by society. The challenge is to portray realistic pictures of later life that capture important variations among older Canadians.

The Study of Aging

The study of aging intersects with many areas of sociology including inequality, the family, health, social policy, demography, and social problems. In many instances, the study of aging picks up where some other substantive areas leave off. For example, family issues (see Chapter 10, Families) such as marriage in later life, intergenerational ties between older parents and adult children, the sibling ties of adults, and the family involvements of single and childless persons tend to receive limited attention in courses and books on the family. But, they are central considerations when studying aging. Exploring such issues expands the family area conceptually. It forces a move away from regarding the family as a fixed structure in a particular location (the household) to viewing family ties as negotiated relationships in an extended family network. In the sociology of health, the focus on the medical model and responses to acute illness has been balanced by concerns about the unique circumstances of older persons. The study of retirement extends our understanding of work and its longer-term consequences. Similarly, the study of stratification (recall Chapter 6, Social Stratification) is enhanced by incorporating age as another system of inequality and by examining the accumulated effects of other sources of inequality, including gender, in old age. As well, the long-term consequences of long-ago events add an additional dimension to social-psychological explorations of the life course.

Sociologists adopt a variety of approaches in their study of aging. Aging may be looked at as a *process* or as the study of *older persons*. Related to this distinction are three separate points of emphasis in sociological research on aging. First, an interest in older persons as a group is often accompanied by an interest in comparing older people with other age groups. Second, when looked at as a process, researchers are interested in examining the changes that are a result of aging, what some have termed **age effects** and others **maturation**. Third, confounding such examinations is the need to determine whether any observed changes are a direct function of aging or of *period effects*. **Period effects** refer to outcomes that result from having been a certain age at a certain point in time (for example, a teenager during wartime) and capture the impact of an historical time or period. The study of age differences can be accomplished using *cross-sectional* data, but the study of age change requires longitudinal data (see Chapter 2, Research Methods). To determine period effects, longitudinal data for several age cohorts are necessary in order to determine whether different cohorts experience similar (supporting age as the reason for the outcome) or different (supporting the influence of historical context) changes over time.

One can also examine aging at an *individual* or *micro* level of analysis or at a social *structural* or *macro* level of analysis. *Micro-level* analysis is concerned with the experience of aging at the individual level. What is it like to be an older person in our community or society? How does one plan for and adjust to retirement? How does one cope with increasing health problems? What is family life like in older age? Addressing questions at the level of *society* is a *macro-level* approach and involves asking questions about the impact of population aging on society, how social structure shapes the experience of aging through such organizing features of social life as gender, the role of society in providing support for older persons, and social policy questions concerning the distribution of benefits (e.g., pensions) based on age. Ideally, theoretical perspectives combine both micro and macro levels of analysis or incorporate bridging concepts that facilitate the connection of one level of theoretical thinking to another (Marshall, 1995a).

Theoretical approaches

Several trends are evident in current theoretical work on the social aspects of aging. They include emphasizing the heterogeneity or diversity of the aged population (some are rich, some poor, some healthy, some not), taking a more critical view of social processes themselves, examining the link between the individual and society (the macro-micro link), and taking a more interpretive view of aging. The *interpretive* perspective views social structure as *socially constructed* and, therefore, subject to change, and emphasizes *individual agency* (our ability to act on our own behalf) in the negotiation of social life. This differs from the *normative* approach, which tends to portray social structure in quite static terms and portrays individuals as fairly passive followers of society's norms and rules. We will consider these issues as we briefly review key theories on aging.

Changes in fashion in sociology are reflected in shifts in theoretical approaches to studying aging over the years. There are several excellent reviews and discussions of aging theory (see Bengtson, Burgess, and Parrott, 1997; Marshall, 1996; McPherson, 1998). Here, we highlight some of the dominant social perspectives of the past sixty years.

The functionalist paradigm of sociology, which took hold in the 1950s and 1960s was represented in the aging field by disengagement theory (Cumming and Henry, 1961). Proponents of **disengagement theory** argued that the withdrawal of older persons from active social life (particularly the labour force) is functional for both the individual and the larger society. Disengaging permits older individuals to preserve their limited resources and energy and allows for their smoother exit from society, without reducing the awkward interruption created by death. **Activity theory** countered disengagement theory by taking the view that the best prescription for a successful old age is to remain active and to take on new activities in later life to supplant those

that have been left behind (Havighurst, 1943). Both perspectives received heavy criticism over the years, especially disengagement theory for effectively putting older people on the shelf for the benefit of society's smooth functioning. However, much of the logic of each perspective is still evident today in arguments about intergenerational equity, avenues for successful aging, as well as ongoing social policy such as mandatory retirement.

Despite taking apparently opposite approaches in their view of what is good for older persons, disengagement and activity theories share the fundamental weakness of treating older persons as a *homogeneous* group. Yet, of all age groups, the old are likely to be the most *heterogeneous* given the time that they have had to accumulate both a broader range of experiences and the effects of intra-cohort differences based on such factors as gender, class, ethnicity, and race (Dannefer, 1987).

A more recent perspective at the micro level is **exchange theory** (Dowd, 1975), an approach that focuses on the relatively weak bargaining position of older persons in their exchanges with younger ones. This inequity violates basic assumptions of exchange, particularly the expectation of reciprocity, the idea that partners in an exchange expect to give and receive in roughly equal measure. Exchange theory introduced the possibility of differential resources among the old, but the focus was on their generally weaker power position vis-a-vis the young. More recent formulations have taken a longer view of exchange by considering reciprocity over a lifetime rather than in relation to immediate exchanges only, reflecting the current popularity of the life course perspective.

The **age-stratification perspective** initiated several strands of theoretical thinking about aging that remain part of current sociological efforts. As originally formulated (Riley, Johnson, and Foner, 1972), this macro-level approach focused primarily on two key concepts: *a stratified age structure* that favours young and middle-aged adults, and the *age cohort* (individuals in the same age group). Each age cohort must make its way through a system of expectations and rewards that are based on age. Hence, society is described as **age-graded**. The approach made explicit the significance of age as a basis for social differentiation, and highlighted the variability of experience among age cohorts, moving

Family Ties and Qualitative Data

The personal accounts of family relationships obtained in qualitative research help bring key themes alive. Some examples from studies of older persons conducted by Connidis (1989–1999) follow.

Intergenerational ties tend to be stronger along the matrilineal (mother) line, and singlehood may be due to strong commitment to the family of origin. A woman talks about her ties to her grandparents, aunts, and uncles: "Mother was from a large family. Dad was from a large family, but he was the youngest of nine and, therefore, his family had all gone. I used to see his sisters once in a while when they came home, but we weren't as close to our father's family as we

were to our mother's. My grandfather and grandmother [mother's parents] used to come to the house and we used to fight about who was going to sleep with Grandma. We just adored her. She was just a darling.... Aunt Kate had never been married and she thought one daughter should stay home and look after the father and mother the way they used to. [A fellow] wanted to marry her, but she said no, that she felt that all her sisters were married and it was her responsibility to look after her mother and father."

The ongoing responsibility toward older parents often continues into retirement. At the same time, retirement can bring opportunities for renewed contact with siblings.

A retired woman observes: "Of course, my husband told me I was always retired; I had never worked since I had the children. I did have a business, but I didn't have to work at it full-time, so it didn't take a lot of time from me. [Retirement] means that Eleanor [sister] and I can spend more time together and we do elder hosteling-we did an elder hostel together before she was ill and we will be doing more, I think, when we get Mother kind of settled. At the present time, that situation is really taking a lot of our time, Eleanor's and mine. I guess we hope that retirement will continue and that it will be a time of doing things together."

the field away from a focus on individual adjustment. At the same time, however, the age-stratification model failed to address diversity *within* age cohorts, and continued the normative tradition of treating individuals as passive followers of age-graded expectations. The perspective did introduce the idea of the life course by stressing cohort flow through the age structure. Recent extensions of the age-stratification perspective have included the concept of *structural lag*, referring to the social structure's failure to respond fast enough to the aging of the population and to the changes in the life course of individuals, such as a lengthy period of retirement (Riley, Kahn, and Foner, 1994; Riley and Riley, 1994). This extension provides a link between micro and macro levels of analysis.

Building in part on Marxist, conflict, and critical foundations, the **political economy of aging perspective** (e.g., see Myles, 1984) takes a macro-level view of how political and economic processes create a social structure that tends to place con-

straints on the lives of older persons. In general, older persons are seen to lose power to varying degrees, depending upon class, gender, race and ethnicity, in a social structure that seeks to maximize economic returns while attempting to honour democratic ideals. One outcome has been to institutionalize retirement as a method of ensuring productivity at the lowest cost, while offering a "citizen's wage" in the form of pension benefits (Myles, 1984). This perspective has the advantages of providing a critical view of social structure in its interpretive treatment of social structure as a creation of political and economic interests and of treating the old as a diverse group. A weakness, however, is the minimization of agency on behalf of the older individual.

The currently popular **life course perspective** seeks to make explicit the link between the individual and society. It has both normative and interpretive roots and is perhaps best thought of as a framework with several linking concepts, compatible with a number of theoretical approaches rather than a theory in its own right (Marshall, 1995b; 1996). The life course involves a series of age-related transitions that occur along a trajectory across the age structure. This approach emphasizes aging as a process, highlighting the connection of older persons to their own life histories, the history of their times, and to younger generations, while connecting their biographies to social structure. Major advantages of this approach are the focus on connections between past and present as well as between generations, the interpretive emphasis on possible disjunction between individual lives and the age structure, the agency of individuals in their attempts to regain control when circumstances change, and the incorporation of institutions such as the family as mid-level institutions that link the individual and society (see Elder, 1991). We can fully understand the lives of older persons only by understanding, first, the social and personal contexts of their aging and, second, their relationships with other age groups. A drawback of the framework is its tendency to treat social structure as a given.

The life course perspective encourages us to connect the lives of older persons to their earlier lives. This is also true of feminist theories on aging in which aging has been described as a women's issue, largely because there are more older women than older men. Feminist theorists emphasize how the life-long gendered nature of social life fundamentally shapes old age. This leads to a particular concern for the effects on women of a lifetime of unpaid labour, erratic labour-force participation, and family obligations in older age. Applications of feminist theory to aging tend to be interpretive and focus on both the macro (e.g., the social construction of gender and gender as a dimension of inequality in old age) and micro levels (e.g., individuals' experiences of caregiving).

Major themes of **critical theory** are woven through several of the perspectives reviewed here, particularly the political economy and feminist approaches. Reflecting a strong interpretive tradition, critical theory focuses on social structure in the study of power, social action, and social meanings that are part of a critique of knowledge, culture, and the economy (Bengtson et al., 1997). As related to aging, this includes examining the social construction of old age and dependency and

of old-age policy. Applications of critical theory also focus on the need to incorporate *praxis* or practical change that benefits older persons when theorizing about aging. Critical theory's characterization of social structure as constraining, and the individual as acting with agency, provides a linking mechanism between macro and micro levels of analysis (see Marshall, 1996).

Finally, the *symbolic interactionist* perspective, more recently referred to as the **social constructionist perspective**, is also influential in theoretical approaches to aging, especially at the micro level. This interpretive approach emphasizes the subjective experience of older persons and their ability to exercise agency in negotiations with others. However, interaction takes place in the context of social constructions (e.g., the view of older persons as dependent) that are influential in shaping the outcome of negotiations and our attitudes toward older people.

Studying the experience of aging and the lives of older persons dramatically illustrates the outcome of fundamental features of social structure and of individual initiatives in negotiating that structure. The effect of organizing our society on the basis of gender, class, ethnicity, race, and age appears in bold relief, when we examine the lives of older Canadians. At the same time, as powerful as these organizational forces are, they do not guarantee identical outcomes for everyone in shared circumstances. Instead, individuals negotiate their situations as best they can to meet their preferences, some more effectively than others. Thus, how life is lived in old age can be viewed as the outcome of the lifetime interplay between social structure and individual action.

A profile of older Canadians

While one can draw general conclusions about the aging of Canada's population, it is important to note substantial variations across the country. First, there are provincial differences in the proportion of the population aged 65 and over, ranging in 1998 from a low of 10 percent in Alberta to a high of almost 15 percent in Saskatchewan. These variations are projected to shift over the next twenty years, with estimates for 2011 of a low of 14 percent in Alberta to a high of nearly 19 percent in Newfoundland,

Where Do Older Canadians Live?

The many gender differences among older Canadians are evident in their living arrangements. While 68 percent of men aged 75 to 84 live with a spouse, only 28 percent of women in this age group do so, reflecting primarily their higher rates of widowhood. On the other hand, 44 percent of women aged 75 to 84 live alone, while only 17 percent of men do so. Living alone is generally a preferred option among those who do not have a spouse because it allows for independence. The ability to live alone also reflects the improved financial circumstances of today's elderly when compared with previous generations. When it comes to institutional living, Canada's rates are fairly high. For the same age group, almost 7 percent of men and just over 10 percent of women are in this situation. This compares with 6 percent of men and 16 percent of women who are living with family other than a spouse. While we tend to think that older persons would prefer living with children over living in a facility for seniors, research suggests that many older people would prefer not to, fearing loss of independence and burdening their children (Connidis, 1983).

Source: Statistics Canada. 1996 Census.

Nova Scotia, and New Brunswick. As analyses by census tract show (Moore and Rosenberg, 1997), population aging is greatest in communities characterized by stagnant economies, fewer financial resources, aging in place (local residents stay and grow older), and net migration effects resulting from the exodus of younger residents. On the other hand, the average age of the aboriginal population is much younger than for the total Canadian population, reflecting lower life expectancy, higher rates of some diseases (e.g., heart disease), and poorer services (Wister and Moore, 1998).

The longer lives of women means that, with each successive age group, the ratio of women to men increases. Sixty percent of Canadians aged 75 to 84 years are women, and this increases to 70 percent among those aged 85 and over. Gender differences are also evident in living arrangements. Among persons aged 75 to 84, 68 percent of men but only 28 percent of women live with a spouse. In contrast, 44 percent of women but only 17 percent of men in this age group live alone (Norris, 1996). Finally, income levels of the older population reveal important differences (Statistics Canada, *Aging and Independence*, 1993). The personal incomes of women are far lower than those of men, which means that loss or absence of a spouse leaves women in a far worse financial position than is true of men, with the exception of the single (never married), in which case older women have higher incomes than older men. For widowed women, access to survivor benefits often means an actual increase in *personal* income (but not in household income). These differences reflect the gendered nature of labour force participation among the current elderly, and the greater importance of marital status to women than to men.

The balance of the chapter focuses on three key topics about later life: family ties, health, and work and retirement. As you read each section, consider its connection to the other main topics. You will see that they are highly interconnected, which suggests their mutual importance to social policy, the final topic addressed in this chapter.

Family Ties and Social Support in Later Life

Who is your family? Make a quick list. Now, think about an older person in your family. Who is his or her family? Make a list beside yours. For years a portrait of the family as a husband and wife with two children has been promoted as the "typical" Canadian family (see Chapter 10, Families). How does this compare with your family and those of your older family members? With changes in family

Intimate ties among family members often span generations.

life over the past few decades, this image of the nuclear family has been eroded for all age groups, as growing numbers of families have different compositions (single-parent families; shared-custody families; gay or lesbian parents; childless couples; single adults; as well as two parents and their children). For older persons, the nuclear family in one household has never been an accurate portrayal of family life. We will discuss three key familial relationships of older persons: intimate ties (mostly marriage at present); intergenerational ties (parent-child and grandparent-grandchild ties); and sibling ties.

Intimate ties

Discussions of close ties in older age generally dwell upon marriage, partly because of the traditional focus on the nuclear family. Indeed, among today's elderly, the primary intimate tie is with a spouse.

As a result, there is very limited research on other intimate relations in older age, including short-term liaisons, longer-term relationships, co-habitation outside of marriage, and gay and lesbian partnerships. This neglect in research is, unfortunately, reflected in the review here.

Because a spouse is the most likely source of support among married persons, knowing about the availability of a spouse, the nature of exchanges between spouses, and the limits of the spousal tie for support are central to understanding the social lives of older Canadians. Most older persons (i.e., those 65 and over) are married. Indeed, despite increases in divorce over time, the likelihood of being married is greater among today's older population than it was for the entire twentieth century, primarily because the likelihood of being widowed has gone down. This trend is more marked among women and is due to the greater life expectancy of both men and women and the narrowing of the gap in life expectancy between men and women (Connidis, 1997; 1999a).

At first glance, it appears that older Canadians can look forward to the companionship and support of a spouse in old age. However, there are very important differences based on age and gender in the availability of a spouse. Some researchers distinguish between the *young-old* and the *old-old* in order to capture the heterogeneity of experience among those aged 65 and over. The fact that women outlive men combines with our custom of women marrying men older than themselves to make widowhood much more common among women. These variations by age and gender are reflected in the 1996 data presented in Table 9.1.

As age increases, the likelihood of being married decreases, while the probability of being widowed increases for both men and women. Note, however, that for women, marriage is the modal (more common) experience among the youngest age group (65 to 74) only, while marriage remains the modal experience for men of all age groups, including those aged 85 and over. For women over 75, the most common experience is to be widowed.

Note also that, so far, only a small percentage of older persons is divorced, although the percentage who have ever divorced is higher as some of those included under "married" in Table 9.1 were previously divorced. However, in 1990, only 12 percent

TABLE 9.1   Percentage Distribution of Marital Status by Age and Gender, Canada 1996

Age	Married	Widowed	Divorced/Separated	Single
WOMEN				
65–74	55	32	8	6
75–84	30	58	4	8
85+	10	79	2	10
MEN				
65–74	79	8	7	6
75–84	71	18	5	6
85+	51	39	4	7

Source: Adapted from Connidis (1999).

of men and 8 percent of women aged 55 and over were in a second or subsequent marriage following either divorce or widowhood (Gee, 1995). Nonetheless, trends indicate that growing proportions of Canadians will enter old age divorced, though not to the extent that media coverage of divorce would lead us to expect. As well, while remarriage means a partner in older age for some, it does not necessarily erase the consequences of divorce for relationships with children and grandchildren, as will be discussed later.

Marriage in the later years

One consequence of living longer is that our relationships with family members are also lasting longer. This applies to those who stay married to a first spouse. There is some debate about the long-term course of marriage. Some argue that marriages follow a curvilinear pattern, with happiness and marital satisfaction greatest in the early and later years. Several parallels between these two phases of marriage may explain this pattern. For both young and old partners there is a heightened sense of appreciation about having a partner, in the first case because the partner is newly acquired, and in the second because both partners have witnessed others lose a spouse. In both phases of marriage,

spouses are usually free to be attentive to each other, without the immediate competing responsibilities of dependent children. Finally, both young and old couples share the need to carefully assess and expend their financial resources together.

Others have argued that the apparent curvilinear trend in marriages is a function of relying upon *retrospective* data (information obtained by asking older persons to reflect on their satisfaction with marriage over time). When couples are asked about the current state of their marriage at different points over the course of their relationship, instead of following a curvilinear pattern, marital satisfaction decreases, especially among women (Vaillant and Vaillant, 1993). Other studies of marital satisfaction that rely on comparing different cohorts suggest that the curvilinear pattern is due to cohort differences that are not identified in cross-sectional data. In a study of five cohorts, marital satisfaction decreases for each successive cohort (Glenn, 1998).

Later-life marriages serve as a key source of companionship and support. Other changes accompanying aging affect the marital tie. The emptying of the nest in middle age represents a positive change to most marriages, with parents free to enjoy the success of launching their children, participation in chosen activities, and each other. However, for some couples, children either served as a diversion from a bad marriage that is unmasked once the children leave or provided a reason for staying together that no longer applies. In these cases, the departure of children may be the precursor of divorce.

Retirement also reshapes the marital tie. To date, more is known about the impact of male retirement on traditional marriage than about the effect of either male or female retirement on the marriage of dual-job couples. We do know that the retirement decision of women is affected by their marital status. Married women are likely to retire early in order to retire at the same time as their usually older husbands. This, of course, has consequences for the economic benefits that women receive in retirement by shortening what was already a shorter career with fewer benefits than typically experienced by men. For some women, leaving a job early may be a source of some resentment, as many older women only re-entered the labour force after staying at home to raise children and were just hitting their stride as they reached retirement (Martin Matthews and Brown, 1987).

On balance, marriage following retirement tends to be positive but, among the current elderly, does require a transition as the previously employed husband finds a niche in his new social world and his wife finds room for her partner in her long-term household patterns. For those in reasonable health and with adequate incomes, retirement can be a time of particular contentment. Conversely, the minority for whom work served as a primary source of identity and a diversion from intimacy may discover a hollow relationship in retirement.

The impact of caring

If one is married, a spouse is the most likely source of help, support, and caring. Women are more likely than men to find themselves in the role of caring for an ill spouse, because they are more likely to outlive their partner. Thus, data on who cares for whom can give the misleading impression that women are neglected by their husbands when, in fact, a key reason that women rely more heavily on other sources of support is that they no longer have a spouse. However, while both men and women come to the aid of their partners, the kind of aid they give and the consequences of giving it differ.

Experiencing the long-term illness of one partner in a marriage can have multiple consequences. First, of course, is the sorrow of serious illness. A mutual sense of loss and the need for support by one partner can actually enhance the *interdependence* of the marital tie, bringing rewards to both partners in terms of the quality of their relationship, in the form of a renewed sense of emotional closeness. At the same time, both providing and requiring care can be stressful. Men are more likely than women to employ a management style of care, making sure that care and support are delivered, but not necessarily personally. Women, on the other hand, tend to provide more extensive care, including the personal hands-on care that men are more likely to delegate to others (Brody and Schoonover, 1986). This reflects the gendered nature of family life in which women typically feel more obliged than do men to provide all forms of support to family members, including their partner. This difference may be the key reason that women experience more stress than do men when caring for a partner. More generally, the well-being of women is tied more closely to the well-being of those to whom they are close than is true of men.

As well as the immediate demands of care-giving, the emotional challenge of facing the physical and/or mental decline of a long-term partner is stressful. For those caring for a partner suffering from dementia, there is the particularly difficult situation of simultaneously caring for and mourning the loss of the partner as the spouse becomes a different person from the one known over the years.

Widowhood and divorce

Losing a husband or wife has both subjective and objective consequences (Martin Matthews, 1991). On the subjective level are the feelings that accompany loss and one's identity in the world as an individual rather than as a member of a couple. On the objective level are changes in such tangibles as finances and the social and practical skills of the partner. The period of bereavement that follows the death of a spouse is a process of about four years during which a new identity as a widowed person evolves. If widowed when older rather than younger, the adjustment is easier. As one might

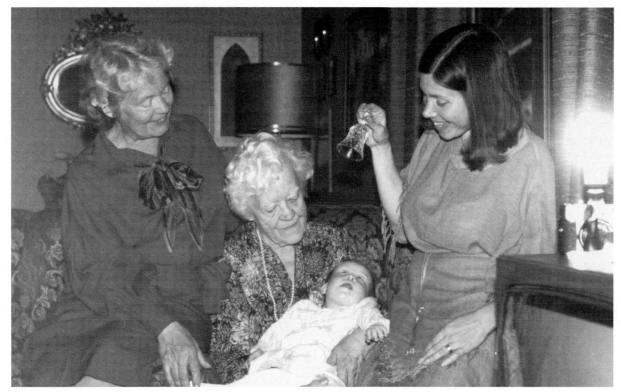

Intrgenerational ties have been the focus of much research on aging.

expect, there are variations by gender. Because women are more likely to be widowed, they are also more likely to have a network of widowed friends and family, particularly sisters, who can share their experiences and provide companionship. Widowed men, on the other hand, have fewer male counterparts but have a larger pool of available women for potential companionship or remarriage. For both men and women, however, remarriage rates have been falling (Burch, 1990).

The gendered nature of social and family life (see also Chapter 10, Families) is reflected in the fact that widowed women are far more likely to be financially deprived than either their married counterparts or widowed men. They are also more likely to have an active network of family and friends, having invested in nurturing these ties over a lifetime. Widowed men often miss the networking skills of their spouse and suffer greater isolation as a consequence of widowhood. While widowhood

is ranked as the most stressful of life transitions, most older persons make a successful personal adjustment to this change in status. This form of resilience is often rewarded with the unjust consequence of a lifetime of inequality that leaves substantial numbers of widowed women financially strapped in old age.

As is true of all ages, the proportion of older divorced persons is increasing, but the numbers are still quite small (see Table 9.1). Relatively little is known about the experience of being divorced in later life. Typically, divorce occurs earlier in life than does widowhood, so the study of divorce in old age is more likely to focus on the longer-term consequences of divorce than the transition from marriage to divorce. Like widowhood, there are feelings of loss and loneliness following divorce. As well, there are similar gender differences in later life, with older divorced men being a particularly isolated group, in part because of the traditional awarding of child custody to mothers. At the same time, while divorce is costly to both men and women, divorced women typically suffer greater financial hardship than other women and than divorced men, and do not have the same benefit entitlements in older age as do widowed women. One aspect of divorce that has received recent attention is the consequences of divorce for intergenerational relationships, discussed later in the chapter.

With the likelihood of divorce rising substantially for younger generations, the impact of divorce over the life course and across generations, not just on young children and recently divorced adults, is a particularly important topic. The challenge of remaining married in the current context of longer lives and higher expectations is noted by one commentator:

[W]hen lifetimes are as much as one-third longer than they used to be, it becomes very difficult to sustain romance for the duration of a marriage...[a] situation made even worse by the fact that...[t]he perfect couple now must be everything to one another-good providers, super sexual partners, best friends, stimulating companions- roles that earlier generations turned to others to fulfil (Gillis, 1996: 151).

The single (never married)

Those who never marry tend to be marginalized when it comes to family ties. Because single persons have tended also to be childless, they are excluded from the traditional family focus on spousal and parent-child ties. Yet, single persons may play very active family roles and, ironically, their obligation to their family of origin often precluded marriage, for women especially (O'Brien, 1991). The proportion of single older persons has remained fairly stable over time, but there is evidence of rising rates of singlehood among younger Canadians. Among older single persons, the gendered nature of family and work was a key reason for singlehood among women. Women who wanted a career had to choose between work and marriage rather than combine the two. As well, then as now, daughters were more likely than sons to meet the obligation of caring for older parents, a responsibility that often overrode forming their own unions.

There is more known about single women than men, but both require further study. Single women have been described as "la crème de la crème" because they tend to have higher levels of education and occupational prestige than their married counterparts. Single men, on the other hand, tend to compare less favourably to their married counterparts. Despite the far more positive image of being a "bachelor" than being a "spinster," it is single men and not women who appear to be isolated in older age. In general, single older persons have adapted to singlehood over their lifetimes, with friends, siblings, and parents serving as important sources of companionship and support. Nonetheless, when compared with married persons and with parents, today's older single persons are less likely to have extensive support available to them when needed. Gaining a better understanding of other family ties, such as those between siblings, between parents and their adult children, and between aunts or uncles and their nieces and nephews will also provide insight into the place of single individuals in family life throughout the life course.

Other intimate ties

Little is known about the intimate relationships of long- or short-term co-habiting couples, of gay and lesbian couples, or of those in less committed relationships in older age (what would traditionally be termed "dating"). Concerning gay and lesbian ties, the failure of Canadian legislation to formally and fully support their relationships (Carter, 1998) limits the extent to which such ties are public, as they cannot be made "official." The likelihood of keeping bonds hidden is higher in the older population, who grew up in a time when the stigma of homosexuality was far greater than it is today. Much research is needed on the nature of such unions and, more generally, the lives of gay and lesbian individuals in old age. Some suggest that dealing with the challenge of being a homosexual in a heterosexist society actually leaves older gay and lesbian persons better equipped to deal with the challenges of aging (Friend, 1991).

Intergenerational ties

Intergenerational ties have been the focus of much research on aging, motivated in substantial measure by concerns regarding who looks after older persons (a concern shared by researchers who identify more personally with adult children than with older parents). Two approaches to studying intergenerational relationships have dominated North American research. The *solidarity perspective* (Roberts, Richards, and Bengtson, 1991) focuses upon the extent to which ties exist between generations. Key criticisms of this approach include the limited discussion of what low solidarity means for familial relations between the generations, the tendency to emphasize consensus, and the failure to deal with conflict and contradiction in familial ties (Luescher and Pillemer, 1998).

A substantial body of research on adult-child/ older-parent relationships takes a *social problems approach* in documenting the shortcomings of older persons' social networks, the burdens of providing care, the conflicts that may ensue between older parents and their children and, more generally, the negative impact of the ups and downs of old age on the parent-child relationship. This perspective tends to heighten the negative stereotype of old age in its overemphasis on the problematic features of intergenerational ties.

A recent third approach to intergenerational ties conceptualizes them as *ambivalent*, with family members torn between feelings of love and obligation, competing interests for their time, and a social world that places contradictory demands upon them (e.g., the competing expectations of individualism and filial obligation towards, or of work vs., family, Luescher and Pillemer, 1998). Addressing how such fundamental ambivalence is resolved involves a conception of familial ties that emphasizes interaction, negotiation between family members, and the possibility of both solidarity and conflict in familial bonds. The combined impact of the social structure (e.g., gender-based expectations of appropriate roles in and outside the family), family history, and personal objectives can be observed in the creation of *legitimate excuses* for avoiding obligations toward family members (Finch, 1989).

Relations between older parents and their adult children

The reduction in fertility rates has led many to conclude that we will have a crisis in informal support because there will be growing numbers of older persons who do not have children and growing numbers of adult children who do not have siblings with whom to share the responsibilities of supporting their parent(s) (see Chapter 15, Demography and Urbanization). Yet, an examination of family size since 1961 shows that the shift in fertility is due primarily to a decline in the number of women who are having five or more children (Connidis, 1997; 1999). As of 1991, the proportion of ever-married women aged 45 and over who had no or only one child was actually lower than for preceding cohorts, while the proportions having two or three children were up.

Some older people, particularly women, outlive some of their children and, therefore, it is useful to know how many living children older persons have. In 1996, among women of all marital statuses aged 75 to 84, 12 percent had no children, 11 percent one, 23 percent two, and 54 percent had three or more children. Thus, as before, most older persons have living children. The question is, what kind of relationship do they have with them?

Older parents tend to have quite active ties with their children, and daughters and sons serve as important support persons when they are needed. At the same time, parents are also significant support providers to their adult children, a fact that is often downplayed in debates on intergenerational equity that focus on government transfers (Stone, Rosenthal, and Connidis, 1998). A realistic portrayal of parental ties with adult children should emphasize exchange and reciprocity over the life course. Exchanges of material goods favour adult children (that is, older parents give more to their grown children than they receive from them). Older parents often provide housing to their adult children (the refilling of the empty nest following job loss, marital separation, or unemployment of the adult child as well as long-term support for children with various disabilities or chronic conditions), and offer various forms of instrumental assistance including caring for grandchildren. More generally, adult children can benefit from the experiences of their older parents, learning from them as they experience such life transitions as marriage, the arrival of children, or widowhood (Connidis, 1989). As well, problems such as alcoholism and marital separation experienced by adult children have an ongoing impact on the lives of their parents (Pillemer and Suitor, 1991).

Nonetheless, as older parents age and experience functional declines, their children are crucial sources of support, particularly among women who are more likely to have no spouse available and are more likely to have cultivated strong ties with their children over their lifetime. The gendered nature of family life is again reflected in the fact that daughters are more likely than sons to provide assistance to their parent(s), including daughters who are in the labour force. Among labour-force participants, unmarried women give more hours of help and are more likely to be primary caregivers than any other gender and marital status combination (Connidis, Rosenthal, and McMullin, 1996).

When daughters are unavailable (there are none, they live far away, or they have other demands that must take precedence), sons do step in. Daughters and sons tend, however, to take a different approach to negotiating care. Daughters are more oriented to consulting siblings about how to meet the needs of their parents, while sons are more likely to deal directly with their parent (usually mother) in determining how much and what type of support is needed. While daughters provide more hands-on care than do their sons, the approach of sons may actually benefit older parents because it fosters independence (Matthews and Heidorn, 1998). A key difference between daughters and sons, parallelling differences between husbands and wives, is that sons are more likely to use a management style of care, ensuring that help is provided though not necessarily by them. A similar difference is emerging among women, with those in the labour force more likely to use this management style than are homemakers, who provide more of the help personally.

Labour-force participation has not meant an abdication of parental support but rather a shift in how it is provided. This shift poses a serious policy challenge. Needed services must be in place for orchestration by adult children, particularly

daughters who, thus far, are combining the responsibility of labour-force participation with care of older parents and, for some, children as well (Martin Matthews and Campbell, 1995; Martin Matthews and Rosenthal, 1993). A key issue is the responsibility that employers should assume to accommodate the situation of the worker responsible for a frail parent.

Rising rates of divorce in both generations also have long-term consequences for the parent-child relationship. The divorce of parents, whether it occurs when children are young or adult, has negative effects on relationship quality and the amount of contact and support exchanged once parents are older, especially between fathers and their children (Cooney and Uhlenberg, 1992; Kaufman and Uhlenberg, 1998). In turn, the divorce of children may limit their ability to assist their parents at the same time as it increases the need for and provision of support from older parents. Maternal grandmothers, in particular, are often central players in the care received by their grandchildren following their daughter's separation or divorce (Gladstone, 1987; 1988).

Childless older persons

In a pronatalist country such as Canada, the childless tend to be ignored in examinations of family life and to be treated, implicitly, as less fulfilled than parents. As well, childlessness tends to be treated as an issue during the childbearing years, not in older age, except for the concern that those without children are lacking a primary source of informal support and will thus require more state-funded formal assistance in old age. Research tends to show little difference between older childless persons and parents in subjective well-being, life satisfaction, loneliness, social participation, or social support (Connidis, 1992; 1994; 1996; McMullin and Marshall, 1996). This indicates successful adjustment to childlessness over the life course by most older persons.

How do older persons view childlessness? When asked to discuss this topic, older persons report both advantages and disadvantages to being childless (Connidis and McMullin, forthcoming). The four main advantages are fewer worries and problems, financial benefits, greater freedom, and career flexibility. The three major drawbacks are lack of companionship, being alone, and loneliness; the missed experience of parenting; and an assumed lack of support and care when older. There is no question that childlessness does have repercussions for support. For example, institutionalization in old age is more likely among women, the non-married, and the childless. Yet, childless people who report loneliness and lack of support are no more likely, actually, to be lonely or lacking in support than those who do not. Thus, the view that children fend off loneliness and guarantee support may be more a function of accepting a cultural bias about the potential support of children than of actual experience. As was true for the unmarried, we need to know more about the family ties of those without children.

Siblings

Limited attention has been paid to the nature of sibling ties beyond childhood. About 80 percent of persons aged 65 and over have at least one living sibling and this will continue to be true in the foreseeable future. The availability of siblings in later life is one basis for exploring the potential of this relationship. As well, siblings have several unique features that may enhance the complementarity of sibling relationships with other family bonds. For most of us who have siblings, our brothers and/or sisters will be our longest-lasting family tie when we reach old age. Unlike a spouse or children, siblings have known us since early childhood and served as our training ground for negotiating peer relationships. Unlike parents and children or grandparents and grandchildren, siblings are horizontal rather than vertical ties, making them more egalitarian. Sibling relationships tend also to be more voluntary and less obligatory than is true of the assumed responsibilities of parents to children, children to parents, and spouses to one another. Siblings connect us with our past and are ideal companions for reminiscence, a favoured pastime in old age.

Siblings tend to have quite close ties in older age. These close bonds in older age often follow a somewhat fallow period in sibling ties during adulthood, when careers are being launched and commitments to others made. Among persons aged 55 and over, 70 percent say that they are somewhat, very, or extremely close to at least one of their siblings (Connidis, 1994), and among those 65 and over, nearly 80 percent describe at least one sibling as a close friend (Connidis, 1989b). Emotional closeness to siblings increases with age among those aged 55 or more and is greater among women than men (Connidis and Campbell, 1995). These emotional connections are evident in the fact that siblings often serve as confidants in later life and are a particularly significant part of older single women's confidant networks (Connidis and Davies, 1990; 1992; Campbell, Connidis, and Davies, 1999). Emotional closeness also increases both personal and telephone contact with siblings, both of which are higher among women than men (Connidis and Campbell, 1995).

How do key life transitions affect the sibling tie? Qualitative research shows that, among those affected by the transition, marriage has varied effects ranging from making sibling ties closer to inhibiting closeness and contact, usually depending upon how a sibling views his or her in-law. However, when siblings have children, divorce, or are widowed, if there is any change in the sibling tie it is positive, leading to greater emotional closeness, more contact, and greater support from siblings (Connidis, 1992).

Another important transition in sibling ties is often triggered by their parents' need for support. The poor health or death of a family member tends to bring siblings emotionally closer to one another. Interesting dynamics in sibling ties are evident when examining how siblings negotiate who will support parents (Matthews and Heidorn, 1998; Coward and Dwyer, 1990). For both men and women, having sisters increases the likelihood that help to parents will be shared with others (Connidis, Rosenthal, and McMullin, 1996). Families of two sisters share the care of parents most equitably, whereas in families with more sisters, two of them will provide most of the help, with periodic assistance from the other sisters. In families with brothers and sisters, sisters provide most of the care, with only occasional or no help from brothers. Men in families of only brothers tend to work out supportive arrangements directly with parents, rather than with one another. Finally, siblings who are emotionally closer tend to share parental care more equitably and also to be more accepting of inequities in support when they exist.

What about support among siblings in older age? While most older persons do not report actually receiving help from their siblings, the majority perceive siblings as potential support providers, should the need arise (Connidis, 1994). Marital and parental status make a difference; siblings are more important as providers of support to the widowed, single, and childless (Campbell, Connidis, and Davies, 1999). At the same time, single, widowed, and divorced siblings are also more likely to be willing to *offer* support to their siblings, if needed. In sum, sibling relationships remain important across the life course, both in their own right and in terms of support received by older parents from their children. Leaving your parents' home to live on your own might include an important transition in your sibling ties.

Aging and Health

The health of the older population has improved steadily over this century, as reflected in longer life expectancy as well as subjective indicators that show that the majority of older persons consider themselves to be in good to excellent health (McPherson, 1998). While women continue to outlive men, the gap is narrowing, and lifestyle changes among women (more smoking, alcohol consumption, and driving in particular) are already taking their toll in elevated rates of lung and heart disease and deaths among women. Despite the fact that women live longer than men, women have higher rates of morbidity (illness) than men, controlling for age (Gee and Kimball, 1987; McPherson, 1998).

Social concerns regarding aging and health include the provision of health care, alternatives to institution-based care, and the disruption of social roles due to poor health. Balanced against these are individual-level concerns about maintaining good health, burdening others and losing personal autonomy, the economic costs of lengthy health care, chronic illness, and the illness of close family members. There is no question that aging brings with it physiological decline. The five senses (sight, hearing, touch, taste, and smell) become less acute and strength and endurance wane as muscles lose their mass, and lung capacity decreases. These represent normal aging processes and must not be mistaken for illness outcomes. For example, sensory decline can lead to confusion, which can be corrected by augmenting the sense (e.g., with glasses or a hearing device). If misperceived as the first signs of dementia, however, the response of others may be quite different.

Lest this message be taken too far, any decrement should not be assumed to be a function of age until other possible explanations have been eliminated. An important consideration is whether limitations incurred with age are a function of disuse. Research on the benefits of physical activity shows that half of what used to be viewed as normal decline with age is actually a result of not using muscle and bone tissue, leading to their degeneration and loss of function (Seniors Directorate, 1995). Physical activity among seniors enhances psychological well-being, heart function, and bone strength; reduces the pain and stiffness of arthritis, the risk of colon cancer and high blood pressure; and helps maintain a healthy weight. These benefits are possible at any age, so a history of a sedentary lifestyle is no reason not to start getting active in old age.

Perhaps no issue rouses concern about population aging more than the assumed escalation of health costs as more people grow old. With age, the number of chronic ailments increases, and older people often experience more than one condition simultaneously. The most common chronic illnesses are arthritis, hypertension, heart-related illness, respiratory problems, and diabetes (McPherson, 1998). The accumulated risk of life-threatening diseases also takes its toll. These are not matters to be taken lightly and there is no point in pretending that older persons are just as healthy as any other age group (Matthews, 1993). But the key question to a sociologist is the extent to which such physical decline and health problems represent functional decline and shape interaction with significant others. Addressing this question allows us to more properly address the health concerns of older persons and the costs of an older population to the health care system. Recent research indicates that those aged 65 and over contribute disproportionately to health care costs in the last year of life because their mortality rates are higher, not because costs per older person for such care are higher (Demers, 1998).

The decline in the senses alters the symptoms of illness as well. Less likely to feel pain or to experience a rise in temperature, a similar illness does not trigger the same response in older persons, making it harder to diagnose. Similarly, the nature of illness is different in older age and is much more likely to be chronic than acute. Thus, unlike younger people who are likely to arrive in hospital requiring short-term treatment for an acute illness, older persons require a focus on care rather than cure. For these reasons, there has been an ongoing concern that our health care system move away from the traditional medical-model focus on cure, and toward a care-centred approach requiring the training of more specialists in geriatric medicine, nursing, and other allied professions.

There is a risk of misdiagnosing or mistreating illness in older people, based on our assumptions about old age and on transferring our understanding of symptoms based on younger persons to older ones. According to a recent issue of the *Canadian Family Physician* (May, 1999), depression is often not diagnosed among the elderly, in part because their symptoms are taken as part of being an older person. Consequently, necessary medication or therapy are often not forthcoming. On the other hand, in institutions, where depression rates are as high as 50 percent, medication may be relied on too heavily as a method for managing caseloads that exceed available staff time. Without the political will and public funding to change institutional settings, the real root of the problem, this situation is likely to persist and potentially worsen as more Canadians reach the oldest ages, when the probability of institutional care is greatest.

Good public policy requires health promotion initiatives rather than responding to illness only (Marshall, 1994). For an aging population this includes augmenting community-based support, recognizing that most support to older persons is provided either by older persons themselves (self-care) or by their family, friends, and neighbours. Thus, all age groups have a shared interest in strategies that improve the health of older Canadians.

Government Income for Older Canadians

There are several sources of state-supported income for older Canadians. These include:

* The Canada/Quebec Pensions Plan (CPP). Based on contributions made from earnings in the labour force. Eligibility is 60 to 64 for early retirement, 65 for normal, and up to age 70 for late retirement. Recent changes allow one parent (mother or father) to claim a Child Rearing Drop-out Provision for children born after December 31, 1958, if the parent dropped out of the labour force to be the child/ren's primary caregiver up to the age of 7. If qualified, the claimant receives a credit toward their CPP benefits.

* Old Age Security Pensions (OAS). General eligibility for a full pension is having lived in Canada for a total of 40 years after the age of 18.

* Guaranteed Income Supplement (GIS). An income-tested supplement for Old Age Security Pensioners with limited incomes. (Some studies use qualifying for GIS as an indicator of poverty.)

* Spouse's Allowance/Widowed Spouse's Allowance. Low-income-based benefits available to the 60- to 64-year-old spouse of an Old Age Security Pensioner or to widowed persons aged 60 to 64. (The Widowed Spouse's Allowance has sparked some controversy on the grounds that divorced and single women do not have access to similar benefits despite the fact that divorced women are at least as financially insecure as are widowed women.)

Source: *Human Resources Development Canada.*

Retirement

Retirement can be examined at both the individual (micro) and societal (macro) levels. Issues of interest at the individual level include personal planning for retirement, the decision to retire, and adjustment to retirement. At the societal level, topics include social policy and legislation regarding retirement and security, the impact of social and economic trends on retirement (e.g., labour-force participation rates, aging of the population, levels of employment), and the impact of retirement on society (e.g., costs of publicly funded pensions; the balance of public- and private-sector responsibility for providing retirement benefits). Examining retirement at both levels of analysis requires considering the impact of such factors as the organization of work and family, gender, health, income, and the economy.

At the macro level, a major concern in Canada is determining how to meet the costs of a growing number of retirees. Central to this issue is determining the appropriate balance between public (social) and personal (individual) responsibility for the welfare of Canadians in old age. It is generally agreed that the two basic objectives of our retirement income system—"ensuring both an adequate basic income for all seniors (the anti-poverty objective) and an adequate standard of living in retirement when Canadians left the labour force (the earnings-replacement objective)"—have not been met (Battle, 1997: 521). The outcome of considerable debate on revising income policy for seniors and retirees has been to take a moderate view by simply tinkering with the existing system. Consequently, the retirement income system continues to be imbalanced because only relatively well-off labour-force participants can rely on private sources of retirement income through occupational pensions and registered retirement savings plans. Meanwhile, "the majority of Canadians depend upon the public parts of the pension system for most or all of their retirement income. Yet public pension programs were not designed to achieve on their own the earnings-replacement objective" (Battle, 1997: 525). Recent changes to the retirement income programs mean, on balance, an increase in contributions by labour-force participants and a decrease in benefits for those under 65 years of age as of December 31, 1997.

Over the years there has been considerable debate about mandatory retirement. This debate (Guppy, 1989) reflects the ongoing tension between *individual justice* (emphasized by proponents of flexible retirement) and *comparative justice*, or group rights (emphasized by proponents of mandatory retirement). In support of *mandatory retirement* is the argument embedded in disengagement theory that a uniform age of retirement ensures the smooth exit of older persons from the labour market, freeing a predictable number of positions for younger persons to fill. Another advantage of mandatory retirement, some argue, is that the need to create assessment techniques of job performance and of having to inform workers that they are no longer capable of performing their job and, therefore, must retire, are avoided. Instead, all workers can retire with the belief that they have retired only by virtue of being a given age, not because they are no longer competent. Those who favour *flexible* retirement hold the view that all adults should have the right to employment and that, particularly in the absence of adequate financial support in old age, the state should not have the right to deny access to income. Mandatory retirement violates principles of individual justice by forcing everyone to retire regardless of ability and desire to continue working.

Canadian law generally supports age-based mandatory retirement, usually at the age of 65. For some occupations, for example, an airline pilot, a younger age can be set if age can be shown to be related to job performance. Most older workers are good workers, and job performance benefits from experience (National Advisory Council on Aging, 1992). However, reaction time and acquiring new skills tend to take longer as we age. There have been some successful appeals of mandatory retirement (e.g., professors at the University of Manitoba) but these are exceptions, and appealing on the basis of the Charter of Rights' protections against discrimination based on age has usually not been successful.

While the typical mandatory age of retirement and the age of entitlement to full government pension benefits is 65, the average age at retirement has been lower than this for some time—62 for men and just under 61 for women in 1996 (Norris, 1999). Initially, this trend reflected an increase in voluntary early retirement, as growing numbers of workers chose to leave the labour force before the mandatory age of retirement (primarily men because they were more likely to be lifetime earners and, therefore, to have pension benefits that made retirement possible). More recently, early retirement has been actively encouraged through incentive programs designed to free jobs for younger persons in a labour market that is glutted with baby-boomers. However, pressure to raise the age of pension entitlement (to ensure that there are enough labour-force participants) is likely to occur as baby-boomers reach retirement age.

Accruing deficits and a weak economy have had similar effects in encouraging cost-saving efforts such as downsizing, prompting employers to force exit through layoffs, creating growing numbers of involuntary retirees. Forced early retirement has substantial consequences for retirees and their families. The shift in identity from being retired to unemployable, the negative consequences for retirement income, and the negative effect on health of forced early exit detract from the retirement years for both the retiree and his or her family (Marshall, 1995a, 1995b; Guillemard, 1996).

The experience of retirement is intricately tied to the experience of work, including salary and benefits, length of employment, full- versus part-time employment, and the nature of employment (e.g., self-employed versus employee; white- versus blue-collar). Prior to any of these issues is whether one spent all or much of a lifetime in paid versus unpaid labour. Historically, the majority of Canadian men have been labour-force participants until full retirement at age 65 or older. However, trends over the past few decades indicate that men are leaving the labour force earlier, some by choice and some following a failure to find new employment after a layoff. For example, among men aged 55 to 64, 80 percent were in the labour force in 1971 compared with 65 percent in 1991. Among those aged 65 to 69, 37 percent were still working in 1971 versus 16 percent in 1991.

Among women, the trends have generally been in the opposite direction, except among those aged 65 and over where the numbers have always been low (12 percent in 1971 versus 10 percent in 1991 for women 65 to 69 years old). The dramatic increase in women's labour force participation over this century is evident among those aged 45 to 54, of whom 41 percent were in the labour- force in 1971 compared with 72 percent in 1991. Corresponding figures for women aged 55 to 64 in 1971 are 33 percent versus 42 percent in 1991. Labour-force histories vary among women according to age, with today's older women much more likely than younger women to have interrupted their employment for lengthy periods to stay at home with their children.

Among those engaged in paid labour, there are substantial differences in the amount of pension support available through work. When compared with men, women of all ages are more likely to interrupt their paid work to care for family, to be employed part-time rather than full-time, and to be in jobs with poorer pension benefits. Thus, one must delve deeply into labour-force participation data to get an accurate picture of the respective positions

The proportion of people who are 65 years and older, currently about 12 percent, is more than double that of fifty years ago.

of men and women at work and, consequently, in retirement. A critical question when you consider any job is, What is the pension package? Over a lifetime, this can mean much more in real dollars and in old-age security than a higher salary with no or few pension benefits.

The nature of work for most Canadians makes retirement attractive. Most retirees enjoy retirement, appreciating the time available to engage in chosen activities, to spend time with children and grandchildren, and to travel. Of course, these pursuits require reasonable health and financial security. Retirement is more difficult for those who have fewer financial resources, who did not develop interests and/or friendships outside of work, who relied heavily on their job for a sense of self-worth, and who are in poorer health (McDonald and Wanner, 1990; McPherson, 1998). The gendered nature of social life makes these factors apply differently to men and women. Today's older men tended to invest quite heavily in their jobs, while today's older women invested more heavily in their families. Thus, the retirement experience at present

tends to be gendered as well; men are more likely to face the challenge of finding alternatives to work as a source of activity, identity, and social contacts. Women, on the other hand, have developed ties with family and friends outside the work domain, but are more likely to face the serious challenges of inadequate financial resources in retirement. The cumulative effects of the gendered division of labour are thus felt in retirement. To the extent that the experiences of men and women as labour-force participants and family members become more parallel, these differences in retirement may diminish in the future, to the benefit of both men and women.

Shifts in the economy can have a particularly dramatic impact on the financial welfare of retirees, because the vast majority of them are on fixed incomes. Thus, if inflation is high and interest rates low, the net effect is to reduce the incomes of many older persons. When inflation is low and interest rates high, incomes stretch further. The economy also shapes views and policies about appropriate retirement ages (high unemployment generates

Pension Benefits and Same-Sex Couples

The recent Supreme Court of Canada decision allowing partners of same-sex unions to entitlements following separation, parallelling those of married and common-law heterosexual couples, has caused quite a stir, from dismay among those promoting traditional family structures to pleasure among those who believe the ruling is long overdue. This represents an example of relying on litigation as a way of obtaining rights for gay and lesbian partners in the absence of legislative change by politicians (Carter, 1998). The failure of politicians to make legislative changes to grant gay and lesbian partners access to spousal pension benefits has also led to litigation, which, so

far, has been unsuccessful. A major obstacle is the federal Income Tax Act, which does not allow extension of pension plans to same-sex couples. However, in part based on anticipating that it would be only a matter of time before the government would be forced by successful litigation to provide pension benefits to same-sex couples, on May 25, 1999 the government passed a bill allowing the retroactive claim of a $30-billion surplus in the public service pension plan, to be used in a variety of ways by the government. The opposition parties voted against it as an inappropriate money grab. However, the bill was also fraught with controversy within the Liberal Party because

some of the money is to be spent on same-sex benefits, and six backbenchers refused to support the bill. Ironically, so did Svend Robinson, one of Canada's two openly gay members of Parliament. Opposing the bill on the grounds that appropriating the surplus amounted to theft, Robinson was quoted as saying, "I would do anything to vote for equal pensions for gay and lesbian people. It hurts terribly to vote against that part of the bill but...I'll swallow my pain and I'll vote against the bill and I'll fight for equal pensions another day." (London Free Press, May 26, 1999, p. A7.)

pressure for a lower retirement age, low unemployment for a higher retirement age) and pension benefits (the current pressure to lower benefits is based on assumptions of a slow economy and a large number of future retirees).

Social Policy and Future Directions

Reflect on the material that you have just read and see if you can think of some policy implications. How does one turn information into the basis for sound policy? This is the challenge before policy-makers and researchers when they are asked to link research findings with policy recommendations. Research findings do not in themselves offer clear directives for policy. Instead, our biases about what kind of society we want to have influences our view of what constitutes good policy decisions. In comparisons with the United States, Canada has been described as a country that favours a more collective (rather than individual) solution to problems, as is evident in universal social programs such as health care (Clark, 1993). However, this orientation has been eroded over the past few years as some programs are no longer universal (e.g., child allowance, referred to as the "baby bonus") and others place much heavier emphasis on individual responsibility (e.g., independent contributions to a registered retirement savings plan; earlier discharge from hospitals to informal care at home).

What position one takes on the balance between individual versus social responsibility will determine the extent to which government-based programs are supported as a means of dealing with social issues, including an aging population. Years ago, Mills (1959) made this distinction by talking about *private troubles* versus *public issues*. Treating social issues as private troubles means that the ultimate responsibility for dealing with a given situation rests with the individual and his or her significant others. Conversely, if one takes a public-issues approach, the focus is on developing collective solutions to the challenges that citizens face. A particular issue may have elements of both. For example, in the case of widowhood, getting through the period of bereavement is very much a private trouble, and there are limits to what any social policy can do to alleviate this fact. The greatest strength is likely to be drawn from oneself and close family and friends. Yet, some of the consequences of widowhood are socially constructed and require social solutions. A clear case in point is the financial setback suffered by many women after their husbands die, a consequence of a social world built upon a gendered division of labour in which women depend upon their partners for financial security. This outcome can be dealt with as a public issue on several possible fronts such as better survivor benefits for widows, paying for domestic labour so that women can secure their own financial future, and income entitlements in older age that are not based on work history or marital status.

Taking a broad view is essential to forming good social policy. One dilemma in focusing on older people when considering policy options is the failure to consider the implications for older persons of other generations' situations. For example, we have seen the very important role played by adult children in providing support to their older parents. However, the high labour-force participation rates of both men and women make caring for older parents a greater challenge than it once was. Public policies and initiatives in the private sector that support employee efforts to care for older family members enhance the probability and quality of care provided by children. Life for both generations is improved as older persons receive support from loved ones, and children are relieved of the stress that can be associated with providing such support. At the moment, the general absence of such policies in the workplace means that employees are paying a substantial price in terms of their own work history in order to aid their parents. This is particularly true of women, who are likely to use holiday time to provide care, to miss employment opportunities, and to forfeit promotions as strategies for balancing care and work (Martin Matthews and Rosenthal, 1993). The irony is that these short-term costs persist in the long term, as these women enter their own old age less financially secure than they would have been otherwise and, in turn, unduly reliant on others and the government for support. Thus, supporting younger persons benefits older ones. Similarly, providing support directly to older persons alleviates pressures on younger family members. Consequently, older persons should not be considered the only beneficiaries of age-based policies.

The heavy reliance of the government on the family (which translates predominantly into a reliance on women) to take care of its older members has been an ongoing concern in several Western nations (Myles, 1991; Walker, 1991). The current focus on deficit reduction and cost savings escalates this concern because of its consequences for social programs. As we have seen, the family continues to be the primary source of support for older persons, even today when the majority of women are in the labour force. Thus, the family does not represent an untapped resource. Yet, cutbacks in service provision are placing greater demands on the family at precisely the same time as the combination of labour-force participation and changes in the family (e.g., rising divorce rates, more single-parent families, and high unemployment rates) make it more difficult for family members to increase their level of support.

Another compelling reason for assuming public responsibility for the older population is our requirement that most older persons must retire (the self-employed are an exception here). Having withdrawn their access to financial livelihood in order to provide jobs for younger persons, there is surely an unspoken agreement to offer economic and social support to ensure a reasonable old age. Yet, as we saw in our discussion of retirement, it is the rare Canadian who can expect to sustain the same standard of living in retirement as he or she enjoyed while working.

Historically, there has been disproportionate attention paid to the help given to older persons. While this has been corrected somewhat in the literature on informal support, the current debate about intergenerational equity has involved a renewed focus on the receipt of support by older persons, this time in the form of government transfers. Discussions of intergenerational equity focus on the equatability of funds expended by the governments on different age groups in the population (e.g., build a new school or a home for the elderly). Those who engage in generational accounting argue that the old are receiving more

than their share at the expense of the young and that measures should be taken to make public transfers more equitable, in part to avoid inter-generational conflict (Corak, 1998). Critics of this position take the view that such accounting procedures suffer from their narrow focus on government transfer payments and on one point in time, and they argue that one must take a life-long perspective, consider the contributions made by the older population over time, and include informal transfers (Marshall, 1987; McDaniel, 1997; Stone, Rosenthal, and Connidis, 1998). Moreover, studies of public opinion indicate that Canadians are willing to spend more in tax dollars to support our older citizens (Northcott, 1994).

Looking ahead

As baby-boomers age, so too will Canada's population, peaking in 2041. After that time, our population will actually become younger, and we will be facing quite different challenges. In an era dominated by unemployment, it is difficult to envisage a time when older workers will actually be encouraged to remain in the labour force, but this is anticipated because so many Canadians will be leaving the labour force as baby-boomers retire. Generally, the older population will be healthier, wealthier, and, if not wiser, more educated, as successive cohorts reach old age. Yet, concerns remain regarding the financial situation of retirees, particularly women who, despite increases in the years spent in paid work, will continue to have poorer pension benefits and a longer period of time in old age than do men.

Changes in labour-force participation among women, declines in labour-force participation for older men, and increases in divorce rates for all age cohorts, will mean shifts in the family ties of older persons. Divorce among both the older generation and their children have the long-term effect of diminishing the amount of informal support and emotional closeness between parents and children, especially between fathers and their offspring (Connidis, 1999; forthcoming). Such general trends will affect the lives of older Canadians. Two outcomes may be the increased importance of siblings and of building relationships with other family and non-family ties.

Increased labour-force participation by women has meant turning to new forms of childcare that go beyond the realm of the family. This shift may leave women more prepared to seek similar alternatives for their older parents and for themselves in old age. The resulting demand for formal sources of support can be met by government and by the private sector provided, in the latter case, that older persons enjoy a better financial situation in the future.

As Canadians continue to live longer and healthier lives, we can also complement our attention to the genuine needs of some older people by considering the contribution that Canadians can continue to make in their older age. Our current customs are predicated on a time when the age of 65 represented a long life. Today, Canadians who live to 65 can expect to live another 18 years. Nine of these years are typically disability free, followed by three years of slight, three years of moderate, and three years of serious disability (National Advisory Council on Aging, 1999). This has been the basis for distinguishing between the third and fourth ages, the third age characterized by retirement, independence, and good health, and the fourth representing a period of growing vulnerability. The challenge before us is to formulate research projects and social policy that address methods of enhancing opportunities for those in the third age to capitalize, personally and socially, on their improved circumstances while meeting the needs of growing dependency during the fourth age.

An anticipated period of retirement, the ongoing availability of family to most older persons, and the general improvement in health combine to enrich the experience of old age for Canadians. This includes more active participation in physical activities, travel (including to see family), and other leisure pursuits at an unprecedented rate. Yet, while the general picture is rosy, a substantial minority of older persons face serious restrictions in the lives that they can lead. Many of these constraints can be alleviated by better social policy designed to more effectively meet the needs of particular pockets of older persons including: women, those without family ties, the poor, immigrants, and the physically and intellectually challenged. Aiding these older persons requires redressing current inequities among the old and longstanding inequities among

all Canadians based on age, gender, class, race, ethnicity, and sexual orientation.

The challenge to researchers is not only to provide useful information. Indeed, we have accumulated a wealth of facts regarding aging and old age. Important contributions can be made by researchers in two additional ways. First, researchers who engage in stock-taking through reflective and analytical syntheses of existing information help clarify what we know and what we need to know. Second, delving beyond the facts by examining the processes that create them and by applying and developing theory allows us to turn information into understanding.

Remember the older person you pictured at the beginning of the chapter? Do you see that person's life any differently now? What does your own old age look like? You are aging and the actions you take now will shape your future as an older person. This chapter has introduced you to a very rich area of sociology. The more that you understand about aging issues, the better prepared you will be for your own aging and old age, for appreciating the situation of older persons close to you, and for contributing wisely to the ongoing debate about how to respond to an aging population.

Summary

Canada's population is aging, due mostly to the decline in birth rates of the past few decades. In 2000, twelve percent of Canadians were 65 years or older. A realistic picture of old age leads us to reject the negative stereotype of this stage as a time of loss, as well as the positive stereotype that tends to equate successful aging with youthfulness. Sociologists seek to understand aging at both the societal and individual levels, examining the balance between social structural forces and the experiences of older persons themselves. Theories on aging have progressed over the past twenty years, and the best of them emphasize heterogeneity among older persons, the role of power and conflicting interests in shaping aging across the life course, and the ability of older individuals to exercise agency over their lives.

Women generally outlive men, creating one basis for the quite different life experiences of older men and women. Older women are more likely to experience old age on their own, while older men are most likely to be married. The greater financial resources of men than women in later life reflect a lifetime of difference due to socially constructed opportunities based on gender. The majority of older men and women have children and siblings, relationships that loom larger in the lives of women, in part because they are less likely to have a spouse in old age. Rising rates of divorce will change the experience of being unattached in older age, given that divorce has different implications for family ties than does widowhood.

The private domain of the family is under strong pressure to provide support for all members in need, including those older persons who require care. A key policy issue is the extent to which we, as Canadians, judge it appropriate for the fate of older persons to rest heavily in the hands of family members who generally care for one another, but who find themselves overextended with competing commitments to different generations and to work as well as family. While older Canadians are enjoying better health than ever, the oldest-old, the fastest-growing age group in our population, experience high levels of chronic illness.

QUESTIONS FOR REVIEW AND CRITICAL THINKING

1.   Gender is a critical organizing feature of social life. Discuss three ways in which the accumulated effects of gender are apparent in older age by comparing the experiences of older women and men.

2.   Besides the theoretical perspectives discussed in this chapter, are there other sociological theories that you think would enhance the study of aging? What are they and why?

3.   Dealing with widowhood was provided as an example of an age-related transition that has elements of both a private and public nature. What are two other examples of age-related transitions that involve both personal and social responsibility? Which measures do you think should be taken in order to deal effectively with your examples as public issues?

4.   This chapter covered three main topics related to aging: family ties, health, and retirement. Discuss five ways in which these topics are interrelated.

KEY TERMS

activity theory, p. 231

age effects, p. 230

age-graded, p. 231

age-stratification perspective, p. 231

critical theory, p. 233

disengagement theory, p. 231

exchange theory, p. 231

geriatrics, p. 228

gerontology, p. 228

life course perspective, p. 232

maturation, see age effects

period effects, p. 228

political economy of aging perspective, p. 232

social constructionist perspective, p. 233

SUGGESTED READINGS

Selections from Butterworth's Monograph Series on *Individual and Population Aging*:

Connidis, Ingrid Arnet. 1989. *Family Ties and Aging;*

McDonald, Lynn and Richard Wanner. 1990. *Retirement in Canada;*

Keating, Norah. 1991. *Aging in Rural Canada;*

Martin Matthews, Anne. 1991. *Widowhood in Later Life;*

Chappell, Neena. 1992. *Social Support and Aging.*

These selections provide extensive overviews of various topics in aging, with a focus on Canadian content. The books are central to a sociological examination of aging.

Marshall, Victor W.

1996   "The state of theory in aging and the social sciences." Pp. 12–30 in R.H. Binstock and L.K. George (eds.) *Handbook of Aging and the Social Sciences* (4th ed.). San Diego, CA: Academic Press.

This article provides an excellent overview of theoretical development regarding the social aspects of aging.

McPherson, B.D.

1998. *Aging as a Social Process: An Introduction to Individual and Population Aging* (3rd ed.). Toronto: Harcourt Brace.

This text provides a comprehensive introduction to the many facets of studying aging and old age.

See also key journals in the aging area. These include: *Canadian Journal on Aging; Journals of Gerontology: Social and Psychological Sciences; The Gerontologist; Ageing and Society; Research on Aging; Journal of Aging Studies;* and *International Journal of Ageing and Human Development.*

WEB SITES

http://www.mbnet.mb.ca/crm/ca/scip/ advoc.cag1eng.html

Canadian Association on Gerontology

Canada's national association is multidisciplinary and includes a Social Sciences Division.

http://www.geron.org

Gerontological Society of America

The national association of the United States has a Behavioral and Social Sciences Division.

http://www.nih.gov/nia/naca.html

National Advisory Council on Aging, Ottawa (Health Canada).

This site has much useful information on aging in Canada.

Social Institutions

Social institutions are structures organized around the performance of central activities in society. They include the beliefs, values, and norms concerning the manner in which a society's needs should be met and the groups that serve these needs. Important activities such as marriage, reproduction, and the raising of children, for example, are generally conducted within families. The acquisition of a particular sense of the meaning of life can take place within religious institutions. Finally, the media can have a powerful influence over our day-to-day lives and our perceptions of the world. This next section examines these social institutions.

We introduced social differentiation by saying it was both a cause and an effect of social phenomena. The same could be said about social institutions. As causes, institutions can influence culture, norms, values, and roles. Certain institutions, especially families, religion, and the media, socialize individuals to acquire culture. Religious institutions define what is and what is not deviant, and the media may affect the reactions, if any, to that deviance. The same two institutions may provide a platform for the birth and development of social movements.

In turn, institutions are affected by cultural variations and by social differentiation. For example, stratification rank and race or ethnicity affect the type of family life individuals experience, and their religion. Finally, institutions affect one another, as when the media affect family and religious values. Thus, there is extensive interdependence among the various institutions, and important links between institutions, culture, and socialization. All contribute to the structure of social life, which impinges on individuals and affects their behaviour.

Because the concept of institution entails the ideas of serving social needs, or getting the tasks of society accomplished, institutions are often portrayed as structures built upon consensus. Yet, there is also conflict between and within each of these institutions, as when religion clashes with the media over proper entertainment standards, or when religious groups seek to intervene in what some see as family decisions. As you have done elsewhere in the book, keep in mind alternative explanations when you read a functionalist, conflict, symbolic interactionist, feminist, or other explanation. Ask yourself what a sociologist with a differing perspective might say.

Families

Roderic Beaujot

Introduction

It is already evident from the previous chapters that the study of families is an important part of the study of society. The chapter on culture introduced examples from the sociology of families: definitions of "mother," an explanation of sexual jealousy, and the existence of incest taboos in almost all societies. It was also pointed out in the chapter on socialization that much of socialization takes place in families, while the chapter on gender shows that fundamental attitudes toward family and gender roles are closely related. And in the last chapter you saw the importance of family ties in later life.

Two further points underscore the place of families in the study of society. First, families are the social arena in which most people spend most of their lives. Thus, if we want to find out how people live and how their lives are organized, it is important to know something about what happens in their families. Second, as one of the institutions of society, families affect and are affected by other social institutions. For example, an economy based

on a high degree of job mobility requires the geographic mobility of families, and it may also require that individual families be more self-sufficient and less dependent on kin or relatives left behind. Thus, the economy can affect families. In turn, the actions of families can affect economic institutions. For instance, when people decide to have fewer children, consequences are soon felt in the industries that supply baby products. Much later, there will be repercussions in the housing market (less demand for housing) and on the growth of the labour force (fewer workers). In some regards, family and economic questions are evolving together, with families seeking to have all adults in the labour force, a consequent increase of part-time and non-standard work, and the 24-hour economy accommodating the complex lives of families.

While the study of families is important for an understanding of society, at least two factors make this study difficult. First, virtually all of us have lived in families, and we are frequently too willing to make generalizations about families based on our own limited personal experience, making it difficult to take an objective look at actual family behaviour. The second difficulty is that family behaviour is generally considered private. Consequently, as researchers we are often barred from studying families in their natural settings. When we can observe them, much of normal family behaviour may be camouflaged-consciously or unconsciously altered by family members-making it hard to reach reliable conclusions.

We shall begin this chapter with definitions of marriage and related family terms and then highlight some of the differences and uniformities in family patterns across societies. This will remind us of some of the variations in family behaviour and of the necessity of viewing families against the background of the larger society. Family change will be described and then interpreted through theoretical perspectives that consider both the evolving role of families in society and the changing importance of families in individuals' lives. We then consider family questions over the life course, including socialization for marriage, childbearing and childrearing, and marital breakdown. The final section considers the general question of change and continuity in family patterns in the recent past and immediate future.

Definitions of Marriage and Family

Marriage can be defined as a commitment and an ongoing exchange. In noting that marriage includes a commitment, we mean that it involves a more or less explicit contract that spells out the rights and obligations between partners. The commitment can be defined at either the personal or social level. At the personal level, it means that marriage is undertaken with considerable seriousness. At the social level, it is a type of social contract, meaning that certain customs and laws govern the processes of entering into or leaving a marriage. Even the dissolution of cohabitation now involves laws concerning children and property.

In noting that marriage includes ongoing exchanges, we wish to stress that it involves a continuing interdependence between spouses. It is useful to distinguish two types of exchange, the expressive and the instrumental, terms we saw in Chapter 7, Gender Relations. The **expressive exchanges**, or emotional dimension of marriage, include love, sexual gratification, companionship, and empathy. The **instrumental exchanges**, or task-oriented dimension, include earning a living, spending money, and maintaining a household. In virtually all marriages, expressive and instrumental exchanges take place. However, in some circumstances the economic dimension may be more important (e.g., a farming couple who act as an economic unit), while in others the expressive level may be foremost (e.g., a childless working couple whose marriage involves mostly companionship).

Marriages do not just happen; they have to be maintained as ongoing exchanges. In the process, one partner may provide more of some things (e.g., income), while the other partner provides more of others (e.g., empathy). Such sharing will continue if the partners see some level of equity in the exchanges, so that each finds marriage to be rewarding. If such complementarity is not perceived, then the exchange, and in fact the marriage, may break down.

A **family** can be defined as two or more people related by blood, adoption, or marriage (legally sanctioned or otherwise), and who reside together. There are two crucial aspects to this definition of a family: the persons must be related in some way and they must customarily maintain a common residence. If they are not related, they form a household and not a family. If they are related but not living together, they are kin and not a family as defined here. Kin may live in close proximity, and there may be considerable social and economic integration among them, but they are not considered a family unless they live in the same dwelling.

Variability in Family Patterns

As indicated in Chart 10.1, there are considerable differences across societies in matters related to marriage and family structure. To demonstrate this variability, we shall consider three aspects of the family: number of partners in the marriage, sex codes, and emphasis on a nuclear family versus a kinship network.

CHART 10.1   Family Terms

Family and kin

Family	Two or more people related by blood, marriage, or adoption and residing together
Nuclear family	A family that includes only spouses, and any unmarried children
Single-parent family	A family consisting of one parent and one or more children
Common-law union	A nuclear family consisting of partners who are not legally married, with or without children
Reconstituted family	A nuclear family with children from a prior union of one of the spouses
Blended family	A nuclear family that includes children from more than one marriage or union
Extended family	A family that includes more than spouses and unmarried children (e.g., grandparents, married children, other relatives) living in the same residence
Consanguine family	A family organization in which the primary emphasis is on the biological relatedness (e.g., parents and children or brothers and sisters), rather than on the spousal relationship
Kin	People related by blood or marriage

Choice of partners

Exogamy	Partner must be chosen from outside a defined group
Endogamy	Partners must be members of the same group

Number of partners

Monogamy	Marriage involving only two partners
Polygamy	Marriage involving more than two partners
Polygyny	One man married to two or more women; husband-sharing
Polyandry	One woman married to two or more men; wife-sharing
Group marriage	Marriage involving two or more men and two or more women

Descent

Patrilineal	Descent traced unilaterally through the male line; the individual is related only to the father's relatives
Matrilineal	Descent traced unilaterally through the female line; the individual is related only to the mother's relatives
Bilateral	Descent that follows both the male and female lines; the individual is related to both parents' relatives

Residence

Patrilocal	Couple takes up residence with the husband's parents
Matrilocal	Couple takes up residence with wife's parents
Neolocal	Couple resides alone

Authority and dominance

Patriarchal	Males are the formal head and ruling power
Matriarchal	Females are the formal head and ruling power
Equalitarian	Equal dominance of males and females

Number of partners in the marriage

There are four possible compositions of the marriage group: **monogamy, polygyny, polyandry,** and **group marriage**. (For definitions of these terms, see Chart 10.1.) From anthropological data gathered in various societies, however, it is clear that historically some marital arrangements have been found with greater frequency than others.

Monogamy is without question the most prevalent marital form, representing the majority of marriages in almost all societies. At the same time, 75 percent of the world's societies (but not 75 percent of the world's population) appear to accept polygyny. This figure is based on a classic study by Murdock (1957), who compiled anthropological and sociological information from 565 societies—data known as the World Ethnographic Sample. For example, polygyny is quite common in West Africa and is an option in most Muslim or Islamic countries. In Senegal, about a third of married men and close to half of married women are in polygynous unions. When polygyny is common, moreover, it is associated with a wide gap in the average age at marriage. It is men who are more established and consequently older who are able to marry young women. Also, most women are married rather than single, divorced, or widowed. When doing field work in Sierra Leone, I worked with a 20-year-old man whose father had sixteen wives in his lifetime. This man was now 65 and married to twelve wives, but considering marriage to two other young women. In some other countries, such as in Muslim North Africa, where polygyny is permitted, it is rather rare. Turkey and Tunisia are Muslim countries that have forbidden polygyny.

Polyandry is relatively rare. A present-day example where polyandry continues but is on the decline involves the Jaunssari of the Himalayas. As in most other cases where polyandry has been observed, it is brothers who share a wife. The prospective bride has a choice to accept one man as her husband or to accept the man and his brothers. The women largely are in charge of the agricultural activities, while the men work in surrounding urban areas. The main explanation for the practice is that it prevents the land from being subdivided into parcels that would be too small for subsistence. Polyandry enables the inheritance to stay within the male line, without being fragmented among brothers.

Group marriage is similarly rare. Although no longer the case, it was for a time practised among the Nayar in Southern India. At or before puberty, each girl was given a "ritual husband," but the couple's obligations to each other were mostly of a ceremonial nature, partly because the men in this society acted as mercenary warriors for neighbouring kingdoms and were often absent. After marriage, women could receive any of the men of the neighbourhood group as sexual partners. At the birth of a child, one or more of them had to acknowledge paternity and pay for the delivery of the child. If no man came forward, it was assumed that the father was either of a lower caste or a Christian, and the woman was put to death (Gough, 1959).

Sex codes

The regulation of sexual behaviour outside of marriage also varies. In a sample of 158 societies, Murdock (1960: 265) found that premarital intercourse was permitted in 41 percent of societies, conditionally approved in 27 percent, mildly disapproved in 4 percent, and forbidden in 28 percent. Thus, the majority of societies at least tolerated premarital intercourse. An example of a particularly relaxed attitude is that of Trobriand Islanders, the users of magic discussed in Chapter 3, Culture, among whom premarital coitus was taken for granted (Malinowski, 1929). In this group, sex was seen as a natural expression of personality, and thus it was considered natural to let children begin their sexual activities at an early age with a number of partners. After puberty, each person tended to form a more permanent relationship with a person of the other sex. If the association continued, the couple was expected to marry.

In general, extramarital coitus is more stringently prohibited than is premarital coitus. However, this too varies, since it was freely allowed in 3 percent of societies, conditionally permitted in 13 percent, and socially disapproved but not strictly forbidden in 3 percent (Murdock, 1960: 265). Even where it is forbidden, many people consider adultery to be acceptable as long as its existence remains a secret.

Consanguine versus nuclear bonds

A final type of variability in family patterns that can be highlighted is that between consanguine and nuclear family bonds. A consanguine family is based on extended biological relatedness, while a nuclear family involves spouses and any unmarried children. All societies recognize both, but vary considerably in the importance they accord blood versus spousal bonds.

In tribal societies the consanguine family is generally paramount. The kinship group is often the most important group in society. Kinship may predominate in all spheres of life: groups based on kin ties are also economic units for production and consumption, political units with regard to power, and religious units with an emphasis on ancestral worship. The Yoruba of Nigeria provide a good example of the importance of consanguine bonds in a tribal society. Communal residence and occupational cooperation would be endangered among the Yoruba if men listened to what their wives said rather than to what their brothers and fathers said:

In fact...relationships between spouses, even in monogamous marriages, are not very strong in traditional Yoruba society and parents do not exclusively focus their attention on their biological children. Even in 1973 only one-third of Yoruba spouses slept in the same room or even ate together (admittedly indexes of affection regarded as less significant by Yorubas than by outsiders), and fewer still identified the person to whom they felt closest as their spouse, while children were commonly brought up by a number of kinsmen (Caldwell, 1976: 340).

Networks of relatives are important in this type of society. They provide economic security, increase the number of allies in the political sphere, and increase the number of people who can attend family ceremonies. Both reproduction and marriage are at a premium in such tribal societies. The advantage of having many offspring is the fact that, from a very young age and throughout the lives of their parents, children provide a variety of services. The advantage of marriage is that it increases the number of alliances with other kin groups. Since the marriages are for the benefit of the kin rather than for the couple, they are usually arranged by parents.

In the nuclear family, the kin network continues to exist but is considerably less important. The emphasis is on the spousal bond, and thus it is important that the spouses choose each other rather than become joined through a parentally arranged marriage. Relations within the nuclear family are much more important than the relations among kin. Couples are less concerned with ancestors and kin than they are with their own children. In fact, they are likely to "spoil" their children, in the sense of giving them more care and wealth than they can ever expect in return. The emphasis is also on having a smaller number of children so that each of them can have the best possible chance in life.

We could go on stressing the variability in family patterns. For instance, we could talk about the various traditions regarding who is permissible as a spouse and the various outlooks on marital

In the nuclear family, the kin network exists but is less important than the bond between spouses.

dissolution. There are also subcultural variations in Canadian families—for instance, the distinctiveness of Hutterite, Inuit, French, or Chinese families. Other evidence of diversity includes the existence of common-law unions, single-parent families, blended families with children from more than one marriage or union, and gay or lesbian marriages (see the boxed insert on "Gay and Lesbian Relationships").

We have focused on three elements of diversity: number of spouses, sex codes, and consanguine versus nuclear bonds. It is important as well to note the elements of uniformity in this diversity: (1) although polygyny is accepted in many societies, most marriages are in fact monogamous; (2) although there are different orientations towards premarital and extramarital sex, reproduction and

Gay and Lesbian Relationships

Comparisons between heterosexual and homosexual relationships indicate that there are many similarities. [There are few] differences in adjustment or general lifestyle patterns.... If we want to describe what goes on in a relationship between two homosexual individuals-what makes for the success of the relationship and what may lead to problems-we do not have to use a different language. We can use the same terms as we would in describing a relationship between two heterosexuals. In our intimate relationships, we are all much more similar than we are different.

It would, however, be foolish to claim that there are no differences between homosexual and heterosexual relationships. Homosexual couples still face considerable social stigma and legal barriers. Legally, [throughout the U.S.] homosexuals are prohibited from marriage, which creates difficulties for tax returns, joint ownership of property, guardianship/adoption of children, pension plans, insurance coverage, and wills. On the other hand, the social psychology of AIDS may have strengthened gay men's motivation to establish enduring relationships.

Source: *Sharon S. Brehm, 1992.* Intimate Relationships. *New York: McGraw-Hill (pp. 138–41). Reproduced with permission of The McGraw-Hill Companies.*

sex are generally controlled for the benefit of families; and (3) although some societies emphasize consanguinity and others the nuclear family, both always are in existence. A number of other uniformities in family patterns also exist, as we discuss below.

Uniformity and Family Patterns

Importance of marriage

Most societies place a high premium on marriage. Marriage is important, at least for reproduction and socialization of the young, and the majority of adults are expected to fulfill these roles. In effect, most people are motivated towards marriage or living in an enduring relationship as the preferred state of adult life. Other aspects of culture that imply a premium on marriage include the expectation that the parents of a newborn be in a state of union, the discouraging of activities that impinge on marriage, particularly adultery and homosexuality, and the dim view taken of marital dissolution. In *Embattled Paradise*, Skolnick (1991: 220) concluded that there is now more tolerance for variation, but lifelong heterosexual marriage with children remains the preferred cultural norm in North America.

Incest taboo

The incest taboo, prohibiting sex and marriage for close biological relatives, is another feature that is almost uniform across societies. The exceptions to this rule are so rare that some have called the incest taboo a cultural universal (see also Chapter 3, Culture). The taboo reinforces the family in two ways. First, restricting legitimate sexual activity to spouses prevents sexual rivalry from breaking up the family. Second, the requirement to marry outside of the nuclear family enlarges the kinship network through alliances with other families. Mead reported the following imaginary dialogue from an Arapesh informant whose friend wanted to marry his own sister:

What? Do you not want brothers-in-law? If you marry another man's sister and another man marries your sister, you have two brothers-in-law. If you marry your own sister, you have none. With whom will you visit? With whom will you talk? With whom will you hunt? (Mead, 1971: 52).

Importance of inheritance

Another virtual uniformity is the importance of inheritance, a fact that partly explains the premium that is put on marriage and reproduction. A marriage involves much more than the two spouses; families are also joined over generations, partially by the passing on of property. The inheritance that links generations produces social relationships that will continue into the future.

In concluding this section on uniformities in family patterns, it is important to note that there are exceptions to these uniformities. Although nearly all societies put a high premium on marriage, those undergoing extensive social change present some deviations from this pattern. In the Israeli kibbutz, for example, the family was seen as endangering communal solidarity, and was thus given little importance; the marriage ceremony was reduced to the simplest ritual, and children did not eat or sleep with their parents. In Communist Russia, marital dissolutions became very easy to obtain and, for members of the political élite, extramarital sex was not considered a serious transgression.

Certainly, no society requires that all adults be married all the time. The incest taboo is almost universal, yet there are exceptions, and the taboo does not necessarily prevent incestuous behaviour. Moreover, while inheritance along family lines is the general rule, this practice can be interrupted in times of revolutionary change.

Family Change

Historical transformations in families can be described in terms of two transitions: first a long-term change that brought about smaller families, and subsequently a more rapid change that increased flexibility in marital relationships (Lesthaeghe, 1995). The first transition occurred over the period of about 1870 to 1950, and involved a change in the economic costs and benefits of children, along with a new cultural environment that made it more appropriate to control family size. In effect, this transition changed family dynamics surrounding fertility (see Chapter 15, Demography

and Urbanization) from an emphasis on child quantity to a focus on child quality.

In discussing the second transition in Western countries (1960 to the present), Lesthaeghe (1995) proposed that it is useful to consider three sub-stages. The first, from about 1960 to 1970, involved the end of the baby-boom, the end of the trend toward younger ages at marriage, and the beginning of the rise in divorces. The second, from 1970 to 1985, involved the growth of common-law unions and, eventually, of children in cohabiting unions. The third stage, since 1985, brought forth a levelling off of divorce levels, an increase in post-marital cohabitation (consequently a decline in re-marriage), and a plateau in fertility due in part to higher proportions of births after age 30.

Table 10.1 presents some statistics that capture these trends in the Canadian case. In terms of the first stage, the average births per woman had reached a peak of 3.9 in 1957 before declining to 2.2 in 1971. The median age at first marriage declined over this century to reach a low of just over 21 years for brides and 23 years for grooms in the early 1970s, then increased to ages 26 and 28 for women and men respectively in 1996. The law permitting divorces on grounds other than adultery dates only from 1968. For every 100 000 married women, there were under 200 divorces in each year over the period 1951–1966 compared to 1000 in 1976 and 1200 in 1996.

Turning to the second stage, Statistics Canada census data showed that some 0.7 percent of couples indicated that they were living common-law in 1976. The 1996 census determined that 13.7 percent of couples were cohabiting. The proportion of births occurring to women who are not married, and who are largely cohabiting, increased from 9 percent in 1971 to 36 percent in 1996.

As regards the third stage, by 1990, half of divorced persons aged 30 to 39, and more than a third of those aged 40 to 49, were in cohabiting relationships (Dumas and Péron, 1992: 50). Besides the stable fertility of 1.7 births per woman over the period 1980–1996, the proportion of births occurring to women aged 30 and over increased from 19.6 percent in 1976 to 43.7 percent in 1996.

These changes in births, marriage, cohabitation, and divorce brought fewer children, but also a

TABLE 10.1   Summary Statistics on Family Change, Canada, 1941–96

	1941	1951	1961	1971	1976	1981	1986	1991	1996
Total fertility rate (average births per women)	2.8	3.5	3.8	2.1	1.8	1.7	1.6	1.7	1.6
Median age at first marriage									
Brides	23.0	22.0	21.1	21.3	21.6	22.5	23.9	25.1	26.3
Grooms	26.3	24.8	24.0	23.5	23.7	24.6	25.8	27.0	28.3
Divorces per 100,000 married couples	–	180	180	600	990	1180	1302	1235	1222
Common-law couples as a percent of all couples	–	–	–	–	0.7	6.4	8.2	11.2	13.7
Briths to non-married women as a percent of all births	4.0	3.8	4.5	9.0	10.9	14.2	18.8	28.6	36.3
Births to women aged 30+ as a percent of all births	35.6	36.2	34.1	21.6	19.6	23.6	29.2	36.0	43.7
Lone-parent families as a percent of all families with children	9.8	9.8	11.4	13.2	14.0	16.6	18.8	20.0	22.3

Notes: For 1941–71 births to non-married women are designated as illegitimate births. Data for 1995 are shown as 1996 for divorce and births to non-married.
Source: Beaujot (1999). Reprinted by permission of Broadview Press.

higher proportion of children who are not living with both biological parents. In particular, lone-parent families as a proportion of all families with children increased from 11.4 percent in 1961 to 22.3 percent in 1996.

The data also confirm the uniqueness of the 1950s as a period between the two broad transitions mentioned earlier. Various authors have observed that this was a period when life was family centred. Not only was this the peak of the baby-boom, but it was also a period of the marriage "rush," as marriage occurred at young ages, and high proportions of persons married at least once in their lives. It was possibly a "golden age of the family," where many families corresponded to the ideal of domesticity, especially in the suburbs, and consequently there was less variability (Skolnick, 1996: 134–41).

Subsequent research has made it clear that not all was ideal in this golden age. Isolated housewives in particular experienced what has been called the "problem with no name." Since the task of maintaining the home had been assigned to

women, men became less competent at the social skills needed to nourish and maintain relationships (Goldscheider and Waite, 1991: 19). The idealism of the time also introduced blinders regarding some realities of family life, including violence and abuse. Given a general denial that such things could ever occur in families, there was little recourse for the victims of violence. There was also a lack of autonomy, especially for women, to pursue routes other than the accepted path. Childless couples were considered selfish; single persons were seen as deviants; working mothers were considered to be harming their children; and single women who became pregnant were required either to marry or to give up the child to preserve the integrity of the family. For instance, in the 1950s, four out of five Americans described persons who did not marry as neurotic, selfish, or immoral (Kersten and Kersten, 1991; Wilson, 1990: 99). In Canada, sentiment was strong to move women out of the labour force once their contribution to the war effort was complete. The following magazine quotation is an example of the subtle pressures put on women to return to a more traditional family form:

> What will they [women workers] demand of [postwar] society? Perhaps—and we can only hope—they'll be tired of it all [working outside the home] and yearn in the old womanly way for a home and a baby and a big brave man (*Maclean's*, 15 June 1942; as quoted in Boutilier, 1977: 23).

The restriction on alternative lifestyles did mean that there were few single-parent families, and consequently the pain associated with this kind of variability was limited. In hindsight, we can nonetheless observe that pent-up problems were preparing the way for the second transition, which started in the 1960s.

Theoretical Perspectives on Family Change

The phenomenon of family change has been addressed through two broadly competing explanations. We shall consider families both at the macro level, as a societal institution, and at the micro level, as the social arena in which people spend most of their lives. At the macro level, we shall consider changes in instrumental exchanges, and at the micro level, changes in expressive exchanges. The macro or structural perspective considers the relations of families to other parts of society, and tends to see a reduction in the role of families. The micro or cultural perspective looks within families, and observes in particular the greater importance of the expressive dimension. Both perspectives effectively argue that the family is weaker, either because it plays fewer roles in society, or because families easily fall short of satisfying high expectations for personal fulfillment.

Macro or structural explanations

Structural functionalism, defined in earlier chapters, maintains that changes in any one part of society affect other parts, and that each part of society serves some function for the whole. From this perspective, it has been argued that family and kin groups had a larger number of functions in pre-industrial societies (e.g. Goode, 1977). In those societies, besides being the chief units of reproduction and socialization of the young, families were also the units of economic production, and sometimes of political action and religious observance. Family groups performed many of the essential activities of the society: production, distribution, consumption, reproduction, socialization, recreation, and protection. For the most part, living space, workplace, and childrearing space were the same. Individuals depended on their families to cope with problems of age, sickness, and incapacity. In particular, the overlap between family and economy meant that economic activities occurred in family relationships. For the most part, only through membership in a family did people have a claim on membership in the broader society.

Industrialization and modernization (see Chapter 16, Social Change) brought *structural differentiation* and, increasingly, separate structures in society came to have specific functions. There was a substantial increase in the role of nonfamily institutions such as factories, schools, medical and public health organizations, police, and commercialized leisure. The family lost many of its roles in economic production, education, social security, and care of the aged.

Consequently, according to the functionalist view, long-term changes in the family are related to societal changes, especially changes in economic structures. Families have become less central to the organization of society. This reduced role allowed for more flexibility in family arrangements. For instance, the growth of wage labour for the young undermined parental authority and removed barriers to early marriage. More broadly, families have become weaker institutions, in the sense of having less cohesion, fewer functions, less power over other institutions, less influence on behaviour and opinion, and consequently less importance (Popenoe, 1988). This can be called *de-institutionalization* in the sense that there are fewer constraints on family behaviour. For instance, families have less control of the sexual behaviour of adolescents and are less involved in the socializing of children. Note that in some other areas of life there have emerged more constraints on behaviour, for instance, smoking in public places, throwing out garbage, or sexually abusive behaviour at work. That is, not all areas of life have seen diminished constraints on individual behaviour.

In terms of the more recent transformations, the functionalist explanation pays attention to the shift to a service economy, which increased the demand for women's involvement in paid work (Chafetz and Hagan, 1996). Until the 1960s, the division of labour encouraged a reciprocal state of dependency between the sexes. Economic and policy structures discouraged women from participation in the labour force, and thus the family was based on a breadwinner model, where wives were dependent on their husbands' incomes, and husbands were dependent on wives for the care of home and children. The expansion that occurred in the labour market, as of the 1960s, involved especially jobs that might be seen as extensions of women's unpaid work, particularly in clerical work, teaching, nursing, and other services. This put pressure on women to postpone marriage as they extended their period of education and invested in their work lives. For both young women and young men, marriage became less important as a means of structuring their relationships and understandings, and consequently cohabitation became an alternative. Women's greater self-sufficiency broke the dependency associated with the breadwinner model. Women became less dependent on marriage, making divorce and cohabitation more feasible alternatives for both sexes.

With respect to children and childbearing, trends can be related to the two broad transitions in the family cited earlier. In the first transition, 1870–1950, children lost their economic value to parents as economic activities depended less on work within the family, including the labour of children. That is, the economic role of children changed from that of producer to that of dependent. In addition, social security replaced the family as the basic welfare net in the face of economic hardships and incapacity. Thus the economic reasons for having children were seriously undermined. In the second transition, since 1960, children became a "cost" to employed women. However, these economic and structural explanations are not definitive. According to economic logic, there should be hardly any children, yet the most common family size involves two children.

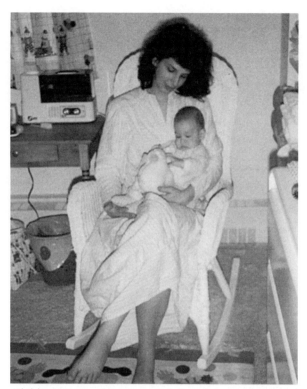

Childrearing restricts women's labour-force activities and disrupts their earning continuity.

Micro or cultural explanations

Other explanations of family change have looked *within* families, proposing that expressive activities have become increasingly important (e.g., Shorter, 1977). While in the past the family was held together because people needed each other for survival, family relations have become based on the need for emotional gratification. Families have become centres of nurture and affection; individuals seek emotional support from families as a retreat from the achievement-oriented struggles of the outside world. This places heavy demands on family relationships, which may not always fulfill people's expectations. People are more prone to abandon family ties when their emotional well-being is not satisfied.

It has been suggested that in nonindustrial societies individuals obtained much of their emotional gratification through an involvement with religion and community. To use Durkheim's terms, these societies were held together by *mechanical solidarity*, a sense of belonging and immediate identity with the surrounding community (see Chapter 16, Social Change). In the industrial world, societies are held together more by *organic solidarity*, by a division of labour whereby individuals are dependent on each other's specialized abilities. But such societies are also competitive and impersonal, providing individuals with less psychological support and security, and less of a sense of identity. In the transition from a nonindustrial to an industrial society, families became considerably more important as sources of emotional gratification, affective involvement, and a sense of personal identity for individuals.

Roussel (1989) suggested that the decades of the 1970s and 1980s involved a cultural change wherein people became less interested in living up to external norms and more interested in living up to what they themselves wanted. Marriage changed from an institution to a "projet de couple" where people can follow their own drummer. In many other areas of life, it is not possible to increase the freedom from external norms. For instance, workplaces and bureaucracies must set limits on the variability of individual behaviour. On questions like child abuse and environmental protection, we now accept a higher level of social restrictions on behaviour. However, in the areas of family behaviour, it has become possible to live with less social constraints. Legislative changes making divorces easier and equating cohabitation with marriage also signified a greater acceptability of alternate sexual and marital arrangements.

This is not to imply that family behaviour was, in the past, constrained by strict norms, while people are now free to do as they please. Cultural norms continue to operate; all societies will constrain individual behaviour in such crucial areas as sex, family, and procreation. The greater acceptability of individualism and self-fulfillment has relaxed, but not removed, the normative context of these behaviours.

Other persons who have written about the long-term changes in the family speak of a movement from institution to companionship (Burgess et al., 1963), while children were transformed from duty-bound workers to emotionally precious objects (Coltrane, 1998). These perspectives imply a loosening up of relationships and a greater priority to emotional gratification. To use Durkheim's terms, the family has changed from a unit of survival where relationships are based on a "division of labour," to a unit of "mechanical solidarity" based on a sense of common identity. Obviously, sentiment is a weaker basis for relationships than is instrumentality, and the need for continuous gratification puts heavy, and sometimes contradictory, demands on relationships. Spouses are expected to give each other the autonomy necessary to develop their potential, but at the same time to "be there for each other." Likewise, each is to develop his or her potential, yet remain the person that one once married.

Other authors have used similar frameworks. For Kettle (1980), the parents of the baby-boom were a "dutiful generation" committed to sacrificing themselves for groups beyond themselves, while their children are now a "me generation" with high expectations of success and personal gratification. This is sometimes called "affective individualism." Based on Giddens, Hall (1996) uses the concepts of "pure relationships" and "reproductive individualism," which refer to relationships that are based on personal choice rather than normative considerations, and reproduction that is oriented to self-fulfillment (see also Jones et al., 1995). Others have called this a collaborative model of marriage, based on few children, attributing high value to the quality of spousal relationships, and involving instability due both to the complexities of the collaborative endeavour and to the greater ability of partners to seek alternatives (Goldscheider and Waite, 1991; Oppenheimer, 1994).

In summary, the last century and a half has seen changes wherein many of the functions previously performed by families have been transferred to the larger society, and, at the individual level, there was a change from meeting instrumental needs to meeting expressive needs. Families became more important as a source of emotional gratification for individuals. While, in the past, families were held together partly because people needed each other for survival, today people still say that they need each other, but now it is for the emotional gratification that marriage and family can provide. As a result, families are quicker to break apart when individual members do not find a particular arrangement to be gratifying.

Anticipating Marriage and Mate Selection

Having examined variability and uniformity in family patterns, and family change, let us now look more closely at family questions over the life course. This section starts with an overview of the average life course, then considers questions of socialization for marriage, dating, premarital sex, home leaving, cohabitation, love, and mate selection.

Family behaviour over the life course

Using data from the 1995 General Social Survey, Table 10.2 summarizes the median ages at which various family life-course events have occurred for birth cohorts 1916–20 to 1971–75. The patterns are rather uniform. Over the birth cohorts 1916–20 to 1941–45, there was a general downward trend in the age at home leaving, first marriage, first birth, last birth, and home leaving of the children. Conversely, the subsequent cohorts have experienced an upward trend. In the cohorts of the 1920s to 1940s, the tendency was not only to marry early, but over a relatively narrow range of ages (Ravanera and Rajulton, 1996; Ravanera et al., 1998a, 1998b).

The proportion of first unions that involved cohabitation increased over the cohorts, to levels above 50 percent for those born after 1965. The separations within 25 years of marriage are also on a continuous upward trend, from 5 percent in the 1916–20 cohort to 36 percent in the 1951–55 cohort.

At the same time, over the period of mid-life, that is ages 30 to 54, the proportions of marriages that have ended have ranged between 18 and 20 percent over the cohorts born between 1911 to 1950 (Ravanera and Rajulton, 1996: 174). In addition, the most common events between these mid-life ages are the birth of a last child or a child leaving home. Consequently, there is much continuity. The change involves a higher proportion of separations among marriages that have ended, and divorces occurring

sooner in the life course, before children leave home. Ravanera and Rajulton concluded that the life course between ages 30 and 54 is characterized by stability rather than crisis.

There have also been changes in the extent to which some *typical* patterns have been followed (Ravanera et al., 1994). For instance, the pattern of leaving home, getting married, then having a first child reached a peak in the 1931–40 cohort at 65.6 percent of men and 65.8 percent of women. In the 1961–70 cohort, only 26.3 percent of men and 23.2 percent of women followed this pattern. These authors conclude that the younger cohorts have not yet established a path or sequence that can be called typical.

Important changes have therefore occurred in the typical marital life cycle from pre-modern to modern times. The years of childbearing have been reduced, and a new and often happy stage of the empty nest has emerged, between the marriage of the last child and the death of one of the spouses. The increased life expectancy and the decreased family size of today's societies also present a very different context for family life. In earlier times family life patterns were subject to sudden changes, since death so often interfered in the family life cycle. Orphanhood, once a common experience, is now rare. The increased rate of survival of parents means that the nuclear family can now be much more self-sufficient. Under high mortality conditions, it was very risky to depend on the nuclear family alone.

In the mid-nineteenth century, only 6 percent of couples would have celebrated their fiftieth wedding anniversary, compared with 39 percent under 1981 mortality conditions. Couples now live a longer life together, changing the meaning of "till death do us part." When romantic love was introduced into Western civilization as the basis for marriage, the promise to "love each other for life" had a vastly different time horizon. When young lovers make a similar promise today, they probably do not realize that it likely will be for almost fifty years. Even when divorces are entered into the calculation, the average duration of marriage is thirty years (Nault and Bélanger, 1996: 36, 42). An unhappy marriage is probably more likely to be broken when one has the prospect of a long life to

TABLE 10.2   Ages at Various Family Life Transitions, Birth Cohorts 1916–20 to 1971–75, Canada, 1995

	Birth Cohorts											
	1916–20	1921–25	1926–30	1391–35	1936–40	1941–45	1946–50	1951–55	1956–60	1961–65	1966–70	1971–75
Median Age at Home Leaving												
Men	22.9	22.0	21.9	21.2	21.8	22.0	21.8	21.5	21.8	22.7	23.2	23.6
Women	21.8	21.6	21.0	20.6	20.1	20.3	21.0	19.9	20.6	20.9	21.2	21.6
First Union												
Men	26.6	25.7	25.2	24.8	25.0	23.6	23.8	24.4	24.5	25.2	25.1	–
Women	23.4	22.9	22.0	21.9	21.7	21.4	22.0	21.5	21.8	22.7	22.7	22.9
First Marriage												
Men	26.6	25.7	25.2	25.0	25.1	23.6	24.0	25.6	26.4	28.7	–	–
Women	23.4	22.9	22.0	21.9	21.8	21.6	22.2	22.1	23.3	25.3	26.1	–
First Birth												
Men	29.6	28.8	28.6	27.3	27.7	26.5	27.5	29.3	29.9	31.2	–	–
Women	26.2	25.0	23.9	23.5	23.5	23.3	25.4	25.6	26.3	27.8	27.8	–
Last Birth												
Men	38.0	35.6	35.8	33.6	33.5	32.5	32.5	33.7	33.2	32.1	–	–
Women	35.6	34.5	33.7	31.8	30.1	29.8	30.6	30.3	31.0	30.6	–	–
First Child's Home-Leaving												
Men	49.4	47.5	48.1	47.0	48.4	47.9	49.3	–	–	–	–	–
Women	45.4	45.0	44.6	43.3	43.7	45.1	48.0	–	–	–	–	–
Last Child's Home-Leaving												
Men	57.6	56.8	59.2	57.1	57.2	–	–	–	–	–	–	–
Women	56.7	57.1	56.3	53.0	54.6	–	–	–	–	–	–	–
Mean Number of Births												
Men	2.9	3.1	2.6	2.9	2.5	1.9	1.9	1.5	1.5	–	–	–
Women	3.3	3.6	3.4	3.3	3.0	2.3	1.9	1.8	1.7	–	–	–
Cohabitations as Percentage of First Unions												
Men	1.9	3.2	1.8	4.4	6.3	9.3	16.1	30.3	39.3	49.9	67.1	–
Women	0.3	1.0	2.6	1.6	2.9	9.2	13.5	25.0	35.9	47.5	55.3	76.6
Proportions Separated within 25 years of First Marriage												
Men	0.03	0.05	0.09	0.09	0.17	0.24	0.27	0.39	–	–	–	–
Women	0.06	0.06	0.10	0.13	0.14	0.29	0.30	0.34	–	–	–	–

Source: Beaujot, 1999 (1995 General Social Survey). Reprinted by permission of Broadview Press.

Couples now live a longer life together: the average duration of marriages that do not end in divorce is close to fifty years.

"endure." Thus, the instability caused by death has been replaced by the personal instability of the marital relationship itself.

Socialization for marriage

To be properly socialized for any role, one needs the motivation to practise the appropriate behaviour, the ability to perform the requirements of the role, and the knowledge of what is expected. With regard to marriage, the overwhelming majority of people are *motivated* to be married or to live in an enduring relationship. In terms of practice and *abilities*, dating provides various relevant experiences. However, unmarried individuals may have difficulty learning about what is actually *expected* of marriage partners, insofar as other people's marriages are generally private. In addition, most people anticipating marriage are very confident, believing that their good intentions will be sufficient to ensure a successful union. As a consequence, they do not seek out information.

The problem of lack of knowledge is further complicated by the fact that, traditionally in our society, boys and girls tend to be socialized differently. Mostly through their peer groups, adolescent girls become adept at interpersonal communication and in the language and actions of romantic love. The male subculture, however, is more sexual and achievement-oriented. As Skolnick (1996: 216) further observes, the order of priorities is reversed between the sexes: "If boys like sex more than they like girls, little girls like boys much more than they like sex."

Boys and girls may have different stakes in entering courtship. The stakes may be higher for girls, since, at least around the late teens and early twenties, marriage may represent a more important life goal for them. For males, marriage becomes an important life goal at a later stage. In addition, boys and girls seek different things from courtship. One might say that boys seek physical intimacy while girls seek love and commitment. Courtship partly involves each gender training the other to be more responsive to what each wants and expects. Boys train girls to see sex as part of a relationship, while girls train boys to see love and commitment as part of a relationship.

Dating and premarital intercourse

Waller (1937) described dating on a U.S. campus during the Depression in a way that may sound slightly exaggerated, but which remains relevant today. He felt that dating was a more or less explicit (often conflict-filled) bargaining relationship, in which each person tried to get the best possible deal. Dating, like marriage, can thus be seen as involving exchanges. In a sense, people who are dating can bargain even harder than those who are married, since they are not formally committed to each other. For instance, if the dating partners are not equal in their desirability as dates, then the one with the higher "rating" has more power in the bargaining and can exploit the other party. Another feature of the dating process, according to Waller, is the "principle of least interest." This means that the less involved person has more power because he or she has less to lose if the relationship ends. The trick then is to remain uncommitted, but to pretend to be committed in order to get the partner committed.

Sex before marriage, as a specific aspect of dating, has also received considerable attention from sociologists of the family. Hobart (1993) studied attitudes and behaviour regarding premarital sex of students in ten postsecondary institutions in 1988. He inquired both about attitudes (what do you think is right for males and for females?) and about behaviour (what have you done?). Table 10.3 presents some of the results. It is useful to consider the extent to which these findings support "old moralities" or "new moralities" of sexual behaviour.

There are several **premarital sexual standards** by which people judge the acceptability of premarital sex. Among these, there are two old moralities: the **abstinence standard**, which forbids premarital sex, and the **double standard**, which grants men premarital sexual licence but expects premarital virginity of women. The data show that about 10 percent of the students favoured the abstinence standard. In addition, there is very little difference in the sexual activities that a given respondent considers appropriate for males and

females, indicating that the double standard is also not very prevalent.

The two new moralities of sexual behaviour receive somewhat greater approval among Hobart's respondents. The **love standard** regards sex as a physical expression of love and sees premarital sex as acceptable when love or strong affection is present. The **fun standard** views sex as primarily a giving and receiving of sexual pleasure; intercourse is acceptable as long as the partners are willing. The love standard receives the greatest support, since slightly more than half of students consider premarital intercourse to be acceptable if the partners are in love. About a third of students indicate that intercourse is acceptable even though the partners are not particularly affectionate. These respondents thus subscribe to the fun standard of sexual behaviour.

There are a few notable attitude differences between males and females in the study, with females more likely to support the love standard and males the fun standard. For instance, 42 percent of men compared with 23 percent of women subscribed to the fun standard. At the same time, little difference between males and females is in evidence when actual behaviour is concerned.

TABLE 10.3   Attitudes Toward Sexual Intercourse and Incidence of Various Sexual Experiences, By Sex of Responent, 1988, in Percentages

	Males %	Females %
Abstinence standard	10	9
Love standard	48	68
Fun standard	42	23
Has never petted	7	8
Has experienced intercourse	74	78
Engaged to all intercourse partners	1	2
In love with all intercourse partners	26	23
Number of Respondents	940	946

Source: Adapted from Charles F. Hobart (1993: 60, 62).

Hobart showed that, between the sexes, the percentage experiencing premarital intercourse per se has, over the years, roughly equalized. Other studies indicate that 25 percent of youth in Grade 9 have had sexual intercourse, and the figure reaches 50 percent somewhere between Grades 11 and 12 (Wadhera and Millar, 1997: 15). Based on the 1994-95 National Population Health Survey, 44 percent of persons aged 15 to 19 had at least one sex partner in the previous year (Galambos and Tilton-Weaver, 1998). Of those who were sexually active, about a third had two or more partners, and some 40 percent had used a condom only "seldom or sometimes."

The long-term increase in permissiveness can be related to general changes in gender roles (see Chapter 7, Gender Roles). Various historical examples have led sociologists to conclude that premarital sex codes are more permissive when women have greater equality and are subject to less occupational differentiation. As women become less dependent on marriage for their major source of status, it is less necessary for them to keep sex out of the dating relationship in order to exchange it for the marriage contract. Sex and marriage, then, have become less closely linked for both men and women. Reliable birth-control methods have greatly enhanced this separation, and it would appear that the fear of disease, including AIDS, has not encouraged a return to more conservative standards.

Home leaving

After having declined decade by decade, the average age at home leaving started to rise in the late 1970s, producing what some have called a "cluttered nest" (Ravanera et al., 1995; Boyd and Norris, 1998). In addition, some children have returned home after having left for a period of time, a pattern very rare in the past. For instance, at age 20 to 24, 50.4 percent of women and 64.3 percent of men were living with parent(s) in 1996, compared to 33.6 and 51.4 percent respectively in 1981 (Boyd and Norris, 1998).

There are clearly *economic* factors at stake, such as the difficulty of "Generation X" or the "Generation on Hold" to establish itself in the labour market (Côté and Allahar, 1994; see also Chapter 3, Socialization). Not only are younger generations

spending a longer period at school, but students also now have a greater likelihood of finding appropriate postsecondary education near home. Economic factors are also relevant to the observation that young people who are trying to get established through a first job are more likely to return home (Wister et al., 1997). Also, Lapierre-Adamcyk et al. (1995) found that economic factors play a larger role for men's than for women's home leaving.

However, there are also *cultural* factors that have probably made parental homes more suitable to older children as the generation gap has declined. Parents have developed more flexible and tolerant attitudes toward their adolescent children. For instance, in the United States in the 1960s, the typical first sexual experience occurred in a car, while, in the 1980s, it was more likely to occur in the parental home, admittedly when the parents were away. The importance of cultural factors can also be demonstrated by the observation that children are less likely to be living at home when the parents are more religious, re-married, or from certain ethnic groups (Wister et al., 1997; Boyd and Norris, 1995).

While there may be some problems of lack of independence, Boyd and Norris (1995) observed that later departure of children presents various advantages in terms of parental investment in children. In this context, it is significant that average age at home leaving is latest in intact families. As is also evident in the case of an absent parent, sharing across family members, and consequently investment in children, is more likely to occur within households than across households. If parents have separated, children are most likely to live with their mother, except if she has established a new relationship. In effect, children tend to prefer living with a father who is not in a relationship over a mother who is in a new relationship (Boyd and Norris, 1995).

Cohabitation

While some common-law unions have always existed in the case of persons who were not allowed to marry, the modern phenomenon of cohabitation started with university students, especially in Scandinavia and North America, in the 1960s. The behaviour then spread to professional classes in the 1970s and subsequently to much of the population.

Initially, cohabitation was often a short pre-honeymoon period. It then became a longer period that most often led to marriage but sometimes resulted in separation. It has become the normal form of entry into unions for persons who are single, but especially for the previously married.

In Canada, only 2 percent of persons born in 1934–38 began their life as a couple through cohabitation, compared to 53 percent of persons born 1959–63 (Lapierre-Adamcyk, 1989). At the 1996 census, 13.7 percent of all couples were cohabiting, compared to 6.4 percent in 1981 (Statistics Canada, *The Daily*, 14 October 1997: 3). For unions that were formed in 1970–74, 17 percent were cohabitations, compared to 57 percent of unions formed in 1990–95 (Turcotte and Bélanger, 1997: 8). At ages 30 to 39 in 1991, over a quarter of single persons and a third of divorced persons were cohabiting (Péron et al., 1999).

To a certain extent, less formal relationships are simply being substituted for marriage. Yet, in some respects, cohabitation is not a true replacement for formal marriages. By comparing various characteristics of cohabiting people with those who are single and those who are married, Rindfuss and VandenHeuvel (1990) found that the cohabiting were more similar to the single than to the married. Surveys show that people who are living together often do not consider themselves married, and that cohabitation can be viewed as an *alternative to being single* or as a *prelude to marriage*. However, there are increasing numbers who do consider cohabitation as an *alternative to marriage*, and by 1996, 47 percent of common-law unions involved children, sometimes from a previous relationship. Le Bourdais and Marcil-Gratton (1996) proposed that cohabitation may well be on the way to losing its marginal status

and acquiring more stability. That is, it could be becoming more like marriage, with a similar long-term commitment, only less legal. On the other hand, they suggested that it may also signal less commitment and a desire for more flexibility in relationships. In effect, attitudes on liberal and permissive orientations imply that common-law unions are more likely to be "pure relationships" that do not fit an institutional mode (Hall, 1996). In particular, they correspond to a liberal or choice model that accepts contractual obligations but not necessarily lifelong commitments (see the "Cohabitation" box).

Given the difference in the meaning of cohabitation, Dumas and Bélanger (1997: 150) have considered six types. The largest category, representing 36 percent of the total, are *stable unions* without commitment, defined as lasting three or more years but having no children. This category is more common for older persons. The second largest category, which has increased in importance and represents 18 percent of cohabitations, is called *unstable unions*, defined as lasting less than three years with no marriage and no children. The categories of *prelude to marriage* (11 percent) and *trial marriage* (16 percent) are persons who marry within a year or within three years respectively, but do not have children until marriage. Both of these categories have declined, so that the proportion of cohabitations that were converted to marriages within three years declined from 36 to 21 percent of the total. Finally, 15 percent are classified as *substitutes for marriage* in the sense that a child is born within three years and the couple remains unmarried for at least another six months following the birth. Based on these analyses, the authors

Cohabitation as an Insurance against Separation?

The lack of understanding associated with some common-law unions also probably underlies their greater likelihood of violence. The probability of assault is 19 percent for young common-law couples compared to 5 percent for young married couples (Bunge and Levett, 1998: 15). Some of this is attributed to difficulties that men can experience with insecure relationships, especially if they also have insecurity associated with unemployment and low income.

conclude that common-law union is no longer a trial period of living together, but increasingly a substitute for marriage.

Researchers such as Leridon and Villeneuve-Gokalp (1994) in fact see the generalization of cohabitation as the most radical change that has occurred to families in the past twenty years. Cohabitation is displacing marriage as a form of first union, and its duration is increasing. While cohabitation could be interpreted as simply an alternative form of entry into unions, it has also transformed premarital, marital, and postmarital relationships. It signals flexibility in unions, which also has significant consequences for children.

Homogamy in mate selection

In everyday conversations about mate selection, two contradictory principles often emerge: "opposites attract" and "like marries like." Clearly, most people do choose someone different from themselves in that they choose someone of the other sex. Beyond that, the idea that opposites attract receives little research support.

There is more support for **homogamy**, the idea that people marry others like themselves. Among marriages occurring in 1990, more than half in each of the following groups married others of the same religion: Jewish, Mennonite, Pentecostal, Jehovah's Witness, Catholic, Eastern Orthodox, and other Christian and non-Christian groups. Even those whose religion was "unknown or not stated" were more likely to marry someone who was in the same category (Statistics Canada, *Marriages*, 1995). Moreover, a study in the United States found that both the education of potential marriage partners and the social class of their parents remain important in mate selection, but that education has become more important in homogamy than social class (Kalmijn, 1991).

The general conclusion, then, is that most people are likely to marry someone who is pretty much like themselves in most social and economic characteristics, and who has similar things to exchange in the marriage bargain. This departs considerably from the romantic notion that love and marriage are individualistic and that everyone has an equal chance of falling in love with everyone else. Note also that this is an average tendency;

obviously, some marriages involve partners who are very different from each other.

The timing and propensity to marry

One example of dissimilarity between married partners—that is, of **heterogamy**—occurs with respect to age. On average, women marry at a younger age than men. In some societies, the age gap is quite large, with the ideal considered to be a five- to ten-year difference. In Canada, the difference in the median age at first marriage is two years, having declined from a difference of about three years in the 1960s, and four years in the early part of the century. Among the currently married population, the 1990 General Social Survey found that in 51 percent of cases the man is two or more years older, and in 38 percent of cases he is three or more years older (McDaniel, 1994: 21). In contrast, only 6 percent of women are two or more years older than their husbands. At the same time, 41 percent of couples are within two years in age.

Although at two years the gap is small, it has considerable sociological relevance. A younger person is likely to be less experienced at taking responsibility and leadership, and to have achieved less in economic or career terms. Taken together, these differences mean that for most couples a wife will tend to be of lesser status than her husband, a condition known as the **mating gradient**. In the average marriage, the husband will tend to earn more money, partly because he is older and more established. As a consequence, for the benefit of the total family income, his job may be given priority when some aspect of family life affects the spouses' jobs. In other words, the family is more likely to move for the sake of his job than for hers, and the wife is more likely than he to withdraw from the labour force for the sake of the children. If the wife's income is lower, which is usually the case, it often seems to make sense to proceed in this fashion. What this means, of course, is that the slight disadvantage with which the wife started, because she is younger, can become entrenched over the course of the marriage.

Until the beginning of the twentieth century, marriage patterns involved relatively late age at marriages and significant proportions who did not marry (Gee, 1986). Over the first six or seven decades of this century, except for a slight reversal in the 1930s, marriages were occurring earlier in people's lives, and higher proportions were getting married. Then suddenly these trends reversed. In 1972 the median age at first marriage was 21.2 for brides and 23.4 for grooms, but by 1996 it had risen to ages comparable to those at the turn of the century, at 26.3 for women and 28.3 for men. In 1965, 30.8 percent of first-time brides were under 20 years of age, compared to 4.7 percent in 1995. Within given cohorts, later marriage is also associated with higher socioeconomic status (Ravanera et al., 1998a; 1998b).

Not only is marriage occurring *later in life,* but it is also happening with less frequency. In the early 1970s, for example, over 90 percent of adults could be expected to marry at some point in their lives, compared to under 75 percent in the early 1990s (Nault and Bélanger, 1996). The changes in entry into first marriage are partly a function of more cohabitation. However, especially under age 35, the combined proportion married or cohabiting has declined appreciably between the 1981 and 1996 censuses (Beaujot, 1999). As achieved characteristics, particularly education and occupation, play an increasing role in the lives of women, the timing of the transition to marital relationships is delayed while stable work careers are being established. Women's greater economic independence also allows them to search longer for the right person (Oppenheimer, 1994). For both sexes, marriage has become less central to the transition to adulthood and to the set of roles that define adult status.

Goldscheider and Waite (1991) found that *employment* today predicts marriage especially for men, but also for women. Many people probably consider that two jobs are needed to marry. The time needed to establish these two jobs may well

Not Living in Union and Living Alone

In 1971, 15 percent of women at ages 25 to 34 were neither married nor cohabiting, compared to 30 percent in 1991. For men at these ages, the proportion who are not in union has increased from 21 to 39 percent. That is, even when cohabitation is included, living in relationships is down compared to levels experienced over the last fifty years (Beaujot, 1995: 40).

A larger proportion of people are now living alone. For the whole population aged 15 and over, 12 percent were living alone in 1996. By age group, the figures are 10 percent or lower until age 55, but they reach 48 percent at ages 85 and over (Statistics Canada, *The Daily,* 14 Oct. 1997). Between 1991 and 1996, living in union decreased for all age groups (Bélanger and Dumas, 1998). Among the reasons suggested for increased singlehood are the following: young people are postponing living together, common-law relationships are breaking up much more frequently than marriages, marriages of young people are breaking up earlier than those of previous generations, and the tendency to remarry after divorce or widowhood is declining.

Living alone is particularly predominant among older women, including 42 percent of those over 65. There is an increase in widows living alone, but that is a function of life expectancy, and not due to the disaffection with family living. In addition, elderly persons living alone are not necessarily isolated (Stone, 1988). Even elderly who have never married have family and friends with whom they are involved in exchanges (Strain, 1990). The evidence would indicate that, while co-residence of elderly persons with their children has declined, they remain in contact with their families.

At younger ages, while there is a delay in leaving home, significant numbers are in relationships. At ages 21 to 44 in France, between a quarter and a third of single persons indicated that they were in a stable love relationship (Leridon and Villeneuve-Gokalp, 1994: 51). In Canada, the high approval of premarital sex would also imply that young people are not excluded from relationships. For instance, at ages 18 to 34, 90 percent approve of premarital sex (Bibby, 1995: 69).

be an important part of the delay of marriage. Analyzing the propensity to marry among American cohorts marrying in the 1970s and 1980s, Sweeney (1997) also found that economic prospects are positively related to marriage for both men and women, suggesting, that men and women have come to resemble one another in terms of the relationship between economic prospects and marriage.

Using longitudinal data from the United States, Goldscheider and Waite (1991: 60-84) further analyzed important aspects of the transition to marriage and its differential dynamics for women and men. Men who have experienced the dissolution of their parents' marriage are more likely to marry, while women in this circumstance are less likely to marry. Similarly, the experience of *non-family living* as an adult increases the probability for men to marry but decreases the probability for women. It could be that men who have lived on their own are more attractive because they have become more adept at domestic work, while women who have lived on their own do not want to lose the associated independence.

Marital and Family Interactions

Having considered socialization for marriage, premarital interaction, mate selection, and marriage, we can now move into the study of some specific aspects of marital and family interactions, some of which were introduced in Chapter 9, Aging. We will consider marital structures, single-parent families, childbearing, and children.

Marital structures

Just as marital life cycles differ cross-culturally and over time, so too do **marital structures**. Scanzoni and Scanzoni (1988) identified four historical North American marital structures based on the positions

What Contributes to the Relative Marital Power of Spouses?

Relative power of spouses, although very difficult to measure, is an important aspect of marital interactions, especially from a conflict perspective. The relative power of spouses depends in part on their respective interpersonal abilities, but it is also structured, largely in favour of males, by broader social factors. For example, the power of a wife is lowest when she is at home with young children and highest when she is working. When she is not totally dependent on her husband, she has more bargaining leverage and thus more power in family decisions.

It is possible that the very definitions of love that are accepted in our culture promote the power difference between men and women. Rossi (1985) proposed that our definition has been feminized—it is taken to refer to expressive questions, emotional closeness, and verbal self-disclosure, including disclosure of one's weakness. The more instrumental side of love, that is, doing things together or helping one another, is less likely to be defined as love. As an example, in one study a husband was asked to show more love for his wife and decided to wash her car. While that was instrumental help, it was not accepted as a sign of love by the wife or by the researchers. Rossi therefore concluded that the accepted definition of love tends to exaggerate women's dependency on the relationship, while men's dependency is repressed. She proposed that a more androgynous kind of love, one that combines expression and practical help, would acknowledge that there is interdependence of men on women, as well as of women on men, in relationships.

and roles of spouses: *owner-property, head-complement, senior-partner/junior-partner,* and *equal partners.*

The **owner-property marriage** is mentioned mainly for historical reasons. In this structure the man, in effect, owns his wife, who is legally his property; the two are one, and the one is the husband. The expressive element in this type of marriage is rather unimportant. While this marriage structure is not very equitable, it does involve clear rights and duties on the part of spouses. (See the boxed insert, "What Contributes to the Relative Marital Power of Spouses?")

A **head-complement marriage** is one in which the wife is "the other half," expected to find meaning in life largely through her husband and family. In making decisions, the husband must take into account the wishes of the wife as complement. The husband has basic responsibility for earning the family income and the wife for the care of the home and family. The expressive side of marriage is important here, as spouses are expected to find pleasure in each other's company and to offer each other emotional support. While this type of marriage structure is decreasing, a significant number of marriages in Canada still fit this description. For instance, among married women aged between 25 and 44, some 16 percent had not been part of the labour force in the year and a half before the 1991 census, compared with under 4 percent of married men in the same age group. In 1976, 57 percent of husband-wife families with children under 16 involved only the father as earner, and another 2 percent had only the mother earning (Marshall, 1998: 10). By 1997 the number of families with the father as the only earner had declined to 26 percent, while those with the mother as the only earner had increased to 6 percent.

A **senior-partner/junior-partner marriage** is a variant of the above, with the wife having more independence than in the previous case because both husband and wife are employed. However, the husband contributes the larger share to the family income, and the wife has basic responsibility for the family and household. Since many women combine work and motherhood, they seek jobs that make it easier to have interruptions, to work part time, or to combine with household duties (Desai and Waite, 1991). Over the past three decades, this senior-partner/junior-partner arrangement has likely become the most common of the four marital categories. While 60 percent of husband-wife families in 1995 where one spouse was working found both spouses working in 1991 (Statistics Canada, *The Daily* 12 May 1998: 15), women largely remain the junior economic partners within the family. The average contribution of wives working full time amounted to 39.9 percent of family income in 1990 (Rashid, 1994: 16, 17). Substantially more wives than husbands work part time. In terms of the unpaid work of housework and childcare, when both are working full time, men contribute about 40 percent and women 60 percent of total hours (Beaujot, 1999).

Finally, the **equal partners marriage** involves spouses who are equally committed to their jobs and who share in household and family tasks equally. A small though growing minority of marriages fit this description. In fact, families where the wife earns more than the husband amounted to 25 percent of husband-wife couples in 1993, compared to 11 percent in 1967 (Crompton and Geran, 1995). In a third of these cases, the husband was unemployed or looking for work sometime during the year. Harrell (1995) also found that the greater the wife's contribution to total family income, the more likely it was for the husband to be involved with cooking and cleaning the house.

It is important to note as well that, although the equal partner arrangement occurs in only a minority of families, equality of partnership rights is enshrined in law. For example, in Ontario, the Family Law Reform Act says that "it is necessary to recognize the equal position of spouses as individuals within marriage and to recognize marriage as a form of partnership" (Ontario Family Law Act, 1990). The act goes on to indicate that, as a default condition, family assets are to be divided in equal shares upon the breakdown of a marriage. Generally speaking, these conditions also hold for persons who have cohabited for three years, or for those who are cohabiting and have a child.

The traditional marital structures pose various problems: women's dependence on men's employment brings insecurity to women and heavy pressures on men. Nonetheless, many models are likely to continue to coexist. Furstenberg (1995), for instance, observed that the symmetrical family, in which both partners contribute more or less equally to economic and domestic activities, is "more prevalent as an ideal type than an actual arrangement." Despite the fact that the dual-earner model has become the norm, most families could be described as "neo-traditional" because the major responsibility for paid and unpaid work remains divided along traditional gender lines.

Single-parent families

Just as marriages can take a number of alternative forms, so too can families. The largest increases in the 1980s have, in fact, involved nontraditional family forms, including common-law unions and single-parent families. Together, these two forms made up 26.3 percent of Canadian families in the 1996 census.

Families with only one parent made up 22.5 percent of all families with children in 1996. In 1971 most one-parent families were led by a widowed parent. In contrast, by 1991 the separated or divorced constituted 60 percent of the total, with another 18 percent involving a never-married parent (Lindsay, 1992: 17). The proportion of male-headed families among the lone-parent families has been stable, amounting to 16.9 percent in 1996. Over the course of life, the experience of single parenthood is in fact quite common, representing a lifetime probability of 34 percent for women and 23 percent for men (Péron et al., 1999: 124, 181). For those who have lived a lone parent episode, 92 percent have left this state within 20 years, with about a quarter of cases involving the departure of children and three-quarters the formation of new unions.

Compared with currently married women of the same age, female lone parents are more likely

Families with only one parent made up 13 percent of all families in 1991, and over 80 percent of those were led by a female parent.

What Are the Challenges and Rewards of Single-Parenting?

In 1991, 13 percent of families in Canada were single-parent families; among those, 82 percent consisted of a mother with children and 18 percent of a father with children. In 1994, the average income of two-parent families with children in Canada was $62 000, compared with $28 000 for female-led and $41 000 for male-led one-parent families. In the excerpt that follows, Cherlin notes the problems associated with the lower standard of living of single-parent families, as well as some of the non-economic rewards of single-parenting.

Saddled with sole or primary responsibility for supporting themselves and their children, single mothers frequently have too little time and too few resources to manage effectively. There are three common sources of strain. One is responsibility overload: single parents must make all the decisions and provide all the needs for their families, a responsibility that at times can be overwhelming. Another is task overload: many single parents simply have too much to do, with working, housekeeping, and parenting; consequently, there is no slack time to meet unexpected demands. A third is emotional overload: single parents are always on call to give emotional support to their children, whether or not their own emotional resources are temporarily depleted.

Moreover, divorced and separated women who are raising children often find that their economic position has deteriorated. Many of those who were not employed in the years preceding their separation have difficulty reentering the job market.

As a result of their limited earning power and of the low level of child support, single mothers and their children often experience a decline in their standard of living after a separation.

[Yet] to be sure, life in a single-parent family also has its rewards, foremost the relief from marital conflict. In addition, single parents may gain increased self-esteem from their ability to manage the de- mands of work life and family life by themselves. They may enjoy their independence and their close relationships to their children. Some writers argue that women are particularly likely to develop an increased sense of self-worth from the independence and greater control over their life they achieve after divorce. ...

Less is known about long-term adjustment to divorce. ... [But] the amount of contact between children and their noncustodial fathers is shockingly low. In the 1981 National Survey of Children [United States], half of the children from maritally disrupted homes who were living with their mothers had not seen their fathers in the last year. Just one-sixth of these children, who were then age 12 to 16, were seeing their fathers as often as once a week.

Source: Andrew J. Cherlin, 1992. Marriage, Divorce and Remarriage. Cambridge: Harvard University Press (pp. 73–75, 79–80). Copyright © 1981, 1992 by the President and Fellows of Harvard College. Reprinted by permission.

to have lived in common-law relationships, to have had their children earlier, and to have less education (Ravanera et al., 1995; Moore, 1987). In effect, they must raise children while facing a double disadvantage of lack of support from a spouse and fewer job skills. McQuillan (1992) found that between 1971 and 1986, as participation of married women in the labour force increased, the income gap between single-parent and two-parent families grew. (See the boxed insert "What Are the Challenges and Rewards of Single-Parenting?")

Thus, family structures affect men and women differently. In particular, men are more likely to be in relationships, while women are more likely to be living with children. Both of these factors present relative economic disadvantages for women.

Childbearing

Childbearing is a part of marital interaction that deserves special attention, especially given the considerable changes since World War II in the ease with which couples can control their reproduction. In fact, few aspects of family behaviour have changed so fundamentally as the extent and effectiveness of control over marital fertility.

Just as marriage can be regarded as involving ongoing instrumental and expressive exchanges, so too the advent of children can be analyzed through the consideration of what they bring to the marriage in terms of "values" and "costs." The value and cost of children are here considered broadly to include both economic (instrumental) and non-economic (expressive) components. At the economic level, children are very costly, since they are largely dependent on their parents and do not contribute to family income. Gauthier (1991) calculated the direct costs to age 18 of a first child, excluding childcare, at $165 000 for a higher income family and $68 000 for a lower income family (in 1996 dollars). The average costs for three children would be $250 000. This figure rises to $500 000 if one includes childcare and indirect costs associated with lower labour-force participation.

The non-economic costs and values of children are more difficult to determine. Children are costly in the sense that parents have less time and energy for themselves. Children are sometimes emotional and psychological burdens; parents worry about them and have to put up with various inconveniences, ranging from a messy place at the table to a dented car fender. On the positive side, children do offer certain advantages: people's status as adults can be more firmly established when they are parents; having children can provide a sense of achievement, of power and influence, of continuity beyond death; children provide immediate pleasure in the form of fun, excitement, and laughter in the home.

However, the value and cost of children do not cover the whole dynamics of childbearing. People are not completely free in the decision to have children (see Chapter 15, Demography and Urbanization). There are often also normative influences that encourage couples to have children. This influence can be stronger in some groups than in others. The fact that fertility in Quebec was higher than in the country as a whole until the 1960s can be partly explained by normative influences that stressed "familism" in traditional French Canadian communities. There was considerable normative

pressure on parents to have large families to preserve the French fact in Canada. This changed in the 1960s as community influence, through the Roman Catholic Church, became less intense and parents became more concerned with the cost of children. French Canadians are now more likely to have fewer children in order to take advantage of the new opportunities for social mobility that have opened up for them since the Quiet Revolution of the 1960s.

Although the level of fertility in Canada has gone down, most couples want to have children. According to the 1995 General Social Survey, some 12 percent of women born between 1927 and 1951 had no live births. While childlessness is probably increasing, only 15.6 percent of women aged 40 to 44 in 1990 had no children (Beaujot, 1995: 54).

Childrearing

Not only do most couples want to have children, they generally take the childrearing role seriously. But while parents want to do a good job, they are faced with the considerable difficulties inherent in the role itself, at least as it is defined in our society (LeMasters and DeFrain, 1989). For instance, the parenthood role offers no margin of error; parents are expected to succeed with every child. In addition, parents cannot easily quit. They can escape from an unhappy marriage, but not from parenthood. In other words, they are supposed to keep trying, even if they know they are failing. Another problem is that parenthood involves being totally responsible for other human beings, yet not having full authority since other agencies also have an influence on what happens to the children. Finally, although there are high standards for the performance of the parenthood role, there is no one established model to follow and little training available. That is, raising children remains the preserve of the amateur.

Perhaps as a result of these difficulties, couples with young children at home are more likely to be dissatisfied with their marriages than are childless couples or those whose children have left home. Eichler (1988: 181) argued that the strain involved in raising children may have increased recently because children are dependent longer, while at the same time there are fewer adults per household, along with fewer children who can keep each other busy. Yet, while marital satisfaction is lower when there are children at home, marital stability is higher. That is, couples with young children are less likely to separate, and marriages with no children are the most prone to divorce (Waite and Lillard, 1991).

Given the difficulties of childrearing, it is predictable that many parents feel frustrated when things do not go well, and that some parents transfer this frustration on to the children in the form of child abuse. The variables now being uncovered that seem to be related to child abuse include parental immaturity, unrealistic expectations, lack of parental knowledge, social isolation, unmet emotional needs, and the parents' own abuse as children. A precipitating crisis then sets the abuse in motion. Moreover, there is in effect a general propensity to abuse, in the sense that adults have much power over children, including the legitimate use of physical strength to impose their authority. Since, as we have proposed, most parents also have high expectations for their children, abuse can occur when these expectations are somehow frustrated, especially if violence is seen as an acceptable form of family interaction.

Family change and children

Given the delay in marriage and childbearing, the family units into which children are born have changed. In the early 1960s, 25 percent of births were *first births*, compared with 44 percent in the early 1980s (Marcil-Gratton, 1988). Consequently, greater proportions of children have "inexperienced" parents. With fewer brothers and sisters, they also have *fewer older siblings*. For instance, half of the generation born in the early 1960s had two older brothers or sisters, compared with one-fifth of those born twenty years later. One in five had a brother or sister ten or more years older, compared with one in twenty for the later generation. That is, fewer births, and their concentration over a shorter time in the lives of adults, implies more potential parental resources per child, but it also means that children have less opportunity to interact with and learn from siblings.

The family lives of children have also been affected by the changing propensities for cohabitation and separation. In the early 1960s, 95 percent of children were born in marriages, compared with 64 percent in the mid-1990s (see Table 10.1). What has changed is not the births to single mothers, but *births to cohabiting couples*.

Among children born in the early 1960s, 8 percent were either born to a *lone parent* or experienced the separation of their parents by age 6, compared with 22 percent for those born in the mid-1980s (Table 10.4). By age 16, more than a quarter (27 percent) of the 1971–73 birth cohort had experienced similar conditions. The experience of lone parenthood is occurring earlier and earlier in the lives of children and now applies to more than a fifth of children by age 6 (Marcil-Gratton, 1998).

Of children who were born in a two-parent family, 20.5 percent experienced lone parenthood by age 10, and 60 percent of these had also experienced a *step family* as a second major family change, all by age 10. Marcil-Gratton concluded that children are born into increasingly diversified families, even over the birth cohorts 1983–84 to 1993–94 who are being followed by the National Longitudinal Survey of Children and Youth.

There are also very strong differences in the experience of lone parenthood depending on whether or not the parents had ever cohabited. For instance, by age 6 in the 1987–88 cohort, among children born to two-parent families, 8 percent had experienced their parents separation if the respondent had never cohabited, but 25 percent if they had cohabited (Table 10.4). The proportion experiencing the separation of parents by age 6 reaches 43 percent if the parents cohabited and never married (Marcil-Gratton, 1998: 18). Consequently, the family life of children born to parents having ever cohabited involves more change and it is particularly unstable (Marcil-Gratton, 1998).

Many children therefore live through a *diversity of family trajectories*. Cohabitation, births outside of marriage, increased divorce, and family reconstitution either through cohabitation or marriage, all these trends represent reduced family stability for children. While family reconstitution often provides children with multiple parents, it does not lessen the instability. For instance, stepfathers can be rather important to the lives of children, and men invest more in non-biological children who are present than in biological children who are absent (Marsiglio, 1998). However, the

TABLE 10.4 Cumulative Percentage of Canadian Children Experiencing Family Disruption, by Cohort

	Age		
	6	16	20
Proportion born to a lone parent or experiencing separation of parents			
1961–63 birth cohort	7.8	19.8	24.2
1971–73 birth cohort	13.0	27.3	–
1981–83 birth cohort	18.1	–	–
1987–88 birth cohort	22.6	–	–
Of children born to two-parent family, proportion experiencing separation of parent			
Parent never cohabitated			
1971–73 cohort	6.0	19.5	–
1981–83 cohort	8.0	–	–
1987–88 cohort	8.1	–	–
Parent ever cohabitated			
1971–73 cohort	18.0	53.2	–
1981–83 cohort	23.1	–	–
1987–88 cohort	24.6	–	–

Source: Beaujot (1999). Reprinted with permission of Broadview Press.

father is replaced by a man who has no common genealogy and no common durable status. Stepfathers largely remove themselves from the lives of step-children if they are no longer living with the child's mother (Kaplan et al., 1998). Goldscheider and Waite (1991) observed that many bad marriages also result in poor parenting, and consequently divorce can be a benefit to children. However, they also note that many other parents with marital problems can parent effectively. Overall, however, it would appear that children are less likely than parents to benefit from divorce and remarriage.

There are clearly strong variations in the economic well-being of children by family type, with markedly lower income for single-parent families, especially in comparison with two-income families (Rashid, 1998: 15). Consequently, the divergence of family types is accentuating the economic inequality across children. This is illustrated by comparing children in the top and bottom income quintiles (Figure 10.1). For children under 18 who are in the top quintile, 93.9 percent are in families with married parents, 4.8 percent are with cohabiting parents, and 1.3 percent with a lone

parent. In contrast, children in the bottom quintile include 44.1 percent with married parents, 7.8 percent with cohabiting parents and 48.1 percent with a lone parent. Other data confirm that increasing proportions of poor children are from lone parent families. For instance, those living with one parent comprised 21 percent of poor children in 1971 but 50 percent in 1996 (Beaujot, 1999).

In summary, some of the family changes have benefitted children. Smaller family sizes, later ages at parenthood, and greater proportions of two-income families mean that parents are more likely to have the necessary resources to care for children. However, the other change of greater propensity of parents to separate has largely had a negative consequence. Coleman (1988) analyzed the situation of children in terms of financial, human, and social capital. Children in lone-parent families are more likely to have relative deficiencies on all three levels. The financial capital is easiest to document, as indicated above. The reduced human capital involves fewer adults and consequently less total available education and experience from parents. Social capital refers to relationships to other family

FIGURE 10.1   **Distribution of Children Under Age 18 Whose Families are in the 1st and 5th Income Quintiles, by Family Environment,[1] 1990**

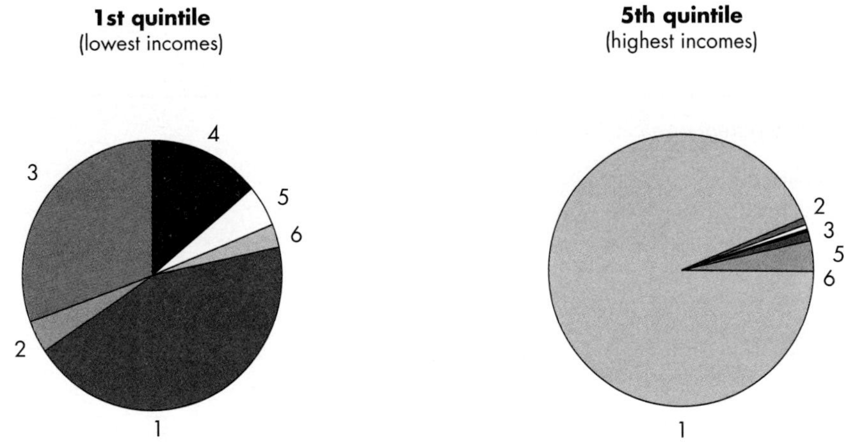

1st quintile
(lowest incomes)

5th quintile
(highest incomes)

	1st quintile (lowest incomes)		**5th quintile** (highest incomes)	
1. Married couples	44.1%	(8.1%)	93.9%	(18.2%)
2. Lone fathers	4.1%	(0.8%)	0.7%	(0.1%)
3. Lone mothers, separated, divorced or widowed)	30.0%	(5.5%)	0.6%	(0.1%)
4. Never-married lone mothers	14.0%	(2.6%)	–	(0.0%)
5. Common-law couples, both spouses never married	5.0%	(0.9%)	1.1%	(0.2%)
6. Common-law couples, at least one spouse ever-married	2.8%	(0.5%)	3.7%	(0.7%)

– nil or zero
[1]In brackets is the percentage each group represents of all children under age 18.

Source: *Péron et al. (1999); Statistics Canada,* Report on the Demographic Situation in Canada, 1997, *Catalogue No. 91-209.*

members beyond the household and to other members of the community. Here again, one parent is likely to provide fewer of such relationships for children.

Marital Breakdown

Having considered selected aspects of marital interaction, we turn our attention in this section to marital breakdown. We have proposed that a marriage involves ongoing instrumental and expressive exchanges and that it involves a form of commitment. How can we use this recognition of exchange and commitment to help us understand divorce trends?

The most observable ways in which families have changed are in terms of entry into unions and exit from marriages, both of which imply greater flexibility in relationships. Having analyzed cohabitation, there remains a higher to exit rate through separation rather than widowhood.

Separation and divorce have certainly increased since the 1960s, but it is also important to appreciate that the most common situation is for people to be married only once. For instance, at ages 30 to 54 in 1990, some 10 percent are never married, another 10 percent are formerly married, 67 percent are married or cohabiting with no previous marriage, and 12 percent are married or cohabiting after a previous marriage (Beaujot, 1995: 42). In terms of family units, the 1995 General Social Survey found

FIGURE 10.2   **Cumulative Proportions of Separations by Length of Union, per 1000 Unions of Each Type, Canada, 1995**

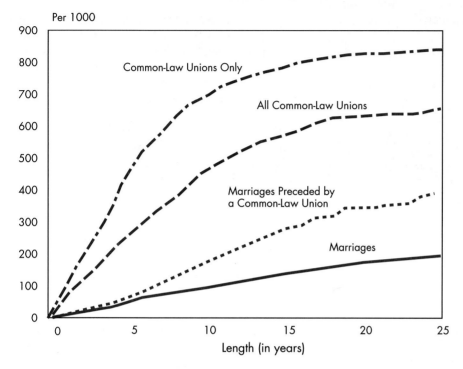

Source: Bélanger and Dumas (1998: 41); Statistics Canada, General Social Survey, Catalogue No. 11-612.

that 70 percent of families with children include both biological parents, while 22 percent involve only one parent and 8 percent are step-families with one biological parent and a step-parent (Statistics Canada, 1997, *Scan*).

Nonetheless, it is estimated that at least one-third of marriages taking place in the last two decades will end in divorce within 25 years (Péron et al., 1999). This estimate is taken from the observation that among persons who married in 1968–69, 29.3 percent had divorced within 25 years (Dumas and Bélanger, 1996: 35).

Given the prevalence of cohabitation, along with its longer duration, sometimes as a substitute for marriage, it is useful to look at the separation of unions of various types (Figure 10.2). The separations in effect vary considerably according to the type of union. After 25 years, 20 percent of marriages not preceded by cohabitation have separated. This compares to 40 percent of unions

that involved a marriage preceded by cohabitation, almost 65 percent of unions that started as cohabitations, and close to 85 percent of cohabitations that did not involve marriages. Even after five years, there are significant differences, with half of unions having dissolved if they involved cohabitations that were not converted into a marriage, compared to only 5 percent dissolution for unions that started as a marriage not preceded by cohabitation.

In their analysis of the *transition to divorce*, Goldscheider and Waite (1991: 104–106) found that the risk of divorce in the U.S. is greater when one's parents have separated, or when parents have higher education. However, higher education for husbands reduces this risk, as does higher husband's earnings. Canadian data show similar patterns (Balakrishnan et al., 1993). Higher men's incomes reduce divorce. Women with higher incomes have higher divorce prospects. Divorce propensities are particularly high for those who married at a young age and who had premarital births. Furthermore, those marrying young are more likely to be downwardly mobile, especially if the wife is pregnant at the time of marriage, because this detracts from the possibility of pursuing further education. Divorce is also higher for couples raising stepchildren, for those who have a larger age difference at marriage, and for persons whose parents had separated (Hall and Zhao, 1995). Divorce levels are also higher at lower levels of socioeconomic status. A lower income means that the instrumental exchanges in the marriage are less rewarding, making the prospect of divorce less negative for working-class individuals.

In analyzing "what holds marriage together," Trost (1986) proposed that most of the bonds have declined. The legal bonds have been redefined to permit divorce by mutual consent. Two-income families mean less economic interdependence. Fewer children means weaker bonds through parenthood. At the expressive and sexual levels, expectations are higher and consequently there is a higher likelihood that people's expectations are not met.

Decrease in instrumental functions

It should be quite evident by now that there has been a decrease in the instrumental functions fulfilled by families. Thus, families have less to hold them together. This is particularly true in the economic domain, where families now involve considerably less economic interdependence. For the wife, it is much easier to get out of an unhappy marriage if she is employed and in a senior-partner/junior-partner marriage than if she is in a head-complement marriage. Moreover, if she receives less of her status from marriage, the prospect of moving out is less negative. Stated differently, the greater independence of women makes the divorce alternative more viable.

Considering instrumental functions helps us to understand several other things about the incidence of divorce. Divorces are less likely to occur when there are young, dependent children because the family is more economically interdependent at that time. Indeed, both childless couples and those in the empty nest stage have higher risks of divorce (Rowe, 1989).

Importance of the expressive dimension

We have argued that marriage now is seen much more as an arrangement for the mutual gratification of participants. Spouses now expect more from families in terms of intimacy and interpersonal affect. In addition, individual well-being and self-fulfillment are seen as important values. Families are expected to serve individual needs, rather than individuals serving family needs. Therefore, divorce may be more prevalent today because it represents a natural solution to marriages that do not serve the mutual gratification of the persons involved. For instance, 88 to 95 percent of respondents to the 1995 General Social Survey consider that divorce is justified if there is "lack of love and respect from the partner," "unfaithful behaviour," or "abusive behaviour" (Frederick and Hamel, 1998: 8). Still, Ambert and Baker (1988) found that significant

Love has become more important as the focus of marriage in the twentieth century, while economic considerations have lessened.

numbers of people were regretting their decision to divorce. In a third of separations, the partners had no serious grounds for divorce. Some divorces happen because of circumstances that have little to do with marriage, such as problems at work, mid-life crises, or continuing emotional problems. Other divorces are due to "taking a risk" with an affair that ultimately does not lead to a permanent relationship.

One of the most consistent findings in divorce research is that the probabilities of divorce are higher for those getting married at an early age. For women aged 35 to 49, the probability of marital dissolution among those who married at 19 years of age or younger was almost twice as large (26 versus 14 percent) as that for those who married at the age of 25 or older (Balakrishnan and Grindstaff, 1988). The same applies to the risk of dissolution of common-law unions, which are higher for those entering unions at young ages or if there was a conception before the union (Turcotte and Bélanger, 1998: 19–20). There are several reasons for the higher divorce levels among those marrying young; some were discussed in the previous section. The lower income associated with youth means that the instrumental exchanges may be less rewarding. Regarding the expressive dimension, one can hypothesize that, as these young married persons mature, they find their spouses have been poor choices and they do not receive the expected gratification. It may even be that, for persons marrying at younger ages, emotional gratification is particularly important. Early marriage may have been a way of escaping an unrewarding situation in their original families. If the expressive dimension is especially important to them, they will be more likely to separate if this dimension is not working.

The higher incidence of divorce for second marriages can be seen in this light as well. The lowest dissolution rate is for marriages involving two previously single people, while those involving a divorced woman and a single man or two divorced persons have the highest failure rates (Dumas, 1990: 28). Persons who have already divorced are more likely to see marriage in terms of mutual gratification and to leave a marriage that is not rewarding.

It is clear that the rejection of one marriage is not to be confused with the rejection of marriage per se. Persons getting divorced are generally not doing so because they do not want to be married; instead, they do so because they find the exchanges with a particular partner to be unrewarding.

Redefinition of the marital commitment

Obviously, divorce would be less common if everyone frowned on it and if the legal restrictions were formidable. But there has been a significant change in the attitudes towards divorce in Western societies. The social stigma attached to marital dissolution has lessened considerably and people now accept that divorce occurs frequently among the "normal" population. There has also been considerable change in the definition of acceptable grounds for dissolving marital commitments. Until 1968, adultery was the only grounds for divorce in Canada. The 1968 Divorce Act extended the grounds for divorce to include both fault-related grounds and marriage-breakdown grounds. Fault-related grounds include adultery and other sexual offenses, prolonged alcohol or drug addiction, and physical and mental cruelty. To obtain a divorce on these grounds, there must be an injured party who brings the other spouse to trial, which then finds him or her guilty. As of 1986, divorce under marriage-breakdown grounds can occur after spouses have lived apart for one year, for whatever reason.

Table 10.1 indicates quite clearly the jump in divorce levels with the advent of the 1968 Act. Part of this jump includes the backlog of separations that occurred before 1968. Even taking this into account, there still has been a great increase in divorce since 1968. Life-table techniques that extrapolate on the basis of the data from a given year suggest that there has been a stabilization of divorces between 1986 and 1991 at slightly more than 30 percent of marriages (Nault and Bélanger 1996: 18). The comparison of divorces by duration of marriage also suggests that there may be the beginnings of a decline in the propensity to divorce (Bélanger and Dumas, 1998: 35). In part, this may be because marriages are becoming more selective, with more cohabitation and less marriage. Compared to other countries, Canadian divorce rates are higher than in Japan, France, or Germany, roughly the same as those of Sweden and the United Kingdom, and considerably lower than in the United States.

The Family in Crisis?

We often hear reference to the family being in a state of crisis. In a book entitled *The Canadian Family in Crisis*, John F. Conway stated his reasons for believing this is so.

Conway viewed the family as undergoing a major transition, from the traditional patriarchal family (dominant since industrialization) to an egalitarian family, and argued that, while this transition is underway, the family is in a state of serious crisis. This crisis partly involves the family's ability to do what it is supposed to do: support children, women, and men.

Recent social, economic, and technological changes have brought about this crisis. In particular, there are various contradictions between the move towards gender equality and the assumptions of the traditional patriarchal family based on complementary husband and wife roles.

According to Conway, without adequate childcare we see many of the consequences of this crisis in the lives of children who are subject to the insecurity of family breakdown and absent fathers. We see the vulnerability of children in the numbers who are abused, living in poverty, or even committing suicide. In effect, the family is not providing the support that children need.

Other consequences of the crisis are felt by women who are caught in various contradictions. In particular, they are expected to be involved in the labour force, yet the work world is not ready to accept them on an equal footing with men. At home, some are abused and more are fatigued as they perform a double duty, because husbands are not taking on an equal share of housework and childcare. Many women decide to move out of a marriage in order to resolve some of the conflict, but that brings the additional problems of single parenthood, especially poverty.

Conway proposed that men are also subject to some of the consequences of the crisis in the family. He said that they have a sense of unease, that is, they are not sure what is expected of them. They too are suffering from the contradictions between the traditional and the egalitarian assumptions. In some ways, they are also subject to a double burden in terms of work and family life, expected to give a hundred percent to career achievements yet also expected to do more at home. In addition, many men are separated from their children and miss the basic human interactions with children that they consider to be an important part of family life.

While Conway saw that the family is in crisis, he was optimistic because he argued that the void created by the death of the traditional family, which arose during industrialization, will be filled by an egalitarian family. While the whole book is about family difficulties, he ends with the concept of a "joyous funeral" for the family's previous form. At the same time, much social change would be needed to bring about this egalitarian family. In particular, for women there is the need for equality in the work world, that is, pay equity and employment equity. For children, there is the need for support mechanisms, in particular daycare, while parents are at work. For both mothers and fathers, there is the need for various changes, such as parental leave and flexible worktime, to enable a better accommodation between roles inside and outside the family.

What do you think about Conway's interpretation and propositions? Is it true that the family is in a state of crisis? Will an egalitarian family resolve the conflicts between the world of work and the private world? Will an egalitarian family be more stable?

Source: Adapted from R. Beaujot, 1995. "Review of John F. Conway, *The Canadian Family in Crisis*," Journal of Comparative Family Studies 26: 284–86.

Anticipating Future Change and Continuity

There has been considerable change in family patterns over the last few decades. The family continues to thrive as an important social institution, although in a variety of forms. Families may not play the same roles, or as many roles as in the past, and they are not as permanent, but they remain crucial to the lives of most people.

There is a greater amount of flexibility and diversity in what is defined as acceptable with regard to marriage and family living. This fluidity has especially been observed in terms of entry into relationships through cohabitation, and the greater frequency of exits through separation and divorce. Other elements of flexibility in family living include the greater acceptability of single parenthood, childlessness, reconstituted and blended families, and gay marriages. The following reflection of a minister after performing a gay marriage indicates this openness to alternate forms of intimacy:

Gay people have the same desire for happiness and ought to have the same right to happiness in our society as heterosexuals. And one of those rights is the chance (with the same lack of guarantees of success or permanence we all struggle with) to create a marital relationship of depth and love (Strong et al., 1983: 340).

With all these changes, some have suggested that "the family" is in crisis (see the boxed insert "The Family in Crisis?"). While some may regret the erosion of traditional family values, others see these changes as liberating. For instance, divorce is often a solution to a poor marriage; and later marriage and lower fertility are liberating, for women in particular (Beaujot, 1990).

For the majority of people, there also remains considerable continuity in family patterns. There is no evidence that marriage, or at least the desirability of durable relationships, is going out of style. The level of divorce has gone up significantly, but it is best viewed as a form of family reorganization. Although the proportion of adults living alone has increased, this mostly applies to persons who are not yet in a relationship, or older people who have been married.

Although separation and divorce are a much more common family experience, estimates imply that close to seven out of ten will experience a lifelong relationship. Childbearing has also gone down, but there is little rejection of parenthood per se.

Perhaps the largest change relates to the liberation of gender roles. While, on average, husbands continue to earn more of the family income, there has been considerable move to more equality in terms of labour-force participation, some equalization in the propensity to work full time, and in a quarter of couples the wife earns more than the husband. Perhaps the greatest difficulty is the resistance to a more equal sharing of the unpaid family work. Nonetheless, there are also examples of change in this caring dimension, in terms of both attitudes and behaviour (Beaujot, 1999).

The study of examples that depart from the typical patterns helps us to understand that there are possibilities for change in these gendered processes associated with caring activities. Coltrane (1996) predicted an increase in future sharing because sharing is more likely to occur in the following conditions: wives who are employed more hours and more attached to their jobs, women earning more of the total household income and especially co-providers, wives negotiating for change and relinquishing control over managing the home and children, more ideological support for gender equality, husbands employed fewer hours, fathers who are involved in the care of infants, and smaller family sizes. In addition, women who delay parenting and who are remarried are more likely to be able to negotiate a more equitable arrangement.

This unlinking of gender and caring may well be crucial to changing gender relations in the broader society, to the reproduction of the population, and to family well-being. In particular, this is the evolution that would bring "new families" based on companionate marriages where spouses are co-providers and co-parents, and where the default condition would be the sharing of responsibility for children in the case of separations. Just as the largest change in the past thirty years has involved women's earning activities, perhaps the next thirty years will see changes in men's caring activities.

Summary

A family is two or more people related by blood, marriage, or adoption, and who reside together. Marriage involves a commitment and ongoing expressive and instrumental exchanges between partners. A look at various cultures shows uniformity in family patterns in some aspects, such as the incest taboo, but variability in others, such as monogamy and polygyny. Thus, there is much variety and complexity to family behaviour, and it is necessary to view family questions against the background of the larger society. This variety is also visible when we look historically at family change. For example, the Industrial Revolution introduced a greater separation between the economic sphere of "public" activity and the "private" family sphere.

In the theory section, we attempted to understand some of the historical changes in families through both macro and micro considerations. The macro perspective has highlighted the structural differentiation through which families no longer perform some of the functions that they previously provided for the larger society. On the other hand, a look inside families at the micro level shows that families now play a more important role in the emotional gratification of their individual members.

In the section on anticipating marriage and mate selection, we first noted that socialization provides little systematic knowledge regarding expectations from marriage. Also, boys tend to be socialized towards the sexual, and girls towards the emotional, aspect of heterosexual relationships. Dating was described as an exchange or bargaining situation in which the person with the most to offer has the most power. Within this dating "environment," moreover, there are several normative standards in existence. As we saw, the abstinence standard has decreased, while the love standard, or permissiveness with affection, is the most representative of postsecondary-school students. We saw as well how love plays an important role in mate selection in our society, partly because everyone expects to fall in love. This is certainly not the only factor operating; homogamy is also important, with similar people getting married to each other more often than those who are different in social, economic, and physical characteristics. In addition, the woman in a marriage is often younger than the man. This age gap tends to entrench traditional gender-role differences.

In terms of marital interactions, the empty-nest stage is an important and relatively new stage in the life course. Another new stage is a premarital one involving young people living together before marriage. Considering the structure of marriage, it was suggested that an important proportion of Canadian marriages are of the head-complement type, in which the husband has basic responsibility for earning the family income and the wife for care of the home and family. The largest category is the senior-partner/junior-partner type, in which the wife contributes to the family income and the husband helps with home and childcare. However, there is growth in the equal-partner or role-sharing egalitarian model.

Regarding childbearing, it was shown that children are expensive and that people are having fewer of them. There has been a weakening of the norm that childbearing is an essential part of marriage. Nonetheless, most couples have children and want to perform well in the difficult job of childrearing.

The rising level of marital breakdown was related to the decrease in instrumental functions played by the family, the increase in the importance of the expressive dimension in marriage, and the changing definition of the commitment.

Finally, while there is a larger variety of family forms today, including especially common-law unions and single-parent families, there is also much continuity in the family patterns, with high priority for living in enduring relationships and having children. Just as the biggest change in the past thirty years has been associated with women's earning activities, there is some basis to anticipate that the future will show important changes in men's caring activities.

QUESTIONS FOR REVIEW AND CRITICAL THINKING

1. There are a number of alternatives to the traditional husband/wife/two-children family, e.g., homosexual union, reconstituted family, patrilocality, and polygyny. Choose several alternatives and describe the strengths and weaknesses of each with respect to both instrumental and expressive functions.

2. Talk to your friends and try to determine how much expectations about mate selection and marriage vary by gender.

3. Are children better off in modern families than in the past? Which would you rather live in?

4. How likely is it that in the future men and women will equally share caring activities in families?

KEY TERMS

abstinence standard, p. 268

double standard, p. 268

equal partners marriage, p. 274

expressive exchanges, p. 254

family, p. 255

fun standard, p. 268

head-complement marriage, p. 274

heterogamy, p. 271

homogamy, p. 271

instrumental exchanges, p. 255

love standard, p. 268

marital structures, p. 273

marriage, p. 255

mating gradient, p. 271

owner-property marriage, p. 274

premarital sexual standards, p. 268

senior-partner/junior-partner marriage, p. 274

Note: Other important terms are defined in Chart 10.1, p. 256.

SUGGESTED READINGS

Ambert, Anne-Marie
1992 *The Effect of Children on Parents.* New York: Harworth.
While most studies consider how parents affect children, Ambert considers the two-way relationships between parents and children, as well as the relevance of the broader social context. Children clearly have considerable effects on parents, and these are often not properly recognized.

Beaujot, Roderic
1999 *Earning and Caring in Canadian Families.* Peterborough: Broadview.
This focus on the earning and caring activities of families provides a synthesis of research on family change, with an anticipation that more couples will adopt family models of co-providing and co-parenting.

Coltrane, Scott
1998 *Gender and Families.* Thousand Oaks, CA: Pine Forge Press.
Taking a social constructionist approach, and with much richness of historical detail, the author considers that family and gender are forged together.

Conway, John F.
1997 *The Canadian Family in Crisis.* Toronto: James Lorimer.
This book considers how family change is having an impact on the lives of children, women, and men. Relevant public-policy considerations are offered for improving people's lives in a variety of family forms.

Goldscheider, Frances K. and Linda J. Waite

1991   *New Families, No Families?* Berkeley, CA: University of California Press.

The authors consider that, unless families evolve toward new models of more egalitarian relations, many people will abandon families. This thesis provides a background on which to consider the determinants and consequences of family behaviour.

Péron, Yves, Hélène Desrosiers, Heather Juby, Evelyne Lapierre- Adamcyk, Céline Le Bourdais, Nicole Marcil-Gratton, and Jael Mongeau

1999   *Canadian Families at the Approach of the Year 2000.* Ottawa: Statistics Canada cat. no. 96-321, no. 4.

This census monograph considers family change and the changing family relations of women, men and children, on the basis of an abundance of data and analysis.

WEB SITES

http://www.yahoo.com/Society_and_Culture/Families

Yahoo! Society and Culture: Families

The perfect resource for anyone doing research on family issues, this site provides links to dozens of sites worldwide dealing with a range of topics, from fatherhood to dating and marriage, to parenting generally.

www.du.edu/~cbrown/soci2210

Sociology of Families: A Guide to Online Databases

This site is maintained by the Penrose Library at the University of Denver. It contains a number of useful links to the main online databases listing current social science research dealing with many aspects of family life.

SAINT GABRIEL OF THE SORROWFUL VIRGIN

Religion

Lorne L. Dawson

Introduction

I am a baby-boomer, part of the single largest generation of people born in North America (1946–1966). When I was born, Canada appeared to be a very religious nation. Most Canadians attended church services with some regularity, and almost everyone was baptized and got married in a church. A great many Canadians contributed money to religious charities, volunteered their time and labour to a wide variety of religious organizations, and participated in an array of social activities centred on their church. Religious leaders carried real influence in the affairs of their communities. Come election time in the 1950s and early 1960s, Canadian politicians still were careful to not offend the churches, as studies showed that people's religious orientation was still the single strongest indicator of how they would vote.

In these respects, there were few differences between Canadians and Americans, and between Canadians and much of the rest of the Western world. As North American families achieved new levels of affluence after the World War II, they moved to the suburbs and built new churches at an unprecedented rate. Look around you, at your own community, and you will see the result: churches, and their associated auditoriums, schools, and community centres.

Moreover, reflecting our heritage and the dominant patterns of immigration to that point, Canada was a Christian nation, and it thought of itself as such. This was an integral part of our identity until the 1960s. In the first decades after the founding of this nation in 1867, during the Victorian era, it is no exaggeration to say that Christianity exercised a profound influence "on both the character of the nation and the Canadian character" (O'Toole, 2000: 67). There was a remarkable uniformity to the religious life of Canadians, since all but a tiny minority of people belonged to either the Roman Catholic Church, the United Church of Canada, the Anglican Church, or the Presbyterian Church. These churches worked to bolster the middle-class values, norms, and goals favoured by the majority of Canadians. They helped to extend God's blessing to the status quo and to exhort Canadians to strive harder to achieve greater prosperity and social respectability. They also helped to temper the disruptive effects of industrialization and urbanization (see Chapter 15, Demography and Urbanization, and Chapter 16, Social Change), and played an important role in creating the culture of concern for the social welfare of all that distinguishes Canadian public life from the politics of free-enterprise individualism in the United States.

The only significant religious division in the nation was between the Catholics and the Protestants, and in some parts of the country the traditional animosities between these groups were perpetuated. As a Protestant boy in small town Ontario, I fought snowball fights with the Catholic kids at the school bus stop. As the Catholics attended "separate schools," I never really knew them, even though they were my neighbours. But the differences did not run deep, and by high school and university many of us were friends. In fact I would marry a Catholic without really giving it much thought. Canadians had learned long ago to accommodate these religious differences and to fashion a public world that did not significantly discriminate between Protestants and Catholics. Canada struck a balance between its founding elements, the English and the French, and the Protestants and Catholics long ago. Like most North Americans, we prided ourselves on leaving behind the serious conflicts over religion that plagued the "old world" (e.g., the sectarian violence of Northern Ireland). In the "new world," many of our ancestors fervently believed, there was the opportunity to lay the foundation for a truly Christian society.

In my own lifetime things clearly have changed. There is, of course, some important continuity with the past. Two-thirds of Canadians still belong, at least formally, to one of the four denominations noted above. Only a small percentage of Canadians do not identify themselves as Christians, though that number is growing fairly rapidly as the predominant patterns of immigration shift increasingly from Europe to the countries of Asia and Africa. But like the majority of my generation, I never have attended a church service with any regularity. Levels of participation are even lower for generations younger than my own. In the late

1940s and early 1950s about 60 percent of Canadians attended church weekly. For Catholics the figure was as high as 83 percent. By the mid-1990s only 20 percent of Protestants and about 30 percent of Catholics attended church with any regularity. Across North America, levels of religious participation began to plummet in the 1960s as many baby-boomers rebelled against "the establishment," and about half of this huge demographic group chose to follow the ethic of the counter-culture, to "turn-on, tune-in, and drop-out." Since the 1980s many have returned to the churches, as they married and started to raise their own families. In fact recent surveys suggest that attendance levels may even be rebounding somewhat (Bibby, 1995). But the benefits of this growth are not being reaped, for the most part, by the churches the baby-boomers left. The traditionally dominant mainstream and liberal denominations have been losing ground to more conservative brands of religiosity. In fact, south of the border, as most Canadians are aware, conservative or *fundamentalist* Christian churches, stressing more literal adherence to Biblical teaching, have also grown rapidly, exerting a strong influence on the cultural and political life of that society. In the United States, however, the real decline in religiosity experienced in the 1960s and early 1970s proved to be temporary. Overall, the levels of church attendance, and other indicators of religious participation, like private prayer, have remained remarkably steady for over fifty years. About 40 percent of Americans report attending church weekly, for example, and 72 percent report praying weekly. Only 48 percent of Canadians say they pray weekly (Grenville, 2000). By all conventional measures, Americans have continued to be much more religious than Canadians.

Over the last fifty years, Canada has become an increasingly secular society. The influence of religious symbols, ideas, and organizations on both the daily life and public affairs of this nation has waned dramatically. A Gallup poll done in 1955, the heyday of religious growth, found that 68 percent of Canadians felt that "religion as a whole is becoming a greater influence in Canadian life." By 1995, only 17 percent of Canadians would say the same (Bibby, 1995). Appearances, however, can be deceiving. Canadians continue to hold tenaciously to their traditional religious affiliations and,

TABLE 11.1   Weekly Religious Service Attendance in Canada 1975 through 1995

	1975	1985	1995
Nationally	**31%**	**28%**	**25%**
Roman Catholic	**45%**	**37%**	**30%**
Quebec	49%	31%	24%
Outside Quebec	41%	40%	38%
Mainline Protestant	**23%**	**16%**	**19%**
Anglican	24%	16%	17%
United Church	28%	13%	20%
Conservative protestant	**40%**	**60%**	**64%**
(e.g., Baptist, Pentecostal)			

Source: Bibby (1995), p. 125. Reprinted by permission of Stoddard Publishing Co. Limited.

The Phenomenon of *The Celestine Prophecy*

Most Canadians now believe they live in an essentially secular society and in irreligious times. But, if this is the case, how can one explain the phenomenal success of Redfield's novel *The Celestine Prophecy*? Here is an adventure tale, recording one American man's quest for spiritual enlightenment while journeying through Peru, and becoming one of the most successful books in modern publishing. In hard cover, *The Celestine Prophecy* spent more than three years on the New York Times best-seller list; it was the best-selling book, worldwide, in 1996. The sequel, *The Tenth Insight: Holding the Vision*, became an instant bestseller as well, and the success of both has prompted the creation of taped *Experiential Guides* and pocket-sized books designed to help readers keep in touch with the lessons learned from the novel. The commercial success of Redfield's work is all the more remarkable, considering that he first published the book himself and sold it from the trunk of his car.

In the novel, Redfield tells the story of an American writer who hears of a mysterious ancient manuscript found in Peru. The manuscript describes nine spiritual insights into the true nature of the world and the untapped potential of humanity. The writer, who narrates the story, follows an impulse, leaves for Peru, and becomes ensnared in a web of intrigue. No one has seen the full manuscript, recently discovered in the ruins of an unknown civilization. A group of people, scattered throughout Peru, are studying fragments of the manuscript and actively pursuing the rest. Some of these seekers are scientists, some are priests, some are other Americans and Europeans, and some are people of suspect motivation. As these individuals read the manuscript, they begin to experience a dramatic transformation of their consciousness, acquiring spectacular new insights into the nature of the world, themselves, and humanity, as well as gaining new psychic powers. The Peruvian government, pressured by the Catholic Church, attempts to suppress the manuscript and arrest all who know it, because it fears the manuscript will undermine the authority of Christianity. In reading the story, we follow the narrator as he moves from adventure to adventure, slowly acquiring a knowledge of each insight, until he and some companions finally out-wit the Church and the government's soldiers and experience the ninth insight, in the ruins where the mysterious manuscript was first found.

Given the tremendous popularity of the novel, I was rather surprised and disappointed when I belatedly read it. The storyline itself is quite simple, and things are presented in a parable-like manner. Redfield, a therapist and not a writer by profession, gives us an overly linear,

continued

almost blow-by-blow, account of what people said and how they acted. Each of the spiritual insights of the manuscript is discovered by the narrator, in the correct sequence, as a result of a series of miraculous coincidences. What we are to learn from each insight is clearly outlined. The characters in the story are underdeveloped, I thought, and seem to be serving too obviously as props for an unfolding exposition of ideas. Beyond the obvious suspense created by the sequenced revelations, I found it difficult to become emotionally engaged in the story. Presumably other readers would disagree with this assessment. In any event, it is evident that the lack of stylistic finesse and realism did little to impair the book's enormous appeal. But if the success of the book is not rooted in its success as a novel, then it must be the nature of the message it delivers that is consequential. This possibility increases the salience of the book for sociologists of religion.

The Celestine Prophecy, like a great many other similar books published about spirituality today, should be treated as a significant source of data about the popular religious sensibilities of many North Americans and Europeans. Intellectually, scholars may wish to scoff at these popular forms of religiosity. But socially, their significance cannot be denied, especially in a world dominated by the mass media. Without ever advertising itself as such, *The Celestine Prophecy* provides an ideal illustration of the common elements of a new configuration of quasi-religious practices known as the New Age Movement (see Heelas, 1996; Hanegraaff, 1996). The diverse array of groups involved in this movement stress the sacredness of the self and various processes of self-discovery that have either been invented or recovered from numerous traditional and usually marginalized cultures of the world (such as the Native American, Celtic, or Tibetan). Full self-realization is linked to the salvation of the world from various grievous errors of humanity, ranging from the pollution of the environment to the suppression of our true psychic powers. The transformation of the self, it is believed, will bring about the collective and radical evolutionary advance of human nature, thereby ushering in a New Age. In popular awareness, the New Age Movement is associated with such practices as yoga, meditation, forms of group-encounter psychotherapy, the use of crystals for healing, macrobiotics, reincarnation, channelling, the reading of auras, telepathic contact with civilizations from other worlds, astral projection, and so on. Through the activities associated with the New Age Movement, spirituality is being reintegrated with the contemporary world in ways that are thought to be compatible, ultimately, with the established ethos of science. Spirituality is identified with gaining a personal understanding of extraordinary, yet largely natural forces, that science simply fails to adequately grasp. Accordingly, the more esoteric theorizing of scientists is often used to justify the claims of New Age practitioners. The scientists may object, but the public is fascinated with the possibilities presented, and more concerned with expanding the meaningful order of the mundane world in which they must spend most of their lives.

when questioned, they continue to display a relatively strong interest in religious and spiritual issues. The number of Canadians who claim to believe in God, or to have personally experienced God in their lives, is as great now as at any other any time in our past. We live in a secular society, yet we tend increasingly to believe in such things as "near-death experiences," contact with spiritual beings (e.g., angels), and reincarnation (Bibby, 1987; 1993; 1995). On any given Sunday, the churches in Canada may be relatively empty, but billions of dollars are spent every year on religious literature in North America.

Popular books like *The Celestine Prophecy*, a "New Age" novel of spiritual intrigue and revelation, or the three volumes of Welsch's *Conversations with God*, have topped the bestseller lists in Canada and the United States for years. As Bibby (1987; 1993; 1995) concluded from his comprehensive surveys of religion in Canada, the number of Canadians who readily express some spiritual needs clearly exceeds the numbers involved in organized religions, of any kind. So what is happening?

Are Canadians becoming less religious? Is religion destined to disappear from the modern world, and the Canadian experience typical? Is the

TABLE 11.2   The Beliefs of Canadians (percentage responding "definitely" believe in or "think so")

	1975	1980	1985	1990	1995
In God	89	85	83	82	81
Miraculous healing	–	–	–	–	74
Divinity of Jesus	71	69	79	75	72
Life after death	73	69	65	68	71
Heaven	–	–	–	70	67
Angels	–	–	–	–	61
Hell	–	–	–	46	49
Have experienced God	47	43	44	43	43
Near-death experiences	–	–	–	–	74
Spirit world contact	–	–	–	39	43
Will be reincarnated	–	–	–	24	27

Source: adapted from Bibby (1995), pp. 131 and 132. Reprinted by permission of Stoddard Publishing Co. Limited.

According to Bibby, Canadians are now likely to treat religion as an assortment of consumer items from which they can choose at will.

continued interest in the supernatural and the spiritual merely a cultural remnant of a bygone era? Or are we in the midst of a significant shift in the nature of North American religiosity? Throughout this century, most sociologists anticipated that religion would be displaced and decline into insignificance as societies modernized. But the United States, that most modern of all nations, has remained a surprisingly contrary case. This stark fact, along with the other kinds of counter-indicators detected in Canada and elsewhere, is leading a growing number of sociologists to believe that religion will continue to be an important element of our societies for the foreseeable future. Complete secularization seems unlikely. Industrialization, urbanization, the growth of science, education, and the state, have all effected a permanent change in the forms and functions of religion as a social institution. But it seems that religiosity and modernity can coexist. How this is the case and for how long is another matter, as are the consequences of these changes for other aspects of the social order. As you will see in this chapter, these are some of the basic issues sociologists are struggling to understand through the detailed study of the many forms of religious life around us.

Studying Religious Life Sociologically

In light of the central role religion has played in shaping and guiding social relations throughout history, sociologists have been concerned with questions about the role and long-term fate of religion for years. The founding figures of sociology—Marx, Durkheim, and Weber—all paid extensive and careful attention to the study of religion in their work. The perceptive theoretical insights they developed continue to inform the sociological analysis of religion, laying the foundations for contemporary discussions. Living in the late nineteenth and early twentieth centuries, they recognized how changes in religion were indicative of the larger social transformations accompanying the disruptive transition from a premodern to a modern social order. Today, sociologists are equally intent on understanding the

transition from a modern to a postmodern society. Are these social changes, and our responses to them, being reflected once again in the changing nature of the religious life of Canadians? To even begin to answer this question, we must first pause to consider a few special features of the academic study of religion.

Perennial problems in the study of religion

In trying to understand religion from a social-scientific perspective, scholars have found themselves repeatedly struggling with three interrelated methodological questions: How can we study religious experience? How can we define religion? How can we measure *religiosity*, the act of being religious? Each of these questions is the subject of long, complex, and still largely unresolved debates (see, for example, Idinopulos and Yonan, 1994; Idinopulos and Wilson, 1998). But for our purposes, it is sufficient to specify a few key points.

Studying the religious experience

Many of the greatest scholars of religion have long argued that religious experience, in its essence, is unique (Eliade, 1969). It cannot be explained in terms of anything else, and most certainly not the kinds of things that social scientists can measure, compare, and criticize. The "religious" is, as Otto (1917) said, "wholly other." Yet every religious tradition has asserted the truth, importance, and power of this essentially non-empirical feature of human existence. In the face of the fervent claims made for the core experience of religion, most sociologists of religion have adopted a position of methodological "detachment." They do not seek to determine the truth or falsity of religious assertions about the **supernatural**, or that which lies beyond day-to-day experience. The task of sociology is to detect and gauge the nature and significance of the human consequences of such claims and experiences. For the purposes of sociological analysis, it can remain an open question whether the gods or God exist; that is matter for the philosophers and theologians to debate. Sociologists will confine their attention to those aspects of people's religious life that can be observed and maybe even measured in some way.

But such a stance is not always satisfactory for some religious leaders and scholars of religion. By formulating explanations of religious behaviour that do not consider the causal role of the transcendent in human affairs, it is argued, many sociologists develop theories of religion that are crucially incomplete or even contrary to the judgments of the religious themselves. Only insiders to the experience, or even to a particular faith tradition, can provide a full and accurate account of religious life (e.g., Smith, 1959). There is undoubtedly some truth to these objections. But claims to a privileged way of knowing for one group of people over against another are counter to the dictates of science (as conventionally understood), because they cannot be empirically tested and compared. With reason, social scientists are suspicious of the conscious and unconscious temptation to seek truth while speaking from a stance of emotional commitment to things known on faith. Today, most sociologists of religion attempt to be much more sensitive to the nature and possible truth of the claims made by the people they study. Out of respect for the unique character of religious experience, they strive to develop ever more subtle conceptualizations of religion and refined instruments of research. In the end, however, they continue to define their task by their prior adherence to the standards of contemporary research.

Defining religion

The great diversity of things that people have held to be holy or sacred through the centuries and across the world poses another fundamental problem for sociologists of religion. What is it that we are studying? No one has ever been able to fashion a definition of religion capable of achieving a consensus of support in the scholarly community. As a rule of thumb, the numerous attempts made to define religion tend to be either substantive or functional in nature.

Substantive definitions of religion emphasize what religion "is," by focusing on some crucial and presumably universal feature of religious activity. A classic illustration of this substantive approach is provided by Tylor (1903), the eminent British anthropologist, who suggested that religion be defined as "belief in Spiritual Beings." He is the

same man who provided an early definition of culture in Chapter 3, Culture. On first glance, this simple definition of religion seems plausible enough. But in fact most scholars have found it to be too exclusive. In the first place, many object to the stress placed on belief. Belief is only one aspect of religion, and in many religions, both old and new, belief is secondary to various forms of action and practice. Contemporary Wiccans and Neo-Pagans (adherents of witchcraft), for example, practice similar forms of magic and ritual, yet their beliefs are tremendously diverse. Participation in rituals takes precedence over knowledge of certain beliefs in these traditions. The stress on beliefs reflects an ethnocentric bias, moreover, one that is characteristic of the codified religions of the modern Western world. It is Protestants in particular, who tend to identify being religious with belief in the teachings of the Bible. Secondly, many Wiccans and Neo-Pagans, like many Buddhists, simply reject the reality of supernatural beings. Such a belief is optional for many Wiccans and other Neo-Pagans, and the Theravada Buddhists of southeast Asia (and elsewhere) formally deny the existence of God and eternal souls. Are these groups to be excluded from the study of religion? In most other important regards, these systems of beliefs and practices certainly seem to be religious. Finally, like most substantive definitions of religion, Tylor's definition suffers from an additional problem. It relies on a term that is itself in need of further definition. What, we should ask, constitutes a "spiritual being"? The term "spiritual" is ambiguous at best.

Functionalist definitions of religion focus on what religion "does," and they tend to suffer from the reverse limitation: they can be too broad and inclusive. The American sociologist of religion Yinger (1970) framed a well-known functionalist definition of religion: "Religion [is] a system of beliefs and practices by means of which a group struggles with [the] ultimate problems of human life." Certainly this approach could encompass both the Wiccans and the Buddhists, along with most other conventional religions. But these terms of reference make it difficult to differentiate between religion and various other "functional equivalents" to religion in society. Some people may throw themselves quite whole-heartedly into the service of some cause, like the fight for political freedom or an attempt to save the environment. Or they may dedicate themselves to a psychological quest for true self-understanding. They may derive much of their understanding of the world, and a sense of ultimate meaning and worth, from engaging in these activities. But is this the same as being religious? They may be quite "religious-like" in their devotion to these endeavours. But in the last analysis, what do we gain by conceptually blurring the boundaries between religion and a host of other kinds of somewhat similar activities? Here, too, we tend to encounter the additional problem that the definitions entail further definitional problems. In this case, we might ask, what constitutes an "ultimate" problem of life?

In most cases, to be frank, sociologists of religion work with a rather commonsensical definition of their subject matter, and, when pressed, defend the definition best suited to their present research interests. They work at all times, however, with an appreciation of the intrinsic limitations of any one definition of religion. As Weber observed, it is simply realistic to acknowledge the largely open-ended character of religion as a subject of study. This said, as a working definition I will simply suggest that a **religion** is a system of beliefs and practices about transcendent things, their nature, and their consequences for humanity. The transcendent refers here to some level, type, or dimension of reality that is thought to be intrinsically different from, and in some sense higher or beyond, our ordinary experience of the world. I favour, as you can see, a rather simple, substantive approach to the definition of religion (see Dawson, 1987).

Measuring religiosity

Given the difficulties sociologists have in coping with the core experience of much of religious life, and in defining religion, it should come as no surprise that measuring how religious people are, their *religiosity*, is problematic as well. Survey researchers regularly ask people about their religious affiliations, levels of attendance, belief in God, and so on. But as almost everyone recognizes, if only from personal experience, the answers to these questions can be poor indicators of how truly religious people are. Some people attend religious services with great regularity, but do not seem to put their religion into practice in their daily lives.

Others strike us as being really very pious or spiritual, though they rarely attend any organized religious services. Religiosity is a complex blend of states of mind, attitudes, and behaviours, and people can be religious in several ways. An adequate measure of religiosity should access information about all the aspects and ways of being religious. With this in mind, Glock and Stark (1965) recommended inquiring into at least eight dimensions of religious life that assess: (1) the *experiential*, whether people think they have had contact with the supernatural; (2) the *ritualistic*, level of participation in public rites; (3) the *devotional*, level of participation in activities like praying or saying grace before meals; (4) *belief*, the degree to which they agree with the doctrines of their faith; (5) *knowledge*, their degree of recognition and understanding of the beliefs of their religion; (6) the *consequential*, the effects of their religion on their everyday life; (7) the *communal*, the extent to which they associate with others members of the same religion; and lastly, (8) the *particularistic*, the degree to which they think their religion is the one and only true path to salvation.

Mystics reject the world that is perceived with their senses as illusory, and seek a passive endurance of earthly trials and tribulations through a learned detachment.

This kind of multidimensional approach has stimulated a great deal of research. As is now widely appreciated, a person may score high on any one or cluster of these dimensions and thus appear to be very religious, while also scoring low on other dimensions, in seeming contradiction of this religiosity. In studies of Canadians and Americans, for example, high levels of church attendance are not necessarily accompanied by a very sound knowledge of the basic doctrines and religious texts of Christianity, i.e., there is only a weak correlation between the ritualistic and knowledge dimensions. Much can be learned then about both the style and the degree of the religiosity of individuals, groups, and whole societies, by devising survey and interview questions that measure each of these dimensions. The design of these research instruments can be quite complicated, however, and pose additional problems. Glock and Stark tended to use quite conventional criteria to measure each dimension in their work on American piety. This had at least two undesirable consequences: first, unconventional religious practices, like the belief in astrology, were simply excluded from their study altogether; second, a bias towards a more conservative style of Christianity was implicitly built into their measurement scales. At every point, then, the sociology of religion is dogged by the conceptual difficulties posed by the sheer diversity of ways in which people can be religious.

Sociologists have tried to devise various other ways to obtain a multidimensional measure of religiosity that minimize some of these problems. Davidson and Knudsen (1977), for instance, sought to keep the issues of the style of religiosity and the extent of religiosity distinct by employing two sets of criteria: one that measures various dimensions of religious orientation and another that measures various dimensions of religious commitment. Questions dealing with specific beliefs, the tendency to particularism, the ethical applications of religion to life, communal involvements, and religious knowledge, highly variable between religious traditions, are used to gauge the religious orientation of someone or group. Questions about the character of religious consciousness and participation are used to gauge the degree of religious commitment of someone or group to their religious orientation, whatever it may be. Studies

employing this approach have found a strong correlation between the two dimensions of religious commitment, consciousness and participation, but only a weak correlation between religious orientation as a whole and religious commitment. Clearly no one style of religion is inherently more "religious" than another. In fact, there is usually only a weak correlation between the dimensions of religious orientation itself, suggesting that there is little or no coherence to belief systems. This is an interesting result in its own right.

No matter how one chooses to measure religiosity, however, every approach is plagued by the problems of self-reporting. Hadaway, Long-Marler, and Chaves (1993; 1998), and others, have found serious discrepancies between the levels of church attendance Americans commonly report to pollsters and the actual number of people they could count in the pews of a selected sample of Protestant and Catholic churches. In general, people are inclined to provide researchers with answers that exaggerate their religiosity because of the normative character of religious life in the United States, and probably in Canada as well. It is still often thought to be socially desirable to be at least somewhat religious, especially in the United States, so people wish to put their best foot forward in dealing with questions on this topic. Attempts to measure religiosity can call our attention to such issues, but they cannot resolve them (see Finke and Stark, 1992). For some answers, sociologists must turn their attention to classical theoretical explanations of religion.

The Insights and Issues of Classical Theory

The founding figures of sociology were interested in the study of religion because they were interested in understanding the forces of social stability and change in society. More specifically they were interested in understanding what was happening to their own European society as it was jolted from the traditional order of things into the modern world. They realized that religious beliefs and practices had exerted a crucial influence over the daily affairs and social structure of all known societies to that time. In the world of premodern society, the very configuration of space and time reflected an opposition of things *sacred* (heavenly) and *profane* (earthly). The order and significance of the human environment and experiences was mapped against the holy places and holy times of each culture. The human understanding of the root issues of life, from the meaning of birth and death, through how we should understand the phenomena of the natural world, to the determination of who should rule and why, was shaped by religious principles and revelations. With the birth of modernity (from about the seventeenth century onwards), all this began to change dramatically as science, technology, and democratic and secular systems of government emerged and became the dominant forces in society. Marx, Durkheim, and Weber had diverse responses to these changes and they focused on different aspects of the role that religious beliefs and practices played in promoting and resisting the social changes associated with modernity. But they all recognized the importance of the sociology of religion to the discipline of sociology as a whole.

Marx: Religion and ideology

Marx's radical sociology was focused on the critique of capitalism. At the heart of the modern social system was the exploitive economic system of the capitalists, and, in Marx's eyes, the primary social function of religion was the legitimation of the rule of the capitalists. In every age, he believed, religion served to justify the rule of one class over another, either as divinely ordained or as part of the natural order of things. With the Communist revolution, and the end of class antagonism, Marx argued, the need for religion would disappear, and religious institutions would simply wither away just like the state (recall Chapter 6, Social Stratification).

Fundamentally, Marx (1818–1883) proposed—quite scandalously—that humanity had not been created in the image of God, as the Bible said. On the contrary, the gods or God had been created in the image of humanity. The beliefs and teachings of religion, he stated, are comforting illusions designed to compensate people for the sacrifices and misery of their present lives with promises of rewards for good behaviour in another life. In his colourful and

famous phrase, religion is "the opium of the people" (Marx, 1972 [1844]: 38). The quest for religious virtue subdues the mind, like a powerful narcotic, distracting people from developing a critical appreciation of the real source of their deprivation: their economic and political exploitation at the hands of a dominant class. In their struggles with temptation and sin, religious people give powerful expression to their distress, and yet misunderstand it. In their visions of heaven they acknowledge the inadequacies of this world, but misidentify the reasons for their disappointment.

Historically the ruling class, to the extent that it too was religious, was equally deluded. They were eager to apply their resources to the support of this illusion because the church usually encouraged humble obedience to the authorities. Throughout history, Marx asserted, religions favoured the status quo, to the direct financial benefit of themselves and the secular rulers of this world. In Marx's words, Christianity declares "all vile acts of the oppressors against the oppressed to be either the just punishment of original sin and other sins or trials that the Lord in his infinite wisdom imposes on those redeemed" (Marx, 1972: 74).

For Marx, then, the critique of religion is a first and necessary step in the emancipation of humanity. But to really liberate the masses in the modern world from the seductive and particularly dehumanizing tyranny of capitalist wage-slavery, he argued that scholars must turn their attention from religious concerns to the analysis of the social, political, and economic systems.

Durkheim: Religion and social solidarity

Durkheim, while no more religious than Marx, recognized a greater purpose for religion in society. Seeking to help create a stable modern state in France during the social and political disruptions of the late nineteenth and early twentieth centuries, Durkheim was keenly interested in understanding the processes that held societies together, that kept them unified and strong in the face of adversity and change. Throughout his life, this central concern led him to the study of religion.

In the past, he believed, religious beliefs and practices had protected the moral integrity of social relations. They worked to hold the egoistic impulses of the individual at bay, while cultivating an altruistic inclination to serve the needs of the group above those of the individual. Unlike Marx, then, Durkheim had no interest in dismissing religion as an unnecessary illusion. On the contrary, he was worried about what might happen to the social solidarity of society should religion wane in the modern world. But like Marx, Durkheim sought a natural and not a supernatural explanation for the persistence of religious convictions. He did not doubt the reality and the power of religious experience. He did doubt, however, that people properly grasped the source of this experience. It is not God or the gods that inspire the religious convictions of humanity, but the experience of *society* itself.

Durkheim's life-long interest in religion culminated in his *The Elementary Forms of Religious Life* (1965 [1912]). In this book he devised a theory of religion based on the study of what was then thought to be one of the simplest of religions, that of an Australian aboriginal group, the Arunta. The information available to Durkheim was seriously flawed and much that he said about the Arunta is now considered to be mistaken. But this deficiency has done little to diminish the lasting impact of his perceptive insights into the more general nature and functioning of religion. With his study of aboriginal religion in mind, Durkheim defined religion as "a unified system of beliefs and practices relative to sacred things...which unite into one single moral community...all those who adhere to them" (1965). This definition combines both substantive and functional elements. Concern with the sacred is the substantive element that differentiates religion from other activities, while functionally, religion is to be identified with the social processes that create a sense of community. In a rather circular manner, these elements are both assumed and supposedly demonstrated by Durkheim's theory of religion.

Durkheim began his analysis of religion with a fundamental observation or assumption that then posed a problem which he, in turn, addressed with another observation or assumption. The most distinctive trait of traditional religious life, Durkheim stipulated, is the division of all things into two opposed categories: the *sacred* and the *profane*. The **sacred**, Durkheim said, is that which

is set apart and treated with special awe and respect. What is sacred in any society is highly variable, and, as Durkheim acknowledged, almost every kind of thing has been sacred for someone at sometime, from particular trees and rocks, to blessed spaces within magnificent temples, particular writings, or the stars in the heavens. The sacred, whatever it may be, is thought to possess a tremendous and unique power that requires people to take special care in its presence. The sacred provides a kind of fixed point in reality, around which all else, or the **profane** circulates. Religious systems place people in controlled contact with the sacred in order to call upon its power to protect them from the vicissitudes of profane life. But, Durkheim asked, "what has been able to lead men to see in the world two het-erogeneous and incompatible worlds, though nothing in sensible experience seems able to suggest the idea of so radical a duality?" (1965). The answer, he proposed, is to be found in another elemental fact of religious life. Religion, unlike the mere practice of magic or superstition, is always a group activity. It is a social phenomenon and, like the religion of the Arunta, deeply concerned with the regulation of the internal and external relations of the group. In traditional societies, religious rites are almost always associated with special times of collective festivity. In the repetitive performance of these group rituals, the Arunta and others, Durkheim thought, encounter the true experiential basis for their belief in the reality and power of the sacred.

Durkheim observed two features of being in the presence of things deemed sacred. First, devotees are moved by feelings of heightened strength. "The believer who has communicated with his gods is not merely a man who sees new truths...he is a man who is stronger. He feels within him more force, either to endure the trials of existence, or to conquer them" (1965). Second, believers feel that this strength comes from sharing in a power that is both outside of themselves and greater than themselves, and capable of acting upon them with or without their consent. There is a real basis for both beliefs, Durkheim reasoned, but it is not the one that religious people interpret it to be. By participating in the concerted action of a group, in the performance of a religious cult of worship and sacrifice, individuals are bringing themselves into intimate contact with two powerful aspects of social life itself: what Durkheim called the *collective conscience* and *collective effervescence*. The carefully orchestrated and solemn acts of ritual have a disciplining effect on people, directing the attention of participants to the ideals and sentiments they share with their group. They are lifted for a time out of the limited horizon of their own personal preoccupations, and exposed through highly condensed symbols, gestures, and stories to an intuitive grasp of the collective wisdom of their society—to the **collective conscience**. This moving reaffirmation of their heritage and their secure place in a larger cultural whole is, Durkheim argued, both invigorating and reassuring and all the more so because the sheer numbers of people involved and their physical closeness has their own psychological effect upon them. Caught up in the emotional and almost contagious energy of a crowd, people will often experience levels of enthusiasm, ecstasy, pride, and fear quite out of keeping with their solitary

Durkheim believed that the power the sacred seems to have over the minds of individuals is really the power the group has over the minds of individuals.

experience. This sense of **collective effervescence** can inspire, for a time at least, a sense of quite superhuman strength in each individual, like soldiers entering battle or participants in large political rallies or sporting events. More on this topic will come in Chapter 14, Social Movements.

The social experience itself, then, contains the properties of religious experience, as understood by Durkheim: the sense of being carried away and strengthened by some force external to and much greater than oneself. The people involved in these collective rituals misattribute the power they feel to the sacred objects, symbols, and mythical entities invoked in the rituals. But this mistake did not perturb Durkheim. Through the practice of the religion, the members of a group are bonded together, and the uplifting effect of this bond serves to perpetuate their feelings of empowerment, and hence, in endless circular fashion, their continued belief in the things deemed sacred and their social solidarity. Sociologically, it is the unifying result that mattered to Durkheim. The primary function of religion then, in Durkheim's theory, is the promotion of social solidarity through the ritualistic and symbolic creation and periodic re-enactment of a social identity. If society is "the soul of religion," as Durkheim said, it is because religion can also be said to be the soul of society. At least such has been the case throughout most of human history. In worshipping the sacred, people are reconfirming their dependence on and commitment to society itself.

Weber: Religion and rationalization

Weber provided us with one of the most profound and comprehensive sociologies of religion. His works reflect a encyclopaedic knowledge of religious traditions worldwide and the historical circumstances of their development. Yet in some respects Weber's abiding interest in religion was merely a by-product of his initial and chief concern: the origins and nature of modernity. In examining such institutional manifestations of modernity as capitalism, bureaucratic administration, and the creation of autonomous legal systems (see Chapter 13, Work and Organizations), Weber believed he could detect a common and essential feature of modernity: an *ascetic* ethic of vocation. Unlike their medieval counterparts, the people involved in the creation and operation of the early systems of modern commerce, government, and law, performed their tasks with an unprecedented diligence and lack of concern for their immediate material benefit. The first capitalists, Weber argued for instance, differed from traditional merchants because they would forgo spending the profits they earned on new luxuries in favour of reinvesting the profits in their businesses. By adopting this more **ascetic** approach, and denying themselves the pleasures of the material world, they prospered as their investments earned them greater profits and they accumulated capital. This approach to their work, their **vocation**, Weber concluded, provided the motivational heart of the spirit of capitalism that emerged from western Europe to transform the world.

But how, Weber asked, did this rather unnatural ascetic ethic of vocation arise? Noting the disproportionate number of Protestants over Catholics involved in business and related professions in his own times, Weber argued that the ascetic impulse underlying capitalism may be the unique legacy of the Protestant Reformation. He developed this idea in his famous book *The Protestant Ethic and the Spirit of Capitalism* (1958 [1904]), where he traced the spirit of capitalism to the probable psychological effect of two doctrines introduced by the Protestant reformers who broke with Catholicism in the sixteenth century: Martin Luther's concept of the *calling* and John Calvin's *doctrine of predestination.*

Seeking to break the hold of the Catholic Church on the people of Europe, Luther, the leader of the Reformation, proposed that all people, and not only priests, are called to the service of God. *Lay* people—ordinary churchgoers—have a **calling** to fulfill in the faithful completion of their secular tasks as farmers, lawyers, miners, or whatever. This calling was comparable in importance to that of the monk praying in his cell. Acceptance of this idea extended divine providence into the details of the daily life of everyone. It tended to make Protestants more methodical in their labours and careful and honest in their dealings with others, for fear of falling into sin. But the full force of this more methodical and ascetic approach to life only emerged later in the Reformation with the teachings

of Calvin, in particular his **doctrine of predestination**. Stressing the omnipotence and the omniscience of God, Calvin argued that the ultimate status of believers, whether they are saved or damned, is something God has predetermined. Individuals can do nothing to either know or change their predestined status without calling into question God's supremacy. It is not appropriate for lowly and largely sinful humans to question the ways of God. Thus the Catholic belief in the power of good deeds, confession, or the sacraments, was illusory.

Faced with such a severe view of our fate, Weber speculated that many ordinary Protestants were driven to find solace in some covert sign of their salvation. For these truly religious people, the uncertainty of their destiny would be an agony. Protestant pastors were advised to tell their parishioners to work hard at their lay callings, have faith in their fate, and avoid the doubts about salvation that are the temptation of the devil. Idle hands, they were repeatedly told, are the devil's helpmates. So with time, and through sheer hard labour, success in one's worldly calling became an unofficial sign that one was saved. But this success could stand as a sign of God's favour only if one did not indulge in the ostentatious displays of wealth that signified one had succumbed to the contaminating pleasures of the flesh. Thus to secure individual peace of mind and social prestige in their communities, the early Protestants were induced to lead relatively humble and industrious lives, faithfully reinvesting their profits in their businesses. In this ironic way, then, out of deep religious devotion and need, the motivation was provided for the endless cycle of accumulation and reinvestment so pivotal to the rise of capitalism. With time and mounting material success, this new spirit of capitalism would itself succeed the Protestant ethic (the ethical orientation towards work as a divine calling) as the motivational wellspring of modern society.

Other factors, Weber well knew, also had to be in place for the development of capitalism, from the invention of something as simple as double-entry bookkeeping, to the growth of large pools of free labourers, the invention of steam engines and other machines, and the discovery of new markets around the world (see also Chapter 6, Social Stratification, and Chapter 16, Social Change). But the presence of these elements was insufficient in themselves, Weber argued, to generate the capitalist system. He explored his suspicion that something like the Protestant ethic of vocation must be present for capitalism to emerge in a series of sweeping comparative studies of the other great civilizations of the world, the Indian, Chinese, and Islamic. Each of these societies might have developed capitalism, he reasoned, if elements of their religious history had not critically hindered this possibility. These studies led Weber to a broader conception of the significance of the ascetic ethic of vocation, and of religion in general. The modernization of Europe, and then the rest of the world, was interpreted by Weber as the result of a long and worldwide process of *rationalization*, one that just happened to reach a crucial juncture in the European context. The development of religious ideas has been instrumental to this broader process of rationalization.

For Weber a society is more *rational* if it displays a more specific and systematic approach to the acquisition and spread of ideas and information,

the creation and enforcement of social norms and sanctions, and the development and implementation of means of motivating social commitments. In practical terms the lives of modern peoples are relatively more rational because they are relatively more orderly, controlled, and efficient. In Weber's reckoning, being more rationalized is not necessarily a good thing. In fact, Weber lamented (1958 [1904]), modern individuals are "specialists without spirit, sensualists without heart." Yet, paradoxically, it is religion that helped to bring this pattern of development to fruition. Throughout the ages the human need to live in a meaningful world, and to take a consistent and unified stance towards it, prompted the creation of ever more elaborate systems of religious speculation. Religion responded in particular to the need to explain pain and suffering, especially the seemingly irrational suffering of the innocent and the just. For millennia the religious explanations humans devised were on a small scale and largely magical and "this-worldly" in nature. People sought and received temporary

Legitimating Religion in Contemporary Society

The traditional legitimating task of religion is being disrupted by two new realities of religious life: *privatization* and *pluralism*. In the past, people almost automatically practised the faith of their families, and in largely the same way as their parents and grandparents. Over the course of the twentieth century, religious beliefs and practices have become a private matter—a matter of individual choice. But as religion becomes increasingly private, it cannot be called upon to support a truly common and transcendent universe of meaning and order. Likewise, it is becoming more difficult to convince oneself and others of the absolute truth of one's faith, that one's reli-

gion is something more than a mere preference, in the face of the growing plurality of religions available in most Western societies. In these societies the old has become new again with the revival of various Neo-Pagan practices from medieval times; the East and West are being integrated with ever greater presence of Hindu, Buddhist, and other traditions in North America and Europe; and all the established religions are being confronted with new competition from innovated faiths, ranging from the Mormonism, to Scientology and Eckankar. In these circumstances, when most public institutions and day-to-day social contacts no longer reinforce one's beliefs,

religion loses its taken-for-granted quality. Instead, for both the exponents and potential followers of many religions, religion becomes more like a product to be sold, using the latest marketing techniques, to an increasingly wary public of religious consumers. Can such commoditied religions perform the primary function of religion effectively? Alternatively, will other religions elect to retreat from the conditions of the modern world in order to still perform this function effectively, if at the cost of cutting themselves off from the source of new members and hence any real chance of growing and influencing contemporary society?

relief from their periodic misfortune through the ministrations of shamans and priests. But as societies grew in size and became more complex, religions evolved into more ascetic and "other-worldly" systems of ideas in which special meanings were attributed to sufferings (e.g., they stemmed from original sin or bad karma), and release from suffering was tied to notions of a continued life in another realm altogether. These evermore complex religious theories of the world and its ultimate meaning were accompanied by an elaboration in systems of social control. In the worlds of the great salvation religions of the last few thousand years, social control was increasingly identified with self-control. To be saved was to live a morally correct life in every sense. Mere obedience to the law, to customs, was not enough. The gods of the great world religions saw into people's hearts. They demanded a purity of both thoughts and deeds. In this way, both the conception of the world and behaviour in it were made more orderly, in Weber's terms, more rational. That is the primary function of religion, and whenever the desire for meaning, order, and justice was frustrated by growing discrepancies between the institutionalized explanations of a society and the actual experiences of its people, the stage was set for the emergence of a new religious prophet and the further religious rationalization of the world. That is what had happened with the rise of Christianity in the Roman world, and again with the Protestant Reformation in feudal Europe.

Understanding the forms of religious life

Most of the work done in the sociology of religion, particularly since World War II, has been dedicated to the empirical study of specific aspects of religious life. Researchers have sought to either accurately describe the great diversity of ways in which people are religious or to discover how religion has interacted with other specific aspects of social life. Thousands of studies have been done to determine how religious beliefs and practices influence or are influenced by such other features of our social existence as racial prejudice, mental health, sexual attitudes, and political preferences. In other words, researchers have been exploring ways in which religion operates as either an *independent* or the *dependent* variable in the shaping of our societies (see Chapter 2, Research Methods). Likewise, a strong need persists to simply acquire reliable information about the size, nature, and functioning of an enormous variety of religious groups, ranging from such mainstream organizations as the Catholic Church or the Lutherans through more recent and rapidly growing groups like the Mormons (Church of Jesus Christ of Latter-day Saints) and the Pentecostals. In the last few decades, for example, a lot of research has been undertaken into the nature of new religious movements (or cults) like the Unification Church (i.e., the Moonies), Krishna Consciousness, Scientology, or Wicca (i.e., contemporary witchcraft). The seemingly sudden conversion of many well-educated, middle-class, young people to these alternative religions, beginning in the 1960s, stirred up a great deal of controversy (see Dawson, 1998a). So did the shocking mass suicides and murders perpetrated by members of the People's Temple (1978), the Branch Davidians (1993), the Solar Temple (1994, and again in 1995 and 1997), Aum Shinrikyo (1995), and Heaven's Gate (1997). Using questionnaires, interviews, and participant observation, sociologists have striven to analyze, classify, and explain the various forms of religious life currently available.

In simply classifying religious groups, sociologists have traditionally taken their lead from an initial distinction drawn by Weber (1958 [1904]) between *church* and *sect*, and further developed by Troeltsch (1931). The church/sect typology, as it is known, has been modified in myriad ways, creating a confusing array of types and subtypes of religious organizations. Here we need only consider a few of the most basic and popular schemes.

As framed by Troeltsch, with only the Christian tradition in mind, the church/sect dichotomy is commonly thought to entail the following characterizations. **Churches** are organizations into which people are born and baptized as infants. Membership is involuntary. **Sects** are voluntary organizations to which people usually convert, frequently as the result of very emotional experiences. All kinds of people usually can and do belong to churches; they are inclusive and their membership is heterogeneous. Sects tend to be much more homogeneous in their membership, drawing disproportionately from the underprivileged elements of society. This situation often reflects the fact that sects are created by schisms within a church that is aligned with the dominant social structure. The beliefs and practices of sects, then, tend to be more radical and ethically stern than those of churches, and constitute an act of protest against the values of the rest of society. Sects tend to be exclusive: individuals must meet and maintain certain clear requirements to belong. Sectarians perceive themselves as an elect, and those who contravene the group's precepts are subject to expulsion much more readily than in churches. The leadership of churches is usually hired or appointed on the basis of special educational qualifications. It operates within a hierarchical and impersonal administrative structure. Sectarian leadership tends to be charismatic, and, in line with this feature, sects tend to have smaller, more democratic, and personal organizational structures. In theology and liturgy, churches are inclined to be dogmatic and ritualistic. Sects reflect a more inspirational, volatile, and even anti-ritualistic orientation.

This fundamental distinction has been expanded to encompass a wider array of additional types of religious groups. In one well-known formulation Yinger (1970) proposed a sixfold typology, based on two criteria: how inclusive or exclusive a group is and how much attention it gives to the integration of its members into the dominant society. In order of decreasing inclusiveness and decreasing attention to integration, Yinger distinguishes between the **universal church** (e.g., the Roman Catholic Church), the **ecclesia**, that is, the established national church (e.g., the Church of England or the Suni Islamic faith of Saudi Arabia), the **denomination** (e.g., Presbyterians or Baptists), the *established sect* (e.g., Jehovah's Witnesses or Christian Science), the *sect* (e.g., Pentecostalist churches or the Worldwide Church of God), and the **cult**, a closed religious system in which the members often live, work, and worship in close proximity (e.g., the Unification Church or Scientology). These kinds of categories have been subdivided further by other sociologists (see Dawson, 1998a).

Why do Cult Suicides Happen?

Thirty-nine members of Heaven's Gate killed themselves in Rancho Santa Fe, California. Why? Five more members of the Solar Temple committed suicide in Saint-Casimir, Quebec. Why? We cannot really say with precision, but we can say more than is commonly supposed.

Each of these tragedies stems from the interplay of a rather complex set of external and internal factors. The external factors—such as the nature and levels of hostility, stigmatization, and persecution experienced by a group—vary widely and make comparisons difficult. But analysts have linked at least three internal features of new religious movements to the outbreak of violence: apocalyptic belief systems, heavy investments in charismatic leadership, and processes of social encapsulation. These are among the prime conditions necessary for the eruption of major incidents of cult-related violence, though they may not be sufficient to predict this violence.

In each of the recent cases, *apocalyptic* beliefs-prophecies about the ultimate end of human history—played a crucial role, structuring and motivating the acts of those who died. The Book of Revelation presents a terrifying narrative of the world's destruction, laced with obscure symbolism and exotic imagery. Since the early Christians, in every generation there have been those who eagerly awaited the end and the return of Christ. In their eyes the events of their own times conform to those prophesied and they have prepared to face the tribulations foretold and to meet their Maker. This was the case with the Branch Davidians in Waco. For the Solar Temple and Heaven's Gate, another element was added to the mix; an eclectic blend of occult and new-age beliefs drawn from the lore, for example, of the medieval Knights Templar, alternative forms of medicine, and a belief in the reality of UFOs and alien interventions in human history.

A number of behavioural consequences commonly follow from

these apocalyptic beliefs. First, anticipation of the apocalypse tends to a questioning of conventional norms and rules, even the law itself. What good are the codes of inadequate humanity in the face of the ultimate acts of divine justice and retribution? The righteous will not require the force of law to live in peace and joy, and the evil is destined to perish. Second, serious anticipation entails preparing to deal with violent times and the persecution of the righteous. Weapons must be secured and defenses prepared (building shelters, storing supplies, generally training to be self-sufficient). These preparations set the stage for actual violence, as people look for evidence to confirm their fears and legitimize their plans.

This leads to a third behavioural consequence: The emotionally volatile conception of one's fate bolsters the common tendency to "demonize" perceived enemies. Opponents are portrayed as being capable of the most heinous acts, and thus they can be resisted with extreme force. Fourth, a life lived in serious expectation of the end tends to instill a level of enthusiasm that blinds sound judgement.

Yet tens of millions of Americans seriously hold apocalyptic beliefs today, and they are not violent. It is the association of this world view with a messianic charismatic leader—a man or woman who identifies the signs of the apoca-

lypse with the events of his or her own life—that makes the difference. The authority of such leaders is founded in a deeply personal relationship of extraordinary faith and trust. But this kind of authority is intrinsically precarious. Even the success of their own group poses a threat, for it diminishes the amount of personal contact and dependency crucial to the maintenance of charisma.

To counteract this loss of authority, charismatic leaders often revert to strategies that reinforce the destabilizing effects of an apocalyptic world view. By instituting sudden shifts in doctrines and policies, for example, they seek to reassert their superiority, forcing some of the old guard to the margins while elevating new people to power. Similarly, these leaders will initiate a progressive escalation of the demands on members for service and sacrifice to the group, as a test of their loyalty and commitment. Close relationships among followers are disrupted to prevent alternative sources of power from arising. The demonization of "outsiders" is extended, crises are invented and dissidents are expelled to galvanize the solidarity of the group and its focus on the leader.

This struggle to overcome the precariousness of charismatic authority leads to a progressive intensifying and aggrandizement of the leader's power, along with the increased homogenization, depen-

dency, and social and physical isolation of the followers, setting the conditions for some of these leaders to indulge the darker desires of their subconscious.

In such a cycle, the new religions that are subject to these tendencies will become ever more extreme in their beliefs and practices and suspicious of others, while the surrounding society will become ever more repelled by or hostile to these groups. Socially and physically, new barriers to meaningful contact and feedback will be erected. A process of social encapsulation will set in. The Solar Temple worked hard to increase the symbolic distance between its spiritual élite and the uninitiated.

As the gulf between the group and the rest of society widens, it is increasingly difficult for the members to gauge whether their behaviour is becoming too bizarre and maladaptive. In the absence of alternative views, and in the face of a perceived threat of dissolution or final promise of rapture, the ultimate solution may be invoked: the "transit" to another world of the Solar Temple and Heaven's Gate. In most cases, this will not happen; but with greater public awareness and appropriate vigilance, it need never happen.

Source: Dawson (2000). Originally published in The Globe and Mail, 31 March 1997. Reprinted with permission.

In each case, it must be recognized that religious groups may be transformed. As Niebuhr observed in *The Social Sources of Denominationalism* (1929), as sects develop they tend to become more like churches. New generations are born to the faith and socialized into the set ways of the community, and

the original sense of protest against the norms of the dominant society fades from memory. Likewise, if a cult manages to grow, it may take on the features and increased stability of a sect. In either case, the movement towards establishment may spawn new acts of religious dissent, and hence more new sects or cults. Religious history often seems to be the tale of an endless cycle of birth, transformation, schism, and rebirth of religious movements.

In the end, the strengths and weaknesses of the various typologies are open for debate. So is the classification of specific groups. Are the Mormons, for example, a cult, sect, established sect, denomination, or even church? The answer will depend on whom you ask, what period of history you have in mind, and in what part of the world. In the context of southern Ontario, the Mormons may be viewed as a sect, but a denomination or even an ecclesia in the state of Utah. Despite some differences of opinion, however, sociologists still use the basic church/sect/cult typology in their analyses and discussions.

Contemporary Conceptions of Religion: Secularization

Building on the insights of Durkheim and Weber, sociologists like Wilson (1982) and Luckmann (1982) have argued that the process of rationalization works against the interests and power of traditional religions in society, by reducing the scope of the functions of religion. Where once almost all aspects of social life fell under the influence, if not direct rule, of religion, over the last several centuries ever larger segments of daily life have been segregated from religious authority and relegated to other institutions. Such a transfer of authority accompanied the sequential development of independent economic, political, medical, educational, recreational, and even family institutions. This process, of what sociologists call *institutional differentiation*, not only stripped religious institutions of their manifest power in social affairs, but also subverted the many latent or unintended functions that religions have long performed. Although offering assurance of ultimate salvation has been a primary function of many religions, before the Industrial Revolution, religion was also the primary agency of social cohesion and social control in society, the chief source of knowledge about the world, the foundation of personal and group identity, and a major force for the cultivation, expression, and regulation of emotions. In the traditional village of

Within an established church, religious experience is highly ritualized and almost intellectual in nature.

the past, the church was the hub of social life. These functions are now the prerogative of national governments, legal systems, science, public education and health systems, professional sports, and the mass media and entertainment industry.

In this most fundamental way, contemporary society has been *secularized*, and few sociologists would disagree. Yet, as indicated earlier in this chapter, there is significant disagreement about whether these and other developments are destined to bring an end to religion altogether, as anticipated by Marx. Contemporary opinions have been influenced heavily by a recent and seminal theory of religion that epitomizes the subtle but important differences in the way **secularization**, the process by which sectors of society are removed from the domination of religious institutions and symbols, can be interpreted. It was advanced in the 1980s by the American sociologists Stark and Bainbridge (1985; 1987).

Stark and Bainbridge's theory of religion

Stark and Bainbridge's (1985, 1987) theory of religion took a pessimistic reading of the future of religion and sought to fashion a simple, deductively structured theory of religion, one that would explain why religion persists all the same. To this end, they sound a theme that is increasingly being heard in the literature: many scholars may be mistaking the secularization of certain traditional forms of religious life for "the doom of religion in general" (1985: 3).

Stark and Bainbridge's theory of religion grows out of the combination of four simple premises. The first is that any meaningful discussion of religious phenomena must ultimately be anchored in a definition of religion that straightforwardly acknowledges the pivotal role played by some reference to the *supernatural*. Religions, they argued (1985: 5), "involve some conception of a super-natural being, world, or force, and the notion that the supernatural is active, that events and conditions here on earth are influenced by the supernatural." Some scholars are inclined to see many phenomena and processes in this world as religious, even though they lack any explicit reference to the supernatural (e.g., the life-consuming commitment of certain radical environmental or animal-rights activists). But, in the last analysis, these phenomena and processes are still only deemed to be like "religions" by virtue of the comparison made with certain past and persisting forms of activity that explicitly do refer to the supernatural, practices that unquestionably are "religious" in the eyes of almost everyone.

The second premise of Stark and Bainbridge's theory is the oft-repeated maxim that "humans seek what they perceive to be rewards and try to avoid what they perceive to be costs" (1985: 5). It is this simple utilitarian adage that reasonably accounts for most human action, including religious acts.

The third premise is that the rewards people seek are often scarce, both in an absolute and a relative sense, and throughout human history some of the most desired rewards seem to be things that are not readily available at all, like life after death or an end to suffering.

The fourth and final premise is that, in the absence of some real rewards, people often create and exchange what Stark and Bainbridge called *compensators*, promises of reward at some later time or in some other place, which range from the specific to the highly general. When a parent promises a future trip to the amusement park to a child in exchange for chores done around the house, a specific compensator is being invoked. The promises of a happy life, knowledge of the meaning of life, or immortality, common to the religions of the world, are obviously very general. These most general of compensators can be provided only, Stark and Bainbridge asserted, through the assumption of the intervention of some supernatural agency.

Combining these four simple premises, Stark and Bainbridge (1985: 8) proposed that religions should be viewed as "human organizations primarily engaged in providing general compensa-tors based on supernatural assumptions." Seen in such a light, they think there is little reason to be pessimistic about the future of religion. For history suggests that "so long as humans intensely seek certain rewards of great magnitude that remain unavailable through direct actions, they will be able to obtain credible compensators only from sources predicated on the supernatural. In this market, no purely naturalistic ideologies can compete. Systems of thought that reject the supernatural lack all means to promise credibly such rewards as eternal life in any fashion. Similarly naturalistic philosophies can argue that statements such as "What is the meaning of life?" or "What is the purpose of the universe?" are meaningless utterances. But they cannot provide answers to these questions in the terms in which they are asked" (1985: 7–8). Implicitly, like Weber before them, Stark and Bainbridge posited that humans inherently need to live in a meaningful world and neither the wonders of modern science nor the material abundance of advanced industrial societies have displaced this need and the consequent quest for supernatural reassurances. The configuration of the possible reassurances offered, of course, is another matter. Religion, in their opinion is changing, not dying.

Secularization is indeed happening, but Stark and Bainbridge (1985: 429–430) introduced an important qualification to their acceptance of this fact. Continuing the economic imagery introduced by Berger (1967), they proposed that secularization is a constantly occurring element of all "religious economies," and not a unique attribute of the contemporary world. The process of secularization is part of the primary dynamic of religious economies, a self-limiting process that engenders religious renewal and not the sheer demise of religion. Properly understood, secularization refers to the periodic collapse of specific and dominant religious organizations as a consequence of their becoming more worldly, more accommodating to the nonreligious aspects of their cultural contexts. Contrary to Berger (and most other sociologists), in this more limited sense, secularization should not be confused with the loss of the need for general supernatural compensators. The reverse is true. It is the failure to provide sufficiently vivid and consistently supernatural compensators that accounts for the decline of established religions.

When religions become stagnant, when their rituals and beliefs become dead and hollow formalities disconnected from any moving personal experiences, there are two possible socioreligious responses: *revival* and *innovation*. Stark and Bainbridge associated the revival option with the formation of sects, and the innovation option with the formation of cults. Sects tend to be splinter groups from mainstream traditions that are seeking to revive what they think to be the original or pure spirit of the religious tradition they are rebelling against. Cults tend to introduce a more unconven-

tional mode of religious expression, one which tends to depart altogether from the dominant traditions of the churches that are being secularized. With time, Stark and Bainbridge thought, some sects and cults will come to replace the existing and weakening forms of religious expression. They will become the new denominations.

From this basic theory, Stark and Bainbridge (1987) deduced a complex series of propositions about the nature and dynamics of almost every imaginable aspect of religious life. One particular proposal that Stark developed further with his colleagues Finke and Iannaccone has attracted a great deal of attention and controversy (e.g., Finke and Stark, 1992; Stark and Iannaccone, 1994; Finke, 1997). Stark and Bainbridge argued that increased pluralism will increase the levels of religiosity and affiliation in any society. This point of view has come to be known as the "supply-side" theory of religious growth. The name stems from the premise that religious pluralism entails increased competition between religious groups, which encourages religious leaders (i.e., the suppliers of religion) to strive harder to attract and retain followers. It is this increased effort, Stark and Bainbridge proposed, and not some increased consumer demand for religion, that explains why a country like the United States is so much more religious than other Western nations. The United States was founded on the principle of religious freedom, as enshrined in the first amendment of its Constitution, and it has long experienced significant religious pluralism.

The Fusion of "Old-Time Religion" and Psychology

The rise of the New Christian Right in the United States since the late 1970s signifies a rather surprising revival of "old time religion" with its characteristic

emphasis on evangelism (i.e., spreading the gospel), the inerrancy of the Bible, and so-called traditional family values. The fundamentalist-led Southern Baptist

Convention is now one of the largest Protestant denominations in the United States, and across the nation the more conservative forms of Christianity have been growing at the expense of the more liberal and once long-dominant denominations like the Congregationalists, Methodists, and Episcopalians. In times of uncertainty and moral flux, many people seem to want religions with a clear and certain conception of what is good and bad and how to behave in the face of the growing temptations of contemporary life. They also want churches where the religion is deeply felt and experienced in a context of strong and uncluttered worship and preaching. They want the greater sense of community often found in such churches, as well as the blatant reinforcement provided for the virtues of the American way of life. As frequently noted by commentators, there is a marked element of resistance to modernity in these communities. There is a strong desire to place things firmly within a sacred context once again, to balance a scientific education with renewed Bible studies, modern medical practice with belief in the power of prayer. These new evangelicals and fundamentalists are, on the whole, members of a rising and prosperous middle class in the American south, mid-west, and elsewhere. Unlike their predecessors, they are now, more often than not, urban, relatively well educated, and make their living in the worlds of business and the professions, and not by the labour of their hands. They are the children of modernity and privilege, yet they crave the old style of religion.

But success brings curious consequences. Twenty years into the turn to the right in American religion, the sheer numerical prevalence and rising socioeconomic status of these people is producing signs of a greater accommodation to modernity, just as sociologists would expect. As Niebuhr argued long ago, in his classic study *The Social Sources of Denominationalism* (1929), the sectarian forms of religion tend to drift, with increases in size and the passage of time, into more the moderate forms of denominationalism. Is this developmental shift happening even more quickly today? One of the changes that may be indicative is the rise and growing acceptance of Christian psychotherapy (as noted by sociologists like Wuthnow [1994] and journalists like G. Niebuhr [1997]). A growing number of evangelical Protestants are coming to think that psychological insights and therapy can be stripped of their anti-religious overtones and delivered from a Christian perspective. Among the books on Christian living, one now can find guides on how to overcome co-dependency, manage stress, and live free of guilt. Enrollments are up in psychology courses at evangelical seminaries, and chains offering psychological services (New Life Clinics) have opened to satisfy the needs of a conservative Christian clientele. Therapeutic concerns are being discussed on religious radio and television programs, and 12-step recovery programs, modelled on Alcoholics Anonymous, are being sponsored and housed by conservative churches. Elements of this religious self-help movement can be seen in the spectacular success of the televised services and publications of Robert Schuller's Crystal Cathedral, and the popularity and controversy of the Promise Keepers, an evangelical men's movement.

Critics fear that the turn to the language of the therapist in the pulpit and the pew of even conservative churches will undermine the authority of the very theology of strict moral accountability and salvation by God's grace that seemingly led to the triumph of the New Christian Right in the first place. Is the glorification of God and the deep cognizance of one's own sinfulness that lie at the base of conservative Protestantism congruent with a preoccupation with psychological well-being, happiness, and self-esteem? As Niebuhr (1997) pointed out: "In voicing their concerns, [religious] critics of the Christian psychology movement are in effect raising a larger question: in the interaction of organized religion and the broader society, who is transforming whom?" Will the intrusion of psychology inevitably have a secularizing effect? Or, alternatively, is there now reason to believe that the faith of the people is strong enough to use psychology, and other aspects of science, without seriously impeaching the intellectual, emotional, and social grounds of that faith? Is the turn to a measure of Christian psychology simply a healthy organizational adaptation, another manifestation of the more holistic tenor of the times? Only time and the careful study of specific religious developments, like the theological and social effects of the support groups run in the churches, will tell us what we need to know.

Source: *Lorne L. Dawson, 1999. Written for this volume.*

Can Religion Make People Happier and Healthier?

A 1994 study focused on whether depth of faith and quality of religious experience has an impact on physical and psychological health. The study involved nearly 300 students at The University of Western Ontario, some of them affiliated with Christian faith groups on the campus and others not. The "affiliated" students, numbering 172, belonged to groups associated with the Anglican, Christian Reformed, Lutheran, Roman Catholic, and United Churches, as well as three major interdenominational fellowships-Campus Crusade for Christ, Intervarsity Christian Fellowship, and Navigators. A comparison group of 127 "non- affiliated" students was selected from undergraduate sociology classes. The sample was deliberately chosen this way, not to be a representative sample of university students, but to ensure the inclusion of students of different faiths and varying levels of religious commitment. In addition, only Christian groups were selected, to minimize the effects of other explanatory factors, such as cultural differences, on the findings.

Using a detailed self-administered survey form, the students answered a number of questions about their physical and emotional health, stress, beliefs and values, religious practices, and faith experiences. The data revealed that both groups of students had encountered a number of stressful events in the six months prior to the study. The affiliated group, however, reported slightly fewer events and, more importantly, they experienced significantly less stress re-

lated to those events than the non-affiliated students. On a standard measure of happiness or emotional well-being, the affiliated students also scored significantly higher, and believed themselves to be healthier than their non-affiliated counterparts; they were also less likely to have visited their family physicians, walk-in clinics, or hospital emergency rooms during the six months before the study. In terms of overall life satisfaction, the affiliated students were more content with all aspects of their lives and more likely to be involved in volunteer activities, both in their church communities and in the larger society.

The affiliated and non-affiliated students were similar in self-esteem (how much they like themselves) and mastery (how competent they feel)-two personality traits that help people deal with stress. What really made the difference, then, for the affiliated people? Was it simply belonging to a religious group or was it something else? Was it going to church? Prayer? Having a personal relationship with God? Having a strong spiritual orientation? Making a financial commitment to the church, either currently as a student or in the future? In fact, all of these dimensions were significantly associated with better physical and emotional health. It does seem, then, that there are important benefits to be gained from a strong faith.

A second study, conducted in 1997, using qualitative methods, focused on the mechanisms through which religious faith enhances personal well-being. In-depth inter-

views were held with 26 Christians, both men and women, ranging in age from 16 to 82; these individuals varied in occupation, marital status, income, and denomination. Despite these variations, there was a great deal of consistency in their views about how faith helped them to deal with the problems they faced in their everyday lives. They indicated that the sense of community derived from their church "families" was an extremely important contributor to their well- being, as was the feeling of hope that permeated their faith. They reported that their beliefs provided a framework for decision-making and for interpreting and understanding events in their lives. They found that the rituals and practises of their churches gave them structure and comfort in daily life. Their belief in eternal life gave them a sense of hope, even when things were going badly around them. Taken together, all of these mechanisms seemed to contribute to an overall feeling of peace in their lives.

While the similarities between these spontaneous reports from individuals and classical sociological theories are quite remarkable, no direct causal interpretation that would suggest that people ought to join the nearest religious organization can be made. Nor do the results of this study negate the general trend towards declining service attendance and religious commitment in Canadian society.

Source: B. Gail (Frankel) Perry, 1999. Written for this volume.

In most European countries (e.g., Britain, Germany, Sweden, and France) on the other hand, various forms of religious monopoly have existed for centuries. In these highly regulated religious economies, where alternatives to the established religions are discouraged, if not suppressed, and where the clergy of the established churches enjoy the security of direct government support for their parishes, religion has been allowed to wither on the vine. It has become static and unresponsive to the changing demands of religious consumers. It is this failure of supply, more than the changes in the religious market, that most directly accounts for the near complete secularization of western Europe.

Does this theory do a better job of explaining why the rates of regular religious practice differ so much between the United States and Europe? At present the jury is still out. Considerable empirical evidence has been accumulated in support of this proposal (see e.g., Finke, Guest, and Stark, 1996; Finke, 1997) but so have some telling critiques (see Olsen, 1999). What about the Canadian situation? Canada represents an interesting test of these theories of religion and secularization. We share much of our religious heritage and cultural environment with the United States. Yet, as indicated at the beginning of this chapter, the religious life of contemporary Canadians seems to be diverging from that of the Americans and moving towards the European model. What does the Canadian case tell us about these theories and thus about the future of religion in general?

Thinking further about religion in Canada

Canada clearly presents a hybrid case, that simultaneously demonstrates the utility and the limitations of the Stark and Bainbridge theory. In England, for example, the Anglican Church, also know as the Church of England, has long been the established church. Non-Anglicans were a disadvantaged minority in most sectors of British society until well into this century. In Germany, the Lutheran church is supported by tax dollars, and only fifteen other religions are legally recognized as religions (though hundreds of others exist). In both nations, despite state support for the churches, regular religious practice has fallen to about 10 percent. In the United States, as indicated, under conditions of religious free enterprise, the level of regular practice has stayed at about 40 percent for decades. In Canada, where no formal establishment of religion has existed since the mid-nineteenth century, levels of regular practice have declined to about 20 to 30 percent. But Canada's colonial history has produced what the British sociologist Martin (2000) called *shadow establishments*. In English Canada, the extended political ties with Britain made the Anglican and Presbyterian churches predominant amongst the social, political, and economic élites of Canada. In Quebec, the Catholic Church virtually ruled supreme, in defence of French Canadian culture, from the time of the English conquest to the 1960s. Things changed dramatically in Quebec following the Quiet Revolution of the 1960s (also see Chapter 14, Social Movements). With the rise of a secular form of Quebec nationalism, the state expanded its responsibilities, displacing the church from important social functions (e.g., health care and education) that it had continued to perform long after other churches had abandoned them in the rest of Canada and elsewhere. With this belated change, the European model of secularization has been repeated in Quebec. The end of the virtual monology of the Catholic Church did not open up the religious economy of the province to new religious competition and growth. Rather, in the space of three decades (1960-1990) the people of Quebec went from being one of the most religious populations in the world, by conventional measures like church attendance, to being one of the least religious populations. English Canada, where the presence of the shadow establishments was balanced by a greater measure of denominationalism, was less religious to begin with and has been secularized at a slower pace and to a lesser extent. But it, too, now seems to be emulating the European, more than the American, path of religious development. At this point, however, it is too difficult to clearly specify what might really be accounting for the differences between Quebec and the rest of Canada, and Canada and the United States. The Stark and Bainbridge approach is suggestive, but the situation is more complex.

Exploring the differences in religiosity between the United States and Canada, for example, the

Canadian sociologist Reimer (1995) found evidence to support the supposition, long held by others (e.g., Wilson, 1966; Luckmann, 1967), that Americans are not nearly as religious as they appear. A generalized commitment to basic religious ideas and at least modest church attendance seem to be synonymous with the American way of life. It is a part of the American culture and not necessarily an indication of greater or more sincere religious conviction. Fewer Canadians attend church, but Reimer (1990: 7) found that these Canadians display higher levels of orthodoxy in their beliefs and practices than their American counterparts. What is more, the differences between the levels of orthodoxy recorded for Americans who do and do not attend church are much lower than for Canadians. In other words, church attendance seems to be less relevant to the determination of the moderate orthodoxy, displayed by most Americans, than it is to the determination of the relatively higher religiosity of Canadians. Fewer Canadians may be religious, but they are more truly religious. The religiosity of

Americans, on the other hand, tends to be, as the American pollster Gallup stated, "broad, but not deep." It seems that the higher levels of church attendance in the United States may be a product of the cultural values to which all Americans are socialized, and not some true difference in the religiosity of the peoples of Europe, Canada, and the United States. In other words, the differences in the levels of secularization between these three areas of the world may be more the result of cultural differences than differences in the structure of their religious economies.

Thinking about these and other kinds of cultural and historical complications, another Canadian sociologist of religion, Beyer (1997; 2000), called the quest for some "master trend" in the development of religion in modernity into question. Stark and Bainbridge's theory should be superceded, he argued, by a recognition that several different, regionally specific, developmental patterns may occur, and that there is a third option: **invisible religion**. This is a term Luckmann (1967) introduced to describe the kind of pervasive, non- institutional-ized, and highly individualistic religiosity or spirituality practised by so many modern people. For example, reading the empirical evidence of alternative patterns of secularization, with these

Canadians continue to maintain, at least officially, a religious identification with the faith of their parents.

three forms of religiosity in mind, Beyer suggested that at least three different developmental patterns are emerging for religion in the modern world. In Europe, where churches have historically been at the centre of religious life, religious change has not produced a switch to denominations. Rather, religious change has been expressed through the enhanced presence of invisible religion that complements the continued presence of churches. Contrastingly, in the United States, denominations persist as the dominant form of religious life, but again with a growing co-presence of invisible religion. In Canada, as indicated, the European accommodation to modernity has been replicated in Quebec, while the rest of Canada has displayed a mixed version of the European and American realities. Most Canadians inhabit a religious environment of denominations and invisible religion, but the dominance of denominationalism is less than in the United States. In each case, Beyer observed, two things stand out: the co-existence of different religious forms and the strong presence of invisible religion. These observations are congruent with the religious trends that other sociologists have been noting, with an eye to the future of religion.

Religion in the Twenty-First Century

Many sociologist have been drawn to the study of what is new in religion. In Stark and Bainbridge's terms, a great deal of attention has been paid over the last several decades to aspects of religious revivalism (i.e., sects) on the one hand, and religious innovation (i.e., cults) on the other. In the United States in particular, but elsewhere in the Western world as well, the single greatest area of religious growth has been amongst groups like the Mormons, Seventh-day Adventists, and the Pentecostal and Charismatic movements. Likewise, there has been an explosion of new kinds of religion, ranging from Asian-based meditational traditions through to New Age trance-channelling groups, in western Europe and North America. It is difficult to gauge the number of people involved in the latter types of

groups, unlike the millions of people known to have been swept up in the surge of Pentecostal and Charismatic activity worldwide. Estimates of the numbers with some involvement in cults range from as low as 1 percent to as high as 10 percent of the population. It is the sheer existence, however, of thousands of truly new and unusual religions, no matter how small most of these groups may be, that points to a shift in the religious sensibilities of Western societies. The cultural significance of these groups, as the harbingers of true religious and cultural pluralism, clearly exceeds their present demographic impact.

In studying both kinds of groups, many sociologists are detecting a structural similarity in the kind of religiosity favoured, one that seems to transcend the differences in the specific beliefs and practices of the groups. Moreover, the similarities noted seem to be in line with broader shifts appearing in the religious consciousness of most Americans and Canadians. The new religions seem to be only the most explicit manifestations of a more implicit pattern of change in our society as whole (see e.g., Lucas, 1992; Roof, 1996; Dawson, 1998b).

Christianity and the Confrontation with Modernity in Canada

Since the advent of the twentieth century and the decline in popular adherence to things religious, Christian churches throughout the Western world have made a concerted effort to make centuries-old religious teaching speak with greater authority to the problems of modern life. Some observers of these efforts have argued that the response to modernity has ultimately been driven by a narrow preoccupation with institutional survival. Others see church adaptation as motivated by more genuine concern for the salvation of humankind. Regardless of motive,

however, there is little question that the innovations in church thinking and action in recent years—such as those apparent within the Catholic Church in the wake of the Second Vatican Council (1962–65)—signal a dramatic change from traditional church postures.

The confrontation with and reaction to modernity by the Christian churches has been as much apparent in Canada as elsewhere. Here, the significant changes in society and politics since Confederation have been coupled with a dramatic decline in many forms of church participation—most notably atten-

dance at religious services. In Quebec, especially, the traditionally high church-attendance rates for the predominantly Roman Catholic population have eroded markedly, with the most visible drop occurring in the aftermath of that province's Quiet Revolution.

In response to this new reality, many Canadian churches have moved gradually, but with determination, to reassert their place within Canadian society. For some, this has meant reaffirming and advertising a fundamentalist agenda,

continued

based upon a more literal interpretation of the Bible, in order to attract those who may feel adrift in the societal milieu of today and desire a return to more traditional forms of religion. The Pentecostal churches in particular have benefited from this approach. Even within Catholicism, the rapid growth of the conservative charismatic movement, with its emphasis upon direct personal contact with the spiritual, has raised more than a few eyebrows.

Still other churches, especially those larger institutions within the mainstream of the religious market, have moved to adapt to the new Canadian reality in a more "liberal" fashion, choosing to focus on the injustices of modern capitalism. As early as the 1930s, in fact, a concern for social justice appeared on the agenda of several Protestant church groups in western Canada. This "Social Gospel" was influential in the formation of the CCF, the forerunner of the NDP. Today, many of the Protestant churches carry on this tradition, speaking out on controversial social issues such as unemployment, Native rights, and, most recently, the environment.

In the Catholic Church as well, an intensive campaign was begun in the late 1960s to make Canadians more aware of the problems faced by the socially disadvantaged. In a series of statements released by the Canadian Conference of Catholic Bishops, that Church soundly criticized capitalist economics, and spoken out strongly in favour of affordable housing, the right to employment, and a more just distribution of income.

There is no question that the more liberal position adopted by those churches has attracted a new following and won much applause. Nevertheless, in some respects, the recent focus on social-justice issues has had some unanticipated and largely undesired results. For example, during the 1980s, the decision taken by the leadership of the United Church of Canada to support the ordination of gays and lesbians precipitated an unprecedented exodus of church members—many of whom were already dissatisfied with the organization's liberal politics. Informal estimates suggest that upwards of forty congregations and some 10 000 members had left the church by

1990. Some of the Catholic bishops' more controversial statements, such as their 1983 statement "Ethical Reflections on the Economic Crisis," have consistently drawn criticism from a number of Catholic and non-Catholic economists, politicians, and theologians. Moreover, the concern for social justice within the institutional church has hardly met with overwhelming enthusiasm among laypeople—so much so that there is today increasingly a turn to more moderate political commentary on the part of Canada's bishops.

Whether or not the churches' innovations-conservative or liberal-manage to reaffirm the relevance of the spiritual in modern Canadian society remains to be seen. For the time being, however, as Bibby's (1993) research has shown, many Canadians simply may remain content to relegate faith-related matters of whatever quality to the periphery of their daily lives, and turn to religion only when necessary to mark important events in the life cycle, such as marriage or the birth of children.

Source: W.E. Hewitt, 2000. Written for this volume.

There are roughly six interrelated features of this new religious consciousness:

(1) There is an emphasis on individualism. Not only is religion increasingly thought to be a matter of personal choice, the focus of concern is on what involvement can do for the individual. The social or group implications or benefits are quite secondary. Correspondingly, the primary motivation for participation lies with the development of personal identity, and the sacred is identified with a reality interior to the self, not exterior.

(2) There is an emphasis on religious experience. The demand for a moving religious experience has been democratized. It is no longer thought to be the preserve of the religiously virtuous. Rather, people wish to be moved intellectually and emotionally by their dealings with the sacred. Mere belief and passive faith are no longer enough.

(3) There is a more pragmatic approach to questions of religious authority and practice. Both aspects of religious life are linked now more than ever to the actual provision of worthwhile religious

experiences for individuals. Religious leaders must display their skills with some regularity. They cannot rest on their credentials.

(4) There is a greater tolerance for other religious systems, rooted in a greater acceptance of the relativism of all religious perspectives. In fact this tolerance often crosses over into a pragmatic **syncretism**, in which beliefs and practices from different traditions are integrated into new systems.

(5) There is a greater emphasis on a holistic approach to life. The traditional dualisms (either/or) of Western culture are either rejected or reduced in scope and significance. This applies to the dualisms of God and humanity, the transcendent and the immanent, the spiritual and the material, humanity and nature, the mind and the body, male and female, good and evil, and science and religion.

(6) There is a greater suspicion of institutionalization and a preference for more organizational openness. Networks of small, grass-roots communities are favoured, to protect the focus on the individual and the here and now, over the formation of bureaucracies justified by claims of efficiency.

None of these features of the new emerging religious consciousness is particularly new in itself. All these features have precedents in the religious history of the West, and the turn to individualism, experience, and pragmatism is rather characteristic of American culture. It is the convergence and strength of these trends that has attracted attention. Will these trends persist and produce a lasting transformation in the form and style of religion practised by Canadians? Will the individualistic invisible religion of so many Canadians take on more visible forms and displace the denomination and the church? Predicting the future is a foolish endeavour, especially with so subtle and volatile a subject as religion. But these trends mirror developments in many other aspects of Canadian lives (e.g., how we work, play, educate ourselves, and engage in politics), and this continuity suggests the trends will last and be consequential.

Summary

We began this chapter by talking about how the conventional religious life of Canadians is changing. Canada was once quite a religious country, but it has been secularizing at a quite rapid pace since the 1960s. This is especially and most surprisingly the case in the province of Quebec. On the one hand, this decline in the fortunes of mainstream religion has brought Canada in line with more long-term developments in western Europe, though we are still more religious than the Europeans. On the other hand, it is putting us increasingly at odds with our close neighbours, the Americans, who continue to be quite religious. Whether this pattern of development will continue, and why, are open questions and the subject of much research. In all three regions, Europe, Canada, and the United States, however, surveys also reveal a continued belief in God and other supernatural phenomena, as well as an active interest in such religious or spiritual questions as the existence of life after death or a greater purpose to life. As a result, most sociologists now doubt that modern societies are destined to be completely secular. Rather it seems we are in the midst of some fundamental change in the form and functioning of religion.

Marx, Durkheim, and Weber, all recognized long ago that changes in the fate of religion were indicative of other sweeping social transformations. Thus each sought to understand something of the fundamental nature and functioning of religion. The social-scientific study of religion, however, entails grappling with three perennial methodological problems: How can we study a phenomenon whose ultimate nature is thought to elude empirical assessment? How can we define religion? How can we measure the religiosity of people? In each case, whether we choose to use a substantive or a functional definition of religion, a multidimensional measure of religiosity or not, it is difficult to capture more than a partial image of the rich and complex nature of human religious experience and activity.

In line with his critique of capitalism, Marx captured the primary role of religious beliefs and institutions in the legitimation of the status quo. He portrayed religions as human creations serving the vested interests of ruling classes by deceiving the masses about the true source of their deprivation, and persuading them to accept their fate as divinely imposed. More comprehensively, Durkheim captured how religion plays a crucial role in the creation and maintenance of social solidarity through the detailed study of the religious life of Australian aboriginals. Individuals and groups are strengthened in their capacity to persevere in the face of the trials and tribulations of life by participating in the religious rituals through which society worships itself in symbolic guise. Alternatively, Weber captured the ways in which religion acts, often unintentionally, as a powerful agent of social change. Seeking the origins of the spirit of capitalism, Weber argued that the Protestant Reformation represented the culmination of a religiously inspired process of rationalization that gave rise to the first true capitalists. In particular he pointed to the combined psychological impact of the doctrines of the calling and predestination in rendering worldly success a sign of salvation.

As the functions of religion are diverse, so are its forms. Sociologists have tried to capture some of this diversity with the development the church/sect typology. Framed in different ways by different theorists, this typology identifies how religious groups vary in terms of their degree of formality, institutionalization, and integration with the dominant society, with churches being the most formal, institutionalized, and integrated groups, and cults the least.

The contemporary debate about the forms and functions of religion is still framed very much by Stark and Bainbridge's theory of religion. They adopted an essentially optimistic view, positing an ongoing need in every society for the kinds of general compensators based on supernatural assumptions that religion uniquely offers. We are not witnessing the end of religion, they argued, just the slow demise of the form in which religion has been delivered for the last few centuries. In general, religions actually succeed better, they reasoned, in an environment of religious competition. Taking a supply-side view of religious growth, they argued that it is monopoly and not pluralism that undermines faith.

Applying the Stark and Bainbridge approach to Canada produces ambiguous results. The Canadian situation is marked by both monopolistic and pluralistic elements. In general, studies by Canadian sociologists suggest that the historical reality of religious development in Canada, the United States, and Europe is more complicated than the Stark and Bainbridge model implies. Cultural differences are important, and in each case we have the coexistence of different forms of religion along with the strong presence of invisible religion. This invisible religion is indicative of a broader shift in religious sensibilities that some sociologists of religion think is emerging. The new religious consciousness entails a greater emphasis on individualism, personal religious experience, pragmatism, tolerance and syncretism, holism, and organizational openness.

QUESTIONS FOR REVIEW AND CRITICAL THINKING

1.   To what extent, in your view, have the various forms of practical and theoretical reason (e.g., science, technology, or the law) taken over the role traditionally played by religion in society? Have you noticed any signs of continued or renewed interest in religious and spiritual concerns among your friends, or in your community?

2.   When you have participated in a religious service, baptism, marriage, or funeral, did you experience some of the elements of the collective conscience and collective effervescence discussed by Durkheim? If so, describe the feelings you experienced.

3.   Design a small empirical study to test some aspects of the Stark-Bainbridge theory of religion.

4.   Attend a religious service of a religion at a different level of institutionalization than your own. What differences can you note? Is what the chapter says about institutionalization borne out?

KEY TERMS

SUGGESTED READINGS

Dawson, Lorne L.

1998 *Comprehending Cults: The Sociology of New Religious Movements*. Toronto and New York: Oxford University Press.

This small book provides a comprehensive overview of the results and insights of the social-scientific study of new religions since the onset of the cult controversy in the 1970s. The discussion is organized in terms of six questions: What are cults? Why did they emerge? Who joins them and why? Are converts brainwashed? Why do some cults become violent? What is the cultural significance of the cults?

Finke, Roger and Rodney Stark

1992 *The Churching of America, 1776–1990*. New Brunswick, NJ: Rutgers University Press.

This award-winning book traces the development of religion in the United States, giving a good overview of the religious history of the common people of this most uniquely religious nation. The authors also explain and demonstrate many of aspects of the influential theory of religion developed by Stark and Bainbridge, in particular the supply-side theory of religious change.

Hewitt, W.E. (ed.)

1993 *The Sociology of Religion: A Canadian Focus*. Toronto: Harcourt Brace.

This is an edited volume with contributions by some of Canada's best-known sociologists of religion. The book deals not only with the principal theoretical issues within the field, but offers detailed descriptions of the state of religion in Canada today.

Weber, Max

1958 [1904–5] *The Protestant Ethic and the Spirit of Capitalism*. New York: Scribners.

One of the most accessible classical studies of religion, this seminal book seeks to demonstrate how religious ideas can have profound and often unanticipated consequences for social life. Weber presents the controversial thesis that Protestantism has been central to the rise of the capitalist economic ethos that has come to dominate life so much throughout the contemporary world.

WEB SITES

www.adherents.com

Religion Statistics

Ever wanted to know how many Hindus live in Canada? What percentage of the world is Catholic? This is the site for you. Search world religions by name and location and find statistical information on all types of faith groups from around the world.

www.web.net/~ccchurch/index.html

The Canadian Council of Churches

This site contains information on an organization representing Canada's main Christian faiths. Links to its various working groups, such as the Commission on Justice and Peace, and various ecumenical organizations, are provided.

Media

Nick Dyer-Witheford

Introduction

In recent popular films such as *Matrix* or *eXistenZ*, characters find themselves plunged into artificial worlds created by video games and computer networks, trapped in environments where image and reality are indistinguishable. It is ironic that such fables are presented to us by Hollywood, perhaps the most powerful of all creators of illusory worlds. But, oddly enough, we find today's social theorists flirting with very similar concepts. The postmodern thinker Baudrillard suggested we inhabit a "hyper-reality" in which the simulations created by television screens, theme parks, and digital technologies are just as—or even more—real than the rest of our social experience (1983: 2). How do you know, he might well ask, that you are really reading this book, rather than just having a virtual experience of doing so? Most sociologists would rapidly pull back from this philosophic abyss. But however wild such speculations may seem, they do identify an important aspect of society: the degree to which our experience is influenced by ever more powerful forms of media.

The term *media* comes from the Latin, medium, meaning "in the middle." In seventeenth- and eighteenth-century English, "medium" could mean a connection between two things, or a way of conveying something from one place to another (Williams, 1983: 203). People spoke of newspapers as a "medium" for communicating ideas to the public. This then became shortened to "media," the plural of the word. The press, and later radio and television, were often referred to as "mass media," suggesting the way these means of communication addressed a large, anonymous, and in many ways unknown audience. Today, when we talk of media, we generally include print publications—newspapers, books, and magazines; telecommunications-such as the telegraph and telephone; broadcast technologies, like radio and television; cable television; domestic electronic devices like video games and CD players; and an array of new digital means of communication, including computer networks such as the Internet.

Think about how successive waves of new media have altered everyday life. Only a few generations ago, most people had very little information about events any distance from where they lived. When such news did arrive, it was with an enormous time lag. In 1814 the British fought a deadly battle with the Americans at New Orleans, taking thousands of casualties, simply because news of a peace treaty had not completed the weeks-long journey across the Atlantic. Today, media technologies have accomplished what Marx (1973: 525) called the "annihilation of space by time," as the near-instantaneous transmission of messages around the globe makes physical distance less and less of a barrier to communication.

Consider also the ways media have reshaped our leisure time. Anyone who has visited a heritage house or historical site from the nineteenth century will have noticed how little packaged entertainment the inhabitants had. No Nintendos or PlayStations for them! Without televisions, CD players, or video games, they depended on reading aloud, or they made up games, or gave their own live performances of music and song. As you will see from Table 12.1, our leisure time today is much more heavily devoted to technologically based amusement. Just watching television is a major occupation of most people in North America, and indeed around the planet. In this sense, our lives have become increasingly *mediated*—more reliant on a technically sophisticated, socially organized communication apparatus that conveys, filters, and constructs our experience. Some theorists try to catch this aspect of our society by saying that we now inhabit a "mediascape" (Appadurai, 1990) or "datasphere" (Rushkoff, 1994) that is as much a part of our environment as the landscape or biosphere.

In this chapter, we review some of the approaches sociologists and communication scholars take to analyzing this aspect of our existence. We review theoretical models and the information society, and then consider the nature and scope and the media and audience reactions to it. We further consider the recent phenomena of globalization and cyberspace.

TABLE 12.1   Percentage of Canadian Households Owning Media Equipment

	1982	1987	1992	1995	1996	1997
Radio	98.7	98.8	98.8	98.9	98.7	98.7
Television	84.6	94.3	97.4	98.5	98.5	98.7
Cable Television	59.1	67.7	71.5	73.4	74.0	73.7
VCR	–	45.1	73.6	82.1	83.5	84.7
Camcorder	–	–	10.1	14.9	16.1	17.7
CD Player	–	–	27.1	47.4	53.4	58.1
Home Computer	–	–	20.0	28.8	31.6	36.0
Modem	–	–	–	12.1	15.5	21.5
Internet Connection	–	–	–	–	7.4	13.0

Note: Statistics Canada recently released 1998 figures for the percentage of households with Internet connections, which rose to 22.6%.
Source: Statistics Canada, 1998. Household Facilities and Equipment, Catalogue No. 64-202-XPB. Statistics Canada, 1999. The Daily, Catalogue No. 11-001, 15 July.

Was There a Gutenberg Revolution?

The theories of McLuhan and similar thinkers are closely tied to the idea of the "Gutenberg Revolution." In this story, the invention of the mechanical printing press by Jonathan Gutenberg in fifteenth-century Europe triggered a whole set of far-reaching cultural changes. For example, national identity was encouraged because print standardized the way language was used and stamped out local dialects; scientific reason blossomed because of the possibility of easily communicated and reliable knowledge, and so on. This view of how media technologies change whole cultures is important today, because the idea of an information revolution assumes computers and telecommunications will make transformations in our own culture.

But was there really a Gutenberg revolution? One fact that complicates the story is that the Chinese had invented the basic components of the mechanical printing press long before it appeared in Europe. Yet it was not widely adopted. A conservative ruling class, concerned about the effects on social stability, suppressed its use. In one way, this seems to reinforce the idea of the press as a change agent. But in another way it alters the picture, because it suggests that technological innovation alone is not enough to create cultural transformation without the right political and economic context.

Another problem is that the introduction of the printing press did not, in and of itself, increase literacy. The spread of reading had to await a number of other innovations. Some of these were technical, like the changes in the process of making paper that made the mass production of books and newspapers economical. But even more important were social innovations, like the gradual introduction of mass education. In fact, it was not until the mid- to late-nineteenth century that literacy rates in Europe and North America began to rise significantly.

We should remember that there are still large numbers of people who do not read and write. It is estimated that some 880 million adults in developing countries have never been taught these skills. Even in the industrial world, there may be as many as 200 million who do not actually use what little they have learned in these areas. This is 550 years after Gutenberg. On the eve of the so-called information revolution, one of the most basic social needs is not for computer literacy, but for the magic skills of reading and writing. None of this is to say that media technologies are insignificant in making cultural change. But it is to insist that social institutions are important, too.

Sources: *Adapted from Cook (1995); Castells (1997); Fjortoft (1999).*

The Information Society: Technological Change

In the Introduction, Chapter 1, you briefly encountered the ideas of McLuhan, arguably Canada's most famous social theorist. In his (1964) view, media can be seen as extending or amplifying the capacities of our sense organs, for example as extensions of our capacities to see and hear. The significance of any new medium is that it alters the balance or "ratio" between the different senses—and so alters the way in which individuals understand the world and organize their lives.

McLuhan's (1967) most famous slogan is "the medium is the message." By this he simply meant that it is the form of communication, not its content, that is important. According to this theory, if you are watching TV it is relatively insignificant whether you are tuned-in to *South Park* or *The National*, "trashy" drama or "improving" educational programs. What is crucial is that you are watching TV rather than reading a newspaper or listening to radio, or carrying on a face-to-face conversation. The mind-shaping factor is the medium itself.

Drawing on the work of earlier theorists, McLuhan proposed three great stages in the development of media. The first was the oral, spoken culture of traditional or "tribal" societies. The second was the era of the written word, whose supremacy was signaled by the invention of

Gutenberg's mechanical printing press in the late Middle Ages. The third is the current era of the electronic media. McLuhan, writing the 1960s, focused on television as the main example of this era. Many later commentators think his ideas are even better demonstrated by computer networks (Poster, 1990).

In McLuhan's view, each shift in the means of communication alters attitudes, institutions, patterns of behaviour, and modes of thinking. Oral societies were relatively balanced and harmonious. Language did not dominate any other sense, but took its place alongside other ways of expression such as touching, music, and dance. Reliance on speech implied small-scale communities, spatially close, based on face-to-face interpersonal exchanges, rather than large, anonymous structures.

All this changed with the advent of writing and, in particular, with the printing press. McLuhan associated print with abstract reason, and the growth of regimented social structures. Once something is written down, it can be separated from the context in which it originates, split-off from the speaker in a way the spoken word can not be. Because writing, unlike speech, is a relatively difficult skill to acquire it can be monopolized by castes or guilds of specialists who work in the service of bureaucratic or military empires. Writing enables the organization of vast, centralized administrative systems dependent on uniform sets of laws and rules.

McLuhan said that the dominance of a printed world fostered a one-sided human development in which all the senses were subordinated to intellectual capacities encouraged by reading. Print was linked to excessive rationality, linear thinking, and a split between head and heart. People in print-dominated societies, such as those in the developed world, were abstracted from the reality about them, regimented in their approach to life, and cut off from the richness of experience.

With the advent of electronic media, however, the situation changed again. Television, because it involves sight and sound, reintegrates the balance between the senses. Unlike print, it is image-based, emotionally exciting, and involving. The effect, McLuhan argued, is to "retribalize" humankind, restoring the immediacy and intimacy that had once existed in small-scale pre-print societies, but now

on a planetary scale, creating the "global village" (1964: 87).

McLuhan (unlike some of his disciples) was not a naive optimist. There is a dark side to his writing. Because media are extensions of our senses, when the dominant form of media changes, it is like a physical alteration to our species' biology. What has happened with electronic media is that our nervous system, our ability to transmit information, has been externalized, lodged outside the body at the interface with technology. We've been turned inside out. Understandably, McLuhan said, such a radical surgery can send the patient into shock, bringing huge social stress and disruption.

Nonetheless, most people have taken from McLuhan's work a sense of technological progress towards a more cooperative and harmonious society. Planetary webs of communication will dissolve boundaries between ages, nations, genders, and classes and enable humankind to form a single world community. Some passages of McLuhan's descriptions of the "global village" are filled with a sense of spiritual unity. Several people have linked this to his Catholic religious background and suggest his thought amounts to a theory of salvation through better media.

This vision of the new electronic culture fit very well with another popular idea of the time about media—that we are moving into a "postindustrial" or "information" society. The most influential proponent of this idea was the sociologist Daniel Bell. In *The Coming of Post-Industrial Society* (1973), he argued that North America was witnessing the appearance of a new type of society, to be fully visible "in the next thirty to fifty years"—that is to say, sometime around the year 2000. He called this society postindustrial to distinguish it from the "industrial society," which had characterized the last two to three hundred years, and the "pre-industrial" or agricultural society of the preceding centuries.

The main force driving the shift to the "postindustrial" society was the advance in scientific knowledge, which was now being systematically organized to create new wealth-producing technologies. This was associated also with other changes: a shift from a manufacturing to a service economy; a move from manual jobs to more technical work; increasing capacities to forecast the trends of social change; and a new "intellectual technology" of computerized systems. The result would be a society "organized around knowledge for the purpose of social control and the directing of innovation and change" (1973: 20). The birth pangs of this new society would inevitably involve dislocation, anxiety, and resistance to change. But the postindustrial-era society could, Bell argued, be a time of extraordinary promise—one that would finally escape from the poverty and class division of the old "industrial" society.

Bell emphasized the role of the media in making the new system. In a famous passage, he wrote of an "information explosion" arising from scientific advances and a:

Growing demand for news, entertainment, and instrumental knowledge, all in the context of rapidly increasing population, more literate and more educated, living in a vastly enlarged world that is now tied together, almost in real time, by cable, telephone and international satellite…and that has at its disposal large data banks of computerized information (1980: 526).

Putting the ideas of Bell and McLuhan together, we can make a tidy three-step model of social change. Preindustrial agricultural societies with their oral culture are replaced by industrial societies dominated by print media. These in turn give way to postindustrial societies with their electronic media. Many social theorists, futurists, and media pundits have adopted this vision. Some follow Bell in calling the new order "postindustrial society." Others talk of the "web society" (De Kerckhove, 1997) or "the network society" (Castells, 1996). But the most common term is the **information society** (Masuda, 1981).

Whatever the name, the basic idea is that the world is moving towards a new stage of civilization. The prime cause for this shift is the invention and diffusion of information technologies-machines that transfer, process, store, and disseminate data. The most important of these are computers and telecommunications, though some theorists also include biotechnologies that manipulate genetic code. These machines play a role in the "information revolution" equivalent to the steam engine and railway in the nineteenth-century "industrial revolution."

In general, this transformation is seen as a good thing. The promises include great increases in prosperity as new technology improves productivity, a decrease in the need for routine manual labour in favour of more creative and interesting jobs, a broader dissemination of knowledge, and, consequently, the potential for a more democratic and participatory society. Thinkers who celebrate the information society are not unaware of possible problems. Technological unemployment, intrusive surveillance, and electronic crime are all acknowledged as real perils. But they are represented as problems of adjustment, temporary setbacks, or avoidable hazards on what remains an ascending path, the next stage in the march of progress. At the extreme, some of these thinkers see the information revolution marking not only a new phase in human civilization but a new stage in the development of life itself, with forms of artificial intelligence as silicon-based successors to humanity (Kurzweil, 1999; Dewdney, 1998).

A great deal of this optimism is focused around new media technologies, for example, computer networks, fax, cell phone, and satellite television. These are seen as increasing people's choice of information sources and channels of communication. Because some of these technologies (such as the Internet) bring with them the capacity for a two-way, rather than one-way, communication, they enable citizens to be transmitters as well as receivers of information—active producers, not just passive consumers. The result, information-society theorists claim, is personally empowering and politically democratizing. The upbeat tone of such predictions is caught by one of McLuhan's collaborators, De Kerkhove (1997: xxxi):

With the common nervous system and senses of the world population now in the care of satellites, and with machines approximating the condition of mind and the minds of humans connecting across time and space, the future can and should be more a matter of choice than destiny.

Underlying many such prophecies is the idea that the real force propelling social change is the introduction of new tools and machines, including new media. Economic, cultural, and political transformations are seen as following behind. This concept is known as **technological determinism**.

Sometimes it leads to very blunt assertions: "because print standardizes communication, it leads to a conformist mentality" or "since computer networks are decentralized, they make society more democratic." Other versions are more subtle. But the overall tenor of the information-society argument is that change in technology is the driving force behind historical change. This idea is clear, powerful, and attractive. No one can deny that by pointing to the rapid pace of technological development, particular in media, theorists such as Bell and McLuhan put their finger on a vital pulse of our time. But precisely because their voices are so persuasive, it is important to look at these ideas critically. See Chapter 16, Social Change, for a broader discussion of change issues.

The Political Economy of Media

A contrasting perspective is provided by the **political economy of media**. Instead of focusing just on technological changes, this approach situates the media in relation to issues of power and wealth. Sociologists who study the political economy of media look at the social institutions that govern the production, distribution, and consumption of information. They are interested in who controls access to the means of communication, and how that control is used to solidify or subvert social power (Mosco, 1996).

As soon as power is mentioned, you may immediately think of government's control of media—and with good reason. In most social systems, the élites or classes that exercise state power regard control over channels of communication as crucial to maintaining their position (Innis, 1950). Conversely, groups challenging the established regime have consistently seen access to the media as critical to mobilizing support for their cause. Media have therefore been centrally involved in conflicts over state power.

Much of our thinking about media has historical roots in such a struggle (Keane, 1990). In eighteenth-century Europe and North America, monarchical and aristocratic regimes attempted to limit access to the new media of the day (printed books and

newspapers) by taxation, and to control their content through censorship. The revolutionary forces that would give rise to parliamentary democracy—mostly middle-class radicals and working-class movements—fought fierce battles in the subterranean world of coffee-house conversation, clandestine bookstores, street-corner pamphleteering, and illegal newspaper printing. These struggles for freedom of assembly and freedom of the press have marked our society. Today, the existence of what is sometimes called a "public sphere," where opinion and discussion can circulate without government interference, is regarded as a central element in liberal democracy (Habermas, 1989).

Even in these democracies, however, government plays an important role in organizing media. Radio and television broadcasting have been arenas of high involvement. To avoid chaos on the airwaves, government regulates the allocation of channels. But beyond this, the reach and pervasiveness of broadcasting systems mean they are often seen as affecting society at large, and therefore the proper concern of government. For example, the provision of reliable news, impartial election coverage, or high-quality children's programming is often seen as a "public good" that should be provided even if it is not commercially profitable. Conversely, violent or sexually explicit radio or TV programs have been suspected of having damaging effects that warrant a higher degree of governmental regulation than print media. Broadcast systems are also often seen as crucial to maintaining national identity. In Canada, for example, the attempt to preserve our culture from invasion via the airwaves by U.S. commercial media led to the creation of national, public broadcasting corporation (the CBC) and various "Canadian content" regulations.

The media systems of liberal democracies are often sharply contrasted with the state-controlled media of totalitarian or authoritarian regimes. Hitler's dramatic use of radio in the 1930s alerted many people to the capacity of broadcast mass media to shape opinion in the service of a political agenda. This example, and that of the Soviet Union under Stalin, have given us the image, unforgettably captured in George Orwell's *1984*, of the state that uses the media both to transmit propaganda to its citizens and to gather information about them through ceaseless surveillance. One of the great

The sector comprised of media, telecommunications, and computer industries is the largest and fastest-growing component of the global market.

hopes associated with the idea of an information revolution is that easy-to-use, speedy, decentralized means of communication will be **technologies of freedom** that empower citizens and make despotic top-down state control of media more difficult to maintain (Pool, 1983). The fall of state socialism seems to provide some support for this idea. Secretly printed or photocopied *samizadat* books and pamphlets, illegal radio stations, underground music, and computer networks all played an important part in undermining authoritarian regimes of the Soviet Union and Eastern Europe. In China, student revolt in Tienanman Square received global publicity from satellite television. But this did not stop the government from crushing the revolt; in fact, it used the television footage to identify and pick up political suspects (Wark, 1994).

A number of political economists of media, some influenced by Marx, others with different backgrounds, challenge the idea that communication systems in liberal democracies are in fact "free." Under capitalism, the means of production—the

technologies and raw resources required to make socially useful things—are privately owned, and organized to make a profit. This is also the case with the means of communication. TV, newspapers, film, radio, books, magazines, video, and other media, by and large, constitute a vast commercially operated **culture industry** (Adorno and Horkheimer, 1972: 120). This is a vital part of the capitalist economy. If one counts media, telecommunications, and computer industries as a single sector, it is today the largest and fastest-growing component of the global market.

In many fields of media, there is a high *concentration of ownership*, as the largest companies control a high proportion of the market. In North America, and indeed globally, film production is dominated by the major Hollywood studios (Paramount, Twentieth-Century Fox, Warner, Universal, Disney, Columbia); the recorded music business by "the big six" (Warner Music, Sony Music, PolyGram, BMG, EMI, MCA); and computer operating systems by a single giant—Microsoft, despite legal challenges. In a Canadian context, we can think of the leading role of Rogers and Shaw in cable television, and of the Southam empire in newspapers. A famous study by Bagdikian (1997) documented the intensification of this trend. He observed that in North America there are some 1,500 daily newspapers, 11 000 commercial radio stations, and 11 800 cable systems; when one adds in magazines and book publishers, network TV affiliates, and movie studios, over 25 000 media entities in all. But most are small, local, and subsidiary to or dependent on larger companies. In each field—film, TV, newspapers—there are a handful of "dominant corporations" that among them control more than 50 percent of the market. When Bagdikian published the first edition of his book in 1983, there were fifty dominant media corporations; by 1997 this had sunk to twenty-three. Moreover, although in the past, such companies usually specialized in one type of media, today the most powerful combine interests in many different areas to form vast media conglomerates (see boxed insert "Media Conglomerates).

Why should we be concerned about commercial media, concentration of ownership, and conglomeration? As Liebling, a famous American journalist, once remarked, "Freedom of the press is guaranteed only to those who own one." Many media analysts argue that commercial ownership introduces serious distortions into communication systems (Schiller, 1999; Garnham, 1990). The owners of the communications companies are members of a class of people—capitalist owners—who have a very particular interest in seeing society run in a way that allows them to continue reaping profits and wielding power. They will use their control over the means of communication to direct the flow of news and entertainment to support the social order.

They will screen out reports sympathetic to alternative regimes, or about activities that threaten their interest, such as trades unions, poor people's movements, or environmental organizations. For example, outrages committed by regimes or movements hostile to U.S.–style capitalism are extensively reported and criticized, but similar or greater atrocities committed by regimes sympathetic to U.S. state and business interests are massively neglected (Chomsky and Herman, 1988).

Media Conglomerates

A large corporation that controls a number of subsidiary companies is often called a conglomerate. Conglomerates can organize themselves through both horizontal integration and vertical integration. *Horizontal integration* refers to a corporation that controls several different enterprises in the same business, all producing the same thing. Media examples would be a newspaper chain, like Southam, or the group of cable companies owned by Rogers. *Vertical integration* exists where a corporation owns different stages or steps in a related economic process, so that companies under the same owner supply and consume each other's products. For example, a film studio that makes movies, owns a chain of cinemas that exhibit these films, and also controls the video-rental stores that sell these films and a cable network that shows them on television would be vertically integrated. Vertical integration can be very powerful, because control of several steps in the production process can block new competitors from entering the field by denying access

to crucial production facilities or market outlets.

Political economists of media distinguish between *general conglomerates* and *communications conglomerates*. A general conglomerate has interests in communications that are matched by or exceeded by its involvement in other industries. Two striking examples are General Electric, which owns NBC television, and Westinghouse, which owns CBS and also has major interests in cable televisions and publishing. These cases are significant because in both these cases, the major companies are heavily involved in nuclear power and weapons production—controversial areas on which impartial news coverage might be considered important.

A **communications conglomerate** operates mainly within the media sector. There is an intensifying tendency for media corporations to aims for control of as many different media as possible: news, magazines, radio, television, books, motion pictures, cable systems, satellite channels, recordings, videocassettes, and chains of

movie theatres. In addition, these giant companies, although nominally competing with each other, often actually collude through joint ventures and strategic alliances or by sharing members on their boards of directors.

Some of these companies are very big indeed. Time Warner is the largest media conglomerate in the world. Its total value exceeded the combined gross domestic product of Jordan, Bolivia, Nicaragua, Albania, Laos, Liberia, and Mali, and that was before it merged with AOL and then EMI. It is the largest magazine publisher in U.S., one of the largest book dealers in the world, runs the second-largest cable-TV operation, owns one of the six major Hollywood studios—and these are only a fraction of its total holdings.

These concerns are so vast that Time Warner could commission one of its journalists to write a novel, publish the book, market it through a Time Warner book club, review it in Time Warner magazines, and make it into a Time Warner movie, which in turn could be the source of further reviews and interviews and feature stories before being broadcast on Time Warner cable television. In the media business, this practice of using material from one aspect of a firm's operation in altered form in its other owned media is known as *synergy*.

Many of these mammoth conglomerates are transnationals, that is, based in one country, typically the United States, Japan, or a Western European nation, but operating in many others. The power of these entities raises obvious concerns about the displacement of economic power beyond the control of nation state governments, and the potential for censorship and control of information.

Anxieties about corporate control often focus on the power wielded by the individual owners of these giant conglomerates. The quintessential modern media mogul is Rupert Murdoch. His News Corporation owns over 130 daily newspapers, including the *Times* of London and the *New York Post*, the U.S. Fox television network and twenty-two television stations covering 40 percent of the U.S. population, Twentieth Century Fox film studios, the book publisher Harper Collins, and major satellite broadcasting operations in Europe, Asia, China, and Latin America (again, that's only for starters . . .) Murdoch was an ardent support of Margaret Thatcher, whose electoral success many political analysts partially at-

tribute to the support of his British newspaper empire. Murdoch is accused of exercising similar clout in national elections in Australia, and in city politics in New York. Ironically, he has even become a pop-culture icon: an evil media mogul clearly based on Murdoch is the villain of a recent James Bond film. But although the personal power wielded by such corporate barons is a real issue, concentrating on individual owners may actually obscure the larger problem posed by the overall system of commercial media ownership.

Sources: *Adapted from Bagdikian (1997); Herman and McChesney (1998); Barnouw (1997).*

According to this line of analysis, commercial media will favour entertainments that keep people in a buying mood and distract them from social criticism. Although nominally competing with one another, such media empires in reality act in collusion to maintain the dominance of a worldview or ideology. The apparent multiplicity of media outlets and channels celebrated by information revolution theorists is thus deceptive, because all transmit a common "corporate-speak" that hides issues of labour exploitation, social injustice, and ecological destruction in favor of an air-brushed depiction of happy consumerism.

Media Audiences: From Couch Potato to Co-Creator?

Up to this point, we have talked about media as a technology, and as an instrument of state and market power. But neither of these perspectives deals with media audiences. For a long time, the assumption of much mass-media theory was that

the audience was indeed just a mass—inert and manipulated. This was the perspective of the "effects" school, so-called because it assumed a linear, cause-and-effect connection between media messages and people's behaviour. Thus it was supposed that TV images of violence instill in people a predisposition to act violently. If radio stations broadcast messages favouring a particular political party, this makes people vote for that party, and so on. Such a view drew support from a bizarre episode in the early history of radio. In 1938 CBS broadcast, in prime time, a dramatized version of H.G. Wells's science-fiction story about a Martian invasion of earth, *War of the Worlds*. Thousands of Americans panicked, fleeing their homes and phoning emergency services, so convinced were they of hearing reports of a real event. This seemed to demonstrate a very direct connection between media content and audience behaviour.

This is sometimes called the **hypodermic model**, because it sees media as "injecting" audiences with messages that make them act in a certain way (Lasswell, 1927). The association with drugs is not accidental. In this perspective, media tend to be regarded as a dangerous and addictive narcotic and the audience as passive zombies or glassy-eyed dupes. Such a view is shared by both conservatives, who hold the media responsible for the breakdown of family and religious values, and from left and liberal critics, who see media as instruments of capitalist indoctrination.

Although this view is intuitively appealing, it has some serious problems. For example, it has been notoriously difficult to isolate the supposed effects of media from a host of other social influences, such as social class or gender roles, which are always simultaneously working on people. Moreover, in practice most studies have shown a variety of responses to specific messages, rather than uniform "mass" effects. It is also worth noting that few media researchers believe that media have taken over *their* minds; television zombies or "vidiots" are always other people.

These difficulties led some social scientists to search for new frameworks that credited media audiences with a more active role. The **uses and gratifications model** began to ask not "what do the media do to people" but "what do people do with the media." They looked, for example, at how watching television sports or crime shows might allow one individual to relieve frustrations with work, or introduce a sense of excitement into the life of another, or provide someone else with topics for conversation with friends or workmates. They examined how responses to media were altered by talk and discussion among viewers and listeners (Blumler and Katz, 1975). Rather than expecting all in a mass audience to be affected in the same way, this perspective opened the issue of media reception to a variety of response and interpretation according to differences of personality or psychology. The problem with these studies was that they did not say very much beyond the fact that varied individuals would respond differently to any given TV or radio program. It lost sight of media as a social institution. If the "effects" school depicted the media audience as identical and mindless clones, the uses and gratifications approach suggested it was just an aggregate of individualistic responses.

A new step came from the **cultural studies** school. This originated with British Marxist researchers who were interested in popular culture as an arena where contending cultural codes and agendas were in conflict. Mass media were sites where capitalist businesses tried to promote the values of consumerism, and governments to assert the need for law and order, respect for authority, and good citizenship. It was by distributing these messages that these groups consolidated their leadership or control over society. But the media were also a zone where these values and identities could be opposed and subverted. This process involved not only how programs were produced, or "encoded," but also how they were received or "decoded" (Hall, 1980).

One example the early cultural studies theorists examined in some depth involved television news. They concluded that the news is not just a neutral, objective window on the world. Rather it is a carefully constructed interpretation of reality, involving politically laden choices, selection, framing, exclusion, and prioritization. Suppose a newscaster begins a broadcast with a statement like, "In a turn of events that significantly worsens Canada's spiraling debt crisis, Wall Street traders sold Canadian dollars." This endorses the view that there really is a debt crisis—as opposed to, say, a rather routine economic fluctuation. Its position— at the beginning of the news—declares that this "crisis" is the most important thing in the world for viewers to know about that evening. If it is then followed by a clip of government ministers asserting the need for cutbacks to meet the crisis, the construction of the news implicitly endorses a certain line of economic policy as "common sense."

So far this sounds like some of the political economic models of how media reflect the interests of state or corporate power. But cultural study theorists went on to give these ideas a new twist. They said that what happens to the news depends on how the audience decodes it. People watching the news might accept the "dominant" interpretation, in effect saying, "Yes, there really is a debt crisis; we have to restore competitiveness, and social services have to be cut." But instead they might come up with a "negotiated" reading that accepts the broad picture laid out by the program, but with some qualification or modification relating to their own position and interests. For example, a student or teacher might accept the general idea of belt-tightening measures, but add that "education is not

Media Filters

A controversial analysis of the way corporate media shape world views was presented by the celebrated linguist Noam Chomsky and his co-author, political economist Edward Herman. They noted that one nightmare of society is the image of thought control—a world in which powerful institutions shape perception of reality, an accusation made about totalitarian societies. But what if it happened here? In fact, they argued, U.S. media, although apparently free, do control the thought of the populace, and increasingly the Canadian populace, by the operation of five "filters":

1) the size, concentrated ownership, owner wealth, and profit orientation of the dominant mass media firms.

2) the reliance of media on advertising as their primary income source.

3) the dependency of the media on information provided by business, government, and "experts" funded and approved by these established sources.

4) "flak"—that is, the ability of corporations and governments to discipline media by threatening expensive lawsuits in response to critical coverage.

5) "anti-communism" as a national secular religion and ideological control mechanism. (This was written at the time when the Cold War was still on [1988]. You might want to think of what has replaced "communism" as U.S. society's chief political bugbear-perhaps "terrorism"?)

Chomsky and Hermann tested their thesis by comparing U.S. media coverage of human rights atrocities around the globe in areas from Indonesia to El Salvador and Guatemala to Lebanon. They found that outrages committed by regimes or movements hostile to U.S.-style capitalism are extensively reported and criticized, but similar or greater atrocities committed by regimes sympathetic to U.S. state and business interests are massively neglected. They concluded that the U.S. media act on a "propaganda model"—one that is actually as, or

even more, effective in controlling public opinion than media in overtly authoritarian societies.

Of course many people strongly disagree with Chomsky and Herman. Some critics dismiss them as "conspiracy theorists"; others claim that their work focuses on a handful of special cases, or underestimates the independence of editors and reporters. Others say that while their theories have some truth with respect to the traditional mass media such as television or newspapers, the growth of alternative sources, such as the Internet, is enough to counterbalance the corporate influence. Nonetheless, their work is a serious challenge to complacency about the fairness and freedom of our own media system. You can see a good presentation of Chomsky and Herman's views in the film *Manufacturing Consent*, which is itself an interesting demonstration of the way independent media can be used to contest mainstream views.

Sources: Adapted from Chomsky and Herman (1988); Herman (1998).

---

the place to cut because we need a trained workforce." Finally, a viewer might make an "oppositional" reading, which rejects the dominant message completely. This would be the case of someone who watched the news and said, "What debt crisis? This is just the corporate agenda for cutting our social programs and wages and increasing their profits."

The cultural studies researchers put these ideas to the test by showing news broadcasts to groups of people from different socioeconomic groupings—managers, management trainees, shop stewards,

trade-union members, students from various institutions—and analyzing their responses (Morely, 1980). They found that the managers tended to accept dominant readings of the news. Rank-and-file trade-union members and students came up with negotiated meanings. Shop stewards and immigrant students produced oppositional readings from the left of the political spectrum, and management trainees made oppositional reading from the right.

What the news meant could not be decided just on the basis of how it was produced. It also depended on how it was received. This is not to say the program was just an ink blot an audience could make anything of. It had a definite structure that favoured a "preferred reading." But viewers are not blank slates waiting to be inscribed with whatever message is transmitted. Rather, they are active agents of interpretation and criticism.

The cultural studies approach differed from the effects school; it also was distinguished from the "uses and gratifications" school insofar as it suggested that variations in decoding could be related to collective factors, like class or ethnic or gender background. Today a whole school of media analysis rejects the idea of audiences as "couch potatoes" and depicts them as creative coparticipants in the construction of meaning (Fiske, 1994). This concept has been applied to many different kinds of programs-not just news, but also to less overtly political and more entertaining media products.

There have, for example, been several studies of the audience activity generated by *Star Trek* (Jenkins, 1994). In addition to their famous conventions, the program's fans, known as "Trekkies," generate a stream of newsletters, books, and discussion groups. These, in effect, constantly add to, reinterpret, and rewrite the 'official' *Star Trek* story. Audiences thus start to "poach" on producers' control over their characters, by investing them with an alternative life—perhaps one that more closely reflects some of the issues audiences find important. Much of this activity has been taken by women and often elaborates on the role of female characters, or adds dimensions of personal relationships that are missing in the TV drama. Each can be seen as an attempt to transform the series from the somewhat traditional masculine-dominated, science-fiction genre in which it was originally cast. Interestingly enough, with the introduction of a female captain, these negotiated readings actually seem to have succeeded in altering the predominant version of *Star Trek* culture.

By showing that people can respond to and reinterpret media in different ways, such **active audience theory** has made a crucial addition to media theory. And it has shown that this activity can be a significant element in struggles over cultural authority. But it is also important to acknowledge the limitations of this perspective. In focusing on the micro choices we make in interpreting media, it is easy to lose sight of the macro structures that shape their overall agenda (Brunsdon, 1997). Concentrating too much on alternative readings of a single episode of, say, *ER* or *The X-Files* can actually make us lose sight of the way all these readings are situated in a framework dictated by television networks' need to attract advertising audiences. A balanced media analysis needs both to acknowledge the power of the meanings inscribed by media producers, *and* to recognize how these meanings can be challenged and changed by viewers and readers in the act of reception.

Gender and the media

Much of the most interesting recent work on these issues of media production and reception has focused around issues of gender. One of sociology's major contentions has been that our identities as male or female, heterosexual or homosexual, are not biologically given but, to some degree, socially constructed. The images and messages distributed through the media play a crucial role in this process. A moment's reflection will suggest to you how images from television, film, video, and music define what we consider attractive or sexy, "truly" masculine or feminine looks and behaviour, or the "typical" conduct or appearance of gays and lesbians.

Many studies have been devoted to the media's role in perpetuating the social subordination of women. Feminist sociologists have argued that men have generally commanded access to the most powerful means of communication of the age. For example, think of the monopoly of predominantly male clerics over reading and writing in the medieval period (Spender, 1995). Despite the prominence of female stars and performers in the contemporary media, a number of studies suggest that, behind the scenes, men continue to occupy a majority of the crucial positions in media ownership, management, and production. Given this, it is perhaps hardly surprising that media are full of stereotypical images and messages that support masculine control over women (see also Chapter 7, Gender Relations). For example, Mulvey (1977: 21), the film theorist, argued that mainstream Hollywood films are constructed for the pleasure of the "male gaze," which makes women objects of voyeuristic spectacle. If all channels of communication disseminate such images, the information revolution is obviously of little good to women.

At the same time, however, media have been identified as a crucial arena in which sexist images and messages can be changed (Allen, Rusk, and Kaufman, 1998). Some of the most interesting debates in this field have focused on "soap operas"—television dramas that deal with everyday events of family, domesticity, and romance. These have long been regarded as typically "female" programs, in contrast to "masculine" news, sports, or action movies. Indeed, the "soaps" were so-called because such shows were at first sponsored on radio by Proctor and Gamble, a producer of domestic cleaners and detergents, to attract the female viewers to whom their products could be advertised.

Advertising

If you were asked what you saw on television last night, you might give the name of a few programs (unless you were studying for your sociology exam). But you probably would not mention the ten, twenty, or one hundred advertising spots you were exposed to. Advertising is such fundamental part of our media system, that we usually take it completely for granted.

Advertisers buy space from media companies to advertise their products to an audience. The sale of such space provides the lion's-share of many media companies' incomes. Newspapers get 75 percent of revenues from ads, general-circulation magazines 50 percent, commercial broadcast TV almost 100 percent, and cable television around 20 percent. Even the media we do not think of as advertising-based, such as film, are involved in practices like product placement, for example, featuring actors drinking an identifiable soft drink. On the latest communication media, the Internet, World Wide Web sites are full of advertising streamers and sidebars inviting you to click on them.

All this means that advertising is very big business. In constant dollars, global expenditures have risen by 30 percent in the last decade, and it is forecast to increase at rates faster than general economic growth for some time to come. This activity is led by a handful of advertising agencies based in New York, London, Paris, and Tokyo. One of these, Saatchi and Saatchi of London, has offices in eighty countries and buys 20 percent of all commercial time in world television. A recent Pepsi Cola TV commercial was reportedly seen by one-fifth of the human race. While advertisers aim at big global markets, they are also becoming more precise. Broadcast radio and TV carry advertisements to general audiences, but media like cable TV and the Internet allow corporations to target smaller, more specific, and lucrative segments of the market.

When one thinks of the Nike "swoosh," Calvin Kline models, Roger's advertisements for its "Wave" Internet service, or McDonald's "golden arches," it is clear that advertising is a major force in our culture. It offers images and messages that enter our perceptions of good fun, sex, technology, food, and just about everything else under the sun. Liess,, Kline, and Jhally (1986) spoke about this process as the creation of a discourse "which bonds together images of persons, products, and well-being." Advertising is a form of communication in which people's sense of identity is strongly associated with particular preferences for consumer goods.

There is, of course, enormous debate as to whether this is positive or negative. Advertising's supporters say that it provides a source of funding that assures the media of independence from government and funds free television programs for large numbers of people. They say that, despite occasional abuses, advertising plays a valuable role in informing the public about the availability, merits, and competing prices of goods. They argue that advertising's images are just our society's version of a more general process by which people across all cultures define their sense of identity and status via material possessions. And they point out that many ads are creative and entertaining.

But critics say that the costs of advertising are born by consumers at the point of purchase of advertised goods, where they becomes part of the final price. They say the need to procure advertising

continued

influences the content of the media. Sometimes an advertiser will specify what content may or may not accompany their ad. But, more generally, dependence on advertising revenues orients media to "lifestyle" issues that encourage people to spend on fashion, holiday, homes, and toys, and away from hard news or controversial topics that might break the "buying mood." Advertising revenues encourage media to cater to the affluent consumers advertisers are most interested in reaching, excluding the views and interests of those who do not have buying power. On top of all this, critics accuse advertising of making people acquisitive and fostering "false needs." They say advertisements encourage unrealistic and unattainable expectations about lifestyle and body-image, promote some very dangerous practices, like smoking, and, by constantly exhorting us to consume, contribute to the load our economy places on the environment.

Wherever you stand on these issues, one thing about which there is no doubt is that advertising is everywhere. It is estimated than in North America a child may well see thirty to forty thousand commercial messages a year. Try a thought experiment. Think of all the ads you saw or heard yesterday—in newspapers, on radio and television, on billboards and signs, and on the Internet-from the time you got up to the time you went to sleep. Then imagine that all these images and slogans had been exhorting you, not to buy things, but to, say, recycle used products, reduce world poverty, or follow a particular religious faith. Think about what it would do to your mind to be surrounded by a media system that depended on those kinds of message. Then you will probably understand what Williams(1980) was getting at when he called advertising "the propaganda of capitalism."

Sources: *Adapted from Leiss, Kline, and Jhally (1986); Williams (1980); Frederick, (1993); Herman and McChesney (1997).*

This was part of a larger pattern. When media-based advertising got into full swing in the early twentieth century, women were very rapidly targeted as a key audience (Spigel, 1994). In the gendered division of labour associated with industrial production, men went to work and women stayed at home to labour in the house (recall Chapter 7, Gender Relations). Women did most of the shopping. They were also responsible for organizing and operating the new domestic appliances, from gas stoves to washing machines and vacuum cleaners, which were changing the household from a site of subsistence activities to a centre of consumption. Advertising was mobilized to win popular acceptance for these innovations, targeting women in campaigns that drew on traditional images of beauty, domesticity, and incompetence, but tied them in a quite new way to the acquisition of goods. "Soaps" were among the programs designed to support these campaigns. They were structured to fit the rhythm of a housewife's work, scheduled to punctuate the day with a break, but designed, to allow distracted viewing.

For a long time, soap-operas were regarded as the epitome of trivial mass media, and dismissed by male critics as mindless entertainment. Insofar as they were discussed, they were often criticized as vehicles by which women were passively indoctrinated into conventional domestic roles—as "good" wives and mothers (Mattelart, 1986). These assumptions were, however, challenged by researchers who studied actual soap-opera audiences (Ang, 1985). They found that such viewers were far from being mere sponges that absorbed what was presented to them. They interpreted and discussed what they watched, and sharply distinguished fantastic from realistic areas of the program. There was an enormous variety in what characters' viewers liked and identified with. Women viewing soaps did not show much sign of passive indoctrination in domestic virtue. A significant number identified not with the conventionally "good" heroines, but with the female villains who disrupt and destroy the stability of the nuclear family. They were sometimes quite open about how this expressed their hostility about domestic subordination.

The plot lines of these shows became topics for conversation among soap-opera watchers, which served as a forum for working out or discussing views about fidelity, monogamy, marriage, abortion, and homosexuality. Soap operas require an understanding of the nuances of human relationships, and the subtleties and significance of domestic interaction. Rather than being just vehicles for patriarchal ideology, soaps were a rich and potentially diverse symbolic resource out of which women constructed scripts for everyday life and affirmed important aspects of everyday life that men in general overlook or disparage.

A different but related approach to the gendering of mass media looked at the control of both technology and time in domestic settings. A study of working-class families in England examined the effects of gender in terms of power over TV program choice (Morely, 1986; 1992). The instrument of this power is the remote—which customarily sits on the arm of Dad's chair. Men usually have ultimate say over which programs are watched. The women do not operate the VCR to any great extent, relying on husbands or children to work it for them. This technological control (or lack of it) is important because men and women have distinct program preferences. Men choose factual programs (news, current affairs, and documentaries) while women prefer fiction. When men like fiction, they want what they deem realistic situation comedy, and reject the fantasy of romance and soaps. Men like news more than women, but insofar as women watch news they gravitate towards local content they consider relevant their own lives and that of their families, such as crime reports.

There are also gender differences in style of viewing. Men practice uninterrupted, silent viewing. For women, watching TV is usually done while performing at least one other domestic task or social activity. Solo viewing is a "guilty pleasure" only to be indulged when the rest of the family is not there. Men plan their viewing much more systematically than women. They also talk much less about TV with friends than women. Thus even if women watch less, with less-intent viewing styles, it is nonetheless a more collective activity than for men, despite the fact that men watch more attentively.

These different viewing styles are, the researchers argued, not biologically fixed attributes, but rather have to do with the cultural and economic shaping of female and male roles. The dominant model of gender relations is one in which the home

is defined for men primarily as a site of leisure, in distinction from the industrial time of their employment. For women, the home is primarily a sphere of work, whether or not they also work outside the home. Television viewing is therefore something men are better placed to do whole-heartedly, and which women seem only to be able to do distractedly because of their continuing sense of domestic responsibility. Significantly, some of these patterns—such as control of the remote—change when women are wage earners and men are unemployed (Morley, 1992).

Of course, the gendered division of labour on which soap-opera TV culture was first founded has slowly been eroding. This process has been both reflected and reinforced by changing media images of women. In the 1960s and '70s, women became increasingly rebellious against stereotypes. Feminist analysis accused advertisers of portraying women only in sexualized, decorative, and subordinate roles, physically passive, emotionally dependent, and intellectually incompetent (Freidan, 1963). Reactions against such derogatory and demeaning images included defacing advertisements, product boycotts, picketing, legal cases, and attempts by women inside of the media industries to alter advertising practices.

Perhaps in response to this media activism, the last two decades have seen some significant alteration in the patterns of representation of women (and men) in television advertising, and the programs it supports. Although there are still plenty of images of smiling housewives and seductive sex mannequins, a growing proportion of consumer-goods advertising stresses women's expanding opportunities for achieving success and equality. TV is full of new images: professional or career women, sublimely self-confident and secure, poised, effortlessly beautiful, independent, and successful—liberated, yet feminine and romantic. Analysts are divided as to the significance of this shift. Some see this as emancipatory. Others believe that "super-woman ads" simply create a yet more demanding ideal image of femininity, in which women have to be professionally successful, caring mothers, and stunningly good looking all at the same time (Goldman, 1992).

There is, however, little doubt that both within individual ads and across the entire span of advertising a more complex cultural construction of gender identities is gradually emerging. Increasingly, men are targeted for a similar range of fashion, cosmetic, and exercise regimes (Kervin, 1990). To some extent, advertisers' representation of domestic work has also changed; it is not unusual today to see images featuring fathers taking care of children. There has also been some alteration in the predominantly heterosexist codes of advertising. Homosexuality was long taboo to the advertising agencies. Outside of publications or programs specifically aimed at the gay or lesbian communities, overtly homosexual representation is still largely excluded. Some analysts, however, argue that certain media—for example men's fashion magazines—now practice "gay window advertising" (Clark, 1995: 490). This doesn't make explicit reference to homosexual desire (male or female) but offers opportunities for readers to perceive it if they want to, thus creating a space for formerly inadmissible sexual preference.

At the same time, the gender codes of primetime television programming have also shifted. It is now common in both soap operas and situation comedies to see champions of "macho" sexist values held up as figures of fun or criticism. Programs such as *Roseanne* have played an important role in giving a public discussion to hidden crimes such as domestic violence and childhood sexual molestation (Rowe, 1994). The on-screen "coming out" of the central character of the comedy *Ellen* was widely regarded as landmark in making lesbianism more publicly acceptable in North America. Even the television show *Baywatch*, notorious for its displays of idealized heterosexuality, was caught up in such change when the decision of its world-famous star, Pamela Lee Anderson, to remove her breast implants provided a catalyst for discussion about cosmetic norms of female beauty. These examples show how media constitute a public forum for negotiation and discussion of gender identity in a society whose sexual codes are currently in a state of flux (Newcomb and Hirsch, 1994: 503).

These changes may be a direct result of the critique of media stereotyping made by women's organizations and gay and lesbian movements. But there is another factor. Changes in advertising's representations of women and sexual minorities correspond to major economic shifts. Since the mid-

century, more and more women have entered the paid workforce, and thus gained independent control of their income. This has given advertisers and media producers an incentive to appeal to potential female buyers on a new basis. Similarly, alterations in the acceptability of homosexuality in media come at least in part from corporate recognition that the gay and lesbian community constitutes a demographically attractive consumer market (Lowe, 1995). The striving of women and sexual minorities for more equitable media treatment may thus be achieved because, while "sex sells," it is just as important that "money talks."

Violence in the Media

An issue where sociological analysis is at the centre of fierce public controversy is that of media violence. Representations of violence abound in our culture. Many popular books, comics, film and television, and, most recently, video games, involve the depiction of death and injury. Thrillers, detective shows, westerns, war films, horror shows, and even many cartoons all, although in different ways, hinge on violent encounters. The relationship, if any, between this simulated mayhem and the actual incidence of murder, assault, and other violent crimes is hotly debated. Indeed, as one writer observed, the topic of television violence alone "may qualify for some sort of world record" in the number of research studies devoted to it (Cashmore, 1994: 59).

Those who believe media violence promotes real-life violence base their argument on the intuitively appealing idea that people learn from media. Repeated exposure to media representations of violent acts provides models for behaviour that may later, under the right conjunction of circumstances, be acted out for real. This is especially the case when the violent acts are glorified or glamorized, or when those perpetrating them do not suffer any negative consequences—as with shows or games that celebrate killers who get away scot-free. Proponents of this point of view have been able to make a good case that the types of violence represented are becoming more graphic and extreme—consider the decapitations and disemboweling common in many recent films and games. Not surprisingly, such concerns tend to focus on the

The role of television in the socialization process is the subject of ongoing debate.

effects of media violence on children and adolescents, who are believed particularly vulnerable.

However, skeptics have a number of counter-arguments. Though the idea that we learn by media example is an attractive one, there is a contrary and equally intuitive theory about the psychological effects of violent spectacles. This says that vicariously experiencing aggression provides a *substitute* for actually expressing it, and acts as a sort of "safety valve." We can call this the **surrogate theory**. So, if you have had an unpleasant confrontation with the boss, going home and playing a few levels of a gory video game such as *Quake* is more likely to work off the frustration and help you calm down than inspire you to check into work next day with a semi-automatic. Further, it is often argued, the idea that media violence is some recent and awful invention is nonsense. Our myths and stories have always found fascination in the violent and gruesome; a glance at traditional children's fairy stories will reveal enough cut-off fingers, beheadings, and general cruelty to keep even Freddy Kruger happy. These stories have played an important and useful part in coming to terms with the "dark side" of our psyches. If we are searching for the causes of violent crime, the skeptics say, there are much more important places to look than media: poverty, drugs, family disintegration, the availability of guns, and so on.

But the critics of media violence come right back with rebuttals. Media industries themselves seem to subscribe to the idea that they are modelling actual behaviour. On what else is advertising, on which television relies for its revenues, based, other than learning by watching? Moreover, to suggest that video games and films are no more dangerous than traditional stories ignores their new level of technological realism and immediacy. In an influential book, Grossman (1995), a psychologist and military officer, pointed out that exposure to elaborate simulations of violence is precisely the way armies increase the deadliness of their soldiers. He suggested that the proliferation of violent video games and films amounts to a sort of informal training to kill, administered to a youthful population.

Faced with this array of arguments, all plausible, yet totally contradictory, what is a media analyst to do? The answer may seem obvious: set up an experiment to test the competing hypotheses. The media violence debate is, however, a startling demonstration of just how difficult it is to convincingly test sociological theories. Many researchers have tried to demonstrate the effects of media violence on experimental subjects. An early, famous experiment was conducted in the 1960s in which two groups of children were shown different pieces of film in which a human interacted with an inflatable, three-foot doll—known as the "Bobo doll." In one film, an adult beats Bobo with a mallet; in the other, Bobo is treated gently. After watching the film, children were left alone with a similar doll. The group who had seen the gentle film treated Bobo nicely, while those who had viewed the violent film gave him a distinctly rough time. Bandura, Ross, and Ross (1963) claimed the children's behaviour had been learned through simple observation and mimicry.

Subsequently there have been many similar but more sophisticated tests. The majority, though by no means all, conclude that exposure to media violence leads to effects such as **desensitization—**

A New Media Industry: Video Games

New technologies are constantly spurring the creation of new media industries. One of the most dramatic recent examples is video and computer gaming. Three decades have seen their transformation from a whimsical invention of bored Pentagon researchers into the most rapidly expanding sector of the entertainment industry. The U.S. video-game business is now generally seen as larger than the Hollywood box-office. Around 35 million North American households, between 30 to 40 percent of the total (and a much higher proportion of those with children), own a video-game system, while another 10 to 20 percent rent or share them. Globally, the value of the industry is estimated at between $10 and 20 billion.

The first digital game, *Spacewar*, was created on the mainframe computers of defense related researchers at U.S. universities. In 1972 Bushnell commercialized this innovation, launching Atari, the company that made the first home console system, an 8- bit mini-computer connected to a TV screen. With games such as *Pong* and *Asteroid*, Atari introduced video gaming to millions of households, and spawned scores of imitative companies. In 1984, however, the U.S. industry experienced an overproduction crisis, destroying consumer interest with a glut of inferior games. Thousands of unsold cartridges were bulldozed into landfill sites in Nevada, and the U.S. industry was all but extinguished.

Its revival was the achievement of a Japanese playing-card and electronic novelty company, Nintendo. In the 1970s Nintendo licensed video-game technology from U.S. producers, then developed its own consoles, and finally took control of the Japanese industry. In the mid-1980s, it invaded the North American market. Nintendo fostered video-game culture not just with cheaper and better game-playing machines, but by lavish promotional ventures, magazines, phonelines, and Disney-style licensing deals. By the early 1990s, its signature character, the Italian-American plumber Mario, had a higher name recognition among U.S. children than Mickey Mouse.

Eventually, in a classic instance of the technological leapfrogging that drives the industry, a challenger, Sega, introduced a newer, faster, 16-bit console. It supported this with an aggressively "cool" campaign of television advertising, aimed at older boys—a demographic targeting underlined by Sega's violent games, such as the notorious heart-ripping version of *Mortal Kombat*, which Nintendo, with its carefully chosen family image, had avoided. Although Nintendo dominated North America and Japan, Sega found a toehold in the growing European market, and support from a variety of independent software developers who resented Nintendo's strict licensing agreements.

Throughout the early 1990s, the Sega-Nintendo game wars drove the business to new technological improvements, evermore extravagant promotional techniques, and a steadily increasing share of leisure expenditures. This drew the attention of the truly giant multimedia corporations to the sector. Sony, the consumer electronics behemoth entered the market with its 64-bit PlayStation console. The industry experienced a short slump in 1993–94, caused by consumer hesitancy to invest in such "next generation" systems, but then resumed its growth. There is currently a three-way fight for corporate dominance in the console gaming field. Sony, the industry leader, reportedly has its PlayStations in one in eight U.S. homes, and derives 25 percent of its entire corporate profits from this machine and its associated games, with Nintendo in second place, and Sega a distant third. At the same time, digital play is rejoining its roots in the larger computer industry. Computer games, playable on a PC, rather than on a console connected to a television, accounted for many of the most popular interactive games of the 1990s, such as *Myst* and its sequel, *Riven*. Games now account for about 30 percent of all PC software sold at retail in the U.S.

Digital play is now central to North American popular culture. Lara Croft, the shapely digital heroine of the hit game *Tomb Raider*, experienced via the forty million PlayStation consoles sold worldwide, became among the hottest of current media celebrities. All the major Hollywood film studios have investments in or alliances with digital gaming enterprises. *Super Mario Bros, Mortal Kombat*, and *Tomb Raiders* become the stuff of films, television programs, and books, while films like *Jurassic Park, Blade Runner, Titanic*, and television shows such as *Beavis and Butthead* and *South Park* migrate into game format. George

Lucas's *Star Wars* franchise series has been converted into a series of successful games, and his software production company LucasArts also makes other games.

This may be only a beginning. Online gaming, played by connection to the Internet, has become increasingly important. Virtual communities formed around games such as *Quake* and *Ultima* are eagerly scanned by business analysts as areas of experimentation with e-commerce. Many commentators believe that digital gaming will play a major role in the commercial development of computer-mediated communication, and tout it as a "killer application" in the wave of interactive entertainment that will transform leisure time across the planet. At the same time, many aspects of video games—their frequent violence, supposedly addictive qualities, and tendency to attract boys and men rather than women and girls—crystallize some people's worst fears about a digital world.

making the subject less sensitive to real violence (Drabman and Thomas, 1974) or to **disinhibition**—inclining the subject to shed barriers towards physical expression of aggressive feelings (Berkowitz, 1975). There are, however, some that support the alternative "surrogate" theory of dissipated or reduced aggression. All, however, find a considerable range of variation in responses to violent programs. And they also find many cultural and context-bound variations, for example, with very different results from tests carried out in the USA, Israel, and Finland. To make things even more difficult, two researchers discovered intensification in aggression among children following extended viewing not only of violent cartoons, but also of *Sesame Street*. This suggests it is not the content, but the pace of a show-or perhaps even the very nature of television as a medium—that is aggressively stimulating. Lots of fast colourful action, rather than images of fighting and injury, may be the crucial factor (Cashmore, 1994: 66).

The problem with all these experiments, however, is that leaping from findings in a highly controlled laboratory to conclusions about real-life behaviour is risky. There are a host of other influences at work on people shaping attitudes towards violence—including family, school, gender, and class. It is very difficult indeed to control for these variables, to isolate the effects of, say, television. Even if we discover that people who watch a lot of violent television behave more aggressively than those who do not, what we have demonstrated is a correlation, not a causal relation (see Chapter 2, Research Methods). We have shown that the two things are associated with each other, not that one leads to another. Watching violent media and behaving violently could both be the products of a third factor. Perhaps, for example, lonely, alienated, depressed people like watching violent TV and are also more likely to be violent because they are lonely, alienated, and depressed.

Responding to these complexities, researchers have built more and more elaborate theories of the relation between media and real violence, such as the *reciprocal effects* model (Eron, Huesmann, Lefkowitz, and Waller, 1972). According to this, TV provides cultural scripts on which people model their behaviour. But so do many other features of the environment. What scripts are actually played out depends on the interaction of these influences. If children live in homes in which domestic violence is commonplace, or in a rough neighbourhood, they may pay greater attention to a violent script offered in the media, remember it, and maintain it for future use. So media violence may contribute to real-life violence in some contexts, but not in others. There is a link between simulated violence and outright aggression, but it is cumulative and variable, built up in an interplay with a variety of other influences. Sophisticated as this model is, when it comes down to policy decisions as to whether certain types of media violence should be banned, it does not provide clear-cut answers.

In this quagmire, there is one research program that stands out by virtue of its clear design and long-term investigation. It is the study of the so-called **cultivation effect**, conducted by Gerbner at the Annenberg School of Communication in

Philadelphia. This started in the late 1960s when the assassinations of the Kennedys and of Martin Luther King had raised public concern about violence in America to one of its periodic peaks. This study had a two-part methodology. First, Gerbner and his associates conducted a systematic analysis of the "message system" of television. They focused not on individual programs, but rather on the overall content of television, doing round-the-clock viewing. Using detailed coding systems, they charted the content of what they saw, to find out what the world depicted on television was like. They found it had a lot more men than women, more young people than old, more professionals and law enforcement officers than manual workers. It was also a very violent world. In the 1980s, for example, Gerbner and his crew found that "crime in prime time is at least ten times as rampant as in the real world. An average of five to six acts of overt physical violence per hour involves over half of all major characters. Yet pain, suffering, and medical help rarely follow this mayhem" (Gerbner, Gross, Morgan, and Signorelli, 1987: 445).

The researchers then took a sample of viewers and asked them questions about their perceptions of the world, to find out how closely they reflect the potential lessons of TV. How far are the apparent facts of television accepted as truth? Dividing viewers into heavy, average, and light viewers, they found that on many issues the assumptions, beliefs, and values of heavy viewers are quite consistent and differ systematically from those of light viewers in the same demographic group. They termed this tendency for heavy viewers to adopt a similar or homogenous world-view mainstreaming (Gerbner, Gross, Morgan, and Signorelli, 1987: 441). In particular, heavy viewers tend to believe that the real world is a far more "scary" place than light viewers do. Those who watch more television express greater interpersonal mistrust, perceive the world as "mean," and endorse statements that reflect fear and vulnerability.

Gerbner concluded that TV systematically "cultivates" certain perceptions of the real world, hence the term "cultivation effect." He did not assert that the heavy TV viewers' apprehensive view of reality would necessarily translate into violent behaviour. But he did suggest that as people see a violent world portrayed on TV they may become fearful, demand protection, and welcome the use of force by police and other authorities. They may re-create the world as television depicts it. We should note that this part of his analysis is speculative. Moreover, some of the statistical techniques used by Gerbner have been seriously challenged. Nonetheless, his research remains one of the most sustained, systematic attempts to demonstrate how media violence affects our perception of the world.

None of this, however, establishes an indisputable causal connection between media and real-life violence. So many attempts have been made that, perhaps in desperation, statistical sociologists are now doing **meta-analysis**—studies of studies—trying to unify the evidence from many different surveys and tests within one unified mathematical framework. A recent attempt claims to have found that while there is a statistically significant relationship between media exposure and aggressive behaviour, less than one-half of one percent of criminal violence can be explained as a media effect (Paik and Comstock, 1994). Even if we credit this finding, the conclusions we draw will probably vary: is the difference so small as to be insignificant, or is any increase in potentially lethal violence too much (Ryan and Wentworth, 1999: 60)? Opponents of censorship or regulation can easily argue that critics of media violence have not met the burden of proof. And even if there is some slight evidence about negative effects of media violence, they say, it is too slender to warrant the abridgement of valued social rights such as freedom of expression.

Those who demand an unequivocal connection will be waiting for a long time. No sensible researcher in the field would pretend that media are the sole—or even primary—cause of real-life violence. If media studies are to inform policy decisions on the issue, the question has to be what action is appropriate in an uncertain, complex, and tangled situation. A strict innocent-until-proven-guilty approach will not favour intensified regulation, since there will always be room for reasonable doubt about media culpability. On the other hand, in some fields—such as ecology—we are beginning to deal with more complex and probabilistic models of risk assessment. Perhaps some of these will prove appropriate for dealing with violence in the cultural environment (for more on this issue, see Chapter 4, Socialization).

Policy decisions about the controlling media violence are, however, not taken on the basis of academic studies. Indeed, from a sociological view, the issue of how these decisions are arrived at is perhaps just as interesting as that of the effects of media violence. In North America recent dramatic instances of deadly in-school violence—particularly in white, middle-class schools—has stirred a spate of public concern about what is now often termed "toxic culture." On the one side are coalitions of teachers, parents, religious groups, and real or potential victims of violence who believe their lives, or those of their children, are endangered. On the other are defenders of artistic and intellectual freedom, and media producers protecting very profitable revenue streams derived from violent shows and programming. In the atmosphere of alarm following the 1999 school shootings in Littleton, Colorado, and Taber, Alberta, politicians are under considerable popular pressure to introduce intensified rating systems or outright bans on some types of violent media content. Victims, or their relatives, launched legal suits for civil damages against films such as *Natural Born Killers* and *The Basketball Diaries*, which contain scenes similar to actual shootings, and against books and video games they believe inspired their assailants. One largely unnoticed but important consequence of these cases has been to raise the insurance costs for makers of violent films and games (Quill, 1999: 17). In the long run, these financial factors may have more results than moral exhortations or scholarly research: the actual effects of media violence remain uncertain, but the response of media industries to threats to their profits is more predictable.

One World: Media and Globalization

We have seen that one of McLuhan's most powerful predictions was that advances in communication technology would lead to the creation of a "global village," a planetary community united by electronic media. In some ways, this promise "appears" to be fulfilled. There is no doubt that new media enable images and messages to be transmitted around the world at a speed and over distances unimaginable

a century ago. We are accustomed to seeing live news broadcasts of horrifying or inspiring events from points as distant as Baghdad, Belgrade, and Beijing. Events like World Cup soccer finals, watched by billions on television sets, do seem like mediated global community experiences. Recently, these developments have been cited as evidence of a globalizing process in which media play a crucial role in integrating the planet economically, politically, and culturally.

However, global integration is not the same as global equality. Just as there are vast differences in the material resources available to different sections of the global population, so there are massive disparities in the distribution of media resources. You may be familiar with the observation that if the world was one village of 1000 people, 200 would receive 75 percent of the village income, and 200 receive less than 2 percent. To this we would add that the top 200 inhabitants would have 100 phones and 100 TVs, while the bottom 200 would only have two of each. Of the computers in the village, 90 percent would be owned by the top 20 percent of the population. At least 500 people in the village would never have made a phone call in their lives (Frederick, 1993; Golding, 1998). Media resources are massively concentrated in the developed world (see Table 11.2). There are more phone lines in Manhattan or Tokyo than in the whole of sub-Saharan Africa. As Hamelink (1990) put it, the planetary information society is characterized by an **information imbalance** that gives some people much better capacities to produce, record, process, and distribute information than others.

Some analysts see the ever-expanding reach of global media as a weapon of **cultural imperialism**. European nations once directly occupied colonial territories in Africa, Asia, and Latin America. But today, it is argued, the "developed" nations—most notably the United States—exercise a more insidious but equally effective long-distance, neocolonial control through economic and cultural means. A major aspect of this neocolonial regime is that developing nations are swamped by Western cultural imports: films, television programs, music, newspapers, and magazines. Indigenous ways of life are overwhelmed by an electronically transmitted global culture whose content is, in fact, determined at the centre of the world system, and

TABLE 12.2   Communication Facilities in the Main Global Regions

Region	Books Published per Million Inhabitants (1991)	Daily Newpapers per Thousand Inhabitants (1992)	Radios per Thousand Inhabitants (1993)	TV Sets per Thousand Inhabitants (1993)
Africa	20	16	173	39
North America	365	143*	982*	406*
Asia	70	63	179	69
Europe	802	267	628	3990
Developed Countries	513	279	968	494
Developing Countries	55	44	178	60
World	160	96	350	154

*for America as a whole
Source: Adapted from Golding (1998: 75). Reprinted by permission of Monthly Review Foundation.

whose advertisements and entertainment are geared to promote dependence on Western consumer goods and political systems.

Recently, however, the cultural imperialism concept has been critically reexamined (Tomlinson, 1991). The idea of Western media indoctrinating people in the developing world depends on a very passive view of media reception, of precisely the sort rejected by "active audience" theory. In a famous study, Liebes and Katz (1993) looked at viewers' responses to the U.S. soap opera *Dallas*, a program often seen as typifying North American greed, materialism, and sexual promiscuity. They examined the reactions of a variety of ethnic groups in Israel—Arabs, newly arrived Russian Jews, Moroccan Jews, and *kibbutz* members—and also conducted a comparison study in Japan. They found a wide diversity of interpretations and reactions. Some viewers "read" the show in a way to make its events consistent with norms of their own culture, for example, reinterpreting personal relations to make them fit their own codes of sexual propriety. Others recognize the difference between the values of *Dallas* and that of their own cultures, but see the program as a critique, rather than a celebration, of consumerist values, exposing the superficiality and misery of its characters' lives.

This finding seems to contradict the idea that Western media impose uniform values on international audiences.

It has also been suggested that the concept of U.S. cultural imperialism has been overtaken by the increasingly diversified international patterns of media ownership. Morely and Robins (1995: 14) listed the twenty largest global audio-visual companies: only six are based in the U.S., six are Japanese, seven European, and one Australian. Moreover, what were once regarded as "Third World" countries like India, Brazil, and Mexico have developed large television and film industries. Nor is it clear that transnational media corporations have an attachment to any particular national culture. When Rupert Murdoch's News Corporation entered the Asian satellite-TV market, it first attempted to win the Indian sub-continent with North American-style programming. But when this failed to attract audiences, the transnational giant entered into an alliance with a small Indian company—Zee TV—which produced a massively successful blending of MTV style shows with Hindi popular music (Thussu, 1998). Examples such as these suggest that global media are quite willing to cultivate and ally themselves with local talent, providing it can be made profitable.

Such developments suggest that what is happening is more complex than cultural imperialism. Rather than a one-way stream of media messages from the West to the rest, what is occurring is a two-way process of **hybridization** (Martin-Barbero, 1993; Morely and Robins, 1995). If reliance on standardized Hollywood products is one key strategy by which media corporations establish a world presence, another is the selling of exotic cultural items for cosmopolitan North American consumers. At the same time, people all over the planet are adapting, improvising, and changing media products, appropriating them to create novel and unexpected forms. An example would be the emergence of various sorts of "world music"—reggae, ska, bhangra, ethno-pop—that can variously be described as "Western pop-stars appropriating non-Western sounds, as Third World musicians using Western rock and pop, or as the Western consumption of non-Western folk music" (Wallis and Malm, 1984: 15).

All this has led some proponents of the cultural imperialism thesis to revise their arguments. In the "not yet the post-imperial era" Schiller (1991) agreed that while American cultural imperialism is not dead, it no longer adequately describes the global cultural condition. What it has given way to is a new form of transnational corporate cultural domination. The problem with this new order is not that it imposes one national culture on the planet but that it absorbs a variety of regional, national, and ethnic idioms into a single, placeless consumerism, in which anything can find a place—at a price. What this global commercial order squeezes out is any form of cultural production that is not for sale. Whereas before art was created in diverse contexts, as an expression of religious devotion, political protest, or communal togetherness, in the world market it has one overriding role: to be a profitable commodity.

This process does not unfold without conflict. Barber (1995) suggested that global media are caught up in a cultural contest he terms "Jihad versus McWorld." "McWorld" is the placeless, global consumer capitalism we have just described. "Jihad" refers to movements asserting traditional religious, ethnic, or nationalist identity. (It is important to note that Barber is not just talking about Islam. His concept of "Jihad" could also include

Christian or Hindu fundamentalism, or Serbian or Québécois nationalism). The faith or place-based movements of Jihad fiercely resist the dominance of the secular, commercial McWorld. Clearly, the giant infotainment corporations are among the most potent forces of McWorld. But, ironically, nationalist and religious forces also use new media. One can think of the way in which video cassettes spread the message of the Islamic revolution in Iran, or of the role of evangelical radio and television in creating fundamentalist Christian communities in North America. In Barber's view, the new planetary mediascape thus promises to be swept over by contradictory currents of both global and local identity.

Cyberspace: The Internet and the information highway

Of all recent developments in media, none has provoked more interest than the emergence of networks of computer-mediated communication, and in particular, the global network of networks, the Internet. The connection of computers and telecommunication allows messages to be sent with unprecedented speed and scope. Although in reality these messages exist only in electronic impulses stored in computer memories and whizzing through fibre-optic cables and satellite links, we often speak as if they existed in some distinct, new dimension. We talk of **cyberspace**—a term invented by Gibson, the Canadian science-fiction author (1984: 51).

The first steps in the construction of cyberspace were taken in the late 1960s by the U.S. Defense Department in its attempt to build a communications system that could survive nuclear war. Later, it used the same technologies to connect university research centres working on military research. In an unforeseen development, the faculty, students, and systems managers extended the network beyond its original scope, connecting more and more sites into the main backbone, and using it not only for research, but to exchange email, chat in electronic discussion groups, play games, and generally explore the new technology. Eventually, in the 1980s, the military withdrew and set up its own, separate system, leaving what had become the Internet to be managed by a decentralized collection of civilian users (Hafner and Lyon, 1996).

Internet use has exploded—in 1999 there were probably more than 100 million Internet users worldwide.

The result was a system that in many ways seems to realize the most radical dreams of democratic communication. Unlike one-way, centralized broadcast systems, with all programs sent from a radio or television station, the Internet is a decentralized system, with many participants, all capable of transmitting as well as receiving, allowing not just one-to-one but one-to-many communications. Although initially the Internet was a text-based system, depending on the on-screen display of words typed on a keyboard, by the 1990s the development of the World Wide Web brought both image and audio capacity. In North America and Europe, universities and other big institutions that pay a flat rate for their Internet connection are offering relatively large numbers of people access for little or no cost. The more affluent sectors of society can connect from home.

On this basis, Internet use exploded in a way totally unforeseen by its early pioneers. In 1970 there

had been fewer than a hundred people using the Internet. By the early 1980s there were only about 20 000. It is extremely difficult to find an accurate census of today's Internet population. Not only may several people be using a single computer connection or e-mail account, but many of the firms and organizations making estimates have a vested interest in optimistic calculations. However, it is probably fair to say that that as of 1999 there were more than 100 million Internet users worldwide, with continuing rapid growth (Matrix Information and Directory Services, 1998).

This activity in cyberspace has attracted considerable attention from professional and amateur sociologists. One of the most influential theories is Rheingold's (1993) idea of **virtual community**. The roots of his thinking go back to the German sociologist Toennies who argued that modern society was characterized by a loss of "we feeling" that exists in traditional communities and being replaced by an impersonal, faceless association typical of industrial, urban life. We shall return to this topic in Chapter 16, Social Change.) According to Rheingold, what people are searching for in virtual interactions is a way of reversing this tendency to isolation. They are migrating into cyberspace in pursuit of a "togetherness" lacking in a society fragmented into malls, freeways, and corporate workplaces. They are searching not just for information but for relationship.

Rheingold and other cyberspace enthusiasts suggested that virtual communities have advantages over ones based on physical presence. People can connect on the basis of mutual interests, rather than accidents of geographic proximity. Because they cannot see one another, they do not form prejudices about others on the basis of race, gender, age, national origin, and physical appearance. The anonymity of online relationships gives the opportunity to experiment with a more flexible, and fluid sense of self, exploring roles and personae that they might not feel free to express "in real life" (Turkle, 1995; Bruckman, 1996). Impressed by the capacity of computer networking to overleap censorship and political restriction, Rheingold and others hope for the growth of an "electronic civil society" reviving direct participation in political life and overcoming the remoteness many people feel from electoral democracy.

Others are more skeptical. They point out that the loss of physical presence in cyberspace makes it easy to misinterpret communication, opens enormous possibilities for deception, and removes many of the commitments and constraints that compel people to act more or less responsibly in face-to-face situations. This leads to the frequent eruptions in online discussion groups called *flame wars* in which people go on long and vicious harangues against people who have offended them. It can also lead to more bizarre problems. A study by Dibbell (1996) documented a "rape in cyberspace" when a member in a role-playing cyber community used his superior programming powers to inflict sexually humiliating behaviour on other participants' virtual personae. This violation of "netiquette" caused the victims serious psychological distress. It also raised a host of problems about how to expel the offender from the virtual community he had abused, and prevent his return under another virtual identity.

Critics of the virtual-community concept say that the more time people spend as "mouse potatoes," in front of computer screens, the more face-to-face community will deteriorate (Lockhart, 1997). In this view, rather than providing a replacement for the crumbling public realm, virtual communities actually contribute to its decline. Although cyber-communication may reinforce social relationships among like-minded individuals, those groups will have a decreasing need or opportunity to interact with other members of the larger society. One recent U.S. study seems to support these concerns (Kraut and Lundmark, 1998). The researchers found 160 people in Pittsburgh who had never been online before, put computers in their homes, tracked their Internet use, and then used psychological questionnaires to measures alterations in their emotional well-being. They discovered a statistically significant connection between hours online and intensified feelings of loneliness and depression. The researchers suggested that, in spending time on the Net, people were trading the "strong" social bonds of face-to-face friendships and relationships for the "weak" ties of the disembodied online realm. It is also the case that the lonely and depressed may be more attracted to the Net.

Although the debate over these issues will continue for some time, it appears that focus in cyberspace is rapidly shifting from "virtual community" to **virtual commerce**. The corporate sector did not pioneer the exploration of computer-mediated communication, but the unexpected growth of the Internet roused intense commercial interest. What signalled this development was the U.S. government's announcement of its National Information Infrastructure initiative, which would reorganize the already-existing but tangled web of fibre-optic copper wires, cable-radio waves, and satellites into a comprehensive, integrated network or **information highway** (Besser, 1995).

Business is interested in this highway: to connect customers with suppliers, monitor its employees, eliminate jobs, cut travel costs, and gather competitive data. Telephone, cable, video, and software companies are preparing to colonize cyberspace with their "killer" applications—video-on-demand, tele-gambling, pay-per-computer games, and infomercials (Gates, 1995). The experiments of companies such as the online bookseller Amazon.com, and the even more successful online pornography business, have stirred interest in all kinds of "e-commerce." It is widely speculated that some sort of fusion of the TV and personal computer will provide an entry point into the home for all these commercial digital services (Gilder, 1994). But to many, the so-called highway seems too close to the late-nineteenth-century U.S. railway development, complete with informational "robber barons" (Schiller, 1999)

It is, however, important to note that, despite the intensifying commercialization of the Internet, it continues to provide expression for a diversity of interests. Some of these are opposed to the corporate agenda. In 1994 peasant farmers in a remote province of Mexico launched a revolt against conditions of poverty and social injustice that they believed were being worsened by international free-trade agreements. This movement—the Zapatistas—succeeded in attracting worldwide attention to their cause by distributing their communiqués on the Internet (Cleaver, 1994). The use of similar online tactics by social movements in Canada and elsewhere across the world contributed to the defeat of a pro-business trade agreement, the Multilateral Agreement on Investment. International women's groups concerned about poverty and labour conditions have also been active in computer networking

(Sreberny, 1998). Incidents such as these suggest to some observers that computer networks may be less easily controlled by business interests than radio and television (Waterman, 1998).

Certainly, it is now apparent that cyberspace, far from providing easy solutions to social dilemmas, is as complex as any terrestrial society. In its early days, the Internet was often referred to as an "electronic frontier." Today, there is an ongoing debate about the appropriate reach for "law and order" on this frontier. The issues provoking this debate include "hacking"—virtual trespass and theft; destructive computer "viruses"; online "hate speech" and pornography; and digital invasions of privacy by individuals, corporations, or government (Friedman, 1997; Grossman, 1997). These issues are made more difficult because of the transnational nature of the Internet, which makes it extremely difficult to police. One possibility is that the Internet will persist as an area of relatively unregulated communication activity, with both the freedoms and problems this implies. Another is that the need to cope with such issues will be among the forces propelling our civilization towards more global institutions.

It is, however, important to realize that, on a world scale, very few people are in cyberspace. Even in Canada, one of the most "wired" nations on earth, in 1997—the latest year for which reliable national figures are available—only 17 percent of households had an Internet connection (Statistics Canada, 1998). Moreover, access is strongly associated with differences in income, gender, and ethnicity. Users tend to be drawn from the most affluent sections of society, with more men than women in cyberspace, and ethnic minorities under-represented. Although access rates are growing, and the gender imbalance diminishing, there is a significant digital divide that excludes major sections of the population from cyberspace because of barriers of cost, education, and time. Once we take a planetary perspective, these obstacles become vast. Less than 3 percent of the world's population is online. In this respect, we may be dealing not with a World Wide Web that links our planet's inhabitants together, but with a "World Wide Wedge" that splits them apart according to access to the globe's most advanced communication systems (Golding, 1996).

Predictions for the Future

Fears that civilization would collapse due to the "Y2K bug" (programming errors that disable computer systems from properly processing third-millennium dates) are a thing of the past. What of the future of information and the media? Over the last two decades, predictions about the "information highway," "500-channel universe," or "wired world" have become commonplace. These prophecies have often been optimistic in estimating the speed of such developments, because they tend to disregard the size and risk of investments required to construct new media systems, and the real barriers-in terms of expense, education, and habit—to their widespread public acceptance.

Because of futurist's failures to take these factors into account, it is sometimes tempting to dismiss their promises as just so much "hype." This would be a mistake. The commercial and cost-saving opportunities presented by new means of communication are so attractive to corporations and government that we can expect to see continuing innovation and applications in media technologies, and huge pressures and incentives to weave these inventions into the fabric of everyday life—in at least in the affluent, "developed" world.

Rapid expansion of "e-commerce"; the fusion of phone, television, and computer into various forms of multipurpose domestic communication devices—such as "Web TV" (combining both many digitalized channels and the capacity to "surf" the Internet or World Wide Web); the proliferation of hand-held and personalized computing devices, interlinked by wireless technologies; the emergence of new forms of simulation-based entertainment (of which today's video games are only a pale shadow); the elaboration of "virtual universities" and "telehealth" systems, orienting both education and medical consultation around computer-mediated communications—all these are very much in the cards now being played by corporate and state planners. If the game goes as they hope, then our lives will be dramatically changed; not necessarily transformed overnight, but nevertheless altered irrevocably and deeply by a series of incremental shifts in our habitual, daily ways of communicating. For example, it is quite possible that, within a decade, texts such as this will have a diminishing role in an education system increasingly oriented around various forms of online delivery.

However, we should never assume that this multiplication of media channels and information technologies amounts in any simple way to social "progress." One of the most extreme and attractive promises of the prophets of "information revolution" is that new media will create of a sort of group-mind or world-brain. In this story, the enhanced capability of the planet's six billion or so inhabitants to easily and speedily circulate information and ideas will significantly improve our collective capacity to solve some the formidable problems facing us, such as the preservation of the biosphere, the avoidance of nuclear/chemical/biological war, the elimination of poverty and disease, and the direction of our genetic future.

There seem at least two formidable barriers to the fulfillment of this dream. The first is the extraordinarily uneven social distribution of the new media. Even within advanced capitalist societies, the "digital divide" among "haves" and "have-nots" is significant; on a planetary scale, it is a gaping chasm. Without a systematic redress of these inequalities, connection to the information revolution will become a sign of global privilege, and access to communicational wealth will be seen as a source of intensified division, rather than enlarged community. The second obstacle involves the nature of the content filtered through the new media channels. Insofar as the emerging global media system is being formed primarily by commercial interests, it contains strong tendencies to select in favour of content that encourages, or at least does not challenge, the daily habits on which consumer capitalism depends. Advertisements, info-tainment, and politically innocuous content will predominate, while issues such as our ecological crisis and global inequality, though not completely excluded, will be marginalized and drowned out by the exhortations to buy and have fun. In this case, advanced communication systems may make us more oblivious to, not more aware of, the future dangers confronting humankind. Only if alert planetary citizens contest these tendencies to inequality and indoctrination will our new global media system contribute to the creation of a true collective intelligence.

Summary

We began this chapter by looking at the vision of an information revolution, and its promise of a world transformed by better communications technology. To many, computer networks seem like the fulfillment of this vision. The Internet and the information highway represent the latest stage of a process that, over a couple of centuries, has taken us from a predominantly oral culture, through the spread of print literacy, and into an era of electronic and digital culture. In many respects these rapid changes have meant huge increases in knowledge, creativity, and enjoyment for millions of people—a point we hope this chapter has sufficiently acknowledged.

At the same time, however, we want to sound a note of caution about the unqualified optimism often expressed about the information revolution. It is important to look not just at technological changes, but at the political economy of media. Control over the means of communication has always involved massive vested interests and intense social conflict. In liberal democracies, our political traditions make us at least somewhat alert to issues of governmental censorship and state direction of media systems. But it is perhaps harder for us to grasp the blind spots and blockages that arise from a market-driven media system, dominated by multinational conglomerates operating on a purely commercial basis. It is in this area that some of the most important critical media studies are now being done.

In studying issues of ownership and control, it is important not to lapse into simplistic notions about media audiences. We saw how straightforward models of media effects, which portray people as passive victims of indoctrination, have been challenged by theories that ascribe a much more active role to audiences in interpreting and criticizing what they read, hear, and see. The cultural studies school of media theory suggests that dominant values encoded in media products can be opposed or subverted by such audience decoding. This is a valuable corrective to notions of monolithic mind-control by media owners. In emphasizing the creativity of audiences, cultural studies theorists sometimes bend the stick too far the other way. But it is clear that media meanings must now be understood as arising not just in production, but also in reception.

We went on to see how these issues played out in some concrete cases. Studies of gender in media have shown that the major means of communication—historically controlled mainly by men—have played an important role in maintaining patriarchal authority. But they also show how media can become a site of struggle. Women have reappropriated and reinterpreted texts and programs that might seem just to confirm their subordinate roles and domestic identities. Through campaigns of media activism, and because of increasing independent economic power, women and also sexual minorities have, over the last few decades, significantly altered the regime of sexual stereotypes transmitted by the mainstream media-even if this process sometimes seems painfully long.

The issues of on-screen and in-print violence show how difficult it can be to conclusively determine the social effects of media. Both critics of media violence and their opponents have strong intuitive arguments as to why representations of violence may or may not lead to real-life aggression. Although the huge volume of research on the topic probably suggests *some* linkage, decades of sociological and psychological work have failed to give a definitive answer to the question, largely because of the difficulty of separating the effects of media from all the other potential factors causing real-life violence. This is a case that indicates how far public-policy decisions about media need to be informed by a recognition of the many unknowns in the media environment.

We went on to place media in a global context. Here, the paradoxes of the information revolution are clearly revealed. In complex ways, new communications technologies *are* making something of a global village, creating exciting transnational cultural cross-fertilizations and dramatic accelerations in the circulation of knowledge. But there are also staggering inequities in the distribution of information resources. Nowhere is this clearer than in the case of that ultimate information-age media, computer networks. Here we have to simultaneously hold in mind two apparently contradictory tendencies. On the one hand, the Internet is, in its speed and ease of communication, a truly global media. On the other, its use is at the moment limited to a very thin and by-and-large highly privileged strata of the planet's population. Our civilization has the technological power to create a real universality of communication. But a market economy rations and stratifies access to media according to purchasing power in a way that sharply divides the global population. This tension between the technological potential for truly global communication and the limitations our economic system places on such networks may eventually prove to be the central issue of the information age.

QUESTIONS FOR REVIEW AND CRITICAL THINKING

1.   Which model of audience behaviour best fits your own experience as a media watcher and listener—the "active audience" concept or the "hypodermic model"?

2.   Take several of your favourite television shows. To what degree do you think they reinforce or challenge gender stereotypes? Can you think of some ways to test this?

3.   Do you think that the media you encounter in daily life adequately inform you about the issues of global poverty and inequality? What factors shape their coverage of such matters?

4.   Have you discovered "virtual community" on the Internet? Is it possible to have a real relationship in cyberspace?

KEY TERMS

active audience theory, p. 330

communication conglomerates, p. 326

cultivation effect, p. 337

cultural imperialism, p. 339

cultural studies, p. 328

culture industry, p. 325

cyberspace, p. 341

desensitization, p. 335

disinhibition, p. 337

hybridization, p. 341

hypodermic model, p. 327

information highway, p. 343

information imbalance, p. 339

information society, p. 323

meta-analysis, p. 338

political economy of media, p. 324

surrogate theory, p. 335

technological determinism, p. 323

technologies of freedom, p. 325

uses and gratifications model, p. 328

virtual community, p. 342

virtual commerce, p. 343

SUGGESTED READINGS

De Kerkhove, Derrick

1997 *Connected Intelligence: The Arrival of the Web Society.* Toronto: Somerville House.

The author, who studied with McLuhan, updates his mentor's work in this charming and balanced example of the argument that the information revolution is changing civilization for the better.

Dewdney, Christopher

1998 *Last Flesh: Life in the Transhuman Era.* Toronto: HarperCollins.

A discussion of the effects of technology on civilization, not only the Internet and mass media, but also genetic engineering and robotics, as they lead us to the posthuman era.

Friedman, Matthew

1997 *Fuzzy Logic: Dispatches from the Information Revolution.* Montreal: Vehicule Press.

This excellent account of Internet culture illustrates the contradictory social implications of digital technology and puts them in a Canadian context. It includes discussions of cyber-sex, censorship, and net-activism.

Herman, Edward and Robert McChesney

1997 *The Global Media: The New Missionaries of Corporate Capitalism.* London: Cassell.

A clear and comprehensive political economy of media in the era of capital globalization, it identifies the dominant corporations and discusses the policies that have brought them to supremacy.

Spender, Dale

1995 *Nattering on the Net: Women, Power and Cyberspace.* Toronto: Garamond.

The book analyzes how men have often attempted to monopolize newly developing means of communication, but also show how women have persistently found ways of overcoming this exclusion.

WEB SITES

www.realaudio.com
Real Audio
Go to this site to download software for tuning in to live broadcasts. The site also provides links to hundreds of radio and television stations from around the globe.

www.mediawatch.ca
Mediawatch
This site provides a view of Canadian media through a female lense. The site also allows visitors to make their views on the media known, by facilitating direct contact with media corporations, retailers, and advertisers.

Social Organization

This last section of this text focuses on social organization in its various aspects. Types of organizations, their sources, and their impact on society are discussed in Chapter 13, Formal Organizations and Work. Special attention is paid here to the world of work, where people spend much of their lives. As we shall see, organizations, whether they be formally (bureaucratically) structured-as in the case of religious institutions or even the media-or based upon a more informal structure-like families-have an especially important influence on human behaviour.

Chapter 14 examines social movements. Their origins are attributed to various sources, including subcultural groups wanting a better position in society, religions trying to create a different social order, political groups seeking power, or members of certain social strata hoping to change the distribution of power and privileges. Collectively, however, social movements share a desire to achieve their goals through change. If successful, most will end up looking like the bureaucracies described in Chapter 13. Some may even become conservative oligarchies, with leaders more interested in maintaining their power than in achieving the original goals of the movement. In both instances, new social movements may emerge and the process may be repeated once more.

Demography and Urbanization, examined in Chapter 15, looks at the factors that determine the size and composition of the population of a society, including social institutions, social differentiation,

even cultural values. For instance, religious and political values have been important in Quebec's encouragement of population growth, which is seen as a means of maintaining the size of the francophone population in Canada. Population variables, in turn, affect most other areas of society. As an example, population size partly determines stratification patterns, since it influences chances for mobility. Probably the most obvious consequence of population growth is increased urbanization. The distinctions between city, town, and rural areas are many and they affect a whole range of social phenomena, from crime to longevity.

Despite their seeming permanence, all forms of social organization are subject to change, the subject of our last chapter. The sources and patterns of change in social systems throughout history have been the subject of much study and debate. As you will see, there are many ways to understand change, with theorists focusing on differing spheres and levels of change. In this last chapter, emphasis is placed on broad changes in economics and politics. By understanding how societies change in these fundamental areas of social organization, we may be better equipped to predict the future.

This examination of social organization completes your introduction to sociology with a Canadian focus. Although presented last, it is a most important area of concern. As you read the chapters, note how the forces discussed are important determinants of the social structure, which, in turn, influences and shapes the behaviour of individuals.

Work and Organizations

Jerry P. White

Introduction

If we look at the many societies in today's world, and those that have inhabited our geosphere over the millennia, we see a striking similarity. From the very complex to the very basic, societies all expend a majority of their creative and intellectual energy sustaining themselves in their natural environment. This chapter explores this basic social process, commonly defined as the world of work. We will introduce you to a new way of defining this activity and show you both how humans are unique in their approach to work and how work has had a unique effect on them. We will look at the evolution of work, how it is organized and whether work is satisfying or a major drudgery for Canadians. You may never think about work in the same way again.

What Is Work?

When we talk about work, we have to make a distinction between using things that already exist in the environment, those provided by nature, and the process of transforming aspects of the environment to make them useful. If a person came across a stream by chance and drank some water from it, that act would not be considered work. If, however, that person were searching for water, dug a well, and then purified the water to take a drink, this would involve a great deal of work.

Work then may be defined as changing physical materials (manual work) or mental constructs/ideas (intellectual work) so as to make these materials and/or ideas more useful to the producer. Many animals, whether beavers, bears, or bees, can be seen working, transforming something in order to live. It seems then that all animals, including humans, share this activity. However, it is not what animals share that is of interest to the sociologist, but what is different between humans and other animals. As Braverman (1974) noted, although the bee constructs with a precision that may shame an engineer, human work is different in two ways.

To begin with, humans conceptualize the end product before they even pick up a tool. Cabinet-makers see their cabinets in their minds before a

Transforming Nature, Transforming Ourselves

The apes that most resemble us have a similar posture to humans and hands they can use much as humans do. There are, however, differences. The human brain is larger in areas where conception and fine work originate, compared to apes. Washburn (1960) seized on this difference and on anthropological findings to develop the hypothesis that in humans these enlarged areas of the brain, where conceptual work is performed, have grown throughout the evolutionary process, while the areas where instinctively driven behaviours are controlled have been suppressed and eventually lost. This withering of instinctually driven activities creates our humanity.

Humans are also one of the very select animal groups to use tools to make tools, an ability closely linked to the growth of their brains. The Washburn thesis essentially argues that humans have quickly evolved as they worked with tools. He fur-

ther hypothesized that it is the process of work, the labour process, that develops the human capacity of conceptualization, and that this ability to conceptualize led to more work with tools, which led in turn to a further growth of abilities (1960: 61–72). Thus, as we transform nature, we transform ourselves. Let us look at an example of how the process may have worked.

In ancient China, several thousands of years ago, there existed a marginally self-sufficient village. The villagers had few contacts with others down river, except for purposes of intermarriage. Each year, there were droughts in late summer and floods in the spring. To stop the flood-then-drought cycle that plagued the area, the villagers eventually built a dam in a local river to divert some water. This prevented flooding and saved water for the dry season, a transformation of nature. What were the accompanying social changes that took place in the society of the village?

First there were health improvements, which translated into a dramatic drop in infant mortality. Also, each year, larger numbers of older residents of the village survived. There was also a surplus of food, which eventually led to trade with surrounding villages, more sharing of experiences, and wider intermarriage. The existence of a surplus forced the village to develop laws to decide who would get the extra food and laws to determine disputes over the surplus. New skills and jobs were developed, as carts had to be built to haul the surplus, and distribution of food had to be organized to feed these small industry workers who were no longer engaged in agriculture directly. A police (army) was then drawn from the population to guard trade goods en route. We could continue, but as you can see, the transformation of the natural state, i.e., the diversion of the river, led to many social changes and the growth of human potential.

---

single nail is pounded into the wood. This makes them superior to any animal that builds an intricate shelter. Conceptualization is a process known to exist only in the higher-order animals and might be thought of as an inner television screen where humans play out their ideas, a place where they see, think, and adjust these ideas. If I ask, have you ever seen a hail storm or felt the wind? you can call up memories of these phenomena and see the storms or feel the wind again. If you are a carpenter and I ask you to build something that you have never seen, you would listen to my description and create an image or set of ideas for this new object to guide you in the building of it. This is conception.

Secondly, human work is purposive and conscious. It is not performed by instinct (Braverman 1974). *Instinct* or instinctive abilities are like genetically programmed motivations, coded at birth, and designed to satisfy certain needs, expressed as relatively inflexible patterns of activity triggered by a stimulus.

Human beings create things not by instinct, but by what exists in their thoughts, based upon learning. Braverman (1974: 47) cited an experiment where scientists studied the behaviour of the South African weaver bird, which builds a complicated nest of sticks and hair. Five generations of the birds were bred from eggs initially taken from the wild, and the generations were kept away from the traditional nesting materials and other weaver birds. There was no way the sixth generation of birds could have learned how to make the nest. Yet when these pairs were released, they immediately went in search of sticks and hair and constructed a typical weaver nest. The only explanation is that the birds "learned genetically," that is, they must have had a pattern etched in their brains acquired with the genetic material passed on in the reproductive process. As animals evolve, we do see more evidence of an ability to learn complex tasks. Dolphins and apes, for instance, perform many very difficult tasks. It has not been demonstrated, however, that the higher-order mammals, except humans, are able to conceptualize. Rather, it appears that our close relatives still have a major portion of their lives determined by instinctive responses.

Why, in the end, are we so different? Evolution plays a great role. It is the evolutionary process that led to what we might call human work, activity that is conscious, purposive, and directed by conceptual thought. Our ability to communicate symbolically through language enables this difference. Indeed many scientists argue that the growth of language, in fact, created a strong selective pressure for more agile intellect. Put simply, we can say that language, tool use, and brain size developed together, reinforcing and increasing the growth in one another. We have seen how we, as humans have

developed, in part, through work. Now let's look at the work of modern human beings.

Where We Work: The Many Faces of Organizations

Whether we are out in a field cultivating with fellow tribes people in Namibia or on an assembly line in Windsor, we are part of an organization. Organizations come in two main types: formal and informal. There are some important differences between them that we should understand as sociologists.

Formal organizations, to begin with, have a division of labour and are set up to achieve a goal or goals. The reason they are established is to make work more efficient, although they may not succeed at this task. Corporations, schools, government agencies, and even political parties are examples of formal organizations. Formal organizations are among the most common forms of organizations found in the world today and run some of the most complex of human activities. A hospital, for example, is responsible for providing care to the ill. This is not a simple task; it involves admitting people, feeding them, facilitating the diagnosis of their problems, keeping patients clean, and much more. The hospital is also a place where health-care professionals learn to perform their duties and

The Iron Law of Oligarchy

Michels, in his book *Political Parties* (1915), argued that an **iron law of oligarchy** exists such that even in democratic organizations, be they socialist or capitalist, rule by the many will inevitably become rule by the few.

How does this occur? Basically it has to do with the hierarchy of authority found in any bureau-

cracy. While it does lead to efficiency, those at the top also tend to develop a monopoly on the knowledge and skills required to run the bureaucracy. This is what happened even under communism (in countries such as the former Soviet Union), with party members forming an élite and then taking privileges for themselves that they did not give to others.

These ideas also find support in studies of various labour unions. Leaders do not want to step down and tend to remain in office for long periods of time. On the other hand, where the job vacated is of a high status, stepping down is more frequent, as might be found in medical and legal associations.

where education of patients and families is undertaken, involving coordination and communication among its many employees, the technology, and the outside world. There is a whole branch of sociology dedicated to the study of how formal organizations achieve their goals.

Often, formal organizations function like bureaucracies, with rigid rules and plans (see the boxed insert on "Weber and Bureaucracy") but these rules cannot anticipate every problem. When we

examine an organizational chart, it cannot account for all the activities, actions, and interactions that take place in a formal organization. The informal rules and groups of people that arise to meet the challenges of complex day-to-day life are known as the informal structure of an organization or simply **informal organization**.

This informal structure of an organization is made up of the activities that people engage in that are not prescribed by the rules but they find

Weber and Bureaucracy

The study of organizations has been a specialized part of sociology since its inception as a social science. Early sociologists like Weber (1921) spent a great deal of energy trying to understand organizations and particularly something he called **bureaucracy**, a special type of complex organization characterized by an explicit set of rules and a hierarchy of authority. We often think of more common characteristics like "red tape," but every bureaucracy, whether a church or a political party, shares these common characteristics:

1. *Specialization and a division of labour.* Bureaucracies employ experts with job titles and job descriptions that indicate what they do in the organization. The members of the organization specialize and are responsible for carrying out their duties in an effective manner.
2. *Hierarchy of authority.* We might think of this as the power structure or chain of command. The members of the bureaucracy report to people who have "higher" positions than they, and who in turn, supervise others "below" them.

3. *Rules and regulations.* Written rules and regulations establish authority within the organization, and the fact that they are standardized ensures that activities become more standardized as well. This allows new members to learn what to do and how to do it more efficiently and ensures that people in the organization know both what is expected and what is not allowed.
4. *Impersonality.* Interactions in a bureaucracy are supposed to be based on the rules not personal feelings or attitudes. Officials are expected to interact with subordinates based on the office they hold not on how they might feel about them.
5. *Technical competence, careers, and tenure in the office.* Candidates for a job are to be evaluated based on their ability to do the job they are being hired to do. There should be set qualifications that are considered for all the candidates, and favouritism, family connections, and all other subjective factors should have no effect on the hiring process. Once hired, a

person should progress through a career, based on job performance and seniority in the job.
6. *Communications should be formal and written.* This provides a clear record of what has been done and who made the decisions. This record helps a bureaucracy to avoid repeating errors as well as the proliferation of verbal commands that can be misunderstood, misinterpreted, or even denied if there are problems that develop.

Bureaucracy represents quite a difference from less formal organizations with their "less rational" structures and small informal groups that lack structures. The ideal bureaucracy seems to regulate everything in a very rational way. It is important to keep in mind that in real life the people in the bureaucracy often subvert this perfection, bringing in their personal biases and ideas. As in all formal organizations, an informal organization develops alongside the formal one.

necessary in order to carry out their tasks. The informal organization thus arises within the formal one as the need arises. If we think back to our hospital example, we know that nurses are supposed to enter into a computer file (formerly write down in charts) at the nursing station all the information that they discover about a patient. However, the day is frantic for most nurses and they can rarely get to all their "charting." Nurses thus rely on word of mouth to convey information to the next shift. They also may pass on information about doctors who are particularly ill-tempered or new ways of doing work that have proven effective. The communications system of the hospital, therefore, has a formal organizational side, including charting and computers, as well as an informal side, which is personal communications.

Informal networks, as the case of the example of nursing, can be very positive, but these types of informal structures can be dysfunctional as well. Rumour mills can target individuals or new management programs and cause harm through false information and accusations. Informal systems are also more easily transformed than formal ones. Symbolic interactionism (see Chapter 1) concentrates on how organizations are socially constructed, and thus are constantly changing. An example is *negotiated order theory*, developed by Corwin (1987: 107), which assumes that organizational structures emerge from the meaningful interactions of persons who are negotiating with and navigating among each other. Negotiated order theorists point out that individuals create temporary agreements and informal understandings with co-workers to facilitate the completion of their job or even to make work more pleasant. This means that any organization is not a static, set pattern but rather a temporary, ever-changing body developed through the negotiation of its members.

The Evolution of Modern Work

The development of human work has been a long and complex process but it is possible to identify patterns, key aspects of the changes, occurring as part of the process. The transition from simple agricultural production to complex industrial production and the accompanying increase in the division of labour are of particular interest to us as sociologists.

The division of labour

In modern society, individuals have become much more dependent on each other. Whereas before industrialization people were more self-sufficient, growing their own food and making their own clothes, now they have to go to stores for food and clothing. They need others to grow, harvest, package, and deliver their food, and still others to make and sell them clothing. We call this interdependence a division of labour; in Chapter 1, you read of Durkheim's attempts to trace this process.

There are two types of division of labour. In the earliest human societies, hunters and gatherers' families divided jobs, with women typically gathering (primarily because of child-raising requirements), and men hunting (as they had more mobility). This is what we call the **social division of labour**. As we moved from hunter-gatherer societies to more complex societies, we increased the social division of labour and now depend on many others to provide the goods and services we consume. However, there is another type of division of labour.

In the more traditional and less complex societies, non-agricultural work involved the acquisition of a skill known as a *craft*. These skills were learned in an apprenticeship process in which students or apprentices performed all aspects of a job. If students wished to be carpenters, they would learn the various aspects of the craft by watching a journeyman carpenter and doing all the aspects of the job "carpentry" over several years. The knowledge required was quite extensive. As societies evolved, these wide, knowledge-based crafts disappeared and in their place came many more specialized and less broadly skilled occupations. In effect, one large job was divided into several parts, and a worker no longer performed the whole job, but was trained to do only a part of the larger activity. The concurrent move away from agriculture, in which the dominant pursuit was farming, to the modern society, in which the dominant work involves some form of production of goods and services, created the context for this process of subdividing single, large, skilled jobs into many job parts. The division of a single job into many parts is called the **detailed division of labour**. A good example of the detailed division of labour is modern shoemaking, where the production of a shoe is divided among a dozen people, some who cut, some who glue, and some who sew. Most sociologists say that different forms of the social division of labour date back millennia and are therefore a natural process, a normal development of complex society. The detailed division of labour, however, is a more modern occurrence and is even seen to be of a potentially destructive process. Let us briefly examine how both work and the economy have developed in our century.

Industrialization

By the turn of the century, the industrial revolution had given rise to a mass production of goods. The traditional type of society, in Europe and North America, which depended on a majority of its

people producing for their own use, was coming to an end, and in its place came industrialized society. Industrial sociology has a long and rich history in terms of the scientific study of the rise of industrialization. In the nineteenth century, Karl Marx warned that as capitalism developed, it would create social discontent, which in turn would lead to the working class taking control of the entire social system (see Chapter 7, Stratification). Durkheim (1895) studied the division of labour and wrote that it would lead to *anomie*, a social problem where people would feel atomized and experience a sense of normlessness. In the late nineteenth century, Weber, and others who followed, argued that social conflicts would arise due to industrial bureaucratic changes. We will examine some of these problems later in the chapter.

The rise of scientific management and Fordism

The turn into the twentieth century brought even further changes in the work process, related to

By the turn of the century, in Europe and North America, industrialization was replacing the traditional type of society which depended on a majority of its people producing for their own use.

scientific management and *Fordism*. **Scientific management**, sometimes called Taylorism, after its inventor Fredrick Taylor, involved the application of principles aimed at eliminating inefficiencies. Taylor made a detailed study of the production processes and the individual jobs involved in these processes. He then broke down these processes and jobs into smaller and simpler tasks. These tasks could then be measured and translated into steps, procedures, and formulae. Workers could be more easily trained to perform them, and controls, such as measuring output or direct supervision over the workers, could easily be put in place. His study led to a system of management that forced workers to perform in set, repetitive ways. Scientific management, as a system of organization, was not interested in the well-being of those who did the work, but was aimed at achieving maximum output. Taylor actually introduced his program into only one steel plant in the U.S., but in fact his method influenced many areas of mass production, in particular, auto production. Henry Ford adapted Taylor's ideas when he designed his auto plants to use special machinery and the assembly-line work system. **Fordism** (Wood, 1994) simply means mass production for a mass market using these assembly-line methods.

Responses to Ford and Taylor

Sable (1982) argued that both Taylorist principles and the Fordist system were seen by the captains of industry as the wave of the future. However, they could not indefinitely play that role for a couple reasons. As productive as the Fordist approaches to mass production were, they only worked when products were standardized, that is, made uniform. If products had to be made in small numbers (small-batch production), perhaps due to changes demanded by consumers, then the process was not very efficient. Savings in the Fordist system are dependent on the production of mass quantities on the assembly line. In the later part of our century, we have seen a move to such small-batch production where manufacturers make smaller quantities, altering sizes or colours (or whatever characteristic) to capture niches in a more specialized consumer market.

The other problem that industrialists had to face came from those who did the work. The unions and individual workers resisted these new systems. Individual workers, forced to work under scientific management, were absent from work more often than individuals working under any other system of management; unions fought scientific management. The problem was that scientific management tried to make people into machines, and people rebelled. Monotonous, repetitive work, with no creativity or input from workers, caused resentment.

This raises an important issue. We said above that humans are conceptual beings whose special skill or attribute is to think and plan in a purposive way and then produce that which they have planned. These new systems thus challenged a central feature of our humanity by taking much of the thinking and conceptualizing out of the work process. Indeed, Taylor stated in his book *The Principles of Scientific Management* (1906) that all "brainwork" must be removed from the shop floor and placed in the hands of management. An emergent resistance to these new systems—through strikes and absenteeism and even sabotage—may, in large part, have been the result of the fact that these systems were not geared to the needs and abilities of the participants. Rather they created work environments that were more akin to "instinctive" work than to conceptual work.

Another problem arose as well. People want to be productive and make contributions to the society around them. They also believe they should get rewards for that commitment to the social good. In post–World War II society, particularly in Canada and the U.S., an understanding developed among those who owned business and industry, those who worked in those businesses and industries, and the State (government). This **social contract** was based on the economics of John Maynard Keynes. Essentially, the contract, or socially accepted understanding, was that if you work hard and produce more goods and services each year, the economy will grow. Such growth means an increasing return on investments to the owners of capital, and increases in the standard of living for the people who work and create this production. Government would ensure stability in the social, political, and economic system by creating policies to move toward full employment. And finally, those who earn their living from wages or salaries would not need to fear unemployment, because their jobs would be secure so long as the economy grew, or at least maintained itself.

The Great Depression of the 1930s indicated the need for such a social contract. The post–World War II prosperity in North America delivered some of the promises of the social contract. Standards of living rose and unemployment stayed relatively low in the 1950s and 1960s as the productivity of industry climbed substantially. This rosy situation was not without significant problems, however, nor did it last forever. Before we pursue what happened to the social contact in the 1990s, let us take a brief look at the problems that have arisen in the work relations in our society, given the way it has organized work outside the family over the last quarter-century.

Work: Satisfying or Alienating?

Karl Marx was the first sociologist to explore systematically the problems of work. He wrote in his *Economic and Philosophic Manuscripts of 1844* ([1848], 1964) that the detailed division of labour would destroy the creativity of work, making it dull and boring. It was not just the repetitive nature of the work process, but the loss of control over work that was the key problem for Marx. He pointed out that although the workers and peasants in traditional societies worked long, hard hours and their life was difficult, they were in control of *how* they worked. They had skills and controlled the use of them, making decisions over how to employ their abilities. This gave workers a measure of satisfaction and well-being concerning their place in, and their contribution to, society. Industrialization, on the other hand, was leading to a situation in which workers were increasingly directed on how and when to do what task, what Marx called **alienation**. This alienation separates workers from the decisions concerning how and when to work, what to make, and how to relate to other workers involved in the production. Alienation, in this sense, is not simply a psychological problem but a structural one. It is a problem rooted in the real relationships between the managers and the managed, the "deciders" and the "doers." If we think back to what differentiates

Marx argued that alienation of the worker is endemic in capitalist society.

humans from other animal forms, it is this purposive and conceptual nature, which is an essential part of our development as intelligent beings. The way work is organized in modern society often denies people the right to labour in a conceptual way, causing them to feel alienated or separated from their essence (White 1990; 1993).

In contrast to Marx's views that the problem with work in modern society is the lack of control over that work, Durkheim (1965; 1966) saw anomie (normlessness) and the breakup of integrated communities as the distinguishing feature and problem in the emerging modern society. This change resulted in strikes, the sabotage of machines, and even revolutionary activity, and was a reflection of the fact that people were not committed to the new role of mass-production worker. Durkheim saw these actions as a reflection of the lack of commitment to the norms of the new society and the separation people felt from that society as they moved from the collective sameness, which characterized traditional societies, to the modern divisions of labour that made each person's life so separate and different from others in their society.

Instrumentalism

Work, in modern society, is often reduced to simply a means to an end. How often have we heard "Thank God it's Friday" because the work week is over? How often have you discussed others jobs with them and found them saying they do not like their job, but must stay with them to pay the bills? This feeling that you work only to earn money so you can enjoy your non-work life represents a problematic relation to one's work. Goldthorpe (1969) found in his classic studies that some workers respond to the alienating aspects of our work situation in an **instrumentalist** fashion. People often think that if they have to work under monotonous and undesirable conditions then they had better be paid well, so they can enjoy their leisure time. This is a problem because work is supposed to be fulfilling and represent an aspect of what makes us human, as we discussed above. Yet the reality of some work is that it is simply a means to an end, and an onerous activity.

Other social scientists find that many workers resist these undesired aspects of work, and often would like to change the organization of work to make it more fulfilling. Thompson (1989), summarizing a wide range of sociological research, concluded that most people actively resist anti-conceptual work and control systems (see also Rinehart, 1996). White (1993) found, in Canada, that even professionals with a high dedication to their jobs, such as nurses, often exhibit resistance behaviours, striking or quitting their jobs to oppose the degradation of control over their own work activities. Let us look closer at this aspect of work.

Resistance and consent work

In every work relationship, those who carry out the tasks have consented in one way or another to be there and do their job. If they had not consented to work under the set conditions, there would be no workers to observe. Yet, except in the most ideal circumstances, these same workers will harbour some level of discontent with the safety conditions, the pay, the supervision, or a thousand other things, and will act on that discontent in minor or major ways. We call this resistance. **Resistance** is used to describe an action(s) aimed at either passively or actively slowing, reversing, avoiding, or protesting management directions or strategies in the workplace. Resistance can manifest itself on any scale, from millions of workers launching general strikes to gain political change, as in Ontario's general strikes against Harris, to small groups protesting a supervisor's order.

Individuals in a workplace learn how and when to consent to work, as well as when and how to resist. The workgroup and its members formulate the conditions under which they will comply/consent to work based on how, over time, they perceive the gains and/or losses involved in that decision. Salaman (1986) noted that the rewards that different groups of workers expect will vary based on what the workers have come to share in terms of norms, values, and knowledge. In the same way that a society develops a culture, workers in a workplace develop a work culture.

When will workers decide to resist openly? In the simplest utilitarian terms, it is when the rewards for consenting to a situation are insufficient and the losses attached to resistance (pay loss in a strike for example) are too great in comparison to the problems they will experience by not changing the situation. The key to determining when the rewards are insufficient and/or the potential of loss is too great to bring about compliance lies in what Willmott (1990: 56) identified as the link between general identity and resistance: "the potential for resistance arises when subjects are constituted whose experience and self-understanding are denied or undermined by the demands being placed upon them." Therefore, if the group has a great deal of commonality, there is greater chance they will respond together to resist the work organization they face. The group whose "basic self-fulfillment" is denied is likely to resist unless the resistance will clearly lead to a loss of something that the group considers valuable. For example, assume management increases the assembly line speed by 10 percent. The workers would discuss their response to the change and probably decide that this change was making work a bit frantic and unpleasant, but they could do it. Let us say that they also believe that the only way to reverse the speedup is to call a strike, but management might then shut down the plant and they would lose their jobs. In this case, the group may opt to bend to the power, to consent to the situation. The fact that they choose to comply, does not extinguish resistance. The potential loss of jobs simply changes the nature of the resistance; they may simply delay their resistance for a time. Therefore, it is best to see resistance and consent as two processes that coexist within every work relationship. Every workplace and group of workers will have ongoing dissatisfactions that may erupt into different forms of resistance. Work generates resistance on a continuous basis. Even in the situation where the workers have walked out, let us say in a strike, there is still some consent. Those workers are seeking to come to an agreement with the management. They want to find a way to come back to work but wish to set terms that are, within their shared understanding, fair from a utilitarian point of view.

Unions and resistance

In Canada, people in a definable workplace or group of workplaces can join together in associations called **unions**. The legal or official role of the union is to represent the collective group of workers in negotiations with the employer to get a contract. The behaviour of both the union and management are circumscribed by labour laws, sometimes called trade-union acts, determined separately in each province in Canada.

The origin of unions in Canada may be traced to the 1800s, when overseas immigrants brought with them their societies and clubs to our shores. Often these organizations provided the major organized opposition to poor working conditions in those early years. Russel (1990) reported that the first Canadian unions existed prior to 1827, mainly in the Maritimes, and by the 1830s both Upper and Lower Canada had many unions operating among craft workers (carpenters, shipwrights, tailors, and shoemakers, for example). These unions attempted to regulate wage rates and exert influence over labour supply through the apprenticeship system and had some success in these endeavours (Palmer, 1983).

There were many differences between these early unions and their modern descendants, however. The first unions were voluntary organizations, which meant that they had to work hard to keep members, operating in a way to maintain the support of the people they served. These unions were also largely illegal, thanks to laws such as the Masters and Servants Act and Anti–Combines Act, which defined workers as servants and gave employers far reaching powers to control them (Keally, 1973). By the end of the nineteenth century, unions had won the right to be legally present in the workplace and the Canadian state was entering a new period of **industrial relations**, which included the creation of a Federal Department of Labour. The twentieth century or modern approach by government to unions and industrial relations can be generally described as one of intervention in disputes between labour and management, aimed at diffusing conflict, to ensure as little disruption to the economy as possible.

It was actually not until World War II that unions got the security they needed to guarantee their longevity. To avert an auto strike during the war, Supreme Court Justice Ivor Rand ruled that employers in unionized companies, not the unions themselves, must collect union dues and hand over these funds to the unions. This ruling, in effect, made every worker in a unionized workplace a member of the union, and each worker had to pay for the union's services. The unions were now free to concentrate on developing their organizing and servicing skills.

The subsequent growth of unions in Canada can be linked to a series of conditions. The new management systems we discussed above, such as Taylorism, job insecurity, and the history of poor working conditions with long hours, all contributed to an increase in union membership. There are many complicated reasons why workers may choose to unionize their workplace. The simplest way to understand the growth of unions, sociologically, is to think of them as a response to powerlessness experienced by the individual worker. A single worker has very little power to negotiate with a company. If there are fewer issues that pose a problem for the workers in a workplace, i.e., there is less resistance, then it is less likely workers will choose to become unionized. If there are very

Nurses Protest Change in Their Work

It was 1988 and nurses were leaving the profession, opting for part-time work and/or going on strike. What was causing this situation? A sociological study of the attitudes of nurses and a review of the relevant documents clarified the problem. In this study, White (1993) argued that there was a dramatic change going on in the kinds of work nurses were doing and in the nurses' workplace. The drive to cut costs in hospitals was leading to a change in what hospital personnel were being asked to do. The crisis over the lack of nurses thus was due in part to the changing role of nurses—the time, the place, and the content of their nursing work. White concluded that the expectations of nurses, or their expectations of what nurses are and do, had been challenged. "They had been challenged by managerial strategies, provoked by a fiscal crisis of the state, that have created a new regime of work" (White, 1993: 128). Nurses told the researcher that they were no longer allowed to do the job they were trained and wanted to do. Their response, according to White, was to resist the changes through strikes, quitting, or moving to part-time work. As one of the nurses interviewed for the study said, "We have felt powerless to make changes in our hospitals. When you want to deliver a first- rate service and feel good that you have really helped make people well or more comfortable but you can not because someone or something is stopping you then...you have to take action" (White, 1993: 119).

important problems, then there is a greater chance that employees will unionize.

The system of industrial relations in Canada

In Canada, the process of forming unions, reaching collective agreements over salaries and working conditions, and solving disputes where management and labour cannot agree is often referred to as our industrial relations system. Figure 13.1 provides an overview of the system, which is made up of the contextual environment, the actors, bargaining, and strike processes and outcomes.

The contextual environment refers to the laws as well as the political, social, and economic situation in the country. The context has an effect on the entire system. For example, if the economy is very depressed, jobs will be scarce and unions will be in a weaker bargaining position. If the law does not permit a strike—as is the case for some hospital workers, police, and firefighters—there is little pressure for the two sides to come to an agreement. The actors in the system are simply labour (unions) and management, obliged by the law to negotiate and who do so with the aim of coming to a contract settlement (outcome). If they cannot come to a settlement, they must resolve their impasse, and this could mean finding a third party like an arbitrator to facilitate a resolution.

Well over 97 percent of all contracts that come up for renegotiation are settled without a strike. This means that on the surface it would appear that the system works. However, there is much more to understand in the process. For the system to work, there must be three sets of protected and enforced rights. These are: 1) the right to organize a union in an atmosphere free of coercion; 2) the right and responsibility to engage in meaningful negotiations for a contract; and 3) the right to resolve impasses that arise in the negotiations. If any of these rights are denied or subverted, the system cannot work in the interests of its stakeholders, which are the workers in the workplace, the owners and managers, and the people of the country as a whole.

What can subvert these rights? A right to organize can be subverted if management threatens workers in the workplace with job loss if they join a union. To prevent this, Canada has enacted laws to protect the right to organize, preventing management from threatening union supporters and unions from coercing people to support it. The right to

FIGURE 13.1   **The System of Industrial Relations in Canada**

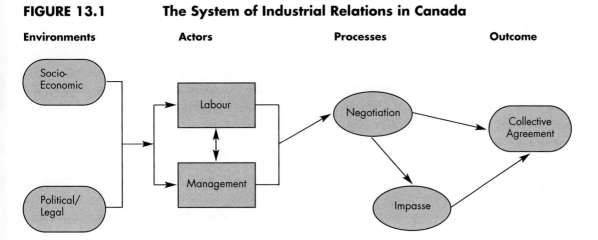

Unions, Labour, and Voting Behaviour

You have read in this chapter about the world of work and the struggle of workers to increase their control over the labour process. The issue here is whether shop-floor resistance is translated into politics and specifically voting behaviour. Looking at the news, it is clear that there is often a split between the NDP, "the party of the worker," and unions. In Ontario many never forgave Bob Rae for introducing the "Social Contract," which rolled back public-sector wages and overrode many collective agreements. Some continue to take out that anger on current leader Howard Hampton. Federal NDP leader Alexis McDonough talks about being more friendly to business so as to ensure a

Canadian working environment that can compete with the much cheaper labour costs of our NAFTA partners, creating another schism. What does the research say?

There is much cleavage in the voting of Canadians. Regionally, apart from the obvious example of the Bloc Québécois, Reform is strong only in the west, while the Liberals rule most of the east, at least federally. Provincial results show the NDP to be largely a party of the west, with the notable exception of Alberta. But is there a class vote?

Comparisons with other nations reveal Canadians (and U.S.) workers to be relatively unpolarized, certainly much less so than in places like Great Britain and the

countries of Scandinavia (Nieuwbeerta, 1996). But there is some, depending on how class is measured. Using income or education to measure social class shows little cleavage; occupation shows a bit more; but union membership and an egalitarian ideology, both related to class, do predict a vote for the NDP (Nakhaie and Arnold, 1996).

Finally we should add that there are other potential sources of cleavage—religion, and gender for just two examples—and times when there is great consensus. Non-francophones of all classes, ages, and ethnicities opposed granting of special rights to Quebec in the 1992 Referendum (Douilly, 1993).

meaningful negotiations may also be nullified. If management really does not want a union in its business, it can simply refuse to negotiate with the union and in that way subvert the system. We have laws in place that demand that both union and management negotiate in good faith or run the risk of having the government intervene.

Lastly, even when the two sides have tried, in good faith, to come to a collective agreement, there are times when they cannot succeed. The system must protect the right to choose different *impasse procedures*. In Canada we often try to "cool down" the sides through mediation, where a government appointee tries to help find some common ground. There are options in some settings to choose an arbitrator, who is a legally appointed and jointly agreed-upon judge of sorts, who will decide what the contract will say. The other option is the withdrawal of labour, which can take many forms such as a strike, a work slowdown (sometimes called working to rule), sit-downs, information pickets, or other legal actions. Management can also "go on strike," an action called a *lockout*. In Canada it is the perceived threat of a loss that encourages the two sides to settle. Management fears losing markets and sales while having to pay for the loans and upkeep of their facilities. Union members fear economic hardship as they will have no pay during the strike. The resources of the union as a whole are severely drained during conflicts as they give strike pay, cover staff expenses, and collect no dues. These fears are the reason why so many contracts are negotiated and work goes on despite the ever-present dissatisfactions that breed resistance in the workplace.

In short, there are, in every jurisdiction, laws that set rules for almost every aspect of union/management relations. These industrial-relations laws determine how to organize a union, how to get rid of one, when and how a union may strike, how a management can lock workers out, and even how negotiations must be conducted. The stated purpose of these laws is to make the industrial-relations system work. Still, often it is political partisanship that leads governments to change labour laws. To many conservative governments, unions represent a hindrance to the creation of wealth and expansion of business interests. Conservative governments have changed laws to make unionization of workers more difficult (Giddens, 1991: 612-13). More social-democratic governments, on the other hand, will sometimes try to protect unions, as they see them as allies and a part of the social fabric of protection for the less powerful in society. Laws can change as governments shift back and forth due to election results.

Unions have had a difficult time over the last decade. The economic recessions, worldwide restructuring of production, and deficit cutting by governments have led to massive layoffs of unionized workers. In the United States, for example, there has been a severe drop in union memberships (Jenson, 1993). Unions in other Western countries, particularly in Europe, have also faced declines (Mumme and Laxer, 1998: 1). Canadian unions have not seen the dramatic declines in numbers that other countries experienced. Membership figures show that unions represented 31.0 percent of the workforce in 1997, only slightly down from a high of 33 percent in 1990. Canadian unions then, have largely held their own. In some sectors, they have actually grown. The reason for this is that many of the unions, like the Canadian Union of Public Employees or the Canadian Auto Workers, have actively organized new members and developed new unionization strategies (White and Pupo, 1994).

Why do people resist at work?

A strike is a temporary work stoppage by a group of workers used to express a grievance or enforce a demand. When one person phones in sick, when she/he is actually just angry about an issue, this is not a strike, but a form of resistance. When workers quit, sabotage a machine, put a virus in a computer, they have engaged in an act of resistance. The causes of these actions are important to determine, and generally we have to take each incident separately to discover exactly why it happened. But as sociologists, we can draw some general lessons. They are that people: 1) are more likely to resist if they do not understand what is going on; 2) will resist changes that they feel jeopardize their security; and, 3) are more likely to resist practices and regulations that are forced upon them.

The key to reducing conflict in the workplace and thus resistance is to reduce insecurity and increase education and information. People will generally cooperate and comply with new systems and procedures if they have a stake in the development of these changed systems. People are more likely to accept new working conditions if they have participated in the selection of the system, learned about it before having it thrust upon them, or if they realize the actual consequences it will have for their job and employment. The Taylorist systems aimed to take all decisions from the worker and put them in the hands of the manager. Thus scientific management almost guaranteed that there would be resistance.

Since Taylor's time, newer types of management approaches have been developed that claim to give more power to the people who do the work. These have shown up under many names, such as Total Quality Management and Continuous Quality Improvement. However the success of such programs is doubtful, and analysts are already indicating that the new systems are not functioning as well as had been claimed (Wells, 1986). Too often the promise of involving employees in the decision-making process gives way to hidden plans to cut labour or seek other efficiencies (Armstrong et al., 1996). Although these systems, which originated in Japan, were successful in that country, they have not been successful in North America (Rinehart et al., 1998), partly because Japanese society is much more collectivist and open to managers and workers sitting down together and sharing ideas. In North America there has been a long tradition of mistrust between management and labour.

The Matsushita Electric Company is guided by collective values that transform Japan's industries into communities.

The End of the Social Contract and the Changing Nature of Work

The social contract, discussed earlier in the chapter, born out of the Depression and realized to a degree in the 1950s, no longer exists in the 1990s. This is one of the most important changes in the structure of the work relationship in Canada and has led to the other changes.

The social contract ceased to operate with the development of the new attitude and actions of business and government concerning job security and full-employment policies. The term **downsizing** is now commonplace. This is a process by which a firm reduces the number of employees as much as possible, while trying to keep returns on invested capital at the same level or preferably higher. Downsizing in the private sector obviously creates higher unemployment rates in Canada, as well as making employees nervous about job security. All levels of government, too, have laid off many civil servants, claiming that a debt crisis is forcing cuts in programs. Gone, then, is the job security that comes with working hard and being productive, and gone too is the social contract.

It is not that Canadian workers have not been productive. Canada started the 1980s with one of the hardest working, most productive workforces in the world, and maintained its productivity over the years. Still, in 1996, the Canadian Auto Workers (CAW) went on strike against General Motors (GM). The CAW argued that its workers had been working faster and more productively and that auto workers had been increasing profits at GM. It asked GM to agree that so long as the CAW workers remained productive and so long as GM remained profitable that GM would not lay off workers. GM, however, wanted to out- source jobs to make profits even higher, which meant they would hire outside companies, who pay their workers less, to do some of the jobs now performed by their own employees.

This example illustrates the effect that the change in the social contract has had on job security in Canada. In the past ten years, we have also seen a general flattening of wages and salaries in Canada. Many analysts are coming to the conclusion that there is actually a decrease in the standard of living

for a majority of the population, even with the change to two incomes, which may well be linked to the decline in employment and the work restructuring that has proceeded since the end of the social contract (Yalnizan, 1998).

The globalization of production

In the 1980s, in addition to downsizing, other changes took place that affected the world of work. There has been a **globalization of production**, which means that companies now look worldwide for the most profitable place to set up production. Before, one would see companies producing primarily in their home nation states. Teeple (1995) wrote that this was a form of nationalism. However, with the new social and economic order, companies are less nationalistic. But while the newly emerging areas of the world are able to offer cheaper labour and attract some companies, they do not have either the educated workforce or the infrastructure (telephones, roads, power, clean water, etc.) that a country like Canada offers. However, these new potential production sites create competition, so that companies looking to invest in Canada demand that Canadian workers be willing to work for lower wages than they had in the past. This is how globalization can affect wage levels and standard of living in developed countries like Canada.

Bond-rating agencies and mutual-fund stock organizations have also had quite an effect. Bond-rating agencies have demanded that governments cut social programs and stay away from full-employment policies if they want a good credit rating to borrow money. This also leads the Canadian government away from the social contract. Mutual-fund managers have placed a lot of value on companies that downsize, even though there is no firm evidence that downsizing is profitable. In fact, if an organization moves too quickly to downsize, there are no benefits at all.

Canada has experienced other changes in this post-social-contract, globalized world. For example, changing labour laws have generally made unionization more difficult (Haiven et al., 1992). A new approach to regulations with increased opening of the Canadian labour market to unregulated market forces has also taken place. Free-trade agreements with the United States and Mexico have forced Canada to drop some of the programs that protected certain workers' jobs and change how we regulate workplaces, in some cases. Moreover, rapid reduction in government spending has resulted in a loss of jobs in the public sector and a decline in social programming like Employment Insurance.

The decline of the social contract has thus had quite an effect on the world of work. We asked the question earlier about whether there has been a new kind of social contract being negotiated to take the place of the old. The answer to that question appears to be no. Essentially, the promises of the old social contract are gone and nothing has emerged to take its place.

Unemployment

There are several interrelated changes that are creating higher unemployment than perhaps necessary in Canada, including: 1) the decline of mass production with the move to more of the small-batch form of production; 2) the movement of jobs to developing countries where labour costs are lower; and 3) the move to less government intervention and the reduction of the civil service.

Thus there are large numbers of those who wish to work, but are not able to find work. The 1990s have seen record levels of unemployment lasting for extended periods of time. If we look at Table 13.1, we see that unemployment has gone up in industrialized countries since the end of the social contract. For the late 1980s and 1990s there has been close to 10 percent official unemployment. But even

this percentage does not count all those who want a job but cannot find one. If people give up, because they have to go on social assistance, for example, they are not counted in the official figures.

Unemployment is a negative phenomenon from several vantage points. It is very costly to a society like Canada. The need to give families and individuals living assistance is the more obvious expense of unemployment, but we also lose these people's contributions in terms of work and taxes. Additionally, the health costs of the unemployed are generally higher than those employed, and the emotional problems that plague those excluded from work can lead to family violence as well as drug and alcohol abuse.

Are there solutions to unemployment?

It is possible to deal with the reduction of jobs in different ways. In the near future, Canada will certainly be forced to come up with some solutions to handle the new world of work and unemployment. For example, it may have to examine spreading around the work that does exist, through shortening the work week, making working careers shorter, restricting overtime work, and creating new forms of job sharing. The common theme of these approaches is the assumption that the amount of actual work society requires will not increase but is likely to continue to decline. These proposals are becoming reality today. We have seen the hours in the work week drop in Canada from 44 hours to 37 hours over the span of this century. In some countries like France, there are laws that restrict annual overtime (Giddens, 1991: 630). The Supreme Court of Canada has upheld the right of organizations to demand that their employees retire at a set age (usually 65 years) and we are seeing a trend as well for earlier retirement with buyout packages. Job sharing, where two people divide one job, is becoming a more widespread practice. Some even prefer it to part-time work, since both employees receive benefits like pensions and dental care.

Some argue that we should seek to try to develop new ways of organizing work so that those who provide jobs allow employees to have real involvement in decisions, with clear cooperation between partners in the work taking place. As we discussed at the beginning of this chapter, human beings need to contribute to society, through

Table 13.1	Average Unemployment in Selected Countries 1964–73 and 1983–95	
Country	1964–73	1983–95
Canada	4.23%	9.69%
France	2.23%	9.74%
Italy	5.48%	10.33%
United Kingdom	2.94%	9.78%

Source: OECD Main Economic Indicators 1965 through 1996. Copyright OECD.

Bad Times Ahead with New Labour Law

The following is from an editorial written by the author and published in the Hamilton Spectator *on 17 January 1999.*

I had resolved to tell the Minister of Labour, Flaherty, that the changes he and the Mr. Harris were planning to make to the laws governing unions were a grave mistake. But I was left on hold and Bell was the only winner as the minutes ticked by and I had to hang up. I couldn't get through to Flaherty, but I can tell you these changes to the labour legislation are not appropriate and everyone is going to pay the price for these mistakes.

Once a year I stand in front of the Masters of Public Administration class at The University of Western Ontario and for the better part of a day I try to explain that labour relations is a system. When you unbalance any part of the system, you risk a complete breakdown. Three parts of that system must be protected to preserve the peace and stability that allow Canada's economy to move along. First, working men and women must have the right to join together in a union to bargain collectively. That right has to be protected from intimidation or threat. The second part that must be protected is bargaining. We have laws that say both union and management must try to find agreement through bargaining in "good faith." And when agreements can't be reached, the third part of the system we must protect is that both unions and managements have recourse to sanctions, such as lockouts and strikes, to get their opposites to come to a settlement. These three rights act as pillars that support the whole labour relations system.

Does this system work? Every year thousands of contracts are bargained and signed. Millions of people head off to work under agreements that are mutually decided between union and management. No strike, no fight, just find the common ground and get on with it. Given the limitations of our capitalist system, the labour relations process works very well.

But let's look at what is being done by Mike Harris. His government changes take away some powers from the Labour Relations Board (LRB) which acts as the "court" on union-management affairs. The new law takes away the LRB's previous right to certify a group of workers as a union when it finds that an employer has broken the law and tried to intimidate employees from unionizing. The Labour Minister, Mr. Flaherty, says it is undemocratic to force unionization on a workplace. But in this case the law was there to allow people the right to unionize if they wish without fear of reprisal. The LRB didn't intervene unless people had their democratic right to unionize seriously undermined.

So how will these changes affect working men and women in this province? For the majority of people who work for honest, law-abiding employers, it won't change anything. But what the new law will do is encourage the dishonest, non-law abiding, anti-union employers to take actions against their employees who want to explore the idea of unionizing. The proposed changes will actually undermine democratic rights and encourage improper behaviour. They do not serve to enhance our democratic ideals.

How will the labour movement react to these changes? No one knows for sure, although I can predict that the labour movement will take actions to oppose these changes. I am also sure we are going to see the tactics in union organizing campaigns change, and thus it is only a matter of time until serious trouble erupts somewhere.

The Harris Government also proposes to interfere in the collective bargaining process, to make it easier for some employers to contract outside workers to do the jobs now done by employees in the company or institution. They plan to interfere in big projects to create special agreements between unions and companies. Contracting out and special arrangements between managements and unions are matters that should be dealt with between the employer and the union in negotiation. That is how our system works. This government is meddling with the second pillar that holds up the system of industrial relations.

It appears to me that the changes being made by the government are ill conceived and will damage our industrial relations system at a time when we need stability to get people back to work and labour peace in order to get the economy working to capacity. These moves by the Government are going to lead to work disruptions as collective agreements are undermined, and civil protest as the right to unionize is undermined. I fear we are witnessing the decline of democratic rights for workers and unions and it will have a terrible price tag.

working, in order to feel a sense of involvement and feel complete. Work that allows people to participate in decisions and achieve goals that they set, is the kind of contribution that people need to make in order to grow.

Gorz (1982), a French sociologist, expressed another view. He argued that it does not make sense to seek full employment or to try to gain more control over the work process. Work, he argued, is organized according to methods that are efficient and must be left that way so that business can compete in the world. People must be freed from work to enjoy life, and it is in the non-work pursuits where people will find fulfillment. But can they accomplish this through non-work? Can work be turned into a necessary evil and our fulfillment come totally from outside-work activities? It remains to be seen. It is clear that non-work in the form of underemployment, i.e., working fewer hours than desired, may pose a real problem for many, a problem for which society will have to seek solutions. In these cases, non-work will certainly not be part of the solution.

The Future

As we enter the third millennium and are living in a society where technological innovation occurs so quickly, is sometimes difficult for us to adapt. We are living in a time when technology means that one worker can produce the large numbers of goods and services that used to take many people to produce. Yet this capacity is somehow turning into a real problem. How can we have all this ability, yet find insufficient work for our highly motivated, highly educated workers? This exclusion from work costs society billions of dollars in social assistance, lost productivity, and lost tax revenue. Unemployment leads to more health costs and a range of other expenses. Thus it is the "lack of work" problem that is foremost on the agenda for the study of work in the new millennium.

But we will also have to face two other major issues that will profoundly affect our society. The first will be the imbalance between resistance and consent. The current economic situation makes it possible that we will face many serious workplace problems that generate great dissatisfaction, but where the resistance does not lead to an overt action. People fear the loss of their jobs, and in many cases this fear prevents resistance from becoming overt. The lack of disruption to production and the lesser numbers of strikes in the first half of the 1990s may reflect people's understanding that the potential losses of resistence outweigh the potential gains, given current rates of high unemployment. But this can only be a temporary phenomenon. These pent-up problems will likely come out in new and old forms of resistance over the next decade.

A last issue that faces us is how to organize the work that has to be done. Will we move to increasing the skill of workers and the discretion they may show in deciding how work is to be carried out, or will we move backwards towards the models that derive from scientific management, where control over work by those whose profits are at stake is the number one concern? If we choose the latter, we run the risk of dehumanizing the work, and creating evermore conflict that may be met with resistance. If we choose the former, those who actually do the work will gain more control in the workplace, leading to less dissatisfaction for workers, but we will have to alter many deeply entrenched notions of "who has the right to decide workplace issues" in order to make it work. That may be very difficult for those sectors of the Canadian population who now have ownership and control of the segments of the economy.

Summary

We began the chapter by defining work as the transformation of materials or ideas so as to make them more useful to the producer. Unlike the work of animals, which is often instinctual, human work is conceptualized and purposive. In the world of human work there coexists a formal, perhaps bureaucratic, and an informal, structure, one which is more easily transformed. The result is that any organization is not static but an ever-changing body developed through the negotiation of its members.

A distinction was then made between a social and a detailed division of labour, the latter a more recent and potentially harmful phenomenon, arising out of industrialism. Scientific management, on paper, seems to be an ideal way to maximize production, but there are costs as well, among which alienation of labour is perhaps the greatest. Labour resistance, from strikes to working only for the money, are common outcomes of this alienation.

The role of unions in this resistance was outlined, followed by a discussion of the system of industrial relations peculiar to Canada. The chapter ended with a discussion of globalization of work and its effect on workers in Canada. Particularly singled out were downsizing and unemployment.

QUESTIONS FOR REVIEW AND CRITICAL THINKING

1.   We learned that humans are endowed with a conceptual ability and that this has played a part in our evolution. We also learned that the scientific management system of Frederick Taylor took the conceptual "thinking" out of work. Is it possible that these management systems make work more like that of lower animal forms and therefore less "human"? Do you think that people's resistance to these management systems is related to this removal of "thinking" from the work process?

2.   Are you and the students around you very instrumental in your views about the jobs you are seeking; i.e. are you most interested in money, or are you looking for something you will enjoy first and foremost? How do you and others justify your choices?

3.   It is predicted that most of you will change jobs three to five times during your lifetime. Based on what you have learned in this chapter, discuss why this is happening.

4.   What is the difference between Durkheim's notion of anomie and Marx's concept of alienation?

5.   The number of people who are members of unions in Canada has not decreased significantly in the last decade. This is a different trend than what we see in the USA or even parts of Europe. Why do you think Canada is different in this regard?

KEY TERMS

alienation, p. 357

bureaucracy, p. 353

detailed division of labour, p. 355

downsizing, p. 364

Fordism, p. 356

formal organizations, p. 352

globalization of production, p. 364

informal organization, p. 353

industrial relations, p. 359

instrumentalism, p. 358

iron law of oligarchy, p. 352

resistance, p. 358

scientific management, p. 356

social contract, p. 356

social division of labour, p. 354

unions, p. 359

work, p. 350

SUGGESTED READINGS

Duffy, A., D. Glenday and N. Pupo (eds.)

1997   *Good Jobs, Bad Jobs, No Jobs: Changing Work in a Changing North America.* Toronto: Harcourt Brace.

This edited text examines key issues in the private, service, and public sectors of work. Authors trace the new realities of working life, providing empirical and theoretical commentaries on the evolving economy and labour markets.

Hall, Richard

1987   *Organizations: Structures, Processes and Outcomes.* (4th ed.) Englewood Cliffs, NJ: Prentice Hall.

A good contemporary analysis of division of labour, formal structure, and hierarchy in organizations. The book, as the title implies, is sensitive to the need to study structure, process, and outcomes in organizations.

Krahn, Harvey, and Graham S. Lowe (eds.)

1993   *Work, Industry and Canadian Society.* (2nd ed.) Scarborough: Nelson.

A comprehensive introduction to the sociology of work and industry from a Canadian perspective.

Rinehart, James

1996   *The Tyranny of Work.* (3rd ed.) Toronto: Longman.

A concise Marxist analysis of alienation in contemporary work organizations and workers' attempts to assert themselves.

WEB SITES

www.yorku.ca/reserch/crws

Centre for Research on Work and Society

This site posts the latest research working papers and provide links to work-related research sites.

http://cupe.ca/resources.html

Canadian Union of Public Employees

This union site has a dictionary of union and industrial-relations terms that is very interesting and useful to students and professionals alike. The site also links to many union research studies and publications.

Social Movements

Samuel Clark

Introduction

When we employ the term *social movement*, we are usually referring to a large group of people trying to bring about or resist social change. They may want to make a small change, such as diverting an expressway that threatens an old residential community; or they may want to make a very large change, such as dismantling the existing political system or transforming the established economic order. They may, like pro-lifers or members of the anti-pornography movement, be concerned with values and morals; or they may, like the Social Credit and CCF, be concerned primarily with economic issues.

The first part of this chapter reviews the various ways in which sociologists have studied social movements and related kinds of social behaviour. In it we shall outline five different theoretical approaches to the subject. In the second part, we shall turn to an analysis of several specific Canadian social movements, adopting a more descriptive and less theoretical tone.

Five Theoretical Approaches

Collective behaviour

One way of approaching the subject of social movements is to include them in a broader category of human activity known as **collective behaviour**. As sociologists use this term, collective behaviour occurs when a large number of people do not accept some of the prevailing values, norms, and/or leaders in a society. They are unwilling to tolerate things the way they are, or they do not follow normal routines and may even try to persuade others not to follow them as well. They advocate or engage in activities that sociologists would call less "institutionalized" or structured, when compared with conventional, routine behaviour.

As we shall see, sociologists differ widely over the kinds of activity that should be grouped together under the heading of collective behaviour. The most common practice, however, has been to include such diverse phenomena as panics, crowds, fads, crazes, and publics, along with social movements, on the grounds that they are all relatively unconventional. Let us examine these types of behaviour. We will begin with the least institutionalized form of collective behaviour—the panic—and then return to a discussion of social movements, the most institutionalized form.

A **panic** occurs when people are overcome by fear or apprehension, and try to save themselves or their possessions by taking immediate action. The term usually implies that such action is rash and impulsive, and that it involves a flight or withdrawal from a situation perceived to be dangerous. People rush to escape from a burning building; they hurry to remove their savings from a bank that appears to be on the verge of collapse. In most panics, there is little if any social control. As a rule, no leaders emerge to direct the collectivity, and there are no generally accepted norms about how people should conduct themselves.

A **crowd** is a temporary grouping of people in physical proximity. No sociologist would claim that all crowds should be placed in the category of collective behaviour. Many crowds are conventional, or casually emerge in the course of conventional behaviour. People waiting for a bank to open or watching a street performer are examples. But some crowds depart sharply from the routine, as when a fight breaks out among fans at a soccer game, or demonstrators are attacked by a group representing an opposing viewpoint. Many people regard such crowds as highly emotional, irrational, and fickle, but sociologists are no longer happy with such assumptions.

A **fad** is an unconventional practice that spreads rapidly and is adopted in a short period of time by a large number of people. A fad is essentially a social norm, but one that is to some degree unusual and departs from the widely accepted norms in a particular society. The best-known kinds of fads are clothing fashions; but furniture styles, varieties of food, and types of leisure activities may also become fads. By definition, a fad is temporary. If it persists for more than one or two years, we no longer call it a fad, but refer to it as conventional behaviour.

A **craze** is a special kind of fad, one that involves unusually intense commitment and enthusiasm, and is inevitably regarded as very strange and perhaps offensive by other people. Some crazes consist of outlandishly unconventional acts, for example running naked through spectator events (popular in the 1970s), while other crazes involve a commonplace pattern of behaviour carried to excess, such as marathon dancing (popular in the 1930s). In either case, a craze requires a level of commitment that is not necessary for most fads.

A **public** is a large and, usually, dispersed group made up of persons who share an interest in the same thing. They may hold similar views or they may sharply disagree. Those Canadians who are concerned about the dangers of nuclear energy constitute a public in Canada today, as do those interested in professional hockey, the depletion of the ozone layer, Celine Dion, poverty, the government deficit, solid-waste disposal, drug addiction, or the health-care crisis. We can learn about the views of publics by studying public-opinion polls, the results of political elections, calls to phone-in shows, letters to newspapers, media interviews, etc.

Finally, a **social movement**, as we have said, is a large collectivity of people trying to bring about or resist social change. Sociologists generally assume that it is the best organized and most institutionalized type of collective behaviour. Whether or not this is true, social movements are certainly more likely to have associations that coordinate the activities of their supporters. Sociologists now refer

A social movement is a large collectivity of people trying to bring about social change. The environmental movement is one prominent example of recent years.

to these as SMOs (social movement organizations). The degree of participation of members in SMOs is the most important characteristic that distinguishes social movements from other forms of collective behaviour. These SMOs may even possess a formal or semiformal structure consisting of leaders, a division of labour, and rules that regulate the conduct of members. Often we find that a large social movement is promoted by a number of SMOs. This has been the case with the women's movement, both in its early phase, before and after the turn of the century, and in the more recent phase, since the 1960s (Prentice et al., 1988: 170; Adamson, Briskin, and McPhail, 1988: 7–8).

A number of different versions of the collective behaviour perspective have emerged over the years, successively building on one another. We shall discuss several of the most influential theories within this tradition, taking them in order of their appearance in the literature.

Blumer and social contagion

One of the earliest proponents of the collective behaviour approach was Blumer, whose classic statement appeared in 1939. He was largely concerned with the behaviour of unconventional crowds, which he saw as driven by social contagion—a concept previously used by the French writer LeBon (1960 [1895]). In Blumer's words, **social contagion** refers to "the relatively rapid, unwitting, and nonrational dissemination of a mood, impulse or form of conduct" (1951 [1939]: 176). An idea, belief, or perception (often a fear) spreads through a group of people much like an epidemic. This happens as a result of a special kind of social interaction in which human responses become magnified as they move back and forth between interacting persons. You start getting nervous; that makes people standing beside you nervous; this in turn makes you more nervous; and so on.

Blumer called this interstimulation **circular reaction**. He contrasted it with "interpretative" behaviour, in which people do not allow themselves to become excited by one another, but instead thoughtfully interpret the actions of others before acting upon them. Circular reaction, as opposed to interpretative behaviour, generally arises when something (e.g., a natural catastrophe, such as a flood or earthquake) has disturbed the established ways in which people are accustomed to doing things. Or it may occur during those periods of history when people acquire new desires or impulses that cannot be satisfied through conventional behaviour.

Blumer's work has had enormous impact on the subsequent study of collective behaviour, but it has also evoked considerable criticism, especially in recent decades. Two objections in particular stand out. First, there is insufficient empirical evidence to demonstrate that circular reaction is more characteristic of collective behaviour than it is of routine behaviour, or even that such a process really exists. No one has yet developed a means of identifying and measuring circular reaction. Second, the idea of contagion exaggerates the unanimity of collective behaviour; it implies that participants are swept up in a common mood and respond similarly. Many writers have called this assumption into question, suggesting that, even within the same crowd, people may vary in both their attitudes and their behaviour.

Smelser's theory of collective behaviour

Without a doubt, the most ambitious work on collective behaviour in American sociology is Smelser's classic *Theory of Collective Behavior* (1962). While most sociologists influenced by Smelser have not been willing to accept his comprehensive and systematic theory in its entirety, many of Smelser's specific concepts and arguments have proven useful.

For Smelser, collective behaviour is essentially an attempt to alter the social environment. More precisely, he argued that we should apply this term when we find people trying to change their environment on the basis of a special kind of perception called a **generalized belief**. Generalized beliefs are oversimplified notions; like magical beliefs, they portray the world in terms of omnipotent forces, conspiracies, or extravagant promises. For example, a radio broadcast in 1938 called The War of the Worlds incited a serious panic in the New York area by creating a generalized belief that the earth was being invaded by beings from another planet.

There are a variety of changes that people might want to make in their social environment. Smelser used this variety to distinguish among different types of collective behaviour, such as panics, crazes, and social movements. He also made a distinction between two types of social movements: "value-oriented" movements, which try to change values; and "norm-oriented" movements, which seek to change social norms. According to Smelser, whether or not collective behaviour occurs—and if so, what type—depends on a number of conditions, including the strains or problems plaguing a society, the nature of the generalized belief, and the factors that precipitate or provoke the collective behaviour.

Two principal kinds of criticism have been levelled at Smelser's book. The first claims that his theory is little more than a set of concepts related to one another by definition. He does not, critics point out, get very far by defining a value-oriented movement as one in which people seek to change values, and then hypothesizing that a generalized belief among people that a certain value should be changed will give rise to a value-oriented movement. Yet this kind of circular logical deduction forms the bulk of Smelser's theory. The second criticism, which focuses particularly on the notion of generalized beliefs, takes Smelser to task for claiming that the motivations and aims of those who engage in collective behaviour are the illusions of irrational minds. In actual fact, Smelser did not take such an extreme position, but it is certainly true that his concept of generalized belief implies a measure of irrationality. Although critics have often distorted Smelser's argument, they have nevertheless identified some serious weaknesses in it.

Emergent norm theory

This theory was developed by Turner and Killian (1957) and deals principally with crowd behaviour, as did Blumer's work. Unlike Blumer, however, they argued that there is a great diversity among those who participate in a crowd. Not all members of a crowd, for example, do the same thing; nor do they all think the same way. Indeed, in many cases a large portion of a crowd has serious doubts about what the crowd is doing, and some might even disagree. And yet they frequently go along, or at least stand back and let the crowd carry on. Why?

The answer, if you accept **emergent norm theory**, is that they are under the impression that most others in the crowd are in agreement. They perceive, rightly or wrongly, that a consensus exists about a specific action that should be taken—for example, that an accused rapist should be lynched, that police arresting a man should be resisted, or that a university building should be occupied. As a result, they may conform to what the crowd is doing. Indeed, sanctions might even be imposed on those who fail to do so. When this happens-that is, when people start to conform to the apparent will of the crowd-then we can say that a new norm is emerging.

Game theory

The propositions of game theory (recall Chapter 1) are similar to those of emergent norm theory. Again the focus is on crowds, which are presumed to be highly diverse, and to consist of many members who are hesitant to participate (Berk, 1974a; 1974b; Granovetter, 1978). Yet there is a difference in emphasis between these two theories. Those who take a game theory approach are critical of the notion of emergent norms; they claim that it assumes people conform automatically and without thinking. **Game theory**, in contrast, assumes that people behave rationally in crowds. Members of a crowd conduct themselves on the basis of the relative pay-offs and costs of an activity.

According to game theory, the effect of a crowd on an individual is not that it induces an irrational hysteria or euphoria (as most earlier writers implied), but that it alters the pay-offs and costs of certain kinds of behaviour. A crowd can make it easier to do something that is usually costly. The probability, for instance, of getting arrested for breaking into a store, for attacking an immigrant, or for running naked through a classroom is greatly reduced if you are not the only person doing it. Indeed, it is even possible that in the presence of a crowd normally costly activity may be rewarded. One's status in a group could be raised if one were the first to charge a police blockade or to throw a punch at an opposing demonstrator. In extreme cases there might be penalties imposed on those who do not follow the crowd. We should not underestimate how often people may go along with collective behaviour out of fear that otherwise they might lose status among their friends, or perhaps even be attacked themselves.

Legacy of the collective behaviour approach

The theories of collective behaviour just discussed have become less acceptable in the past twenty years. Many sociologists are now quick to point out the weaknesses of this tradition. One repeated objection is that most writings on collective behaviour give insufficient attention to **social structure** and the particularities of social structure. Collective behaviourists convey the impression that what is important is much the same in all societies, in any historical period, regardless of differences in social structure.

Orderly Riots

It is now recognized that crowds are not as wild and senseless as was once thought. There is often a logical pattern to their activities, including the choice of victims for their violence. In some cases the behaviour of the crowd can be highly structured. E.P. Thompson has argued that English food rioters in the late eighteenth century were following the values and norms of a traditional "moral economy," which dictated that the food requirements of the local population be met before grain could be exported from a district. The conduct of many such crowds could be highly restrained and was often perfectly legitimate within the traditional social order.

It is the restraint, rather than the disorder, which is remarkable; and there can be no doubt that the actions were approved by an overwhelming popular consensus. There is a deeply felt conviction that prices ought, in times of dearth, to be regulated, and that the profiteer put himself outside of society. On occasion the crowd attempted to enlist, by suasion or force, a magistrate, parish constable, or some figure of authority to preside over the taxation populaire. In 1766 at Drayton (Oxon.) members of the crowd went to John Lyford's house "and asked him if he were a Constable—upon his saying 'yes' Cheer said he sho'd go with them to the Cross & receive the money for 3 sacks of flour which they had taken from one Betty Smith and which they w'd sell for 5s a Bushel"; the same crowd enlisted the constable of Abingdon for the same service. The constable of Handborough (also in Oxfordshire) was enlisted in a similar way, in 1795; the crowd set a price—and a substantial one—of 40s a sack upon a waggon of flour which had been intercepted, and the money for no fewer than fifteen sacks was paid into his hands. In the Isle of Ely, in the same year, "the mob insisted upon buying meat at 4d per lb, & desired Mr Gardner a Magistrate to superintend the sale, as the Mayor had done at Cambridge on Saturday sennight." Again in 1795 there were a number of occasions when militia or regular troops supervised forced sales, sometimes at bayonet-point, their officers looking steadfastly the other way. A combined operation of soldiery and crowd forced the mayor of Chichester to accede in setting the price of bread. At Wells men of the 122nd Regiment began by hooting those they term'd forestallers or jobbers of butter, who they hunted in different parts of the town—seized the butter—collected it together—placed sentinels over it—then threw it, & mix't it together in a tub—& afterwards retail'd the same, weighing it in scales, selling it after the rate of 8d per lb...though the common price given by the jobbers was rather more than 10d.

It would be foolish to suggest that, when so large a breach was made in the outworks of deference, many did not take the opportunity to carry off goods without payment. But there is abundant evidence the other way, and some of it is striking. There are the Honiton laceworkers, in 1766, who, having taken corn from the farmers and sold it at the popular price in the market, brought back to the farmers not only the money but also the sacks; the Oldham crowd, in 1800, which rationed each purchaser to two pecks a head; and the many occasions when carts were stopped on the roads, their contents sold, and the money entrusted to the carter.

Source: *E.P. Thompson, 1971. "The moral economy of the English crowd in the eighteenth century." Past and Present (pp. 112–13).*

Second, this theoretical interpretation pays little attention to interest groups and to conflict among such groups. Some sociologists argue that much of what is called collective behaviour is simply the activity of people in conflict; and yet the concept of conflict almost never appears in the collective behaviour literature.

Finally, a number of critics object to the argument that collective behaviour is non-institutionalized. They point out that people may participate in collective behaviour in order to defend values they have held for years, and they may do so in a relatively conventional manner. This is often true of social movements. We shall discuss a good example of this in the second part of this chapter, when we look at the historical roots of French Canadian nationalism. Other examples include the pro-life and anti-pornography movements. Even crowds can acquire a conventional character. Rioting can become a tradition, such as the storming of a football field after the final game of the year, or clashes with police stemming from yearly marches or festivities. An example frequently cited by critics of the collective behaviour approach is the food riot that was common in western Europe during the late eighteenth and early nineteenth centuries. Typically, these rioting crowds followed well-established norms and sought to defend time-honoured values (Rudé, 1964; Thompson, 1971) (see the boxed insert on "Orderly Riots"). Cases such as these have led many writers to question the fundamental assumption of this approach: that the distinguishing feature of collective behaviour is its relative non-institutionalization.

Social breakdown

There is a widespread supposition in sociological writings that social unrest occurs when established institutions are disrupted or weakened. As a consequence, so the argument goes, people are left "uprooted" and become susceptible to the appeal of a social movement. This notion appears in many different theoretical approaches to our subject, including the collective behaviour tradition just discussed. But we shall treat it separately and call it the **social breakdown approach**.

This perspective owes a considerable debt to Durkheim's notion of **social integration**, the attachment of individuals to social groups or institutions. We saw in Chapter 1 how social disintegration could help explain suicides. Durkheim also used it to account for economic conflict in Europe at the turn of the century (Durkheim, 1949: 2). Breakdown arguments may be formulated in several ways. Most common in sociology are the following sorts of assumptions.

1. The probability of social unrest is greatest in those places or countries where intermediate institutions (educational institutions, political parties, trade unions, etc.) are either absent or not functioning properly. These institutions integrate people into society and thus restrain rebellious behaviour. For example, perhaps the reason more social unrest is found in many Latin American countries than in Europe is that intermediate institutions are stronger in countries such as Denmark or Switzerland.

2. The probability of social unrest is high during periods of rapid social change (especially during rapid industrialization and urbanization) because such change disrupts and weakens traditional institutions. This kind of argument has been used to explain political turmoil in many developing countries and former Soviet-bloc countries today.

3. The people most likely to participate in social unrest are those who are relatively alienated, uprooted, or socially maladjusted. They are individuals who, for some reason, are poorly integrated into social institutions, perhaps even dismissed by others as misfits. Activists in the women's movement have been regarded this way, both in its first phase and in the more recent phase. Cartoons at the turn of the century portrayed feminists as unseemly and offensively self-assertive.

It is best to postpone some of the criticisms of this approach until we discuss the remaining theoretical perspectives. At this point we can simply offer one general remark. Although it is true that intermediate institutions may restrain rebellious behaviour, it is also possible for them to promote social unrest. Think of the role that universities, political parties, and labour unions have played in promoting the separatist movement in Quebec.

Relative deprivation

This is the simplest and most straightforward theoretical approach to social movements, and probably comes closest to your own common-sense explanation. It says that people will turn against existing social arrangements when they are most unhappy with them. Concepts such as *discontent* and *dissatisfaction* have been used to describe popular feelings of this kind. According to this point of view, if the level of discontent rises in a society, people are more likely to rebel.

Numerous reasons can be given for increases in discontent. The most generally accepted in sociology is that they occur when people are experiencing **relative deprivation**, or a gap between what people believe they have a right to receive (their expectations) and what they actually receive (their achievements). A popular view today is that people are most likely to participate in social unrest when their expectations for advancement are frustrated. This situation is even more likely to generate unrest than one in which their welfare is actually deteriorating.

The idea of rising expectations has been around for a long time. It is probably most often associated with the French statesman and historian Alexis de Tocqueville, who wrote a famous study on the origins of the French Revolution (1955 [1856]). De Tocqueville's explanation of the Revolution consisted of several different lines of argument, but he is most remembered for his claim that the Revolution occurred when economic conditions were relatively better and political repression less severe than in earlier periods. He also pointed out that support for the Revolution was greatest in comparatively prosperous parts of France. He suggested that prosperity and political freedom, far from satisfying people, simply raise their expectations further. And then he drew the conclusion so often quoted: "Thus the social order overthrown by a revolution is almost always better than the one immediately preceding it, and experience teaches us that, generally speaking, the most perilous moment for a bad government is one when it seeks to mend its ways" (1955 [1856]: 176–77).

In spite of its intuitive appeal, some serious questions can be raised about relative deprivation theory. Again you will find it easier to understand them after we have discussed the collective action approach. Nevertheless, we can make a preliminary observation here. The relative deprivation approach makes the mistake of focusing primarily on the conditions that immediately precede a social movement or a revolt. There is an assumption that, if we can identify and understand discontent just before an uprising, then we have explained the uprising itself. Relative deprivation explanations of the French Revolution concentrate on social conditions and the popular mood as they emerged in the late 1780s. But what if people had been just as dissatisfied in earlier years and yet did not rebel? If this were true, relative deprivation theory might be doing little more than identifying precipitating factors.

Collective action

The fourth theoretical approach contrasts sharply with the first three. It conceives of social movements in a very different way. To begin with, it rejects the concept of collective behaviour and the whole idea that a social movement is relatively non-institutionalized. Instead, it argues that social movements (as well as crowds and many other forms of social unrest) belong to an even broader category of human behaviour called collective action (Tilly, Tilly, and Tilly, 1975; Tilly, 1978).

It is necessary to define this term carefully, since it can easily be confused with collective behaviour, which has quite a different meaning. Collective *behaviour* refers to relatively non-institutionalized conduct, that is, conduct that departs from the ordinary and routine. In a Canadian neighbourhood, a group of young people wearing rings in their tongues is collective *behaviour*. In contrast, **collective action** covers both institutionalized and non-institutionalized activity. It can best be defined as the pursuit of a goal or set of goals by a number of persons. Thus it includes a wide range of social phenomena. A terrorist organization kidnapping a diplomat, a group of neighbours cleaning a park, the members of a trade union seeking to raise their wages, a group of students doing a class project-all are examples of collective action.

Collective action is always occurring. Every day, people participate in collective efforts of some sort, within their family, at their place of work, or in a voluntary association. But not all collective action is the same. Its character varies tremendously, and this variation is what we should study, according to this theoretical perspective. Each of the preceding theoretical approaches was developed essentially to explain variations in the *amount* of social unrest. Collective action theorists suggest that we can understand much more by studying and explaining variations in the *character* of social unrest. How does collective action differ from one society to another? How does its character change over time within the same society?

Let us take an example. Suppose we are doing a study of the native peoples' movement in Canada during the 1990s. If we were to adopt one of the theoretical approaches described above, we would ask ourselves why protest among Indians and Inuit increased during this period. We might look for rising expectations in the Indian and Inuit population, or a breakdown in their traditional institutions, or perhaps the emergence of a new norm or generalized belief.

If, on the other hand, we were to adopt a collective action approach, we would be inclined to see the recent movement as part of a tradition of collective action by native peoples in Canada. We would emphasize that this movement was by no means their first effort to defend their interests. We would point out that native peoples have a significant history of collective action, especially in the western provinces. We would insist on asking, therefore, how the recent movement differed from earlier movements. How did collective action by native peoples change in terms of numbers and kinds of people participating, in terms of goals, and

in terms of methods used to achieve those goals? In answering these questions we would discover, among other things, that a much younger and generally more educated native population has become involved, and that the objectives and strategy of collective action have become less defensive and more offensive. We would learn that natives have developed more skilled leadership, which is able both to organize Indians and Inuit and to defend their legal rights. And we would see that the movement has become more unified across Canada, though many divisions persist.

In addition to describing changes in the character of collective action, those who adopt this theoretical perspective also try to explain why such changes occur. To do this they examine the underlying social bonds and divisions in the society, and endeavour to understand how these structural conditions change over time. For each historical period, one needs to determine the particular combinations of people that are likely to engage in collective action. The job is to identify two kinds of factors: first, *cleavage factors*, which tend to separate people from one another or set them at odds; and second, *integrating factors*, which pull people together in social groups so that they can engage in collective action, whether or not collective action actually occurs. A basic argument of the collective action perspective is that both cleavage and integrating factors are necessary conditions for social movements to occur.

Notice in this regard that the collective action approach has borrowed a concept from the breakdown perspective—the concept of integration—but has broadened its application. When breakdown theorists talk about integration, they mean

TABLE 14.1   Dominant Perspectives on Social Movements in Europe and North America, 1950s to 1990s

	Dominant perspectives in the 1950s, 1960s, and early 1970s	Dominant perspectives in the late 1970s, 1980s, and 1990s
Europe	Collective action, especially Marxism	New social movements
North America	Collective behaviour, breakdown, and relative deprivation	Collective action, especially resource mobilization

The rise in collective action by Canada's Native population can be interpreted in many ways. Does it relate to a break-down in traditional Native institutions? Or to the emergence of more skilled leadership in the Native community? Or is there some other fundamental cause?

integration into established groups and institutions that support the status quo. Integration, as far as they are concerned, always impedes social unrest. Advocates of the collective action approach, however, are referring to integration into any kind of group or institution, whether or not it supports the established order. In other words, they assume that social integration forms the basis for any kind of collective action, radical or conservative, rebellious or loyalist. This assumption challenges the basic tenets of the breakdown approach.

The collective action approach also runs counter to relative deprivation theory. Collective action theorists are extremely critical of the emphasis placed on discontent as a condition for social unrest. They insist that discontent, though perhaps a necessary condition, is not a sufficient condition for social unrest. In other words, its presence alone

does not ensure that social protest will occur. Even a very high level of discontent is not, by itself, enough to generate protest. Discontent must be mobilized. The people who are dissatisfied have to come together and get organized to act collectively. Their goals must be defined; they must be persuaded to join forces; and their activities have to be coordinated.

The weakness of the discontent approach, according to this alternative line of reasoning, is that it treats mobilization as non-problematic. It assumes that people will automatically mobilize if their level of dissatisfaction is high. The collective action perspective firmly rejects such a supposition, and argues, on the contrary, that mobilization is problematic, indeed far more problematic than discontent. Reversing the emphasis, collective action theory claims that enough dissatisfaction is generally present in any society to cause social unrest, provided it can be mobilized. But the mobilization of discontented populations is extremely difficult. Consequently, the argument goes, when protest does materialize, often it is not because the level of dissatisfaction has risen, but rather because conditions for the mobilization of discontented people have improved.

Resource mobilization

An important body of literature within the collective action perspective focuses on the means by which people are mobilized in collective action. The concept of mobilization may be familiar to you. The word is frequently used outside sociology. One often speaks of mobilizing people to fight wars, vote for certain political candidates, search for lost children, collect donations for charity, clean up the environment, and so forth. In all of these contexts, one is describing the commitment of resources to a goal or objective to which they were not committed before. At a particular time, people are organized to engage in a specific collective activity. The term **mobilization**, it is essential to understand, is not meant to denote the *creation* of new resources but rather the *transfer* of resources from one kind of collective action to another. A fundamental assumption of the resource mobilization approach is that getting resources transferred is an organizational problem, and as such should be studied using concepts developed for the analysis of social organizations in general.

Let us now identify some more specific conditions that assist mobilization. One is an appropriate *ideology*, or **frame**—that is, a set of beliefs that helps people to interpret and explain their world and that provides the basis for collective action. The term was developed by Goffman (1974), but adapted for the study of social movements by Snow and others (Snow et al., 1986; Snow and Benford, 1988 and 1992). In resource mobilization theory, the function of a frame is to identify a problem, diagnose it, attribute blame, and offer a solution. Common perceptions among members or potential members of a movement also facilitate the coordination of their activities and direct them towards a common goal.

An underlying frame can emerge spontaneously (that is, without anyone trying to create it) in a culture, but frames are usually brought to bear on a specific issue consciously and intentionally by social movement leaders. These leaders often have to struggle against alternative frames promoted by the dominant institutions in a society or by the leaders of opposing groups. The gay and lesbian movement has had a particularly difficult time in struggling with opposing frames in society.

The success of any organizational activity also depends on whether members possess an *effective means of communicating* with one another. People have to become aware of their common interests or goals, to agree on action to achieve these goals, and to coordinate their efforts. Discontented groups that possess or are able to acquire channels for communication (particularly access to mass media) are more likely to become mobilized than those without such channels.

A network of *cooperative relationships* serves a similar purpose. A cooperative relationship is a normal social relationship involving some kind of cooperative activity. Examples might be people working as a team on a job, spending free time together in a voluntary organization or social club, or participating in the same youth gang, trade union, church, or political party. If relationships of this kind exist among discontented people, communication is greatly facilitated. Cooperative relationships can also serve as the basis for persuasion and influence. None of the other theoretical approaches gives sufficient attention to the question of how people become involved in a social movement. The answer is that they typically join through the influence of a friend or acquaintance.

Those who have studied resource mobilization have come to place considerable emphasis on the effects of **selective incentives**. The term refers to the benefits that a person can derive from belonging to an association or joining a social movement. These incentives are what motivate people to pay the costs of joining the movement. Generally, the most common selective incentive is fellowship with other activists. In some cases, the prestige of a position of leadership in a social movement, and the media publicity that may go with it, can also be rewarding to participants. Some movements are also able to offer more material rewards, such as salaries, travel expenses, insurance discounts, or appointment to government office.

A social movement is easier to organize if leaders have *financial resources* to promote its activities. Money can buy media time, pay for members to travel, provide compensation for the work that members devote to the cause, and meet other expenses of collective action. Many social movements collapse simply because they run out of money. Those movements that have access to funds, particularly a relatively affluent body of supporters or potential supporters, will survive longer. In Canada, government grants have been an important source of funds for some movements, such as the women's movement and the environmental movement.

As a result of the need for framing, leadership, a means of communicating, cooperative relation-ships, and financial resources, social movements are much more likely to mobilize successfully if they can build on existing groups, organizations, or institutions. Literature on the emergence of political movements in western Canada between the wars has generally emphasized this point (Thompson and Seager, 1985: 231, 234; Finkel, 1989: 30). The organizational base of urban movements in Montreal in the 1960s, like most other urban movements in North America, consisted of existing neighbourhood organizations (Hamel, 1991: 101–102). The women's movement that emerged in the late 1960s and early 1970s built on a range of existing or developing organizations. On the more conservative side, the movement built on established organizations, such as the National

Contemporary women's organizations, like the National Action Committee on the Status of Women, build on already existing or developing organizations. Joan Grant-Cummings (centre) is shown here celebrating her victory to become the Committee's new president.

Council of Women, the Canadian Federation of Business and Professional Women's Clubs, the Canadian Federation of University Women, the National Council of Jewish Women, and the YWCA; on the more avant-garde side, the movement built on the new left movement and student radicalism, including student separatist bodies in Quebec (Prentice et al., 1988: 331–34, 346, 354–56; Adamson, Briskin, and McPhail, 1988).

Populations vary in the resources to which they have access. Some social groups lack resources of their own and can only be mobilized if leaders and resources come from the outside; that is, they depend on external resources. Other groups have more of their own internal resources. In the course of its history, a movement may develop its own resources and thus become more independent (Pichardo, 1988). Although the native movement in Canada obtains funds from the government, it has also developed more internal resources as a result of successful land claims.

Again, let us note the difference between this line of reasoning and a breakdown argument. Theories of breakdown, if you recall, assert that a social movement is most likely to occur when social institutions are weak; breakdown theories also claim that those who participate are, as a rule, socially isolated. The collective action literature, in contrast, emphasizes the need for organizational structures to furnish leadership and framing, and to provide channels for communication and a network of cooperative relationships. According to writers on collective action, the breakdown of institutional structures will decrease rather than increase the probability of social unrest, and those who are socially isolated are least likely, not most likely, to participate.

It is also interesting to see differences in the way collective action theory and relative deprivation theory explain the fact that it is not usually the most disadvantaged groups in society that engage in social movements. Relative deprivation theory solves this puzzle by saying that it is relative rather than absolute deprivation that makes people angry. Collective action theorists, in contrast, argue that only people who are better off have the resources to organize a social movement and impress their demands on authorities. This is why the poorest do not rebel.

Marxist explanations of social movements

The collective action perspective has been significantly influenced by Marx and Marxist writers. Long before sociologists began to talk about collective action or resource mobilization, Marxists had taken what we would now call a collective action approach. During the period in which collective behaviour, breakdown, and relative deprivation were the dominant approaches in North America, Marxism was more influential in Europe.

Marxists have never been interested in social movements in general. They like to study revolts that could lead to major overhauls in the whole way in which political and economic functions in a society are carried out—that is, the entire existing order. According to Marxists, such revolts fall into two categories.

The first consists of revolts that lead to the overthrow of feudalism. These are called *bourgeois revolts*. The major two in which Marxists have been interested are the English overthrow of Charles I in the seventeenth century and the French overthrow of Louis XVI in the eighteenth century (in which each king lost his head). Although the French revolt is, of course, called the French Revolution, the English do not like to call theirs a revolution; it is known as the English Civil War. Both revolts supposedly undermined the political power of the feudal lords and increased the political power of a rising bourgeois class. Some Marxists argue that this transfer of political power was a consequence of economic and structural changes taking place in the society, while other Marxists argue that this transfer of political power facilitated the economic structural changes. Neither argument has received much support from non-Marxist historians.

The second category of social movements includes those that Marx hoped would eventually lead to the overthrow of capitalism. These are primarily the labour and socialist movements of the nineteenth and twentieth centuries. As mentioned in Chapter 6, Social Stratification, Marx identified two underlying causes of these movements. First, the capitalist system creates increased exploitation, which intensifies discontent among the mass of the population and opposition to the capitalist system. Second, the capitalist system polarizes classes, brings workers together physically in crowded urban centres and in factories, provides improved means of communication among them, and in other ways creates better conditions for the mobilization of workers in collective action, including the development of class consciousness. It is this part of the Marxist thesis that has had considerable influence on the collective action approach.

More recently, many Marxists have been influenced by the writings of an Italian communist of the early twentieth century, Antonio Gramsci, who spent many years in prison jotting ideas down on paper, which were subsequently published as his *Prison Notebooks*. Gramsci argued that the proletariat needs, even before the fall of capitalism, to build a new order in which it establishes proletarian **hegemony**. Here the term "hegemony" refers to the domination of a class or alliance of classes over others, not only economically but politically and culturally. A precondition for the revolution of the working class, in Gramsci's view, is the replacement of bourgeois hegemony with proletarian hegemony. For example, the high value placed on profit and economic growth would have to be replaced by other values in order to undermine bourgeois hegemony. He referred to the achievement of prerevolutionary proletarian hegemony as a "war of position," as opposed to a direct attack on the capitalist system, which he called a "war of movement." One of the significant contributions of Gramsci has been to persuade Marxists of the importance of non-economic struggles, including ideological struggles, against the existing order.

Status movements

Some of the movements studied as forms of "collective action" are status movements. The term "status" has been used in a variety of ways, but here it denotes positive or negative social evaluation. It is synonymous with prestige or esteem. Status is a type of power, the power to command respect. It is derived from the possession or presumed possession of characteristics that people admire or are told they should admire. How people are treated depends on their status. Usually (but not always) high status enables a person to obtain better treatment. (For a more complete discussion of the conceptualization of status see Clark 1995: 15–18.)

Status varies greatly in the extent to which it is institutionalized, that is the extent to which stable norms and values regulate the distribution of status and the rights and duties associated with it. Throw several 5-year-olds together and status quickly comes to have an effect on their interaction, but it is not well institutionalized. In most other contexts, the institutionalization of status varies between this extreme and situations where it is rigidly controlled. When status is well institutionalized it becomes a position in a status hierarchy with certain rights and obligations. Most people hold both institutionalized and non-institutionalized statuses, and it is possible for them to lose one more than the other—non-institutionalized status more than institutionalized status (a king who comes to be regarded as a fool) or vice versa (a king who is forced to abdicate but is still highly respected). Status may even be institutionalized in law, in which case it becomes a "legal status."

Examples of institutionalized statuses in Canada today are woman, man, adult, child or minor, juvenile, student, native, citizen, immigrant, WASP, and visible minority. A distinction has been made in sociology between "status communities" and "status columns" or "blocs" (Turner 1988: 12–13). The former refers to enduring communities that have lived together over long periods of time, sharing language, culture, and other attributes. Native communities in Canada provide examples of status communities. Status columns or blocs are organizations or associations in which people come together for specific purposes. Feminist organizations, organizations for the protection of refugees, pensioners' associations, and gay and lesbian organizations are all examples of status columns or blocs in Canada today.

The collective action approach has called attention to deficiencies in some of the earlier schools of thought. However, it is itself by no means safe from criticism. Not surprisingly, it has been chastised for ignoring discontent or motivation, or for taking them for granted. It is frequently claimed that it over-emphasizes calculating, strategic, instrumental, rational, goal-oriented action, to the neglect of non-calculating, expressive, emotional, impulsive, or passionate human behaviour. It has been lambasted for neglecting culture and psychological forces, and for ignoring the role of social movements in giving people a collective identity and meaning to their lives. And it has been criticized for giving insufficient attention to non-political movements. More surprisingly, it has also been accused of neglecting ideology, major social changes, and structural conditions. (One or more of these criticisms can be found in Scott, 1990; Canel, 1992; Gamson, 1992; and McAdam et al., 1996b.) An important part of the collective action literature could also be accused of taking a functionalist cookbook approach to social movements—for some sociologists, studying social movements has become primarily a matter of developing a list of conditions for their emergence, continuation, spread, and success.

The Marxist perspective on social movements has been criticized primarily on two grounds: first, for over-emphasizing the importance of economic factors in social processes; and second, for neglecting movements that are not based on class. There has been a tendency among Marxists to focus almost all of their attention on working-class movements.

Postmodernism and the new social movements

The first three approaches (collective behaviour, breakdown, and relative deprivation) sought to develop generalizations about social movements that would be valid in most times and places. The collective action perspective generally gives more attention to differences in time and place. Without rejecting generalizations altogether, the fifth approach we shall discuss is also more interested in understanding social movements in a particular time and place—the last half of the twentieth century in western Europe and North America.

This approach is based on the assumption that Western society has changed significantly from what it was like in the nineteenth century and the first half of the twentieth. The earlier period is often referred to as "industrial" or "modern" society, while the more recent period is called "postindustrial" or "postmodern" society. This new society has given rise to "new social movements"—movements that result from new conflicts, new problems, or new forces (Luke, 1989; Hamel, 1991). The major new social movements are the student, urban, feminist, environmental, and gay and lesbian movements.

This approach emerged primarily in Europe in reaction to the Marxist approach. It rejected the earlier emphasis on class-based movements, or at least the Marxist emphasis on the working class as the only class that could bring about fundamental change. Thus, this literature was reacting against the previously dominant approach in Europe just as in North America the collective action approach was reacting against the previously dominant approaches—collective behaviour, breakdown, and relative deprivation theory.

The new social movement approach is based on two overlapping bodies of literature regarding the nature of late twentieth-century society: (1) the postmodern literature; and (2) the postindustrial literature.

Postmodernism means a lot of different things to different people, but in sociology it means primarily a rejection of all the scholarship that has sought to explain "modernity" (as evidenced in western Europe and North America in the nineteenth and twentieth centuries). The scholarship that is rejected includes the major sociological theorists—Marx, Weber, and Durkheim—and all those who have been influenced by their work. Postmodernists focus on differences and discontinuities; they denounce positivism and stress indeterminacy; and they reject large, all-embracing theories, interpretations, or explanations—what they call "metanarratives" or "totalistic" theory, theories that try to explain everything.

This literature is highly diverse, encompassing a large number of contradictory claims about what postmodern society is like. It is possible to find postmodern writers asserting that postmodern people are cynical, sceptical, amoral, individualistic, spontaneous, selfish, self-gratifying, relaxed, and/or light-hearted. Gone is the serious, committed, ideologically motivated class warrior of Marxism; in postmodern society we have less confidence in the superiority of our convictions. Class, some postmodernists insist, is no longer the principal basis for collective action.

In addition, people who were formerly ignored, who were "voiceless," come to be heard, or should come to be heard, in a postmodern society. There is a rejection of authority and of the separation that has been made between high arts and mass culture. Some postmodern writers suggest that struggles over culture have replaced the struggles over production that dominated modern or industrial society. There is general agreement that postmodern society is disconnected and fragmented (Huyssen, 1986; Connor, 1989; Rosenau, 1992).

According to the *postindustrial* literature, during the last half of the twentieth century there has been a shift in the centre of production from resource extraction (agriculture, mining, lumbering, and so forth) and heavy manufacturing (building ships and trains) to light high-tech industry, communications, and information-based production. The manufacturing, working class plays a less important role—white-collar workers and the middle class a more important role—in post-industrial production. Growth depends on science and other kinds of knowledge more than on capital accumulation and investment. Domination is achieved not through economic and political repression, but through hyper-consumption, technological progress, seductive integration, and mass manipulation. The mass media and the advertising industry are the major instruments of this postindustrial integration and manipulation (Marcuse, 1964; Touraine, 1971; Luke, 1989).

What all these arguments lead to is the assertion that the distinctive characteristics of postindustrial or postmodern society have created distinctive characteristics in the social movements that have emerged in this society. The new social movements are more concerned with values and culture than were the old working-class movements. Counter-culture and opposition to the conventional is praised in a "romance of the marginal" (Connor, 1989: 228). The pop-art movement sought to collapse the distinction between high and low art, and between art and everyday life (Huyssen, 1986). Most new social movements are anti-authority. Although there is considerable disagreement on this point, some have argued that new social movements are less political than the old movements. There is more agreement that they are less economic. New social movements represent the formerly unrepresented, often involving a variety of groups and issues. The middle class plays a greater role than the employed working class. New social movements are characterized by spontaneity, fragmentation, decentralization, and discontinuity. These characteristics are well illustrated in the Montreal urban movements studied by Hamel (1991 and 1995).

The most common criticism of the new social movement approach is that the so-called "new social movements" are not so new. Feminist movements, youth movements, and even the environmental movement can be found in earlier periods. Many writers have pointed out, as well, that not all movements in the nineteenth and early twentieth centuries were working-class movements; there is nothing new about non-class movements. It has also been claimed that new social movements are not, in general, less political than earlier social movements. Critics have also charged that differences among new social movements have been disregarded. And the new social movement literature has been attacked for ignoring class (Scott, 1990; Canel, 1992; Adam, 1993).

A major criticism of both postmodernism and the new social movement literature is that it is ethnocentric, specifically Eurocentric, and that it is fixated on middle-class experiences (Gamson, 1992). Both journalistic and academic literature on tattooing, for example, has been castigated for ignoring class differences in tattooing and for being taken in by the promoters of middle-class tattooing, who pretend that respectable and artistic tattooing is replacing ugly and offensive "biker" tattooing (DeMello, 1995).

A final word in defence of each approach

Like the people they study, sociologists are prone to fads and fashions. As already indicated, some of the above approaches are now out of favour. This is not to be deplored so long as their contributions are not cast aside. It would be a mistake, for example, to dismiss the abundant research carried out by students of collective behaviour just because we cannot accept certain parts of their argument. In particular, it would be a serious error to throw away the concept of institutionalization just because we find some collective behaviour that does not seem to be less institutionalized than routine behaviour. Social behaviour does in fact vary in its degree of institutionalization. Panics, crowds, and social movements may not always be less institutionalized than the behaviour we encounter daily, but most often they are. What we need to do is study the degree of institutionalization of any social activity in which we are interested, whether it has generally been classified as collective behaviour or not. Institutionalization should be taken not as a given but as a variable that we want to measure and explain, and whose consequences we need to understand. Whatever its errors and omissions, collective behaviour theory does make a contribution to our knowledge on the subject.

Similarly, theories that explain social movements as a result of social breakdown should not be totally rejected. This literature is not so much incorrect as incomplete. It is perfectly reasonable to assume that social disorganization or breakdown raises the probability of protest or rebellion, so long as we specify the social ties that are breaking down. If people are well integrated into institutions that support the established order, then there is indeed little chance that they will engage in movements that challenge that order; and the likelihood that they will rebel against established institutions does increase if their integration into these institutions weakens. What breakdown theory has ignored, as we have seen, is that people have to be integrated into groups of some kind in order to be mobilized for collective action. People who are wholly disorganized, completely uprooted, and alienated may engage in antisocial behaviour, but they will not form social movements. Thus, the ideal condition for rebellious action is the integration of a large number of people into strong institutions or structures that are themselves "alienated" from the established order (Pinard, 1968).

Although relative deprivation cannot alone account for the rise of a social movement, we must somehow explain motivation. Motivating factors are more diverse than most sociologists have recognized. We need to take into account not only relative deprivation, but also other factors that could motivate a person to join a movement, such as moral outrage, an expectation that the movement will be a success, and selective incentives. We must above all explain what makes people angry, because anger is usually the major reason that people engage in protest activities. This is what relative deprivation theory tried to do, and to a considerable extent it succeeded, if at the expense of ignoring much else.

Many of the criticisms that have been made of the collective action perspective apply primarily to the resource mobilization approach, not to the collective action perspective as a whole. This is true of the claim that the approach over-emphasizes calculating, strategic, and instrumental action; that it neglects ideology, macro processes, and structural conditions; and that it takes a functionalist cookbook approach to social movements. Many of these criticisms can be overcome, and some are being overcome. There is an increasing recognition in the resource mobilization literature of the importance of motivation and culture (McAdam et al., 1996a).

The major strength of the collective action perspective is that it gives more emphasis to the uniqueness of societies than do the theoretical orientations to which it was reacting. It seeks most of all to identify and explain what is dissimilar about collective action at different times and in different places. Writers in this perspective would insist that most of what is significant about collective action varies from one society to another.

In an important respect, this is the major strength of the new social movement approach as well. It is true that the writers in this school have ignored movements outside western Europe and North America, but at least they have never claimed that they are explaining all social movements. What they have wanted to do is to develop a perspective that would help them best understand the movements that were emerging in the society in which they lived. They believed this could not be done with general theories.

Canadian Social Structure and Collective Action

The remainder of this chapter is devoted to social movements in Canada and the social conditions underlying them. We shall not endeavour to apply or test the theoretical approaches discussed above. We shall, however, adopt the general framework provided by the collective action approach. To help understand the conditions that have given rise to social movements in Canada, we shall look for sources of integration and cleavage in the social structure. A **social cleavage** is a division based on age, class, ethnicity, etc., that may result in the formation of distinct social groups. An effort will be made to explain how the social structure has provided certain groups in the Canadian population with the solidarity and resources necessary for building and maintaining collective action.

Although similar social cleavages can be found in many societies, every society is unique in two ways. First, the relative importance or intensity of different types of cleavage varies from one society to another. In some societies, class cleavages are more divisive than ethnic cleavages, while in others the reverse is true. Second, the relationship among cleavages differs from one country to another. In some societies, people who belong to the same social class may be opposed to one another because they belong to different ethnic groups. In other societies, ethnicity may coincide with class divisions and serve to reinforce them. The final "topography" that emerges from these patterns will be unique to a particular society and will determine the character of its collective action.

In Chapter 6, Social Stratification, we listed a number of patterns of differentiation that underlie Canadian social structure and give rise to unequal ranking or status hierarchies. Some of these same patterns of differentiation also divide Canadian society into identifiable groups on which collective action has been based. We shall outline, very briefly, those patterns of differentiation that have had the most effect on collective action.

Age   In virtually all societies, profound differences exist in attitudes, lifestyle, social relationships, and access to resources between the young and old (recall Chapter 9, Aging). This is no less true in Canada. Indeed, age differentiation may be more pronounced in an advanced industrial society such as ours than in other types of societies, as a result of changes in family structure and the expansion of educational institutions that intensify and prolong differences between youth and older members of the population. These educational institutions also serve to increase the integration of young people as a group, by helping to bring them together and providing a milieu for the development of youth cultures. This integration in turn can provide the basis for the mobilization of collective action by young people, and on their behalf. A consequence, most obvious in the 1960s and 1970s, has been the appearance of a variety of youth movements in Canada and in several other industrialized societies.

Movements by the elderly have been less common, but are not unknown. An illustration in Canada was the mobilization of large numbers of people against the de-indexing of the Canadian old-age pension in 1985. As their proportionate size in the population grows, we may see more political activity by senior citizens, but thus far collective action by the elderly has been limited.

Class   In Canada, as in most societies, class has a significant effect on collective action. This is especially the case whenever people of the same class position have developed integrative structures that help to mobilize their collective activities. Labour unions can provide such integration. The long and bitter history of labour strife is indicative of the great impact of class differentiation on collective action in this country. Also important is the influence that class has on collective action when it coincides with other major sources of social differentiation. The labour movement in Quebec, for example, owes much of its strength to a special combination of ethnic, regional, and class solidarities.

Ethnicity   In Chapter 8, Race and Ethnic Relations, we discussed in detail the numerous and often deep racial and ethnic divisions found in Canadian society. It is frequently the case that people who belong to different ethnic groups also differ in attitudes, interests, and social relationships, while those who belong to the same ethnic group often share these attributes. The result, as we shall see in a moment, can be an extremely effective social base for the organization of collective action.

Region   A number of factors have served to create deep regional divisions in Canada. The vast geographical expanse of the country, the fact that different parts of it were settled at different times, and the economic disparities that exist among regions have all promoted regional cleavage. Modern means of communication and considerable mobility in the population serve to mitigate these divisions to a degree, but there remain sharp social and cultural differences from one part of the country to another. In some cases there is also, within a particular region, a strong measure of social cohesion and group feeling. Collective action in Canada has repeatedly shown signs of these regional divisions and solidarities.

Rural or urban residence   The cleavage between rural and urban groups usually diminishes in advanced industrial societies as the two sectors become culturally and economically assimilated. There always persists, however, a fundamental opposition in interests between rural and urban populations. That division remains especially pronounced in Canada as a result of our tendency to exploit or abandon rather than transform many of our rural areas as the country becomes more industrialized. One can find large rural areas in Canada that are economically depressed, relatively depopulated, and socially isolated from the larger urban society. Inevitably, rural-urban differences have had an impact on collective action in Canada.

Gender   This is the most unpredictable of these six patterns of differentiation. On the basis of their sex, women are assigned separate roles in our society, most obviously those of housekeeper and child-raiser (see Chapter 7, Gender Roles). On the same basis, they were once denied equal political and economic rights. On the other hand, men and women typically share attitudes, interests, and social bonds through the marriage and kinship structure. These have served to mitigate the gender cleavage, and at the same time to undermine the integration of women as a group by creating strong cross-gender ties. Consequently, in spite of the feminist movement, women are far from united in collective action.

We shall now provide a further discussion of two of the above patterns, the regional and ethnic divisions. We shall consider the way in which these sources of integration and cleavage have shaped the character of collective action in Canada.

Regional cleavage

Geographical disunity in Canada has resulted not only from the vast distances that separate people living in different parts of this country, but also from the fact that, for various reasons, regional variations have tended to coincide with other kinds of differences.

Most obviously, regional diversity coincides with economic functions. Some parts of the country are manufacturing centres; others are largely agricultural; and still others supply natural resources. In addition, and partly as a consequence, there are substantial inequalities in wealth and income from one province to another, particularly between western Canada and the Atlantic region (see Chapter 6, Social Stratification). Further, ethnic groups are not evenly distributed throughout the country (see Chapter 8, Race and Ethnicity). The most obvious concentration is that of French Canadians in the province of Quebec, but we can find other patterns of variation. For example, outside of Quebec, the percentage of persons claiming British ancestry varies widely, from close to 90 percent in Newfoundland and Prince Edward Island to about half in Manitoba and Saskatchewan. The regional cleavage is also associated with rural/urban differences; certain provinces are much less urbanized than others. In 1991 the percentage of the population living in rural areas ranged from 63 percent in the Northwest Territories, 37 percent in Saskatchewan, 41 percent in the Yukon, and over 40 percent in each of the Atlantic provinces to only 18 percent in Ontario and 22 percent in Quebec (Statistics Canada, 1992, 1991 *Census of Canada*).

Given this variation, it is not surprising that values and attitudes have differed from one province to another. Public opinion surveys have routinely shown significant differences among provinces on a wide range of issues. A poll conducted in 1992 indicated that the percentage of persons favouring a decrease in immigration ranged from 58 percent in the Atlantic provinces to 35 percent in Quebec (Canadian Institute of Public Opinion, 1992).

These and other differences among regions have had a profound impact on the character of collective action in this country. Social cleavage between regions, combined with social integration within regions, has resulted in collective action that tends to be weak and divided nationally, while often strong regionally. Canadians have considerable difficulty getting together and doing things as a nation. Most organizations to which they belong, whether political, economic, or social, are geographically disconnected. Inevitably, social movements tend to attract support from specific parts of the country. Even a national movement, such as the women's movement, can vary greatly from one province to another (Adamson, Briskin, and McPhail, 1988: 8, 28). And many social movements in Canada have directly reflected the grievances and animosities that some areas have felt towards others.

Prairie movements

The best-known regional movements in Canadian history are those that appeared primarily in the Prairie provinces between the two world wars. They are by no means the only movements with a regional basis, but since they have received the most scholarly attention, we shall illustrate the effect of regional cleavage on collective action by briefly describing these movements.

The Prairie movements emerged on a social foundation that was formed by divisions of both class and region. A highly diversified population settled in the Prairie provinces in the late nineteenth and early twentieth centuries; yet out of it there soon developed a remarkably unified social group loosely based on agriculture. We must be careful, however, not to overstate this point. In addition to conflicts of interest between farmers and other sectors, there were significant divisions among farmers themselves, most notably as a consequence of differences in the size of their farms, type of agriculture, and their ethnic origin. We should also recognize that other social groups contributed to Prairie movements besides farmers. Still, farmers were critical and, in comparison with most other groups in Canadian society, those in the Prairies possessed considerable solidarity and cohesion. They were brought together by common problems and a common position in the social structure. The majority were engaged in the production of the same crop, namely wheat, and were therefore simultaneously affected by its success or failure. Their fortunes rose and fell collectively, and this served to integrate them as a group, facilitating their political mobilization.

At the same time, other factors divided them from the rest of the country. No doubt the great physical distances that separated Prairie people from those living in other parts of Canada helped to alienate them. More important, however, was a fundamental opposition of interests. Western

farmers were forced, as a result of tariffs, to buy expensive goods manufactured in eastern Canada, yet they had to sell their wheat on an unprotected international market. Furthermore, the marketing of this wheat was, in their perception at least, controlled by urban and eastern business interests, and the terms of trade were maintained in favour of those business interests.

The first significant collective effort by western farmers was the struggle against the grain-elevator companies. The Territorial Grain Growers' Association was formed just after the turn of the century and became the Saskatchewan Grain Growers' Association in 1905. This body, along with other cooperative organizations established in this period, formed an effective base for increased political activity by farmers, which accelerated around 1910 and was directed primarily against tariffs. One of the most active new political associations was the United Farmers of Alberta, which brought together two smaller bodies in 1909. There was also the Canadian Council of Agriculture, which pressed the federal government for tariff reform.

The Progressives The war effort helped to restrain the call for tariff reductions, but Prairie residents expected that, once the war was over, substantial reductions would be legislated. When this did not occur, a new wave of agitation developed. A dissatisfied group of politicians formed the National Progressive Party, which shocked the nation in 1921 by capturing sixty-five seats in the House of Commons.

Nationally, the Progressive movement did not survive long as an independent political force. Part of the explanation usually given for this decline emphasizes two factors: the Progressives were split into two groups, known perhaps simplistically as the "Alberta faction" and the "Manitoba faction." While this lack of unity is certainly part of the story, we should not overlook the fact that the Progressives, though by no means restricted to one region of the country, drew their strength primarily from the Prairie provinces. In British Columbia, Quebec, and the Maritimes, the Progressives had little support; in Ontario the movement's objectives were different from those in the west (Thompson and Seager, 1985: 31–34). They could, and in fact did, win some significant concessions from the major parties; but—given the regional distribution of their

There is a long history of collective action on the Canadian Prairies. The general strike that shut down the city of Winnipeg for six weeks in 1919 was one of the most dramatic instances.

support—they could not themselves become a major national party. By 1926 the National Progressive Party largely had been absorbed into the Liberal Party.

At the provincial level, the situation was altogether different. Within certain provinces, farmers and their allies were able to dominate politics and elect governments generally committed to representing their interests. This became true in all three Prairie provinces in the 1920s: farmers' parties were elected in Alberta and Manitoba, and a Liberal government sympathetic to agrarian interests held power in Saskatchewan. As a consequence, while considerable dissatisfaction with the federal government persisted, western farmers were less discontented with their own provincial governments in this period. They remained so until the Great Depression.

Social Credit In 1935, under the leadership of former preacher William Aberhart, a new political party—the Social Credit Party—took power in the province of Alberta. It is not hard to understand why a movement of this kind should find support among self-employed farmers, particularly during a severe economic depression. Obtaining credit—always a serious problem for farmers—was especially difficult at this time, and it was primarily this difficulty that Aberhart's movement promised to solve. The theory of social credit assumes that economic stagnation results from a shortage of credit in an economy, and that this shortage can be overcome by the distribution of monthly cash dividends to all citizens. The program appealed as well to other classes in Western society, particularly the urban working class, whose members were also suffering from the Depression (Bell, 1990).

Regina Manifesto

One of the most interesting and significant documents in Canadian history is the CCF program adopted at the First National Convention in Regina, July 1933. Here are the opening paragraphs of that declaration.

The CCF is a federation of organizations whose purpose is the establishment in Canada of a Co-operative Commonwealth in which the principle regulating production, distribution, and exchange will be the supplying of human needs and not the making of profits.

We aim to replace the present capitalist system, with its inherent injustice and inhumanity, by a social order from which the domination and exploitation of one class by another will be eliminated, in which economic planning will supersede unregulated private enterprise and competition, and in which genuine democratic self-government, based upon economic equality will be possible. The present order is marked by glaring inequalities of wealth and opportunity, by chaotic waste and instability; and in an age of plenty it condemns the great mass of the people to poverty and insecurity.

Power has become more and more concentrated into the hands of a small irresponsible minority of financiers and industrialists and to their predatory interests the majority are habitually sacrificed. When private profit is the main stimulus to economic effort, our society oscillates between periods of feverish prosperity in which the main benefits go to speculators and profiteers, and of catastrophic depression, in which the common man's normal state of insecurity and hardship is accentuated. We believe that these evils can be removed only in a planned and socialized economy in which our natural resources and the principal means of production and distribution are owned, controlled, and operated by the people.

The new social order at which we aim is not one in which individuality will be crushed out by a system of regimentation. Nor shall we interfere with cultural rights of racial or religious minorities. What we seek is a proper collective organization of our economic resources such as will make possible a much greater degree of leisure and a much richer individual life for every citizen.

This social and economic transformation can be brought about by

political action, through the election of a government inspired by the ideal of a Co-operative Commonwealth and supported by a majority of the people. We do not believe in change by violence. We consider that both the old parties in Canada are the instruments of capitalist interests and cannot serve as agents of social reconstruction, and that whatever the superficial differences between them, they are bound to carry on government in accordance with the dictates of the big business interests who finance them. The CCF aims at political power in order to put an end to this capitalist domination of our political life. It is a democratic movement, a federation of farmer, labour, and socialist organizations, financed by its own members and seeking to achieve its ends solely by constitutional methods. It appeals for support to all who believe that the time has come for a far-reaching reconstruction of our economic and political institutions. ...

Source: Walter Young, 1969. The Anatomy of a Party: The National CCF, MCMXXXII–LXI. Toronto: University of Toronto Press (pp. 304–5).

Aberhart charged that eastern business élites were controlling and manipulating the economy to serve their interests. They tried, he claimed, to restrict the supply of money and to create a dependence on credit institutions from which they profited. As fashioned by Aberhart, social credit ideology was unmistakably anti-establishment (Finkel, 1989: 34–35). It appealed to western farmers and workers who wanted to believe that their troubles resulted from the control of the economy by eastern financial interests.

CCF At approximately the same time as Social Credit, a very different kind of movement also appeared in the west. The Co-operative Commonwealth Federation (CCF) was founded in the 1930s and eventually won a provincial election in Saskatchewan in 1944.

The surprising thing about the CCF is that its official platform was socialist, which seems a curious ideology with which to seek the support of self-employed farmers. And yet a socialist wing had been active within the farmers' movement in Saskatchewan well before the arrival of the CCF, so the CCF did not come to Saskatchewan as a foreign import. Moreover, the CCF carefully presented its program to appeal to farmers. It de-emphasized those parts of socialism that would offend their sense of free enterprise, while it stressed aspects that were plainly in their interest. The party was forced, for example, to moderate and eventually abandon its call for land nationalization, but most farmers were not put off by the idea of state regulation of the marketing of their produce, or by the nationalization of transportation and natural resources.

We should be careful not to attach too much significance to ideological differences between the Social Credit party and the CCF. Though these differences were real, in each case the program was moulded to suit the interests and demands of western farmers. Moreover, sharp differences in the ideologies of two new parties formed in two western provinces do not necessarily mean that there were great ideological differences between the people of each province. To argue, for example, that most people in Alberta were further to the right than those in Saskatchewan is to ignore the fact that many of these same Albertans voted for a radical farmers' party (the United Farmers of Alberta) in the early 1920s, when the Liberal Party still held power in Saskatchewan. And there is certainly no compelling reason to believe that Saskatchewan voters were indeed endorsing socialism when they voted for the CCF in 1944.

The significance of these movements does not lie in their respective ideologies; it lies in their relationship to the social groups on which they were based. Both Social Credit and the CCF, as they took shape in western Canada, should be seen as collective efforts by members of a particular region to find political formations that represented their special needs. These needs were markedly different from those of most other Canadians and were not-at least in their eyes-being met by the national political parties.

This same sentiment was responsible for the emergence of a new political force in the west during the late 1980s. Under the leadership of Preston Manning, the Reform Party of Canada was founded to give westerners an alternative to the major political parties. As long as the Liberals under Trudeau formed the government in Ottawa, westerners could vote for Progressive Conservatives in order to express their dissatisfaction with Ottawa. When, however, the Conservatives assumed office in Ottawa and took actions that were unpopular in the west, such as introducing the Goods and Services Tax and supporting some of the demands of Quebec, many westerners turned to the Reform Party. Its first major breakthrough was the election of Deborah Grey to the House of Commons in a March 1989 by-election, followed later in the year by the success of Stanley Waters in an Alberta poll to choose a nominee for a Senate appointment. The founders and early supporters of the movement espoused an unmistakably right-wing ideology, but the party has broadened its policies in an effort to attract voters further to the left, including discontented supporters of the NDP. Yet it has remained very much a regional party. In the federal election of 1993, it won fifty-two seats, all but one of them in western Canada. In the federal election of 1997, it won sixty seats, but none outside western Canada.

Ethnic cleavage

Ethnic diversity in Canada coincides with many other differences. We have already discussed in Chapter 6, Social Stratification, variations in socioeconomic status found among ethnic groups. We have also observed a tendency for ethnic groups to be distributed unevenly among provinces. And in Chapter 8, Race and Ethnic Relations, we saw that, even within the same city, considerable ethnic residential concentration is likely. These differences in socioeconomic status and residential patterns would alone be enough to create social distances between members of distinct ethnic groups. But additional factors, particularly dissimilarities in values, have served to intensify ethnic cleavages in Canadian society.

The consequences of ethnic divisions for the character of collective action in Canada are evident at almost every level. The country abounds in ethnic institutions—schools, religious groups, clubs, and other voluntary associations. Many social movements are affected by ethnic diversity. For example, the current women's movement has not overcome divisions between French-speaking and English-speaking women, and separate organizations have been formed for some minorities, such as native women and black women (Prentice et al., 1988: 355–56, 396–98, 405).

In addition, a number of social movements in Canada have arisen from ethnic divisions. The largest and most successful are nationalist movements in the province of Quebec. We have already mentioned some of the most important differences (in education, occupation, and income) that have helped to reinforce divisions between French- and English-speaking Canadians. We could add to this list differences in language, religion, and values.

Native peoples

Great as the cleavage is between the French and the English in Canada, it is less than the cleavage that isolates the Indians and Inuit from the rest of the society. Almost whatever variable is being considered—cultural values, income, occupation, or geographical separation—differences between native peoples and other Canadians are no less, and indeed are often greater, than differences separating the French and the English.

The history of collective action by indigenous peoples is, as noted earlier, much longer than is often assumed. It is important not to underestimate the courage and sophistication of native leadership in the past. Still, all things considered, what is perplexing is the weakness and ineffectiveness of native movements until the 1990s. Why was this the case? Why did the English-French cleavage generate more significant collective action than the much greater cleavage between native peoples and other Canadians?

Part of the answer is simply numbers. When the British took control of Quebec in the eighteenth century, the native population vastly outnumbered the French in the territories that now make up Canada. Since then, however, the French have generally enjoyed strong population growth, while native peoples have, until recently, suffered a serious demographic decline. As a result, the French

have had the benefit of much greater numerical strength than the native population.

Yet the French have had other advantages as well. We need to think back to the theoretical approaches discussed earlier and recall the factors that underlie collective action. These include not only cleavage factors, but also integrating factors, which pull people together and make it possible for them to organize in collective action. If people are to engage in collective action, it is not enough for them to be separated by cleavage factors from other members of society; they must also be united among themselves. Only in this way can they be mobilized.

The main obstacle to collective action by Indians and Inuit was a distinct lack of such integrating factors. Separated and alienated from other Canadians as they have been, they did not themselves form a cohesive group. They were subdivided most obviously by language and cultural differences, but also by geographical dispersion and artificially imposed administrative distinctions (e.g., status versus non-status Indians, and treaty versus non-treaty Indians). Until the 1990s, considerable factionalism characterized collective action by Indians and Inuit in Canada. Put together with several other organizational weaknesses (the absence of a large educated middle class to provide leadership, a lack of material resources, and political apathy within the indigenous population), this factionalism allowed other Canadians, until lately, to rule the Indians and Inuit without serious opposition.

Gradually, however, the organizational basis for native collective action has improved. Ironically, the assimilation of native peoples into Canadian society has promoted integrating factors. Linguistic and cultural differences within the native population have declined. More advanced means of communication and transportation have made it easier for native peoples in different parts of the country to coordinate activities. National conferences of native peoples have become more common. As already noted, a more educated and more effective leadership has emerged. The financial resources of natives have increased through state assistance and favourable land claims. And native peoples have more and more come to see themselves as a unified group, even though historically that had not been the case. Native peoples were just as discontented fifteen years ago, thirty years ago, and even sixty years ago as they are now. What has changed is their organizational capacity to engage in more aggressive and national collective action than they could have in the past.

Nevertheless, the social conditions for collective action have been more favourable for French Canadians for most of this century, and to a large extent remain so. Whereas native peoples are dispersed across the country, most francophone Canadians live in one province. Whereas native people comprise a great many cultural groups, francophones generally belong to a single cultural group, which has its own historical tradition, a unifying religion, and a common language. And whereas native peoples are separated into a great number of different communities with unconnected institutions, francophones possess numerous unifying institutional structures, including their own provincial government. To be sure, major sources of cleavage exist within Quebec society, most notably class and generational divisions. However, there has always been sufficient cultural

and structural integration to facilitate the mobilization of effective collective action.

Quebec nationalism

There is a widespread misconception among English-speaking Canadians that nationalism in Quebec is something new. Unless defined very narrowly, French Canadian nationalism can be traced back to before Confederation. The movement for responsible government that emerged in Upper and Lower Canada in the first half of the nineteenth century was, for French Canadians, both a campaign for reform and a struggle against British political domination. Although Confederation tied French Canadians to the rest of British North America, it also gave them a separate province in which they constituted the majority, and in which, it was assumed, they would be able to protect their distinct culture. Indeed, the participation of francophones in Confederation can legitimately be interpreted as an expression of French Canadian nationalism, albeit a nationalism based on totally different premises than that found in Quebec today.

Language, Guardian of the Faith

Henri Bourassa is widely regarded as the greatest nationalist leader in the history of French Canada. His nationalism emphasized the importance of preserving traditional Quebec culture, above all its religion. In La langue, gardienne de la foi, he asserted that the French language embodies the Catholic religion more than does any other language and that this gives French Canadians a unique mission in the world.

Our special mission, we French Canadians, is to carry on in America the struggle of Christian France, and to defend against all opposition, if

necessary against France herself, our religious and national heritage. This heritage does not belong to us alone: it belongs to the whole of Catholic America, and constitutes a centre from which radiates inspiration and light; it belongs to the entire Church, for which it is the principal source of strength in this part of the world; it belongs to all of French civilization, for which it is the only port of refuge and mooring place in this immense sea of Saxon Americanism.

We are the only ones, let us not forget, who are capable of fulfilling this mission in America. French Canadians and Franco-Americans represent the only large group, the

only nation of the French race and language outside Europe....

But if we want to defend our intellectual and national heritage, which belongs to French people everywhere, we must do so without disturbing the harmonious relationship between our social duties and our divine calling.

Let us fight not merely to preserve our language, or to preserve our language and our faith; let us fight for our language in order better to preserve our faith.

Source: Henri Bourassa, 1918. La langue, gardienne de la foi. Montreal: Bibliothèque de l'Action française (pp. 49–51).

Confederation certainly did not mean a decline in the determination of French Canadians to protect their society from assimilation into the larger English-speaking culture. Almost throughout the period since Confederation, nationalism as an ideology has been popular among the Québécois. It has been articulated and advanced by countless French Canadian intellectuals, and has been espoused, in a diversity of forms and with varying degrees of emphasis, by most Quebec politicians. Until the 1950s, Quebec nationalism tended to be conservative and at times oriented towards preserving the past. Although the material benefits of industrialization were welcome, **la survivance**— the survival of French Canada as a distinct society— was to be achieved primarily by keeping people loyal to traditional values. It was assumed that support of the traditional culture was the best way to maintain a distinct French Canadian society. It was also generally assumed that this survival could be guaranteed within Confederation simply by guarding the provincial rights that Confederation had granted.

Throughout this period, the majority of French Canadian nationalists hesitated to advocate separation from the rest of Canada. Many were "dual" nationalists, who stood for both provincial autonomy and the dissociation of Canada from Great Britain. The most representative advocate of this brand of nationalism was Henri Bourassa. Although Bourassa was not opposed to the industrialization of Quebec, the underlying theme of his politics was the preservation of traditional French Canadian culture, in particular its religion. At the same time, he was an ardent Canadian. In 1903 his adherents organized the Ligue nationaliste, with the double objective of promoting the independence of Canada and safeguarding the rights of French Canadians.

Writers such as Tardivel and Groulx were representative of a more separatist brand of nationalism. Abbé Groulx was the most influential nationalist intellectual after Henri Bourassa. A historian at the Université de Montréal, he articulated a nationalism that was conservative and religious. He extolled the destiny of the French Canadian "race," stressing the importance of their traditional culture and calling on his people to resist the forces of modernization that were threatening them.

Henri Bourassa was an ardent dual nationalist. He believed strongly in both provincial autonomy and Canadian independence from Great Britain.

Yet, as Groulx himself came to realize, it was not in fact possible for French Canada to insulate itself from the forces of modernization. During the very years in which he lived and wrote, the kind of society he lauded was being undermined as a rural decline and growing urbanization seriously threatened the traditional nationalist strategy. In various ways, modernization brought French Canadians into greater contact with Anglo culture. It also created monstrous pressures on them to assimilate into the English-speaking world, at least if they wanted to enjoy the material benefits of industrial society.

Although this process actually began around the turn of the century, the nationalist strategy for keeping French Canada distinct did not reflect the change until much later. Even when nationalist leaders became conscious of the seriousness of the threat-and they certainly were conscious of it by the time of the Depression, if not earlier—they were still reluctant to alter their approach to *la survivance*.

In the 1930s and 1940s they experimented with various ideas, but they did not come up with a realistic solution to the danger that urbanization and industrialization posed.

The reasons for the lag in the development of their thinking are complex, but certainly a major factor was the conservatism of French Canadian élites, even while urbanization and industrialization were taking place in their province. Members of the élite continued to look to the past for the model of the ideal society, and they generally opposed any significant expansion of the public sector, particularly if it threatened to interfere with the traditional functions of the Roman Catholic Church in spheres such as education and welfare. This "anti-statism" is most often associated with the *Union nationale* government of Maurice Duplessis, premier of Quebec from 1936 to 1939 and again from 1944 to 1959. More than any other individual, Duplessis symbolizes the era of conservative nationalism in Quebec.

Meanwhile, changes in the social structure of Quebec continued to undermine the traditional culture. By 1961 the number of people of French origin who could be classified as rural had fallen to 29 percent, and only 13 percent were living on farms (Posgate and McRoberts, 1976: 48). As the economy of Quebec developed along the same lines as the economy of the rest of North America, the traditional basis for distinctiveness in Quebec was eroded. French Canadian leaders began to realize that they were going to have to fight even harder to prevent Quebec from melting into the larger society that surrounded it. At the same time, urbanization and industrialization were gradually creating a new French élite in the province, whose members rejected the basic premises of conservative nationalism. New leaders emerged who did not idealize the past and were unwilling to accept the traditional opposition to the expansion of the public sector. This new élite has appropriately been called the "bureaucratic middle class" (Guindon, 1964). It was composed of educated employees in both private and public bureaucracies, most notably in state organizations and educational institutions. These bureaucracies had grown substantially in number and size after World War II to meet the needs of urban Quebec, but their power and further expansion were being frustrated by those who clung

to the old nationalism. The closing years of Duplessis's premiership saw increasing opposition to his government and ideological ferment in the province (Coleman, 1984).

When Duplessis died in 1959, he was followed by premiers who were prepared to make greater concessions to this new bureaucratic middle class. Paul Sauvé, who succeeded Duplessis as leader of the Union Nationale, and Jean Lesage, who headed a Liberal government from 1960 to 1966, oversaw a dramatic shift in the orientation of politics in Quebec. They led governments that were not so reluctant to expand the role of the state in the lives of the people of the province. The educational system was reorganized to train French Canadians better for participation in an advanced industrial society and to reduce the power of the Church; the delivery of social services was rationalized and expanded, and again the power of the Church was curtailed; new institutions to define French Canadian culture were established; state control over natural resources was increased; and the labour code was overhauled.

The **Quiet Revolution**, as this new approach came to be called, had profound implications for the character of Quebec nationalism. A basic assumption of French Canadian nationalism had always been that only French Canadian leaders—be they religious or political—could be trusted to look after the interests of their people and to safeguard their distinct culture. So long as a relatively minor role was assigned to the state, the best strategy was simply to maintain tight control over the provincial government while resisting any encroachments by the federal government. This had been the course pursued by the majority of French Canadian intellectuals and politicians until the Quiet Revolution.

But when a new attitude towards the state began to win acceptance, the basic principles of *la survivance* inevitably underwent a change. Nationalists who believed in the Quiet Revolution felt it imperative to do more than just protect the existing powers of the provincial government; *la survivance* now appeared to depend on an extension of these powers. Within Quebec, the new nationalists sought to expand the powers of the provincial government at the expense of other institutions, most notably the Church. Within the larger political framework, they tried to expand these powers at the expense of the federal government. Unavoidably, the Quiet Revolution gave rise to increased conflict between the governments of Ottawa and Quebec City. During the Duplessis years, federal-provincial conflict had been largely avoided by Duplessis's simple refusal to cooperate with federal programs. Under Lesage and his successors (Johnson, Bertrand, and Bourassa) an intense struggle developed between federal and provincial politicians over the powers of their respective governments.

This new nationalist orientation also provided the basis for the rise of the separatist movement in Quebec. Indeed, it has been argued that separatism is simply a logical extension of the Quiet Revolution, carrying its philosophy a step further, to the conclusion that the expansion of the power of the state in Quebec cannot be achieved within Confederation. To obtain the powers needed to modernize Quebec—and to keep this modernization under French control—almost complete autonomy is necessary.

As always, a stimulus for Quebec nationalism is fear of assimilation. French Canadians were adopting the individualism, pragmatism, and materialism of the North American economy and society. Through educational institutions and the media, North American culture was reaching almost all parts of the province. Ironically, the very policies and programs of the Quiet Revolution contributed to this threat. They promoted the integration of the economy of Quebec with that of North America. They standardized education in Quebec so that it looked more like education elsewhere on the continent. As the reforms of the Quiet Revolution were introduced and the Church relinquished many of its traditional functions, only language remained to distinguish French-speaking society from the larger society that surrounded it. Many Québécois turned to separatism out of fear that French Canada would not survive (Coleman, 1984).

They also turned to separatism as a result of the relative deprivation they felt in the 1960s and 1970s. The Quiet Revolution raised expectations that could not be fulfilled. In particular, French Canadians resented the fact that the business élite in Quebec continued to be largely English-speaking and that, when they talked to English-speaking

people, they still had to do so in English. It was they, the francophones, an overwhelming majority in the province, who had to speak the other language.

Although the Parti Québécois won provincial elections in 1976 and 1981, their goal of sovereignty association—which would have effectively given Quebec political independence while retaining economic and other ties with Canada—was defeated in the referendum of 1980. Subsequently, support for separatism declined until 1990, when it experienced a major revival. Many French Canadians were horrified when some municipalities in Ontario passed English-only resolutions for their jurisdictions and when members of the Association for the Preservation of English in Canada trampled on a Quebec flag. And the struggle over the Meech Lake Accord made many in Quebec feel rejected by the rest of Canada. They had little sympathy with English-speaking Canadians who opposed Meech Lake because it weakened the central government in Canada. They also could not understand the concern of English-speaking Canadians over the treatment of anglophones in Quebec. The majority of Québécois still believed their language and culture were in peril and that they had to secure the political power necessary to defend them against the vastly greater numbers of anglophones in North America.

In the federal election of 1993, the Bloc Québécois won fifty-four seats in the House of Commons and became the Official Opposition. In 1994 the Parti Québécois became the provincial government of Quebec. This set the stage for the Quebec referendum on sovereignty in October 1995, in which the voters rejected sovereignty by a narrow margin: 50.6 to 49.4 percent. In other words, the 1995 referendum was a tie game. Precisely for that reason, however, it has come to mark the beginning of a new phase in the struggle over Quebec. The province is now clearly split in half. On the one side are French Canadians living outside the Montreal and Ottawa regions; they are predominantly in favour of greater sovereignty for Quebec. On the other side are the anglophones, allophones (those of neither French nor British ancestry), and French Canadians living in the Montreal and Ottawa regions, most of whom are opposed to greater sovereignty for Quebec, or at least opposed to total independence, which they believed that voting Yes

As Parti Québécois premier of Quebec, Lucien Bouchard works closely with the separatist Bloc Québécois, the federal party of which he was once leader.

in the referendum would have led to, even though the referendum did not in fact put the question of total independence to the voters. Whether or not this means that the rural-urban cleavage in Quebec is now shaping the independence struggle, it is clear that separatism is no longer based primarily on the Quebec urban middle class.

Although nationalist sentiment in Quebec is not a new phenomenon, it has repeatedly changed in character. Its social basis, its ideology, and its objectives have gone through a number of transformations. Many francophones in Quebec no longer see themselves as an ethnic minority, but rather as a nation that, like other nations, is entitled to its own state (du Pays, 1996). "French Canadian" nationalism has given way to a more territorially based "Quebec" nationalism, in which the ideal is to build a new nation in North America embracing all Quebeckers (Rocher, 1996).

In the 1998 provincial election, the Parti Québécois won a solid majority of seats, but received only 42.7 of the popular vote, slightly less than the Liberals. These results have discouraged the Parti Québécois from holding another referendum on sovereignty. Obviously, however, we cannot assume that Quebec separatism is a dying movement. The future will bring more struggles between separatist and federalist forces in Quebec, the results of which are impossible to predict.

Social movements of the future: The politics of status

In addition, what kind of social movements will the future bring us? Many sociologists believe that it will be more "new social movements." For them the environmental movement is the prototype of the future. We would suggest that, instead, it is more likely that status movements will come to predominate.

Until recently, status movements in Canada have been uncommon. The most significant was the suffragette movement in the early decades of the twentieth century. During the past several decades, in most Western societies, there has been a significant increase in the number of status movements. This is perhaps true in Canada to a greater extent than anywhere else, as a result of the Charter of Rights and Freedoms of 1982. Section 15 of the Charter assures equality of rights for a variety of groups. Initially it gave protection to only a small number of groups, but it allowed the courts to add groups to the list. When Section 15 came into effect in 1985, the federal government offered funding to groups who wanted to take advantage of its provisions (Brodie 1996: 254–5). Not surprisingly, the Charter encouraged the formation of a large number of interest-litigation groups: the Canadian Disability Rights Council, the Canadian Prisoners' Rights Network, the Equality of Rights Committee of the Canadian Ethnocultural Council, Equality of Gays and Lesbians Everywhere, the Women's Legal Education and Action Fund, and the Charter Committee on Poverty Issues (Brodie 1996: 254). Eventually the Supreme Court limited protected constitutional status to groups that are "discrete and insular minorities" or groups that have historically suffered social disadvantage. Yet it also determined that immigrants awaiting Canadian citizenship merit "protected" status, and a number of courts have deemed homosexuals to be a protected group (Brodie 1996: 255–6).

These movements represent a new (though not altogether unprecedented) development in status rights. In earlier centuries, status groups claiming special treatment usually justified it on the basis of the high prestige they enjoyed or thought they should enjoy. Thus the European nobility claimed special privileges, such as exemption from taxation, on the basis of their alleged military and/or moral superiority. Property-owning males who enjoyed the exclusive right to vote in the nineteenth century claimed it on the basis of their alleged capacity for more responsible judgment. In contrast, status groups in Canada are now beginning to claim special treatment on the basis of the inferior position to which they have been assigned. Of course, they do not accept the validity of that inferior position and want their prestige to be raised. Yet they are basing their claim to special treatment on a supposed inferior, not superior, position.

Although a proliferation of protected status groups will dilute the advantages of the Charter of Rights and Freedoms for any single group (Brodie 1996), it is nonetheless likely that status movements will come increasingly to dominate the scene in Canada during the twenty-first century. If a certain status group has gained advantages, or is perceived to have gained advantages, at the expense of another status group, a possible recourse for the latter is to organize its own status movement. Thus movements have been formed by divorced men to challenge what they perceive to be the preference that the judicial and legal system has shown toward women in marital breakups, especially with regard to their respective rights and obligations toward the couple's children. A number of movements have also emerged to challenge discrimination against white males in recruitment practices. And a few small movements have even sprung up to protect heterosexuals from purported discrimination.

Summary

The first part of this chapter examined five different theoretical approaches to the study of social movements. It began with the collective behaviour perspective, which was long the dominant theoretical school in North American sociology. This approach assumes that social movements are less institutionalized than ordinary behaviour, and it studies them along with other types of relatively less institutionalized events, such as panics, crowds, and crazes. Several different versions of this perspective were examined: an early statement of the argument by Blumer, Smelser's theory of collective behaviour, emergent norm theory, and game theory.

The discussion then turned to the breakdown theory that social unrest occurs when institutions that normally control and restrain human behaviour are weakened. The third theoretical perspective presented was the relative deprivation approach. It makes the intuitively appealing argument that social unrest is most likely to erupt when a sharp increase develops in the difference between what people receive and what they think they have a right to receive.

The fourth approach takes a different tack by placing social movements in a broad category of events called collective action. Most advocates of this position emphasize the need to study how social unrest—indeed, how any kind of collective action—varies from one society to another, and how it changes in character over time. They also attempt to explain these variations in terms of the structural conditions that underlie and shape collective action, particularly those conditions that facilitate mobilization. This theoretical approach is critical of other perspectives for giving insufficient attention to how people acquire the capacity to act collectively.

Finally, postmodernism and the new social movement approach sought to explain the particular movements that have emerged in postmodern or postindustrial society in western Europe and North America, placing more emphasis on the importance of culture than other perspectives.

The second part of the chapter shifted to a general, and necessarily brief, examination of collective action in Canada. A very short outline was given of the principal cleavages and integrative bonds that have shaped the character of collective action in this country. Movements in western Canada were then described as examples of collective action built on regional cleavage, and the unrest among native peoples and Quebec nationalism were discussed as examples of collective action resulting from ethnic cleavage. Finally, it was suggested that status movements will predominate in Canada in the twenty-first century.

QUESTIONS FOR REVIEW AND CRITICAL THINKING

1. Many studies have shown that the level of social unrest usually increases in a society during the transition from a nonindustrial to an industrial social organization, and then declines thereafter. How true is this for Canada? Given what you have just learned about theories of relative deprivation, breakdown, and collective action, how do you think each approach would explain the Canadian case?

2. What types of people do you think are likely to join a radical left organization, a right-to-life association, a feminist group, or a gay-rights body? Are they really alienated, uprooted, and poorly integrated into social institutions, as the social breakdown approach suggests?

3. The collapse of communism in eastern Europe has led many people to believe that Marxism is dying, both as a basis for organizing political, economic, and social structures and as an intellectual tool for understanding society. Is Marxism still useful for understanding social movements?

4. Some argue that hyper-consumption, technological progress, seductive advertising, and mass manipulation have limited the ability of social movements to emerge in Canada. Do you agree with this view or not? Why?

5. To what extent have regional social movements in Canada eclipsed class-based movements?

KEY TERMS

circular reaction, p. 372

collective action, p. 376

collective behaviour, p. 370

craze, p. 380

crowd, p. 371

emergent norm theory, p. 373

fad, p. 371

frame, p. 379

game theory, p. 373

generalized belief, p. 372

hegemony, p. 382

mobilization, p. 379

panic, p. 371

public, p. 371

Quiet Revolution, p. 395

relative deprivation, p. 376

selective incentives, p. 379

social breakdown approach, p. 375

social cleavage, p. 385

social contagion, p. 372

social integration, p. 375

social movement, p. 371

social structure, p. 374

la survivance, p. 394

SUGGESTED READINGS

Carroll, W.K. (ed.)

1997   *Organizing Dissent: Contemporary Social Movements in Theory and Practice: Studies in the Politics of Counter-Hegemony.* (2nd ed.) Toronto: Garamond.

An excellent collection of articles on social movements. While all articles discuss social movements in general, some include an analysis of a specific Canadian movement.

McAdam, Doug, J.D. McCarthy, and M.N. Zald (eds.)

1996   *Comparative Perspectives on Social Movements: Political Opportunities, Mobilizing Structures, and Cultural Framings.* Cambridge and New York: Cambridge University Press.

A collection of articles representing the cutting edge of collective-action theory, including some revisions to earlier versions.

McRoberts, Kenneth

1988   *Quebec: Social Change and Political Crisis.* (3rd ed.) Toronto: McClelland and Stewart.

The book is one of the better introductory surveys of society and politics in Quebec.

Prentice, Alison, Paula Bourne, Gail Brandt, Beth Light, Wendy Mitchinson, and Naomi Black

1988   *Canadian Women: A History.* Toronto: Harcourt Brace.

A good history of women in Canada, covering both the changing role of women in our society and collective efforts by women to improve their condition.

Tilly, Charles

1978   *From Mobilization to Revolution.* Reading, MA: Addison-Wesley.

Tilly is the leading exponent of the collective action approach. This book is not easy reading, but it is important for anyone interested in the study of social movements.

WEB SITES

www.citizenscoalition.org
The National Citizens' Coalition
Social movements come in a variety of forms and are oriented to numerous causes. At this site, learn about the NCC, a group of citizens with a neoconservative orientation.

www.canadians.org
The Council of Canadians
At the other end of the political scale is the Council of Canadians, which advertises itself as "a progressive voice on key national issues." Read about current economic and social issues affecting Canada from a left-of-centre, nationalist perspective.

Demography and Urbanization

Kevin McQuillan and Danièle Bélanger

Introduction

Because Canada is a large country with a relatively small population, daily life here does not seem to be affected by population the way it is in countries like China and India. Yet when it comes time to seek a job, find a partner, or save for retirement, population questions turn out to be of considerable significance for Canadians. **Demography** is the study of population; it examines how the size, structure, and rate of growth are affected by rates of fertility (births), mortality (deaths), and migration (movement).

   While such demographic variables have far-reaching effects on most aspects of social life, demographic factors do not operate on their own. Their influence often comes about through their interaction with other social, cultural, and economic factors. In this chapter we shall briefly examine how population affects social life, and how, in turn, social factors influence population. In doing so, we shall concentrate on the population of Canada, and how demo-graphic factors have influenced its evolution. As part of this discussion, we also consider urbanization, the trend of residing in cities and towns.

The course of world population growth

To put population growth in Canada in context, let us first look at world population growth. As we do so, we realize that since migration only moves people around, only two factors are relevant: the number of births and the number of deaths. Two simple measures, the **crude birth rate** (CBR) and the **crude death rate** (CDR), have been devised by demographers to help us understand how births and deaths determine the rate of population growth. They are calculated by dividing the number of births (deaths) occurring in a population in a given period of time (usually one year) by the total size of the population (best measured at the mid-point of the year), and expressed per thousand population.

Classical Views on Population

Scholars have examined population issues since the earliest times. But the beginnings of a modern approach to demography date from one man and one piece of writing, *An Essay on the Principle of Population* by Thomas Malthus. The essay was first published in 1798 and immediately attracted considerable public interest. Malthus wanted to create a stir and thus had produced a provocative account of the role of population in human society. He was very critical of the optimistic ideas prominent among other Enlightenment scholars (see Chapter 1). In contrast to their views, he painted a deliberately bleak picture of humanity's future. Societies may experience considerable technological and social progress, he agreed, but population growth would always be a problem.

In Malthus's view, human nature is marked by two basic needs or drives: the need to eat, and what he termed "the passion between the sexes." As a result, he argued, an increase in the supply of food can produce only a temporary improvement in the standard of living, because it also produces an increase in population size, which then eats up any increase in food. The growth of population can only be stopped by what he termed **positive checks** to population—war, famine, and disease.

Not surprisingly, Malthus's essay drew considerable critical attention, and as a result Malthus greatly expanded the book in later editions and softened his vision of the future. Human society could avoid the punishing effects of positive checks to population growth by taking steps to limit the number of births. For Malthus, an Anglican

minister as well as a scholar, this did not mean the use of contraceptive practices, referring to them as "improper arts." Instead, he advised people to postpone marriage until they could provide for the children that would be born to them. Only by using this **preventive check**, as he called it, could society avoid going through an endless cycle of population growth followed by insufficient food and rising mortality. Malthus, we might add, followed his own advice. He married in 1804 at the age of 38, and had only three children.

Malthus's ideas on population and society seem outdated today. Technological progress, at least in the industrialized world, has expanded food supplies far beyond the levels Malthus could have imagined. And the spread of modern means of birth control has meant that some modern societies even experience population decline. Still, for many countries in the developing world, rapid population growth still poses a major challenge to their ability to improve their standard of living. Moreover, in language that might have been borrowed from Malthus, modern environmentalists argue that we must stop exhausting natures resources before nature intervenes with a new series of positive checks to growth.

Among the earliest and most forceful critics of Malthusian ideas was Marx, calling his essay "schoolboyish" and "a superficial plagiary" (Marx, 1906: 675). Marx felt Malthus blamed the poor for their desperate state, because they produced children they could not afford to care for. For Marx, as you read in Social Stratification, Chapter 6, the source of poverty

lies not with the poor themselves but with the inherently oppressive character of capitalist societies. Capitalism needs a surplus population or what Marx called "a reserve army of labour" to restrain the wage demands of workers. Workers will be less likely to striike, for example, if a surplus population of unemployed is available to replace them. Thus over-population is a good thing for the capitalists. Indeed, if workers followed the advice of Malthus and strictly limited the size of their families, capitalists would, Marx argued, respond by replacing workers with machines, creating a new class of unemployed workers. So long as capitalism exists, Marx believed, so would unemployment and thus the appearance of overpopulation. Only the transition to an economy built on socialist principles would eliminate unemployment and make clear that nature can provide for all.

Marx's ideas continue to influence contemporary analysts of population questions. Some less-developed societies, for example, argue that their problems lie less in the size of their populations than in the unequal relations between rich and poor countries. The solution to poverty in the countries of Africa, Asia, and Latin America, they argue, requires not population control (though this may sometimes be helpful) but rather a fundamental change in the economic relations between rich and poor countries. More specifically, fairer prices for the exports of developing societies and greater access to investment capital and modern technology will bring greater benefits than population control to the developing world.

The CBR in the world today is approximately twenty-four per thousand, while the CDR is only nine per thousand (United Nations, 1999: 95). The fifteen persons per thousand difference between these two rates is a measure of how fast the population is growing per year, and known as the **rate of natural increase**. Fifteen per thousand people is equal to 1.5 percent.

Prior to the seventeenth century, human populations tended to grow very slowly, or not at all, with any increase usually offset by periods of decline due to famine, disease, and war. With the eighteenth century, however, European societies began to tackle a variety of economic and technological problems (see Chapter 16, Social Change) which in turn allowed a period of sustained population growth. Then with increased industrialization and even higher standards of living in the nineteenth century, the pace of demographic growth began to quicken. From the one billion figure of 1800, world population grew to two billion persons in 1920, three billion by 1960, four billion by 1975, five billion in 1987, and six billion in 1999. To understand the current pace of growth, the world population will grow this week by an amount roughly equal to the population of metropolitan Vancouver.

While tracking the rate of world population growth is important, we have to remember that 1.5 percent is just an average, concealing the tremendous variation in population growth rates in the different parts of the world. In countries like Canada, the rate of natural increase is low, 0.5 percent. In many countries of Eastern Europe, including Russia and Hungary, the rate is negative; more

In the Western world of the nineteenth and early twentieth centuries, birth rates were approximately twice death rates—stage two of the demographic transition.

people die than are born. By contrast, in some countries of Asia and Africa, population is growing very rapidly. In Niger, for example, the rate of natural increase is 3.4 percent. At that pace, the population will double in just twenty years (United Nations, 1999: 98).

Demographic Transition Theory

What lies behind such differences in population patterns? One answer comes from **demographic transition theory**. Built on the experience of the currently developed societies, the theory suggests that societies pass through a three-stage process of change. In the first stage, population grows slowly because high birth rates are balanced by high, if fluctuating, death rates. In this stage, typical of Western societies before the Industrial Revolution, the average woman gives birth to a large number of children, perhaps five or six on average. This high rate of childbearing is offset, however, by a high level of mortality. As many as one in four babies does not live to see its first birthday, and others die in childhood due to famine and disease. If these societies are to survive, a high level of fertility is thus essential.

In these nonindustrial societies, moreover, children are a valuable resource. From an early age, they contribute to the family by doing various household chores, and as they age their value increases. They can be particularly important as a

---

Family Life and Child Mortality in Eighteenth-Century France

Demographic transition theory emphasizes the effect of high rates of infant and child mortality on fertility. Faced with the prospect of one or more of their children dying, families opted to have a large number of children, as the following example shows.

Husband: HESS, Sebastien
Birthdate: January 4, 1732   Deathdate: October 10, 1792
Wife: MULLER, Anne Marie
Date of Birth: July 3, 1729   Deathdate: January 27, 1801
Marriage Date: January 19, 1751

Children	Birthdate	Deathdate
Anne Marie	April 2, 1755	January 6, 1761
Sebastien	April 17, 1759	February 20, 1761
Marie Marguerithe	November 22, 1761	March 26, 1762
Anne Marie	June 6, 1763	June 29, 1791
Sebastien	May 29, 1768	June 13, 1768
Catherine Marguerithe	April 20, 1770	December 23, 1845

In this example, drawn from the church records of a village located in northeastern France, the couple had six children, four of whom died in infancy or early childhood. A fifth died at age 28, and as a result only one child was alive at the death of the parents. Note also the interesting pattern of names. It was the custom to have a child named after each parent. When the child carrying that name died in childhood, the name was "reused" for subsequent children, a practice that many in today's societies might consider unacceptable.

Source: *Example based on the parish registers of baptisms, marriages, and burials contained in the* Archives départementales du Bas-Rhin, *Strasbourg, France.*

source of support for their parents in old age. In addition, children in such societies are far less costly to raise than those in industrial societies. Schooling, if it exists at all, is limited to several years of basic training and is often confined to parts of the year when children's labour is not needed by the family. As a result, children's economic contribution to the family quickly comes to outweigh their cost. To the average couple, then, having children makes good economic sense and, given the high risk of children dying in childhood, producing a large number of children is a good way to insure that at least a few of them survive to adulthood, and thus to their parents' old age.

Societies move into the second stage of the transition, one marked by a combination of high birth rates and declining death rates, as a result of industrialization and the development of a modern economy and the enormous changes in living conditions that come with them. A higher standard of living combined with improvements in sanitation and health gradually reduce death rates, especially for infants and children. But this decline in mortality rates is not immediately matched by a decline in the birth rate. Transition theorists suggest that families take some time to adapt to this new situation. Religious beliefs frequently forbid the use of birth control, and producing a large number of children is still often seen as a mark of social status. As a result, birth rates often remain high for a generation or so after mortality rates begin to decline, and thus societies experience a period of rapid population growth.

The persistence of low mortality gradually convinces couples that they do not need to have a large number of births to ensure several surviving children. Thus eventually societies pass into the third stage of the transition in which birth rates begin to decline significantly. Moreover, continuing economic and technological change greatly reduces the economic value of children while simultaneously increasing their costs. Childhood in today's industrial societies is no longer spent at work but in school, and the period of schooling has been constantly increasing, during which parents are expected to provide for their offspring. What this means for society as a whole is a new balance between birth and death rates, and a population that grows slowly or not at all. Returning to our question

of why currently developing countries experience much faster population growth than countries like our own, transition theorists would respond that these countries are simply further behind in the transition process. While Western countries have entered the final stage of the transition, lesser developed societies are still in stage two. Transition theorists predict that as these societies continue to develop, they too will pass into the third stage, and the population problem will be solved.

How accurate is this view? Do populations naturally tend toward a position of zero population growth? Whether this occurs depends on two questions. First, does transition theory accurately reflect the past experience of Western societies? And second, will that Western experience be repeated in currently developing countries? Let us begin with the experience of Western countries.

There is little question that societies like Canada passed through a transition. Women in the past gave birth to far more children, and death rates have plunged dramatically over the last two centuries. There is some question, however, about the mechanisms responsible for this transition, as posited by transition theorists. Some critics, for example, pointed out that France experienced significant change in birth and death rates *before* the beginning of widespread industrialization (Knodel and Van De Walle, 1986). Others pointed to parts of Germany where the birth rate actually began to decline *before* the infant mortality rate did. Fewer children, they argued, enabled parents to provide a better standard of care, leading to lower rates of infant and childhood death.

Such issues have important consequences for social policy. If, as transition theorists claim, industrialization is a necessary condition for a decline in the birth rate, then that and not family-planning initiatives should be the first goal for Third World societies. If on the other hand, people adopt birth control methods when they become available, even before the beginning of widespread economic development, as some critics of transition theory have suggested, then the emphasis should be on birth control not industrialization.

Turning to the second question, even if the transition theory provides a good explanation of the experiences of past Western societies, its applicability to currently developing societies may still be limited because the situation they face is very different from the one faced by Western societies. First, their decline in mortality has been much faster than was true for societies like our own. Here the death rate fell gradually over the last century due to gradual improvements in the standard of living and, more recently, advances in public health and medical care. In many developing societies, however, the introduction of Western-style public health programs has succeeded in very rapid reductions in the death rate. In Mexico, for example, life expectancy increased from 39 years around 1940 to almost 72 years today; in Canada, it took more than a century to achieve a similar amount of progress.

Second, birth rates are much higher in many developing societies, (particularly in sub-Saharan Africa) than those of past Western societies because in many developing societies marriage is nearly universal and occurs at a younger age than was true in the Western experience. This means that women will have a longer time period to produce children. As a consequence, while the rate of natural increase in European societies probably never surpassed 2 percent, in some developing societies today, the rate of natural increase has approached 4 percent per year, which means a doubling of population in just seventeen years.

Finally, the population of many developing societies is already much larger than was true of Western societies. For countries like ours and the United States and even some European societies, land and resources were abundant and the spur of population growth probably encouraged more rapid development. But can Bangladesh, for example, with a population of 123 million living in an area less than half of the size of Newfoundland, deal with a doubling of its population over the next generation, while birth rates gradually fall into line with reduced death rates?

The points raised in the preceding paragraphs suggest currently developing societies face more acute population problems than did currently industrialized societies. It needs to be pointed out, however, that the resources available to devote to these problems are greater as well (Caldwell et al., 1997). While the decline of fertility in Western societies occurred before the development of modern, efficient means of contraception, and usually in the face of pro-natalist opposition from major social in-

stitutions such as government and religion, in contrast, in countries such as China, Singapore, and Thailand, governments have been enthusiastic supporters of birth control. The most striking example is the case of China where the government has used coercive means to try to bring about the spread of the "one-child family" (Johnson et al., 1998). In Thailand, also, in the 1960s, women had, on average, more than six children. Today, they have fewer than two. Thus just as death rates frequently declined more rapidly in developing societies, in several cases birth rates have fallen dramatically as well, unlike what had occurred in places like Canada.

In sum, then, transition theory is a flawed explanation of population trends. It can best be seen as a guide to the factors that must be considered when examining long-term changes in population patterns, factors discussed in the sections which follow.

Factors Affecting Population Growth

Fertility

Fertility measurement

We have already discussed the crude birth rate (CBR), which provides a general measure of the rate of childbearing in a population. Useful as it is, the CBR has a major limitation. It considers childbearing in relation to the entire population and not in relation to those capable of having children. If women of childbearing age decline as a proportion of the total population, perhaps because a society is aging, the crude birth rate will decline even if the average woman continues to have exactly the same number of children.

To avoid this problem, demographers have developed some simple alternatives to the CBR. One is an **age-specific fertility rate**, obtained by dividing the number of births to women of a given age by the total number of women of that age in the population. Since only women of childbearing age are included, the problem of changes in the makeup of the total population is avoided. These rates have two additional benefits. One is that we can observe changes in the age pattern of fertility. For example, although the overall level of fertility may not be changing, fertility rates may be decreasing among younger women but increasing among older women. Second, if we add up the age-specific rates for women across the childbearing years, we arrive at an estimate of the average number of children a woman will bear in her lifetime if she experiences the current age-specific rates of fertility. This measure, which is of great importance in demography, is called the **total fertility rate** (TFR), and may be expressed per woman (e.g., 1.7 children per woman).

Before leaving the question of measurement, one further distinction is worth introducing. The measures discussed so far—the CBR, age-specific fertility rates, and the TFR—are all based on information gathered at one point in time. For example, the TFR for 2000 is computed by relating the number of births in the year 2000 to the number of women of childbearing age in 2000. Such measures are referred to as **period measures** because they refer to a particular period of time. But what if, for some reason, 2000 produces an unusually small crop of babies. The age-specific rate will correctly inform us of this slowdown in births, but if we attempt to use it as an indicator of the total fertility rate, we will be misled.

To deal with this problem, demographers have developed a second approach to measuring behaviour known as the *cohort approach* (Ryder, 1965). The basic principle is very simple. All people who share a common starting point belong to a particular cohort. Thus, if you were born in 1980s, you are a member of the 1980s birth cohort. The members of these cohorts can then be observed over time and their behaviour recorded. For example, women born in 1955 are at the end of their childbearing years, and we can record the total number of children born to them. The result is a *cohort total fertility rate* of women. Unlike period measures, it is unaffected by year-to-year fluctuations in births. Since the **cohort measure** shows the number of children women of a particular cohort ultimately produce, it makes no difference whether they have those children early in life or delay them until later. In that sense, it is a truer picture of the fertility behaviour of women. This does not mean that cohort measures are necessarily better than period measures, however. For some purposes, e.g., the need for portable classrooms, it is more important to know about year-to-

year changes in fertility. Thus it is best to see period and cohort measures as complementary, providing information from two different perspectives.

Social and biological factors affecting fertility

The term *fecundity* refers to the biological potential to bear children; for example, Prime Minister Chretien was the eighteenth in a family of nineteen children. Demographers use the term *fertility* to refer to the actual childbearing of a woman or group of women. Thus, a woman may be fecund (able to give birth to a child) but not fertile (she has not yet given birth to a child). On the whole, fertility rates tend to fall well below the biological maximum and not only in modern, industrialized societies. There are a variety of reasons for this. First, most societies have developed practices and customs that, often unintentionally, tend to limit fertility (Weeks, 1996: 101). In Western societies, the most important is the influence of marriage patterns on childbearing. Until recently, childbearing outside of marriage was uncommon. And since marriage usually occurs well after the beginning of a woman's childbearing years, many years of potential childbearing were thus "lost." From a biological viewpoint, later marriage limits fertility. Other practices also can unintentionally reduce fertility levels well below their biological maximum. For example, breastfeeding acts as a natural contraceptive by suppressing ovulation, thus reducing the likelihood of the nursing mother becoming pregnant. In some developing societies, breastfeeding may extend up to two years, increasing the length of time between births and thus reducing fertility. Indeed the World Health Organization promotes intensive breastfeeding of infants for six months as a way to enhance the child's and mother's health, and as a means to space births and reduce family size. In the Philippines, for example, where the Catholic Church discourages the use of modern contraception, efforts are made to promote breastfeeding, along with other natural methods, as a socially acceptable way to prevent pregnancy (Mangahas, 1994).

In our society, the most important fertility-reducing practice is the use of modern forms of contraception. While past research had pointed to significant historical differences among women from different religious and ethnic backgrounds in their use of contraception, the use of contraception today is almost universal among married couples in Canada (Wu and Martin, 1999). Moreover, sterilization is the most popular method of contraception among married couples, while unmarried women are most likely to use the pill. The data on sterilization are especially striking; sterilization rates in Canada are significantly higher than in other modern societies with similar population structures.

Finally, an important factor affecting fertility is abortion. The use of abortion varies tremendously among countries, reflecting differences in laws, population policies, reproductive health services, as well as social attitudes towards voluntary pregnancy termination. Generally speaking, where abortion is legal, available, and socially acceptable, rates are higher. Socialist countries for instance, have a tradition of providing wide access to legal abortion services at low cost. In Russia, it is estimated that one-half of all pregnancies are ended by an abortion (Henshaw et al., 1999). Asian countries, such as Japan and Korea, also have very high abortion rates, partly because there are fewer moral and religious objections to abortion than in countries such as the United States and Canada. In other countries, like Vietnam, abortion rates may be higher partly because women have few options available to them to avoid conception, while abortion services are widely available (Bélanger and Khuat, 1998).

In sum, marriage patterns, breastfeeding practices, contraceptive use, and abortion are four very important and measurable factors explaining variations in fertility across time and among societies. Demographers commonly refer to them as *proximate determinants* because they act *directly* on fertility. In contrast, other factors such as the level of education or income indirectly affect the number of children families have. More educated women, for instance, have fewer children not because they are more educated *per se*, but because they tend to marry later and use contraceptive methods more effectively. Depending on social, cultural, and economic factors as well as population policies, a country may achieve a decline in fertility with different combinations of the four proximate determinants.

Fertility in developed societies

Table 15.1 shows period total fertility rates for a number of industrial societies. Not surprisingly, the data indicate that fertility rates in these countries are relatively low. Since a total fertility rate of slightly more than two children per woman is necessary to avoid population decline, we can see that most advanced societies now face the prospect of a natural decrease of population and, in the absence of immigration, a decline in their total population.

If we compare the evolution of birth rates in the various societies, we see that while all now experience relatively low fertility, there are nevertheless important differences among them. Some countries, such as Italy and Germany, have been experiencing a fairly steady downward drift of their fertility rate. In other cases, Sweden, for example,

---

TABLE 15.1   Total Fertility Rates for Selected Industrialized Nations, 1950–1995

Country	1950–55	1960–65	1970–75	1980–85	1990–95
Canada	3.72	3.61	1.97	1.71	1.74
U.S.A.	3.45	3.31	2.02	1.92	2.05
Sweden	2.21	2.33	1.89	1.68	2.01
Italy	2.32	2.55	2.28	1.64	1.24
Germany	2.16	2.49	1.64	1.43	1.3
France	2.73	2.85	2.31	1.8	1.7

Source: United Nations, World Population Prospects: The 1996 Revision, New York: United Nations, 1998: 274–276.

the fertility rate has increased in recent years after having reached a low level during the 1980s. Fertility rates in the U.S. and English Canada have followed a kind of roller-coaster pattern in the decades since the end of World War II. In both cases, fertility rates rose sharply in the 1950s, creating the phenomenon known as the baby-boom. Rates then plunged dramatically, reaching their lowest points in the late 1970s before turning upward in the 1980s. But, in recent years, the two countries have followed different paths. While the Canadian rate has once again declined, hitting a new low of 1.56 in 1997 (Statistics Canada, 1999, *The Daily*, June 16: 5), the American rate continued to increase, and, in 1996, stood at 2.04 (U.S. Bureau of the Census, 1998: 79) the highest total fertility rate in the Western world.

Among the factors influencing recent Canadian fertility patterns is the changed timing of child-bearing. The postwar period saw a shift toward younger childbearing. Couples married younger, and this usually meant an earlier start on child-bearing. Recently, however, age at marriage has been rising, and there is often a long delay between marriage and the birth of the first child. Thus, in 1997, 31 percent of first-time mothers were over 30 years of age (Statistics Canada, 1999, *The Daily*, June 16: 5). The increasing presence of women in higher education and their growing involvement in the labour force lie behind this shift to later childbear-ing. Many women probably feel it is better to es-tablish themselves in a career before taking on the commitments involved in having children. Some of the recent increase in fertility in countries like Sweden and the United States may reflect the births occurring to those women who had postponed hav-ing children.

Another significant trend is the weakening of the link between marriage and childbearing (Rindfuss and Parnell, 1989). In Canada, for exam-ple, as late as 1960, only 4.3 percent of children were born to unmarried mothers, with a large propor-tion of these children given up for adoption shortly after birth. In recent decades, however, the propor-tion of children born to non-married women has risen sharply. In 1996, 31 percent of births in Canada as a whole, and 53 percent of births in Quebec, oc-curred to unmarried women (Statistics Canada, 1999, *Annual Demographic Statistics 1998*: 169). The circumstances surrounding these births may vary greatly, of course. In some cases, the child may be

The Course of Canadian Population Growth

The British North America Act, Canada's basic constitutional document, requires a census of the country to be taken every ten years. In 1966, however, the fed-eral government decided that a de-cennial census was insufficient for keeping track of Canada's rapidly changing population and decided to hold a census every five years. The information contained in these censuses provides a detailed por-trait of our national population, not simply a count of the number of people in the country but also data on a wide variety of characteristics, including ethnicity, occupation, ed-ucation, and income. A census was conducted on May 14, 1996. It showed that the total population of the country reached 28 846 761 in 1996, an increase of 5.7 percent over the 1991 total of 27 296 859.

Not surprisingly, the rate of growth varied significantly across the country. British Columbia, with an increase of 13.5 percent, was the fastest growing province, while Ontario was in second place with an increase of 10.8 percent. Newfoundland, on the other hand, was the only province to lose popu-lation in this period, and at the time of the census the province's popula-tion stood at just 551 792. The Maritime provinces, Manitoba, and Saskatchewan all grew slowly, while the rate of growth in Ontario and Alberta surpassed the national average. These trends reflect a long-term pattern of movement to-wards the west. While the Atlantic provinces' share of Canada's popu-lation declined from 11.6 percent in 1951 to 8.1 percent in 1996, the proportion of the population in Alberta and British Columbia rose from 15 percent in 1951 to 22.3 percent in 1996.

born to a couple in a stable cohabiting relationship, while in others the birth may occur to a woman on her own, with no support, financial or otherwise, from the father. Data from the 1996 census show that more than half of Canada's lone- mother families with a child less than 18 years old lived below the poverty line (McQuillan and Belle, 1999).

One of the best researched topics in demography is differential fertility, or the association between traits like income, level of education, or ethnicity, for example, and family size. In Canada today, the factors affecting childbearing are rather different than those that played a leading role in the past (McVey and Kalbach, 1995). For older generations of Canadians, characteristics such as ethnicity and religion were very important. For women born between 1917 and 1921, Catholic women had an average of 3.8 children while Protestant women had an average of only 2.7 children. When we turn to more recent generations, however, we find that the effect of factors like religion has decreased. For women born in the post-World War II era, there is no significant difference between Catholics and Protestants. Members of some smaller religious groups(e.g., Mormons, Pentecostals) do still have significantly larger families, but, given the small proportion of the population belonging to these denominations, the effect on overall Canadian fertility levels is small (McVey and Kalbach, 1995: 285).

While the effect of religion is now limited, education continues to exert an important influence. To be sure, virtually all Canadian women today are likely to produce a relatively small number of children. But it is also true that the longer women continue education, the smaller the number of children they are likely to have. According to the 1991 census, women over 45 years of age with less than nine years of completed schooling had given birth to an average of 3.8 children, while those who had completed university had borne only 2.2 children (Statistics Canada, 1993, *1991 Census: The Nation—Fertility*: 163). While these differences may be reduced among younger generations of Canadian women, it seems unlikely they will disappear entirely.

Fertility in developing societies

Few if any topics have attracted as much attention from demographers as fertility patterns in developing societies. In reviewing this research, the first thing that becomes apparent is the great variability in behaviour among developing countries. While it may have made sense to speak of a Third World fertility pattern in the '60s, as the data in Figure 15.1 make clear, we cannot do so any longer. All the countries listed there experienced fertility rates in the early sixties that appear high by Western standards. But over the last generation, these countries have followed a variety of paths. Let us look at a few of them to gain some clues as to the sources of fertility decline in the developing world.

South Korea is perhaps the most outstanding example of a society that has experienced both rapid economic growth and rapid fertility decline. Indeed, some argue that it makes little sense anymore to speak of Korea as being a developing country. A rising standard of living, growing urbanization, and industrialization have transformed the country and brought about a shift to a fertility pattern similar to that of Canada or other Western countries. It is a near perfect example of the kind of change predicted by demographic transition theory.

Thailand provides a somewhat different example, one favoured by those who emphasize the importance of cultural factors in producing fertility decline. Thailand experienced rapid economic growth in recent years; by some accounts, it had one of the fastest growing economies in the world during the 1980s (World Bank, 1992). Yet fertility decline has seemed to leap ahead of economic development. Although income levels are still low by Western standards and much of the population remains in rural areas, the total fertility rate is similar to that found in Western societies. Clearly the growing economy influenced this process, but some analysts argue that particular features of the Thai culture played an important role as well. The majority of the population is Buddhist, a religion that has raised no objections to the spread of contraceptive use. Moreover, women in Thai culture have considerable autonomy, particularly in comparison with women in many other developing societies (Knodel et al., 1987). Thus the Thai case demonstrates that where a culture is open to fertility control, birth rates may decline significantly, even before the society achieves a high level of development.

The third example of large-scale fertility decline, China, presents another strikingly different pattern. In this case, the impetus to fertility decline

FIGURE 15.1   Total Fertility Rates for Selected Developing Countries, 1960–65 and 1990–95

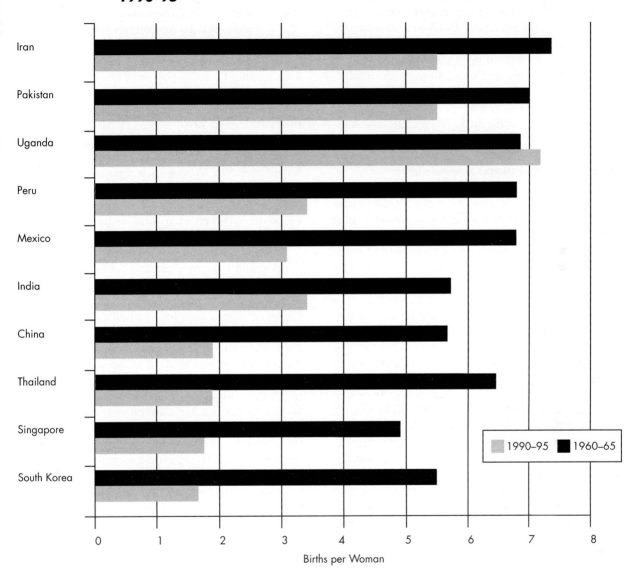

Births per Woman

Source: United Nations (1996: 274–276).

came from the government. Since the early 1970s, the Chinese government has introduced a series of evermore stringent fertility policies, culminating in the introduction of the one-child family policy in 1979. This policy uses a series of incentives and penalties to induce couples to have only one child. There is little doubt that the policy has been effec-

tive, but it also raises important ethical as well as practical questions, such as would it work without coercion? Also, the policy should not be seen has having been uniformly enforced and successful. In urban areas, for instance, the policy was more strictly enforced than in most rural areas (Li, 1995). In the rural areas, compliance with the policy was low, and many families found ways to be granted permission to have a second or third child (Li, 1995).

In fact, in 1989, the policy was revised to allow rural families whose first-born child was a daughter to have a second child. A preference for sons, followed by sex detection of the fetus and sex-selective abortion (East-West Centre, 1995) institutionalize discrimination against girls. Ethical discussions arise today over China's one-child policy about the "missing girls" (recall the boxed insert on this topic in Chapter 7, Gender Relations). While the press has given much attention to abandonment and infanticide of female infants, data reveal that many of the missing girls were born and are alive, but that families have simply not registered their birth in order to avoid consequences (Yi et al., 1993).

A second group of countries demonstrate a pattern of more moderate fertility decline. As the data in Figure 15.1 show, countries like Mexico, Peru, and even India have experienced important changes in fertility. Yet those rates still remain well above those needed for a halt to population growth. Indeed, given the relatively low mortality rates in many of these nations combined with their young populations, their populations continue to grow rapidly. During the 1990s, for example, the rate of natural increase in Mexico was 2.2 percent.

The remaining nations in Figure 15.1 reflect a pattern of continuing high fertility. Although there is considerable diversity in the group of high fertility countries, the majority are found in Africa and in the Islamic world, and these rates are not the simple result of lack of access to contraception. Women in these countries demonstrate knowledge of contraception and often indicate they have at times used various contraceptive methods. At the same time, they express a desire to have what we would consider a large number of children. Analysts point to a combination of economic and sociocultural factors as leading to this pattern of high fertility. In many parts of Africa where families are engaged in subsistence farming, children continue to be economically useful to their parents, much as they used to be in Western societies (Weeks, 1996: 135). Even in urban areas, children can contribute to family income from an early age through unskilled work or by providing childcare for younger siblings. Cultural factors appear to contribute to the persis-

tence of high fertility as well. In many societies, particularly where women's roles centre largely on the family, producing a large number of children adds to a woman's stature within her family and community. For men as well, being the father of a large family may be seen as both adding to their prestige and augmenting the power of the their family or lineage within the community. Having at least one son may be especially important, and this may influence decisions about having more children. Often these views are reinforced by religious values that either support high fertility or oppose the use of fertility control. Where such a powerful combination of economic and social supports for high fertility exist, birth rates may remain high despite the influx of Western ideas and official attempts to lower the birth rate.

Given this diversity of experience among Third World countries, are there any definite conclusions we can draw about the course of fertility? Many analysts would suggest two. First, while the link between economic development and fertility decline is not a simple one, it does appear that once a society achieves a high level of economic development, birth rates decline to near or below replacement level (Watkins, 1986). Secondly, on an individual level, there appears to be a strong connection between education for women and lower fertility (Weeks, 1996: 146). A variety of studies have shown that women in developing countries with at least a high-school education have significantly smaller families, pointing again to the significance of economic development for population change.

Mortality

Mortality measurement

Each of us will die; demographers are interested in when. One aspect of this question is what demographers call *longevity*, the maximum length of years any human can live. No one to our knowledge has lived to be 150 years old. In fact, longevity has probably changed very little over the centuries. Mortality change has come about not because of a lengthened life span, but because a far greater proportion can now expect to survive to what we consider to be old age. Recent data suggest that almost 90 percent of young Canadians can expect to celebrate their sixty-fifth birthday (Statistics Canada, 1995: *Life*

Tables, Canada and the provinces, 1990–92); reaching retirement age is now the norm.

As with fertility, we shall briefly consider the problem of measuring mortality, before discussing the factors associated with mortality change. Since death, unlike childbirth, is a certainty for all of us, one might think that measuring mortality would be an easier task. Unfortunately, this is not so, and in this chapter we can only introduce some important aspects of the problem. We have already discussed the crude death rate (CDR), which relates the total number of deaths to the total size of the population. As is obvious, however, the risk of dying varies greatly by age. For example, the likelihood of a death in any year among a group of nursing-home residents is far greater than the likelihood among a group of university students. As we saw in Chapter 9, Aging, the proportion of Canada's population in the older, high-risk age categories is growing, and this will raise the CDR. This does not mean, of course, that health conditions are deteriorating. As a result, other measures are needed to understand the changes in the risk of mortality at various ages.

As was true with fertility, the first are **age-specific death rates**, calculated by dividing the number of deaths to persons of a given age by the total number of persons in that age cohort. Such rates can be used to construct what demographers call a **life table**, a statistical model which estimates the number of years persons of a given age can expect to live. One specific by-product of the life table is called the **expectation of life at birth**, the average number of years a group of newborns can expect to live if current mortality risks prevail throughout their lifetime.

Table 15.2 provides data on expectation of life at birth for a number of developed and developing societies. Note that in all developed societies, life expectancy is now well above 70 years and, for women, often surpasses 80 years. Developing countries too have experienced considerable progress in recent years. For most countries in Asia and Latin America, expectation of life at birth is now more than 60 years. The lowest levels tend to be found in the less developed societies of sub-Saharan Africa, where life expectancies below 50 years are not uncommon. Worse, high rates of HIV infection in a number of these countries have caused life ex-

TABLE 15.2   Expectation of Life at Birth for Males and Females, Selected Countries, 1995–2000

Country	Male	Female
Canada	76.1	81.8
United States	73.4	80.1
France	74.6	82.9
Italy	75.1	81.4
Switzerland	75.3	81.8
Mexico	69.5	75.5
Chile	72.3	78.3
Bolivia	59.8	63.2
China	68.2	71.7
South Korea	68.8	76.0
Bangladesh	58.1	58.2
Nigeria	50.8	54.0
Ethiopia	48.4	51.6

Source: *United Nations,* World Population Prospects: The 1996 Revision, *New York: United Nations, 1998: 332–357.*

pectancy to decline in recent years. The U.S. Bureau of the Census estimates that the AIDS epidemic may drive expectation of life at birth in countries such as Botswana, Malawi, and Zambia to less than 40 years by 2010 (U.S. Bureau of the Census, 1999: 57).

Mortality change

As we saw earlier, past Western societies experienced very high mortality rates. In some cases, expectation of life at birth was as low as 25 years. Remember that this is an average figure; it does not mean that the majority of the population died in their early adult years. On the contrary, then as now, the early adult years were among the safest in life. Indeed, the risk of death is highest in infancy and early childhood, declines throughout later childhood and adolescence, and then gradually rises throughout the adult years to again reach high levels in older age.

The Effect of HIV/AIDS on Life Expectancy

Given the poor quality of the data, particularly in the countries most affected by the virus, until recently the demographic impact of AIDS was difficult to estimate. But in the 1990s, the commitment of many governments to monitor the disease, combined with the work of international and nongovernmental organizations, has greatly increased our knowledge of the demographics of this devastating pandemic. Using sophisticated demographic techniques, demographers can now estimate the dramatic impact of AIDS on mortality indicators.

Too much remains unknown about the epidemic in large countries such as China and India for accurate estimates of the demographic impact of AIDS worldwide. Still, since it began, the United Nations estimates that by 1998 over 33 million people had been infected with HIV and that nearly 14 million had died of AIDS (UNAIDS, 1998). In sub-Saharan Africa, where some of the most af-fected countries are located, up to 5 percent of the adult population carries the HIV infection, and impact on life expectancy is dramatic. In Botswana, for instance, life expectancy at birth was only 40 in 1998, but would have been over 60 without AIDS. In Kenya, life expectancy was reduced by 18 years due to AIDS. Many of these drops in life expectancy are attributable to the fact that large numbers of deaths are concentrated among infants and children under age 5. In Zimbabwe, for instance, the risk of dying under age 5 more than doubled in 1998 because of AIDS (123.4/1 000 instead of 50.5/1 000). To name only a few, Cameroon, Ethiopia, Nigeria, South Africa, and Malawi also suffer important demographic losses due to AIDS. In other parts of the developing world, AIDS will seriously affect life expectancies at birth in Brazil, Guyana, Haiti, Honduras, Burma, Cambodia, and Thailand. High mortality levels due to AIDS, however, will not be suffi-cient to bring about population stabilization or decline, even to the most affected countries. While the disease reduces growth rates, they are, and will remain, positive due to high fertility rates (U.S. Census Bureau, 1999).

In Canada, HIV/AIDS does not affect enough people to substantially affect life expectancy at birth. In fact, since 1993 the number of new cases reported has steadily declined. This decrease may be attributed to a lowered incidence caused by an increase in awareness of its causes, as well as reporting delays and under-reporting. As of December 1998, a total of 43 347 positive HIV tests and 16 236 AIDS cases had been officially reported since the beginning of the epidemic. The number of people who died of AIDS peaked in 1995 with 1 420 deaths but was under 200 in 1998. That is not to say that the epidemic is under control in Canada; monitoring and awareness continue to be of crucial importance (Health Canada, 1999).

Probably the first reason for mortality decline, you might think, is the growth of quality medical care. As is often true in demography, however, the obvious cause is not the right one, for mortality rates were already falling in most Western countries in the last half of the nineteenth century when medical knowledge was modest, to say the least, and only a small proportion of the population had any contact with doctors or hospitals. For example, the death rate from tuberculosis declined steadily throughout the late nineteenth and early twentieth century although no effective medical treatment was devised until the 1930s. What then caused the initial fall of mortality in Western societies? Most observers point to a variety of causes, but chief among them are an improving standard of living, including better nutrition, and the growth of effective public health and sanitation measures. Better nutrition allowed people to survive once-fatal diseases, and in the process, they often developed immunity to further outbreaks of the same disease. In recent generations, medical advances have produced further progress in the fight against mortality but, in most Western societies, life expectancy had already reached 60 or higher before medical care began to exert a real influence.

While medicine's contribution to lower mortality in Western countries has been modest, this is not true for developing countries. What is striking about the data in Table 15.2 is that the figures are relatively high even for countries that remain very poor. In Bangladesh, for example, where Gross National Product per capita is only $270, compared to $19 290 in Canada, (World Bank, 1999: 190), life expectancy is over 56 years, a figure attained in Canada only in 1920s. One reason for this is that many developing countries have been able to import advances in medical care and public health that had occurred over a long period of time in places like Canada all at once. As a result, death rates have often fallen very rapidly even in the absence of widespread economic development.

Differential mortality

As we saw in the section on fertility, differences in fertility levels among various groups in Canada have been declining over time. We might have expected to discover the same situation when studying mortality. Yet recent research on mortality patterns in Canada and other industrial countries show not only the persistence of differences in life expectancy between social groups, but, in some cases, a widening of those differences. Here we briefly note some of the most significant differences uncovered:

1. Undoubtedly the most significant is the difference in expectation of life between males and females. As the data in Table 15.2 demonstrate, in all industrialized societies (and in most developing ones as well), women outlive men, often by a significant amount. A variety of factors explain the difference. In one way or another, most centre on the different social roles and behaviour of men and women. Some touch on differences in exposure to risk. Women, for example, have historically been employed (inside or outside the home) in situations that entail lower risks of mortality whether through accident, stress, or environmental factors.

On average, women in Canada outlive men by about seven years, and female rates of mortality are less than male rates for virtually every age category.

Other explanations focus on coping strategies. Studies in Canada and elsewhere, for instance, reveal a greater tendency for women to respond effectively to illness by seeking medical help. As women's roles change and become more similar to traditionally male roles, will the advantage held by women in life expectancy shrink or even disappear? The most recent data available suggest that, in recent years, life expectancy for men has been growing faster than for women, though a gap of 5.8 years still remains (Bélanger and Dumas, 1998: 77). Only the future will tell us whether this is the beginning of a shift towards greater equality in the risk of dying.

2. A second difference concerns variation in expectation of life by marital status. Again, studies from a variety of nations have shown that married persons enjoy a significant advantage over single, divorced, or widowed persons (Adams, 1990). The difference is larger for males, but marriage provides some advantage to women as well. One possible explanation for this situation centres on what is called a *selection hypothesis*. What this means is that the difference we see between the married and unmarried may not be a result of differences in their situation, but rather a result of differences in the characteristics of those who marry and stay married versus those who do not. To take an obvious example, alcoholics may be more likely to divorce than non-alcoholics and also more likely to die younger as a result of alcohol abuse. The difference in life expectancy between the married and divorced would reflect the influence of this factor, not the divorce itself. In general, though, while selection factors cannot be ruled out as contributing to the advantage enjoyed by the married, most research seems to point lifestyle differences between the married and non-married as carrying the most weight. The married state is seen as characterized by a more orderly, stable style of living, entailing fewer health risks and perhaps better care when problems occur.

3. A third important category of differences involves class and ethnic variations in mortality. Even in countries like Canada, which boasts universal medical insurance, important differences in life expectancy by social class remain. One study suggested that while class differences have declined in recent years, the difference in life expectancy between the highest and lowest income groups is still 3.7 years (Wilkins et al., 1990). Similarly, ethnic group membership also is associated with differences in life expectancy. French-English differences, once marked, have largely disappeared (Nault, 1997:39), but native peoples in Canada continue to suffer significantly higher death rates, despite some progress in recent years (MacMillan et al., 1996). As in all these situations, no one factor can be identified as responsible for these differences. Most research on the problem identifies two groups of factors that lead to the observed differences. One group reflects the economic and social deprivation these groups experience: poorer quality housing and nutrition, greater environmental risks of disease and accidents, and poorer quality medical care. A second group focuses on behavioural differences by social class or ethnicity, noting that members of disadvantaged groups are more likely to engage in behaviours that carry high health risks. Rates of smoking and drug use tend to be higher among persons from poorer backgrounds (Millar, 1996; Health Canada, 1998). Taken together, these factors create an enduring pattern of difference in the health and mortality of different segments of our population.

Migration

Defining migration

Any growth in global population can be measured using only fertility and mortality rates. When we examine national or regional patterns of population growth, however, we need to consider the movement of people into or out of these regions. Demographers refer to this type of movement across legally defined boundaries as **migration. Internal migration** refers to movement across boundaries within countries. A young person from Nova Scotia who takes a job in British Columbia and establishes permanent residence there is an internal migrant. Since most nations allow people to move about freely within their borders, studying internal migration is difficult since often there is no legal record of the move.

By contrast, international migration, which involves crossing a national boundary, is almost always regulated by law, and governments typically collect statistics on the number of persons entering (and sometimes the number leaving) the country. Such data, however, generally miss illegal immigrants and, as with many issues in sociology, so we need to remind ourselves that official statistics present only a partial view of the topic under study.

International migration

Canada, the United States, and indeed all the Western Hemisphere are lands developed largely by immigration. Since the seventeenth century, immigrants from Europe and elsewhere have poured into the Americas, transforming forever the character of these lands long inhabited by a variety of native peoples. Relative to the small size of the population at the time, the numbers arriving were huge. According to the 1911 census, Canada's population totalled just over seven million people, but in the years 1911–1913 more than one million, mostly European, immigrants arrived (Beaujot, 1991: 105). Many of these, it is true, quickly moved on, most to the United States. Yet the many who stayed helped develop Canada's empty lands and swelled the populations of the country's still small cities and towns.

The period between World Wars I and II, including the Great Depression, was marked by much lower levels of immigration, but after 1945 immigration to Canada again increased. Thousands of Europeans uprooted by war and the economic chaos that accompanied it, looked here for the chance to start a new life. And though, as we shall see, the origins of the persons coming have changed, Canada continues today to be a country open to immigration. In no year since World War II has Canada accepted fewer than 70 000 immigrants, and in 1997, 216 000 new immigrants arrived (Bélanger and Dumas, 1998: 84). Proportionate to the size of its population, Canada continues to be one of the leading recipients of immigrants in the world.

Given Canada's colonial links, first to France and later to Great Britain, it is not surprising that the earliest immigrants to Canada came from these nations (see also Chapter 8, Race and Ethnic Relations). As political and economic changes occurred, however, the origins of immigrants to Canada constantly changed, and very often these

changes were unwelcomed by the resident population. When thousands of Irish immigrants fled to Canada in the nineteenth century, for example, many were met with open hostility. Later, as the number of immigrants from the British Isles declined, Canada began to turn to central Europe as a new source of people. Again, there was a reaction against people who spoke a different language and were seen as too different to fit into Canadian society. In recent years, the sources of immigration to Canada have once again changed. Canada's newest immigrants are increasingly likely to come from countries in the developing world, particularly in Asia. With many countries in the world suffering from poverty and political conflict, the number of potential immigrants to Western countries is very high.

An important, if sometimes unspoken, concern of Canadian immigration policy is the settlement of Canada's open spaces. Despite the huge size of Canada, our population is concentrated in a small portion of our territory. More than half of our population live in the Windsor-Quebec City corridor alone; that area plus Winnipeg, Calgary, Edmonton, and Vancouver account for almost three-quarters of Canada's population. Governments have often hoped to use immigration to bring people to underpopulated parts of the nation. On the whole, such policies have failed. Immigration did help to settle the largely empty lands of the prairies in the early part of the century when land-hungry immigrants from central Europe settled in Manitoba, Saskatchewan, and Alberta. In recent years, however, the majority of immigrants have been drawn to the economic and commercial centres of the country, with more than 60 percent saying they hope to settle in Toronto, Vancouver, or Montreal (Bélanger and Dumas, 1998: 86).

As Canadians, our interest in international migration tends to concentrate on the inflow of people to our country. But for the developing countries that send us immigrants, migration is also a source of concern. In the nineteenth century, the outflow of European emigrants to the Americas was almost certainly a benefit for both the sending and receiving countries. Emigration helped to ease the population pressures felt by European countries experiencing rapid growth and industrialization and drawing ever-larger numbers of migrants to their cities. For the developing world today,

The 1991 census showed that 16 percent of the Canadian population is foreign-born.

however, the benefits of international migration are not so clear. Given the rate of population growth in the developing world, the number of migrants who leave is too small to make much of a difference. The population of India grows by about fifteen million people per year, or roughly twenty times the number of immigrants admitted by Canada and the U.S. in recent years. Moreover, the tendency of industrialized countries to admit only those with a high level of skill and education often means that the developing countries are robbed of the skilled persons most needed for their own development. The balance, of course, is not completely negative. Immigrants often send money to help relatives back home, and this inflow of funds can be valuable for the economy of these countries. Nevertheless, it is not surprising that developing countries have often raised the question of interna-

tional migration when arguing for better treatment in their dealings with the industrialized world.

Internal migration

Canada, like all highly developed societies, has a very mobile population. Almost half of Canadians change their residence at least once during the five-year period between censuses, though only about 5 percent change their home province (Che-Alford and Stevenson, 1998: 15). While individuals move for a variety of reasons, economic factors play a primary role. In Canada, this has most often meant Ontario and British Columbia have been the greatest recipients of internal migrants. Examining migration data for the period from 1970 to 1996, Bélanger and Dumas (1998: 103) showed that British Columbia has been a consistent gainer of population through internal migration, and Ontario and

"Who Are the Movers?"

While mobility is an important feature of the Canadian population, not all groups in the population are equally likely to move. Demographers note that the decision to migrate normally involves a calculation about the likely rewards that will come from a move to a new location, balanced against the costs involved in the move. It is not surprising, then, that the propensity to migrate is strongly related to age. Figure 15.7 shows the interprovincial migration rates for different age groups in the population (data derived from Statistics Canada, *Annual Demographic Statistics 1998*, pp. 232–33). It is

young adults who are most likely to make the decision to set off for another province. At younger ages, the rewards available in the form of better jobs and higher incomes are especially attractive. Just as important, young people are not encumbered by some of the obligations that may discourage others to move. For example, they are less likely to own homes or have children who will complain about changing schools or leaving friends. As people reach age 30 and begin to settle down, the likelihood of moving declines. At this stage of life, a variety of commitments means that people will think very carefully before pulling up

stakes for a new community. Migration rates continue to decline with age, though a slight increase is noticeable around the age of retirement. Freed from the obligations of work, some of the newly retired will look for a new setting in which to spend their later years. While economic conditions are usually most important in the selection of a destination, older migrants are often lured by other factors such as climate. The attraction of places like Vancouver Island or the southern United States for older migrants has important implications for a variety of social services such as health care.

Alberta have generally gained more people than they lost. For the other Canadian provinces, the balance of movement has been mostly negative. Quebec lost almost half a million residents since 1970, many of them Anglophones who left in the wake of political changes. Combined with the lower fertility rate in Quebec, the province's share of the national population total declined from 28.9 percent in 1951, to only 24.7 percent in 1996 (Statistics Canada, 1997, 1996 *Census: A National Overview—Population and Dwelling Counts*: 1).

Urbanization

While demographers pay more attention to the growth of populations, they are also interested in the distribution of a population across the territory of countries. One of the most extraordinary developments of the last century has been the increasing concentration of human populations in cities. Why this has occurred and the limits to urban growth

are questions that have intrigued demographers and geographers.

One of the most remarkable features of urban life is that people who live in cities do not produce the most essential item needed for life: food. Thus, the essential prerequisite for the growth of cities is society's ability to produce a sufficient agricultural surplus to allow city-dwellers to spend their time on other types of work. The limited capacity to produce sufficient food and to transport it to the cities before it spoiled limited the growth of urban areas, with even the great cities of the past relatively small by present-day standards. As late as 1700, London and Paris, the largest cities in Europe, likely had populations of just over 500 000 residents, smaller than Calgary is today. Indeed, until at least 1950, more than three-quarters of the human population lived in rural areas (Davis, 1972).

Economic growth and technological development allowed societies to rely on an ever-smaller segment of the labour force to produce the resources necessary for urban living. It also allowed the quality of life in urban areas to improve dramatically. Cities of the past were, to put it mildly, unappetizing places to live. In addition to importing the food, water, and fuel that would support the urban population, cities faced the challenge of ridding themselves of the waste produced by thousands of people living in a confined area. Before the nineteenth century's dramatic improvements in public health and sanitation, cities struggled with problems of sewage and garbage disposal. Human waste was often dumped into the streets and left to be washed away by the rains, ending up in the streams and rivers that were the source of water for drinking, cooking, and washing. Garbage was left to rot, attracting vermin and insects that, in turn, spread disease.

The appalling conditions of life in cities of the past meant that death rates were very high and sometimes reached catastrophic levels. The great plague that struck London in 1665 killed 100 000 people or some 25 percent of the city's population at the time (Wrigley and Schofield, 1981: 82). In light of these conditions, death rates often exceeded birth rates in urban populations, and cities would have grown slowly or even declined were it not for the flow of people moving to the urban areas from the countryside.

Urbanization in developed societies

When demographers examine the growth of cities, they distinguish between urban growth, which refers to the rate of growth of the urban population, and *urbanization*, or the proportion of a society's population that resides in urban areas. In countries like Canada and the United States, not only have cities continued to grow rapidly throughout the twentieth century, but the share of the total population living in cities has continued to increase as well. Stone (1967: 14) estimated that approximately 7 percent of the Canadian population lived in cities of 20 000 or more in the middle of the nineteenth century. Today, more than three-quarters of the population of Canada count an urban area as their usual place of residence.

The period since the end of World War II has seen dramatic growth of Canadian cities, both in the size of their populations and the amount of land they cover. The period has also seen the develop-

ment of a new form of settlement that we commonly refer to as *suburbanization*. The improvement of transportation systems and the growth of automobile ownership allow large numbers of urban residents to live far away from their place of work. This, in turn, leads to the development of new communities on the fringe of cities where families seek more living space and privacy while still retaining the economic and cultural advantages of city life. And although some disadvantaged urban neighbourhoods have been revitalized by young professional couples attracted to the downtown core, the fastest growth continues to occur on the urban fringe. In the period 1991–1996, the population of the city of Toronto grew by only 2.9 percent, while the suburban communities of Newmarket and Richmond Hill experienced rapid growth, increasing by 25.6 percent and 26.9 percent respectively.

The continuing urbanization of the population is an experience Canada shares with other highly developed societies. Where Canada differs is in the dominant role played by its largest metropolitan areas. The "big three" Canadian cities, Toronto, Montreal, and Vancouver, account for an astounding 32.6 percent of the national population. That is far greater than in most other advanced societies. New York, Los Angeles, and Chicago, the three largest American cities, hold just 16 percent of the U.S. population, while Paris, Lyon, and Marseille account for less than 20 percent of France's population. Moreover, the largest Canadian cities have continued to grow rapidly. As Table 15.3 demonstrates, though Montreal has grown slowly in recent years, Toronto and Vancouver continue to be among the fastest-growing cities in the country.

Urbanization in the developing world

In 1950, most urban dwellers lived in Europe and North America. But today, about two-thirds of the world's urban population lives in cities of developing Asia, Africa, and Latin America. According to U.N. projections, over 80 percent of all urban dwellers will live in developing countries in the year 2030 (United Nations, 1998). Not only are cities of the developing world growing rapidly and accounting for more and more of the total urban population, but their sizes have also reached levels unimaginable a few decades

TABLE 15.3   Population of Ten Largest Canadian Cities, 1976 and 1996

City	1976	1996	% Change
Toronto	2 803 101	4 263 757	52.1%
Montreal	2 802 485	3 326 510	15.7
Vancouver	1 166 348	1 831 665	57.0
Ottawa-Hull	693 288	1 010 498	45.8
Edmonton	554 228	862 597	55.7
Calgary	469 717	821 628	74.9
Quebec	542 158	671 889	23.9
Winnipeg	578 217	667 209	15.4
Hamilton	529 371	624 360	17.9
London	270 383	398 616	47.4

Note: Figures refer to the Census Metropolitan Area.
Source: 1976 Census of Canada *Cat. No. 92-806 Table 6;* 1996 Census of Canada *Cat. No. 93-357-XPB.*

TABLE 15.4   The 15 Largest Urban Conglomerations, Ranked by Population Size (in millions), 1950 and 2000

1950		2000	
City	Population	City	Population
New York	12.3	Tokyo	28
London	8.7	Mexico City	18.1
Tokyo	6.9	Bombay	18
Paris	5.4	São Paulo	17.7
Moscow	5.4	New York	16.6
Shanghai	5.3	Shanghai	14.2
Essen	5.3	Lagos	13.5
Buenos Aires	5	Los Angeles	13.1
Chicago	4.9	Calcutta	12.9
Calcutta	4.4	Buenos Aires	12.4
Osaka	4.1	Seoul	12.2
Los Angeles	4	Beijing	12
Beijing	3.9	Karachi	11.8
Milan	3.6	Delhi	11.7
Berlin	3.3	Dhaka	11

Source: United Nations, World Urbanization Prospects, The 1996 Revision, New York: United Nations, 1998: 21.

ago. In 1950, only New York City had more than 10 million people; in the year 2000, more than 15 cities of the developing world have passed the 10 million mark. Among the 15 largest urban agglomerations in the world today, 11 are located in the developing world (See Table 15.4).

Why have the cities of Asia, Africa, and Latin America grown so fast and reached such large populations? While natural increase remains important, it is not the driving force it used to be. For many cities, migration has become the most important factor in accounting for rapid growth. In China, where fertility is now below the replacement level, migration accounts for most of the growth of cities such as Shanghai, Beijing, and Tianjin (Jones and Visaria, 1995). The same holds true for Mexico City, now the second largest city in the world.

Massive immigration from rural to urban areas results from the poor living conditions in rural areas and people's desire to have a better life for themselves and their children. Cities offer better access to basic services such as water and electricity; urban citizens also enjoy better prospects for education, health care, and employment. Overall, city dwellers in developing nations enjoy better lives than their rural counterparts (United Nations Development Program, 1997). If, from your perspective, people's lives in a slum in Calcutta seem unbearable, from their point of view it is likely an improvement from the quality of life in the rural villages of India. This migration to urban areas creates problems for cities, but it is also a problem for rural areas. Migrants are often younger and more educated than non-migrants, and their departure robs the rural areas of

Malthus felt that, if population always increases to the ultimate point of subsistence, progress can have no lasting effects.

Population and Resources: Is Malthus Now Right?

Since the time of Malthus, any discussion of population growth has raised issues of overpopulation, starvation, and the depletion of the world's scarce resources. The rapid growth of the world's population over the last few decades is currently seen by some as an important element in a coming environmental crisis. This perspective has been articulated by many writers but none more convincingly than American ecologist, Paul Ehrlich. In 1968, he wrote *The Population Bomb*, probably the most widely discussed book on population since Malthus's original essay. He predicted a global crisis involving starvation, rising mortality levels, and environmental disaster as a result of the unprecedented population growth that characterized the late 1960s.

In 1990, he and his wife Anne released another book entitled *The Population Explosion* (Ehrlich and Ehrlich, 1990), which argues that the catastrophic events earlier predicted have already arrived. Hundreds of millions have already perished through starvation and malnutrition, world grain production is falling, and quality agricultural land and water supplies are diminishing. Underlying these problems, according to the Ehrlichs, is rapid population growth in developing countries, which places an unsustainable burden on the ecosystem. Given the very high level of consumption in rich countries, even the slow rate of population growth there in recent years contributes substantially to a coming environmental disaster. The world needs not only a halt to

growth but, in their view, a population decline. If each of us does not voluntarily have only one or at most two children, they suggested, governments will eventually move toward the kind of coercive population policy that exists in China.

The Ehrlichs' position is a somewhat more extreme and popularized version of what most demographers would support. Indeed finding someone on the other side of the issue was not easy until the appearance of a book entitled *The Ultimate Resource*, published in 1981 by an American economist (Simon, 1981). Is there a population crisis? Are there too many people? Are resources being used up? Is pollution getting worse? Simon's answer to all these questions is no. For him, scarcity can be measured in only one way-by looking at the price of goods. If the world's scarce resources are being exhausted, their prices will go up. But, he argued, the real price of most resources has been going steadily down. In relation to our salaries, items such as food, oil, and other energy supplies, and the minerals needed to produce consumer goods are cheaper now than ever before. Concerning pollution, for Simon, things have never been better. Cities today are far cleaner than the cities of the past, and the environments of industrialized societies are often cleaner than those of the developing societies. Indeed it is their higher standard of living that makes them more sensitive to pollution and to demand stronger action on the environment. Are there not too many people and

does not population growth make things worse? No, Simon said, people are the "ultimate resource," the source of new ideas that have led to the steady improvement in the human condition. Population pressure leads people to develop new and more efficient ways of doing things.

Can we say which side of this debate is right? Not really, but the two protagonists did engage in an interesting contest (Tierney, 1990). In 1980, Simon offered to bet that resources would be more plentiful in 1990, and thus their real price would decline during the 1980s. He challenged opponents to select resources they felt would become scarcer and thus more expensive. Ehrlich could not resist saying he would "accept Simon's astonishing offer before other greedy people jumped in." He and his associates chose five resources—copper, chrome, nickel, tin, and tungsten— that they felt would appreciate in value over the decade. Who was the winner? Simon, by a clear margin. The real price of all five materials fell during the 1980s, and the same quantities that cost $1000 in 1980 could have been purchased in 1990 for $618. Simon offered the same wager to Ehrlich for the decade of the 1990s, but he and his friends declined. Ehrlich, however, failed to acknowledge defeat. Commenting on Simon's position, he claimed Simon was like a man who had just jumped off the roof of the Empire State building. Asked how he felt as he passed the tenth floor, the man replied "just fine so far."

the talent needed to promote economic and social development, thus increasing pressures to leave.

While urbanization is perceived as entailing numerous benefits for economic development and the well-being of families and individuals, there is a consensus that policies to slow city growth are crucial for social planning. City dwellers face acute problems, many the same problems that cities of the developed world faced over the past few hundred years. Given the very large size of these cities, however, these problems affect more people, and their solutions become more complex.

Providing even the basics of urban infrastructure remains difficult for most cities of the developing world. Urban transport poses a particular problem. There has been an unprecedented increase in private vehicles and paratransit transportation, such as minibuses and microbuses, leading to congestion and contributing to pollution. Water and sanitation are two other critical problems most large cities in the developing world face. The city of Cairo, for instance, has a population of ten million people, but its water and sanitation system is designed to serve two million (Todaro, 1997). While waste removal and recycling are certainly major issues, many cities are struggling with problems of garbage collection. The average amount of garbage not collected ranges between 30 to 50 percent for some cities (United Nations, 1995).

Urban areas in the developing world also display great disparities in income. Extreme poverty is found in slums of most cities, while the centres often look like any other large city of the world, with international hotels renting rooms in American dollars. Buying an apartment in downtown Bombay in India would cost you as much as buying one in Toronto (The Economist, 1995). Today, slum settlements represent more than one-third of the urban population in all developing countries; in many cases they account for 60 percent or more of the total urban population. Better urban planning as well as sustainable rural development are the approaches local governments and international agencies are promoting for dealing with some of these daunting problems (Jones and Visaria, 1995). Keeping fertility low in rural areas in order to alleviate strong demographic pressure is also a priority for reducing migration streams from the countryside to cities.

Age/Sex Structure

Populations differ not only in terms of size and growth rates, but also in terms of their age/sex structure. The rates of fertility, mortality, and migration experienced by a population combine to shape its age/sex structure. Demographers have worked out several useful tools for examining this issue. The simplest and most commonly used is the **population pyramid**, a picture or graphic representation of the composition of a population at a particular point in time. By drawing to scale bars representing the number of persons in each population category (for example, males 30-34 years of age), we get an image of the overall distribution of a population. Once we understand the nature of these graphs, we can tell at a glance important characteristics of a population. In populations with a high rate of fertility, for example, the graph will look like a real pyramid. That is, it will have a broad base and narrow gradually as we move up to the older age categories. Such populations are said to be "young," since a large proportion of the population is in the childhood and adolescent years. In some African countries today, for example, 50 percent of the population is under age 15. In many Western societies, which have been aging rapidly in recent years, less than 20 percent of the population will be under age 15.

Figure 15.2 shows the 1978 and 1998 population pyramids for Canada. The pyramids do not neatly fit the image of a young or old population, because Canada's population has been passing through a period of dramatic change. Look at the size of the bars representing those between ages 14 and 31 in 1978 and 34–51 in 1998. These groups represent those born during the baby-boom and constitute a bulge in the age distribution. The declining fertility rate since the baby-boom has produced the smaller cohorts that follow behind (lower bars on pyramid). One consequence of this is the continued aging of our population, a fact that Figure 15.2 reveals very clearly. If low fertility continues in Canada, our pyramid will gradually take on a block-like appearance. The pyramid will have a narrow base and the width of the bars representing some of the older age categories may actually be wider than those representing the number of children.

Urbanization in the Developing World: Wrestling the Tiger

While cities in the developed world worry about issues such as tax freezes, recycling, and core revitalization, developing world cities are concerned with much more basic dilemmas-most related to their phenomenal growth in recent years.

Consider the case of São Paulo, Brazil, the largest city in South America. Between 1961 and 1993 the municipality of São Paulo tripled in size, from 3.7 million to nearly 10 million, while the greater São Paulo region increased from 4.7 million to over 15 million. As the new century dawns, the number of inhabitants in the metropolitan region will top 17 million (EMPLASA, 1993: II.2. 49–50).

Such rapid growth has given risen to many social problems. One of the most serious of these is poverty. As an industrial and financial centre, São Paulo is the wealthiest city in Brazil (if not all of Latin America). Yet many of its residents survive on very meagre incomes. The median income of male wage-earners, for example, is less than $3600, as compared with approximately $29 000 for larger cities in Canada. Some 35 percent of all families subsist on less than $4500, and about 10 percent on less than $1800 per year.

Another problem is housing. Not only is household occupant-density higher in São Paulo than it is in most Canadian cities, but substandard housing is a serious problem in many areas. Nearly 2 million citizens inhabit precarious shacks in sprawling favelas spread throughout the city. Over 4,000 are without homes altogether (PMSP, 1996: 146–148).

Basic services for the majority of the municipal population are also seriously lacking. In some areas of the city, especially on the periphery, streets are unpaved, and neighbourhoods frequently lack schools and parks. Commuting from outer areas to the city centre and industrial nuclei is also a challenge. The public transportation system is both inexpensive and extensive-well over 3 billion passengers ride the bus or subway in the municipality of São Paulo each year, compared with about 400 million in Toronto. Service, however, is often sporadic, uncomfortable, time-consuming, and sometimes unsafe.

The quality of policing represents still another concern. Municipal and especially state military police maintain a high visibility, but the crime rate remains staggering. From January to November of 1996, police registered 7171 homicides, 101 700 robberies, and 103 200 auto thefts ("Grande SP registra," 1996).

Health care, finally, is seriously inadequate, as indicated by São Paulo's infant mortality rate of 31 per thousand-five times the Canadian rate. Along with a general lack of free public facilities, hospitals and health centres tend to be concentrated in the city core. With only 14 percent of the total population, the downtown region is home to nearly half of São Paulo's 167 health facilities. By contrast, the much poorer eastern periphery, with 28 percent of the population, has less than 1 percent of all facilities (EMPLASA, 1993: II.2. 50; III.2. 23). A lack of sanitary sewers in many regions compounds health problems. In the absence of septic tanks or other waste-treatment strategies, sewage on many streets simply flows down open drainage ditches and eventually into nearby streams and rivers. Often children play freely in these areas.

Currently, efforts are being made by the municipal government to improve living conditions for São Paulo's citizens. Given the city's limited resources, however, it may be some time before services and infrastructure can be brought up to developed world standards.

Source: W.E. Hewitt, 2000. [Written for this volume.]

One other tool demographers use to understand the effects of population age structures is the **dependency ratio**, which relates the number of persons in what are considered the dependent-age categories to the number in the independent or working-age categories. Conventionally, the dependent-age categories comprise those under 15 and over 65, while the working population consists of those

FIGURE 15.2   Age Pyramid of the Population of Canada, July 1, 1978 and 1998

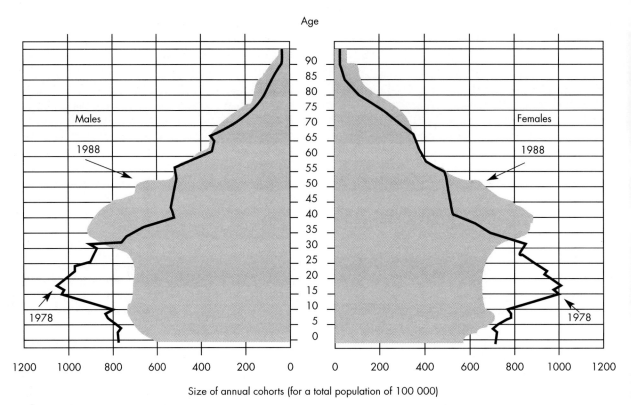

Source: Statistics Canada, 1999. Annual Demographic Statistics, 1998. Catalogue No. 91-213, Statistical Table 1.4.

between the ages of 15 and 64. Developed for making international comparisons, the dividing lines for the age categories do not fit very well with contemporary Canadian reality. Moreover, it treats children and the elderly as being equivalent, although the direct cost to government for caring for the elderly is much higher than for a child. Nevertheless, the measure gives a reasonable indicator of how population change has been shifting the balance between the independent and dependent parts of our population. The data show that the burden of dependency is relatively low in Canada right now. High fertility rates during the baby-boom (many children under age 15) pushed the dependency ratio up during the 1950s and '60s, but since then it has declined and will remain relatively low until the large baby-boom cohorts begin to swell the ranks of the elderly, around the year 2011. At the same

time, the number of persons in the working-age categories will be reduced by the low fertility rates of recent decades. It is the combination of these trends that will put great pressure on governments to provide services to the elderly population, paid for with taxes collected from those in the labour force.

Not only the elderly, but all age groups are affected by changes in the population's age structure. Indeed, one economist argued that the overall changing age structure is the key to understanding social change in recent years. Although his theory is complex, Easterlin's basic message regarding age structure changes can be summarized simply (Easterlin, 1987). He maintained that it is an advantage to be born into a small cohort (in other words, during a period of low fertility) and a disadvantage to be born into a large cohort. Being a member of a smaller cohort, he reasoned, means less competition and thus greater opportunity. By contrast, those born when fertility is high, members of the baby-boom cohorts, for example, face intense competition throughout the life-cycle and reduced chances of success. This occurs because many activities in our society are age-graded. Most people enter university after high school, marry and look for their first house in their late twenties or early thirties, and expect to retire in their sixties. If we are born into a large cohort, there will always be a large number of people wanting to do the same thing we want to do. As a result, it may be harder to get accepted into university or a professional school and harder to find our first job. When we look to buy a house, we find houses are in demand and prices have risen. When we and our fellows retire, we place a strain on pension systems and may have to get by with a lower pension. Selling all of those large houses at the same time may reduce prices. Members of smaller cohorts benefit from the opposite situation.

Although many believe Easterlin pushed his argument too far, cohort size does influence life chances. At the same time, other observers have noted that large cohort size can also work to a group's advantage by giving its members more political and economic weight within society. Businesses anxious to achieve maximum sales will often tailor their products to meet the demand of the largest group of consumers (Foot, 1998). And politicians, anxious to collect votes, may be willing to support programs designed to appeal to the largest bloc of voters. If true, the "disadvantaged" members of large cohorts may be able to offset part of this disadvantage by using their greater weight in society to change the rules of the game, transferring their disadvantage to the cohorts that follow in their wake.

Population in the Twenty-First Century

Demographers do not have a very good record of predictions. Just prior to the baby-boom, many observers were convinced population decline was imminent. One of North America's leading demographers, Frank Notestein, writing in 1953,

believed it would sensible to plan for a world population of just over three billion by the year 2000. As we have seen, the true figure is six billion. Thus, it is best to be modest in making forecasts about the future. However, as we look ahead into the new century, it seems likely that population growth will continue to slow around the globe. All corners of the world have been touched by fertility decline, and past experience suggests that once fertility begins to decline, it seldom changes course. At least in the currently developed societies, discussion will likely turn more the question of very low fertility. With countries like Italy, Spain, Japan, and Canada now experiencing fertility rates well below the level needed to replace the population, people will begin to ask whether this is a problem and if something can be done about it.

Tremendous progress has been made in the control of disease and many other important advances may lie ahead. But the saddest story in the early years of the century will be the toll taken by the spread of HIV/AIDS, especially in southern Africa. Many millions more are almost certain to die in the first decades of the century.

Finally, with slowing population growth and continued population aging, immigration is likely to continue to be a hot political topic. The declining rate of natural increase in countries like Canada means that a larger share of any future population growth will have to come from immigration. The question of how many immigrants to admit and what types of immigrants to seek will remain on the front page in the years to come.

Summary

In this chapter we discussed the trends in population growth at both the global and national level. Our examination of population change has been influenced by the theory of the demographic transition, which sees populations moving from a situation in which both birth and death rates are high to one in which birth and death rates are low. The more economically advanced countries of the world have completed this transition and now experience slow population growth or even decline. In most other regions of the world, the transition is continuing and rates of natural increase are beginning to fall. Nevertheless, global population is likely to continue to increase for some time to come and may eventually reach a total of more than nine billion people.

In Canada, population is now growing slowly. Most women have few children, and life expectancy is rapidly approaching 80 years of age. Demographers expect these patterns to continue, and once the baby-boom generation enters the older age groups, the number of deaths will exceed the number of births in Canada. If Canada's population is to grow in the future, then it will do so as a result of the immigrants who choose to settle here. The distribution of Canada's population is also changing in two important ways. As a nation, we are gradually growing older. Continued low fertility will see this trend continue in the years ahead. And our population is becoming more concentrated in our major cities. The attractions of urban living continue to draw Canadians to the urban centres, leaving much of this very large land very thinly populated.

QUESTIONS FOR REVIEW AND CRITICAL THINKING

1.   Fertility rates are declining or have reached low levels in all major regions of the world. Is overpopulation still a problem with which societies must deal? Should governments attempt to develop and enforce policies to further reduce rates of population growth?

2.   With a fertility rate below replacement level, immigration will place a more important role in shaping the future population of Canada. In what ways will the Canadian population in 2050 differ from our population today?

3.   Canada's major cities, especially Toronto and Vancouver, continue to grow rapidly, while some areas, especially in the Atlantic region, are growing very slowly or not at all. Is this uneven distribution of population a problem for Canadian society? What steps could be taken to deal with these trends?

KEY TERMS

age-specific death rates, p. 413

age-specific fertility rates, p. 406

cohort measures, p. 407

crude birth rate (CBR), p. 401

crude death rate (CDR), p. 401

demographic transition theory, p. 404

demography, p. 401

dependency ratio, p. 425

expectation of life at birth, p. 413

internal migration, p. 416

life table, p. 413

migration, p. 416

period measures, p. 407

population pyramid, p. 424

positive checks, p. 402

preventive checks, p. 402

rate of natural increase, p. 403

total fertility rate, p. 407

SUGGESTED READINGS

Bélanger, Alain and Dumas, Jean

1998   *Report on the Demographic Situation in Canada 1997*. Ottawa: Statistics Canada.

Now appearing on a yearly basis, this series provides up-to-the-minute information on population trends in Canada.

Weeks, John R.

1996   *Population: An Introduction to Concepts and Issues.* (6th ed.) Belmont, CA: Wadsworth.

A readable text that provides a good introduction to the field of demography while also presenting current data on world population trends.

Foot, David K. (with Daniel Stoffman)

1998   *Boom, Bust & Echo 2000.* Toronto: Macfarlane, Walter, and Ross.

The provocative bestseller that argues "two-thirds of everything" is explained by demographics. No book does a better job of showing the practical importance of studying demography.

Simon, Julian

1996   *The Ultimate Resource 2.* Princeton, NJ: Princeton University Press.

An original work that goes against the conventional wisdom by arguing that continued population growth is a benefit to the human species.

Canadian Social Trends

A quarterly publication of Statistics Canada, this social science magazine presents short, readable analyses of current topics of interest with a special focus on social policy issues.

WEB SITES

http://www.city.net

City Net

This site is your gateway to the urban world. Choose a city and explore.

http://www.prb.org

Population Reference Bureau

An excellent site for current world population data. The Population Reference Bureau's World Population Data Sheet can be consulted online. It provides current data on fertility, mortality, and population growth for every country in the world.

http://www.cip-icu.ca/eng/intro.html

Canadian Institute of Planners

This site provides information on dimensions and benefits of urban planning in Canada. There are links, as well, to other related planning sites worldwide.

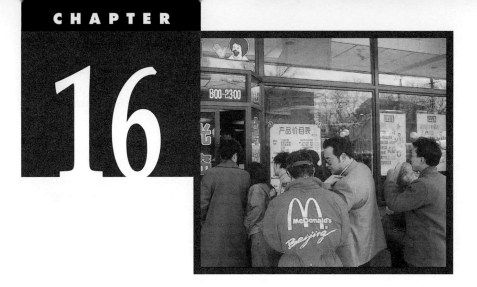

Social Change

Edward Bell

Introduction

Social change is all around you. Even if you are a young adult you will have noticed that things are somewhat different from the way they were when you were a child. When you were born, you were probably delivered by a male doctor. When you were a toddler, your parents or caregivers did not ferry you about in a sport-utility vehicle, talk on a cellphone while driving, or watch NHL hockey in June. High-school students did not wear "Gothic" dress or get to school on their in-line skates. People did not meet in Internet "chat rooms," a majority of university students were men, and virtually every country in the world was in some sort of political or military alliance with either the United States or the Soviet Union.

Ever wonder *why* things change? Sociologists certainly do. In Chapter 14, Social Movements, you saw that one way to learn about change is to examine how large groups of people try to create or prevent it. In this chapter a somewhat different approach will be taken. Instead of focusing on the

people and organizations involved in attempts to produce or hinder change, we shall look at the larger social forces and patterns of interaction that contribute to change. We will also take into consideration innovations like new technologies whose impact on change may be profound but unintended.

In Chapter 1 you learned that sociology itself came into being largely as an attempt to understand the tumultuous social changes that began in Europe and North America in the eighteenth century. When sociology was in its infancy, it seemed as if the foundations upon which human societies had been based were collapsing—a new world was being created by industrialization, and there was a rise of popular democracy. It was in the midst of these developments that the sociological study of social change began. Early sociologists, like their present-day counterparts, disagreed over where the changes were leading and what was causing them. In this chapter you will have a chance to consider the arguments made by both classical and contemporary sociologists concerning those vast changes. You will also take a new look at how sociologists make sense of the changes unique to the present era. Another thing you will learn is that many of the debates scholars engage in concerning social change have not been resolved. This chapter will not attempt to settle those debates, but it will provide you with an introduction to the key issues involved and offer some insights on how to think about them *sociologically*.

You will find that the study of social change, perhaps more than any other area of sociology, requires a comparative and international orientation. For instance, although industrialization and democratization are important innovations, they affect people in different ways and are still largely absent in many parts of the world. You will also learn that some very important changes occurred in human societies thousands of years ago. It will be worthwhile to find out about those changes, because in many ways people are still struggling to adapt to them. We use the term **structural lag** or **cultural lag** to describe this process of adaptation, where parts of a culture catch up with other parts. The extended time frame will also bring into focus the scope and pervasiveness of change in human societies and help to illustrate how certain sociological models and theories can be applied to any historical era.

We will begin our discussion of social change by taking a look at what the original types of human society were like and how these evolved, over time, into the forms with which we are familiar today. Then we shall consider some theories that seek to explain the fundamental changes that occurred over that time. We shall also discuss how Western industrialized countries like Canada have changed in recent decades, and examine the emerging relationship between those societies and the less economically developed nations. Since social change is an ongoing process, we shall conclude with some thoughts on what the future may hold for Canada and other countries.

Early Societies and the Beginnings of Social Change

Our species, *homo sapiens*, has been around in its current form for at least 40 000 years (Chirot, 1994: 1). Genetically and physiologically speaking, we have changed very little over those four hundred centuries. It follows that the extensive changes in the human condition that took place over this period cannot be attributed to human genetic change—we simply do not evolve that quickly (recall Chapter 4, Socialization). Other causes must be considered to determine what happened to us over that time.

Hunting and gathering societies

For the most of the time they have spent on earth, humans have lived in hunting and gathering societies. These are societies that survive by hunting wild game and gathering edible plants; they do not grow their own crops or raise livestock. It has only been since about 8000 BC that humankind has engaged in farming to any significant degree.

What was life like in this original type of human grouping? There was a diversity of experiences and

For most of the time they have spent on earth, humans have lived in hunting and gathering societies. The !Kung Sun of Botswana still do.

cultures among foraging peoples, much of it created in response to variations in the biophysical environment, such as the climate, the animal and plant life available, and the topography. Some societies adapted to harsh environments, like deserts or frigid regions, while others lived in more hospitable surroundings, like tropical islands or lush rainforests. Some led desperate, precarious lives; others did not have to work very hard to survive.

Although there was considerable diversity among hunting and gathering societies, they also had a lot in common. Individual groups or bands tended to be small, on average about forty or fifty people. They were nomadic, usually following a circuitous route, moving when the food supply became depleted. They were deeply spiritual, and a pervasive norm encouraged people to share key resources among the entire group. Many practised abortion and infanticide, and domestic violence and homicide were not unheard of.

Hunting and gathering societies were also characterized by a division of labour based on gender. By and large, women did the gathering of plant products and the rearing of young children, men the hunting. Men tended to be more dominant than women, although there was a rough equality between the sexes. For instance, Shostak states that among the !Kung San of Botswana:

Women's status in the community is high and their influence considerable. They are often prominent in major family and band decisions, such as where and when to move and whom their children will marry. Many also share core leadership in a band and ownership of water holes and foraging areas (1983 [1981]: 13).

In many ways foraging peoples were a lot like us. They were just as intelligent and curious. They had marriage ceremonies and elaborate kinship structures, loved their children, and liked to laugh, sing, and dance. A good story was appreciated, and the best storytellers enjoyed high prestige. But there were also some fundamental differences between hunting and gathering societies and our own. Some people claim that even after thousands of years of existence in more technological societies, some societies still have not adequately adjusted to the "new" conditions created by their departure from a foraging life, another of those lags. For one thing,

there now are states to contend with. The **state**, as defined by Weber, refers to the organization that has a monopoly on the legitimate use of force. Foraging peoples had no formal state. Group decisions were vigorously debated by all who cared to do so, and although the recommendations of some people carried more weight than others, little coercion was applied to dissidents. For example, those who disagreed over the timing or direction of the next migration were free to strike out on their own.

Another difference between hunting and gathering societies and our own is that, in our society, certain groups may acquire more power or wealth than others, and may even exploit people. The absence of these forms of inequality and exploitation among hunter-gatherers can be explained by the fact that these societies had virtually no surplus production; almost all of what they produced was needed to keep them alive. With little left over, once they had consumed the amount needed for sustenance, the exploitation of one group by another was not feasible. The fact that no group had access to weapons unavailable to others also prevented one faction from controlling another (Lenski, Nolan, and Lenski, 1995: 118–20).

Farming societies

Exploitation and pronounced inequalities had their origins in farming societies, first formed some 10 000 years ago. Farming created a sustained economic surplus, which in turn gave rise to the issue of who would have access to the surplus, an issue that remains with us to this day. In the first farming societies, which developed in the Middle East in places like Mesopotamia and Egypt, most of the surplus went to the state and the groups that controlled it. This was the beginning of social stratification in material possessions (economic inequality), a topic introduced in Chapter 6, Social Stratification.

Those who have surplus production at their disposal are able to use some of it to bolster their power. As farming technologies improved and the surplus increased, the people in control of the state became very powerful, usually creating a military organization to protect and further their interests. This greatly magnified a second dimension of social stratification: inequality of power. The historic role of the state in creating and maintaining inequality illustrates the pivotal role it can play in social change, a notion further explored below.

Another thing to note about farming societies is that the status of women in them was usually substantially lower than that of men, particularly in the more technologically advanced groups. Class divisions often crosscut gender inequalities, such that upper class women lived far better lives than male slaves or peasants, but *within* any particular class men usually enjoyed more privileges than women.

The domination of one group by another within farming societies was made more effective once metals were produced and used to make weapons. In early farming societies, only the army had metal weapons, which made it relatively easy for rulers to dominate their people (Lenski, Nolan, and Lenski, 1995: 156-59). But states rarely rely on brute force alone to establish and maintain dominance; they usually make some claim to legitimacy. In early farming societies, state legitimacy derived in part from religious beliefs and ideologies that maintained that the ruler was a god or at least in some special relationship with a god or gods.

The advent of metal weapons contributed to another kind of domination: **imperialism**, the control or exploitation of one society by another, usually by conquest. Although imperialism is often thought of as a European or American phenomenon, there were imperial powers in the Middle East, Asia, and among the indigenous peoples of the Americas long before Europe or the United States emerged as world powers.

The existence of imperialism sheds light on another important point. To understand social change, one must recognize that societies rarely live in isolation from one another. There have always been regional systems of societies, and for several centuries now a world system of societies has been in existence (Wallerstein, 1974). In these systems, a change in one society often leads to a change in another. The shift to farming by some hunter-gatherers, for example, changed the local ecosystem, often causing societies that remained foragers to seek new habitats. And throughout human history, it has been very common for one society to absorb or annihilate another. For example, the indigenous Arawaks of Barbados, a "peaceful and amiable people," were conquered and destroyed by Caribs, who were "fierce and warlike" and practised cannibalism. The Caribs were, in turn, driven from Barbados by the Spanish, who later enslaved them (Hoyos, 1978: 1–13). This sort of scenario has been played out countless times all over the world.

The preeminence of farming societies lasted some 10 000 years. The legacy of the ancient Greeks and Romans, the medieval European societies, as well as the farming societies of the Middle East, Asia, Africa, and the Americas are still with us today. In addition to creating new forms of inequality and dominance, they bequeathed to humanity the major world religions and the cultural and scientific foundations of the modern age.

The modern era

Machines fuelled by inanimate energy sources were first used for commercial purposes in the textile industry in Britain in the late eighteenth century. As the Industrial Revolution progressed, machine production was used for a variety of tasks in an increasing number of societies. The Revolution would eventually transform many countries from agrarian nations into industrial ones, a transformation that reshaped all aspects of their societies. Gender relations, the nature of work, the family structure, race relations, and politics, to name just a few things, would never be the same again.

Some of the foundations of modern ways of thinking also can be traced to developments of the eighteenth century. This was the century of the **Enlightenment** wherein many of the doctrines of the agrarian age were challenged, especially those relating to the forms of domination prevalent at the time. Enlightenment thinkers viewed skepticism as a good thing, saw reason and observation as the best means to acquire knowledge, and proclaimed that people should not be persecuted for what they say or believe, ideas still popular today. The American and French Revolutions, inspired in part by Enlightenment philosophies, challenged the right of hereditary monarchs to rule over their subjects and championed a belief in social equality. Such ideals provided the inspiration for many of the changes that would take place in the next two centuries, although they were rarely put into practice at the time.

Two Perspectives on Change in Early Societies

As in modern societies, the conflict experienced by hunting-gathering and farming societies often resulted in change. Sometimes the conflict and changes were extreme, as in the instances in which one society absorbed or conquered another. The Romans, for example, built a huge empire through conquest, which destroyed or radically altered the lives of the vanquished. Other forms of conflict led to less drastic changes, as when one hunting and gathering society drove another out of a given territory, or when clashes between medieval lords and their monarch resulted in constitutional change. When you are thinking about a social change in any society, it would be worthwhile to ask yourself, "Was this change a result of conflict? If so, what was at stake? Who were the major players? How did one side manage to

prevail over the other?" A related question, one often posed by conflict sociologists, is, "Who benefits from this change?" Seeking answers to such questions is one way to think about social change sociologically. The conflict perspective thus may be used to understand change in early societies.

The functionalist perspective provides another useful way to make sense of change. It can sometimes be used in conjunction with, or in addition to, the conflict approach. Functionalists tend to view change as gradual or incremental, usually focusing on how a particular society becomes increasingly differentiated, and how the growing division of labour meets some kind of need. For example, researchers adopting a functionalist perspective have observed that members of hunting and gathering societies usually did not specialize in a single task. Hunters,

for instance, also made their own weapons; there was usually no one in the society who only hunted or only made weapons. Similarly, the spiritual leaders of the group normally performed all the other tasks expected of people of their gender. The transition to farming, a gradual process that may have taken thousands of years, satisfied a need for a greater food supply and eventually produced the surplus necessary for increased occupational specialization. This specialization, for example among artisans, military personnel, and scribes, in turn contributed to the development of towns and cities. These were profound changes to human societies, changes that cannot be directly attributed to conflict. Another question to ask yourself when considering a particular social change, then, is "Does this change meet some social need?"

With the advent of industrialization and the modern capitalist system it helped to create, the world system of societies, and many characteristics of the societies therein, were drastically altered. By the middle of the nineteenth century, Marx and Engels were well aware of the scope and depth of the social change that had arrived in the wake of modern capitalism. In 1848 they wrote that the modern bourgeoisie:

was the first to show what man's activity can bring about. It has accomplished wonders far surpassing Egyptian pyramids, Roman aqueducts, and Gothic cathedrals; it has conducted expeditions that put in the shade all former Exoduses of nations and crusades (Marx and Engels, [1848] 1979: 83).

Marx and Engels also offered an influential theory of social change, which will be considered below.

How were human societies transformed from small bands of hunter-gatherers into the societies of today? What were the consequences of this transformation? In trying to answer these and other related questions, social scientists formulated a number of formal theories of social change to which we now turn.

Theories of Social Change
Evolutionism

Evolutionism and evolutionary theories of change have a long history in sociology, a history that predates Darwin (Sztompka, 1993: 100). In fact according to Harris, Darwin developed his principles through "an application of social-science concepts to biology" (1968: 122–23). Herbert Spencer (1820–1903), who coined the term "survival of the fittest" and popularized the term "evolution," presented a theory of societal evolution that held sway among English-speaking social scientists from the late nineteenth century until the 1930s (Hamilton, 1996: 206). Darwin was very impressed with Spencer's sociological writings and publicly acknowledged his influence on his own theories (Weinstein, 1997: 28), once remarking that Spencer is "about a dozen times my superior" (Carneiro, 1967: ix).

Spencer wrote that human societies evolve from small, disjointed, undifferentiated groups of people into larger entities composed of heterogeneous, interdependent parts in a manner analogous to the way in which biological organisms develop through the life cycle from single cells into complex organic systems. For example, he noted that hunting and gathering societies (which, as we have seen, have a minimal division of labour) may evolve into societies having specialized, interrelated institutions performing educational, political, kinship, religious, economic, or other functions. This is compared to the development of an organism from a single cell into a creature having interdependent organs such as a brain, heart, lungs, and so on. The development of each aspect of society is explained in terms of the function it fulfills, in particular how it enhances the society's survival potential. For instance, Spencer argued that the monogamy now widely practised in industrial societies came into being in part because over the centuries sex ratios had become relatively even. Nonindustrial societies that frequently engaged in war and sustained heavy losses of soldiers tended to have more women than men, which made polygyny an attractive option; it maximized the society's reproductive potential (all women could have a partner) and offered some care for widows and orphans. Industrial societies tend to have relatively even sex ratios. If a large number of men practised polygyny, many others would be unable to find a wife, a situation not conducive to social peace.

For Spencer, the growing differentiation and integration in human societies results primarily from conflict. Initially at least, societies change and adapt to protect themselves from attack or go on the offensive themselves. Although he loathed war and the social formations and personality traits that accompany it, Spencer believed that civilization would not have evolved without it. He argued that over the centuries societies have increased in size and complexity by conquering other societies and incorporating them into their own. In this way societies evolve from "simple" to "compound" forms, and then to "doubly compound," "trebly compound," and beyond, depending on the number and nature of the smaller societies forcibly brought together. According to Spencer, to reach the highest level, societies must pass through each successive stage of compoundedness. The level of compoundedness is then associated with various societal characteristics such as the amount of social differentiation present, the degree of formalization in law and religious practices, and the level of technological sophistication (Spencer, 1898: 549–56).

In addition to creating societies of increased size and complexity, war is said to be conducive to cooperation within a society, as under the conditions of war all must unite in order to avoid annihilation. For Spencer, it was the increased size, complexity, and internal cooperation generated by war that creates civilization. Nonetheless, he looked forward to the day when war would be no more, believing that such a day will arrive if all societies reach an advanced stage of evolution. As the foregoing discussion illustrates, Spencer's approach to social change incorporated both the functionalist and conflict perspectives, which you have read about in a number of previous chapters.

Spencer also distinguished between "militant" and "industrial" societies, which he presented as two extremes on a continuum; most societies fall somewhere in between (Spencer, 1898: 556–75). The difference between the two types pertains to the degree to which matters of warfare take precedence over economic production. In militant societies, warfare is the main activity; economic production, such as it is, is geared toward waging war. Militant societies allow little personal freedom and have a centralized, powerful, autocratic state; these are seen as necessary for waging war effectively. As the doctrine of "the survival of the fittest" would suggest, those societies that do not tightly control their populations wage war less efficiently and so are more likely to disappear. When militant societies are ascendant, the nations that survive and dominate the world stage are those with coercive political systems and greatest military might.

Militant societies may evolve into the second basic type, the industrial society. In the latter, warfare is less often undertaken. Economic production is not devoted to military ends but is instead conducted as an end in itself. Industrial societies, according to Spencer, also have democratic governments that respect individual rights and freedoms and generally allow people, businesses, and organizations to pursue their interests without interference. Industrial societies are also characterized by equality of opportunity in the acquisition of wealth and power, and tend to value self-reliance, innovativeness, and individual initiative as character traits. For Spencer, respect for individual rights and freedoms in a society is proportionate to the degree to which society is devoted to economic production for its own sake. The relations between economic actors in an open market (voluntary, uncoerced, etc.) is said to generalize to the realm of politics. In a fully mature industrial society, people would be characterized by a "growing independence, a less-marked loyalty, a small faith in governments, and a more qualified patriotism" (Spencer, 1897: 639).

Spencer foresaw a third type of society evolving out of the industrial one. At some future time, economic production would be used neither for the support of a military regime nor for the acquisition of material things as an end in itself. Production would instead provide the things that people need to engage in the "higher activities." These future societies will invert the industrial dogma that "life is for work" into the belief that "work is for life" (Spencer, 1898: 575). Spencer is reluctant to elaborate on this idea but observed that in the industrial-capitalist societies of his time there was an increasing number of organizations and institutions devoted to artistic and intellectual development. He did not have an overly optimistic outlook, however, as he believed that in addition to progress, a worsening of conditions was not only possible in any given society but was as likely to occur as progress. To minimize the chances of regress, he favoured minimal powers for the state, arguing that the greatest good would result if the natural evolutionary process were allowed to run its course without interference. He believed that there was little people

could do to improve the world, but much they could do to foul it up. Spencer was thus the antithesis of the sociologist as "activist," a matter discussed below.

Classical evolutionists like Spencer have been subject to criticism. For one thing, the society-as-organism metaphor popular among them has been called into question. Critics claim that there is just too much inequality, conflict, disruption, strife, and suffering within modern societies to justify a model that assumes that the various organs or parts of society serve the interests of the whole, and do so by interacting in a harmonious, integrated fashion. Also, the implication that some societies are superior to others is seen as offensive and ethnocentric.

Nevertheless, evolutionary theory has enjoyed a resurgence in recent decades. Often termed "neo-evolutionary theory," the contemporary version of this approach maintains that an evolutionary model can be devised that helps to explain social change without the shortcomings of the original. Neo-evolutionists do not maintain that highly industrialized societies are morally, intellectually, or esthetically superior to any other kind of society. The new perspective is also based far more on archaeological and historical data than the nineteenth-century variant (Lenski, 1976: 560–61).

An example of a neo-evolutionary approach is the Lenski's **ecological-evolutionary theory** (Lenski, 1966; Lenski, Nolan and Lenski, 1995). This view maintains that societies are profoundly influenced by their bio-physical and social environments, and that the characteristics of a society are strongly affected by its *subsistence technology*, the technology it uses to acquire the basic necessities of life. The type of subsistence technology employed (either hunting-gathering, herding, fishing, overseas trade, horticulture, agriculture or industry) is said to affect societal characteristics like the status of women, population size, level of urbanization, stratification, kinship, and so on. Human history is divided into four major epochs, according to the type of society politically and militarily dominant at the time: the hunting and gathering era (human origins to about 8000 BC); the horticultural era (roughly 8000–3000 BC); the agrarian age (about 3000 BC–1800 AD); and the industrial age (about 1800 to the present)(Lenski et al., 1995: 84).

One illustration of the effects of the natural environment and subsistence technology presented by Lenski and his co-authors involves a comparison of herding societies (societies that sustain themselves by raising livestock such as horses, cattle, or sheep) and horticultural societies (farming societies that do not use the plow). Herding societies tend to be found in mountainous areas or territories having little rainfall or short growing seasons, regions unsuitable for plant cultivation. They are usually nomadic or semi-nomadic due to the need to have fresh grazing areas for their herds. They also tend to be highly patriarchal, in part because they gain a great deal of their wealth from raids and warfare (a male activity in these societies), and they consider the herding activity itself to be men's work. Women's roles in the society's subsistence activities are minor.

Horticultural societies, by contrast, tend to be found where conditions are more suitable for farming. Horticulture makes roaming about less necessary, especially among the more technologically advanced groups. Consequently, they are less nomadic than herding societies. Horticultural societies also bestow a higher status on women. Women's places in the stratification system are explained, in part, by making reference to their extensive involvement in subsistence activities. In horticultural societies women do virtually all of the planting, tending of crops, and harvesting (Lenski et al., 1995: 138-50, 226–29).

As mentioned, ecological-evolutionary theory also maintains that societies are influenced by their *social* environments in important ways. The social environment refers to those other societies that have an effect on a given society. The effect of the social environment can range from minimal to severe, the last including the destruction of one society by another. The perspective thus incorporates the idea that regional and, later, world systems of societies develop and have an important impact on human history. To illustrate the profound influence that systems of societies can have, Lenski and his collaborators pointed out that the vast majority of human societies that ever existed are now extinct. The extinct societies changed very little over the course of their existence and, as a result, either perished as the biophysical environment changed or were absorbed or destroyed by other societies. In keeping with the evolutionary model, in particular the idea of natural selection, the authors suggested that societies having large populations, complex

Horticultural Societies in Canada

Many studies from different parts of the world have shown that societies relying on horticulture (the cultivation of plants without the use of the plow) have social characteristics very different from those found in hunting and gathering societies, the societal type from which they usually evolve. Horticultural societies tend to have larger populations, more permanent settlements, more material possessions, greater social stratification, and a greater propensity to engage in warfare than hunting and gathering societies. They are also more likely to be matrilineal (tracing descent through the female line).

This pattern appears to hold true for prehistoric horticulturalists in Canada. There is evidence that the Iroquoian peoples, a matrilineal tribe that lived in a area stretching from southwestern Ontario to the St. Lawrence River valley, grew maize 1500 years ago, and several centuries later supplemented this with beans and squash. Over time, horticulture replaced hunting and gathering, to become their primary mode of subsistence. As in other societies that underwent this transition, the Iroquoian population increased-the region in which they lived had the highest population density of any aboriginal area in Canada. The Iroquois lived in relatively permanent villages, some of them containing over 2000 people, in huge multi-family longhouses. The advent of horticulture also appears to have increased the amount of warfare they waged.

Source: Entries "Iroquois," "Longhouse," and "Prehistory" in The Canadian Encyclopedia (2nd ed.). Edmonton: Hurtig, 1988.

social structures, and powerful military organizations have higher survival potential than those lacking these traits, just as in the biotic world animals having certain characteristics—such as white fur in northerly regions—are more likely to survive.

Neo-evolutionists are careful not to take the comparison with biological evolution too far; they best spell out in detail how social evolution differs from its biological cousin. For instance, it is acknowledged that social evolution results in *fewer*, more *similar* societies, whereas biological evolution produces an *increasing number* of *highly differentiated* life forms. In biological evolution, highly complex species often co-exist with the less complex, as when micro-organisms inhabit the human body. But in the social world, less complex societies usually do not fare well amid more complex ones. Also, because social change can result from **diffusion**, the adoption of an innovation by a society that did not create it, important changes can spread rather quickly, just as the use of computers spread rapidly from the United States to hundreds of other societies, including Canada. In the biotic world, physical evolution involves genetic mutation, which can take a very long time. As noted above, our species has not undergone discernible genetic change in over 40 000 years.

A theory of Canadian development that in some ways parallels ecological-evolutionary theory is Innis's **staples thesis** (1956a: 383–402; 1986 [1950]: 2–4). Innis argued that the economic, political, and cultural formation of Canada was shaped by its geography and the natural resources and raw materials or "staples," available for export. The export of fish, furs, lumber, wheat, minerals, and energy products to more highly developed economies—France, then Great Britain, then the United States—formed the basis of the Canadian economy and strongly influenced settlement patterns, communications networks, and our political history. For instance, Innis maintained that "the northern half of North America remained British [after the American Revolution] because of the importance of fur as a staple product" (Innis, 1956a: 391). Our economy at the time of the Revolution, he observed, was centred on the export of fur to Great Britain in exchange for manufactured goods; severing ties with Britain would have put that trading relationship in jeopardy.

"Each staple in its turn left its stamp," Innis wrote, "and the shift to new staples invariably produced periods of crisis in which adjustments in the old structure were painfully made, and a new pattern created in relation to a new staple" (1986 [1950]: 3). He was also mindful of the central role indigenous peoples played in the formation of Canada, especially through the fur trade: "We have not yet realized that the Indian and his culture were fundamental to the growth of Canadian institutions" (Innis, 1956a: 392). An abiding theme of his work is that a reliance on the export of raw materials throughout our history limited Canadian development and made Canada vulnerable to the shifting needs and demands of more populous and developed foreign metropolitan centres.

Developmental theories

Another group of social scientists maintains that human societies develop through a series of stages, although they do not employ all of the arguments offered by the evolutionists. For example, Auguste Comte (1798–1857), the first person to call himself a sociologist, identified three stages that he believed all societies go through: the theological, metaphysical, and scientific or positive stages (Lauer, 1982: 51–55). The stages are based on the predominant way in which knowledge is sought; each approach to knowledge is said to create a certain kind of society or social order. In the theological phase, explanations for physical and social phenomena are sought in the realm of the supernatural. In the metaphysical, people look for explanations in the natural world, using reason to formulate theories of abstract forces. Finally, in the positive period, reason is coupled with the systematic observation of science to produce knowledge of all things. Like most nineteenth-century thinkers Comte believed in **progress**, the notion that social change ultimately leads to improved social conditions. For Comte, the metaphysical and positive stages represented successively higher forms of civilization; progress occurs as societies enter a higher phase. And like most thinkers using the developmental paradigm, he maintained that social change characteristically occurs gradually and incrementally.

As you learned in Chapter 1, Comte believed that sociologists would form a sort of priesthood

Chapter 16   Social Change   439

Conflict and Change in Canada

The conflict approach to social change, which maintains that change often has its origins in social conflict of some kind, is a fruitful perspective for understanding change in Canadian society. Here are some examples of how conflict led to change in Canada:

1) *The conquest of New France, 1759.* With New France's defeat by British forces, Canada embarked on a long history of cultural-linguistic dualism, which remains a defining characteristic of our society, evident today in official bilingualism and the Quebec independence movement. One immediate result of the conquest was a greatly increased British presence in the higher echelons of business and government in the former French colony. Another was the marginalization of several native peoples, no longer needed as allies and warriors in British-French conflicts after the conquest. The conquest also influenced the American Revolution, as the withdrawal of the French army meant that the American colonies no longer needed British protection from French forces. This gave the Americans one fewer reason to remain loyal to Britain. Needless to say, American independence has had a profound effect on Canada over the past two centuries.

2) *World War I.* Morton, the Canadian historian, wrote that this war changed almost every facet of Canadian life. For example, women's voting rights, which were won at the federal level in 1918, grew out of the compelling argument that the service, sacrifice, and competence women showed during the war made them deserving of the vote. Canadian independence from Britain was taken a step further by the war effort, as the Canadian military became increasingly autonomous and Canada was granted a seat in the League of Nations. The war worsened ethnic tensions between British- and French-Canadians, who disagreed over wartime policies such as conscription. World War I also saw the introduction of a new form of government revenue-income tax.

3) *Conflict between employees and employers.* The political rights, wages, working conditions, and benefits that Canadian working people have today are in many ways a result of a long series of conflicts between employees and employers (see also Chapter 13, Work and Organization). In the nineteenth century, the Nine Hour movement fought to have the working day reduced from up to twelve hours down to nine. In 1894 the federal government established Labour Day after decades of labour unrest. By 1944, after many years of struggle, employers were required by law to recognize the union chosen by their employees. In the immediate post-war period, grievance procedures and vacation pay were instituted, another culmination of a long series of conflicts. More recent conflict has resulted in the establishment of maternity leave.

that would guide societies through the transition to the positive state by proposing solutions to social problems and teaching people to think scientifically. This illustrates that, from the beginnings of the discipline, some sociologists not only *analysed* social change but also viewed themselves as *agents* of change. (As you study change, try to determine whether the author whose works you are reading advocates change of some sort.) Most authors writing on the topic present either an implicit or explicit program for social change.

Another early sociologist using the idea of phases of social development was Tönnies, who in the 1880s introduced the concepts *Gemeinschaft* and *Gesellschaft*. **Gemeinschaft**, which means "community," refers to the old agrarian social setting in which people lived in small communities or villages close to their kin and friends, knew their neighbours well, and generally felt a sense of belonging and interdependence. In this sort of milieu, social norms are fairly clear and people tend to obey them. **Gesellschaft**, which means "society" or

Durkheim, Social Change, and the Law

According to Durkheim, the type of society—mechanical or organic—affects all aspects of social life, including the law. In mechanical societies, pressure to conform is strong, and sanctions are *repressive*, not so much to deter the criminal or for retribution, but because the conformist others would become demoralized were this not to happen. They work so hard to follow the collective conscience that not severely punishing the criminal is not acceptable; he or she has attacked the very fabric of what holds the society together. Punishment is necessary to keep the conformists tied to society, and punishment serves as a visible sign of the unacceptability of the deviant. Finally, since there is little division of labour, with all performing similar roles in such societies, no one is indispensable; even capital punishment will not deprive the society of any needed ingredient.

In organic societies, marked by an interdependence, criminal sanctions are *restitutive*. The division of labour is greater, with more diversity, and thus the collective conscience is not as strong. As a result, restitution not repression is the form of punishment. The goal is to right a wrong and then to have the criminal brought back into society, a society that needs him or her for completeness.

"association," describes the social setting that Tönnies believed characterizes large cities once capitalist development has taken place. Here things are more impersonal; relationships and exchanges outside kin groups and close friends tend to lack warmth and intimacy, and the interdependence and community spirit of traditional life are replaced with the pursuit of narrow self-interest. Not surprisingly, Tönnies held that deviance is more common in modern societies. Indeed, Tönnies was one of very few nineteenth-century thinkers who had grave misgivings about what the future would hold for members of industrial societies. Most writers, philosophers, social scientists, and natural scientists of the day believed in progress. It was not until the twentieth century that widespread disillusionment with modernity and its prospects arose (Sztompka, 1993: 24–27).

About a decade after Tönnies drew his conclusions on the effects of industrialization, Durkheim offered a somewhat similar assessment, although his overall view was more optimistic. In preindustrial societies, Durkheim noted, there is minimal division of labour; people's tasks in the economy tend to be similar to those of other people of the same gender. This creates strong bonds between the members of a society and near unanimity on the appropriateness of social norms, especially those rooted in religion. He called this unity-based similarity **mechanical solidarity**.

Durkheim drew attention to the fact that things become rather different once industrialization has taken place. The expanded division of labour, especially in urban areas, creates different experiences and perceptions, which tend to divide people. For example, the world view of a nurse may be quite different from that of a stockbroker. Modern cities attract people from diverse cultural backgrounds, which also detracts from a uniform view of life. Durkheim claimed that, under these circumstances, the legitimacy of traditional norms may be challenged or the norms may become ill-defined, a condition referred to as **anomie**. Deviance, he argued, becomes more prevalent as anomic conditions set in. In the 1930s, Merton adopted some of Durkheim's ideas in creating his anomic theory of deviance (Merton, 1938), presented in Chapter 5, Deviance.

As noted, Durkheim was less pessimistic about how Western societies were evolving than Tönnies, who viewed modernity in decidedly negative terms. For Durkheim, there was always the possibility that **organic solidarity** would hold society together and lead to social progress, a solidarity based on the complementarity or interdependence of positions in modern, complex divisions of labour. For instance, the stockbroker may fall ill and discover the value of the nurse, and the nurse may come to appreciate the stockbroker's contribution to the economic development needed to build hospitals. Durkheim claimed that awareness of this sort of interdependence can unify a society and contribute to genuine social progress.

Historical materialism

Another approach to social change is **historical materialism**. The name derives from the fact that its proponents maintain that material (usually economic) factors are the engine of change. Culture, ideas, spiritual forces, religious beliefs, and all other non-material phenomena are considered to be much less important influences. This view is exemplified in a famous statement made by Marx:

The mode of production of material life conditions the general process of social, political, and intellectual life. It is not the consciousness of men that determines their existence, but their social existence determines their consciousness (1970 [1859]: 20–21).

Marx and his collaborator, Engels, have been the most influential advocates of historical materialism (see also Chapter 6, Social Stratification). The approach they take is **dialectical**, for every thesis there is, built into it, its own antithesis or transformation, in that they claim that societies are constantly changing, and that all societies, except future communist societies, contain conflicts and tensions that eventually lead to their demise. For example, they believed that capitalist society, like all previous social formations, contains the seeds of its own destruction. Their notion of the dialectic also assumed that the social transformation that occurs is not random or arbitrary but, instead, results in higher forms of social organization, and that each new form makes the next one possible.

Marx and Engels divided human history into several periods or epochs, defined according to the way in which economic production is conducted, for example, ancient, feudal, and capitalist epochs. They argued that the mode of production largely determines what form the other aspects of the society will take and that if the mode of production changes, all the other facets of the society will change in a dramatic, fundamental way. For example, if the agrarian mode of production charac-teristic of the Middle Ages is replaced by industrial capitalism, medieval culture collapses. Gone are such things as the divine right of kings, the belief that the aristocracy is the natural ruling class, and the notion that one cannot escape one's station in life. In its place comes capitalist culture: ideological support for open markets and free trade, a devotion to material things and those who acquire them, the belief that capitalist society is the best possible society, and so on. Marx and Engels explained culture as follows:

The ideas of the ruling class are in every epoch the ruling ideas, i.e., the class which is the ruling *material* force of society, is at the same time its ruling *intellectual* force. The class which has the means of material production at its disposal, has control at the same time over the means of mental production...(1973 [1846]: 64).

For Marx and Engels, culture in the broad sense is not neutral, but instead justifies the wealth and power enjoyed by the dominant classes. In their words, "the ruling ideas are nothing more than the ideal expression of the dominant material relationships." For example, they argued that capitalist culture extols the virtues of the bourgeoisie and has the effect of discouraging the rest of the population from changing the system.

The radical change that accompanies a new mode of production comes about through *revolution*. It is through revolution that a new epoch is created. Thus, unlike evolutionary or developmental theorists who claim that societal change often occurs in a gradual, almost imperceptible way, Marx and Engels maintained that sharp, sudden breaks with the past can occur.

Revolution is said to come about through class conflict. This kind of conflict is so central to their theory of social change that they maintained that the "history of all hitherto existing society is the history of class struggles" (Marx and Engels, 1979 [1848]: 79). The clashes between classes are said to be "uninterrupted," a "now hidden, now open fight." Class conflict ends "either in a revolutionary reconstitution of society at large, or in the common ruin of the contending classes." Marx and Engels contended that to understand any era, one must examine the configuration of classes present and try to determine how the most powerful ones dominate and exploit the others, as this will

Marx and Engels suggested that in the modern capitalist era, society is splitting more and more into two hostile camps—the bourgeoisie and the proletariat.

provide clues about the prevailing form of class conflict and the revolution to come.

They described the evolution of social classes as follows. The earliest human aggregates are referred to by Engels as "primitive Communistic society," which have most property in common and so lack class divisions and class conflict. Later social types include ancient societies such as the Romans with their classes of patricians, plebians, and slaves. In the medieval epoch, the aristocracy, local lords, vassals, guild-masters, journeymen, serfs, and others made up the class structure. In the modern capitalist era, the class system left over from the Middle Ages is recast such that a greatly simplified version appears. Instead of the wide assortment of classes found in medieval times, "society as a whole is more

and more splitting up into two hostile camps, into two great classes facing each other: Bourgeoisie and Proletariat" (Marx and Engels, 1979 [1848]: 80). Marx and Engels also described a lower middle class-small tradespeople, shopkeepers, peasants and so on—but this class is destined to "sink gradually into the proletariat" (Marx and Engels, 1979 [1848] 88), leaving only an expanded, wretched proletariat and an increasingly insecure bourgeoisie to battle it out in a socialist revolution.

The final epoch, they believed, will be the communist epoch, a time when all productive property will be owned by society at large rather than by private individuals. Although they had very little to say about what life would be like in this epoch, they implied that it would be free of major conflict, people would have an opportunity to cultivate their true selves, and the state would be very weak. Ironically, they hinted at a state of affairs that bears some resemblance to the future hoped for by Spencer. Marx and Engels shared with him the popular nineteenth-century belief that violence and struggle can have beneficial results. But unlike Spencer, Marx and Engels maintained that social activism can help to bring about better conditions. They claimed that it is not enough to understand society-one must also change it.

Many sociologists over the years have offered criticisms of Marx and Engels's theory of social change. Few today, for example, expect a socialist revolution in advanced capitalist countries, and the collapse of communism suggests that their view of the future was at least somewhat misguided. Marx and Engels remain respected figures in the discipline, but most feel that some modification of their position is in order.

The Weber thesis

Perhaps the best-known challenge to historical materialism written by a sociologist is Weber's *The Protestant Ethic and the Spirit of Capitalism* (1930 [1905]), although confronting "the ghost of Karl Marx" was not his only motivation for writing the book (Hamilton, 1996: 104–06). According to Weber, the notion that change results primarily from economic factors does not provide a complete explanation of social transformation. A more comprehensive account would show how both material factors and culture or ideas interact to produce change. The change he sought to explain was the rise of modern capitalism, a phenomenon that, as we have seen, set in motion a wide range of developments. Weber maintained that even with the requisite technology, markets, banking system, and so on, capitalism would not have developed when and as it did had the necessary cultural characteristics not been present. Those cultural attributes, he suggested, were provided by Calvinism, a Protestant movement formed in western Europe in the sixteenth century. Weber's argument linking Calvinism with the development of capitalism was discussed in Chapter 11, Religion.

Although Weber's thesis enjoys wide popularity in sociological circles, a number of scholars have also raised questions concerning the evidence (or lack thereof) he offered to substantiate his claims (see Hamilton, 1996: ch.3). According to Hamilton, the Weber thesis is just that—a thesis—not a proven account. He showed that several of Weber's key points linking Calvinism with the development of capitalism are open to challenge.

Our discussion of historical materialism and *The Protestant Ethic* (as well as the criticism made of these positions) illustrates how sociologists can disagree about the influence material factors and culture have on social change. When thinking about a particular social change, it would be worthwhile to keep this debate in mind.

The state theory of modernization

Weber's thesis is only one of several offered in the social sciences to explain the rise of capitalism. Another is the **state theory of modernization**, a perspective that is also used to analyze other aspects of modern societies. According to the state theory, the reason why some countries have become wealthy, industrialized nations and others have not is because the state thwarted development in the latter. This view holds that if people are free to produce and exchange goods and services without fear of confiscation, excessive taxation, or other forms of state interference, they will, by pursuing their self-interest, foster development that increases the overall wealth of the society. This unencumbered pursuit of self-interest will produce a dynamic science and technology sector. It is claimed that the potential for such development has existed for centuries, but the norm for most farming societies over the past 10 000 years has been state suppression of economic and intellectual initiative (Chirot, 1985: 183).

Why would rulers in agrarian societies not allow people to freely produce and exchange goods, services, and ideas? First of all, it is important to recognize that agrarian autocrats probably had no idea of the enormity of the changes they were preventing. It was impossible for them to envision the transformation that would have occurred over the long run had they acted differently; they were simply acting in what they perceived to be their self-interest. They saw no need to act differently—expropriation and high taxation produced revenues that were usually sufficient to maintain their society and their place in it. Also, restricting economic activity prevented competing power bases from developing, which might challenge their authority or even destroy their way of life. In addition, the dominant ideologies usually legitimized and supported their rule. To allow open intellectual discourse would leave the official justification for the regime open to challenge.

To illustrate the validity of their theory, scholars adopting this perspective have compared the role of the state in various agrarian societies with what happened in western Europe in recent centuries. McNeill (1982: 25–33) described how a number of privately owned and operated smelters producing iron and steel were constructed in the Chinese provinces of Honan and Hopei around 1000 AD. The smelters were so productive that they made more iron in the year 1078 than England and Wales did in 1788 in the early stages of the Industrial Revolution. The smelters were also quite profitable. They enriched the owners and provided employment for hundreds of workers. However, Chinese government officials tightly controlled the sale of iron weapons, had a long-standing policy of heavily taxing iron production, and in 1083 monopolized the distribution of iron tools. As a result, goods made of iron were sold at artificially high prices, which may have restricted civilian access to them and prevented a further expansion of production. By the twelfth century, iron and steel production had declined precipitously. Athough the historical record is not complete enough to reveal exactly what caused either the boom in iron and steel products or its deterioration, McNeill (1982: 33) stated that:

...governmental policy was always critically important. The distrust and suspicion with which officials habitually viewed successful entrepreneurs meant that any undertaking risked being taken over as a state monopoly. Alternatively, it could be subject to taxes and officially imposed prices which made the maintenance of existing levels of operation impossible.

Chirot made a similar argument, claiming that if the Ming and Ch'ing Dynasties had not been able to exert their dominance over China, the Chinese rather than western Europeans would have been the first to industrialize on a large scale (1985: 183).

How then was the old agrarian practice of state suppression of economic and intellectual affairs broken by the Europeans? How were they, rather than the Chinese, or the Egyptians, or some other group, able to create the first industrial societies? According to Chirot (1985), geographical and political factors were crucial. The temperate climate in western Europe was an inhospitable place for most of the crop-damaging parasites that plagued the other regions of the world where agrarian empires developed; western Europe had sufficient rainfall to make large-scale irrigation unnecessary; and its terrain was not suitable for the nomadic herding societies that pillaged much of eastern Europe, Asia, the Middle East, and Africa. These geographical advantages allowed western European societies to flourish and accumulate considerable wealth compared to other agrarian regions.

The geography of western Europe also contributed to political decentralization, the second major factor cited by Chirot. The region has many small river valleys, which made communication and the conquering of large empires difficult, a situation rather different from China and other non-western European areas. A good many small, independent principalities emerged in Europe, which after the eleventh century competed with each other economically and intellectually. The principalities allowed freedom of movement such that those fleeing religious or intellectual oppression or overtaxation could go from one district to another. This gave people with innovative ideas and practices some chance of survival. In addition, conflicts among the monarch, local lords, urban merchants and artisans, and the Church were such that no single faction could completely control the other three. The urban dwellers often supported the monarch in order to escape the domination of local lords, who were prone to overtaxing them. To gain the favour of the urban classes, monarchs were less controlling and confiscatory toward them, awakening to the fact that it was in the crown's interests to have a well-off group of merchants from which it could draw taxes on a regular basis.

According to scholars taking this perspective, the stalemate that existed between the four contending groups in western European societies allowed for **rationalization**, a condition in which there are formalized procedures that give individual actors a measure of predictability in the outcomes of their actions. Economic rationality, for example, allows people to know the economic outcome of their actions; one can learn the commercial regulations and tax laws and act accordingly. In a non-rational system, one is not sure of what will be allowed and what will not. Maybe one can earn money from a particular commercial enterprise; but maybe the monarch will disapprove and, without warning, confiscate the wealth, as apparently happended in Honan and Hopei. Few are willing to risk time or resources under such uncertain conditions. As a result, economic development is minimal or nonexistent. According to the state theory of modernization, rationality evolved in western Europe because of the limitation of state power that grew out of the stalemate among the four ranks.

It is not claimed that the process of rationalization and the transition to modern capitalism was smooth and straightforward. Adherents of this position maintain that the system took about a thousand years to evolve and that it still retains some non-rational elements.

This explanation for the rise of capitalism illustrates how significant social change may be totally *unplanned* and *unintended*. The monarchs who acquiesced, in their own interest, to a limitation of their power probably would have preferred not to. Similarly, each of the other three groups would have welcomed the chance to dominate society. They agreed to a compromise not to promote rationality, or boost development, or advance the free exchange of ideas, but to salvage what they could from their position in society. The modernization that followed from the compromise was largely unintended.

Once they came into existence, industrial capitalist societies continued to change and evolve. The next section examines how they have changed in recent years. It also explores the modern relationship between industrialized and nonindustrialized societies.

Recent Changes and Relationships Between Societies

The "Great Disruption"

A number of significant social changes have occurred in advanced capitalist societies since the 1960s. One constellation of these changes has been called the "Great Disruption" by Fukuyama (1999). He pointed out that, in recent decades, crime rates have jumped, the number of babies born to unwed parents has increased (in some Scandinavian countries it has reached almost 60 percent of all births), norms governing sexual behaviour have become more permissive, and divorce is much more common. Fukuyama noted that although there are some national variations in these trends, they are clearly present in all western industrialized countries, including Canada. He searched for factors common to all of these societies, to explain the changes in morality.

Fukuyama suggested that these trends were caused by two broad social changes: one cultural, the other economic. With regard to the first, he maintained that, since the Enlightenment, there has been a growing acceptance of individual rights and freedoms and a concomitant decline in the ability of all forms of authority—church, state, and community—to set limits on people's behaviours. Previous forms of social control, he claimed, were rooted in religion but, with the Enlightenment, religion started to lose its effectiveness in this regard. A series of bloody religious wars in Europe had caused various states to increasingly distance themselves from matters of religion and morality, leaving individuals and groups more freedom to decide on their own what moral precepts they would follow. But it soon became apparent that the use of reason espoused by the Enlightenment philosopers was not going to lead to any consensus on moral or religious issues. In the nineteenth and early twentieth centuries, Western intellectuals examined a wide variety of moral rules and codes found in various non-Western cultures. Some of these intellectuals concluded, with Nietzsche, that morality is a social construction, not something based on reason or objective judgment. Others, such as Freud, Dewey, William James, and the behaviourist Watson proclaimed that tight control over behaviour is not necessary for human development and may even be harmful. Both were arguments against a common strict morality. The message propounded by such intellectuals was eventually picked up by the popular media, finding its way into childrearing manuals, educational practices, novels, movies, and television programs.

Fukuyama also claimed that changes in the economies and technologies of Western industrialized countries contributed to the growing individualism. By the 1960s, a significant proportion of the labour force was made up of non-manual occupations, a proportion that continues to rise. Chapter 6, Social Stratification, provides the relevant figures for Canada. As Table 6.1 shows, by 1981 a majority of the Canadian labour force worked in non-manual ("white collar") occupations. The increase in non-manual jobs, Fukuyama contended, led to a rapid increase in the number of women in the paid labour force. He argued that this changed the nature of the marriage bond, as industrial-era marriages had previously been based on the assumption that the husband would provide the family's economic resources while the wife bore children and performed domestic duties. With women

becoming more financially independent, marital breakup no longer meant financial devastation for women, which increased the frequency of divorce. (Changes made to divorce laws at this time were another important influence.) Fukuyama argued that women's enhanced financial independence also contributed to the increase in the number of unwed parents. If a woman can support herself or receive financial assistance from the state if she has a baby, avoiding parenthood outside of marriage becomes less of an issue for both men and women.

Fukuyama was confident that the "disruption" is only temporary. Social and moral life, he claimed, is cyclical. He maintained that human societies usually develop new norms to take the place of old, obsolete ones, and that societies usually return to a more balanced state. He noted that in many Western countries divorce, crime, and births to

Got the Time?

People today seem to be under intense pressure to squeeze more and more activities into their day, with little time left over for rest or leisure activities. In 1992, Statistics Canada data indicated that 52 percent of married mothers and 39 percent of married fathers felt stress, resulting from trying to accomplish too much in too little time (Schachter, 1999: D2). Schachter also described how people in economically developed countries are now more harried than ever. Forty-five-hour work weeks are increasingly common, with many people working over fifty hours. Cities have increased in size, as have commuting distances, which further reduces the time spent in non-work-related activities.

Many employers are demanding that more and more tasks be done

per unit of time. For example, a Canadian nurse recently remarked that her job is now organized like assembly-line work. Bell telephone employees are timed to insure that they move on to the next caller quickly enough. Fear of layoff and a high unemployment rate make it difficult to refuse employer demands.

With both spouses working, which is now the norm, housework now greets the weary worker upon arrival at home. Children's sports and recreational endeavours are now more formalized and organized than ever, which means more non-restful time spent transporting children to and from ballet lessons, hockey practices, music recitals, soccer games, and the like, as well as many hours spent watching them perform.

This sort of frenzied activity is a far cry from medieval times when almost a third of the year was devoted to holidays, which were usually a mixture of religious observance and community social activities. Time was not in the forefront of consciousness in those days—few people even owned clocks, which in any case were big and heavy and hence not portable. Today, of course, most people wear a wristwatch that gives them the time to the second, a reflection of the modern obsession with time.

As I was preparing this chapter, I had to dash off to buy a birthday present for my 7-year-old son. His request? A watch. On the way home from making the purchase, with the watch on his wrist, he repeatedly reminded me that we were late for another engagement.

unwed parents are already declining, although he does not foresee a return to more conservative sexual norms or to a revival of religious orthodoxy.

Although some scientific norms maintain that social scientists should not make value judgments in their work, it happens quite frequently, as it did here. In calling the set of changes he examined the "Great Disruption," Fukuyama highlighted what he perceived to be the negative aspects of the period in question. As you think about social change, you will find that you too will take a moral stand—you will welcome some changes and oppose others. When you come to make this sort of judgment, keep in mind that social scientists are not more qualified than anyone else in matters of morality. You be the judge—feel free to agree or disagree with any moral position offered by a social scientist—but try to learn as much about the topic at issue as you can.

Increased tolerance, rejection of authority

There may be a positive side to the phenomenon Fukuyama described. The loosening of constraints on behaviour in Western societies in some ways has contributed to a greater tolerance of differences. This is evident in the proliferation of different lifestyles, fashions, haircuts, foods, books, movies, and other aspects of social life once forbidden or frowned upon, but now accepted. For instance, there is a growing acceptance of gays and lesbians in society. Polls indicate that a majority of Canadians now believe that same-sex marriages should be legal, and the Supreme Court of Canada has ruled that Ontario's Family Law Act must give homosexual couples the same rights as heterosexual ones when it comes to support payments following the breakup of common-law relationships. There also appears to be greater tolerance and understanding between racial, ethnic, and religious groups in Canada. As noted in Chapter 8, Race and Ethnic Relations, although racism and prejudice have not disappeared here, there is considerable evidence that they have diminished. In 1949, for instance, the Ontario Court of Appeal pronounced that it was perfectly legal for Lake Huron cottagers to ban blacks and Jews from their beaches. Such discrimination would spark outrage today.

The general trend toward individualism and individual rights also has an explicitly political dimension. Newman (1995) argued that Canadians are now less deferential to authority than in years past (see also Nevitte, 1996). We are less likely to follow the lead of political élites, journalists, religious leaders, union officials, the royal family, or any person of power or influence. An example cited by Newman is Canadians' rejection of the Charlottetown Accord in 1992. All the major political parties, the leading newspapers, business representatives, organized labour, aboriginal leaders, even Newman himself-all came out in favour of the accord, yet it was soundly voted down by the Canadian public. One way of viewing this is that Canada is becoming more democratic, or a least more demanding of its political élites.

Trends in academe have in some ways mirrored the rejection of authority that is evident in Canada and other industrialized countries. For instance, in the 1980s and 1990s, **postmodernism** and *deconstructionism* gained favour in some academic circles, as noted in Chapter 3, Culture. Although there is no consensus on what these terms mean, one can discern certain themes expressed by the writers of this genre. One is a moral and epistemological relativism, an adherence to Nietzsche's dictum that there are no facts, only interpretations (Nietzsche, 1910: 12). This is reflected in a questioning of scientific methods of inquiry and notions of truth by postmodernists; among those taking an extreme position, science is given the same truth status as magic. This is a rather radical departure from the Enlightenment philosophers' belief in reason as a means to truth.

Another postmodernist theme is that the traditional canon of Western civilization—the revered books, the great works of art—serve to perpetuate existing forms of domination. Here the message echoes Marx and Engels's belief that "the ruling ideas are nothing more than the ideal expression of the dominant material relationships" (1973 [1846]: 64), with the words "power and gender" added after "material."

While most of the public is largely unaware of these intellectual movements, there is a kind of mass "in your face" rejection of much of what was once considered sacred or at least beyond reproach.

Whether the postmodernist intellectual movements have had an effect on the general public through popularization by the mass media, or the general mood in the population later found academic expression, is difficult to determine. Perhaps both are related to the centuries-old thrust in Western societies toward individualism, towards a lack of trust in the judgments of élites.

Although postmodernist tendencies exist in industrial societies, their impact should not be overstated. Many reject the movement. The idea that there are universal truths about humanity and the natural world is still part of our culture. Shakespeare remains a huge draw among theatre-goers, and his creations are more popular than ever in film. Science still enjoys enormous prestige among the general public and in the university. But the assumption that what is beneficial, relevant, or aesthetically pleasing is or should be the same for all people, or

that one should habitually rely on the judgments of intellectual authorities, is fast disappearing.

Postmaterialism

Another change in industrial societies has been a shift towards postmaterialist values among some segments of the population. Inglehart (1997) studied this phenomenon as part of a larger inquiry into social change. He adopted a general theoretical position comparable to the ecological-evolutionary and historical materialist approaches in that he claimed that cultural, economic, and political changes are closely related, and that once a country industrializes, a predictable pattern of change is likely to follow. For example, he maintained that regardless of location, as capitalist development proceeds, mass formal educational programs are created, women enter the paid labour force in increasing numbers,

Social Needs and Social Change in Canada

Functionalists maintain that social change may result from attempts to satisfy a society's needs. Several significant changes in Canadian society came about this way. Here are some examples:

1) *The creation of the Canadian Broadcasting Corporation (CBC).* The CBC was created in the 1930s to counter the growing influence of American programming in Canada. It was believed that there was a need for a Canadian perspective on culture and world events that was not being fulfilled. Another influence was the need to foster Canadian unity and develop national spirit.

2) *The expansion of the university system in the 1960s and 1970s.* As the baby-boom gen-

eration began to reach adulthood, educators in Canada realized that the existing university system was inadequate to meet the needs of the rapidly increasing student population. As a result, universities expanded enormously, and eight new ones were created. In Quebec, in addition to developing the existing universities, a large system of junior colleges (CEGEPs) was created.

The expansion of postsecondary education in Canada occurred not only because of the increases in the student population. It was also a response to a need for greater economic productivity, as it was widely believed that national education levels and economic pro-

ductivity are related. Another need the expansion addressed was social justice. The universities expanded to allow people of limited financial means greater access to education.

3) *Growth in the personal services sector.* With changing gender roles and a majority of married women of working age now in the paid labour force, many domestic tasks formerly done without remuneration by women are being performed by service workers. Daycare facilities, restaurants, house-cleaning businesses, catering firms, pet-care providers, bakeries, and other service operations have expanded to meet needs formerly satisfied largely by housewives.

families get smaller, gender roles become more similar, and media of mass communication are established.

Values also change. People who grew up during periods of prolonged peace and prosperity have different attitudes and outlooks compared to those who did not. Inglehart argued that individuals born before the post-World War II economic expansion tend to have **materialist values**, which place a high priority on economic and physical security. By contrast, the post-war generations tend to take it for granted that they will not live lives of destitution or be victims of military attack. The latter are more likely to have **postmaterialist values**, which emphasize self-expression, participation in decision-making, belonging, self-esteem, and intellectual and artistic development. Postmaterialists do not reject material well-being; in fact they value it highly. But because they feel secure physically and economically, they place an even higher priority on non-material things (Inglehart, 1997: 34–35). For example, Inglehart linked the environmental movement to the growing preponderance of postmaterialist values—many people now believe that the preservation and enjoyment of the environment is more important than economic development, a view that is far less popular in less economically developed countries. Postmaterialists also tend to place a lower value on the science and technology that makes development possible, which may explain some of the postmodernist suspicion of science mentioned above. Inglehart's research indicates that the proportion of postmaterialists is fairly high in Canada. The percentage postmaterialist minus the percentage materialist in his 1990 sample of Canadians was 14; the same figure for the United States was 6 (Inglehart, 1997: 157).

Inglehart stated that a general sense of security among postmaterialists explains the larger trend toward the rejection of authority. If one's survival is threatened in either an economic, military, or medical way, one is inclined to follow leaders and authority figures. People in societies under military attack, for example, tend to follow the orders given them by military and political leaders. By contrast, people who are secure are not fond of orders and rigid rules, preferring to follow their own ideas.

A similar argument is made to explain the shift away from religious orthodoxy in wealthy coun-

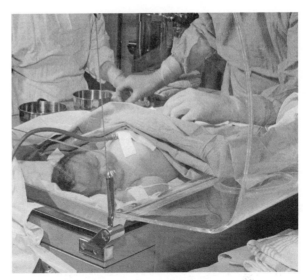

Substantial improvement in medical care since the late 1950s have helpled to reduce Canada's infant mortality rate.

tries like Canada. In post-war industrial societies—characterized by prolonged economic and military security, low infant mortality, advanced medical technology, and long-life expectancy—death or disaster, especially among those who are not elderly, rarely seems imminent. As a result, religious quests are not pursued with the same sense of urgency or despair as they once were. Postmaterialists are interested in matters of spirituality, the meaning of life, figuring out who they are, and so on, but they are not in as great a rush to find final answers as people who grew up in more troubling times. Postmaterialists also differ from materialists in that they are reluctant to develop their spirituality by following absolute rules imposed by someone else, often the standard method offered by established religions.

Having postmaterialist values has some drawbacks. Generally, people with these values have lower levels of overall life satisfaction than materialists in the same country (Inglehart, 1997: 87). It seems that it is more difficult for postmaterialists to meet their expectations with regard to self-expression, participation in government, intellectual development, and so on than for materialists to satisfy their needs for material well-being.

Group rights

Although much of the foregoing illustrates how, since the Enlightenment, Western society has, for good or ill, been increasingly individualistic in orientation, a second somewhat contradictory propensity is also evident. It is a quest for group rights and equality of condition, goals embraced by one faction of Enlightenment thinkers and some of the leaders of the French Revolution (Fonte, 1999). In the nineteenth and twentieth centuries, socialists carried this banner. Recently, those promoting affirmative action programs and various other group-based rights initiatives have adopted this philosophy. The current clash between the two perspectives, individual and group, can be seen in Canada in the controversies surrounding the relevance of race and gender in hiring policies for university positions and other jobs, and in the conflict over language legislation in Quebec (see Chapter 14, Social Movements). When should equity among groups override individual merit as a criterion for advancement?

Globalization and development

Another phenomenon that characterizes current times is globalization. Contemporary societies are now so closely interlinked economically, politically, and culturally that some sociologists argue that the discipline must abandon the country or single society as its primary unit of analysis and embrace "a sociology of world society" (Sztompka, 1993: 86). Economic globalization has resulted in some transnational corporations having revenues comparable to middle-sized countries; financial markets are now international in orientation and effect; more and more countries are embracing free trade. Although Canada's economy has relied on international trade for centuries, the implementation of the Canadian-U.S. Free Trade Agreement in 1989 and the North American Free Trade Agreement in 1994 extended the global reach of our economy.

The globalization of culture is also significant. The rich nations, especially the United States, export their culture to the poorer ones, mainly through television and movies (recall Chapter 11, Media). For example, the American news network CNN is seen around the world, as are American television dramas and comedy shows. English is increasingly the international language of business, tourism, science, and the Internet. American fast-food outlets are found around the world, as is Microsoft computer software. And more and more countries are adopting Western forms of dress. For instance, after years of bitter war with the United States, many Vietnamese have ditched their traditional conical hats in favour of American-style baseball caps (*Globe and Mail*, 17 June 1999: A31).

The arrival of Western culture in non-Western societies can cause resentment. A dramatic illustration of this is the Iranian Revolution of 1979. The Shah, Mohammad Reza Pahlavi, who had acceded to power in the 1950s with the assistance of the American government, had for years welcomed Western investment and culture into Iran, even to the point of discouraging Iranian women from wearing the traditional Muslim headwear. Many Iranians, led by the Ayatollah Khomeini, were outraged at the extent of Western influence and drove the Shah out of power, setting up a traditional Islamic theocracy. Comparable Islamic revivals have occurred in Afghanistan, Algeria, and other countries.

As the example of the Iranian Revolution illustrates, the phenomenon of globalization is closely linked to the issue of Third World economic development. Researchers in the area of development try to determine why the poorer countries of the world have a level of economic development that is so far below that of the industrialized nations, and what can be done to foster economic growth. Researchers are also concerned with the consequences of globalization and development for Third World countries. See the boxed insert "Why Are Some Countries Poor?" for a summary of the different views that have emerged on this topic.

Summary

In this chapter we've examined in broad outline how human societies have changed over the past 10 000 years. Their evolution from hunting and gathering bands to farming societies and finally to industrialized nations produced a number of significant changes, including new forms of inequality, altered gender relations, variations in the power of the state, and urbanization. We also examined

Why Are Some Countries Poor?

Scholars disagree over the issue of why Third World nations are stricken with poverty. According to **modernization theory**, the limited development in the Third World is a consequence of a number characteristics of these countries (So, 1990: 58). They include: traditional cultures that may not be conducive to development; capital shortages; a lack of technological expertise; low levels of education; absence of infrastructure such as roads, bridges, and energy sources; and limited entrepreneurial skills. Advocates of modernization theory tend to view the increasing levels of contact between the industrialized nations and the Third World as favourable, as the richer countries may provide investment funds, technology transfers, field workers, and, above all, the example of their own economies to emulate.

Neo-liberalism holds that international free trade, privatization, the free flow of capital, and minimal government regulation provide optimal conditions for economic development in any country, wealthy or not. People adopting this perspective believe that the lack of development in poorer countries results from too much state ownership and intervention in the economy, along with outright corruption on the part of rulers and government officials. To back up their case, they cite examples of formerly impoverished countries like Hong Kong, Taiwan, South Korea, and Singapore, which experienced rapid economic growth by following neo-liberal principles.

Dependency theory argues that underdevelopment in the Third World is a result of its domination and exploitation by rich industrialized nations. Used primarily to analyze Latin American development, the theory claims that the wealth required for development is usually transferred out of the region to the rich nations. For example, dependency theorists (e.g. Frank, 1967) stated that Latin American countries export mainly raw materials and agricultural products to the developed world, where they are purchased at low prices. The developed nations in turn export expensive finished products to Latin America. These theorists also claim that a large part of the profits acquired by foreign-owned transnational corporations in Latin America are exported to their headquarters in the developed world (So, 1990: 100). Dependency theorists argue that to foster development, the poorer countries are forced to take out loans from the wealthy nations, the interest on which constitutes another drain on their economic well-being. Dependency theorists also maintain that people in impoverished countries suffer at the hands of authoritarian governments that form alliances with domestic and international corporations.

World system theory, developed by Wallerstein (1974), has much in common with dependency theory as it too claims that underdevelopment is caused by the exploitation of the poorer countries by the richer ones, but its unit of analysis is the world as a whole as opposed to a particular region or country. The theory claims that all the countries of the world form a unified system, and that the social conditions in any society can be understood by examining its position in the world system. The nations of the world are divided into three groups. *Core* countries are rich and highly developed, dominating the world both economically and militarily. *Peripheral* countries are poor and weak because they are exploited by the core. *Semiperipheral* countries are in an intermediate position, enjoying some wealth and influence but still under the domination of the core.

Many of the claims made by the theories seeking to explain Third World poverty continue to be debated. Critics of the dependency and world system theories, for example, point out that developed countries trade overwhelmingly with other developed countries, and that therefore the vast majority of their wealth is not generated at the expense of poorer countries. Critics of modernization theory and neo-liberalism argue that these theories tend to overlook or downplay the effect that colonialism had on Third World development.

several theories that seek to account for the changes that occurred, namely evolutionism, developmental theories, historical materialism, the Weber thesis, and the state theory of modernization. Recent changes in Western industrialized countries were discussed as well. These included increases in divorce rates and the number of unwed parents, growing tolerance among racial and ethnic groups, the decline of deference to élites, and the influence of postmodernism and postmaterialism. We concluded with a discussion of globalization and development.

What will the future bring? What will societies look like years, decades, centuries from now? One thing to note in this regard is that social scientists do not have a very good record when it comes to making long-term predictions. Few anticipated some of the most significant changes that occurred in the late twentieth century, such as the rise of feminism or the collapse of the Soviet bloc. Although it is difficult to know what the world will be like in the future, one can be certain of this: in many respects it will be markedly different from the way it is today. Change is always present in human societies, and the rate of change is accelerating.

Those caveats aside, one way to make predictions is to base them on current trends. Using this method, one can expect the division of labour to continue to expand—for the most part, occupational specialization shows no sign of reversing or staying constant. Likewise, the trend toward similarity in gender roles and gender equality, especially in wealthier societies, will probably continue. Liberal democracy, as Fukuyama (1989) argued, no longer has serious rivals in the economically developed world, although the form that democracy will take is open to question. Look for greater democracy in Western countries in the form of increased scrutiny of public officials and more accountability.

The individualism that has been growing over the past few centuries will not abate—in matters of personal taste, self-expression, sexuality, spirituality, and esthetics; the range of choices that are considered acceptable will continue to grow. Developments in biotechnology in areas such as cloning, genetic engineering, and the aging process will likely create new moral dilemmas and may radically alter how we live our lives.

Greater globalization will probably occur, as more countries move away from state ownership and economic regulation toward free trade and open markets. This will likely lead to increased development in some Third World countries.

These predictions are premised on two rather flimsy assumptions. One is that warfare will continue to be localized, a condition that could

Should Rich Countries Cancel Third-World Debt?

One of the biggest obstacles to development faced by poor countries is the huge debt that many of them have incurred over the years to finance various development projects. For example, according to an editorial in the *New York Times* (11 March 1999), Nicaragua pays eleven times as much money to service its debt as it spends on health care.

The vast majority of the debt that poor countries must contend with is owed to governments and government-owned organizations in richer countries. An international movement called Jubilee 2000 has been organized to try to get richer countries to cancel Third World debt. The movement has its headquarters in London, England, and has been endorsed by a number of international celebrities and dignitaries such as Muhammad Ali, Judi Dench, and Archbishop Desmond Tutu. In Canada, demonstrations in favour of cancelling the debt have been held in fifteen cities under the auspices of the Canadian Ecumenical Jubilee Initiative, which has also gathered 650 000 signatures on its petition.

Sources: The New York Times, 11 March 1999; The Globe and Mail [Toronto], 11 June 1999: A17; and 17 June 1999: A21.

literally change any minute. Particularly worrisome is the possibilty of nuclear or chemical warfare. Russia, which has substantial nuclear capability, currently lingers in a state of humiliation and turmoil. China, another nuclear power, feels slighted by the rest of the world and appears to be in the process of attempting a dominance in Asia. There are about a half a dozen states headed by dictators who possess or are developing nuclear and other weapons of mass destruction. And there is always the danger that local territorial disputes like those in the former Yugoslavia, the Middle East, Kashmir, and Tibet will draw the major powers into a larger conflagration.

The second assumption is that the world economy will not sink into depression. This premise is closely related to the first, as economic troubles sometimes threaten democracy or even lead to war. Likewise, war can lead to economic disruption. Although advanced capitalist societies have survived depressions before, they were shaken to their foundations by them. A major danger is that, in conditions of economic crisis, warlike leaders may come to the fore in either the developed or less-developed countries.

Assuming that no catastrophe befalls the world, one of the most perplexing and intriguing questions in the study of global social change surrounds the issue of whether non-Western countries will become culturally similar to us, if they experience advanced levels of economic development. Will Iran, say, or China, become liberal democracies, adopt more equal gender roles, show tolerance for alternative lifestyles, and generally follow the same cultural trajectory towards individual rights and freedoms as Western countries did (at least within their own borders) as they became more economically developed? Or is the whole conglomeration of things that fall under the heading of Western civilization peculiar to the West, something that does not necessarily follow from high levels of development?

Perhaps the thought that others will become similar to us once they have comparable economies is just another example of Western ethnocentrism. Huntington (1996) made this claim. Or perhaps there is, as other social scientists have argued, a universal pattern of cultural and political change that, in the long run, follows upon capitalist development.

QUESTIONS FOR REVIEW AND CRITICAL THINKING

1. What do you think was the most important social change in Canadian society in the twentieth century? How would the two general approaches to change discussed in this chapter, the functionalist and conflict perspectives, explain it?

2. What aspect of Canadian society is most in need of change? List all the positive and negative consequences of the change advocated and then explain why the change has not yet occurred.

3. Do you believe in progress, that as time passes the human condition tends to improve? Explain your answer by presenting a comparison of two different time periods. Be sure to list both positive and negative aspects of both periods.

4. More and more people all over the world are watching Hollywood movies and American television programs, logging on to the Internet, adopting Western styles of dress, and working in capitalist economies. Does this suggest that all countries will eventually have the same basic culture? What might prevent the emergence of a single global culture?

KEY TERMS

anomie, p. 440

cultural lag, p. 431

dependency theory, p. 451

dialectical, p. 441

diffusion, p. 438

ecological-evolutionary theory, p. 436

Enlightenment, p. 433

evolutionism, p. 434

gemeinschaft, p. 439

gesellschaft, p. 439

historical materialism, p. 441

imperialism, p. 433

materialist values, p. 449

mechanical solidarity, p. 440

modernization theory, p. 451

neo-liberalism, p. 451

organic solidarity, p. 440

postmaterialist values, p. 449

postmodernism, p. 447

progress, p. 438

rationalization, p. 444

staples thesis, p. 438

state, p. 432

state theory of modernization, p. 443

structural lag, p. 431

world system theory, p. 451

SUGGESTED READINGS

Chirot, Daniel
1994   *How Societies Change*. Thousand Oaks, CA: Pine Forge Press.
A succinct account of how human societies have evolved from hunting and gathering groups to modern forms. It includes a very useful annotated bibliography at the end of each chapter.

Inglehart, Ronald
1997   *Modernization and Postmodernization: Cultural, Economic, and Political Change in 43 Societies.* Princeton, NJ: Princeton University Press.
Inglehart makes a compelling argument that cultural, economic, and political change are closely related, and that, once a country industrializes, a predictable pattern of changes is likely to follow. The book also offers a good definition of "postmaterialist" values and provides evidence on who holds them and how prevalent they are.

Lenski, Gerhard, Patrick Nolan, and Jean Lenski
1995   *Human Societies: An Introduction to Macrosociology* (7th ed.) Toronto: McGraw-Hill.
An excellent explication of ecological-evolutionary theory from a sociological perspective.

Sztompka, Piotr
1993   *The Sociology of Social Change*. Oxford, UK: Blackwell.
An excellent critical review of the theories and concepts of social change that sociologists have propounded since the birth of the discipline in the early nineteenth century. Sztompka also offers an original contribution, his "theory of social becoming."

WEB SITES

http://www.pbs.org

Globalization and Human Rights

To get the text of a PBS documentary on globalization and human rights, click on "Globalization & Human Rights" at the "Select a PBS Online Web site" box.

http://mason.gmu.edu/~ffukuyam/

Francis Fukuyama and The Great Disruption

This site contains detailed statistical information, for several countries, that illustrates the extent to which divorce rates, births to unwed parents, and other aspects of what Fukuyama calls the "Great Disruption" have increased in recent decades.

Glossary

abstinence standard   the premarital sexual standard that allows no premarital sex (p. 268)

acceptable deviance   deviance which is engaged in by a large proportion of the population and generally tolerated, for example, speeding (p. 101)

acculturation   the learning of the language, values, and customs of a dominant group by an ethnic group; also called cultural assimilation (p. 219)

achieved status   a position in a status hierarchy attained by individual effort or accomplishment (p. 137)

active audience theory   the idea that audiences play an active role in interpreting or decoding media messages, often contrasted with the **hypodermic model** (p. 330)

activity theory   the view that the best prescription for a successful old age is to remain active and to take on new activities in later life to supplant those that have been left behind (p. 231)

age effects   changes that are a direct function of aging; also called maturation (p. 230)

age-graded   a system of expectations and rewards that are based on age (p. 231)

age-specific death rates   an alternative to the crude death rate, obtained by dividing the number of deaths to persons of a given age by the total number of persons in that age cohort (p. 413)

age-specific fertility rates   an alternative to the crude birth rate, obtained by dividing the number of births to women of a given age by the total number of women of that age in the population (p. 406)

age-stratification perspective   a macro-level approach focussed primarily on two key concepts: a *stratified age structure* that favours young and middle-aged adults, and an *age cohort*, individuals who share the same age group (p. 231)

alienation   as developed by Marx, this concept describes the separation of the worker from the product of his labours as well as from the process of work, fellow workers, and even the basic traits of humanity (p. 357)

androcentrism   a bias that involves (1) seeing things from a male point of view or (2) seeing things in a way that reinforces male privilege in society (p. 57)

anomie   a state of normlessness caused by a large-scale breakdown of societal rules (p. 440)

anomie theory   the explanation that views the widespread discrepancy between a society's goals and the legitimate means it provides to achieve those goals as leading to normlessness and eventually to deviance (p. 115)

anticipatory socialization   the learning of attitudes, and behaviours for roles individuals expect to play in the future (p. 89)

ascetic   practising self-discipline with a view to spiritual improvement, especially by living a simple and austere life, doing without such common creature comforts as warm and soft beds, rich foods, or fancy clothing (p. 301)

ascribed status   a position in a status hierarchy that is inherited or assigned (p. 137)

assimilationism   the view that ethnic diversity gradually and inevitably declines as group members are absorbed into the general population, in the process becoming more and more like the dominant group (p. 218)

axiomatic logic   the making of connecting links between related statements for deriving hypotheses (p. 21)

bourgeoisie   the capitalist class, as defined by Marx. The petite bourgeoisie were the small property owners, destined to be swallowed by the larger capitalists. (p. 140)

bureaucracy   a special type of complex organization characterized by an explicit set of rules and a hierarchy of authority (p. 353)

calling   a purpose in life. In a religious context, it is the idea that people have been born to fulfil God's will on earth through their life's work. (p. 301)

chain migration   sequential movement of persons from a common place of origin to a common destination with the assistance of relatives or acquaintances already settled in the new location (p. 195)

church   in sociological usage, the term for religious organizations that are well-established and characterized by an inclusive orientation (i.e., all people who meet certain minimal standards can belong) and involuntary membership (i.e., most members are inducted when still infants) (p. 303)

circular reaction   a special type of social interaction in which responses are reinforced among people. The behaviour of one individual stimulates a response in another person, which in turn reinforces the tendency of the first person, and so on. (p. 372)

class   a set of individuals sharing a similar economic status or market position (p. 138)

class for itself   a Marxian category including people who share the same economic position, are aware of their common class position, and who thus may become agents for social change (p. 140)

class in itself   a Marxian category including people who share the same economic position, but who may be unaware of their common class position (p. 140)

class, status, party   Weber's answer to Marx concerning the bases of social inequality: class is economic, status is prestige, party is political; all three are measures of inequality (p. 143)

cluster sampling   a series of random samples taken in units of decreasing size, such as census tracts, then streets, then houses, then residents (p. 24)

cofigurative culture   those in which social change brought by technological advancement, economic transformation, immigration, war and so forth makes the intergenerational linkage tenuous; as opposed to **postfigurative** and **prefigurative** cultures (p. 91)

cohort measures   measuring demographic data based on segments of the population divided by year of birth (i.e. if you were born in 1985, you are a member of the 1980s birth cohort) (p. 407)

collective action   the pursuit of goals by more than one person. As an explanation of social movements, this perspective looks at integration and cleavage factors and seeks to explain what is dissimilar about collective action at different times and in different places. (p. 376)

collective behaviour   activity in which a large number of people reject and/or do not conform to conventional ways of acting. Behaviour of this kind is often described as less "institutionalized" than ordinary behaviour. (p. 370)

collective conscience   the term Durkheim used to describe the sense people have of sharing in the overall intellectual heritage and wisdom of their culture while participating in religious rituals (p. 101, 300)

collective effervescence   the term Durkheim used to describe the sense of excitement and power people experience when participating in lively events involving relatively large crowds, like a religious revival, a rock concert, or good football game (p. 300)

colonialism   the domination by a settler society of a native or indigenous population. The colonizing society extracts resources from the conquered land, establishes settlements there, and administers the indigenous population, frequently employing violence and a racist ideology. In time, the colonized population suffers the erosion of its traditional culture, economy, and way of life, and usually occupies a subordinate status in the pluralist society of which it has involuntarily become a part. (p. 209)

communication conglomerates   large corporations that combine many different media holdings, or have interests both in media and other industrial sectors (p. 326)

concrete operational stage   the second stage in Piaget's theory characterized by the early use of concept formation and intuition by children (p. 82)

conflict theory   the sociological model that portrays society as marked by competition and/or exploitation. Its three major concepts are power, disharmony, and revolution. (p. 6)

content analysis   a method of analysis that extracts themes from communications, including letters, books, and newspapers (p. 26)

contraculture   a way of life in opposition to, not merely distinct from, the larger culture; also called counterculture (p. 117)

control group   the group of subjects in an experiment that is not exposed to the independent variable, as opposed to the **experimental group**, which is exposed (p. 27)

control variables   variables included in a model of behaviour that are neither independent nor dependent variables. They are controlled or held constant to check on apparent relationships between independent and dependent variables. (p. 27)

correlation   not to be confused with cause, it is changes in one variable that coincide with changes in another variable (p. 34)

craze   an unconventional practice that is adopted by a large number of individuals but is regarded as strange by most people in the society. Crazes are generally more outlandish than fads, and therefore require greater personal commitment. (p. 380)

crime funnel   the process by which the actual number of crimes is reduced through losses attributable to fear, bias, discretion, and human error (p. 108)

critical school (also radical school)   the view that the economic élite is the single major force behind definitions of what is and what is not deviant (p. 103)

critical theory   focuses on social structure in the study of power, social action, and social meanings that are part of a critique of knowledge, culture, and the economy. As related to aging, this includes examining the social construction of old age and dependency and of old-age policy. (p. 233)

cross-sectional research   the type of research that takes place at one point in time as opposed to longitudinal research, which can detect change and demonstrate cause because it takes place over a period of time (p. 34)

crowd   a temporary group of people in reasonably close physical proximity. Only unconventional crowds are included under the heading of collective behaviour. (p. 371)

crude birth rate   a measure devised by demographers to help us understand how births determine the rate of population growth, calculated by dividing the number of births occurring in a population in a given period of time by the total size of the population, and expressed per thousand population (p. 401)

crude death rate   a measure devised by demographers to help us understand how deaths determine the rate of population growth, calculated by dividing the number of deaths occurring in a population in a given period of time by the total size of the population, and expressed per thousand population (p. 401)

cult   a type of non-established religious organization based on voluntary membership. It is usually small and focussed on the esoteric teachings of a charismatic leader. (p. 304)

cultivation effect   the idea that heavy viewing of television leads people to perceive reality in ways consistent with the representations they see on television (p. 337)

cultural element   anything that (1) is shared in common by the members of some social group; (2) is passed on to new members; and (3) in some way affects their behaviour or their perceptions of the world. Three of the most important elements are values, norms, and roles. (p. 41)

cultural imperialism   the imposition of one nation's culture on another, not through direct occupation but by the indirect effects of media influence (p. 339)

cultural integration   the interrelationship of elements in a given culture such that a change in one element can lead to changes, sometimes unexpected, in other elements (p. 52)

cultural lag   the process of adaptation where parts of a culture catch up with other parts (also called **structural lag**) (p. 431)

cultural materialism   a theoretical perspective in which cultural elements are explained by showing how they are pragmatic and rational adaptations to the material environment (p. 62)

cultural studies   a school of research that focuses on how people make meanings in everyday life, sometimes in ways that are resistant or alternative to the dominant values promoted in major media channels (p. 328)

cultural universals   elements of culture found in all known societies (p. 51)

culture   the sum total of all the cultural elements associated with a given social group (p. 41)

culture industry   a term originally used critically to describe the crass, conservative and conformist tendencies of commercially organized mass entertainment, now often used approvingly to refer to business-driven media (p. 325)

cyberspace   the imaginary space or dimension in which we conceive of computer-mediated communication occurring (p. 341)

deductive logic   the derivation of a specific statement from a set of more general statements (p. 22)

defective socialization   socialization attempts that have unintended outcomes or consequences (p. 89)

demographic transition theory   suggests that societies pass through a three-stage process of change (p. 404)

demography   the study of population, examining how the size, structure, and rate of growth are affected by rates of fertility, mortality, and migration (p. 401)

denomination   church-like religious organizations that acknowledge the legitimacy of other religious groups with which they are in competition for members (p. 304)

dependency ratio   relates the number of persons in what are considered the dependent-age categories to the number in the independent or working age categories, conventionally comprised of those under 15 and over 65 (p. 425)

dependency theory   the perspective which argues that underdevelopment in the Third World is a result of its domination and exploitation by rich industrialized nations (p. 451)

dependent variable   the effect in a causal statement, as opposed to the independent variable which is the cause (i.e. other things being equal, if A, then B—B is the dependent variable) (p. 21)

desensitization   a term applied to the alleged tendency for repeated exposure to scenes of media violence to make people increasingly indifferent to or accepting of such incidents in real-life (p. 335)

detailed division of labour   the division of one complete complex task into its sub-tasks. These tasks are than given to different people who can be more easily trained and often paid less in wages or salaries (p. 355)

deviance   a condition or behaviour perceived by society as not normal and at least somewhat disvalued, and thus an acceptable target for social control (p. 99)

deviance amplifying process   an argument stating that punishing individuals for minor forms of deviance may backfire and encourage them to take up more major forms of deviance, even deviant careers (p. 126)

deviant subculture   a group of individuals who share a similar trait that is defined as deviant by the larger culture but that for them is normal and important for their identity (p. 100)

dialectical   used to describe an approach which maintains that for every thesis there is built into it its own antithesis or transformation (p. 441)

differential association   a theory that sees deviance as learned in small-group interaction, wherein an individual internalizes pro-deviant perspectives (p. 125)

diffusion   the adoption of an innovation by a society that did not create it (p. 438)

discrimination   the denial of opportunities, generally available to all members of society, to some people because of their membership in a social category (p. 204)

disengagement theory   view that the withdrawal of older persons from active social life (particularly the labour force) is functional for both the individual and the larger society (p. 231)

disinhibition   the idea that viewing media violence encourages people to shed their restraints against committing real-life violence (p. 337)

disjunctive socialization   socialization processes that lack continuity between socialization contexts, making it difficult for people to make transitions between them or to adjust to new contexts (p. 89)

doctrine of predestination   the belief that an all-knowing and all-powerful God will have known and determined who is religiously saved and damned from the dawn of creation (p. 301)

double ghetto   the dual segregation of women into the pink-collar ghetto of paid labour outside the home and the domestic ghetto of unpaid labour inside the home (p. 185)

double standard   the premarital sexual standard that allows premarital sex for men only (p. 268)

downsizing the process by which a company reduces its labour force to cut operating costs (p. 364)

dysfunctions the occasional minor, temporary disruptions in social life, as defined by functionalists (p. 7)

ecclesia a church that dominates a society or nation and considers itself, ideally at least, to be the sole legitimate religion of that society or nation (p. 304)

ecological-evolutionary theory one that takes into consideration the effects of the biophysical environment, a society's subsistence technology, and interaction between societies (p. 436)

ectomorphs, endomorphs, mesomorphs body types (thin, fat, and muscular, respectively) tested for their relationship to personality and then to crime and delinquency (p. 112)

emergent norm theory an explanation of crowd behaviour that stresses diversity of membership but a perception of consensus, which leads to a new norm expressing the apparent will of the crowd (p. 373)

Enlightenment an 18th-century movement championing free speech, freedom of conscience, equal rights, empiricism, skepticism, and reason (p. 433)

epigenetic in human development theory (like Erikson's), the person is likened to a flower, which has genetically preset stages of growth, the outcome of which depends on how well, or poorly, the environment nurtures it during that stage (p. 70)

equal partners marriage a marriage which involves spouses who are equally committed to their jobs and who share in household and family tasks equally (p. 274)

equilibrium envisioned by functionalist sociologists as the normal state of society, marked by interdependence of parts and by harmony and consensus (p. 7)

ethnic group a people; a collectivity of persons who share an ascribed status based upon culture, religion, national origin, or shared historical experience founded upon a common ethnicity or race (p. 199)

ethnocentrism seeing things from the perspective of one's own culture. It includes the belief that one's own culture is superior to others and the belief that what is true of one's culture is true of others. Two of its major variants as they affect the study of culture are androcentrism and Eurocentrism. (p. 54)

Eurocentrism a bias shaped by the values and experiences of the white, middle class in Western industrialized societies, assuming that these values and experiences are universally shared (p. 55)

evolutionism a theoretical perspective maintaining that social change is in some ways comparable to biological evolution. Change is explained by making reference to societal characteristics that promote survival and help societies reproduce themselves, such as complex social structures, powerful armed forces, and large populations. (p. 434)

exchange theory focuses on the relatively weak bargaining position of older persons in their exchanges with younger ones (p. 231)

expectation of life at birth the average number of years a group of newborns can expect to live if current mortality risks prevail throughout their lifetime (p. 413)

experimental group the group of subjects in an experiment that is exposed to the independent variable, as opposed to the control group, which is not exposed (p. 27)

expressive dimension the set of traits including emotionality, passivity, and weakness, seen by functionalists as associated with the female roles of unpaid wife, mother, and homemaker, particularly as limited to the private sphere (p. 172)

expressive exchanges the emotional dimension of marriage, including sexual gratification, companionship, and empathy (p. 255)

external validity the ability to generalize research results beyond the artificial laboratory experimental situation to the real world (p. 28)

fad an unconventional practice that spreads rapidly and is adopted in a short period of time by a large number of people. Fads are generally less outlandish than crazes, and therefore require less personal commitment. (p. 371)

feminization of poverty the tendency in Canadian society for women at all stages of the adult life cycle to be poorer than men, and to be trapped in lives of poverty (p. 188)

folkways those norms that when violated do not provoke a strong reaction on the part of group members (p. 43)

Fordism A process developed by Henry Ford, designed to effect production of mass quantities of goods to facilitate mass consumption. The assembly line is often the centrepiece of Fordist production. (p. 356)

formal operational stage the fourth stage in Piaget's theory in which people have the ability to use propositional thinking and abstract reasoning in a variety of contexts. This is accompanied by full role-taking capacities—the ability to "project" self and others into hypothetical situations. (p. 82)

formal organization organizations with a clear division of labour and goals. Corporations, schools, government agencies and political parties are examples (p. 352)

frame a set of beliefs that helps people to interpret and explain their world and that provides the basis for collective action (p. 379)

fun standard the premarital sexual standard that approves of premarital sex for either gender, even without love (p. 268)

functionalism a) applied to culture, the theoretical perspective that explains cultural elements by showing how they contribute to societal stability; b) the sociological model which portrays society as harmonious and as based on consensus. Its three major concepts are function, equilibrium, and development. (p. 6, 59)

functionalist definition of religion any definition that uses what religion does (not what it is) as its primary criterion (p. 295)

game theory   an explanation of crowd behaviour similar to emergent norm theory, except that it assumes that people conduct themselves in a "rational" manner and on the basis of relative costs and pay-offs (p. 373)

gemeinschaft   a term used by Tönnies meaning "community," to describe the warm, intimate social relations that he claimed characterized agrarian communities before the advent of industrialization (p. 439)

gender   a social category, involving a continuum of traits ranging from "masculine" to "feminine", referring to the social expectations developed and placed upon individuals on the basis of their biological sex (p. 169)

gender norms   the set of norms specifying appropriate behaviour for males and females; those who violate these norms are generally labelled deviant (p. 169)

gender socialization   the process of acquiring a gendered identity (p. 169)

gendered division of labour   role differentiation in which males and females are segregated, according to their sex, in the spheres of both paid and unpaid labour, according to the belief that certain tasks are more appropriate for one sex than the other (p. 184)

gendered identity   the self as it develops in accordance with the individual's gender and the social definitions of that gender within the larger gendered order (p. 169)

gendered order   the set of structural relations through which individual members of society are accorded differential treatment on the basis of their gender (p. 169)

generalized belief   oversimplified notions that, according to Smelser, give rise to collective behaviour. Generalized beliefs portray the world in terms of omnipotent forces, conspiracies, or extravagant promises. (p. 372)

generalized other   an individual's conception of what is expected and provides a unified basis for self reference (p. 80)

geriatrics   the study of the physiological aspects of aging and the unique health concerns of older persons (p. 228)

gerontology   an interdisciplinary study of aging that involves the physical, psychological, and social processes related to growing older and being an older person (p. 228)

gesellschaft   a term used by Tönnies, meaning "society" or "association," to describe what he believed to be the cold, impersonal, and self-interested social relations typical of industrial cities (p. 439)

globalization of production   the trend of companies looking worldwide for the most profitable place to set up production (p. 364)

grounded theory   explanations that arise from the data collected and which are thus grounded in reality rather than in deductive logic (p. 29)

head-compliment marriage   a marriage in which the wife is "the other half," expected to find meaning in life largely through her husband and family. The husband has basic responsibility for earning the family income and the wife for the care of the home and family. (p. 274)

hegemony   the domination of a class or classes over others, not only economically but politically and culturally (p. 382)

heterogamy   marriage between persons who are dissimilar in some important regard such as religion, ethnic background, social class, personality, or age (p. 271)

heterosexual assumption   the assumption that females and males in our society are exclusively heterosexual; those who are not are labelled deviant (p. 175)

historical materialism   a perspective claiming that fundamental social change results primarily from material, in particular economic, factors. It is often associated with Marx and Engels' theory of social change. (p. 441)

homogamy   marriage of persons with similar physical, psychological, or social characteristics. This is the tendency for like to marry like. (p. 271)

horizontal mobility   movement by an individual from one status to another of similar rank within the same status hierarchy (p. 137)

hybridization   the tendency of international communication flows to create cultural mixes or cross-overs between previously distinct national and ethnic groups (p. 341)

hypodermic model   the belief that media shoot powerful messages into weak, passive audiences, thus directly controlling their behaviour (p. 327)

hypothesis   a statement of a presumed relationship between two or more variables (p. 21)

I and me   the two aspects of Mead's conception of the self. The *I* is the impulsive, creative aspect; the *Me* is more deliberative and cautious of the *I*. (p. 80)

id, ego, superego   the major components of Freud's model of personality. The id is that aspect of personality which is impulsive, selfish, and pleasure-seeking. The ego includes the intellectual and cognitive processes; most of the ego is conscious, and it is guided by the reality principle: ideas and actions are modified to fit actual experiences. The superego consists largely of what is generally called "conscience." (p. 84)

ideology of gender inequality   the widespread belief and understanding that males are superior to females, and that they are therefore more entitled to make decisions, to control resources, and generally to occupy positions of authority (p. 169)

imperialism   the control or exploitation of one country by another, often by conquest (p. 433)

inadequate socialization   incomplete socialization, occurring when a person is not exposed to all experiences necessary to function in certain roles (p. 89)

independent variable the cause in a causal statement, as opposed to the **dependent variable** which is the effect (i.e. other things being equal, if A, then B—A is the independent variable) (p. 21)

inductive logic the construction of a generalization from a set of specific statements (p. 29)

informal organization the informal rules and groups of people that arise to meet the challenges of complex day to day life (p. 353)

information imbalance the disparity between the capacities of the developed and less-developed world to produce and distribute information (p. 339)

information highway a popular term for the integration of computers, telecommunications, and other digital technologies into a society-wide network (p. 343)

information society a new stage of civilization supposedly being brought into being by computers and telecommunications, succeeding the old industrial society (p. 323)

innovation, ritualism, retreatism, rebellion Merton's four deviant adaptations to the problems created when society provides insufficient means to achieve its goals. Innovators find illegitimate means, ritualists water down goals, retreatists give up goals and means, and rebels seek both new goals and new means. (p. 116)

institution a specific set of norms and values that the members of a society use to regulate some broad area of social life (p. 45)

institutional completeness the development of a full set of institutions in an ethnic community that parallels those in the larger society (p. 198)

institutionalized power sometimes called domination, power is institutionalized when it becomes a regular part of everyday human existence, usually because it is established in formal laws or accepted customs (p. 136)

instrumental dimension the set of traits including rationality, aggression, and strength, seen by functionalists to be associated with the male roles of breadwinner and disciplinarian, particularly as limited to the public sphere (p. 172)

instrumental exchanges the task-oriented dimension of marriage, including earning a living, spending money, and maintaining a household (p. 255)

instrumentalism working not for the enjoyment of the job, but for the money and/or material rewards that then translate into life enjoyment (p. 358)

intergenerational mobility movement or change between parental status and a child's status in the same status hierarchy (p. 137)

internal migration movement across boundaries within countries (p. 416)

intragenerational mobility movement by an individual from one status to another in the same status hierarchy during a single lifetime or career (p. 137)

invisible religion the term used by the sociologist Thomas Luckmann to describe non-institutional and private expressions of religiosity in modern, largely secular societies (p. 312)

iron law of oligarchy the premise that even in democratic organizations, be they socialist or capitalist, rule by the many will inevitably become rule by the few (p. 352)

la survivance survival of French Canada as a distinct society (p. 394)

labelling theory the explanation of deviance that argues that societal reactions to minor deviance may alienate those labelled deviant and may cut off their options for conformity, thus leading to greater deviance as an adaptation to the label (p. 126)

learning theory the microsociological argument that individuals act and interact based on their past history of associations, rewards and punishments, and observing and being instructed by others (p. 10)

liberal feminism the view that most structural inequality between women and men can be eradicated through the creation of laws and social policies which will alter power relationships (p. 175)

life course perspective a framework with several linking concepts, compatible with a number of theoretical approaches rather than a theory in its own right. The life course involves a series of age-related transitions that occur along a trajectory across the age structure. (p. 232)

life table a statistical model which estimates the number of years persons of a given age can expect to live (p. 413)

linguistic sexism the tendency to communicate sexist messages, such as male superiority or the assumption that certain roles must be occupied by either males or females, through the use of language (p. 179)

longitudinal research research done over time by participant observers (p. 34)

looking-glass self Cooley's idea that personality is shaped as individuals see themselves mirrored in the reactions of others (p. 79)

love standard the premarital sexual standard that permits premarital sex for persons of either gender if they are in love (p. 268)

marginality the state of having within the self two conflicting social identities; also, the social condition of a minority group that lives on the edge of a society, not treated as a full member of that society (p. 202)

marital structures the four common forms of husband-wife relationships within marriage. Owner-property marriage is a marriage in which the husband owns his wife; in a head-complement marriage the wife finds meaning in life through her husband; in a senior partner/junior partner marriage the wife is employed, but her job and income are less important than her husband's; and in an equal partners marriage both spouses are equally committed to marriage and a career. (p. 273)

marriage a commitment and an ongoing exchange. The commitment can include legal or contractual elements, as well as the social pressures against dissolution. The arrangement includes both instrumental and expressive exchanges. (p. 255)

material culture the physical objects manufactured or used by the members of a society or subculture (p. 45)

materialist values values that place a high priority on economic and physical security (p. 449)

maternal feminism the view that women's real strength lies in their reproductive capacities, and that women's roles as wives and mothers are their true calling and source of status (p. 175)

mating gradient the lesser power of a woman in a typical marriage, partly due to her being younger than her husband (p. 271)

mechanical solidarity according to Durkheim, solidarity based upon unity or sameness within a social group (p. 440)

meta-analysis a research method that extracts statistically significant data from a range of previous studies, here applied in the investigation of media violence (p. 338)

migration movement across legally defined boundaries (p. 416)

minority group a social category, usually ethnically or racially labelled, that occupies a subordinate rank in the hierarchy of a society (p. 204)

mobilization the transfer of resources, particularly human resources, from the pursuit of one goal or set of goals to the pursuit of another goal or set of goals (p. 379)

modernization theory the approach which argues that the limited development in the Third World is a consequence of domestic factors such as traditional cultures that may not be conducive to development, capital shortages, the lack of technological expertise, or the absence of infrastructure such as roads, bridges, and energy sources. (p. 451)

moral autonomy the stage of moral development in which individuals can operate and think independently of authority, rules, and laws as opposed to **morality of constraints** and **morality of cooperation** (p. 83)

moral entrepreneurs people who seek to influence the making of rules and definitions of deviance (p. 103)

morality of cooperation the stage of moral development where one sees rules as products of negotiation and agreement rather than as absolute as opposed to **morality of constraints** and **moral autonomy** (p. 83)

morality of constraints the stage of moral development in which children believe that ethical rules are absolute, coming from some higher external authority, as opposed to **morality of cooperation** and **moral autonomy** (p. 83)

mores those norms that when violated provoke a relatively strong reaction on the part of group members (p. 43)

naturalization of history to take a cultural product and treat it as if it were "natural" (p. 176)

nature/culture dualism the way of thinking that sees females as close to nature and men close to culture (p. 170)

nature versus nurture the debate over the extent to which human behaviour is affected by genetic vs. social factors (p. 72)

neo-liberalism the view which holds that international free trade, privatization, the free flow of capital, and minimal government regulation provide optimal conditions for economic development in any country, wealthy or not (p. 451)

norms relatively precise rules specifying the behaviours permitted and prohibited for group members (p. 42)

ontogenetic stages the stages through which individuals pass as they grow and mature from an embryo through adulthood (p. 81)

operational definition description of the actual procedures used to measure a theoretical concept, as in I.Q. scores being an operational definition of intelligence (p. 22)

organic solidarity according to Durkheim, solidarity based on the complementarity or interdependence of positions in modern, complex divisions of labour (p. 440)

owner-property marriage a marriage in which the husband, in effect, owns his wife, who is legally his property (p. 274)

panic a rapid and impulsive course of action that occurs when people are frightened and try to save themselves or their property from perceived danger (p. 371)

participant observation a research strategy whereby a researcher becomes a member of a group in order to study it, and group members are aware that they are being observed (p. 29)

patriarchy the system of masculine dominance through which masculine traits are privileged and males are systematically accorded greater access to resources and women are systematically oppressed (p. 175)

period effects outcomes that result from having been a certain age at a certain point in time and capture the impact of an historical time or period (p. 228)

period measures measures referring to a specific period of time (p. 407)

pluralism the view that power in modern society is shared among competing interest groups. With respect to deviance, it means that definitions of deviance arise not from consensus, nor from any one group, but from a diversity of sources. Also suggests that ethnic diversity, stratification, and conflict remain central features of modern societies, and that race and ethnicity continue to be important aspects of individual identity and group behaviour (p. 103, 223)

pluralistic society   a social system of coexisting and usually hierarchically ranked racial and ethnic groups, each of which to some degree maintains its own distinctive culture, social networks, and institutions, while participating with other racial and ethnic groups in common cultural, economic, and political institutions (p. 194)

political economy of aging perspective   macro-level view of how political and economic processes create a social structure that tends to place constraints on the lives of older persons (p. 232)

political economy of media   an approach to communication studies that focuses on the power relations governing the production, distribution, and consumption of information (p. 324)

popular culture   those preferences and objects that are widely distributed across all social classes in a society (p. 46)

population pyramid   a picture or graphic representation of the composition of a population at a particular point in time (p. 424)

positive checks   events or circumstances which stop the growth of population, including war, famine, and disease (p. 402)

positivism   the application of natural science research methods to social science (p. 20)

postfigurative culture   those in which the relations between parents and offspring are governed by traditional norms beyond questioning of either parent or child, as opposed to **cofigurative** and **prefigurative** cultures (p. 90)

postmaterialist values   those that place a high priority on non-material things such as self-expression, participation in decision-making, self-esteem, and intellectual development versus (p. 449)

postmodernism   an intellectual movement advocating, among other things, moral and epistemological relativism. It also promotes the idea that science and culture are often forms of domination and control. (p. 447)

power   a differential capacity to command resources and thereby control social situations (p. 136)

praxis   Marx's concept that research should not be pure, conducted just for knowledge's sake, but *applied*, undertaken to improve society (p. 35)

prefigurative culture   those in which the social change is so great that parental life experiences are dated and thus parental guidance is not well regarded by children, as opposed to **postfigurative** and **cofigurative** cultures (p. 91)

prejudice   prejudging people based upon characteristics they are assumed to share as members of a social category (p. 208)

premarital sexual standards   standards by which people judge the acceptability of premarital sex. See also **abstinence standard, double standard, love standard**, and **fun standard** (p. 268)

pre-operational stage   the third stage in Piaget's theory describing how people learn basic logic and social perspective-taking (p. 82)

preventive checks   controlling population by people postponing marriage until they could provide for the children that would be born to them (p. 402)

primary versus secondary sources   the former are records produced by contemporaries of an event, the latter interpretations of primary sources made by others not immediately present at the event (p. 35)

private realm   the realm of unpaid domestic labour and biological reproduction, seen from a functionalist perspective as the preserve of females (p. 172)

profane   quite literally, all that is not sacred. In most cases, the world of everyday, non-religious experience. (p. 299)

progress   social improvement; it can also refer to the belief that social change ultimately results in improved social conditions (p. 438)

proletariat   Marx's word for the working class, the non-owners of the means of production (p. 140)

public   a large and dispersed group made up of persons who share an interest in the same thing. They may hold similar views or they may sharply disagree. (p. 371)

public realm   the realm of paid labour and commerce, seen from a functionalist perspective as the preserve of males (p. 172)

Quiet Revolution   a movement in the 1960s in Quebec to expand governmental powers, decrease Church power, modernize Quebec, and fight vigorously for *la survivance* (p. 395)

quota sample   a selection of people that matches the sample to the population on the basis of certain selected characteristics (p. 24)

race   an arbitrary social category in which membership is based upon inherited physical characteristics such as skin colour and facial features, characteristics defined as socially meaningful (p. 202)

race relations cycle   the four stages, posited by Park, in the relationship between dominant and minority groups. The cycle involves contact, competition, accommodation, and finally assimilation. (p. 219)

racism   an ideology that regards racial or ethnic categories as natural genetic groupings, and that attributes behavioural and psychological differences to the genetic nature of these groupings (p. 203)

radical feminism   the view that equality between the sexes can be achieved only through the abolition of male supremacy. Some **radical feminists** argue for female separatism and the abdication of women's reproductive role as the route to liberation. (p. 176)

random sample   a sample in which every member of the population is eligible for inclusion and individuals are selected by chance (p. 24)

rate of natural increase   a measure of how fast the population is growing per year, based on the difference between the crude birth rate and the crude death rate (p. 403)

rational   anything based on or in accordance with reason. In Weber's usage, the rationality of a social phenomenon depends on how ordered, complex, and effective it is in its functioning.

rational choice theory   the microsociological view that individuals act on the basis of what they expect will help them to achieve their goals, and interact by playing cooperative and non-cooperative games with each other (p. 10)

rationalization   a condition in which there are formalized procedures that give actors a measure of predictability in the outcomes of their actions (p. 444)

reaction formation   Cohen's name for the tendency of working class delinquents to invert middle class values as a form of protest (p. 117)

relative deprivation   the difference between what people believe they have a right to receive (their expectations) and what they actually receive (their achievements) (p. 376)

reliability   the degree to which repeated measurements of the same variable, using the same or equivalent instruments, are equal (p. 22)

religion   a system of beliefs and practices about transcendent things, their nature and their consequences for humanity (p. 296)

replication   repeating a research project in an attempt to verify earlier findings (p. 33)

resistance   an action or actions aimed at either passively or actively slowing, reversing, avoiding, or protesting management directions or strategies in the workplace (p. 358)

role   a cluster of behavioural expectations associated with some particular social position within a group or society (p. 44)

role conflict   a situation in which the behavioural expectations of one role are inconsistent with those of a concurrent role (p. 44)

role system   an interrelated set of social positions in which people share common expectations about desired outcomes as part of a division of labour (p. 88)

role taking   Mead's term for individuals' attempts to put themselves in others' shoes to imagine what they are thinking thus enabling them to see themselves as others see them (p. 79)

rule breakers   those who commit deviant acts but to whom no one responds as if they have done so, either because they are not caught, or if caught, because they are excused for some reason (p. 108)

sacred   those things set apart by society and treated with awe and respect, in many cases because of their association with gods or God (p. 299)

scientific management   a system of management that seeks to transfer control of the work process from skilled workers to the owners and managers of production. It relies on the establishment of a detailed division of labour. (p. 356)

secondary analysis   the examination by a researcher of someone else's data (p. 36)

secondary deviance   that which arises out of the anger, alienation, limited options, and change of self-concept that may occur after a negative social reaction or labelling for primary deviance (p. 127)

sect   a type of religious organization that is characterized by a more exclusive orientation than churches and voluntary membership, as well as a more radical social outlook and rigorous demands of practice (p. 303)

secularization   the process by which sectors of society are removed from the domination of religious institutions and symbols (p. 306)

segregation   the maintenance of physical distance between ethnic or racial groups. Sometimes this term is used to describe the exclusion of minorities from the facilities, institutions, or residential space used by dominant groups, as in South Africa's system of apartheid. At other times, it refers to the residential separation among ethnic or racial populations that may occur for a variety of reasons. (p. 206)

selective incentives   the individual benefits that a person can derive from belonging to an association or joining a social movement. Selective incentives help motivate people to join social movements. (p. 379)

senior-partner/junior-partner marriage   a variant of the **head-compliment marriage**, with the wife having more independence because both husband and wife are employed. However the husband contributes the larger share to the family income, and the wife has basic responsibility for the family and household. (p. 274)

sensorimotor stage   the first stage in Piaget's theory representing the infant's concern with understanding how needs can be met by the external environment (p. 82)

sex   a biological category, either male or female, referring to physiological differences, the most pronounced of which involve the reproductive organs and body size (p. 169)

significant others   persons whose attitudes and opinions affect one's life. Significant others include family and friends as well as persons of high prestige like teachers and celebrities. (p. 80)

social breakdown approach   an approach to collective behaviour that argues that social unrest occurs when established institutions are disrupted or weakened (p. 375)

social category   a collection of individuals who share a particular trait that is defined as socially meaningful, but who do not necessarily interact or have anything else in common (p. 202)

social class   a category of individuals who possess similar economic position as well as group consciousness, common identity, and a tendency to act as a social unit (p. 138)

social cleavage a division (based on age, class, ethnicity, etc.) that may result in the formation of distinct social groups social constructionist perspective emphasizes the subjective experience of the older person and his/her ability to exercise agency in negotiations with others (p. 385)

social constructionist perspective an interpretive approach which emphasizes the subjective experience of older persons and their ability to exercise agency in negotiations with others, also called the symbolic interactionist perspective (p. 233)

social contagion the rapid and uncontrolled spread of a mood, impulse, or form of conduct through a collectivity of people (p. 372)

social contract the socially accepted understanding, sanctioned by government, that if people work hard and produce more goods and services each year, the economy would grow, and thus growth financially benefits both the workers and management (p. 356)

social differentiation the tendency towards diversification and complexity in the statuses and characteristics of social life (p. 135)

social division of labour the division of jobs among people in order to ensure societal survival and prosperity (p. 354)

social facts social sources or causes of behaviour; used by sociologists to explain rates of behaviour in groups as opposed to individual behaviour (p. 2)

social inequality the general pattern of inequality, or ranking, of socially differentiated characteristics (p. 135)

social integration the attachment of individuals to social groups or institutions. Integration depends on a set of sanctions that rewards conformity to the group and punishes nonconformity (p. 375)

social movement a large collectivity of people trying to bring about or resist social change structure. The term "structure" has many meanings, but generally it refers to a stable arrangement or interconnection among parts of a whole. (p. 371)

social reproduction the ways in which societies reproduce themselves in terms of privilege and status (p. 78)

social stratification the structure of inequality in a society.

socialist feminism the view that gender inequality has its roots in the combined oppressiveness of patriarchy and capitalism (p. 176)

socialization the means by which someone is made "fit" to live among other humans (p. 70)

socialization ratio the number of socializers, e.g., teachers or parents, to those being socialized. The lower the ratio (fewer agents), the less the context will change those being socialized. (p. 88)

society a group of people who reside in the same geographical area, who communicate extensively among themselves, and who share a common culture (p. 42)

spurious relationship the appearance that two variables are in a causal relationship, when in fact each is an effect of a common third variable (p. 34)

staples thesis Innis' idea that the economic, political, and cultural formation of Canada was shaped by its geography and the natural resources and raw materials ("staples") available for export. The thesis maintains that a reliance on the export of staples limited Canadian economic development and made Canada vulnerable to the shifting needs and demands of more populous and developed foreign metropolitan centres. (p. 438)

state the organization that has a monopoly on the legitimate use of force in a given territory (p. 432)

state theory of modernization the theory that modern capitalism first emerged in western Europe because the state was relatively weak there. It claims that the state, especially in agrarian societies, has a natural tendency to stifle economic and intellectual development. (p. 443)

status any position occupied by an individual in a social system (p. 136)

status consistency similarity in the ranking of an individual's statuses in a set of status hierarchies (p. 136)

status hierarchy any one of a set of rankings along which statuses are related in terms of their power (p. 136)

status inconsistency dissimilarity in the ranking of an individual's statuses in a set of status hierarchies (p. 136)

status set the combination of statuses that any one individual occupies (p. 136)

stereotypes mental images that exaggerate traits believed to be typical of members of a social group (p. 208)

stigma of excellence a form of deviance based on possessing extremely highly valued traits which sets one aside from the norm (p. 99)

stratum a set of statuses of similar rank in any status hierarchy (p. 136)

structural assimilation acceptance of a minority group by a dominant group into its intimate, primary, social relationships (p. 219)

structural lag the process of adaptation where parts of a culture catch up with other parts (also called **cultural lag**) (p. 431)

subculture a subset of individuals within a society who are characterized by certain cultural elements that set them apart from others in the society (p. 45)

substantive definition of religion any definition that uses some conception of what religion essentially "is," some key characteristic, as its primary criterion (p. 295)

supernatural those things or experiences which appear to be inexplicable in terms of the laws of nature or the material universe (p. 294)

surrogate theory the idea that watching media violence, rather than stimulating real-life violence, provides a substitute or safety valve for aggressive feelings (p. 335)

symbolic interactionism the microsociological perspective which assumes that individuals act and interact on the basis of symbolically-encoded information (p. 6)

syncretism the attempt to reconcile and combine different religious and philosophical views, even ones seemingly in conflict with each other (p. 315)

systemic or institutionalized discrimination discrimination against members of a group that occurs as a by-product of the ordinary functioning of bureaucratic institutions, rather than as a consequence of a deliberate policy to discriminate. Systemic discrimination perpetuates a social, political and economic structure in which some groups are privileged while others are disadvantaged. (p. 205)

techniques of neutralization rationalizations that allow deviants to define their behaviour as acceptable (p. 125)

technological determinism the idea that new technologies drive social change (p. 323)

technologies of freedom a phrase suggesting that computers and other digital technologies empower citizens by allowing them to create and circulate information for themselves (p. 325)

theory a set of interrelated statements or propositions about a particular subject matter (p. 20)

total fertility rate an estimate of the average number of children a woman will bear in her lifetime if she experiences the current age-specific rates of fertility, expressed per woman (p. 407)

triangulation the application of several research methods to the same topic in the hope that the weaknesses of any one method may be compensated for by the strengths of the others (p. 34)

two-category perspectives the view of race relations that sees two hierarchically ranked, separate collectivities in conflict, bound together in a relationship of dominance and subordination within a single society and culture (p. 221)

union an association of people in a definable workplace or group of workplaces whose role is to represent the collective group of workers in negotiations with the employer to get a contract (p. 359)

universal church the term used to characterize very large, international religious organizations seeking, ideally, to include everyone in the world in their membership (p. 304)

urban legends oral stories of the recent past, which, although believed to be true, are actually false and reflect unconscious fears (p. 47)

uses and gratifications model an approach to mass media research that examines how individuals use the media to satisfy emotional or intellectual needs (p. 328)

validity the degree to which a measure actually measures what it claims to (p. 22)

values relatively general beliefs that define right and wrong, or indicate general preferences (p. 42)

variable a characteristic, such as income or religion, that takes on different values among different individuals or groups. Causes are generally called independent variables, and effects are usually called dependent variables. (p. 20)

verstehen the understanding of behaviour as opposed to the predicting of behaviour (p. 30)

vertical mobility movement up and down a status hierarchy (p. 137)

vertical mosaic the hierarchical ranking of ethnic populations in a society (p. 195)

virtual commerce the use of computer networks such as the Internet and the World Wide Web for business purposes, primarily by creating direct links between producers and customers. (p. 343)

virtual community a group of computer users separated geographically but linked together in cyberspace on the basis of shared interests and concerns (p. 342)

work changing physical materials (manual work) or mental constructs/ideas (intellectual work) so as to make these materials and/or ideas more useful to the producer (p. 350)

world system theory the approach which argues that all the countries of the world form a unified system, and that the social conditions in any society can be understood by examining its position in the world system. The nations of the world are divided into three groups: the *core, periphery*, and *semiperiphery*. (p. 451)

Bibliography

Adam, B.A.

1993   "Post-Marxism and the new social movements." *Canadian Review of Sociology and Anthropology* 30: 316–36.

Adamson, Nancy, Linda Briskin, and Margaret McPhail

1988   *Feminist Organizing for Change: The Contemporary Women's Movement in Canada.* Toronto: Oxford University Press.

Adorno, Theodor and Max Horkheimer

1972   *Dialectic of Enlightenment.* New York: Herder and Herder.

Agócs, Carol

1979   "Ethnic groups in the ecology of North American cities." *Canadian Ethnic Studies* 11: 1–18.

Agócs, Carol and Monica Boyd

1993   "The Canadian ethnic mosaic recast for the 1990s." Pp. 330-352 in James Curtis, Edward Grabb and Neil Guppy (eds.), *Social Inequality in Canada: Patterns, Problems, Policies.* (2nd ed.) Scarborough, Ont.: Prentice Hall.

Agócs, Carol, Catherine Burr, and Felicity Somerset

1992   *Employment Equity: Cooperative Strategies for Organizational Change.* Scarborough, Ont.: Prentice Hall.

Akerlind, I. and J. Hornquist

1992   "Loneliness and alcohol abuse: a review of the evidence of interplay." *Social Science and Medicine* 34: 405–14.

Alder, Christine

1992   "Violence, gender, and social change." *International Social Science Journal* 44: 267–76.

Ali, Jennifer and Edward Grabb

1998   "Ethnic origin, class origin, and educational attainment in Canada: further evidence on the mosaic thesis." *Journal of Canadian Studies* 33,1: 3–21.

Allahar, Anton L. and James E. Côté

1998   *Richer and Poorer: The Structure of Social Inequality in Canada.* Toronto: Lorimer.

Ambert, Anne-Marie and Maureen Baker

1988   "Marriage dissolution." In B. Fox (ed.), *Family Bonds and Gender Divisions.* Toronto: Canadian Scholar's Press.

Ang, I.

1985   *Watching Dallas: Soap Opera and the Melodramatic Imagination.* London: Methuen.

Anisef, Paul and Paul Axelrod (eds.)

1993   "Universities, graduates, and the marketplace: Canadian patterns and prospects." Chapter 6 in P. Anisef and P. Axelrod (eds.), *Transitions: Schooling and Employment in Canada.* Toronto: Thompson Educational Publishing, Inc.

Appadurai, A.

1990   "Disjuncture and difference in the global cultural economy." *Public Culture* 2: 1–24.

Arat-Koc, Sedef

1992   "Immigration policies, migrant domestic workers and the definition of citizenship in Canada." Pp. 229-242 in Vic Satzewich (ed.), *Deconstructing a Nation: Immigration, Multiculturalism and Racism in 90s Canada.* Halifax: Fernwood.

Archibald, W. Peter

1978   *Social Psychology as Political Economy.* Toronto: McGraw-Hill Ryerson.

Armstrong, P., H. Armstrong, J. Choiniere, E. Mykalovskiy, and Jerry P. White

1996   *Medical Alert.* Toronto: Garamond Press.

Astin, Alexander W., W.S. Korn, L.J. Sax and K.M. Mahoney

1994   *The American Freshman: National Norms for Fall 1994.* Los Angeles: Higher Educational Research Institute, University of California.

Avery, Donald

1995   *Reluctant Host: Canada's Response to Immigrant Workers, 1896–1994.* Toronto: McClelland and Stewart.

Baer, Douglas

1999   "Educational credentials and the changing occupational structure." Pp. 92-106 in J. Curtis, E. Grabb, and N. Guppy (eds.), *Social Inequality in Canada: Patterns, Problems, Policies.* (3rd ed.) Scarborough, Ont.: Prentice Hall.

Baer, Douglas, James Curtis, Edwrad Grabb, and William Johnston

1996   "What values do people prefer in children? A comparative analysis of survey evidence from fifteen countries." Pp. 299–328 in Clive Seligman, James Olson, and Mark

Zanna (eds.), *The Psychology of Values: The Ontario Symposium.* Vol. 8. Mahwah, NJ: Lawrence Erlbaum Associates Inc.

Baer, Douglas, Edward Grabb, and William Johnston

1993   "National character, regional culture, and the values of Canadians and Americans." *Canadian Review of Sociology and Anthropology* 30: 13–36.

Baer, Douglas, Edward Grabb, and William Johnston

1990   "The values of Canadians and Americans: a critical analysis and reassessment." *Social Forces* 68: 693–713.

Bagdikian, Ben H.

1997   *The Media Monopoly.* (5th ed.) Boston: Beacon.

Balakrishnan, T.R. and Carl Grindstaff

1988   *Early Adulthood Behaviour and Later Life Course Paths.* Health and Welfare Canada: Report for Review of Demography.

Balakrishnan, T.R., K. Krotki, and E. Lapierre-Adamcyk

1993   *Family and Childbearing in Canada.* Toronto: University of Toronto Press.

Bandura, A., D. Ross and S. Ross

1963   "Vicarious reinforcement and imitative learning." *Journal of Abnormal and Social Psychology* 66: 3–11.

Barber, Benjamin

1995   *Jihad vs McWorld: How the Planet Is Both Falling Apart and Coming Together—And What This Means for Democracy.* New York: Times Books.

Barnouw, Erik

1997   *Conglomerates and the Media.* New York: New Press.

Barth, Fredrik

1969   "Introduction." Pp. 9–38 in F. Barth (ed.), *Ethnic Groups and Boundaries: The Social Organization of Culture Difference.* Bergen-Oslo: Universitets Forlaget.

Battle, K.

1997   "Pension reform in Canada." *Canadian Journal on Aging* 16: 519–552.

Baudrillard, Jean

1983   *Simulations.* New York: Semiotext(e).

Beauchesne, Eric

1994   "University degrees put women on equal footing with men." *London Free Press,* October 5: A3.

Beaujot, Roderic

1999   *Earning and Caring in Canadian Families.* Peterborough: Broadview Press.

1995   "Family patterns at mid-life (marriage, parenting and working)." In Roderic Beaujot, Ellen M. Gee, Fernando

Rajulton, and Zenaida Ravanera (eds.), *Family over the Life Course.* Statistics Canada, Catalogue No. 91-543. Ottawa: Minister of Supply and Services Canada.

1991   *Population Change in Canada.* Toronto: McClelland and Stewart.

1990   "The family and demographic change: economic and cultural interpretations and solutions." *Journal of Comparative Family Studies* 21: 25–38.

1979   "A demographic view on Canadian language policy." *Canadian Public Policy* 1: 16–29.

1978   "Canada's population: growth and dualism." *Population Bulletin* 33: 1–48.

Becker, Howard S.

1973   [1963] *Outsiders. Studies in the Sociology of Deviance.* New York: Free Press.

Beisner, M. and W. Iacono

1990   "An update on the epidemiology of schizophrenia." *Canadian Journal of Psychiatry* 35: 657–68.

Béland, Francois and André Blais

1989   "Quantitative methods and contemporary sociology in francophone Quebec." *The Canadian Review of Sociology and Anthropology* 26: 533–556.

Bélanger, Alain and Jean Dumas

1998   *Report on the Demographic Situation in Canada 1997.* Statistics Canada, Catalogue No. 91-209. Ottawa: Minister of Supply and Services Canada.

Bélanger, Danièle and Thu Hong Khuat

1998   "Young single women using abortion in Vietnam." *Asia-Pacific Population Journal* 13: 3–26.

Bell, Daniel

1980   "The social framework of the information society." Pp. 500–49 in Tom Forester (ed.), *The Microelectronics Revolution: The Complete Guide to the New Technology and Its Impact on Society.* Cambridge: MIT Press.

1973   *The Coming of Postindustrial Society.* New York: Basic Books.

Bell, Edward

1990   "Class voting in the first Alberta Social Credit Election." *Canadian Journal of Political Science* 23: 3.

Bem, Sandra

1974   "The measurement of psychological androgyny". *Journal of Consulting and Clinical Psychology* 42: 155–62.

Benedict, Ruth

1934   *Patterns of Culture.* Boston: Houghton Mifflin.

Bengtson, V.L., E.O. Burgess, and T.M. Parrott

1997   "Theory, explanation, and a third generation of theoretical development in social gerontology." *Journal of Gerontology: Social Sciences* 52B: S72–S88.

Bennett, William J.

1994   *The Index of Leading Cultural Indicators: Facts and Figures on the State of American Society.* New York: Touchstone Books.

Berger, Peter L.

1967   *The Sacred Canopy: Elements of a Sociological Theory of Religion.* New York: Doubleday.

Berger, Peter L. and Thomas Luckmann

1966   *The Social Construction of Reality: A Treatise in the Sociology of Knowledge.* New York: Anchor Books.

Berk, R., A. Campbell, R. Klap, and B. Western

1992   "The deterrent effects of arrest: a Bayesian analysis of four field experiments." *American Sociological Review* 57: 698–708.

Berk, Richard A.

1974a   "A gaming approach to crowd behavior." *American Sociological Review* 39: 355–73.

1974b   *Collective Behavior.* Dubuque, IA: Brown.

Berkowitz, L.

1975   "Some effects of thoughts on anti and prosocial influences of media events." *Psychological Bulletin* 28: 410–27.

Besser, Howard

1995   "From Internet to information superhighway." Pp. 59–71 in James Brook and Iain Boal (eds.), *Resisting the Virtual Life: The Culture and Politics of Information.* San Francisco: City Lights.

Best, Pamela

1995   "Women, men and work." *Canadian Social Trends* 36: 30–33.

Bettelheim, Bruno

1959   "Feral children and autistic children." *American Journal of Sociology* 64: 455–467.

Beyer, Peter

2000   "Modern forms of the religious life: denomination, church and invisible religion in Canada, the United States, and Europe." In David Lyon and Marguerite Van Die (eds.), *Rethinking Church, State, and Modernity: Canada Between Europe and the USA.* Toronto: University of Toronto Press.

1997   "Religious vitality in Canada: the complementarity of religious market and secularization perspectives." *Journal for the Scientific Study of Religion* 36: 272–288.

Bibby, Reginald

1995   *The Bibby Report: Social Trends Canadian Style.* Toronto: Stoddart.

1993   *Unknown Gods: The Ongoing Story of Religion in Canada.* Toronto: Stoddart.

1987   *Fragmented Gods.* Toronto: Irwin.

1979   "Religion in Canada." *Journal for the Scientific Study of Religion* 18: 1–17.

Bibby, Reginald W. and Donald C. Posterski

1992   *Teen Trends: A Nation in Motion.* Toronto: Stoddart.

Bland, Roger, Stephen Newman, and Helene Orn

1990   "Health care utilization for emotional problems: results from a community survey." *Canadian Journal of Psychiatry* 35: 397–400.

Bloch, Herbert and A. Niederhoffer

1958   *The Gang: A Study in Adolescent Behavior.* New York: Philosophical Library.

Blum, D.

1997   *Sex on the Brain: The Biological Differences Between Men and Women.* New York: Viking.

Blumer, Herbert

1969   *Symbolic Interactionism: Perspective and Method.* Upper Saddle River, N.J.: Prentice Hall.

1951   [1939] "Collective behavior." Pp. 167–222 in A.M. Lee (ed.), *Principles of Sociology.* New York: Barnes and Noble.

Blumler, J., and E. Katz (eds.)

1975   *The Uses and Gratifications Approach to Mass Communication Research.* Beverly Hills, CA: Sage.

Boutilier, Marie

1977   "Transformation of ideology surrounding the sexual division of labour: Canadian women during World War Two." Paper presented at the Second Conference on Blue-Collar Workers, London, Ontario, May.

Boyd, Monica

1993   "Gender, visible minority and immigrant earning inequality: reassessing an employment equity premise." In Vic Satzewich (ed.), *Deconstructing a Nation: Immigration, Multiculturalism, and Racism in the '90s in Canada.* Halifax: Fernwood Publishing.

Boyd, Monica and Doug Norris

1995   "Leaving the nest? Impact of family structure." *Canadian Social Trends* 38: 14–17.

1998   "Changes in the nest: young Canadian adults living with parents, 1981–1996." Presentation at the Canadian Population Society Meetings, Ottawa, June.

Boyko, John

1998   *Last Steps to Freedom: The Evolution of Canadian Racism.* Manitoba: J. Gordon Shillingford Publishing.

Bozinoff, Lorne and André Turcotte

1993   "Canadians split over effects of working moms." *The Gallup Report*, January 24.

Brabant, S. and L. Mooney

1989   "Him, her, or either: sex of person addressed and interpersonal communication." *Sex Roles* 20: 47–48.

Brake, T.

1980   *The Sociology of Youth Culture and Youth Subcultures.* London: Routledge and Kegan Paul.

Braverman, Harry

1974a   "Labor and monopoly capital: the degradation of work in the twentieth century." *Monthly Review* 26: 1–134.

1974b   *Labor and Monopoly Capital.* New York: Monthly Review Press.

Breton, Raymond

1990   "The ethnic group as a political resource in relation to problems of incorporation: perceptions and attitudes." Pp. 196-255 in Raymond Breton, Wsevolod Isajiw, Warren Kalbach, and Jeffrey Reitz (eds.), *Ethnic Identity and Equality.* Toronto: University of Toronto Press.

1989   "Quebec sociology: agendas from society or from sociologists?" *The Canadian Review of Sociology and Anthropology* 26: 557–70.

1978   "The structure of relationships between ethnic collectivities." In Leo Driedger (ed.), *The Canadian Ethnic Mosaic.* Toronto: McClelland and Stewart.

Breton, R., W. Isajiw, W. Kalbach, and J. Reitz

1990   *Ethnic Identity and Equality: Varieties of Experience in a Canadian City.* Toronto: University of Toronto Press.

Brislin, Richard

1993   *Understanding Culture's Influence on Behavior.* Fort Worth: Harcourt Brace Jovanovich.

Britton, John H. (ed.)

1996   *Canada and the Global Economy.* Montreal and Kingston: McGill Queen's University Press.

Broad, William and Nicholas Wade

1982   *Betrayers of the Truth.* New York: Touchstone Books.

Brodie, Ian

1996   "The market for political status." *Comparative Politics* 28: 253–71.

Brody, E.M. and C.B. Schoonover

1986   "Patterns of parent-care when adult daughters work and when they do not." *The Gerontologist* 26: 372–381.

Brooks, N. and A. Doob

1990   "Tax evasion: searching for a theory of compliant behavior." Pp. 120–64 in M. Friedland (ed.), *Securing Compliance.* Toronto: University of Toronto Press.

Broude, Gwen and Sarah Greene

1983   "Cross-cultural codes on husband-wife relationships." *Ethnology* 22: 263–280.

Brown, M. and B. Warner

1992   "Immigrants, urban politics, and policing in 1900." *American Sociological Review* 57: 293–305.

Brownfield, D. and K. Thompson

1991   "Attachment to peers and delinquent behavior." *Canadian Journal of Criminology* 33: 45–60.

Bruckman, Amy

1996   "Gender swapping on the Internet." Pp. 441–47 in Victor J. Vitanza (ed.), *CyberReader.* Boston: Allyn and Bacon.

Brundson, Charlotte

1997   *Screen Tastes: Soap Opera to Satellite Dishes.* London: Basic Books.

Bulcroft, Kris A. and Richard A. Bulcroft

1991   "The timing of divorce: effects on parent-child relationships in later life." *Research on Aging* 13: 226–243.

Burch, T.K.

1990   "Remarriage of older Canadians: description and interpretation." *Research on Aging* 12: 546–559.

Burgess, E.W., H. Locke, and M. Thomas

1963   *The Family: From Institution to Companionship.* New York: American Book Company.

Burke, R.J.

1991   "Managing an increasingly diverse workforce: experiences of minority managers and professionals in Canada." *Canadian Journal of Administrative Sciences* 8: 108–120.

Buss, David M.

1999   *Evolutionary Psychology: The New Science of the Mind.* Boston: Allyn and Bacon.

Byrne, C., M. Velamoor, Z. Cernovsky, L. Cortese, and S. Loszatyn

1990   "A comparison of borderline and schizophrenic patients for childhood life events and parent-child relationships." *Canadian Journal of Psychiatry* 35: 590–95.

Caldwell, J.C. and P. Caldwell

1997   "What do we now know about fertility transition?" Pp.15–25 in G.W. Jones, R.M. Douglas, J.C. Caldwell, and R.M. D'Souza (eds.), *The Continuing Demographic Transition*. Oxford: Claredon Press.

Caldwell, John C.

1976   "Toward a restatement of demographic transition theory." *Population and Development Review* 2: 321–66.

Calzavara, Liviana

1993   "Trends and policy in employment opportunities for women." Chapter 22 in J. Curtis, E. Grabb, and N. Guppy (eds.), *Social Inequality in Canada: Patterns, Problems, Policies*. (2nd ed.) Scarborough, Ont.: Prentice Hall.

Campani, Giovanna

1992   "Family, village and regional networks and Italian immigration in France and Quebec." Pp. 183–207 in Vic Satzewich (ed.), *Deconstructing a Nation: Immigration, Multiculturalism and Racism in '90s Canada*. Halifax: Fernwod Publishing.

Campbell, L.D., I.A. Connidis, and L. Davies

1999   "Sibling ties in later life: a social networks analysis." *Journal of Family Issues* 20: 114–148.

Canadian Institute of Public Opinion

1992   *Gallup Report*. Toronto: CIPO.

Canadian Press

1994   "Study urged of income disparity." *London Free Press*, March 24: A10.

Canel, Eduardo

1992   "New social movement theory and resource mobilization: the need for integration." Pp. 22–51 in W.K. Carroll (ed.), *Organizing Dissent: Contemporary Social Movements in Theory and Practice: Studies in the Politics of Counter-Hegemony*. Toronto: Garamond.

Caplan, Paula J. and Jeremy B. Caplan

1999   *Thinking Critically about Research on Sex and Gender* (2nd ed.). New York: Longman.

Carneiro, Robert L.

1967   Editor's introduction to *The Evolution of Society*. Chicago: University of Chicago Press.

Carroll, William

1986   *Corporate Power and Canadian Capitalism*. Vancouver: University of British Columbia Press.

Carter, D.D.

1998   "Employment benefits for same-sex couples: the expanding entitlement." *Canadian Public Policy* 24: 107–117.

Cashmore, Ellis

1994   *And There Was Television*. Routledge: London.

Castells, Manuel

1997a   *The Power of Identity*. Oxford: Blackwell.

1997b   *End of Millennium*. Oxford: Blackwell.

1996   *The Rise of the Network Society*. Oxford: Blackwell

Chafetz, Janet Saltzman and Jacqueline Hagan

1996   "The gender division of labour and family change in industrial societies." *Journal of Comparative Family Studies* 27: 187–219.

Chalk, Frank and Kurt Jonassohn

1990   *The History and Sociology of Genocide*. New Haven: Yale University Press.

Chawla, Raj K.

1990   "The distribution of wealth in Canada and the United States." *Perspectives on Labour and Income* 2: 29–41.

Chesney-Lind, Meda

1989   "Girls' crime and woman's place: toward a feminist model of female delinquency." *Crime and Delinquency* 35: 5–29.

Chesney-Lind, Meda and Noelie Rodriguez

1983 "Women under lock and key." *Prison Journal* 63: 47–65.

Chirot, Daniel

1994   *How Societies Change*. Thousand Oaks, CA: Pine Forge Press.

Chisholm, Patricia

1999   "Teens under siege." *Maclean's* May 3: 22–24.

Chomsky, Noam and Edward S. Herman

1988   *Manufacturing Consent: The Political Economy of the Mass Media*. New York: Pantheon.

Christian, Nicole

1999   "Is smaller perhaps better?" *Time* May 31: 19.

Christie, Nils

1993   *Crime Control as Industry: Towards Gulags, Western Type?* London: Routledge.

Christofides, L.N. and R. Swidinsky

1994   "Wage determination by gender and visible minority status: evidence from the 1989 LMAS." *Canadian Public Policy* 20: 34–51.

Chui, Tina, James Curtis, and Edward Grabb

1993   "Who gets involved in politics and community organizations?" Chapter 36 in J. Curtis, E. Grabb, and N. Guppy (eds.), *Social Inequality in Canada: Patterns, Problems, Policies*. (2nd ed.) Scarborough, Ont.: Prentice Hall.

Clark, Danae

1995   "Commodity lesbianism." Pp. 484–501 in
C.K. Creehmar and A. Doby (eds.), *Out in Culture: Gay,
Lesbian and Queer Essays in Popular Culture*. Durham,
NC: Duke University Press.

Clark, P.G.

1993   "Moral discourse and public policy in aging: framing
problems, seeking solutions, and 'public ethics'."
Canadian Journal on Aging 12: 485–508.

Clark, Peter and Anthony Davis

1989   "The power of dirt: an exploration of secular defilement
in Anglo-Canadian culture." *Canadian Review of
Sociology and Anthropology* 26: 650–73.

Clark, S.D.

1975   "Sociology in Canada: an historical overview."
Canadian Journal of Sociology l: 225–34.

Clark, Samuel

1995   *State and Status: the Rise of the State and Aristocratic Power
in Western Europe*. Kingston and Montreal: McGill
Queen's University Press.

Clark, Warren

1998   "Religious observance: marriage and family." *Canadian
Social Trends* Autumn: 2–7.

Clarke, Juanne

1990   *Health, Illness, and Medicine in Canada*. Toronto:
McClelland and Stewart.

Cleaver, Harry

1994   "The Chiapas uprising." *Studies in Political Economy* 44:
141–157.

Clement, Wallace

1988   "The state and the Canadian economy." Chapter 31 in
J. Curtis, E. Grabb, N. Guppy, and S. Gilbert (eds.),
Social Inequality in Canada: Patterns, Problems, Policies.
Scarborough, Ont.: Prentice Hall.

1978   "A political economy of regionalism in Canada."
Pp. 89–110 in Daniel Glenday, Hubert Guindon, and
Alan Turowetz (eds.), *Modernization and the Canadian
State*. Toronto: Macmillan.

1975   *The Canadian Corporate Elite*. Toronto: McClelland and
Stewart.

Clinard, Marshall and P. Yeager

1980   *Corporate Crime*. New York: Free Press.

Cloud, John

1999   "Just a routine school shooting." *Maclean's* May 31:
14–19.

Cloward, Richard and L. Ohlin

1960   *Delinquency and Opportunity*. New York: Free Press.

Cockerham, William C.

1996   *Sociology of Mental Disorder*. (4th ed.) Englewood Cliffs,
NJ: Prentice Hall.

Cohen, Albert

1955   *Delinquent Boys: The Culture of the Gang*. New York: Free
Press.

Coleman, James S.

1988   "Social capital in the creation of human capital."
American Journal of Sociology 94: S95–S120.

Coleman, W.D.

1984   *The Independence Movement in Quebec, 1945–1980*.
Toronto: University of Toronto Press.

Collins, Randall

1979   *The Credential Society: A Historical Sociology of Education
and Stratification*. New York:Academic Press.

Coltrane, Scott

1998   *Gender and Families*. Thousand Oaks, CA: Pine Forge
Press.

1996   *Family Men: Fatherhood, Housework and Gender Equality*.
New York: Oxford.

Comack, Elizabeth and Steven Brickey

1991   *The Social Basis of Law*. (2nd ed.) Toronto: Garamond.

Combes-Orme, T., J. Helzer, and R. Miller

1988   "The application of labeling theory to alcoholism."
Journal of Social Service Research 11: 73–91.

Condry, J. and S. Condry

1976   "Sex differences: a study in the eye of the beholder."
Child Development 47: 812–19.

Conger, Jane and Nancy L. Galambos

1997   *Adolescence and Youth*. (5th ed.) New York: Addison
Wesley Longman.

Conkey, Margaret

1997   "Men and women in prehistory: an archaeological chal-
lenge." Pp. 57–68 in Caroline B. Brettell and Carolyn F.
Sargent (eds.), *Gender in Cross-cultural Perspective*.
Upper Saddle River, N.J.: Prentice Hall.

Connidis, I.A.

Forthcoming   "Anticipating change in family ties and
aging: The implications of demographic trends." In
L.O. Stone (ed.), *The Economic and Social Aspects of
Population Aging*. Ottawa: Statistics Canada.

1999   "The impact of demographic and social trends across
age groups on informal supports for older persons."
Paper presented at the National Seminar on
Demographic Change and Population Ageing.
Moncton, New Brunswick, April.

1997   "Family ties and aging in Canada: continuity and change over three decades." *Lien social et politiques/ Revue internationale d'action communitaire* 38: 133–143.

1994   "Sibling support in older age." *Journal of Gerontology: Social Sciences* 48: S309–S317.

1992   "Life transitions and the adult sibling tie: a qualitative study." *Journal of Marriage and the Family* 54: 972–982.

1989a   *Family Ties and Aging.* Toronto: Butterworths/Harcourt Brace.

1989b   "Contact between siblings in later life." *Canadian Journal of Sociology* 14: 429–42.

1989c   "Siblings as friends in later life." *American Behavioral Scientist* 33: 81–93.

1983   "Living arrangement choices of older residents: assessing quantitative results with qualitative data." *Canadian Journal of Sociology* 8: 359–75.

Connidis, I.A. and L. Campbell

1995   "Closeness, confiding, and contact among siblings in middle and late adulthood." *Journal of Family Issues* 16: 722–745.

Connidis, I.A. and L. Davies

1992   "Confidants and companions: choices in later life." *Journal of Gerontology: Social Sciences* 47: S115–122.

1990   "Confidants and companions in later life: the place of family and friends." *Journal of Gerontology: Social Sciences* 45: S141–149.

Connidis, I.A. and J.A. McMullin

Forthcoming   "Permanent childlessness: perceived advantages and disadvantages among older persons." *Canadian Journal on Aging.*

1996   "Reasons for and perceptions of childlessness among older persons: exploring the impact of marital status and gender." *Journal of Aging Studies* 10: 205–222.

1994   "Social support in older age: assessing the impact of marital and parent status." *Canadian Journal on Aging* 13: 510–527.

1993   "To have or have not: parent status and the subjective well-being of older men and women." *The Gerontologist* 33: 630–636.

Connidis, I.A., C.J. Rosenthal, and J.A. McMullin

1996   "The impact of family composition on providing help to older parents: a study of employed adults." *Research on Aging* 18: 402–429.

Connor, Steven

1989   *Postmodernist Culture: An Introduction to Theories of the Contemporary.* Cambridge: Blackwell.

Cook, Cynthia and Rod Beaujot

1996   "Labour force interruptions: the influence of marital status and the presence of young children." *The Canadian Journal of Sociology* 21: 25–42.

Cook, Scott D. N.

1995   "The structure of technological revolutions and the Gutenberg myth." Pp. 63–84 in Joseph Pitt (ed.), *New Directions in the Philosophy of Technology.* Boston: Kluwer Academic.

1992   "Support from parents over the life course: the adult child's perspective." *Social Forces* 71: 63–84.

Corak, M. (ed.)

1998   *Government Finances and Generational Equity.* Ottawa: Statistics Canada and Human Resources Development Canada.

Cormier, Jeffrey J.

1997   "Missed opportunities: the institutionalization of early Canadian sociology." *Society/Société* 21 (1): 1–7.

Corwin, Ronald G.

1987   *The Organization-Society Nexus: A Critical Review of Models and Metaphors.* Westport, CT: Greenwood Press.

Coser, Lewis

1964   *The Functions of Social Conflict.* New York: Free Press of Glencoe.

Côté, James E.

1992   "Was Mead wrong about coming of age in Samoa? An analysis of the Mead/Freeman controversy for scholars of adolescence and human development." *Journal of Youth and Adolescence* 21: 1–29.

Côté, James E. and Anton A. Allahar

1994   *Generation on Hold.* Toronto: Stoddart.

Côté, James E. and Charles Levine

1997   "Student motivations, learning environments, and human capital acquisition: toward an integrated paradigm of student development." *Journal of College Student Development* 38: 229–243.

1987   "A formulation of Erikson's theory of ego identity formation." *Developmental Review* 9: 273–325.

Coward, R.T. and J.W. Dwyer

1990   "The association of gender, sibling network composition, and patterns of parent care by adult children." *Research on Aging* 12: 158–181.

Creese, Gillian, and Brenda Beagan

1999   "Gender at work: seeking solutions for women's equality." Pp. 199-211 in James Curtis, Edward Grabb, and Neil Guppy (eds.), *Social Inequality in Canada: Pattern Problems, Policies.* (3rd ed.) Scarborough, Ont.: Prentice Hall.

Crompton, Susan and Leslie Geran

1995 "Women as main wage-earners." *Perspective on Labour and Income* 7: 26–29.

Crosby, Faye J.

1991 *Juggling: The Unexpected Advantages of Balancing Career and Home for Women and Their Families.* New York: Free Press.

Cumming, E. and W.E. Henry

1961 *Growing Old: The Process of Disengagement.* New York: Basic Books.

Curtis, B. et al.

1992 *Stacking the Deck.* Toronto: Our Schools/Our Selves.

Curtis, Bruce

1992 "Pre-sociological observation? Maria Edgeworth, Elizabeth Hamilton, and A.A. de Saussure Necker." *Society* 16: 10–19.

Curtis, James, Edward Grabb, and Tina Chui

1999 "Public participation, protest, and social inequality." Pp. 371–386 in J. Curtis, E. Grabb, and N. Guppy (eds.), *Social Inequality in Canada: Patterns, Problems, Policies.* (3rd ed.) Scarborough, Ont.: Prentice Hall.

Dabbs, James

1990 "Testosterone, social class, and antisocial behavior in a sample of 4462 men." *Psychological Science* 1: 209–11.

Dahrendorf, Ralf

1959 *Class and Class Conflict in Industrial Society.* Stanford, CA: Stanford University Press.

Daly, Mary

1974 *Beyond God the Father.* Boston: Beacon Press.

Dannefer, D.

1987 "Aging as intracohort differentiation: accentuation, the Matthew effect, and the life course." *Sociological Focus* 2: 211–36.

Das Gupta, Tania

1996 *Racism and Paid Work.* Toronto: Garamond.

Davidson, James and Dean Knudsen

1977 "A new approach to religious commitment." *Sociological Focus* 10: 151–73.

Davies, Scott

1999 "Stubborn disparities: explaining class inequalities in schooling." Pp. 138–150 in J. Curtis, E. Grabb, and N. Guppy (eds.), *Social Inequality in Canada: Patterns, Problems, Policies.* (3rd ed.) Scarborough, Ont.: Prentice Hall.

Davis, Arthur K.

1971 "Canadian society and history as hinterland versus metropolis." Pp. 6–32 in Richard J. Ossenberg (ed.), *Canadian Society: Pluralism, Change, and Conflict.* Scarborough, Ont.: Prentice Hall.

Davis, Kingsley

1972 *World Urbanization 1950–1970. Volume 11: Analysis of Trends, Relationships, and Development.* Berkeley, CA: Institute of International Studies.

1937 "The sociology of prostitution." *American Sociological Review* 2: 744–55.

Davis, Kingsley and Wilbert E. Moore

1945 "Some principles of stratification." *American Sociological Review* 10: 242–49.

Dawson, Charles

1936 *Group Settlement: Ethnic Communities in Western Canada.* Toronto: Macmillan of Canada.

Dawson, D., B. Grant, S. Chou, and R. Pickering

1995 "Subgroup variation in U.S. drinking patterns: results of the 1992 National Longitudinal Alcohol Epidemiologic Study." *Journal of Substance Abuse* 7: 331–44.

Dawson, Lorne L.

1998a *Comprehending Cults: The Sociology of New Religious Movements.* Toronto: Oxford University Press.

1998b "Anti-modernism, modernism, and postmodernism: struggling with the cultural significance of new religious movements." *Sociology of Religion* 59: 131–151.

1987 "On references to the transcendent in the scientific study of religion: a qualified idealist proposal." *Religion* 17: 227–250.

de Beauvoir, Simone

1953 *The Second Sex.* New York: Knopf.

De Kerckhove, Derrick

1997 *Connected Intelligence: The Arrival of the Web Society.* Toronto: Somerville House.

DeKeseredy, Walter S.

1992 "Wife assault." Pp. 278–312 in Vincent Sacco (ed.), *Deviance: Conformity and Control in Canadian Society.* (2nd ed.) Scarborough, Ont.: Prentice Hall.

Dekker, J., J. Peen, et al.

1997 "Urbanization and psychiatric admission rates in the Netherlands." *International Journal of Social Psychiatry* 43: 235–46.

Demers, M.

1998 "Age differences in the rates and costs of medical procedures and hospitalization during the last year of life." *Canadian Journal on Aging* 17: 186–196.

Denzin, Norman K.

1994   "The art and politics of interpretation." Pp. 500–515 in Norman K. Denzin and Yvonna S. Lincoln (eds.), *Handbook of Qualitative Research.* Thousand Oaks, CA: Sage.

Desai, Sonalde and Linda J. Waite

1991   "Women's employment during pregnancy and after the first birth: occupational characteristics and work commitment." *American Sociological Review* 56: 551–566.

Devor, Holly

1989   *Gender Blending: Confronting the Limits of Duality.* Bloomington, IN: Indiana University Press.

Dewdney, Christopher

1998   *Last Flesh: Life in the Transhuman Era.* Toronto: Harper Collins.

Di Leonardo, Micaela

1991   "Contingencies of value in feminist anthropology." Pp. 140–158 in Joan E. Hartman and Ellen Messer-Davidow (eds.), *(En)Gendering Knowledge.* Knoxville, TN: University of Tennessee Press.

Dibbell, Julian

1996   "A rape in cyberspace." Pp. 448–65 in Victor J. Vitanza, (ed.), *CyberReader.* Boston: Allyn and Bacon.

Dickson, Lovat

1973   *Wilderness Man: The Strange Story of Grey Owl.* Scarborough, Ont.: New American Library of Canada Ltd.

Dobasch, R.E. and R.P. Dobasch

1992   *Women, Violence, and Social Change.* London: Routledge.

Dohrenwend, B., I. Levav, et al.

1992   "Socioeconomic status and psychiatric disorders: the causation-selection issue." *Science* 255: 946–52.

Dowd, J.J.

1975   "Aging as exchange: prelude to a theory." *Journal of Gerontology* 30: 584–594.

Downing, Christine

1989   *Myths and Mysteries of Same Sex Love.* New York: Continuum.

Drabman, R. and M. Thomas

1974   "Does media violence increase children's toleration of real life aggression?" *Developmental Psychology* 10: 418–21.

Driedger, Leo and Richard Mezoff

1981   "Ethnic prejudice and discrimination in Winnipeg high schools." *Canadian Journal of Sociology* 6: 1–17.

Duleep, Harriet and Seth Sanders

1992   "Discrimination at the top: American-born Asian and white men." *Industrial Relations* 31(3): 416–32.

Dumas, Brigitte

1987   "Philosophy and sociology in Quebec: a socio-epistemic inversion." *Canadian Journal of Sociology* 12: 111–33.

Dumas, Jean

1990   *Report on the Demographic Situation in Canada 1988.* Statistics Canada, Catalogue No. 91-209. Ottawa: Minister of Supply and Services Canada.

Dumas, Jean and Alain Bélanger

1997   *Report on the Demographic Situation in Canada 1996.* Statistics Canada, Catalogue. No. 91-209. Ottawa: Minister of Supply and Services Canada.

Dumas, Jean and Yves Péron

1992   *Marriage and Conjugal Life in Canada.* Statistics Canada, Catalogue No. 91-534. Ottawa: Minister of Supply and Services Canada.

Dupré, John

1993   *The Disorder of Things: Metaphysical Foundations for the Disunity of Science.* Boston, MA: Harvard University Press.

Durkheim, Emile

1965   [1895] *The Division Of Labour in Society.* New York: Free Press.

1951   [1897] *Suicide: A Study in Sociology.* Translated by J. Spaulding and G. Simpson. New York: Free Press.

1949   [1893] *The Division of Labor in Society.* New York: Free Press.

Easterlin, R. A.

1987   *Birth and Fortune.* (2nd ed.). Chicago: University of Chicago Press.

Economist

1995   "The most expensive slum in the world." *The Economist* May 6.

Edgerton, Robert B.

1985   *Rules, Exceptions, and Social Order.* Berkeley, CA: University of California Press.

Ehrenreich, Barbara and Deirdre English

1979   *For Her Own Good: 150 Years of the Experts' Advice to Women.* New York: Anchor.

Ehrlich, P.

1968   *The Population Bomb.* New York: Ballantine.

Ehrlich, P. and A. Ehrlich

1990   *The Population Explosion.* New York: Simon & Schuster.

Eichar, Douglas

1989 *Occupation and Class Consciousness in America.* New York: Greenwood Press.

Eichler, Margrit

1988 *Nonsexist Research Methods: A Practical Guide.* Boston, MA: Allen and Unwin.

Eichler, M. with R. Tite

1990 "Women's studies professors in Canada: a collective self-portrait." *Atlantis* 16: 6–24.

Elder, G. H.

1991 "Lives and social change." Pp. 58–86 in W.R. Heinz (ed.), *Theoretical Advances in Life Course Research: Status Passage and the Life Course,* Vol. 1. Weinheim: Deutscher Studien Verlag.

Eliany, Marc

1991 "Alcohol and drug use." *Canadian Social Trends* 20: 19–26.

Engels, Friedrich

1972 [1884] *The Origin of the Family, Private Property, and the State.* Edited by Eleanor Burke Leacock. New York: International Publishers.

Erikson, Erik H.

1968 *Identity: Youth and Crisis.* New York: Norton.

1963 *Childhood and Society.* (2nd ed.) New York: Norton.

Erikson, Kai

1966 *Wayward Puritans.* New York: Wiley.

Eron, L, L.R. Huesmann, M. Lefkowitz, and L.O. Waller

1972 "Does television cause aggression?" *American Psychologist* 32: 237–244.

Farnsworth Riche, Martha

1990 "The boomerang age: don't assume 18-to-24-year-olds are adults." *American Demographics* May: 25–30, 52–53.

Feeley, M. and D. Little

1991 "The vanishing female: the decline of women in the criminal process, 1687–1912." *Law and Society Review* 25: 719–57.

Finch, J.

1989 *Family Obligations and Social Change.* Cambridge, MA: Polity Press.

Fine, Gary Alan

1992 *Manufacturing Tales.* Knoxville: University of Tennessee Press.

Finke, Roger

1997 "The consequences of religious competition: supply-side explanations for religious change." In Lawrence A. Young (ed.), *Rational Choice Theory and Religion: Summary and Assessment.* New York: Routledge.

Finke, Roger, A. Guest and Rodney Stark

1996 "Mobilizing Local Religious Markets: Religious Pluralism in the Empire State, 1855 to 1865." *American Sociological Review* 61: 203–218.

Finke, Roger and Rodney Stark

1992 *The Churching of America, 1776–1990: Winners and Losers in our Religious Economy.* New Brunswick, N.J.: Rutgers University Press.

Finkel, Alvin

1989 *The Social Credit Phenomenon in Alberta.* Toronto: University of Toronto Press.

Fjortoft, Arne

1999 "Challenging the divide." Pp. 402–10 in Anne Leer (ed.), *Masters of the Wired World: Cyberspace Speaks Out.* London: Financial Times.

Fleras, Augie and Jean Leonard Elliott

1992 *Multiculturalism in Canada: The Challenge of Diversity.* Scarborough, Ont.: Nelson Canada.

Fonte, John

1999 "Back to the future." *National Post* [Toronto]. June 19: B7.

Foote, David K.

1998 *Boom Bust & Echo 2000.* Toronto: Macfarlane, Walter, and Ross.

Forcese, Dennis

1997 *The Canadian Class Structure.* (4th ed.) Toronto: McGraw-Hill Ryerson.

Form, William H.

1985 *Divided We Stand.* Urbana, IL: University of Illinois Press.

Foucault, Michel

1978 *The History of Sexuality, Volume 1: An Introduction.* New York: Random House.

Fournier, Elaine, George Butlin, and Philip Giles

1999 "Intergenerational change in the education of Canadians." Pp. 130–137 in J. Curtis, E. Grabb, and N. Guppy (eds.), *Social Inequality in Canada: Patterns, Problems, Policies.* (3rd ed.) Scarborough, Ont.: Prentice Hall.

Fournier, Suzanne and Ernie Crey

1997 *Stolen from our Embrace: The Abduction of First Nation Children and the Restoration of Aboriginal Communities.* Vancouver: Douglas and McIntyre.

Fox, Bonnie

1989 "The feminist challenge: a reconsideration of social inequality and economic development." Pp. 120–67 in R.J. Brym with B.J. Fox (eds.), *From Culture to Power.* Toronto: University of Toronto Press.

Fox, John and Michael Ornstein

1993 "The Canadian state and corporate elites." Chapter 34 in J. Curtis, E. Grabb, and N. Guppy (eds.), *Social Inequality in Canada: Patterns, Problems, Policies.* (2nd ed.) Scarborough, Ont.: Prentice Hall.

Francis, Diane

1986 *Controlling Interest. Who Owns Canada?* Toronto: Macmillan of Canada.

Frank, Andre Gunder

1967 *Capitalism and Underdevelopment in Latin America: Historical Studies of Chile and Brazil.* New York: Monthly Review Press.

Frank, Thomas

1997a *The Conquest of Cool: Business Culture, Counterculture, and the Rise of Hip Consumerism.* Chicago: The University of Chicago Press.

1997b "Let them eat lifestyle: from hip to hype—the ultimate corporate takeover." *Utne Reader* November–December: 43–47.

Franzoi, Stephen L., Jennifer J. Kessenich, and Patricia A. Sugrue

1989 "Gender differences in the experience of body awareness: an experiential sampling study." *Sex Roles* 21: 499–515.

Frederick, Howard H.

1993 *Global Communication and International Relations.* Belmont, CA: Wadsworth.

Frederick, Judith and Jason Hamel

1998 "Canadian attitudes to divorce." *Canadian Social Trends* 48: 6–11.

Freeman, Derek

1983 *Margaret Mead and Samoa: The Making and Unmaking of an Anthropological Myth.* Cambridge, Mass.: Harvard University Press.

Freidan, Betty

1963 *The Feminine Mystique.* New York: Dell.

Frideres, James

1988 *Native Peoples in Canada: Contemporary Conflicts.* (3rd ed.) Scarborough, Ont.: Prentice Hall.

Friedman, Matthew

1997 *Fuzzy Logic: Dispatches from the Information Revolution.* Montreal: Vehicule Press.

Friend, R.A.

1991 "Older lesbian and gay people: a theory of successful aging." In John Alan Lee (ed.), *Gay Midlife and Maturity.* New York: Haworth Press.

Frieze, I.H., J.E. Parsons, P.B. Johnson, D.N. Rubble, and G.I. Zellman

1978 *Women and Sex Roles.* New York: W.W. Norton.

Fukuyama, Francis

1999 "The Great Disruption: human nature and the reconstitution of the social order." *The Atlantic Monthly* May: 55–80.

Furstenberg, Frank F.

1995 "Family change and the welfare of children: what do we know and what can we do about it." In K. Mason and A-M. Jensen (eds.), *Gender and Family Change in Industrialized Countries.* Oxford: Clarendon.

Gabor, Thomas

1999 "Trends in youth crime." *Canadian Journal of Criminology* 41: 385–92.

Gabor, T. and E. Gottheil

1984 "Offender characteristics and spatial mobility: an empirical study and some policy implications." *Canadian Journal of Criminology* 26: 267–81.

Galambos, Nancy and Lauree Tilton-Weaver

1998 "Multiple-risk behaviour in adolescents and young adults." *Health Reports* 10: 9–20.

Gallup, George

1990 *Religion in America.* Princeton, NJ: Princeton Religious Research Center.

Gamson, W.A.

1992 "The social psychology of collective action." Pp. 53–76 in A.D. Morris and C.M. Mueller (eds.), *Frontiers in Social Movement Theory.* New Haven: Yale University Press.

Gamson, William and Andre Modigliani

1974 *Conceptions of Social Life.* Boston: Little Brown and Company.

Garnham, Nicholas

1990 *Capitalism and Communication: Global Culture and the Economics of Information.* London: Sage.

Gauthier, Anne Hélène

1991 "The economics of childhood." In A.R. Pence (ed.), *Childhood as a Social Phenomenon.* Vienna: European Centre for Social Welfare Policy and Research.

Gecas, Viktor

1981 "Contexts of socialization." Pp. 165–199 in Morris Rosenberg and Ralph H. Turner (eds.) *Social Psychology: Sociological Perspectives.* New York: Basic Books.

Gee, Ellen

1986   "The life course of Canadian women: an historical and demographic analysis." *Social Indicators Research* 18: 263–83.

Gee, E. and M. Kimball

1987   *Women and Aging.* Toronto: Butterworths.

Geipel, John

1969   *The Europeans.* New York: Pegasus.

Gelles, Richard J.

1983   "An exchange/social control theory". Pp. 151–165 in David Finkelhor, Richard J. Gelles, Gerald T. Hotaling, and Murray A. Strauss (eds.), *The Dark Side of Families: Current Family Violence Research.* Beverley Hills, Ca.: Sage.

Gerber, Linda

1984   "Community characteristics and out-migration from Canadian Indian reserves: path analyses." *Canadian Review of Sociology and Anthropology* 21: 145–65.

Gerbner, George, Larry Gross, Michael Morgan, and Nancy Signorielli

1987   "Charting the mainstream: television's contributions to political orientations." Pp. 441–64 in Donald Lazare (ed.), *American Media and Mass Culture: Left Perspectives.* Berkeley: University of California Press.

Gero, Joan

1991   "Genderlithics: women's role in stone tool production." Pp. 163–193 in Joan M. Gero and Margaret W. Conkey (eds.), *Engendering Archaeology: Women and Prehistory.* Cambridge, MA: Blackwell.

Gibson, William

1984   *Necromancer.* New York: Ace Books.

Giddens, Anthony

1991   *Introduction to Sociology.* New York: Norton.

1981   *A Contemporary Critique of Historical Materialism, Volume 1: Power, Property, and the State.* London: Macmillan.

1973   *The Class Structure of the Advanced Societies.* London: Hutchinson and Co.

Giffen, P.J., S. Endicott, and S. Lambert

1991   *Panic and Indifference—The Politics of Canada's Drug Laws.* Ottawa: Canadian Centre on Substance Abuse.

Gilder, George

1994   *Life after Television.* New York: Norton.

Gilligan, Carol

1982   *In a Different Voice.* Cambridge, MA: Harvard University Press.

Gillis, J.R.

1996   *A World of Their Own Making: Myth, Ritual, and the Quest for Family Values.* Cambridge, MA: Harvard University Press.

Gladstone, J.W.

1988   "Perceived changes in grandmother-grandchild relations following a child's separation or divorce." *The Gerontologist* 28: 66–72.

1987   "Factors associated with changes in visiting between grandmothers and grandchildren following an adult child's marriage breakdown." *Canadian Journal on Aging* 6 : 117–127.

Glenn, N.D.

1998   "The course of marital success and failure in five American 10-year cohorts." *Journal of Marriage and the Family* 60: 569–576.

Glock, Charles Y. and Rodney Stark

1965   *Religion and Society in Tension.* Chicago: Rand McNally.

Goffman, Erving

1974   *Frame Analysis: An Essay on the Organization of Experience.* New York: Harper.

1959   *The Presentation of Self in Everyday Life.* Garden City, NY: Doubleday Anchor Books.

Golding, Peter

1998   "Global village or cultural pillage: the unequal inheritance of the communications revolution." Pp. 69–86 in Robert McChesney, Ellen Meiskins Woods, and John Bellamy Foster (eds.), *The Political Economy of the Global Communication Revolution.* New York: Monthly Review Press.

Golding, Peter

1996   "World wide wedge: division and contradiction in the global information infrastructure." *Monthly Review* 48: 70–86.

Goldscheider, Frances K. and Linda Waite

1991   *New Families, No Families?* Berkeley, CA: University of California Press.

Goldthorpe, John

1969   *The Affluent Worker in Class Society.* New York: Cambridge University Press.

Goode, William J.

1977   "World revolution and family patterns." Pp. 47–58 in A.S. Skolnick and J.H. Skolnick (eds.), *Family in Transition.* Boston: Little, Brown.

Gordon, Milton

1964   *Assimilation in American Life: The Role of Race, Religion, and National Origin.* New York: Oxford University Press.

Gorman, Christine

1992   "Sizing up the sexes." *Time* 139(3): 36–43.

Gorz, Andre

1982   *Farewell to the Working Class.* London: Pluto.

Gough, E. Kathleen

1959   "The Nayars and the definition of marriage." *Journal of the Royal Anthropological Institute* 89: Part 1.

Gould, Stephen Jay

1981   *The Mismeasure of Man.* New York: W.W. Norton.

Gove, Walter

1990   "The effect of marriage on the well-being of adults: a theoretical analysis." *Journal of Marriage and the Family* 11: 4–35.

Goyder, John C. and James E. Curtis

1977   "Occupational mobility in Canada over four generations." *Canadian Review of Sociology and Anthropology* 14: 303–19.

Grabb, Edward

1999a   "Conceptual issues in the study of inequality." Pp. vii-xxii in J. Curtis, E. Grabb, and N. Guppy (eds.), *Social Inequality in Canada: Patterns, Problems, Policies.* (3rd ed.) Scarborough, Ont.: Prentice Hall.

1999b   "Concentration of ownership and economic control in Canada: patterns and trends in the 1990s." Pp. 4–12 in J. Curtis, E. Grabb, and N. Guppy (eds.), *Social Inequality in Canada: Patterns, Problems, Policies.* (3rd ed.) Scarborough, Ont.: Prentice Hall.

1997   *Theories of Social Inequality: Classical and Contemporary Perspectives.* (3rd ed.) Toronto: Harcourt Brace.

1988   "Occupation, education, and feelings of powerlessness." Chapter 39 in J. Curtis, E. Grabb, N. Guppy, and S. Gilbert (eds.), *Social Inequality in Canada: Patterns, Problems, Policies.* Scarborough, Ont.: Prentice Hall.

Grabb, Edward G. and James E. Curtis

1992   "Voluntary association activity in English Canada, French Canada, and the United States: a multivariate analysis." *Canadian Journal of Sociology* 17: 371–388.

Granovetter, Mark

1978   "Threshold models of collective behavior." *American Journal of Sociology* 83: 1420–43.

Grayson, J. Paul

1997   "Who gets jobs? Initial labor market experiences of York graduates." Working Paper, York University: Institute for Social Research, January.

Greer, Germaine

1992   *The Change: Women, Aging, and the Menopause.* New York: Alfred A. Knopf.

Grenville, Andrew S.

2000   "'For by Him all things were created . . . visible and invisible': sketching the contours of public and private religion in North America." In David Lyon and Marguerite Van Die (eds.), *Rethinking Church, State, and Modernity: Canada Between Europe and the U.S.A.* Toronto: University of Toronto Press.

Groneman, Carol

1995   "Nymphomania: the historical construction of female sexuality." Pp. 219–249 in Jennifer Terry and Jacqueline Urla (eds.), *Deviant Bodies.* Bloomington, IN: Indiana University Press.

Grossman, Dave

1995   *On Killing: The Psychological Cost of Learning to Kill in War and Society.* Boston, MA: Little Brown.

Grossman, Wendy M.

1997   *net.wars.* New York: New York University Press.

Guindon, Hubert

1964   "Social unrest, social class and Quebec's bureaucratic revolution." *Queen's Quarterly* 71: 150–62.

1977   "Class, nationalism and ethnic tension." Pp. 18–28 in Christopher Beattie and Stewart Crysdale (eds.), *Sociology Canada: Readings.* Toronto: Butterworths.

Guppy, Neil

1989   "The magic of 65: issues and evidence in the mandatory retirement debate." *Canadian Journal on Aging* 8: 173–186.

Guppy, Neil and A. Bruce Arai

1993   "Who benefits from higher education? Differences by sex, social class, and ethnic background." Chapter 16 in J. Curtis, E. Grabb, and N. Guppy (eds.), *Social Inequality in Canada: Patterns, Problems, Policies.* (2nd ed.) Scarborough, Ont.: Prentice Hall.

Guppy, Neil, James Curtis, and Edward Grabb

1999   "Age-based inequalities in Canadian society." Pp. 246–257 in J. Curtis, E. Grabb, and N. Guppy (eds.), *Social Inequality in Canada: Patterns, Problems, Policies.* (3rd ed.) Scarborough, Ont.: Prentice Hall.

Guppy, Neil, and Scott Davies

1999   *Education in Canada: Recent Trends and Future Challenges.* Ottawa: Statistics Canada and Nelson Canada.

Guppy, Neil, S. Freeman, and S. Buchan

1988   "Economic background and political representation." Chapter 33 in J. Curtis, E. Grabb, N. Guppy, and S. Gilbert (eds.), *Social Inequality in Canada: Patterns, Problems, Policies.* Scarborough, Ont.: Prentice Hall.

Gusfield, J.

1986   [1963] *Symbolic Crusade.* Urbana, IL: University of Illinois Press.

Habermas, Jurgen

1989   *The Structural Transformation of the Public Sphere: An Inquiry into a Category of Bourgeois Society.* Trans. T. Burger and F. Lawrence. Cambridge, MA: MIT Press.

Hackler, J. and K. Don

1990   "Estimating system biases: crime indices that permit comparisons across provinces." *Canadian Journal of Criminology* 32: 243–64.

Hadaway, C. Kirk, Penny Long Marler and Mark Chaves

1998   "Overreporting church attendance in America: evidence that demands the same verdict." *American Sociological Review* 63: 122–130.

1993   "What the polls don't tell us: a closer look at United States church attendance." *American Sociological Review* 58: 741–752.

Hafner, Katie and Matthew Lyon

1996   *Where Wizards Stay Up Late: The Origins of the Internet.* New York: Simon and Schuster.

Hagan, J. and F. Kay

1990   "Gender and delinquency in white collar families: a power-control perspective." *Crime and Delinquency 36: 391–407.*

Hagan, John

1992   "The poverty of classless criminology: the American Society of Criminology 1991 Presidential Address." *Criminology* 30: 1–19.

1991   The Disreputable Pleasures: Crime and Deviance in Canada. (3rd ed.) Toronto: McGraw-Hill Ryerson.

1988   *Structural Criminology.* Cambridge: Polity.

Haiven, L., S. McBride, and G. Shields (eds.)

1992   *Regulating Labour: The State, Neo-Conservatism and Industrial Relations.* Toronto: Garamond Press.

Hall, David R.

1996   "Marriage as a pure relationship: exploring the links between pre-marital cohabitation and divorce in Canada." *Journal of Comparative Family Studies* 27: 1–12.

Hall, David R. and John Z. Zhao

1995   "Cohabitation and divorce in Canada: testing the selectivity hypothesis." *Journal of Marriage and Family* 57: 421–27.

Hall, G. Stanley

1904   *Adolescence.* Englewood Cliffs, NJ: Prentice Hall.

Hall, Stuart

1980   "Encoding/Decoding." Pp. 128–37 in Stuart Hall, Dorothy Hobson, Andrew Lowe, and Paul Willis (eds.), *Culture, Media, Language.* London: Hutchinson.

Hamel, Pierre

1995   "Mouvements urbains et modernité: l'exemple montréalais." *Recherches sociographiques* 36: 279–305.

1991   *Action collective et démocratie locale: les mouvements urbains montréalais.* Montreal: Les presses de l'Université de Montréal.

Hamelink, Cees

1990   "Information imbalance: core and periphery." Pp. 217–28 in J. Downing, A. Mohammadi, and Annabelle Srebery-Mohammadi (eds.), *Questioning the Media: A Critical Introduction.* Newbury Park, CA: Sage.

Hamilton, Richard F.

1996   *The Social Misconstruction of Reality: Validity and Verification in the Scholarly Community.* New Haven, CT: Yale University Press.

Handleby, J.B., L. Keating, and C.L. Hooper

1990   "A follow-up of Ontario training school boys." Paper presented at Ontario Psychological Association meeting, Feb. 16.

Hanegraaf, Wouter J.

1996   *New Age Religion and Western Culture.* Leiden, Holland: E.J. Brill.

Harman, Lesley D.

1992   "The feminization of poverty: an old problem with a new name." *Canadian Woman Studies* 13: 6–9.

1989   *When a Hostel Becomes a Home: Experiences of Women.* Toronto: Garamond Press.

1985   "Acceptable deviance as social control: the cases of fashion and slang." *Deviant Behavior* 6: 1–15.

Harrell, W. Andrew

1995   "Husband's involvement in housework: the effects of relative earning power and masculine orientation." *Psychological Reports* 77: 1331–37.

Harris, Marvin

1985   *Good to Eat: Riddles of Food and Culture.* New York: Simon and Schuster.

1968   *The Rise of Anthropological Theory: A History of Theories of Culture.* New York: Harper & Row.

Hartnagel, Timothy

2000   "Correlates of criminal behavior." Pp. 95–138 in Rick Linden (ed.), *Criminology: A Canadian Perspective.* (4th ed.) Toronto: Holt, Rinehart and Winston.

Harvey, Pierre

1969   "Pourquoi le Québec et les Canadiens français occupent-ils une place inférieure sur le plan économique?" Pp. 113–27 in R. Durocher and P.A. Linteau (eds.), *Le "Retard" du Québec*. Quebec: Editions Boréal Express.

Hasselback, P., K. Lee, Y. Mao, R. Nichol, and D. Wigle

1991   "The relationship of suicide rates to sociodemographic factors in Canadian census divisions." *Canadian Journal of Psychiatry* 36: 655–59.

Health Canada

1999a   "Social inequality in the health of Canadians." Pp. 300–314 in J. Curtis, E. Grabb, and N. Guppy (eds.), *Social Inequality in Canada: Patterns, Problems, Policies*. (3rd ed.) Scarborough, Ont.: Prentice Hall.

1999b   *HIV/AIDS Epi Update*. Bureau of HIV/AIDS, STD and TB Update Series. Laboratory Centre for Disease Control.

Heelas, Paul

1996   *The New Age Movement*. Oxford: Blackwell.

Heimer, Karen and Ross Matsueda

1994   "Role-taking, role commitment, and delinquency." *American Sociological Review* 59: 365–90.

Helmes-Hayes, Richard

1994   "Canadian sociology's first textbook: C.A. Dawson and W.E. Getty's *An Introduction to Sociology* (1929)." *Canadian Journal of Sociology* 19: 461–97.

Helmes-Hayes, R. and D. Wilcox-Magill

1993   "A neglected classic: Leonard Marsh's *Canadians In and Out of Work*." *Canadian Review of Sociology and Anthropology* 30: 83–109.

Henry, Frances

1999   "Two studies of racial discrimination in employment." Pp. 226–235 in J. Curtis, E. Grabb, and N. Guppy (eds.), *Social Inequality in Canada: Patterns, Problems, Policies*. (3rd ed.) Scarborough, Ont.: Prentice Hall.

Henry, Frances and Effie Ginsberg

1993   "Racial discrimination in employment." Chapter 24 in J. Curtis, E. Grabb, and N. Guppy (eds.), *Social Inequality in Canada: Patterns, Problems, Policies*. (2nd ed.) Scarborough, Ont.: Prentice Hall.

1985   *Who Gets the Work? A Test of Racial Discrimination in Employment*. Toronto: Urban Alliance on Race Relations and Social Planning Council of Metropolitan Toronto.

Henry, Frances, Carol Tator, Winston Mattis and Tim Rees

1995   *The Colour of Democracy: Racism in Canadian Society*. Toronto: Harcourt Brace.

Henshaw, Stanley K., Susheela Singh, and Taylor Haas

1999   "The incidence of abortion worldwide." *International Family Planning Perspectives* 25 (supplement): S30–S38.

Henshel, Richard L.

1990   *Thinking about Social Problems*. Toronto: Harcourt Brace Jovanovich.

Herman, Edward

1998   "The propaganda model revisited." Pp. 191–206 in Robert McChesney, Ellen Meiskins Woods, and John Bellamy Foster (eds.), *The Political Economy of the Global Communication Revolution*. New York: Monthly Review Press.

Herman, Edward and Robert W. McChesney

1997   *The Global Media: The New Missionaries of Corporate Capitalism*. London: Cassell.

Herman, Harry

1978   *Men in White Aprons: Macedonian Restaurant Owners in Toronto*. Toronto: Peter Martin.

Hewitt, John P.

1994   *Self and Society: A Symbolic Interactionist Social Psychology*. (6th ed.) Boston: Allyn and Bacon.

Hiller, Harry H.

1982   *Society and Change: S.D. Clark and the Development of Canadian Sociology*. Toronto: University of Toronto Press.

1979   "The Canadian sociology movement: analysis and assessment." *Canadian Journal of Sociology* 4: 125–50.

Hobart, Charles W.

1993   "Sexual behaviour." Pp. 52–72 in G.N. Ramu, *Marriage and Family in Canada Today*. (2nd ed.) Scarborough, Ont.: Prentice Hall.

Hofley, John M.

1992   "Canadianization: a journey completed?" In Wm. K. Carroll et al. (eds.), *Fragile Truths: 25 Years of Sociology and Anthropology in Canada*. Ottawa: Carleton University Press.

Holmes, Thomas H. and Richard Rahe

1967   "The social readjustment rating scale." *Journal of Psychometric Research* 11: 216.

Homans, George C.

1950   *The Human Group*. New York: Harcourt Brace Jovanovich.

Hou, Feng and T.R. Balakrishnan

1996   "The integration of visible minorities in contemporary Canadian society." *Canadian Journal of Sociology* 21: 307–326.

Hoyos, F.A.

1978   *Barbados: A History from the Amerindians to Independence.* London and Basingstoke: Macmillan.

Huntington, Samuel P.

1996   *The Clash of Civilizations and the Remaking of World Order.* New York: Simon and Schuster.

Hurst, Charles E.

1996   *Social Inequality: Forms, Causes, and Consequences.* (2nd ed.) Boston: Allyn and Bacon.

Huxley, Aldous

1932   *Brave New World.* London: Triad Grafton.

Huyssen, Andreas

1986   *After the Great Divide: Modernism, Mass Culture, Postmodernism.* Bloomington: Indiana University Press.

Ibarra, Herminia

1993   "Personal networks of women and minorities in management: a conceptual framework." *Academy of Management Review* 18: 56–87.

Idinopulos, Thomas A. and Brian C. Wilson (eds.)

1998   *What is Religion? Origins, Definitions and Explanations.* Leiden, Holland: Brill.

Idinopulos, Thomas A. and Edward A. Yonan (eds.)

1994   *Religion and Reductionism.* Leiden, Holland: Brill.

Inglehart, Ronald

1997   *Modernization and Postmodernization: Cultural, Economic, and Political Change in 43 Societies.* Princeton, NJ: Princeton University Press.

Innis, Harold A.

1986 [1950] *Empire and Communications.* David Godfrey (ed.) Victoria: Press Porcépic.

1956   *The Fur Trade In Canada: An Introduction to Canadian Economic History* (Revised Edition). Toronto: University of Toronto Press.

1950   *Empire and Communication.* Toronto: University of Toronto Press.

Isajiw, W., A. Sev'er, and L. Driedger

1993   "Ethnic identity and social mobility: a test of the drawback model." *Canadian Journal of Sociology* 18: 177–96.

Ishwaran, K.

1977   *Family, Kinship and Community: A Study of Dutch Canadians.* Toronto: McGraw-Hill Ryerson.

Jain, Harish, Simaon Taggar, and Morley Gunderson

1997   "The status of employment equity in Canada: an assessment." Paper presented at the 49th Annual Conference of the Industrial Relations Research Association, January 4–6, 1997.

Jenkins, Henry

1994   "Star Trek rerun, reread, rewritten: fan writing as textual poaching." Pp. 448–73 in Horace Newcomb (ed.), *Television: The Critical View.* Oxford: Oxford University Press.

Jenson, J. and R. Mahon (eds.)

1993   *The Challenge of Restructuring.* Philadelphia: Temple University Press.

Johnson, Kay, Huang Banghan, and Wang Liyao

1998   "Infant abandonment and adoption in China." *Population and Development Review* 24: 469–510.

Jones, Gavin W. and Pravin Visaria (eds).

1997   *Urbanization in Large Developing Countries: China, Indonesia, Brazil and India.* Oxford: Clarendon Press.

Juteau, Danielle and Louis Maheu

1989   "Sociology and sociologists in francophone Quebec: science and politics." *The Canadian Review of Sociology and Anthropology* 26: 363–93.

Kalbach, Warren E.

1990   "Ethnic residential segregation and its significance for the individual in an urban setting." Pp. 92–134 in Raymond Breton, Wsevolod Isajiw, Warren Kalbach, and Jeffrey Reitz (eds.), *Ethnic Identity and Equality.* Toronto: University of Toronto Press.

Kalmijn, Matthijs

1991   "Status homogamy in the United States." *American Journal of Sociology* 97: 496–523.

Kaplan, H. and H. Fukurai

1992   "Negative social sanctions, self-rejection and drug use." *Youth and Society* 23: 275–98.

Kaplan, Hillard S., Jane B. Lancaster, and Kermyt G. Anderson

1998   "Human parental investment and fertility: the life histories of men in Albuquerque." In A. Booth and A.C. Crouter (eds.), *Men in Families: When Do They Get Involved? What Difference Does It Make?* Mahwah, NJ: Lawrence Erlbaum.

Kaplan, Marcie

1983   "A woman's view of DSM-III." *American Psychologist* 38: 786–92.

Karambayya, Rekha

1997   "In shouts and whispers: paradoxes facing women of colour in organizations." *Journal of Business Ethics* 16(9): 891–897.

Kates, N. and E. Krett

1988   "Socio-economic factors and mental health problems: can census-tract data predict referral patterns?" *Canadian Journal of Community Mental Health* 7: 89–98.

Katz, Jack

1988   *Seductions of Crime: Moral and Sensual Attractions of Doing Evil.* New York: Basic Books.

Kaufman, Gayle and Peter Uhlenberg

1998   "Effects of life course transitions on the quality of relationships between adult children and their parents." *Journal of Marriage and the Family* 60: 924–938.

Kaufman, Michael (ed.)

1993   *Cracking the Armor: Power, Pain and the Lives of Men.* Toronto: Viking.

Keally, Greg (ed.)

1973   *Canada Investigates Industrialism: The Royal Commission on the Relations of Labor and Capital.* Toronto: University of Toronto Press.

Keane, John

1990   *Media and Democracy.* Oxford: Blackwell.

Kegan, Robert

1994   *In Over Our Heads: The Mental Demands of Modern Life.* Cambridge, Mass: Harvard University Press.

Kennedy, L. and S. Baron

1993   "Routine activities and a subculture of violence: a study of violence on the street." *Journal of Research in Crime and Delinquency* 30: 88–112.

Kennedy, L., R. Silverman, and D. Forde

1991   "Homicide in urban Canada: testing the impact of economic inequality and social disorganization." *Canadian Journal of Sociology* 16: 397–410.

Kent, Stephen

1990   "Deviance labelling and normative strategies in the Canadian 'new religions/countercult' debate." *Canadian Journal of Sociology* 15: 393–416.

Kersten, Karen and Lawrence Kersten

1991   "A historical perspective on intimate relationships." In J. Veevers (ed.), *Continuity and Change in Marriage and Family.* Toronto: Holt, Rinehart and Winston.

Kervin, D.

1990   "Advertising masculinity: the representation of males in Esquire advertisements." *Journal of Communication Inquiry* 14: 51–70.

Kettle, John

1980   *The Big Generation.* Toronto: McClelland and Stewart.

Knodel, J., A. Chamratrithirong, and N. Debavalya

1987   *Thailand's Reproductive Revolution.* Madison, WI: University of Wisconsin Press.

Knodel, J. and E. Van De Walle

1986   "Lessons from the past: policy implications of historical fertility studies." Pp. 390–416 in A.J. Coale and S.C. Watkins (eds.), *The Decline of Fertility in Europe.* Princeton, NJ: Princeton University Press.

Koenig, D.

1991   *Do Police Cause Crime? Police Activity, Police Strength, and Crime Rates.* Ottawa: Canadian Police College.

Kohn, Melvin, A. Naoi, C. Schoenbach, C. Schooler, and K. Slomczynski

1990   "Position in the class structure and psychological functioning in the United States, Japan and Poland." *American Journal of Sociology* 95: 964–1008.

Krahn, Harvey, and Graham Lowe

1998   *Work, Industry, and Canadian Society.* (3rd ed.) Scarborough: ITP Nelson.

Kraut, Robert, and Vicki Lundmark

1998   "The Internet paradox: a social technology that reduces social involvement and psychological well being?" *American Psychologist* 53: 1017–1031.

Krauter, Joseph and Morris Davis

1978   *Minority Canadians: Ethnic Groups.* Toronto: Methuen.

Kubat, Daniel and David Thornton

1974   *A Statistical Profile of Canadian Society.* Toronto: McGraw-Hill Ryerson.

Kurzweil, Ray

1999   *In the Age of Spiritual Machines: When Computers Exceed Human Intelligence.* New York: Viking.

La Prairie, Carol

1990   "The role of sentencing in the over-representation of aboriginal people in correctional institutions." *Canadian Journal of Criminology* 32: 429–40.

Lachapelle, Rejean and Jacques Henripin

1982   *The Demolinguistic Situation in Canada.* Montreal: The Institute for Research on Public Policy.

Langford, Tom and J. Rick Ponting

1992   "Canadians' responses to aboriginal issues: the roles of prejudice, perceived group conflict, and economic conservatism." *Canadian Review of Sociology and Anthropology* 29: 140–166.

Lapierre-Adamcyk, Evelyne

1989   "Le mariage et la famille: mentalités actuelles et comportements récents des femmes canadiennes." In J. Légaré, T.R. Balakrishnan, and R. Beaujot (eds.), *The Family in Crisis: A Population Crisis?* Ottawa: Royal Society of Canada.

Lapierre-Adamcyk, Evelyne, Céline Le Bourdais, and Karen Lehrhaupt

1995   "Les departs du foyer parental des jeunes Canadiens nés entre 1921 et 1960." *Population* 50: 1111–35.

Lasswell, H.

1927   *Propaganda Techniques in the World War.* New York: Knopf.

Lauer, Robert H.

1982   *Perspectives on Social Change* (3rd ed.). Toronto: Allyn and Bacon.

Lautard, Hugh and Neil Guppy

1990   "The vertical mosaic revisited: occupational differentials among Canadian ethnic groups." Pp. 189–208 in Peter Li (ed.), *Race and Ethnic Relations in Canada.* Toronto: Oxford University Press.

Lawrence, Raymond

1999   "Plains Indians Cultural Survival School," *Transition* Winter: 1, 5.

Laws, Sophie, Valerie Hey, and Andrea Eagan

1985   *Seeing Red: The Politics of Pre-menstrual Tension.* London: Hutchinson.

Le Bourdais, Céline and Nicole Marcil-Gratton

1996   "Family transformations across the Canadian/American border: when the laggard becomes the leader." *Journal of Comparative Family Studies* 27: 415–36.

Leacock, Eleanor

1983   "Interpreting the origins of gender inequality: conceptual and historical problems." *Dialectical Anthropology* 7: 263–284.

LeBlanc, M., P. McDuff, et al.

1991   "Social and psychological consequences, at 10 years old, of an earlier onset of self-reported delinquency." *Psychiatry* 54: 133–47.

LeBon, Gustave

1960   [1895] *The Crowd.* New York: Viking Press.

Leck, J.D. and D.M. Saunders

1996   "Achieving diversity in the workplace: Canada's Employment Equity Act and members of visible minorities." *International Journal of Public Administration* 19: 299–322.

Leiss, W., S. Kline, and S. Jhally

1986   *Social Communication in Advertising.* Toronto: Methuen.

LeMasters, E.E. and J. DeFrain

1989   *Parents in Modern America.* (5th ed.) Belmont, CA: Wadsworth.

Lemert, Edwin

1951   *Social Pathology.* New York: McGraw-Hill.

Lenski, Gerhard

1976   "History and social change." *American Journal of Sociology* 82: 548–64.

1966   *Power and Privilege.* New York: McGraw-Hill.

Lenski, Gerhard, Patrick Nolan, and Jean Lenski

1995   *Human Societies: An Introduction to Macrosociology* (7th ed.). Toronto: McGraw-Hill.

Leridon, Henri and Catherine Velleneuve-Gokalp

1994   *Constances et Inconstances de la Famille.* Paris: Presses Universitaires de la France.

Lerner, Richard M.

1976   *Concepts and Theories of Human Development.* Reading, Mass: Addison-Wesley.

Leroux, T. and M. Petrunik

1990   "The construction of elder abuse as a social problem: a Canadian perspective." *International Journal of Health Services* 20: 651–63.

Lesthaegue, Ron

1995   "The second demographic transition in Western countries: an interpretation." In K. Oppenheim Mason and A-M. Jensen (eds.), *Gender and Family Change in Industrialized Countries.* Oxford: Clarendon.

Letkemann, Peter

1973   *Crime as Work.* Englewood Cliffs, NJ: Prentice Hall.

Li, Jiali

1995   "China's one-child policy: a case study of the Hebei Province, 1979–1988." *Population and Development Review* 21: 563–85.

Li, Peter

1998   "The market value and social value of race," Pp. 115–130 in Vic Satzwewich (ed), *Racism and Social Inequality in Canada.* Toronto: Thompson Educational Publishing.

1992   "Race and gender as bases of class fractions and their effects on earnings." *Canadian Review of Sociology and Anthropology* 29: 488–510.

1988   *Ethnic Inequality in a Class Society.* Toronto: Wall and Thompson.

Lian, Jason, and David Ralph Matthews

1998   "Does the vertical mosaic exist? Ethnicity and income in Canada, 1991." *Canadian Review of Sociology and Anthropology* 35, 4: 461–482.

Liebes, Tamar and Elihu Katz
1993   *The Export of Meaning: Cross-Cultural Readings of Dallas.* NY: Oxford University Press.

Lindsay, Colin
1992   *Lone-Parent Families in Canada.* Statistics Canada, Catalogue No. 89-522. Ottawa: Minister of Supply and Services Canada.

Lindsay, Colin, Mary Sue Devereaux and Michael Bergob
1994   *Youth in Canada: Second Edition.* Ottawa: Minister of Industry, Science and Technology.

Link, Bruce
1991   "The stigma of mental illness." Paper read at the Annual Meeting of the Society for the Study of Social Problems.

Link, Bruce and Francis Cullen
1990   "The labeling theory of mental disorder: a review of the evidence." *Research in Community and Mental Health* 6: 75-105.

Lippman, Walter
1922   *Public Opinion.* New York: Macmillan.

Lo, Celia
1995   "Gender differences in collegiate alcohol use." *Journal of Drug Issues* 25: 817—36.

Lockhart, Joseph
1997   "Progressive politics, electronic individualism and the myth of virtual community." Pp. 219–31 in David Porter (ed.), *Internet Culture.* London: Routledge.

Logan, Ron, and Jo-Anne Belliveau
1995   "Working mothers."*Canadian Social Trends* 36: 24–28.

Long, Elizabeth
1997   *From Sociology to Cultural Studies.* Oxford: Blackwell Publishers Ltd.

Lowe, Donald
1995   *The Body in the Late Capitalist USA.* Durham, NC: Duke University Press.

Lowe, Graham
1999   "Labour markets, inequality, and the future of work." Pp. 113–127 in J. Curtis, E. Grabb, and N. Guppy (eds.), *Social Inequality in Canada: Patterns, Problems, Policies.* (3rd ed.) Scarborough, Ont.: Prentice Hall.

Lower, J.A.
1973   *Canada: An Outline History.* Toronto: McGraw-Hill Ryerson.

Lowman, John
1992   "Street prostitution." In Vincent Sacco (ed.), *Deviance: Conformity and Control in Canadian Society.* (2nd ed.) Scarborough Ont.: Prentice Hall.

Lucas, Phillip
1992   "The New Age and the Pentecostal/charismatic revival: distinct yet parallel phases of a fourth great awakening?" In James R. Lewis and J. Gordon Melton (eds.), *Perspectives on the New Age.* Albany, NY: State University of New York Press.

Luckmann, Thomas
1967   *Invisible Religion: The Problem of Religion in Modern Society.* New York: Macmillan.

Luescher, K. and K. Pillemer
1998   "Intergenerational ambivalence: a new approach to the study of parent-child relations in later life." *Journal of Marriage and the Family* 60: 413–425.

Luhmann, Niklas
1982   *The Differentiation of Society.* Translated by Stephen Holmes and Charles Larmore. New York: Columbia University Press.

Luke, T.W.
1989   *Screens of Power: Ideology, Domination, and Resistance in Informational Society.* Urbana: University of Illinois Press.

Lundberg, Olle
1991   "Causal explanations for class inequality in health: an empirical analysis." *Social Science and Medicine* 32: 385–93.

Lupri, Eugen, Elaine Grandin, and Merlin Brinkerhoff
1994   "Socioeconomic status and male violence in the Canadian home: a reexamination." *Canadian Journal of Sociology* 19: 47–73.

Luxton, Meg
1990   "Two hands for the clock: changing patterns in the gendered division of labour in the home." In M. Luxton, H. Rosenberg, and S. Arat-Koc (eds.), *Through the Kitchen Window: The Politics of Home and Family.* (2nd ed.) Toronto: Garamond.

Mackie, Marlene
1991   *Gender Relations in Canada.* Toronto: Butterworths.

MacKinnon, Catharine A.
1989   *Toward a Feminist Theory of the State.* Cambridge, MA: Harvard University Press.

Madoo-Lengermann, P. and J. Niebrugge
1996   "Contemporary feminist theory." Pp. 436–86 in George Ritzer (ed.) *Contemporary Sociological Theory.* (4th ed.) New York: McGraw-Hill.

Males, Michael A.

1996 *The Scapegoat Generation: America's War on Adolescents.* Monroe, Maine: Common Courage Press.

Malinowski, Bronislaw

1954 [1925] *Magic, Science and Religion.* New York: Doubleday.

Mangahas Malou

1994 "The oldest contraceptive: the lactional amenorrheam method and reproductive rights (Philippines)." Pp. 57–68 in Shymala Nataraj et al.(eds), *Private Decisions, Public Debate: Women, Reproduction and Population.* London: Panos.

Marchak, M. Patricia

1990 "Sociology, ecology, and a global economy." *Cahiers de Recherche-sociologique* 14: 97–109.

Marchand, Philip

1989 *Marshall McLuhan: The Medium and the Messenger, A Biography.* Toronto: Random House.

Marcil-Gratton, Nicole

1988 *Les Modes de Vie Nouveaux des Adultes et Leur Impact sur les Enfants au Canada.* Health and Welfare Canada: Report for Review of Demography.

1998 *Growing up with Mom and Dad? The Intricate Family Life Course of Canadian Children.* Statistics Canada, Catalogue No. 89-566. Ottawa: Minister of Supply and Services Canada.

Marcuse, Herbert

1964 *One-Dimensional Man: Studies in the Ideology of Advanced Industrial Society.* Boston: Beacon.

Marshall, Katherine

1998 "Stay-at-home dads." *Perspectives on Labour and Income* 10: 9–15.

Marshall, V.W.

1997 *The Generations: Contributions, Conflict, Equity.* Prepared for the Division of Aging and Seniors. Ottawa: Health Canada.

1996 "The state of theory in aging and the social sciences." Pp. 12–30 in R.H. Binstock and L.K. George (eds.), *Handbook of Aging and the Social Sciences.* (4th ed.) San Diego, CA: Academic Press.

1995a "The micro-macro link in the sociology of aging." Pp. 337–371 in C. Hummel and Christian Lalive D'Epinay (eds.), *Images of Aging in Western Societies.* Proceedings of the 2nd Images of Aging Conference. Centre of Interdisciplinary Gerontology. University of Geneva, Switzerland.

1995b "Social models of aging." *Canadian Journal on Aging* 14: 12–34.

1994 "A critique of Canadian aging and health policy." Pp. 232–244 in V.W. Marshall and B.D. McPherson (eds.), *Aging: Canadian Perspectives.* Peterborough, Ont.: Broadview Press.

Martin Matthews, A.

1991 *Widowhood in Later Life.* Toronto: Butterworths/ Harcourt Brace.

Martin Matthews, A. and K. Brown

1987 "Retirement as a critical life event: the differential experience of women and men." *Research on Aging* 9: 548–71.

Martin Matthews, A. and L. D. Campbell

1995 "Gender roles, employment, and informal care." Pp. 129–143 in Sara Arber and Jay Ginn (eds.), *Connecting Gender and Ageing: A Sociological Approach.* Buckingham, England: Open University Press.

Martin Matthews, A. and C. Rosenthal

1993 "Balancing work and family in an aging society: the Canadian experience." Pp. 96–122 in G. Maddox and P. Lawton (eds.), *Annual Review of Gerontology and Geriatrics* Vol. 13. New York: Springer.

Martin, David

2000 "Canada in comparative perspective." In David Lyon and Marguerite Van Die, eds., *Rethinking Church, State, and Modernity: Canada Between Europe and the U.S.A.* Toronto: University of Toronto Press.

Martin-Barbero, Jesus

1993 *Communication, Culture and Hegemony: From Media to Mediation.* London: Sage.

Marx, Karl

1973 *Grundrisse.* Harmondsworth: Penguin.

1972 "An introduction to the critique of Hegel's *Philosophy of Right*." In K. Marx and F. Engels. *On Religion.* Moscow: Progress Books.

1970 [1859] *A Contribution to the Critique of Political Economy.* New York: International Publishers.

1906 *Capital: A Critique of Political Economy.* New York: The Modern Library.

Marx, Karl and Friedrich Engels

1979 [1848] *The Communist Manifesto.* Markham, Ont.: Penguin.

1973 [1846] *The German Ideology, Part I.* C.J. Arthur (ed.) New York: International Publishers.

Masuda, Yoneji

1981 *The Information Society as Post-Industrial Society.* Washington, DC: World Future Society.

Matrix Information and Directory Services

1998   "More than 100 million Internet users as of January 1998 [Online]." June 29. Retrieved from the World Wide Web: http://www3.mids.org/press/pr199801.html

Mattelart, Michele

1986   *Women, Media and Crisis.* London: Comedia.

Matthews, S.H.

1987a   "Provision of care to old parents: division of responsibility among adult children." *Research on Aging 9: 45–60.*

1987b   "Perceptions of fairness in the division of responsibility for old parents." *Social Justice Review* 1: 425–437.

1993   "Undermining stereotypes of the old through social policy analysis: tempering macro- with micro-level perspectives." Pp. 105–118 in J. Hendricks and C. Rosenthal (eds.), *The Remainder of Their Days: Domestic Policy and Older Families in the United States and Canada.* New York: Garland.

Matthews, S.H. and J. Heidorn

1998   "Meeting filial responsibilities in brothers-only sibling groups." *Journal of Gerontology: Social Sciences* 53B: S278–S286.

Matthews, S.H. and T.T. Rosner

1988   "Shared filial responsibility: the family as the primary caregiver." *Journal of Marriage and the Family* 50: 185–195.

Maxim, Paul S.

1993   "Ethno-religious diversity and local option in Ontario, 1906–14." Paper presented at the International Congress on the Social History of Alcohol, London, Ontario.

McAdam, Doug, J.D. McCarthy, and M.N. Zald (eds.)

1996a   *Comparative Perspectives on Social Movements: Political Opportunities, Mobilizing Structures, and Cultural Framings.* New York: Cambridge University Press.

McAdam, Doug, J.D. McCarthy, and M.N. Zald

1996b   "Introduction: opportunities, mobilizing structures, and framing processes—toward a synthetic, comparative perspective on social movements." Pp. 1–40 in Doug McAdam, J.D. McCarthy, and M.N. Zald (eds.), *Comparative Perspectives on Social Movements: Political Opportunities, Mobilizing Structures, and Cultural Framings.* New York: Cambridge University Press.

McCarthy, B. and J. Hagan

1987   "Gender, delinquency and the Great Depression: a test of power-control theory." *Canadian Review of Sociology and Anthropology* 24: 153–77.

McClelland, David

1961   *The Achieving Society.* New York: Free Press.

McDaniel, S.A.

1997   "Intergenerational transfers, social solidarity, and social policy: unanswered questions and policy challenges." *Canadian Public Policy/Canadian Journal on Aging.* Supplement: 1–21.

McDaniel, Susan

1994   *Family and Friends.* Statistics Canada, Catalogue No. 11-612, no. 9. Ottawa: Minster of Supply and Services Canada.

McDonald, Kevin and Ross D. Parke

1986   "Parent-child physical play: the effects of sex and age on children and parents." *Sex Roles* 15: 367–78.

McDonald, P.L. and R.A. Wanner

1990   *Retirement in Canada.* Toronto: Butterworths.

McDonald, Ryan

1991   "Canada's off-reserve Aboriginal population." *Canadian Social Trends* 23: 2–7.

McGee, Tom

1997   "Getting inside kids' heads." *American Demographics* January.

McKie, Craig

1990   "Lifestyle risks: smoking and drinking in Canada." Pp. 86–92 in Craig McKie and Keith Thompson (eds.), *Canadian Social Trends.* Toronto: Thompson Educational Publishing.

McLuhan, Marshall

1967   *The Medium is the Message.* New York: Bantam.

1964   *Understanding Media: The Extensions of Man.* New York: McGraw Hill.

McMullin, J.

1995   "Theorizing aging and gender relations." Pp. 30–41 in Sara Arber and Jay Ginn (eds.), *Connecting Gender and Ageing: A Sociological Approach.* Philadelphia: Open University Press.

McNeill, William

1982   *The Pursuit of Power: Technology, Armed Force, and Society since A.D. 1000.* Oxford: Basil Blackwell.

McPherson, B.D.

1998   *Aging as a Social Process: An Introduction to Individual and Population Aging.* (3rd ed.) Toronto: Harcourt Brace.

McPherson, Barry

1990   *Aging as a Social Process.* (2nd ed.) Toronto: Butterworths.

McQuillan, Kevin

1992 "Falling behind: the income of lone-mother families, 1970–1985." *Canadian Review of Sociology and Anthropology* 29: 511–523.

McQuillan, K. and M. Belle

1999 "Lone-father families in Canada, 1971–1996." Paper presented at the Annual Meeting of the Canadian Population Society, Lennoxville, Québec, June 9.

McRoberts, Kenneth

1988 *Quebec: Social Change and Political Crisis.* (3rd ed.) Toronto: McClelland and Stewart.

McVey, W. and W. Kalbach

1995 *Canadian Population.* Toronto: Nelson.

Mead, George H.

1934 *Mind, Self and Society.* Charles Morris (ed.) Chicago: University of Chicago Press.

Mead, Margaret

1971 *The Mountain Arapesh III.* Garden City, NY: Natural History Press.

1970 *Culture and Commitment.* Garden City: Doubleday.

1935 *Sex and Temperament in Three Primitive Societies.* New York: Morrow.

1928 *Coming of Age in Samoa: A Psychological Study of Primitive Youth for Western Civilization.* New York: Morrow Quill Paperbacks.

Mendel-Meadow, C. and S. Diamond

1991 "Content, method, and epistemology of gender in sociolegal studies." *Law and Society Review* 25: 221–38.

Menzies, Charles

1999 "First nations, inequality, and the legacy of colonialism." Pp. 236–243 in J. Curtis, E. Grabb, and N. Guppy (eds.), *Social Inequality in Canada: Patterns, Problems, Policies.* (3rd ed.) Scarborough, Ont.: Prentice Hall.

Merton, Robert K.

1957 *Social Theory and Social Structure.* New York: Free Press.

1938 "Social structure and anomie." *American Sociological Review* 3: 672–82.

Miedzian, Myriam

1991 *Boys Will Be Boys: Breaking the Link Between Masculinity and Violence.* New York: Basic Books.

Millar, Wayne J.

1996 "Reaching smokers with lower educational attainment." *Health Reports*, Statistics Canada, Catalogue No. 82-003-XPB. Ottawa: Minster of Supply and Services Canada.

Miller, James Roger

1996 *Shingwauk's Vision: A History of Native Residential Schools.* Toronto: University of Toronto Press.

Mills, C. Wright

1959 *The Sociological Imagination.* New York: Oxford University Press.

1956 *The Power Elite.* Oxford: Oxford University Press.

Milner, Henry and Sheilagh Hodgins Milner

1973 *The Decolonization of Quebec.* Toronto: McClelland and Stewart.

Mirowsky, J. and C. Ross

1995 "Sex differences in distress: real or artifact?" *American Sociological Review* 60: 449–68.

Modell, John, Frank F. Furstenberg and T. Hershberg

1976 "Social change and transitions to adulthood in historical perspective." *Journal of Family History* 1: 7–31.

Mogelonsky, Marcia

1996 "The rocky road to adulthood." *American Demographics* May: 26–35, 56.

Moghaddam, Fathali and Donald Taylor

1987 "The meaning of multiculturalism for visible minority immigrant women." *Canadian Journal of Behavioural Science* 19: 121–36.

Moghaddam, Fathali, Donald Taylor, and Richard Lalonde

1987 "Individualistic and collective integration strategies among Iranians in Canada." *International Journal of Psychology* 22: 301–13.

Moore, E.G. and M.W. Rosenberg, with Donald McGuinness

1997 *Growing Old in Canada: Demographic and Geographic Perspectives.* Statistics Canada, Catalogue No. 96-321-MPE No.1. Ottawa: Minister of Supply and Services Canada.

Moore, Maureen

1987 "Women parenting alone." *Canadian Social Trends* 7: 31–36.

Morely, David

1980 *The Nationwide Audience: Structure and Decoding.* London: British Film Institute.

1992 *Television, Audience and Cultural Studies.* London: Routledge.

1986 *Family Television: Cultural Power and Domestic Leisure.* London: Routledge.

Morley, David and Kevin Robins

1995 *Spaces of Identity: Global Media, Electronic Landscapes and Cultural Boundaries.* London: Routledge.

Morris, Raymond

1991   "The literary conventions of sociological writing in Quebec and English Canada." *Society* 15: 10–15.

Morton, Desmond

1988   "World War I." Pp. 2341–2344 in *The Canadian Encyclopedia* (2nd ed.) Edmonton: Hurtig.

Mosco, Vincent

1996   *The Political Economy of Communication.* London: Verso.

Mowbray, C., S. Herman, and K. Hazel

1992   "Gender and serious mental illness: a feminist perspective." *Psychology of Women Quarterly* 16: 107–26.

Mulvey Laura

1977   "Visual pleasure and narrative cinema." In Karyn Kay and Gerald Peary (eds.), *Women and the Cinema.* New York: Dutton.

Mumme, Carla and Kate Laxer.

1998   "Organizing and union membership: a Canadian profile in 1997." No. 18. Working Papers Series, Centre for Research on Work and Society, York University.

Murdock, George P.

1960   *Social Structure.* New York: Macmillan.

1957   "World ethnographic sample." *American Anthropologist* 59: 664–87.

Muuss, Rolf

1996   *Theories of Adolescence.* (6th ed.) New York: McGraw Hill.

Myles, J.

1984   *Old Age and the Welfare State.* Boston: Little Brown.

1991   "Editorial: women, the welfare state, and caregiving." *Canadian Journal on Aging* 10: 82–85.

Nakhaie, Reza

1997   "Vertical mosaic among the elites: the new imagery revisited." *Canadian Review of Sociology and Anthropology* 34, 1: 1–24.

Nakhaie, Reza, and James Curtis

1998   "Effects of class positions of parents on educational attainment of daughters and sons." *Canadian Review of Sociology and Anthropology* 35: 483–516.

National Advisory Council on Aging

1999   *1999 and Beyond: Challenges of an Aging Canadian Society.* Draft. January.

1992   *The NACA Position on Managing an Aging Labour Force.* Ottawa: Minister of Supply and Services.

National Council of Welfare

1993   "Poverty in Canada." Chapter 9 in J. Curtis, E. Grabb, and N. Guppy (eds.), *Social Inequality in Canada: Patterns, Problems, Policies.* (2nd ed.) Scarborough, Ont.: Prentice Hall.

1990   *Women and Poverty Revisited.* Ottawa: Ministry of Supply and Services.

Nault, François

1997   "Narrowing mortality gaps, 1978–1995." *Health Reports* 9: 35–41.

Nault, Francois and Alain Belanger

1996   *The Decline in Marriage in Canada, 1981 to 1991.* Statistics Canada, Catalogue No. 84-536-XPB. Ottawa: Minister of Supply and Services Canada.

Neallani, Shelina

1992   "Women of colour in the legal profession: facing the familiar barriers of race and sex." *Canadian Journal of Women and the Law* 5: 148–165.

Neuman, W. Lawrence

2000   *Social Research Methods.* (4th ed.) Boston: Allyn and Bacon.

Nevitte, Neil

1996   *The Decline of Deference: Canadian Value Change in Cross-national Perspective.* Peterborough, Ont.: Broadview Press.

Newcomb, Horace and Paul M. Hirsch

1994   "Television as a cultural forum." Pp. 503–14 in Horace Newcomb (ed.), *Television: The Critical View.* Oxford: Oxford University Press.

Newman, Peter C.

1995   *The Canadian Revolution 1985–1995: From Deference to Defiance.* Toronto: Viking.

1981   *The Acquisitors.* Toronto: McClelland and Stewart-Bantam.

Newman, S.C. and R.C. Bland

1987   "Canadian trends in mortality from mental disorders, 1965–83." *Acta Psychiatrica Scandinavica* 76: 1-7.

Niebuhr, Gustav

1997   "God therapy: putting life's trials in a sacred context." *New York Times*, February 9.

Neibuhr, H. Richard

1929   *The Social Sources of Denominationalism.* New York: Henry Holt.

Nietzsche, Friedrich

1910   *The Will To Power: An Attempted Transvaluation of All Values*, Vol.II. London: George Allen & Unwin.

Nobert, Lucie and Ramona McDowell

1994　*Profile of Post-secondary Education in Canada 1993 Edition.* Ottawa: Minister of Supply and Services.

Noh, S., W. Zheng, and W. Avison

1994　"Social support and quality of life: sociocultural similarity and effective social support among Korean immigrants." *Advances in Medical Sociology* 5: 115–37.

Norris, D.

1999　"Demographic outlook for Canada." Paper presented at the National Seminar on Demographic Change and Population Ageing. Moncton, New Brunswick, April.

Northcott, H.C.

1994　"Public perceptions of the population aging crisis." *Canadian Public Policy* 20: 66–77.

Notestein, F. W.

1945　"Population—the long view." Pp. 36–57 in T.W. Schultz (ed.), *Food for the World.* Chicago: University of Chicago Press.

Novak, Mark

1997　*Aging and Society: A Canadian Perspective.* Toronto: ITP Nelson.

O'Brien, M.

1991　"Never married older women: the life experience." *Social Indicators Research* 24: 301–315.

O'Connor, Julia

1999　"Ownership, class, and public policy." Pp. 35–47 in J. Curtis, E. Grabb, and N. Guppy (eds.), *Social Inequality in Canada: Patterns, Problems, Policies.* (3rd ed.) Scarborough, Ont.: Prentice Hall.

Ogmundson, R. and J. McLaughlin

1992　"Trends in the ethnic origins of Canadian elites: the decline of the BRITS?" *Canadian Review of Sociology and Anthropology* 29: 227–242.

Olesen, Virginia

1994　"Feminisms and models of qualitative research". Pp. 158–174 in Norman K. Denzin and Yvonna S. Lincoln (eds.), *Handbook of Qualitative Research.* Thousand Oaks, CA: Sage.

Olsen, Daniel V.A.

1999　"Religious pluralism and U.S. church membership: a reassessment." *Sociology of Religion* 60: 149–173.

Olsen, Dennis

1980　*The State Elite.* Toronto: McClelland and Stewart.

Oppenheimer, Valerie K.

1994　"Women's rising employment and the future of the family in industrial societies." *Population and Development Review* 20: 293–342.

Ortega, S. and J. Corzine

1990　"Socioeconomic status and mental disorders." *Research in Community and Mental Health* 6: 149–92.

Ortner, Sherry

1972　"Is female to male as nature is to culture?" *Feminist Studies* 1 (2): 5–31.

O'Toole, Roger

2000　"Canadian religion: heritage and project." In David Lyon and Marguerite Van Die (eds.) *Rethinking Church, State, and Modernity: Canada Between Europe and the USA.* Toronto: University of Toronto Press.

Otto, Rudolf

1958　[1917] *The Idea of the Holy.* Translated by John W. Harvey. Oxford: Oxford University Press.

Pahl, Robert E.

1969　"Urban social theory and research." *Environment and Planning* 1: 143–48.

Paik, Haejung and George Comstock

1994　"The effects of television violence on antisocial behaviour: a meta-analysis." *Communications Research* 21: 516–546.

Palantzas, T.

1991　"A search for 'autonomy' at Canada's first sociology department." *Society/Société* 15: 10–18.

Palladino, Grace

1996　*Teenagers: An American History.* New York: Basic Books.

Palmer, Bryan

1983　*Working Class Experience: The Rise and Reconstitution of Canadian Labour, 1800–1980.* Toronto: Butterworths.

Park, Robert E.

1952　*Human Communities.* New York: Free Press.

1950　*Race and Culture.* New York: Free Press.

Parliament, Jo-Anne

1990　"Increased life expectancy, 1921–1981." Pp. 64–65 in Craig McKie and Keith Thompson (eds.), *Canadian Social Trends.* Toronto: Thompson Educational Publishing.

Parsons, Talcott

1937　*The Structure of Social Action.* New York: Free Press.

1953　"A revised analytical approach to the theory of social stratification." Pp. 92–128 in Reinhard Bendix and S.M. Lipset (eds.), *Class, Status and Power.* Glencoe, IL: The Free Press.

1951　*The Social System.* Glencoe, IL: The Free Press.

Parsons, Talcott and Robert F. Bales

1955   *Family, Socialization and Interaction Process.* New York: Free Press.

Patai, Daphne

1994   "U.S. academics and Third-World women: is ethical research possible?" In S.O. Weisser and J. Fleischner (eds.), *Feminist Nightmares, Women at Odds.* New York: New York University Press.

Péron, Yves, Hélène Desrosiers, Heather Juby, Evelyne Lapierre-Adamcyk, Céline Le Bourdais, Nicole Marcil-Gratton, and Jael Mongeau

1999   *Canadian Families at the Approach of the Year 2000.* Statistics Canada Catalogue No. 96-321 no.4. Ottawa: Minister of Supply and Services Canada.

Petrunik, M. and C. Shearing

1988   "'The 'I,' the 'me,' and the 'it': moving beyond Meadian conception of self." *Canadian Journal of Sociology* 13: 435–448.

Phillips, Andrew

1999   "Lessons of Littleton." *MacLean's* May 3: 18–21.

Piaget, Jean

1954   *The Construction of Reality in the Child.* New York: Basic Books.

Pichardo, N.A.

1988   "Resource mobilization: an analysis of conflicting theoretical variations." *Sociological Quarterly* 29: 97–110.

Picot, Garnet and Ted Wannell

1993   "Who suffers permanent job loss?" Chapter 13 in J. Curtis, E. Grabb, and N. Guppy (eds.), *Social Inequality in Canada: Patterns, Problems, Policies.* (2nd ed.) Scarborough, Ont.: Prentice Hall.

Pillemer, K. and J. Suitor

1991   "Will I ever escape my child's problems? Effects of adult children's problems on elderly parents." *Journal of Marriage and the Family* 53: 585–594.

Pinard, Maurice

1968   "Mass society and political movements: a new formulation." *American Journal of Sociology* 73: 682–90.

Pineo, Peter

1986   "The social standing of ethnic and racial groupings." Pp. 256–72 in L. Driedger (ed.), *Ethnic Canada: Identities and Inequalities.* Toronto: Copp Clark Pitman.

Platiel, Rudy

1993   "Inuit to sign deal for 'our land'." *The Globe and Mail,* May 25: 1.

Pleck, Joseph

1981   *The Myth of Masculinity.* Cambridge, Mass: MIT Press.

Polakowski, Michael

1994   "Linking self- and social control with deviance: illuminating the structure underlying a general theory of crime and its relation to deviant activity." *Journal of Quantitative Criminology* 10: 41–78.

Ponting, Rick

1998   "Racism and stereotyping of first nations." Pp. 269–298 in V. Satzewich (ed.), *Racism and Social Inequality in Canada.* Toronto: Thompson Educational Publishers, Inc.

Popenoe, David

1998   *Disturbing the Nest: Family Change and Decline in Modern Societies.* New York: Aldine de Gruyter.

Pool, Ithiel de Sola

1983   *Technologies of Freedom.* Cambridge, MA: Harvard University Press.

Pooley, Eric

1999   "Portrait of a deadly bond." *Time* May 10: 14–20.

Porter, John

1980   "Canada: dilemmas and contradictions of a multi-ethnic society." Pp. 325–36 in Jay Goldstein and Rita Bienvenue (eds.), *Ethnicity and Ethnic Relations in Canada.* Toronto: Butterworths.

1965   *The Vertical Mosaic: An Analysis of Social Class and Power in Canada.* Toronto: University of Toronto Press.

Posgate, Dale and Kenneth McRoberts

1976   *Quebec: Social Change and Political Crisis.* Toronto: McClelland and Stewart.

Posner, Judith

1975   "The stigma of excellence: on being just right." *Sociological Inquiry* 46 (2): 141–144.

Poster, Mark

1990   *The Mode of Information: Poststructuralism and Social Context.* Chicago: University of Chicago Press.

Prentice, Alison et al.

1988   *Canadian Women: A History.* Toronto: Harcourt Brace Jovanovich.

Quill, Greg

1999   "Driving up the cost of violence." *Toronto Star,* June 6: D16–19.

Rashid, Abdul

1994   *Family Income in Canada.* Statistics Canada, Catalogue No. 96-318. Ottawa: Minister of Supply and Services Canada.

1998   "Family income inequality, 1970–1995." *Perspectives on Labour and Income* 10: 12–17.

Ratner, A. and C. McKie

1990   "The ecology of crime and its implications for prevention: an Ontario study." *Canadian Journal of Criminology* 32: 155–71.

Ravanera, Zenaida and Fernando Rajulton

1996   "Stability and crisis in the family life course: findings from the 1990 General Social Survey, Canada." *Canadian Studies in Population* 23: 165–84.

Ravanera, Zenaida, Fernando Rajulton, and Thomas Burch

1998a   "Trends and variations in the early life courses of Canadian men." University of Western Ontario. Discussion Paper No. 98-7.

1998b   "Early life transitions of Canadian women: A cohort analysis of timing, sequences, and variations." *European Journal of Population* 14: 179–204.

1995   "A cohort analysis of home leaving in Canada, 1910–1975." *Journal of Comparative Family Studies* 26: 179–94.

Reid, G.M.

1994   "Maternal sex-stereotyping of newborns." *Psychological Reports* 75: 1443–1450.

Reimer, Samuel H.

1995   "A look at cultural effects on religiosity: a comparison between the United States and Canada." *Journal for the Scientific Study of Religion* 34: 445–457.

Reinharz, Shulamit

1992   *Feminist Methods in Social Research.* New York: Oxford University Press.

Reitsma-Street, Marge

1999   "Justice for Canadian girls: a 1990s update." *Canadian Journal of Criminology* 41: 335–46.

Reitz, Jeffrey

1990   "Ethnic concentrations in labor markets and their implications for ethnic inequality." Pp. 135–195 in Raymond Breton, Wsevolod Isajiw, Warren Kalbach, and Jeffrey Reitz (eds.), *Ethnic Identity and Equality.* Toronto: University of Toronto Press.

Reitz, Jeffrey G., and Raymond Breton

1994   *The Illusion of Difference: Realities of Ethnicity in Canada and the United States.* Toronto: C.D. Howe Institute.

Renaud, Marc, Suzanne Doré, and Deena White

1989   "Sociology and social policy: from a love-hate relationship with the state to cynicism and pragmatism." *Canadian Review of Sociology and Anthropology* 26: 426–56.

Renzetti, Claire M. and Daniel J. Curran

1992   *Women, Men and Society: The Sociology of Gender.* (2nd ed.) Boston: Allyn and Bacon.

Rhodes, A. and P. Goering

1994   "Gender differences in the use of outpatient mental health services." *Journal of Mental Health Administration* 21: 338–46.

Rice, Frank P.

1998   *Human Development: A Life-span Approach.* (3rd ed.) Upper Saddle River, NJ: Prentice Hall.

Rice, Patricia C.

1981   "Prehistoric Venuses: symbols of motherhood or womanhood?" *Journal of Anthropological Research* 37: 402–414.

Richer, Stephen and Pierre Laporte

1971   "Culture, cognition, and English-French competition." Pp. 141–50 in Jean L. Elliott (ed.), *Minority Canadians II: Immigrant Groups.* Scarborough, Ont.: Prentice Hall.

Riley, M.W. and J.W. Riley

1994   "Age integration and the lives of older people." *The Gerontologist* 34: 110–115.

Riley, M.W., M. Johnson, and A. Foner (eds.)

1972   *Aging and Society, Vol. 3: A Sociology of Age Stratification.* New York: Russell Sage Foundation.

Riley, M.W., R.L. Kahn, and A. Foner

1994   *Age and Structural Lag: Society's Failure to Provide Meaningful Opportunities in Work, Family and Leisure.* New York: Wiley.

Rindfuss, R.R. and A.M. Parnell

1989   "The varying connection between marital status and childbearing in the United States." *Population and Development Review* 15: 447–470.

Rindfuss, Ronald R. and Audrey VandenHeuvel

1990   "Cohabitation: precursor to marriage or an alternative to being single." *Population and Development Review* 16: 703–26.

Rinehart, J., C. Huxley, and D. Robertson

1998   *Not Just Another Auto Plant.* Ithaca: Cornell University Press.

Rinehart, James W.

1996   *The Tyranny of Work.* (3rd ed.) Toronto: Harcourt Brace.

Rioux, Marcel

1978a   "Bill 101: a positive anglophone point of view." *Canadian Review of Sociology and Anthropology* 15: 142–44.

1978b   *Quebec in Question.* Toronto: James Lorimer.

Ritchie, Karen

1995 "Marketing to Generation X." *American Demographics* April: 34–39.

Roberts, Julian and Thomas Gabor

1990 "Lombrosian wine in a new bottle: research on crime and race." *Canadian Journal of Criminology* 32: 291–314.

Roberts, R.E.L., L.N. Richards, and V.L. Bengtson

1991 "Intergenerational solidarity in families: untangling the ties that bind." *Marriage and Family Review* 16: 11–46.

Rocher, G.

1996 "Préface." In Marc Brière (ed.), *Le goût du Québec: l'après référendum 1995*. La Salle: Hurtubise.

1977 "The future of sociology in Canada." In Christopher Beattie and Stewart Crysdale (eds.), *Sociology Canada: Readings*. Toronto: Butterworths.

1992 "The two solitudes between Canadian sociologists." In Wm. K. Carroll et al. (eds.), *Fragile Truths: 25 Years of Sociology and Anthropology in Canada*. Ottawa: Carleton University Press.

Rohde-Dascher, C. and S. Price

1992 "Do we need a feminist psychoanalysis?" *Psychoanalysis and Contemporary Thought* 15: 241–59.

Roof, Wade Clark

1996 "God is in the details: reflections on religion's public presence in the United States in the mid-1990s." *Sociology of Religion* 57: 149–162.

Roscoe, Paul

1996 "Incest." Pp. 631–34 in D. Levinson and M. Ember (eds.), *The Encyclopedia of Cultural Anthropology*, Vol. 2. New York: Henry Holt.

Roscoe, W.

1991 *The Zuni Man-Woman*. Albuquerque: University of New Mexico Press.

Rosenau, P.M.

1992 *Post-modernism and the Social Sciences: Insights, Inroads, and Intrusions*. Princeton: Princeton University Press.

Rosenberg, Harriet

1990 "The home is the workplace." In M. Luxton, H. Rosenberg, and S. Arat-Koc (eds.), *Through the Kitchen Window: The Politics of Home and Family*. (2nd ed.) Toronto: Garamond.

Rosenberg, M. Michael and Jack Jedwab

1992 "Institutional completeness, ethnic organizational style and the role of the state: the Jewish, Italian, and Greek communities of Montreal." *Canadian Review of Sociology and Anthropology* 29: 266–287.

Rosenfield, Sarah

1982 "Sex roles and societal reactions to mental illness: the labeling of 'deviant' deviance." *Journal of Health and Social Behavior* 23: 18–24.

Rosser, S.V.

1990 *Female-Friendly Science: Applying Women's Studies Methods and Theories to Attract Students*. New York: Pergamon.

Rossi, Alice S.

1985 *Gender and the Life Course*. New York: Aldine de Gruyter.

Rowe, Geoff

1989 "Union dissolution in a changing social context." Pp. 141–64 in J. Légaré et al. (eds.), *The Family in Crisis: A Population Crisis*. Ottawa: The Royal Society of Canada.

Rowe, Kathleen

1994 "Roseanne: unruly woman as domestic goddess." Pp. 202–11 in Horace Newcomb (ed.), *Television: The Critical View*. Oxford: Oxford University Press.

Royal Commission on Bilingualism and Biculturalism

1967 *Report. Book I: The Official Languages*. Ottawa: Queen's Printer.

1969 *Report. Book IV: The Cultural Contribution of the Other Ethnic Groups*. Ottawa: Information Canada.

Rudé, George

1964 *The Crowd in History: A Study of Popular Disturbances in France and England, 1730–1848*. New York: Wiley.

Rushkoff, Douglas

1994 *Media Virus! Hidden Agendas in Popular Culture*. New York: Ballantine.

Rushton, J. Philippe

1988 "Race differences in behavior: a review and evolutionary analysis." *Personality and Individual Differences* 9: 1009–1024.

Russel, Bob

1990 *Back to Work? Labour, State and Industrial Relations in Canada*. Scarborough, Ont.: Nelson Canada.

Ruth, Sheila

1990 *Issues in Feminism*. (2nd ed.) Toronto: Mayfield.

Ryan, John and William W. Wentworth

1999 *Media and Society: The Production of Mass Media*. Needham Heights, MA: Allyn and Bacon.

Sabel, Charles, F.

1982 *Work and Politics: The Division of Labor in Industry*. New York: Cambridge University Press.

494   Bibliography

Sacco, V. and H. Johnson

1990   *Patterns of Criminal Victimization in Canada*. Ottawa: Minister of Supply and Services.

Sacco, Vincent

1992   *Deviance: Conformity and Control in Canadian Society*. (2nd ed.) Scarborough, Ont.: Prentice Hall.

Salaman, Graeme

1986   *Working*. New York: Routledge, Chapman and Hall.

Salutin, Rick

1993   "Men and feminism." *This Magazine* 26: 12–18.

Sampson, R. and J. Laub

1990   "Crime and deviance over the life course: the salience of adult social bonds." *American Sociological Review* 55: 609–27.

Satzewich, Vic (ed.)

1998   *Racism and Social Inequality in Canada*. Toronto: Thompson Educational Publishers, Inc.

Satzewich, Victor and Peter Li

1987   "Immigrant labour in Canada: the cost and benefit of ethnic origin on the job market." *Canadian Journal of Sociology* 12: 229–41.

Scanzoni, Letha and John Scanzoni

1988   *Men, Women and Change: A Sociology of Marriage and Family*. (3rd ed.) New York: McGraw-Hill.

Schachter, Harvey

1999   "The hurrier we go, the behinder we get." *The Globe and Mail,* May 15: D1–D2.

Scheff, Thomas

1984   [1966] *Being Mentally Ill: A Sociological Theory*. Chicago: Aldine.

Schiller, Dan

1999   *Digital Capitalism: Networking the Global Market System*. Cambridge, MA: MIT Press.

Schiller, Herbert J.

1991   "Not yet the post-imperial era." *Critical Studies in Mass Communication* 8: 13–28.

Schissel, Bernard

1992   "The influence of economic factors and social control policy on crime rate changes in Canada, 1962–1988." *Canadian Journal of Sociology* 17: 405–28.

Schlegel, Alice and Herbert Barry

1991   *Adolescence: An Anthropological Inquiry*. New York: Free Press.

Schur, Edwin M.

1984   *Labeling Women Deviant: Gender, Stigma, and Social Control*. New York: Random House.

Scott, Alan

1990   *Ideology and the New Social Movements*. London: Unwin Hyman.

Sellin, T.

1938   *Culture Conflict and Crime*. New York: Social Science Research Council.

Semple, R. Keith

1988   "Urban dominance, foreign ownership, and corporate concentration." Pp. 343–56 in J. Curtis et al. (eds.), *Social Inequality in Canada: Patterns, Problems, Policies*. Scarborough, Ont.: Prentice Hall.

Seniors Secretariat

1995   *Seniors Info Exchange*. 6: 1–30. Ottawa: Health Canada.

Sharp, R.L.

1952   "Steel axes for stone age Australians." *Human Organization* 11: 17–22.

Shaw, C. and H. McKay

1942   *Juvenile Delinquency in Urban Areas*. Chicago: University of Chicago Press.

Sheldon, William

1949   *Varieties of Delinquent Youth: An Introduction to Constitutional Psychiatry*. New York: Harper and Row.

Shore, Marlene

1987   *The Science of Social Redemption: McGill, the Chicago School, and the Origins of Social Research in Canada*. Toronto: University of Toronto Press.

Shorter, Edward

1977   *The Making of the Modern Family*. New York: Basic Books.

Shostak, Marjorie

1983   [1981] *Nisa: The Life and Words of a !Kung Woman*. New York: Vintage Books.

Siggner, Andrew

1986   "The socio-demographic conditions of registered Indians." Pp. 57–83 in J.R. Ponting (ed.), *Arduous Journey, Canadian Indians and Decolonization*. Toronto: McClelland and Stewart.

Silverman, Robert

1992   "Street crime." Pp. 236–77 in Vincent Sacco (ed.), *Deviance: Conformity and Control in Canadian Society*. (2nd ed.) Scarborough, Ont.: Prentice Hall.

Silverman, Robert, James Teevan, and Vincent Sacco (eds.)

2000   *Crime in Canadian Society.* (6th ed.) Toronto: Harcourt Brace.

Simon, J.

1981   *The Ultimate Resource.* Princeton, NJ: Princeton University Press.

Simpson, Sally

1991   "Caste, class, and violent crime: explaining differences in female offending." *Criminology* 29: 115–35.

Skolnick, Arlene S.

1996   *The Intimate Environment: Exploring Marriage and the Family.* New York: Harper Collins.

1991   *Embattled Paradise: The American Family in an Age of Uncertainty.* New York: Basic Books.

Small, Stephen

1998   "The contours of racialization: structures, representation and resistance in the United States." Pp. 69–86 in Vic Satzwewich (ed), *Racism and Social Inequality in Canada.* Toronto: Thompson Educational Publishing.

Smelser, Neil J.

1962   *Theory of Collective Behavior.* New York: Free Press.

Smith, Dorothy

1989   "Feminist reflections on political economy." *Studies in Political Economy* 30: 37-60.

1987   *The Everyday World as Problematic.* Toronto: University of Toronto Press.

Smith, Michael D.

1990a   "Sociodemographic risk factors in wife abuse: results from a survey of Toronto women." *Canadian Journal of Sociology* 15: 39–58.

1990b   "Patriarchal ideology and wife beating: a test of a feminist hypothesis." *Violence and Victims* 5: 257–73.

Smith, Philip (ed).

1998   *The New American Cultural Sociology.* Cambridge: Cambridge University Press.

Smith, Wilfred Cantwell

1959   "Comparative religion: whither—and why?" In Mircea Eliade and Joseph Kitagawa (eds.), *The History of Religions: Essays on Methodology.* Chicago: University of Chicago Press.

Snider, Laureen

1992   "Commercial crime." Pp. 313–62 in Vincent Sacco (ed.), *Deviance: Conformity and Control in Canadian Society.* (2nd ed.) Scarborough, Ont.: Prentice Hall.

1991   "Critical criminology in Canada: past, present and future." In Robert Silverman, James Teevan, and Vincent Sacco (eds.), *Crime in Canadian Society.* (4th ed.) Toronto: Butterworths.

Sniderman, P., D. Northrup, J. Fletcher, P. Russell, and P. Tetlock

1993   "Psychological and cultural foundations of prejudice: the case of anti-Semitism in Quebec." *Canadian Review of Sociology and Anthropology* 30: 242–70.

Snow, D.A., E.B. Rochford, Jr., S.K. Worden, and R.D. Benford

1986   "Frame alignment processes, micromobilization, and movement participation." *American Sociological Review* 51: 464–81.

So, Alvin

1990   *Social Change and Development: Modernization, Dependency, and World-System Theories.* Newbury Park, CA: Sage Publications.

Solomon, R. and T. Madison

1986   "The evolution of non-medical drug use in Canada." In Robert Silverman and James Teevan (eds.), *Crime in Canadian Society.* (3rd ed.) Toronto: Butterworths.

"Spanker spanked"

1995   *Globe & Mail* Feb. 9: A2.

Sparks, Allister

1995   *Tomorrow Is Another Country: The Inside Story of South Africa's Road to Change.* Chicago: University of Chicago Press.

Speer, Tibbett L.

1998   "College come-ons." *American Demographics* March: 41–45.

Spencer, Herbert

1898   *The Principles of Sociology,* Vol.II-2. New York: D. Appleton.

1897   *The Principles of Sociology,* Vol.I-2. New York: D. Appleton.

Spender, Dale

1995   *Nattering on the Net: Women, Power and Cyberspace.* Toronto: Garamond.

Sperling, Susan

1991   "Baboons with briefcases vs. langurs in lipstick." Pp. 204–234 in Micaela di Leonardo (ed.), *Gender at the Crossroads of Knowledge.* Berkeley, CA: University of California Press.

Spigel, Lynn

1994   "Women's work." Pp. 19–45 in Horace Newcomb (ed.), *Television: The Critical View.* Oxford: Oxford University Press.

Spitzer, S.

1975 "Toward a Marxian theory of deviance." *Social Problems* 22: 638–51.

Sreberny, Annabelle

1998 "Feminist internationalism: imagining and building global civil society." Pp. 208–23 in Daya Kishan Thussu (ed.), *Electronic Empires: Global Media and Local Resistance*. London: Arnold.

Stark, Rodney and Laurence Iannaccone

1994 "A supply-side reinterpretation of the 'secularization' of Europe." *Journal for the Scientific Study of Religion* 33: 230–252.

Stark, Rodney and William Sims Bainbridge

1985 *The Future of Religion: Secularization, Revival and Cult Formation*. Berkeley, CA: University of California Press.

1987 *A Theory of Religion*. New York: Peter Lang.

Stebbins, Robert

1988 *Deviance: Tolerable Differences*. Toronto: McGraw-Hill Ryerson.

Steffensmeier, D. and C. Streifel

1991 "Age, gender, and crime across three historical periods: 1935, 1960, and 1985." *Social Forces* 69: 869–94.

Stone, L.O., C.J. Rosenthal, and I.A. Connidis

1998 *Parent-Child Exchanges of Supports and Intergenerational Equity*. Ottawa: Statistics Canada.

Stone, Leroy O.

1988 *Family and Friendship Ties among Canada's Seniors*. Statistics Canada, Catalogue No. 89-508. Ottawa: Minister of Supply and Services Canada.

1967 *Urban Development in Canada*. Ottawa: Dominion Bureau of Statistics.

Stonequist, Everett

1963 "The marginal man: a study in personality and culture conflict." Pp. 327–45 in E.W. Burgess and Donald Bogue (eds.), *Contributions to Urban Sociology*. Chicago: University of Chicago Press.

Strain, Laurel A.

1990 "Receiving and providing care: the experiences of never-married elderly Canadians." Presentation, XII World Congress of Sociology, Madrid, July.

Strasburger, Victor C. and Edward Donnerstein

1999 "Children, adolescents, and the media: issues and solutions." *Pediatrics* 103: 129–139.

Streitmatter, J.L.

1988 "Ethnicity as a mediating variable of early adolescent identity development." *Journal of Adolescence* 11: 335–46.

Strong, Bryan, Christine DeVault, Murray Suid, and Rebecca Reynolds

1983 *The Marriage and Family Experience*. St.Paul, MN: West Pub. Co.

Sumner, William G.

1940 *Folkways*. Boston: Ginn.

Sunahara, Ann

1981 *The Politics of Racism: The Uprooting of Japanese Canadians During the Second World War*. Toronto: James Lorimer.

Sutherland, Edwin

1939 *Principles of Criminology*. (3rd ed.) Philadelphia: Lippincott.

Swan, Neil and John Serjak

1993 "Analysing regional disparities." Chapter 30 in J. Curtis, E. Grabb, and N. Guppy (eds.), *Social Inequality in Canada: Patterns, Problems, Policies*. (2nd ed.) Scarborough, Ont.: Prentice Hall.

Swanson, Guy

1960 *Birth of the Gods*. Ann Arbor, MI: University of Michigan Press.

Sweeney, Megan

1997 "Women, men and changing families: the shifting economic foundations of marriage." University of Wisconsin-Madison: Center for Demography and Ecology, Working Paper No. 97-14.

Sykes, G. and D. Matza

1957 "Techniques of neutralization: a theory of delinquency." *American Sociological Review* 22: 664–70.

Symons, Thomas H.B.

1976 *To Know Ourselves, the Report of the Commission on Canadian Studies*. Vol. 1 and 2. Ottawa: Association of Universities and Colleges of Canada.

Sztompka, Piotr

1993 *The Sociology of Social Change*. Oxford, U.K.: Blackwell.

Tannen, Deborah

1990 *You Just Don't Understand: Women and Men in Conversation*. New York: Ballantine Books.

Tanner, J. and H. Krahn

1991 "Part-time work and deviance among high school seniors." *Canadian Journal of Sociology* 16: 281–302.

Tanner, Julian

1992 "Youthful deviance." Pp. 203–35 in Vincent Sacco (ed.), *Deviance: Conformity and Control in Canadian Society*. (2nd ed.) Scarborough, Ont.: Prentice Hall.

Tarde, Gabriel
1903   [1962] *The Laws of Imitation.* Translated by Elsie Clews Parsons. New York: Henry Holt & Company.

Teeple, Gary
1995   *Globalization and the Decline of Social Reform.* Toronto: Garamond Press.

Temple, M. et al.
1991   "A meta-analysis of change in marital and employment status as predictors of alcohol use on a typical occasion." *British Journal of Addiction* 86: 1269–81.

Templeton, Alan R.
1999   "Human races: a genetic and evolutionary perspective." *American Anthropologist* 100: 632–650.

Thompson, E.P.
1971   "The moral economy of the English crowd in the eighteenth century." *Past and Present* 50: 76–136.

Thompson, J.H. and Allen Seager
1985   *Canada, 1922–1939: Decades of Discord.* Toronto: McClelland and Stewart.

Thussu, Daya Kishan
1998   "Localising the global: Zee TV in India." Pp. 273–94 in Daya Kishan Thussu (ed.), *Electronic Empires: Global Media and Local Resistance.* London: Arnold.

Tierney, J.
1990   "Betting the planet." *New York Times Magazine,* December, p. 52.

Tilly, Charles
1978   *From Mobilization to Revolution.* Reading, MA: Addison-Wesley.

Tilly, Charles, Louise Tilly, and Richard Tilly
1975   *The Rebellious Century, 1830–1930.* Cambridge, MA: Harvard University Press.

Timms, Duncan
1998   "Gender, social mobility, and psychiatric diagnoses." *Social Science and Medicine* 46: 1235–47.

Tittle, C.
1995   *Control Balance: Toward a General Theory of Deviance.* Boulder, CO: Westview Press.

Tocqueville, Alexis de
1955   [1856] *The Old Regime and the French Revolution.* New York: Doubleday.

Todaro, Michael
1997   *Urbanization, Unemployment, and Migration in Africa: Theory and Policy.* New York: The Population Council.

Tomlinson, John
1991   *Cultural Imperialism.* Baltimore: John Hopkins University Press.

Touraine, Alain
1971   *The Post-Industrial Society: Tomorrow's Social History: Classes, Conflicts and Culture in the Programmed Society.* Translated by L.F.X. Mayhew. New York: Random House.

Townsend, Joan B.
1990   "The Goddess: fact, fallacy and revitalization movement." Pp. 179–203 in Larry W. Hurtado (ed.), *Goddesses in Religions and Modern Debate.* Atlanta, GA: Scholars Press.

Troeltsch, Ernst
1931   *The Social Teachings of the Christian Churches*, Vol. 2. Translated by Olive Wyon. New York: Macmillan.

Trost, S.
1986   "What holds marriage together." In J. Veevers (ed.), *Continuity and Change in Marriage and Family.* Toronto: Holt, Rinehart and Winston.

Trovato, Frank
1991   "Sex, marital status, and suicide in Canada: 1951–1981." *Sociological Perspectives* 34: 427–45.

Tuchman, Gaye
1994   "Historical social science: methodologies, methods, and meanings." Pp. 306–323 in Norman K. Denzin and Yvonna S. Lincoln (eds.), *Handbook of Qualitative Research.* Thousand Oaks, CA: Sage. Turner, B.S.

Turcotte, Pierre and Alain Bélanger
1998   "The dynamics of formation and dissolution of first common-law unions in Canada." Ottawa: Statistics Canada.
1997   "Moving in together." *Canadian Social Trends* 47: 7–9.

Turkle, Sherry
1995   *Life on the Screen: Identity in the Age of the Internet.* New York: Simon and Schuster.

Turner, B.S.
1988   *Status.* Minneapolis: University of Minnesota Press.

Turner, Ralph and L.M. Killian
1957   *Collective Behavior.* Englewood Cliffs, NJ: Prentice Hall.

Tylor, Edward
1903   *Primitive Culture: Researches into the Development of Mythology, Philosophy, Religion, Language, Art, and Custom*, Vol. 1. London: John Murphy.

U.S. Bureau of the Census

1998   *Statistical Abstract of the United States 1998.* Washington, DC: U.S. Government Printing Office.

UNAIDS

1998   *AIDS epidemic update: December 1998.* UNAIDS Joint United Nations Program on HIV/AIDS.

United Nations Development Program

1997   *Human Development Report 1997.* New York: Oxford University Press.

Urmetzer, Peter, and Neil Guppy

1999   "Changing income inequality in Canada." Pp. 56–65 in J. Curtis, E. Grabb,and N. Guppy (eds.), *Social Inequality in Canada: Patterns, Problems, Policies.* (3rd ed.) Scarborough, Ont.: Prentice Hall.

Vaillant, C. and G.E. Vaillant

1993   "Is the U-curve of marital satisfaction an illusion? A 40-year study of marriage." *Journal of Marriage and the Family* 55: 230–239.

van Poppel, F. and L. Day

1996   "A test of Durkheim's theory of suicide." *American Sociological Review* 61: 500–507.

Van den Berghe, Pierre

1967   *Race and Racism: A Comparative Perspective.* New York: Wiley.

Waddell, Eric

1986   "State, language and society: the vicissitudes of French in Quebec and Canada." Pp. 67–110 in Alan Cairns and Cynthia Williams (eds.), *The Politics of Gender, Ethnicity, and Language in Canada.* Toronto: University of Toronto Press.

Wadhera, Surinder and Wayne Millar

1997   "Teenage pregnancies, 1974 to 1994." *Health Reports* 9: 9–17.

Waite, Linda J. and Lee A. Lillard

1991   "Children and marital disruption." *American Journal of Sociology* 96: 930–953.

Walker, A.

1991   "The relationship between the family and the state in the care of older people." *Canadian Journal on Aging* 10: 94–112.

Waller, Willard

1937   "The rating and dating complex." *American Sociological Review* 2: 727–34.

Wallerstein, Immanuel

1974   *The Modern World System.* New York: Academic Press.

Wallis, Roger and Krister Malm

1984   *Big Sounds from Small Peoples: The Music Industry in Small Countries.* New York: Pendragon.

Walsh, A. and R. Gordon

1995   *Biosociology: An Emerging Paradigm.* Westport, CT: Praeger.

Wanner, Richard A.

1993   "Patterns and trends in occupational mobility." Chapter 12 in J. Curtis, E. Grabb, and N. Guppy (eds.), *Social Inequality in Canada: Patterns, Problems, Policies.* (2nd ed.) Scarborough, Ont.: Prentice Hall.

Wanner, Richard A., and Bernadette C. Hayes

1996   "Intergenerational occupational mobility among men in Canada and Australia." *Canadian Journal of Sociology* 21: 43–76.

Ward, Martha

1996   *A World Full of Women.* Boston: Allyn and Bacon.

Wark, McKenzie

1994   *Virtual Geography: Living with Global Media Events.* Bloomington, IN: Indiana University Press.

Washburn, Sherman

1960   "Tools and human evolution." *Scientific American* September: 61–74.

Waterman, Peter

1998   *Globalization, Social Movements and the New Internationalism.* London: Mansell.

Weber, Max

1978   [1958] *From Max Weber: Essays in Sociology.* Translated by H.H. Gerth and C. Wright Mills. New York: Oxford University Press.

1921   *Economy and Society: An Outline of Interpretive Sociology,* Vol.1 and 2. G. Roth and C. Wittich (eds). Berkeley CA: University of California Press.

Weeks, John R.

1996   *Population: An Introduction to Concepts and Issues.* (6th ed.) Belmont, CA: Wadsworth Publishing Company.

Weinstein, Jay

1997   *Social and Cultural Change: Social Science for a Dynamic World.* Toronto: Allyn and Bacon.

Weitzman, N., B. Birns, and R. Friend

1985   "Traditional and nontraditional mothers' communication with their daughters and sons." *Child Development* 56: 894–96.

Wells, L. Edward and Joseph H. Rankin

1991   "Families and delinquency: a meta-analysis of the impact of broken homes." *Social Problems* 38: 71–93.

White, J.P.

1992   "The state and industrial relations in a neo-conservative era." Pp 198–221 in L. Haiven, S. McBride, and G. Shields (eds.) *Regulating Labour: The State, Neo-Conservatism and Industrial Relations.* Toronto: Garamond Press.

1990   *Hospital Strike: Women, Unions and Public Sector Conflict.* Toronto: Thompson Educational Press.

White, J.P. and N. Pupo

1994   "Union leaders and the economic crisis: responses to restructuring." *Industrial Relations* 49: 821–845.

White, Lynn

1994   "Coresidence and leaving home: young adults and their parents." *Annual Review of Sociology* 20: 81–102.

White, Pamela

1990   [1986] *Census of Canada: Ethnic Diversity in Canada.* Ottawa: Minister of Supply and Services Canada.

Whyte, William Foote (ed.)

1991   *Participatory Action Research.* Newbury Park, CA: Sage.

Wien, Fred

1999   "Regional inequality: explanations and policy issues." Pp. 270–286 in J. Curtis, E. Grabb, and N. Guppy (eds.), *Social Inequality in Canada: Patterns, Problems, Policies.* (3rd ed.) Scarborough, Ont.: Prentice Hall.

1993   "Regional inequality: explanations and policy issues." Chapter 31 in J. Curtis, E. Grabb, and N. Guppy (eds.), *Social Inequality in Canada: Patterns, Problems, Policies.* (2nd ed.) Scarborough, Ont.: Prentice Hall.

Willmott, Hugh (ed).

1990   *Labour Process Theory.* Houndmills, Basingstoke, Hampshire: Macmillan.

Wilkins, Leslie T.

1964   *Social Deviance: Social Policy, Action, and Research.* London: Tavistock.

Wilkins, Russell, Owen Adams, and Anna Brancker

1989   "Changes in mortality by income in urban Canada from 1971 to 1986." *Health Reports* 1(2) Statistics Canada, 820–003: 137–74. Ottawa: Minister of Supply and Services Canada.

Williams, D., D. Takeuchi, and R. Adair

1992   "Marital status and psychiatric disorders among blacks and whites." *Journal of Health and Social Behavior* 33: 140–57.

Williams, Raymond

1983   *Keywords.* Oxford: Oxford University Press.

1980   *Problems in Materialism and Culture.* London: Verso.

Williams, Thomas Rhys

1972   *Introduction to Socialization.* St. Louis: The C.V. Mosby Company.

Willis, Paul

1977   *Learning to Labour.* Farnborough, Hants: Saxon House.

Wilson, Bryan

1982   *Religion in Sociological Perspective.* Oxford: Oxford University Press.

1966   *Religion in Secular Society.* London: Watts.

Wilson, Edward O.

1975   *Sociobiology: The New Synthesis.* Cambridge, MA: Harvard University Press.

Wilson, J. and R. Herrnstein

1985   *Crime and Human Nature.* New York: Simon and Schuster.

Wilson, Paul, Robyn Lincoln, and Duncan Chappell

1986   "Physician fraud and abuse in Canada: a preliminary examination." *Canadian Journal of Criminology* 28: 129–46.

Wilson, Susannah

1990   "Alternatives to traditional marriage." In M. Baker (ed.), *Families: Changing Trends in Canada.* Toronto: McGraw-Hill.

Wilson, Susannah J.

1991   *Women, Families, and Work.* (3rd ed.) Toronto: McGraw-Hill Ryerson.

Wister, A. and C. Moore

1998   "First Nations elders in Canada: issues, problems and successes in health care policy." In Andrew Wister and Gloria Gutman (eds.), *Health Systems and Aging in Selected Pacific Rim Countries: Cultural Diversity and Change.* Vancouver: Gerontology Research Centre, Simon Fraser University.

Wister, Andrew, Barbara A. Mitchell, and Ellen M. Gee

1997   "Does money matter? Parental income and living arrangement satisfaction among "Boomerang" children during coresidence." *Canadian Studies in Population* 24: 125–45.

Wolf, Naomi

1997   *Promiscuities: The Secret Struggle for Womanhood.* Toronto: Random House.

Wolff, K. (ed.)

1950   *The Sociology of Georg Simmel.* New York: The Free Press.

Wolff, Lee

1991   "Drug crimes." *Canadian Social Trends* 20: 26–9.

Wordes, M. and T. Bynum

1995   "Policing juveniles: is there bias against youths of color?" Pp. 47–65 in K. Leonard et al. (eds.), *Minorities in Juvenile Justice*. Thousand Oaks, CA: Sage.

World Bank

1999   *Knowledge for Development: 1998/99 World Development Report*. New York: Oxford University Press.

1997   *World Bank Development Report*. Washington, D.C.

1992   *World Development Report 1992*. New York: Oxford University Press.

Wotherspoon, Terry (ed.)

1991   *Hitting the Books: The Political Economy of Retrenchment*. Toronto: Garamond.

Wotherspoon, Terry and Vic Satzewich

1993   *First Nations: Race, Class, and Gender Relations*. Scarborough: Nelson Canada.

Wrigley, E.A. and R.S. Schofield

1981   *The Population History of England, 1541–1871*. Cambridge: Cambridge University Press.

Wrong, Dennis

1961   "The oversocialized conception of man in modern sociology." *American Sociological Review* 26: 183–193.

Wu, Zheng and Kelly Martin

1999   "Contraceptive choice in Canada." Paper presented at the Annual Meeting of the Canadian Population Society, Lennoxville, Québec.

Wuthnow, Robert (ed.)

1994   *"I Come Away Stronger": How Small Groups are Shaping American Religion*. Grand Rapids, MI: Eerdmans.

Yi, Sun-Kyung

1991   "Crime statistics based on race promote hatred, board told." *The Globe and Mail*, Aug. 23.

Yi, Zeng, T. Ping, G. Baochang, X. Yi, L. Bohau, and L. Yongping

1993   "Causes and implications of the recent increase in the reported sex ratio at birth in China." *Population and Development Review* 19: 283–301.

Yinger, J. Milton

1970   *The Scientific Study of Religion*. New York: Macmillan.

Young, J. and R. Matthews

1992   *Rethinking Criminology: The Realist Debate*. London: Sage.

Zigler, Edward F. and Irvin L. Child

1973   *Socialization and Personality Development*. Reading, Mass: Addison-Wesley.

Zollo, Peter

1995   "Talking to teens: the teenage market is free-spending and loaded with untapped potential." *American Demographics* November: 22–28.

Name Index

Subject Index

Photo Credits